THE CASPIAN WORLD

THE CASPIAN WORLD

CONNECTIONS AND CONTENTIONS AT A
MODERN EURASIAN CROSSROADS

Edited by Abbas Amanat,
Kevin Gledhill, and
Kayhan A. Nejad

CORNELL UNIVERSITY PRESS
Ithaca and London

The ebook editions of this book are available as open access volumes through the Cornell Open initiative.

Copyright © 2025 by Cornell University

The text of this book is licensed under a Creative Commons Attribution-NonCommercial-NoDerivatives 4.0 International License: https://creativecommons.org/licenses/by-nc-nd/4.0/. To use this book, or parts of this book, in any way not covered by the license, please contact Cornell University Press, Sage House, 512 East State Street, Ithaca, New York 14850. Visit our website at cornellpress.cornell.edu.

First published 2025 by Cornell University Press and Cornell University Library

Library of Congress Cataloging-in-Publication Data

Names: Amanat, Abbas editor | Gledhill, Kevin editor | Nejad, Kayhan A., 1991- editor
Title: The Caspian world : connections and contentions at a modern Eurasian crossroads / edited by Abbas Amanat, Kevin Gledhill, and Kayhan A. Nejad.
Description: Ithaca [New York] : Cornell University Press, 2025. | Includes bibliographical references and index.
Identifiers: LCCN 2025001695 (print) | LCCN 2025412006 (ebook) | ISBN 9781501777172 hardcover | ISBN 9781501781278 paperback | ISBN 9781501781292 epub | ISBN 9781501781285 pdf
Subjects: LCSH: Caspian Sea Region—History | Caspian Sea Region—Politics and government | Caspian Sea Region—Foreign relations
Classification: LCC DK511.C07 C3775 2025 (print) | LCC DK511.C07 (ebook) | DDC 947.5—dc23/eng/20250305
LC record available at https://lccn.loc.gov/2025001695
LC ebook record available at https://lccn.loc.gov/2025412006

Contents

Acknowledgments ix
Abbreviations x
Note on Transliteration xi

Introduction KEVIN GLEDHILL AND
KAYHAN A. NEJAD ... 1

1. The Persianate Caspian: Isolation to Inclusion ABBAS AMANAT ... 16

PART I: EARLY EXPANSION: KNOWLEDGE, COMMERCE, AND DIPLOMACY IN THE EARLY MODERN CASPIAN

2. The Ottoman Empire and the Caspian Sea in the Sixteenth Century MURAT YAŞAR ... 49

3. Papering Over a Diplomatic Gulf: Bureaucracy and Translation between Early Modern Central Asian and Muscovite Courts ULFAT ABDURASULOV ... 66

4. Armenians and Russian Interests in the Caspian Sea, 1660–1795 GEORGE BOURNOUTIAN ... 91

5. Astrakhan and the Caspian Sea in Russia's Early Modern Political Geography GUIDO HAUSMANN ... 113

6. Nader Shah and the Caspian: A Sea too Far ERNEST TUCKER ... 134

7. Follow the Armenians: British Plans for the Caspian in the Eighteenth Century MATTHEW P. ROMANIELLO 151

PART II: ASCENDENCY AND ANNEXATION: EMPIRE-BUILDING, STATE-FORMATION, AND THE TRANSITION TO THE MODERN

8. "Under the Pretense of Trade, They Drew Maps": Qajar Views of Russia and Russian Mapmaking in the Caspian in the Eighteenth Century KEVIN GLEDHILL 169

9. Caspian Forests as Political Setting: A Socioenvironmental Study of the Bābi Resistance at the Fort of Shaykh Ṭabarsi SAGHAR SADEGHIAN 191

10. The Custom of Customs: Licit and Illicit Crossings in the Caspian Sea, 1864–1917 RUSTIN ZARKAR 207

11. The Transcaspian Railroad in the Works of Nikolaĭ Karazin, 1842–1908 ELENA ANDREEVA 227

12. Border Crossings: Iranian Artists in Tsarist Russia and Georgia LAYLA S. DIBA 247

PART III: RESISTANCE TO SUPREMACY: CONTESTING IMPERIAL AND STATE CONTROL ON THE SOUTHERN CASPIAN LITTORAL

13. In the Glocal Crossfire: Russia, Britain, and the Caspian, 1916–1919 DENIS V. VOLKOV 271

14. The Jangal Movement and Regional Revolutionaries in Northern Iran, 1914–1921 KAYHAN A. NEJAD 292

15. "The Persian Gate to Revolution": Bolshevik Networks and Post-WWI Transnationalism in Iran
    ALISA SHABLOVSKAIA   309

16. Pragmatic Elements of Early Soviet Policy toward Iran
    IURII DEMIN   326

17. Maritime Horizons: The Caspian Sea in Soviet-Iranian Relations, 1930s–1980s
    ETIENNE FORESTIER-PEYRAT   350

Bibliography   365
Contributors   403
Index   405

Acknowledgments

The editors express their gratitude to the Persian Heritage Foundation, the American Institute of Iranian Studies, the Farzaneh Family Endowment at the University of Oklahoma, the Yale MacMillan Center for International and Area Studies, and the Parsa Community Foundation at the University of Oklahoma for providing the subvention funding that made the publication of this volume possible.

The editors express their gratitude to the Yale MacMillan Center Program in Iranian Studies, the Edward J. and Dorothy Clarke Kempf Memorial Fund, and the European Studies Council for their financial support for the conference at which the chapters of this book were first presented: "The Caspian in the History of Early Modern and Modern Eurasia" (Yale University, 2019).

Abbreviations

ARDA   Azərbaycan Respublikasının Dövlət Arxivi (National Archives of the Republic of Azerbaijan)
AVPRI   Arkhiv Vneshneĭ Politiki Rossiĭskoĭ Imperii (Archive of Foreign Policy of the Russian Empire)
BL   British Library
D   Delo
F   Fond
GARF   Gosudarstvennyĭ Arkhiv Rossiĭskoĭ Federatsii (State Archive of the Russian Federation)
O   Opis
PSZ   *Polnoe sobranie zakonov Rossiĭskoĭ Imperii*, series 1 (St. Petersburg, 1830)
RGADA   Rossiĭskiĭ Gosudarstvennyĭ Arkhiv Drevnikh Aktov (Russian State Archive of Ancient Acts)
RGAE   Rossiĭskiĭ Gosudarstvennyĭ Arkhiv Ėkonomiki (Russian State Archive of the Economy)
RGASPI   Rossiĭskiĭ Gosudarstvennyĭ Arkhiv Sotsial'no-Politicheskoĭ Istorii (Russian State Archive of Sociopolitical History)
RGVA   Rossiĭskiĭ Gosudarstvennyĭ Voennyĭ Arkhiv (Russian State Military Archive)
RSDLP   Russian Social Democratic Labor Party
SSRI   Soviet Socialist Republic of Iran
TNA   The (British) National Archives
       CAB   Cabinet Office
       FO   Foreign Office
       WO   War Office

Note on Transliteration

This book adheres to the transliteration guidelines of the *International Journal of Middle East Studies* for Persian, with vowel diacritic simplification. It follows Library of Congress transliteration guidelines for Russian and Turkish, with consonant diacritic simplification. For the purposes of readability, well-known names and names with established English spellings have been transliterated without diacritics.

This book adheres to original-language capitalization conventions, except for usages of proper nouns and proper adjectives, all of which have been capitalized in transliteration.

FIGURE 0.1. The Caspian region, eighteenth–nineteenth centuries. Map by Gordie Thompson, Castle Time Mapping.

FIGURE 0.2. Political map of the Caspian region since 1991. Map by Gordie Thompson, Castle Time Mapping.

THE CASPIAN WORLD

Introduction

Kevin Gledhill and Kayhan A. Nejad

Recent years have seen a growing interest in the historical relations between and among the states that surround the Caspian Sea—Azerbaijan, Kazakhstan, Turkmenistan, and especially Iran and Russia. This trend is most noticeably present in the study of the modern period. In English-language scholarship, this new interest offers important correctives to historical framings that emphasize the relationship of the Persianate world to the Middle East and to western Europe but inadequately address the Eurasian dimensions of the region's history. Critically, this work also begins to engage with a well-established literature produced within Russia, Iran, Central Asia, and the Caucasus, especially an extensive body of scholarly works in the Russian language developed in the Soviet period and after 1991.

Despite this, the absence of a clearly defined subfield of "Caspian history" persists in North American and west European scholarship, even as bodies of water such as the Indian Ocean and Black Sea have joined the Mediterranean and Atlantic as major areas of research.[1] Sitting between high mountains to the south and west, hills and desert that extend up to the Amu Darya to the east, and the open steppe to the north, the Caspian may appear more of a barrier than a source of connection. Its precious few natural harbors and major cities, as well as the exposure of ships to storms, lend further credence to this impression.

This book argues for Caspian history as a rich and generative field of study and shows how the Caspian Sea, known in Persian and some Turkic languages also as the Sea of Mazandaran or the Khazar Sea, has historically been a source of both connection and contestation since the early modern period. Covering the history of the Caspian region from the sixteenth century, when large empires like tsarist Russia, the Ottomans, and Safavid Iran began to establish their presence on its shores, through the modern era, the chapters in this book collectively make a case for the existence and significance of this Caspian space, giving definition to its key features. Rather than embracing a binary, state-to-state relations framework (Russia and Iran, Russia and Khiva, Baku and Moscow or Tehran), this volume highlights the Caspian, together with its littoral and adjacent regions, as a distinct space of historical activity and study, one with multisided exchanges and numerous centers.

The field of Mediterranean history suggests itself as a model, but profound differences limit its applicability to the study of the Caspian. Mediterranean history owes its origins to Fernand Braudel, whose work *The Mediterranean and the Mediterranean World in the Age of Philip II* first appeared in French in 1949. Braudel's analysis posits an inherent unity of this sea and its littoral zone, dictated over the long durée by its physical and human geography, the underlying structures of a coherent Mediterranean space. In the medium term, states, economic patterns, and to some extent, religious movements created a more perceptible layer of history (*conjonctures*). Human agency can be seen at the level of short-term events, though these are heavily influenced by the structural factors and *conjonctures* mentioned above.[2] The Caspian Sea is not the Mediterranean: its geography imposes a distinct set of possibilities and limitations, while the linguistic diversity of the region adds a further layer of difficulty to research on the Caspian as a single unit. Thus, a truly long durée study of the region remains elusive, and the idea of a consistent, abiding unity of the region must be tested by further study.

Still, works that followed and responded to Braudel have complicated or challenged aspects of his Mediterranean, suggesting that the sea consists of distinct ecological and cultural microregions with long histories of exchange due in part to crises or shortages experienced locally; alternatively, Mediterranean history has been defined as the history of the sea itself, linked together by distinct phases of intensive contacts and movement between its port cities.[3] Given the variety of climates and terrain in the region, as well as an acceleration in contacts across the Caspian and between it and major imperial and national state-building projects, these models will find some echoes in the early modern and modern Caspian. However, the region's particularities remain and will be evident throughout this book.

The distinctiveness of the Caspian begins with its physical geography. Due to its lack of connection to global oceans, being surrounded on all sides by land, the Caspian is often referred to by geographers and historians as a lake, rather than a "sea" as such.[4] Its waters acquire a somewhat saline quality (though much less so than ocean water) from the soil and minerals carried by the rivers that fill the Caspian. Geographer Xavier de Planhol noted that the Caspian's water levels and surface area have fluctuated significantly over time, but that it is divided into three major basins, with the shallowest and freshest waters around the Volga River Delta in the north. By the late 1980s, the surface area of the Caspian Sea was around 378,400 square kilometers. It is fed by many rivers, and because it has no outlets to other bodies of water, any decreases in its volume or in surface area are driven by evaporation, making it a good indicator of climate in the northern hemisphere over many millennia.[5] Receding waters and lower surface levels in recent decades indicate the impact of climate change on the Caspian, with one study showing a three-meter fall in water levels in the twentieth century and models anticipating much more significant losses of area and depth in the twenty-first.[6]

Plan of the Book

The chapters in this book cannot offer a complete view of the Caspian Sea over the past five hundred years; but taken together, they trace the intersections of state-building projects there with trade, linguistic and cultural identities, artistic production, new religious movements, global conflict, and revolution. Collectively, these chapters aim to sketch out the role of the Caspian Sea as a connecting force, but also as a source of perceived threat from the point of view of its major states. The book also argues for the significance of local interests in defining this space through negotiation with and resistance to powers based in Tehran, Moscow, St. Petersburg, Khiva, Istanbul, and other capitals.

The volume's first chapter, by Abbas Amanat, explores the defining features of the Caspian world as seen from its southern shores from the Sasanian era of pre-Islamic antiquity to the present day. It makes several interventions that help to define the Caspian as a coherent space of historical activity over the longue durée. Amanat demonstrates a pattern of localism and autonomy in the region, bolstered by geographic features including thick forest, separation from the interior of the Iranian plateau by the Alborz Mountains, and few natural harbors. This northern sphere of the Persianate world became an incubator for heterodox religious movements since the arrival of Islam in Iran, placing it at the center of the history of Shi'ism, Bābism, and millenarian and apocalyptic Sufism. In the modern period, the creation of imperial or national states and a Transcaspian economic sphere transformed the region, even as patterns of regional distinctiveness continued to assert themselves.

Following this piece, the work is divided into three distinct sections: the early modern period (1556–1779), the nineteenth century (1779–1906), and a twentieth-century era initiated by the revolutions that occurred in Qajar Iran and the Russian Empire before the First World War. These sections trace the interactions between commerce, ideological considerations, imperial and state-building projects in the Caspian littoral region, and cultural exchange between all sides of the Caspian Sea and adjacent lands.

Part I is titled "Early Expansion: Knowledge, Commerce, and Diplomacy in the Early Modern Caspian." This section begins with the Russian conquest of the post-Mongol Khanate of Astrakhan in 1556 and the emergence of Safavid control over Gilan and Mazandaran in the 1590s. Along with Ottoman campaigns toward the Volga and in Shirvan, the late sixteenth century marks the beginning of an imperial moment in the Caspian Sea, as these three empires attempted to control this space and the flow of commodities through it, while securing their positions militarily on its shores. Despite this periodization, which focuses on the rise of Russia, Iran, and the Ottoman Empire on the horizons of the Caspian world, this section demonstrates the prevalence of local power and the necessity of horizontal negotiation between the imperial centers and local interests. These local elements include but are not limited to Armenian merchant networks and clergy, the rulers of the patchwork of kingdoms in the North Caucasus, Turkic- and Persian-language translators, and diplomats and traders seeking to balance personal interests with state service. The picture that emerges is one of an interconnected Caspian sphere from the mid-sixteenth century to the end of the eighteenth, with the region's few major ports (Astrakhan, Derbent, Baku, Anzali, Astarabad) emerging as cosmopolitan centers that both facilitated the presence of imperial powers and limited the degree of their direct control between the Alborz Mountains and the Volga Delta, the Caucasus and the Amu Darya.

This section opens with a chapter by Murat Yaşar, "The Ottoman Empire and the Caspian Sea in the Sixteenth Century." Using sources from Ottoman state archives, Yaşar reexamines the famed Ottoman campaign against Astrakhan in 1569, including efforts to build a canal between the Don and the Volga to support military operations launched from Crimea. However, Yaşar's chapter tells a larger story that continues over several decades, arguing that the Ottoman central authorities hoped to apply the model of their consolidated control over the Black Sea into the Caspian, in competition with Safavid and Russian rivals. In doing so, the Ottoman state cultivated local partnerships with existing elites, particularly in the North Caucasus, establishing nominal control there and direct rule to the south along the coast into the 1590s. Particular attention is given to relations with the Crimean khan and the shamkhāl of Tarki in Dagestan. These relationships and efforts to maintain garrisons and supply routes into Shirvan and Baku enabled Ottoman victories and even a naval presence in the Caspian during the late sixteenth century. Thus, the Caspian became a site of imperial contestation, but one in which the direct power of distant imperial centers was limited and the ability to project power intertwined with local dynamics.

With the consolidation of Russian control of the entire length of the Volga, Moscow gained access to the Caspian and, via the sea, to markets in Iran, Central Asia, and, its tsars hoped, India. In its diplomatic outreach to these states and its efforts to promote trade, the Russian state often approached the region through intermediaries and in the medium of Turkic languages, rather than the Persian that predominated in court cultures south and east of the Caspian in the early modern era. Ulfat Abdurasulov demonstrates this phenomenon in his chapter, "Papering Over a Diplomatic Gulf: Bureaucracy and Translation between Early Modern Central Asian and Muscovite Courts." He finds a consistent preference for Turkic languages, alongside Russian, in Moscow's Caspian diplomacy. He then traces this trend to the institutional expertise in the Posol'skiĭ Prikaz, the bureaucratic office managing foreign affairs for the tsars before the Petrine reforms. Key interlocutors, including Kasymov Tatars and Central Asian merchants at Astrakhan provided translation services and may have produced the Turkic-dominant idiom of the period. In making this argument, Abdurasulov complicates the idea of a "Persianate world" as viewed from the Caspian and Russia and affirms the significance of partners of Russia's imperial project in the region.

Building on these observations, George Bournoutian addresses the relationship between Russian empire-building and networks of Armenian traders and churchmen from the mid-seventeenth to late eighteenth centuries. In "Armenians and Russian Interests in the Caspian Sea, 1660–1795," Bournoutian shows that Russian efforts at expansion toward the south and east were carried out in order to secure transit trading routes between Asia and western Europe. This project depended on close cooperation with Armenian commercial interests and often required concessions to the political aspirations of Armenian elites. With these priorities in mind, we can understand Peter I's partial backing of Israyel Ori's plan for an Armenian state in the first decades of the eighteenth century. However, this support was ultimately secondary to Russian economic and territorial ambitions, and it proved fleeting. A focus on developing commercial infrastructure drove decision-making in St. Petersburg until the outbreak of war with Qajar Iran in 1804, which ultimately brought direct Russian rule in the Caucasus.

Alongside these partnerships, the court in St. Petersburg and officials of its various administrative bodies attempted to exert direct influence over the Caspian region. One way in which such efforts are evident is in the production of scientific knowledge and cartography. Guido Hausmann analyzes projects in this field in the fifth chapter, "Astrakhan and the Caspian Sea in Russia's Early Modern Political Geography." Hausmann argues that eighteenth-century Russian cartographic expeditions represented a project of the central state to create knowledge of the region in service of the larger goal of expansion toward the south. Still, cartography was a transnational project, carried out by individuals with distinct interests and with connections to European scientific discourses of the early modern period.

In the chapter titled "Nader Shah and the Caspian: A Sea too Far," Ernest Tucker draws on the chronicle histories of the Afsharid rulers of Iran who rose to power following the Safavid collapse and the Afghan, Russian, and Ottoman invasions of 1722. Tucker uses these texts to assess the post-Safavid Iranian military leader and conqueror Nader Shah's (r. 1725/36–47) interests in the Caspian Sea. While primarily based in Khorasan and successful in land-based military endeavors that briefly gave him control over not only the former Safavid lands, but also much of India and Central Asia, Nader was drawn increasingly toward the Caspian Sea for strategic reasons. He hoped to project power via the Caspian over the Turkmens and into Dagestan. He also sought access to the region's commercial potential to develop the area around Kalāt and Mashhad, the closest approximation he had to a capital city. While he came to value the Caspian strategically, his court lacked expertise and worked through intermediaries, most famously John Elton of the British Russia Company, to create naval capabilities in the north. Ultimately, the project of building a northern Iranian fleet ended with the shah's assassination in 1747, and the area became a refuge for rivals, including the Qajars, who later established their rule over all of Iran from their base on the southern shores of the Caspian Sea.

The history of the Russia Company as a whole and Elton, in particular, is one of the most intriguing episodes in eighteenth-century Caspian history. Building on his recent work on the company's relations with Russia and Eurasia, Matthew P. Romaniello examines competing ideas and factions within the Russia Company in its efforts to establish its position in the Caspian trade during the 1730s and 1740s. In the short window between Britain's 1734 commercial treaty with Russia and the expulsion of the company from this route in 1747, the Russia Company's agents promoted a vision of prosperous trade with Iran and Bukhara, picking up where the East India Company had failed in the Persian Gulf. Both Elton and Onslow Burnish advanced this idea in writing for debates in London, where they hoped Parliament would alter the Acts of Navigation. Their legislative agenda would allow imports of Iranian goods to enter Britain via Russia, an activity then prohibited because it competed with other British companies that held monopoly rights for Iranian and Levantine trades. Elton's and Burnish's writings show differing visions, with the former portraying the existing Armenian commercial networks as hostile foes, while the latter saw them as a model to emulate. But as Russia's own growing economic presence in the Caspian removed the need for British partners, Elton's collaboration with Nader's fleet provided British agents looking to maintain their presence in Russia and Gilan with a way to explain the company's failures to maintain support in St. Petersburg. Still, the window for British trade in the Caspian closed as quickly as it had opened.

The second section, titled "Ascendancy and Annexation: Empire Building, State Formation, and the Transition to the Modern," covers the period from the mid-eighteenth century to the beginning of the twentieth. During this period, the many independent poles of authority in the Caspian were consolidated under the Russian Empire (in the west between 1804 and 1859 and to the east of the sea by the 1880s). Qajar Iran emerged from the 1780s as the prevailing power in the south and, for a time, in the Caucasus. During this period, the Russian state accelerated efforts to increase and direct movement through the Caspian, supporting the creation of the Kavkaz i Merkuriĭ steamship line in 1849 and constructing the Transcaspian Military Railroad in Central Asia from 1879 to 1906.[7] Russian and Qajar state power grew but continued to be limited by varying forms of resistance and the geographic realities of the Caspian itself. While Russia clearly became the preeminent power in the region by the end of the Russo-Persian Wars (1804–13, 1826–28), conflicts in the Caucasus and Central Asia continued for decades, and the Caspian became a site of imperial anxieties, as well as connectivity.

This section begins with a chapter by Kevin Gledhill, drawing on many of the themes of the early modern era and the transition to the bipolar Caspian world of the late eighteenth century. In "'Under the Pretense of Trade, They Drew Maps': Qajar Views of Russia and Russian Mapmaking in the Caspian in the Eighteenth Century," he discusses the role of cartography as a tool of Russian imperial expansion from the collapse of the Safavids in 1722. Mapmaking and the production of scientific knowledge preceded the Russian occupation of the western and southern shores of the Caspian Sea during the post-Safavid period and enabled Russia's commercial and diplomatic contacts over the Caspian throughout the eighteenth century. With the rise of Qajar power in Astarabad from 1779, Āqā Moḥammad Khan Qajar strove to balance outreach to Russia for commercial reasons with a deep suspicion of its military presence. Cartography became identified with Russian expansion over the course of the century. Opposition to mapmaking contributed to Qajar officials' decision to arrest the officers of a Russian naval squadron in the southeastern corner of the Caspian in 1781. This was the first major confrontation between Qajar Iran and the Russian Empire, the two states that ruled all sides of the Caspian by the 1880s.

This section continues with a chapter by Saghar Sadeghian, "Caspian Forests as Political Setting: A Socioenvironmental Study of the Bābi Resistance at the Fort of Shaykh Ṭabarsi." Drawing on a wide array of Persian and British sources, Sadeghian probes the environmental and social dimensions of the siege of Fort Ṭabarsi in 1848–49, a major episode of the Bābi uprisings of 1844–53. Sadeghian argues that precipitation, dense forest cover, and underdeveloped road networks in Mazandaran allowed the Bābis to prolong their resistance before their massacre by state forces. As a corollary, Sadeghian applies E. J. Hobsbawm's theory of the "Primitive Rebel" to the defenders of Ṭabarsi, asking how their relations with the local population allowed the Bābis to negotiate difficulties of supply and provision. In so doing, Sadeghian raises original theories on not only the Bābi resistance, but also the proliferation of subsequent rebellious movements on the southern Caspian littoral.

Over the course of the late nineteenth century, the discovery of oil afforded the Caspian region a measure of global importance.[8] The extraction of oil, in turn, gave rise to a powerful labor movement, which both engaged with and challenged other manifestations of political resistance in Baku and beyond. By the early twentieth century, cresting currents of socialism and national liberation had placed the Caspian between—or arguably, at the center of—revolutionary movements that extended from the Caspian to the Russian, Ottoman, and Qajar polities.[9] In his "The Custom of Customs: Licit and Illicit Crossings in the Caspian Sea, 1864-1917," Rustin Zarkar interrogates the material bases of these movements, as well as state efforts to counter them. Drawing on documents from the Central State Archive of the Republic of Dagestan in Makhachkala, Zarkar demonstrates that the movement of contraband from late tsarist Russia to Iran played an important role in the radical turn of political movements on the Caspian littoral, including the Iranian Constitutional Revolution (1905-11). Zarkar argues that, over the course of a half century, the Russian state adapted to the flow of contraband, but only incompletely and ineffectively. In so doing, he makes an original contribution to understanding the political devolution that followed the tsarist collapse.

Elena Andreeva's chapter, "The Transcaspian Railroad in the Works of Nikolaï Karazin, 1842-1908," examines the expansion of Russian power via the Caspian into the Turkmen lands through the works of a late nineteenth-century painter, ethnographer, and traveler. The chapter connects Karazin's work to the construction of the Transcaspian Military Railroad after the 1882 conquest of the region. The railroad established the Russian presence between the Caspian and the Amu Darya and built out the infrastructure of the empire. Andreeva shows that Karazin, who served as a soldier in Central Asia and painted watercolor images of his travels, presented the region to a Russian audience, casting the railroad as a powerful driver of its integration into the Russian Empire and as a civilizing force. These works helped to define newly acquired territories for the public in places like St. Petersburg and Moscow. Advances in the technologies of communication, transportation, and warfare drew the Caspian closer to St. Petersburg and, by the 1920s, to Tehran, but the late nineteenth and early twentieth centuries also saw cultural and artistic production that reflected growing contacts across this region.

In the concluding chapter of this section, "Border Crossings: Iranian Artists in Tsarist Russia and Georgia," Layla S. Diba considers cultural exchange through the Caucasus and western Caspian during the late nineteenth and early twentieth centuries. Focusing on the work of Russian- and Georgian-trained Iranian painters, including Ḥosayn Ṭāherzādeh Behzād and 'Abbās Rassām Arzhangi, Diba argues that the Russian Empire, particularly its Caucasus Viceroyalty and institutions located there, served as a conduit for artistic influences from Europe to reach northwestern Iran. Furthermore, she situates these exchanges within the broader political and cultural history of the period, as one of many forms of exchange via the Caspian world and the Caucasus, alongside other forms of material culture, as well as nationalist and revolutionary politics.

The third and final section, "Resistance to Supremacy: Contesting Imperial and State Control on the Southern Caspian Littoral," probes the breakdown and reconstitution of the state and, with it, the control of the center over the periphery. The Russian Revolution of 1917, arguably the most important episode in the history of the twentieth century, shaped these processes of the Caspian littoral. In subsequent years, a string of independent states emerged in the Caucasus, each to become a Soviet republic by 1922. On the eastern shores of the Caspian, meanwhile, the Bolsheviks moved to quash competing revolutionary and autonomous Turkmen movements and to fully incorporate the region under Soviet control.[10] These efforts placed them in conflict with a coalition of anti-Bolsheviks, including the British Indian forces of Wilfrid Malleson (1918–19).[11] The anti-Bolsheviks' resistance culminated, at least in Soviet historiography, in their execution of the 26 Commissars, Bolshevik and non-Bolshevik socialist leaders who spearheaded Baku's resistance to Ottoman forces before their forced flight across the Caspian in mid-1918.[12] Soviet commemoration of this episode triggered, in turn, decades of anti-Soviet polemics devoted to countering "false" narratives around the Baku Commissars, and especially the question of British responsibility for their deaths.[13]

In the first chapter of this section, "In the Glocal Crossfire: Russia, Britain, and the Caspian, 1916–1919," Denis V. Volkov probes an important episode of Allied intervention in the Russian Civil War on the Caspian littoral. Drawing on Russian- and English-language memoirs as well as archival materials from Russia and the United Kingdom,

Volkov centers the exploits of Colonel Lazar' Bicherakhov (d. 1952) and his role between the Bolsheviks, the British, and the White Russians in Iran after the October Revolution. Volkov demonstrates that Bicherakhov played an outsized and underappreciated part in securing northern Iran for the British, but that ideological divisions complicated the British-White Russian alliance, and eventually doomed Bicherakhov's attempted rapprochement with the Bolsheviks. In so doing, Volkov draws attention to the transient and variable nature of alliances on the southern Caspian littoral, where he argues that state actors discarded allies and clients in pursuit of realpolitik aims.

The impending victory of the Red Army in the Russian Civil War foretold the flight of the White Russian forces from the Iranian north. Partially in an effort to accelerate this process, the Bolsheviks agreed to a unity government with the Jangal Movement of Mirza Kuchek Khan (d. 1921) in May 1920. Kayhan A. Nejad, in his chapter "The Jangal Movement and Regional Revolutionaries in Northern Iran, 1914–1921," questions the movement's ideological evolution in the years before the establishment of this unity government. Nejad asks why, among several rebellious movements across the Iranian north, the Soviets formed an alliance with one built on pan-Islamic principles. More, while most accounts of the Jangal Movement center its coalition with the Soviets, Nejad asks if this shift reflected the ideological bent of the Jangalis before 1920, or a departure from their founding principles.

The Soviet Socialist Republic of Iran, established by the Jangal Movement, may be interrogated either as an adaptation of a northern Iranian revolutionary tradition or as an extension of the Soviet revolutionary front into West Asia and beyond. In her chapter, "'The Persian Gate to Revolution': Bolshevik Networks and Post-WWI Transnationalism in Iran," Alisa Shablovskaia centers the confluence of three loci of Asian revolution in India, the former Ottoman Empire, and the Caspian region, including northern Iran and the independent Azerbaijan Democratic Republic (1918–20). Drawing on a broad array of materials in Russian and Persian, Shablovskaia asks how Soviet Iran policy functioned not in isolation, but rather as one among many linked but semidistinct approaches to revolutionary movements across Asia. As a corollary, Shablovskaia questions the one-way flow of revolutionary dictates from Soviet Russia to Asia, instead demonstrating that Asian revolutionaries made their own contributions to early Soviet policy on the greater Caspian littoral.

Ultimately, Soviet revolutionary designs on Iran faltered in Gilan province. In his chapter, "Pragmatic Elements of Early Soviet Policy toward Iran," Iurii Demin reinterprets what he asserts to be the realpolitik and survivalist underpinnings of Soviet policy in Iran after this episode. Drawing on original documents from the Archive of Foreign Policy of the Russian Federation, Demin argues that the Soviets adopted conventional state-to-state relations with Iran after 1921. Rather than attempting to export socialism, the Soviets instead prioritized commercial and economic agreements with the Iranian government, including fishing concessions in the southern Caspian and mining rights in the Iranian north. In addition to conferring economic benefits to the fledgling Soviet republics, these agreements allowed the Soviets to counterweight British influence in Iran.

For decades after the October Revolution, the Caspian world settled into a period of relative stability, excepting the sovereignty crisis that erupted in Iranian Azerbaijan in 1945–46. This crisis, which stemmed from the autonomist or independent turn of Iranian Azerbaijan after the Second World War, marked the site of one of the first confrontations between superpowers at the outset of the Cold War.[14] The final chapter of this volume, Etienne Forestier-Peyrat's "Maritime Horizons: The Caspian Sea in Soviet-Iranian Relations, 1930s–1980s," centers the broader development of Soviet-Iranian relations beyond this episode. Forestier-Peyrat reconstructs the recent history of the Caspian with attention to the shifting priorities and diplomatic postures of the Soviet and Iranian states. In particular, Forestier-Peyrat traces the evolution of the Caspian littoral from a point of geopolitical conflict to a site where both governments made economic investments and confronted common environmental issues from the 1950s through the 1970s. In conclusion, Peyrat probes the return of political tensions and sovereignty disputes on the Caspian littoral in the 1980s.

The Future of "Caspian Studies"

When evaluating the Caspian region's contemporary history, social scientists have tended to center issues of energy and security, particularly political contestation between regional actors and the confounding role of outside powers. These scholarly focuses reflected the political changes in the Caspian region after the breakup of the USSR. In the 1990s, the sudden diminution of Moscow's power provided an opportunity for nonregional states to exert their influence on the Caspian littoral and to secure access to its supply of hydrocarbons.[15] The United States, in particular, made inroads into the Caspian region both to safeguard energy supplies and to counter Russia's influence in its own "near abroad."[16] More recently, the US invasion of Afghanistan in 2001, the resurgence of Russian influence in the years thereafter, and the efforts of European Union member states to secure hydrocarbons prompted the production of new scholarship on the Caspian region.[17]

Given the nonresolution of conflicts and the need for economic investment in the Caspian, social scientists will likely afford greater attention to China's regional role in the coming years. The Caspian, however, is not only a site for competition between major world powers, as all five littoral states (Iran, Turkmenistan, Kazakhstan, Russia, Azerbaijan) conducted protracted negotiations over its legal status after the breakup of the USSR.[18] In 2018, these efforts finally bore fruit, as the five littoral states agreed to the Convention on the Legal Status of the Caspian Sea, marking a significant step toward the resolution of outstanding, interrelated economic and territorial disputes.[19]

In 2020–23, following the reemergence of hostilities in the Caspian and greater Caspian regions, Iran and the post-Soviet space assumed a renewed importance in global affairs. These developments lie beyond the purview of a historical anthology. Rather, *The Caspian World* asks how, during the early modern and modern periods, the Caspian region emerged as a site for the contestation of and competing visions of power, and for the movement of persons, goods, and ideas. In filling these roles, the Caspian merits study not only as an appendage of adjacent world regions, but also as a unit of historical analysis in its own right.

Notes

1. There are a few exceptions. Several edited volumes have appeared with a focus on the Caspian region. These have tended to address contemporary geopolitical concerns, especially energy, security, and great-power competition. See Moshe Gammer, ed., *The Caspian Region*, vol. 1, *A Re-emerging Region* (London: Routledge, 2004); R. Hrair Dekmejian and Hovann H. Simonian, *Troubled Waters: The Geopolitics of the Caspian Region* (London: I. B. Tauris, 2001). For historical studies, see Guive Mirfendereski, *A Diplomatic History of the Caspian Sea: Treaties, Diaries and Other Stories* (Basingstoke: Palgrave, 2001). In this text, Mirfendereski gives many narrative accounts of episodes from the modern history of the region. This book considers the meaning of the Caspian Sea in the history of Iran since the eighteenth century, with many historical moments used as an opportunity for reflection on the legal and treaty regimes governing

this body of water. N. A. Sotavov identified competition between local powers and larger imperial interests from Russia, the Ottomans, Iran, and western Europe as the defining features of a "circum-Caspian" region in the eighteenth century. Sotavov connected that model to rising Western interest in the region following the collapse of the USSR. See N. A. Sotavov, "The Circum-Caspian Areas within the Eurasian International Relations at the Time of Peter the Great and Nadir Shah Afshar," *Iran and the Caucasus* 5 (2001): 93–100. Bruno de Cordier has written about the role maritime connections played in the integration of Central Asia into the Russian state from the sixteenth to twentieth centuries, arguing that a mercantilist, seaborne economic motive contributed to Russia's southward expansion from the sixteenth century. While contiguous territories were absorbed into the empire in the eighteenth and nineteenth centuries, maritime supply and naval power were an integral part of this process. This is a rare phenomenon in Russian history, outside of Alaska and northern California. See Bruno de Cordier, "Central Asia's Maritime Dimension? The Historical Position and Role of the Aral-Caspian Basin in the Modern Shaping of the Region," *Region: Regional Studies of Russia, Eastern Europe, and Central Asia* 8, no. 2 (2019): 149–72.

2. Fernand Braudel, *The Mediterranean and the Mediterranean World in the Age of Philip II*, vol. 1, trans. Siân Reynolds (London: Fortuna/Collins, 1975), 19–21.

3. For the former view, see Peregrine Horden and Nicholas Purcell, *The Corrupting Sea: A Study of Mediterranean History* (Oxford: Blackwell, 2000). For the latter, see David Abulafia, *The Great Sea: A Human History of the Mediterranean* (Oxford: Oxford University Press, 2011).

4. Mirfendereski, *A Diplomatic History of the Caspian Sea*, 1; Xavier de Planhol, "Caspian Sea i. Geography," in *Encyclopaedia Iranica*, V/1, 48–50, https://www.iranicaonline.org/articles/caspian-sea-i.

5. De Planhol, "Caspian Sea i."

6. Sifan A. Koriche, Joy S. Singarayer, and Hannah L. Cloke, "The Fate of the Caspian Sea under Projected Climate Change and Water Extraction during the 21st Century," *Environmental Research, Letters* 16 (2021): 094024, https://doi.org/10.1088/1748-9326/ac1af5.

7. The steamship line and the movement of Russian naval operations from Astrakhan to Baku helped facilitate economic and logistical integration of the region into the Russia Empire in the mid-nineteenth century; see de Cordier, "Central Asia's Maritime Dimension?," 160–62.

8. John McKay, "Baku Oil and Transcaucasian Pipelines, 1883–1891: A Study in Tsarist Economic Policy," *Slavic Review* 43, no. 4 (1984): 604–23.

9. See the study of Houri Berberian, *Roving Revolutionaries: Armenians and the Connected Revolutions in the Russian, Iranian, and Ottoman Worlds* (Oakland: University of California Press, 2019).

10. Nikolai Alun Thomas, "Revisiting the 'Transcaspian Episode': British Intervention and Turkmen Statehood, 1918–1919," *Europe-Asia Studies* 75, no. 1 (2023): 131–53.

11. Saul Kelly, "'A Man on a Watchtower': Malleson and the British Military Mission to Turkistan, 1918–20," *Middle Eastern Studies* 58, no. 3 (2022): 341–53.

12. The best work on this episode remains Ronald Grigor Suny, *The Baku Commune, 1917–1918: Class and Nationality in the Russian Revolution* (Princeton, NJ: Princeton University Press, 1972).

13. See, for example, Taline Ter Minassian, "Some Fresh News about the 26 Commissars: Reginald Teague-Jones and the Transcaspian Episode," *Asian Affairs* 45, no. 1 (2014): 65–78; Brian Pearce, "A Falsifier of History," *Revolutionary Russia* 1, no. 1 (1988): 20–23.

14. Krista Goff has reinterpreted this episode, demonstrating that regional officials in the Azerbaijan Soviet Socialist Republic partially drove Soviet designs on northwestern Iran. See Krista Goff, *Nested Nationalism: Making and Unmaking Nations in the Soviet Caucasus* (Ithaca, NY: Cornell University Press, 2021); see also the foundational accounts of Touraj Atabaki, *Azerbaijan: Ethnicity and Autonomy in Twentieth-Century Iran* (London: British Academic Press, 1993); Louise Fawcett, "Revisiting the Iranian Crisis of 1946: How Much More Do We Know?," *Iranian Studies* 47, no. 3 (2014): 379–99; Louise Fawcett, *Iran and the Cold War: The Azerbaijan Crisis of 1946* (Cambridge: Cambridge University Press, 1992).

15. Writing in tendentious publications such as *Problems of Post-Communism*, Stephen Blank connected a potential US expansion into the region with advances on other fronts, including Ukraine's contemporaneous overtures to NATO. See Stephen Blank, "The Future of Caspian Security," *Problems of Post-Communism* 50, no. 1 (2003): 10.

16. Jan Adams, "The US-Russian Face-off in the Caspian Basin." *Problems of Post-Communism* 47, no. 1 (2000): 49–58.

17. See, for example, Roy Allison, "Strategic Reassertion in Russia's Central Asia Policy," *International Affairs* 80, no. 2 (2004): 277–93; Rafael Kandiyoti, "What Price Access to the Open Seas? The Geopolitics of Oil and Gas Transmission from the Trans-Caspian Republics," *Central Asian Survey* 27, no. 1 (2008): 75–93; Alec Rasizade, "The Mythology of Munificent Caspian Bonanza and Its Concomitant Pipeline Geopolitics," *Central Asian Survey* 21, no. 1 (2002): 37–54; Catherine Locatelli, "Russian and Caspian Hydrocarbons: Energy Supply Stakes for the European Union," *Europe-Asia Studies* 62, no. 6 (2010): 959–71; Gawdat Bahgat, "Europe's Energy Security: Challenges and Opportunities," *International Affairs* 82, no. 5 (2006): 961–75.

18. Mehrdad Haghayeghi, "The Coming of Conflict to the Caspian Sea," *Problems of Post-Communism* 50, no. 3 (2003): 32–41; Yusin Lee, "Toward a New International Regime for the Caspian Sea," *Problems of Post-Communism* 52, no. 3 (2005): 37–48. When reconstructing these processes, some scholars have devoted attention to trends in Iran's regional engagement, including during the presidency of Mohammad Khatami (1997–2005). See, for example, Edmund Herzig, "Regionalism, Iran and Central Asia," *International Affairs* 80, no. 3 (2004): 503–17.

19. Phoebe Greenwood, "Landmark Caspian Sea Deal Signed by Five Coastal Nations," *The Guardian*, August 12, 2018, https://www.theguardian.com/world/2018/aug/12/landmark-caspian-sea-deal-signed-among-five-coastal-nations.

CHAPTER 1

The Persianate Caspian
Isolation to Inclusion

Abbas Amanat

Studies about the Caspian Sea generally lag behind other major bodies of water in the northern hemisphere or on the Eurasian landmass. Even though the Caspian is the largest lake on earth, situated between Europe and Asia and with many urban centers in its vicinity, it has barely aroused scholarly attention. Today, even though there is a growing body of works in Russian and Persian, there are very few studies in English.[1] Of the Caspian's unique characteristics, one may name rich marine life of which the sturgeon, a survivor of the early Jurassic era, is a well-known example, albeit as a gastronomic luxury available to few. Less known is the endangerment of the Caspian's marine life, caused by overfishing and pollution. In the post-Soviet era, the Caspian has also been the subject of much debate as the countries surrounding it negotiated, or quarreled, over a maritime regime regulating its rich, and as yet largely untapped, oil resources. By the same token, the history of the early modern and modern Caspian has also fallen by the wayside.

The Ancient Memory

Premodern geographical knowledge about the Caspian has predominantly been tied to its southern shores, the coastal provinces of the Persian Empire of ancient times. Archeological evidence from the

Bronze Age, as in the civilizations of Marlik and Amlash belonging to the first millennium BCE, both in Gilan province, are early examples. But findings in the 1960s and 1970s raised more questions about these settlements, their fascinating artifacts, and their interaction with the Caspian rather than offering reliable clues about their society and culture.

Aside from vague mentions in Assyrian sources, the first clear historical reference to the Caspian seems to come from the fifth century BCE Behestun inscription of the Achaemenid ruler Darius the Great. There the Caspian is identified as the Hyrcanian Sea, named after the lush province of Hyrcania on its southern shores (later known as Tabarestān and today as the Mazandaran and Gorgan/Golestan provinces of northern Iran).[2]

Greek sources, even before Herodotus, speculated about the whereabouts of the Caspian and its southern shores. Yet even two centuries afterward, Aristotle in his *Meteorologica* still provides an enigmatic description of the Caspian, presumably for his famous pupil, Alexander of Macedonia.[3] The information nevertheless seems to have been appealing enough to whet the appetite of the young conqueror, who dispatched in 330 BCE an expeditionary force to the Caspian region during the Persian campaign, presumably in pursuit of the last of the Achaemenids, Darius III. The Greek detachment apparently crossed the so-called Gates of Alexander in the northern Caucasus (today's Darband or Derbent in the autonomous Republic of Dagestan in the Russian Federation), where the Greeks faced stiff local resistance. This seems to have given rise to the legend of the Iron Curtain, an imagined defensive barrier that was supposed to keep the biblical Gog and Magog from penetrating further south. The Alexandrian Barrier (*sadd-e sekandar*) offered fuel for much apocalyptic imagination throughout premodern and early modern times.[4]

Even when in late antiquity the Sasanian Empire under Khosrow II (Parviz) constructed a massive defensive barrier on the southeastern corner of the Caspian to fend off northern nomadic raiders, that wall later came to be associated with the Alexandrian Barrier. The Great Wall of Gorgan, as it is known today, second in length only to the Great Wall of China, stretched some two hundred kilometers from the southeastern Caspian shores to the mountains of northern Khorasan. Serving as part of the fortifications for the western and southern Caspian, it was meant to reassert Sasanian control over a region rich in agriculture and vital to the trade of the Iranian interior.[5]

Curiously, the nomenclature for the Caspian Sea, after the enigmatic Caspi people of Transcaucasia, also reflects the awe that the inhabitants along the southern shores felt toward these nomadic raiders. Yet Iranians, and the Persianate people in general, employed various terms to identify the Caspian Sea. *Caspian* seems to have some etymological affinity with the historic city of Qazvin (from Kazbin or Kaspin in earlier renderings), some two hundred kilometers south of the Caspian. The term *Baḥr-e Qazvin* can occasionally be found in medieval Persian and Arabic geographical texts. This is in contradistinction to the Greco-Roman identification of *Caspian* as the nomenclature of this body of water as early as the first century CE. Persian and Arabic geographers often employed the term *Baḥr-e Khazar*, named after the Khazar people and their empire that from the seventh to tenth centuries dominated the Volga basin (and stretched westward to the Crimean Peninsula and eastward to Kazakhstan). Familiarity with the term *Khazar* for Persian and Arabic sources may well be traced to the Khazar trading network that reached southward to Iranian shores. Closer to modern times, however, the Sea of Mazandaran (*Daryā-ye Māzandarān*) gained greater acceptance as the official name of the sea on some Iranian maps and documents even though the term *Daryā-e Khazar* endured to the present.[6]

Defying Inclusion

The impenetrability of the lush forests of the southern Caspian protected Tabarestān from the first phase of the Arab conquest in the late seventh century, as both local dynasties survived and the dialects and cultures of the region also endured. Conversion to Islam from the late eighth century onward was gradual and mostly peaceful, often revolving around a cult of saints and their local shrines. The tomb of Kiā Esmāʻil, a ruler of the minor Bāvandi dynasty in the village of Lājim in the Savādkuh region in central Alborz, is a remarkable case of Perso-Islamic hybridity. The inscriptions around the dome of the shrine are in Middle Persian (Pahlavi) dated as 389 in the Yazdgerdi calendar, and in Kufic Arabic dated 413 AH (1022 CE). This is a rare clue to the survival of the Sasanian legacy some four centuries after the Arab conquest.[7] The same coexistence may be seen in the region's "Arab-Sasanian" coins, whereby the image of a Zoroastrian fire temple appears on the obverse side of Islamic coins displaying Arabic script.[8]

The essential feature in the sustained semiautonomous status of the southern Caspian, stretching from Azerbaijan to Astarabad, no doubt was the distinct terrain that defined the region, and of course its climate. Separated from the Iranian plateau to the south, the high mountains of the Alborz range offered a natural barrier against encroachments. More importantly, the range captured many of the rain-producing clouds coming from the Black Sea and beyond, as well as the moisture generated by the warm waters of the southern Caspian. The substantial rainfall almost year-round made the region exceptionally lush with a temperate climate, plenty of surface water, extensive forests, and open areas for cultivation. By the same token, the Alborz mountain range bars rain-bearing clouds from traveling southward, marking a visible contrast between the northern and southern Alborz and the adjacent alluvial plains. As a result, the southern slopes developed an agricultural regime distinct from the Caspian and its agrarian economy.[9]

The Caspian thus remained somewhat peripheral to sociopolitical life on the Iranian plateau for most of the period prior to the seventeenth century. Even in the semiformal nomenclature of the Safavid and Qajar eras, the Gilan province within the "Guarded Domains of Iran" (*mamālek-e maḥruseh-ye Iran*) was known as the "Frontier Abode" (*dār al-marz*), an indication of its peripheral place prior to the twentieth century. Yet marginality did not prevent the central Iranian state from conquering and reconquering Gilan and Mazandaran, first under the Safavids and subsequently under Nader Shah, and thereafter under the early Qajars. Procurement of silk and rice, among other agricultural products, served as prime motives for the Iranian presence in the Caspian region as far northwest as the Caucasian provinces. Even such health hazards as frequent ravages of malaria had limited impact on such ventures. Modern road construction in the late nineteenth century further incorporated the Caspian provinces into Iran proper, a process facilitated by the fact that the Qajar and the Pahlavi dynasties had both originated in Mazandaran. The growth of foreign trade through Caspian ports, moreover, helped to facilitate the region's inclusion into the Iranian state, at least before the rise of the Soviet Union and the ensuing Cold War. By the middle of the twentieth century, the growth of road and rail networks and a rigorous antimalaria campaign opened up even further the picturesque Caspian coasts to Iranians yearning to enjoy the lush resorts.[10]

By the ninth century, local dynasties from the Caspian region, first the Ziyarids (*Āl-e Ziyār*) and soon after the celebrated Buyids (*Āl-e Buyeh*), came to play a crucial part in northern Iran and beyond. The Buyids, in particular, acquired immense military and political power that stretched beyond western Iran to include Baghdad, the seat of the Abbasid caliphate. During the "Shi'ite Century," as some historians defined the era, the Abbasid caliphate was reduced to a virtual Buyid vassalage. The Buyid "king of kings" (*shāhanshāh*), a title they revived from the Sasanian era, largely relied on the Daylamite mercenaries from the mountainous region of Gilan province to subdue the Sunni-dominated caliphate of Baghdad and patronized instead the Shi'ite learning circles in southern Iraq and in Iran. Celebrated scientists and philosophers, such as Ibn Sina, also benefited from Buyid patronage. The religious affiliation of the Buyids, no doubt, was rooted in their Tabarestān origins, where Shi'ism has long persisted. Although the specific denomination of Buyid Shi'ism is not clearly identified, during their rule Ithna-'Ashari Shi'ite scholarship thrived in Baghdad, as well as in Rayy and in other Shi'ite centers of central Iran.[11]

As the center of Buyid power moved southward, the old Tabarestān preserved something of its autonomy. The agricultural wealth that was generated in the region seems to have attracted Viking traders and other northern European peoples to the Samanid Empire of Central Asia, based in Bukhara, as early as the eleventh century. Caches of Samanid silver coinage were found as far north as Sweden. The connection through the Caspian with northern Europe also attracted Volga Viking raiders of Russian origin who occasionally ransacked southern Caspian shores. Centered around the Volga River basin, these seasonal raids, now almost forgotten, caused havoc and hardship. They also set early precedents for the later Russian gravitation toward the warmer climate of the Caucasus that led eventually to a drive for the conquest of northern Iran.

Predictably, contacts with Russians and with the Nordic people, either because of the raids or trade, triggered some attention in the Persian sources. A rare tenth-century Persian geographical text, *Ḥodud al-'Ālam* (The Regions of the World) by an anonymous author, is one of several early accounts of the period that offers precious details about the Caspian littoral and its human geography. It is remarkable for its breadth of coverage, stretching from North Africa to the outer reaches of Eurasia. Relying on post-Sasanian geographical sources, *Ḥodud* is among the earliest to mention the "Russian prince" (*khāqān-e Rus*) among the rulers of the Nordic regions. Needless to add that here reference to the "Russian prince" precedes by at least three centuries the office of the Grand Duchy of Moscow. The author also offers a least complementary stereotyping of Russians, which no doubt reflects the fears and anxieties of the people of the south Caspian toward the northerners:

> This is a vast country, and the inhabitants are evil-tempered, intractable, arrogant-looking, quarrelsome, and warlike. They war with the all the infidels who live around them, and come out victorious. The king is called Rus-khaqan. It is a country extremely favoured by nature with regard to all the necessities (of life).[12]

Yet an adverse view of Russians does not follow in the text by fear of their expansionism. Prior to the modern era, Russians were considered distant enough so as not to disturb the tranquility of the Persianate world of the south.[13]

A Vibrant Cultural Space

Russia aside, the southern Caspian region retained a foreign, and even fearful, place in the Iranian imagination, as reflected in its ancient Persian mythological geography. In Ferdowsi's *Shāhnāmeh* (the Book of Kings), for instance, Mazandaran's natural beauty lures the Iranian ruler Kaykavus to march to that mysterious territory, whereby he and his army are captured and enchained on Mount Damavand by the White Demon (Div-e Sefid). Subsequently, it was Rostam, the greatest champion of the *Shāhnāmeh* and the guarantor of Iranian sovereignty, who embarked on a hazardous journey for the release of the Iranian king. Over the course of the Seven Trials (*haft khwān*), Rostam sought to complete the last and most arduous: the slaying of the White Demon, the master of Mazandaran, on Mount Damavand. In this highly celebrated deed of his long career, Rostam releases the reckless Kaykavus and his army and brings them back from the hazardous land of demons to the safety of their own territory.

Remarkably, that very Mount Damavand, which was the abode of the White Demon of Mazandaran and a fierce symbol of its autonomy, had been the birthplace of Fereydun, the charismatic founder of the Kayānid Dynasty in the *Shāhnāmeh*. He was nursed and raised by Barmāyeh, a colorful and caring cow, on the slopes of Damavand. Later on, once Fereydun defeats and captures Ẓaḥḥāk, the greatest villain of the *Shāhnāmeh*, the undying usurper, too, is taken to Mount Damavand and enchained there. We may note that Damavand's liminal locale, between the indomitable Mazandaran and the safety of Iran proper, makes it a focal point for messianic hopes and demonic fears.[14]

Yet the southern Caspian served as an incubator for powerful cultural trends that helped to shape Iran proper. As it turned out, it produced some of the most celebrated scholars of the early Islamic era. The historian, Qur'an commentator, and jurist Mohammad Jarir Tabari is but one example. He was born in the town of Amol, close to the Caspian coast, to a Mazandarani mother and an immigrant Arab father. It was in Baghdad of the ninth century that he produced his celebrated universal history, *Tārikh Rusul wa'l Muluk* (History of Prophets and Kings). Within the pages of this work, Tabari paid substantial attention to the ancient Iranian past. It may be argued that the level of detail now known about the Sasanian era would have been impossible to acquire had it not been for Tabari's textual knowledge of the period and his familiarity with remnants of the Sasanian legacy some three centuries earlier in his homeland.[15]

The relative isolation of the southern Caspian also was the birthplace of Tabari's contemporary, the influential 'Abd al-Qāder Gilāni (known to the Arabic sources as Jilāni) also known in Baghdad as 'Ajami (the Persian). Born in 1078 in the vicinity of Reżvāndeh (now Reżvānshahr) south of the city of Rudsar in coastal Gilan, at eighteen he moved to Baghdad. There, as a Sufi shaykh and a staunch Hanbalite, he preached a provocative and infidel-bashing version of Islam to a large following. By the time of his successors, Gilāni came to be recognized as the founder of the Qaderiyeh Sufi order, one of the largest and most influential in the Islamic world.[16]

The fourteenth century witnessed two mystical-messianic movements with ascetic undertones in two corners of the southern Caspian. In contrast to the Sunni Qaderiyeh order, however, both the Horufi movement and the splinter Noqtavi movement were of Shi'i origin and they were both noticeably antinomian. Their message of continued prophetic revelation, in the latter case with a historical awareness of cyclical renewal, also entailed political dissent, especially against the ruling Timurid of the Iranian world and later the Mamluk dynasties of Egypt and Syria. Fazlullah Astarābādi, the founder of the Horufi movement, was born and raised in Astarabad, in the southwestern corner of the Caspian (today's Gorgan), before embarking on lifelong travel around the Caucasus and then to Mashad, Isfahan, and Tabriz. He eventually returned to Shirvan and settled in Baku. The success of his movement among the people of the region predictably brought against him a charge of heresy by the pro-Timurid ulama of Samarqand and Tabriz, and he was executed by the order of Mirānshāh, Timur's son, in 1394.

Fazlullah's claim that his divine incarnation surpassed Islamic prophethood, which was the core of his death sentence, involved sacred dreams and their imaginative interpretation. Also central to his teaching was a system of numerology based on letters of the Persian alphabet (*ḥoruf*), hence the movement's name. The magical values assigned to letters revealed an existential value both in the human microcosm as well as the universal macrocosm. Sacred letters, in Fazlullah's estimation, thus constituted a divine text through which the hidden essences of humanity, both good and evil, were to be divulged. Remarkably, Fazlullah wrote his seminal work, the greater *Jāvidān-nāmeh*, in his native Astarābādi Persian dialect, an indication that his early followers were mainly recruited from his birthplace and the vicinity around the Caspian coast. That he settled in Baku, presumably under the protection of the local Shirvanshahi dynasty, may also explain a distinct sense of Persian awareness that is intertwined with the movement's message. He furthermore may have secured the loyalty of certain elements from among the Ahl-e Ḥaqq (People of the Truth) scattered along the southern Caucasus, northern Azerbaijan, and southern Caspian. The Horufis' self-assumed nomenclature, the "Truthful Dervishes" (*Darvishān-e Rāstguyi*), may indeed indicate an affinity with the rustic communities of the Ahl-e Ḥaqq, which though originally from greater Kurdistan, came to play a seminal role in shaping the socioreligious movements of the Caspian basin from the Horufis to the Safavid and later. As in similar antinomian movements, Fazlullah stressed truthfulness to his dervish followers, a theme already evident in the Caucasus, as for example in the work of the twelfth-century Persian poet Nezāmi of Ganjeh.[17]

After Fazlullah's death, his daughters and sons, his successor, and a large number of his followers fell victim to the Timurids' oppression. They were executed or otherwise perished in the early ravages of the Black Death. By contrast, the Horufi movement survived in pre-Ottoman Anatolia and, shortly thereafter, within the influential Bektashi Sufi order and as far west as in Ottoman Rumelia. Yet early Horufis continued to be persecuted. Among the victims was the celebrated Perso-Turkish poet 'Emād al-Din Nasimi, who was executed on the charge of heresy in 1419 by the order of the Mamluk ruler of Aleppo.[18]

Maḥmud Pasikhāni (d. ca. 1428), formerly a disciple of Fazlullah, was born and raised in the village of Pasikhan in the vicinity of Rasht, today the provincial capital of Gilan. His Noqtavi movement was even more striking in its supra-Islamic teachings than Horufism. Toward the end of his life, he resided at some unspecified location on the banks of the River Aras north of Tabriz. There, in a manner similar to Fazlullah, he attracted followers throughout the western Caspian, stretching from Kurdistan to northern Azerbaijan and the southern Caucasus. His "pointist" doctrine (i.e., *noqtavi* from the word *noqteh*: point) revolved around a remarkable mystico-materialist concept that considered earth, and not the heavens, as the original source of existence and specifically as the point of prophetic ascent and ultimate return. This cycle of creation and salvation was built on an elaborate cabalistic system of points, as building blocks of letters, that shaped words in the book of creation. Maḥmud's self-assumed mission, with a messianic undertone, was to rescue prophethood, and by implication the whole of humanity, from the tyranny of the heavens and return it back to its earthly origin. In Maḥmud's view this would complete a metahistorical cycle that started with the earthly Adam and comes to its fruition in Maḥmud's own prophetic mission. Furthermore, he viewed his mission as the end of the Arabian Islamic cycle and the start of the Persian (*'ajam*) cycle, implying, no doubt, proto-nationalist sentiments.[19]

Remarkably, both the Horufi and the Noqtavi movements evolved in the Caspian domain not far from the Safavid movement, the third and historically the most influential of the messianic movements of late Islamic medieval times. Both Fazlullah and Pasikhāni had their headquarters not far from Ardabil where their near-contemporary, the thirteenth-century Ṣafi al-Din Ardabili, the influential founder of the Safavi Sufi order, was based. He was the son-in-law and disciple of another celebrated Sufi of Gilan, Shaykh Zāhed Gilāni, through whom Shaykh Safi traced the chain of his Sufi authority.

At the turn of the sixteenth century, coinciding with the turn of the ninth Islamic century, Ismaʿil I, the founder of the Safavid dynasty, first uttered his claims to temporal power and divine reincarnation in the Caspian city of Lahijan, east of River Sefidrud. There he was kept in hiding by a group of devotees known as the "Elders of Lahijan" (*Pirān-e Lāhijān*). Like the Horufis and the Noqtavis, the Safavids under the rule of Ismaʿil and his successors gravitated from their south Caspian base to the interiors of Iran, as well as to the cities of the South Caucasus. Yet, in contrast to earlier movements, the Safavid ruler and his militant devotees embarked on a ferocious empire-building enterprise that within a decade came to control a vast territory from eastern Anatolia and the Caucasus to the outer reaches of Khorasan. It has been argued, convincingly, that the Safavi order had its origins in the Ahl-e Ḥaqq communities of western Iran, and even their recruiting of Qizilbash devotees seems, to some extent, to have relied on Ahl-e Ḥaqq loyalties. The rise of the Safavid power was the outcome of more than a century of transformation of a Sufi order first from Sunni into Shiʻi Islam and then into a militant messianic movement with expansionist ambitions. Ismaʻil's forefathers, and his brother, were victims of an enterprise that relied on an army of fervent devotees in the Caspian and Anatolian peripheries to conquer the Iranian center. Under the banner of an ideological empire with Perso-Shiʻi features, Safavids materialized the long-fermenting potentials in the Caspian periphery. These were forces of unification that earlier on manifested themselves, though with much lesser intensity, in the Horufis, the Noqtavis, and in similar messianic trends. The Marʻashi movement of the Gilan province in the latter half of the fourteenth century and the contemporary Sarbedāri movement of northern Khorasan shared with the Horufis and the Noqtavis some Shiʻi messianic impulses that only came to fruition with the rise of the Safavids a century later.[20]

That throughout the late medieval and early modern times the south Caspian was a breeding ground for antinomian movements further confirms the frontier nature of the region. The absence of overt political power, especially during and after the Ilkhanid era, and implicit support for Persian culture by local dynasties of the southern Caucasus, such as the Shirvanshahis, may have been a boost for heterodoxies, especially in the Ahl-e Ḥaqq surroundings. Even after Gilan was conquered in 1592 under ʻAbbas I and incorporated into the Safavid Empire, primarily for silk cultivation, the frontier nature of the land was not entirely lost. As early as the time of ʻAbbas's successor, Shah Safi (r. 1629–42), the Marʻashi revolt let by Gharib Shah Gilāni was one of several revolts the Safavids encountered in the province. That various communities of Georgians, Armenians, Circassians, and other peoples of the Caucasus were forcibly settled in the Gilan by ʻAbbas I and his successors no doubt added to its ethno-cultural diversity, but could have also contributed to the province's peripheral resistance to central authority. Even after the reassertion of the Qajar central authority in the late eighteenth century, there ensued several episodes not only of antistate resistance but anticlerical revolts.

For Slaves and Silk

The northern Iranian frontier space, from eastern Anatolia to southern Central Asia, was home to several autonomous dynasties with prosperous economies and a shared Persianate culture. But centers like Ganjeh, *Iravān* (Yerevan), and Baku were coveted by Islamic empires all through the medieval and early modern times. By the sixteenth century, the region once more was the target of conquest, yet it took the Safavids a full century before they could stabilize their hold over the Caspian provinces. From the time of Isma'il I to 'Abbas I (1501-88), raids on prosperous Georgia and Circassia took precedence over Gilan in part because the Christian Caucasus offered a "legitimate" target under the aegis of Islamic crusade (*ghaza*) for taking white slaves, female and male. The Caucasus also offered chances for plunder, not only of towns and villages but of churches, monasteries, and other religious sites.

In this respect, the Safavids were only matched by their Ottoman neighbors who ravaged the western part of the Caucasus with similar pretexts and objectives. Female slaves from Gorjestān (Georgia) and the adjacent Abkhazia and Circassia populated the harems of the Safavid and Ottoman royalty and the nobility. The captured male stock, however, provided the necessary fighting force in the Safavid slave (*gholām*) army. Up to the early eighteenth century, men of the Caucasian Christian regions also comprised the military elite of Egypt, Syria, and Iraq under the general rubric of Mamluk (pl. *mamālik*, those who are owned, i.e., slaves). Likewise the *gholām* army of the Safavid Empire, which was first introduced under Tahmasb (r. 1524-76) and then expanded under 'Abbas I, was replenished by the arrival of new stocks from the Caucasus. It was this very slave element that wrecked the supremacy of the quarreling Qizilbash military elite, and subsequently allowed the quelling of the Uzbek raids in Khorasan, the recapture of the western Safavid provinces from the Ottomans, the repelling of the Portuguese from the northern shores of the Persian Gulf, the reconquest of Gilan province in 1592, and the buttressing of an otherwise crumbling empire.

The Caspian enterprise of the Safavid era also involved the monopolization of silk cultivation and its export in the southern Caucasus and in Gilan. Under 'Abbas's supervision, the developing silk production of Gilan poured enormous revenues into the state coffers. A precious commodity in high demand, especially in Europe, silk was exported under 'Abbas I and his successors mostly through the English and Dutch East India Companies via the Persian Gulf. The success of the southern trade through the Indian Ocean came in the place of largely unsuccessful attempts by Europeans to access the Persian and Caucasian markets through a northern trading route via the Baltics and the Volga River. It may be argued that in the long run the difficulties in utilizing the northern route, because of the frozen sea and harsh climate in the northern Caspian, gave the southern route a greater advantage that contributed to the decline of the Caspian hub over time. This is all the more striking given that the northern route, if it ever had become fully operational, provided a much shorter distance between the Caspian silk-producing regions and western European markets.[21]

Becoming a "Russian Lake"

Aside from the Baltics or the preference of the British and the Dutch East India Companies for the Persian Gulf route, access to Europe was at the mercy of the Ottomans. They controlled such eastern Mediterranean entrepôts as Aleppo and imposed, for all intents and purposes, a fairly effective trade embargo on the Persian exports. Alternatively, access to northern Europe became increasingly conditioned by Russia, which loomed large in the northern Caspian and along the northern Black Sea littoral. Russian advances in Transcaucasia, which began with invasion of Circassia in 1763 and continued throughout the late eighteenth and early nineteenth centuries, underscored the severity of Russian primacy and, so far as the Safavids were concerned, surpassed Ottoman coercion. The genocidal treatment of the Circassians that involved extensive massacres or mass exile of the population from its homeland, under the rubric of pacification, was an ominous lesson to endogenous peoples of the Caucasus and to the neighboring Safavids and their successors throughout the eighteenth century.[22]

The conquest of Circassia, which linked the northern Caucasus to the shores of the Black Sea, initiated in effect a much larger project of southern Russian expansion. Over the span of one century from the annexation of Circassia, Russia had conquered as far southwest as the Crimean peninsula on the northern shores of the Black Sea, the entire Caucasian provinces of the south Caspian, and soon after the whole of the Central Asian khanates on the eastern flank of the Caspian. The famous Treaty of Küçük Kaynarca (1774) with the Ottomans, the Golestan (1813) and Turkmenchay (1828) Treaties with Qajar Iran, and the Treaty of Edirne (1829) with the Ottomans showed the Russian drive for access to the temperate climate in the south as well as to these highly fertile regions.²³ The Russian advance in effect turned the Caspian Sea, if not its southern coasts, into a liability for the Iranians. Over the course of the eighteenth and early nineteenth centuries successive Iranian governments, all land-bound, had to fend off a menace from the sea, whether the nomadic raids of the Cossacks of the eastern Caspian coasts or the much larger territorial ambitions of the Russian Empires.

Compared to the Mediterranean basin, whereby maritime trade nurtured the exchange of goods, material culture, and ideas, the Caspian basin suffered from stark disadvantages. The often-tumultuous crossing and paucity of deep harbors contributed to the absence of even a modicum of a merchant fleet, let alone a naval force, on the southern Caspian shores. Naval supremacy thus remained entirely a Russian monopoly. By contrast, Mediterranean naval supremacy seldom rested with one power, be it the Ottoman Empire, Habsburg Spain, or Tudor England. Moreover, a dislike for seafaring, almost a cultural thalassophobia, discouraged Iranians from venturing into the Caspian, beyond fishing along the coastal waters. Hesitancy to navigate the length of the Caspian proved to be a serious impediment to Iran's imperial or commercial maritime expansion, an impediment aggravated by the absence of a shipbuilding tradition.

The uninhabitability of the eastern shores of the Caspian was another impediment to the emergence of an integrated Caspian hub. The eastern shores were even less hospitable than the Caspian Sea's often stormy waters. As late as the twentieth century, short of humble fishing villages, there were no notable permanent settlements between the Gulf of Balkan (now Turkmenbashi Gulf in Turkmenistan) and the Gulf of Astarabad (today's Gulf of Gorgan) on the southeast corner of the Iranian coast. A barren extension of the Karakum Desert, the empty lowlands of the eastern Caspian stretch all the way to the interiors of Central Asia. Ashgabat, some five hundred kilometers inland to the east, was the closest center to these shores. Moreover, settlements across the eastern Iranian coasts were not safe from Cossack warlords scattered along the northern Caspian steppes. As early as 1667, Cossack raiders pillaged settlements on Iranian shores or caused havoc eastward in the Central Asian khanates of Kokand, Khiva, and Bukhara.²⁴

By the beginning of the eighteenth century, the Cossacks were brought under Russian control. Yet shortly afterward in 1722, Russia under Peter the Great, taking advantage of the downfall of the Safavid

Empire and the ensuing chaos in its provinces, dispatched an expeditionary force to the Caucasus and occupied the Caspian shores of Azerbaijan (known as Aran, with Baku as its capital), and shortly thereafter marched southward to the Gilan province. The occupation lasted an entire decade before ending in a disastrous withdrawal, largely because of the ravages of malaria.[25]

The emerging security and relative calm that ensued nevertheless encouraged further contacts between the northern and the southern Caspian. Traders and diplomats were active not only along the shores of the Caucasus but across the Caspian north–south axis between Astrakhan, the principle port on the Volga's delta, and ports of Baku, Anzali, and Astarabad. By the middle of the eighteenth century, Iranian trade with Russia visibly thrived, particularly following the conclusion of two peace treaties between Iran and Russia: the 1732 Treaty of Rasht and the 1735 Treaty of Ganjeh. The latter treaty returned the northern Iranian provinces of Gilan, Mazandaran, and Astarabad, then under nominal Russian control, to Iran thanks to the rising fortune of then Nader-Qoli Khan Afshar (later Nader Shah) in exchange for Russian possession of all the territories north of the Kura River in the Caucasus. This indeed was Russia's first permanent territorial gain in the south Caspian.

Nader Shah Afshar (r. 1736–47), witnessing the Russian naval fleet on the Caspian shores, was persuaded to build his own navy not only to counter the Russians but also to support his Transcaucasian campaigns in Dagestan. Thanks to his military acumen, a certain Captain John Elton, an English naval officer, inventor, and shipbuilder who was in Nader's service, built a small Caspian fleet in 1743 with lumber from the forests of Gilan. Irked by the very idea of an Iranian navy, the Russian government, backed by the Russia Company (formerly the Muscovy Trade Company, the first British public company of its kind to be established in London in 1555), opposed the Iranian initiative, and Elton in particular for sharing his naval know-how with the Iranian conqueror. Nader's ambition to build a fleet in the Persian Gulf nevertheless soon took precedence over the Caspian initiative.[26]

Despite offers and threats to lure him to the side of the Russia Company, Elton remained in Iran even after the Afsharid sovereign's assassination in 1747. In the ensuing intense race for power, he came to support Moḥammad Ḥasan Khan Qajar, the powerful claimant to the throne who was based in Mazandaran. Captured by the governor of Rasht, who in the chaotic interregnum after Nader sought to rule autonomously over Gilan, the independent-minded English seaman was murdered in Rasht by the governor, perhaps at the instigation of the Russia Company. Whether this was a joint intrigue of the Russians and the English, after Elton's murder no further effort was made by contenders to the Iranian throne, least of all the Qajars, to develop a Caspian fleet, a reaffirmation of the land-based nature of Iran's imperial enterprise.[27]

Some four decades later, after the demise of the Zands in southern Iran, it was the revenue from this Caspian trade that contributed to the rise of Qajar power in its base in Mazandaran province. Āqā Moḥammad Khan Qajar (later Aqa Mohammad Shah, r. 1786-97), the founder of the Qajar dynasty (1786-1925), at least partially relied on the revenue levied on merchants active in the Russian trade of the Caspian to quell rivals within his own tribe and outside, and to consolidate his power base in Gilan and subsequently over the central Iranian plateau. This was also the first instance in the post-Safavid era that Russian diplomatic intervention, still at the consular level, came to play a part in shaping Qajar Iran. It is important to note that Āqā Moḥammad Khan was one of several Caspian-based local rulers of the period to benefit from the maritime trade with Russia. Yet, it was the Qajar khan who was able to buy off support and allegiance by organizing raids on economic centers in Gilan, where the Russian consulate was based. Distributing Russian trade revenues among his Turkmen troops and other nomadic supporters, he consolidated his power in the north.[28]

By the early nineteenth century, Russian naval supremacy over the Caspian was an unchallenged reality, as was confirmed by article 8 of the 1828 Treaty of Turkmenchay at the end of the second round of Russo-Persian Wars (1826-28). This offered Russia sizable strategic and trade advantages and reduced the chances for a fair commercial exchange with Iran, the only area that mattered to the Iranian side. Of course, the volume of the Caspian import-export trade further increased both with Russia and with the annexed Caucasian provinces lost to Iran. Yet, one way or another, the imperial Russian shadow endured almost to the end of the twentieth century and the collapse of the Soviet Union. The Cold War only added a new layer of self-imposed restrictions and isolation on the Caspian littoral.

Loss of the famed "seventeen Caucasian provinces" was enormous and immediate for Qajar Iran. For one, Iran lost some of the most fertile and agriculturally rich provinces of the Guarded Domains of Persia, and with them a huge drop in the state revenue. In the eyes of its own subjects and in the eyes of European observers, the loss of prestige, especially after 1828, was complemented with the payment of an enormous war reparation in gold, which in effect wiped out the Qajar coffers and bankrupted the state for decades to come (or perhaps to the very end of the Qajar rule). Imposition of a capitulatory regime on Iran under the rubric of the most favored nations and the conclusion of a supplementary trade treaty with Russia, with obvious legal and commercial disadvantages for the vanquished state, added to the ordeal.[29]

As such, the Iranian lamenting of the "loss of navigation rights" in the Caspian after the Turkmenchay Treaty seems rather unrealistic, given the enormity of losses noted above. Even in the latter half of the twentieth century Iran barely maintained a sizable fleet in the north. One can only recall the depth of Naser al-Din Shah's horror aboard a Russian vessel when, on his way back from his European tour of 1873, he experienced a severe storm close to Anzali harbor. That this was serious enough to slip onto the pages of his otherwise carefully edited journal is noteworthy.[30]

Granting economic concessions to Russian individuals and firms was another harsh reality embedded in the Turkmenchay Treaty whereby Iran had to sustain, especially in the late nineteenth century, a number of burdensome concessions. At the time the impact on the local economy of the southern Caspian was probably negligible even though the damage to forestry resources proved to be significant. In 1888 a concession for fisheries in the waters of the southern Caspian, which included the export of Iranian beluga for its famed caviar, was granted to the Russian subject Stepan Lianozov. Pressure by the Russian government on the Qajar monarch Naser al-Din Shah only paid off after the shah succumbed in the same year to British pressure to grant a concession for navigation of the Karun River in the Iranian southwest. A decade later, in 1899, another concession was granted to the Koussis brothers, Greek subjects of the Russian Empire who for some years were active in the export of Iranian timber. The exploitation of the Mazandaran forests was one of the many concessions that Russia and Russian subjects acquired between 1888 and 1905 for banking, railroad construction, and building carriage roads. The Qajar state had little choice but to condone these requests. Seeking access to Mazandaran timber, the British, too, relied on diplomatic pressure and had no scruples bribing Qajar officials or local notables. The initial British success in gaining access to these northern resources nevertheless triggered an imperial rivalry in which the Russians managed to prevail.[31]

Russian concessions brought no major industrial breakthrough in the local economy of the region but proved to be a harbinger of environmental harm. Export trade from the ports of Anzali in Gilan and Bārforush in Mazandaran to some degree helped revitalize the region's local economies. The Russian near-monopoly of Caspian commerce and commercial navigation was only partially offset by limited Iranian exports. In addition to timber these included luxury textiles, cotton, dried fruits, and carpets in exchange for sugar, textiles, manufactured goods, and soon kerosine oil from the refineries of Baku. Greater Russian industrialization in the latter half of the nineteenth century further increased the export of Russian manufactured goods, a successful competitor to the British and European trade of the Black Sea port of Trabzon or the Persian Gulf route. By the 1920s, the bustling Caspian trade came to a standstill because of the Bolshevik Revolution, witnessing near complete standstill after the Second World War.[32]

Irrespective of the twentieth-century Soviet isolation, it may be argued that the Russian conquest of the Caucasus in the nineteenth century engendered visible economic prosperity for the region, better communication, population growth, and general improvement of the government institutions, especially in urban centers such as Tbilisi (Tiflis), Baku, Ganjeh, Shamakhi, Yerevan, and Lankaran. By the 1880s the completion of the Russian conquest of southern Central Asia also triggered new economic and social vitality across the former khanates.

The Caucasian connection in the latter part of the nineteenth century also allowed greater commercial access to European markets for northern Iranian urban centers such as Tabriz and Rasht. Slightly later, contact with Europe through such centers as Tbilisi and Baku allowed constitutional and then socialist revolutionary ideas to take root in northern Iran. Judging by a sizable movement of Iranian emigrants to the Caucasus for trade, education, and as cheap labor in the oilfields of Baku, and their subsequent return to the towns and villages of Iran, the transformative effect of such a trend cannot be overstated. From the 1880s onward, Ashgabat, formerly a minor trading post north of the ancient city of Marv on the northeastern Iranian border, attracted a sizable Iranian population mostly from towns and villages of eastern Iran. A showcase for the Russian modernization project, Ashgabat appealed to Iranian émigrés for reasons of trade and business, but also for its promise of a life free from religious persecution.[33]

It may be argued that the Russian thrust toward the southern Caspian was a foregone conclusion given Russia's military and technological superiority, its efficient methods of imperial domination, and its ability to draw upon the loyalties of Armenians and Georgians of the Caucasus to rule over the Muslim majority. Fueled by ethnic nationalisms, and a naïve sense of comradery with their Russian overlords, most elites within these Christian communities opted for Russian rather than Iranian sovereignty, a decision some of them came to regret once they tasted the rough side of Russian racial superiority. All in all, beginning in the eighteenth century it seemed destined that the Caspian Sea, insofar as its navigation allowed, would become a Russian monopoly, or as it somewhat sarcastically came to be known, "a Russian lake."

Revolution in the Forest

By the early twentieth century and the rise of revolutionary movements worldwide, the Caucasian cities of Tbilisi and Baku served as breeding grounds for radical ideologies, often with socialist undertones, and came to play a crucial part in the revolutionary trends of northern Iran. The ties between the revolutionaries on two sides of a porous border continued into the second decade of the twentieth century.

Revolutionary trends in northern Iran were not without precedent. Aside from the aforementioned heterodoxies of late medieval times, and no doubt with a degree of continuity, Iran of the mid-nineteenth century witnessed the Bābi movement. For at least a decade, the Bābi movement threatened the very stability of the Qajar state, and even more so the Shi'i religious establishment. The makeshift fortress of Shaykh Ṭabarsi, deep in the forests of Mazandaran south of Aliabad (today's Qā'em-shahr), was the site of stiff Bābi resistance in 1848-49 whereby some three hundred followers of Sayyid 'Ali Moḥammad Shirāzi, known as the Bāb, organized a determined resistance against the local government, the supporters of the local clergy, and the growing body of Qajar forces that was dispatched to the province. Displaying a remarkable degree of self-sacrifice, the majority of the Bābis were killed in skirmishes or otherwise were executed after their surrender.

The Ṭabarsi episode, though not the largest among the three major Bābi revolts that occurred almost simultaneously in different parts of Iran, may be considered as the most representative of the messianic spirit that shaped the Bābi movement. Ṭabarsi may be seen as the climax of a process that was in the making for some half a century, since the shaping of the Shaykhi movement, and in a more pronounced fashion since the Bāb's proclamation in 1844 as being the "gate" (the *bāb*) to the expected Shi'i savior (the Mahdi). The Ṭabarsi fighters brought together followers from all walks of life and with a notably wide geographical distribution. Among them were low- and middle-rank clergy, low- and middle-rank merchants and artisans, government functionaries, small landowners, and peasants. Initially they were demanding the release of the Bāb, who by the order of the Qajar state was incarcerated in the fortress of Maku, in the northwesternmost part of the Azerbaijan frontier (and some sixty miles west of Nakhichevan, in the South Caucasus in the present-day Republic of Azerbaijan).

As the Ṭabarsi resistance became more organized, and at the same time more desperate, the Bābis came to view their struggle as an apocalyptic jihad, themselves as a communistic body devoid of private property, and two of their leaders as messianic Mahdis. As they saw it, they were destined to fight and die on behalf of their incarcerated Mahdi, who now proclaimed to be a post-Islamic prophet. After a year of resistance, exhausted and disillusioned, the Ṭabarsi fighters, who defined themselves as the "remnants of the sword," surrendered to the Qajar military chief, and those who refused to repent were massacred.[34]

The Ṭabarsi episode was remarkable not only because it resonated with earlier antinomian movements in the south Caspian, but also because it represented nationwide participation. In later decades of the nineteenth century the Bābis, and later the Baha'is, were poised to become the most audible voices of dissent in Iran's socioreligious arena. In some respects they anticipated the Constitutional Revolution and served as its radical prototype. Moreover, by using the forest as a natural cover against the urban-based umbrages of the government and the Shi'i authorities, they also predicted the Jangal Movement six decades later.

Over the course of the Constitutional Revolution (1905–11), and later in the Jangal Movement (ca. 1915–21), we again witness the Caspian factor, and especially the Caucasian-Azerbaijan connection. In the early stages of the revolution, some affluent Iranian expatriates in Baku who had made their fortunes in Baku and Tbilisi were willing to support compatriots such as Hassan Taqizadeh, the first deputy from Tabriz to the newly founded Iranian Constitutional Assembly (Majles). One of the most influential members of the First Majles, Taqizadeh was originally from Nakhichevan, but was educated in Tabriz and exposed to liberal ideas in Beirut and Cairo.

Later on, the conclusion of the notorious 1907 Anglo-Russian Agreement, which envisioned two "zones of influence" in Iran for the old rivals-turned-allies, further highlighted the place of the Caucasus in defying the agreement's ominous consequences. The Russian-assisted coup of July 1908, and the bombardment of the Iranian Majles and the ensuing civil war, triggered a movement of resistance in Tabriz, and soon after in Rasht, that relied on Caucasian support. The pro-constitutional fighters in Tabriz not only benefitted from the support of the Shaykhi urban quarters but were backed by a Caucasian contingent of Armenian, Georgian, and Muslim fighters, numbering at least three hundred. They were mostly from Tbilisi, then a hotbed of Armenian nationalism and anti-Russian dissidents. That Tsar Nicholas II suppressed the 1905 Russian Revolution had the secondary effect of driving off these fighters south of the border to Tabriz and Rasht. Fighting side by side with their Iranian allies, these fighters were mostly backed by the Dashnak Party of Tbilisi, whose support for Iranian constitutionalists was colored by their anti-Ottoman sentiments, especially in the light of the massacres a decade earlier of the Armenians at the hands of the Ottoman *Hamidiye* regiments. Most members of the Caucasian contingent stayed behind even after the conquest of Tehran in August 1909, only to be driven out during the ensuing power struggle in the Iranian capital. Some perished and others returned, disillusioned, to their homelands.

Of those who stayed behind, one was the influential chief of the Tehran police, Yeprem Khan, who came to play a crucial part in the future survival of the constitutional order. His eventful life story, from early adventures in his birthplace, Ganjeh, to confrontations with the Ottomans and Russians, and to his tragic death in Kermanshah fighting Qajar royalists, demonstrates shared political ideas and sentiments that tied the Caucasus to northern Iran.[35]

The rise of the Jangal Movement during the WWI era and after, and its later conversion into a revolutionary socialist movement, further displayed the radical Caucasian sway. Its leading figure, Mirza Kuchek Khan, originally a student in the Shiʻi madrasas of Rasht and Qazvin, joined the constitutionalists and fought in Rasht during the civil war. Later on, while fighting alongside Yeprem Khan in the 1911 Battle of Gomishtappeh (north of Astarabad) against the Russian-instigated counterrevolutionary force aiming to restore Mohammad ʻAli Shah to power, he was injured and sent off as a captive to Baku. While recovering, he came into contact with members of the Social Democratic Party there, and upon his surreptitious return to Rasht, while under Russian surveillance, he was recruited by the Society of Islamic Unity, the external arm of the Young Turks' pan-Islamic propaganda organ.

With its support, Kuchek set about to organize the Jangal Movement in his homeland in the forests of Fuman, on the southwest corner of the Caspian. Though backed by the Islamic Society and echoing their pan-Islamic objectives, he seemed to have remained sympathetic to the Social Democrats of Baku.

The prospects of a new offensive by forces of the Tehran government, backed by the British Norperforce (North Persian Force), forced the inundated Kuchek Khan to surrender the leadership of the Jangal to pro-Bolshevik elements. It is therefore not surprising that after 1917 and the demise of the Young Turks, the desperate Jangal Movement welcomed such socialist radicals as Ehsān-Allah Khan Dustdār and Ḥaydar Khan 'Amu-Oghlu Tāriverdi. Ehsān-Allah Khan had been born in Mazandaran and participated in the civil war of 1908-9 on the side of the constitutionalists. Thereafter he cofounded a clandestine terrorist group in Tehran before joining the Jangal. As a Bolshevik enabler, Ehsān-Allah was in cahoots with Ḥaydar Khan, an electrical engineer trained in Tbilisi, whose checkered record of sabotage and assassination brought much harm to the Constitutional Revolution.

The Russian Bolsheviks' landing in Anzali in February 1920 proved to be a game changer, strengthening the Jangal's radical contingent at the expense of the moderates. The ephemeral Soviet Socialist Republic of Iran (also known as the Socialist Republic of Gilan) was declared in 1920, a hasty replica of the yet embryonic Soviet Union. Together Ehsān-Allah and Ḥaydar Khan managed to bring ruination to what was left of the Jangal Movement by making it subservient to Bolshevik wishes. Ḥaydar Khan was ambushed and killed in 1921 while trying to reconcile the quarreling wings of the Jangal. Soon after, Kuchek Khan perished in the mountains of Talesh in the western Caspian while fleeing the advancing Iranian troops under Reżā Khan (later Reżā Shah Pahlavi). Ehsān-Allah managed to escape with the evacuating Bolsheviks to Baku, where he resided until 1933. He perished in one of Stalin's purges.[36]

The tragic ends of Yeprem Khan, Ḥaydar Khan, Kuchek Khan, and Ehsān-Allah Khan, among other events, were indicative of the demise of the Caucasian symbiosis with the south Caspian. For years, this symbiosis had been facilitated, among other channels, by migration from Iranian Azerbaijan to the oil fields of Baku at the turn of the twentieth century. Coming to terms with the centralizing Reżā Khan Pahlavi's government in Tehran ensured the end of the region's historic isolation.[37]

For most of its history, the ancient Tabarestān, on the southern shores of the Caspian, remained a semiautonomous region on the Iranian periphery. Its natural setting—lush vegetation and dense forests bordered by the Caspian Sea on one side and by the Alborz range on the other—defined its isolated pockets of ethnicity and inherent rustic religion. The south Caspian's geography allowed some commonalities with its northwestern Caucasian neighbor, but also caused contentious interactions. The South Caucasus, with its distinct ethnoreligious diversity (Georgian, Armenian, Azari, and Kurds, among others), held an elusive political loyalty toward the Iranian center. Like Tabarestān, it also preserved a distinct Persian (and Persianate) culture.

Perhaps the most significant outburst of Tabarestān's political expansion in premodern times was the rise of the Buyid dynasty and its control of central Islamic lands from the middle of the ninth to the middle of the tenth century, an apogee in the classical Islamic period. Once in power, they not only salvaged for themselves the title of "king of kings" (*shāhanshāh*) from the memories of the Sasanian past, but also patronized a brand of Shi'ism indigenous to their homeland. Given its political, military, and cultural sway over the Abbasid caliphate for a whole century, it is not an exaggeration to state that the Buyid Empire was the most significant release of the south Caspian peripheral energies in the early Islamic era.

For the period prior to the early modern era, the south Caspian also preserved its own cultural autonomy. As an intermediary space distinct from the Iranian interior, it offered fertile ground for alternative cultures, often with antinomian features that survived until the modern era. The southern coastal provinces had limited access to the Caucasus via maritime trade. Most, if not all, exchanges with the prosperous eastern Caucasus flowed through the Azerbaijan overland routes. The local dynasties of the Caucasus were strongholds of Iranian culture and often tolerated counter-Sharia trends. The heterodox communities such as the Ahl-e Ḥaqq, stretching from the Caucasus to Kurdistan, also offered fertile ground for messianic movements, with lasting impacts on the whole region. The Safavid movement is a case in point. The messianic instincts that led to the rise of the Safavid Empire may be seen as the second example of the peripheral energy of the south Caspian taking control of the center. With a greater vehemence than even the Buyids, the Safavids' adherence to Shi'ism transformed the Iranian interior.

Even the rise of imperial Russia in early modern times, and its subsequent naval presence in the Caspian, did not entirely arrest the empire-building potential of the south Caspian provinces. Its lasting impact on the trade and diplomacy of the region gradually shifted the power equilibrium in favor of Russia. Russian maritime trade brought a new dynamism to the Caspian that by the late eighteenth century exerted visible influence over Iran's post-Safavid destiny. The rise of Āqā Moḥammad Khan Qajar, whose base was in the southeastern corner of the Caspian, no doubt benefited from Russian presence. Moreover, at least from the early nineteenth century and the annexation of the Caucasus, Russia came to play an important, often intrusive, part in Iran's domestic politics and foreign relations.

Russia also served as a conduit for introducing aspects of modernity to Iran, whether through institutions, commodities, or ideologies. Modernity, furthermore, brought the Caspian provinces of Iran out of isolation and incorporated them into a national Iranian narrative. Nevertheless, relations with these provinces remained secondary to those with Azerbaijan, and especially Tabriz, since contact with Caucasian centers was always overland rather than by sea. The aversion to long-distance navigation in the Caspian remained an inveterate Iranian handicap. Once imperial Russia reached the southern shores, it became abundantly clear to the Qajars that control over the Caucasus, let alone over Central Asia, could not be maintained. The two rounds of Russo-Persian Wars brought the message home (as did the two Herat campaigns against British naval power in the Persian Gulf in 1837–38 and 1854–55). After the loss of the Caucasus, Qajar pragmatism prioritized sovereignty and territorial integrity of its central provinces, and avoided conflict with its formidable imperial neighbor.

The Caucasian provinces were valuable for the high revenue they brought to Iranian state coffers. Yet the Iranian state's hold over these mostly hereditary governorates was fragile at best. The Qajar means and methods of governing were arcane, and despite some modernizing measures under ʿAbbās Mirza, it was difficult for the Qajar state to exert efficient control from afar. The shift of loyalties to the Russian crown, especially by Armenian and Georgian landlords, made it even harder for the Qajars to maintain a semblance of sovereignty. After the conquest, however, the Armenian and Georgian euphoria subsided, giving way to the sober realization that Persian relaxed overlordship was preferable to Russian heavy-handed taxation methods and almost colonial assertion. The Muslim population of the region, too, had condoned the growing social engineering executed through the juxtaposition of ethnic communities and sporadic Russification measures. Yet improved road and railroad communication, the introduction of modern educational and judicial institutions, and a greater degree of calm and security worked in favor of these newly annexed nationalities.

After the Russian conquest, the long-standing Iranian immigration to the Caucasus, as well as cultural exchanges and trade links with Iran, developed further, reaching their height by the end of the century. Cultural ties also evolved, as a number of Caucasian-Iranian hybrid intellectuals, among them Mirza Fatḥ-'Ali Ākhundzādeh with an Iranian émigré background, and 'Abd al-Raḥim Tālebov, originally from Tabriz, exerted some influence over the discourse of modernity among Iranian dissidents. By the turn of the twentieth century, another nonelite Iran-Caucasus symbiosis emerged once a large Iranian émigré labor force from rural Azerbaijan found employment in the oil fields of Baku. Mostly occupying menial jobs, they were less exposed to revolutionary trends in their new surroundings. By contrast, it was the Georgian and Armenian radicals of the Caucasus who brought a revolutionary message to Iranian constitutionalists in Tabriz and Rasht.

Yet even in the postconstitutional era, Iranians hardly warmed to the idea of asserting greater control over the Caspian or over the Caucasus. Rather, the overwhelming concern was the security and survival of Iran proper as an endangered buffer state. The politics of balancing off the two powers, Russia and Britain, continued to preoccupy Iranian nationalists well into the middle of the twentieth century. Even the rise of the Tudeh Party, the prevalence of the secessionist Democratic Party of Azerbaijan in 1945-46, Soviet demand for concession of south Caspian oilfields during the oil nationalization era, and the contingencies of the ensuing Cold War did not essentially change the south Caspian's geopolitics vis-à-vis its northern nemesis. Nor did the Soviet preponderance over the Caucasus region or over the Caspian Sea waters essentially change. What did noticeably change was greater incorporation of the south Caspian into the centralizing Iranian system, which was in contrast to the region's long history of sociopolitical and sociocultural liminality.

Notes

1. See Moshe Gammer, ed., *The Caspian Region*, vol. 1: *A Re-emerging Region* (London: Routledge, 2004), and Moshe Gammer, ed., *The Caspian Region*, vol. 2: *The Caucasus* (London: Routledge, 2004); L. S. Ruban, *Kaspiĭ—more problem* (Moscow: Nauka, 2003). Giuve Mirfendereski, *The Diplomatic History of the Caspian Sea: Theories, Diaries, and Other Stories* (Basingstoke: Palgrave, 2001) is an insightful survey of the political history of the region between the eighteenth

and twentieth centuries. One of the most well-known studies in Persian is Manouchehr Sotudeh's four-part historical geography: *Az Āstārā tā Astarābād*, 1st ed., 5 vols. (Tehran, 1349/1970); 4th ed., 10 vols. (Tehran, 1375–80/1996–2001). For a survey of literature on the Caspian, see Xavier de Planhol, "Caspian Sea i: Geography," *Encyclopaedia Iranica*, V/1, 48–50, https://iranicaonline.org/articles/caspian-sea-i and cited sources. As de Planhol points out, there is a substantial Russian literature on the Caspian covered in Giovanni M. degli Angiolelli, *A Narrative of Italian Travels in Persia in the Fifteenth and Sixteenth Centuries*, ed. C. Grey (London, 1873).

2. See for example F. Herzfeld, *The Persian Empire: Studies in Geography and Ethnography of the Ancient Near East* (Wiesbaden: F. Steiner, 1968), 320–22.

3. Aristotle, *Meteorologica*, text with English trans. by H. D. P. Lee (Cambridge, MA: Harvard University Press, 1952), book 2, chap. 1, 127–29; see also Multiple Authors, "Caspian Sea," *Encyclopaedia Iranica*, V/1, 48, https://www.iranicaonline.org/articles/caspian-sea-index.

4. See for example references to "Alexandrian wall" in the poetry of the celebrated Qajar statesman Abol-Qāsem Farahāni, Qā'im-Maqām II, in Abbas Amanat, "'Russian Intrusion into the Guarded Domain': Reflections of a Qajar Statesman on European Expansion," *Journal of the American Oriental Society* 113, no. 1 (1993): 36–55.

5. Relevant studies include Jebrael Nokandeh et al., "Linear Barriers of Northern Iran: The Great Wall of Gorgan and the Wall of Tammishe," *Iran* 44 (2006): 121–73; Hamid Omrani Rekavandi et al., "An Imperial Frontier of the Sasanian Empire: Further Fieldwork at the Great Wall of Gorgan," *Iran* 45 (2007): 95–136.

6. For nomenclature of the Caspian Sea, see de Planhol, "Caspian Sea i" and cited bibliography.

7. For inscriptions of Lājim Tower (Borj-e Lājim), see H. Reżā'i Bāghbidi, "Katibeha-ye Pahlavi-Kufi-ye Borj-e Lājim," *Nāmeh-ye Irān-e Bāstān* 4, no. 1 (1383/2004): 9–21.

8. See Michael L. Bates, "Arab-Sasanian Coins," *Encyclopaedia Iranica*, II/3, 225–29, https://iranicaonline.org/articles/arab-sasanian-coins and cited sources; Jamshedji M. Unvala, *Coins of Tabaristan and Some Sassanian Coins from Susa* (Paris, 1938); Malek Iradj Mochiri, *Étude de numismatique iranienne sous les Sassanides et Arabe-Sassanides*, vol. 2, rev. ed. (Louvain: Impremerie Orientaliste, 1983).

9. For the physical and ethnographic geography of the southern Caspian, see, for example, Marcel Bazin, "Gilan i. Geography and Ethnography," *Encyclopaedia Iranica*, X/6, 617–25, https://iranicaonline.org/articles/gilan-i-geography and cited sources and Habibullah Zanjani, "Gorgan i. Geography," *Encyclopaedia Iranica*, XI/2, 139–42, https://iranicaonline.org/articles/gorgan-i and cited sources. Both entries have numerous subentries that are also highly informative.

10. Extensive construction of resorts and private villas proved to be a curse, however, given inconsiderate usage of limited resources and environmental pollution of the coastal region and deep in the Caspian forests. Pillage of the Caspian forests for illegal export of timber, for crude methods of charcoal production, and for conversion into cultivated land were among other tragedies

that were sustained by the region particularly since the late decades of the twentieth century. See A. Beiranvand et al., "The Study of Causes and Factors of Illegal Logging in Caspian Forests," *Majaleh-ye Jangal-e Irān* 15, no. 2 (2023): 35-51.

11. For the Buyids, see for example Roy P. Mottahedeh, "The Abbasid Caliphate in Iran" (57-89) and H. Bosse, "Iran under the Buyids" (250-304), in *The Cambridge History of Iran*, vol. 4, *The Period from the Arab Invasion to the Saljuqs*, ed. R. N. Frye (Cambridge: Cambridge University Press, 1975).

12. "Discourse on Rus Country and Its Towns," in V. Minorsky, ed. and trans., *Hodud al-ʿĀlam* (London: Gibb Memorial, 1970), 159.

13. See also Rudi Matthee, "Facing a Rude and Barbarous Neighbor: Iranian Perceptions of Russia and Russians from the Safavids to the Qajars," in *Iran Facing Others: Identity Boundaries in a Historical Perspective*, ed. Abbas Amanat and Farzin Vejdani (New York: Palgrave Macmillan, 2012), 101-26; Oleg A. Nikonov, *Iran vo vneshnepoliticheskoĭ strategii Rossiĭskoĭ Imperii v XVIII v.* (Vladimir: Vladimir University Press, 2009); N. A. Sotavov, "The Circum-Caspian Areas within the Eurasian International Relationships at the Time of Peter the Great and Nadir-Shah Afshar," *Iran & the Caucasus* 5 (2001): 93-100; George A. Bournoutian, "The Role of the Armenians in the Russian Move into the South Caucasus," in *From the Kur to the Aras: A Military History of Russia's Move into the South Caucasus and the First Russo-Iranian War, 1801-1813* (Leiden: Brill, 2020), 237-48.

14. For Rostam's exploits in Mazandaran, see A. Ferdowsi, *The Shahnameh*, gen. ed. E. Yarshater, vol. 2, ed. J. Khaleqi-Motlaq (New York: Persian Heritage Foundation, 1366/1987), 478; English trans. Dick Davis, *Shahnameh: The Persian Book of Kings* (New York: Penguin Classics, 2007), 152-73. In the *Shahnameh*'s mythological geography, Mount Alborz (Alborz Kuh) at times is located elsewhere on the edge of the Land of Iran (Iranzamin). Yet in the story of the White Demon and, to an extent, in the story of Fereydun, it is in Mazandaran.

15. For Tabari's biography, see Franz Rosenthal, *The History of al-Tabari*, vol. 1, *General Introduction and from the Creation to the Flood*, ed. F. Rosenthal and E. Yarshater (Albany: State University of New York Press, 1989). The author's erudite biography nevertheless tends to ignore the significance of Tabari's origins and its place in the historian's worldview. Tabari's own introduction to his monumental history clearly displays his esteem for the Sasanian rule as his ideal example of kingship in his binary of "prophets and kings."

16. For ʿAbd al-Qāder Gilāni, see B. Lawrence, "ʿAbd-al-Qader Jilani," *Encyclopaedia Iranica*, I/2, 132-33, https://iranicaonline.org/articles/abd-al-qader-jilani and cited sources.

17. For the Horufi movement, see A. Bausani, "*Hurufiyya*," *Encyclopaedia of Islam*, 2nd ed., https://referenceworks.brill.com/display/entries/EIEO/COM-0303.xml and cited sources (including works by Helmut Ritter, Edward Granville Browne, Clément Huart, and Sadeq Kiya); Shahzad Bashir, *Fazlullah Astarabadi and the Hurufis*, Makers of the Muslim World Series (London: Oneworld, 2005) and cited sources. The "truthful dervish" appears in Nezami Ganjavi, *Khamseh: Makhzan al-Asrār*, story 47: "Story of the truthful dervish and oppressive ruler."

18. For Nasimi, see M. R. Hess, "Nəsimi, İmadəddin," *Encyclopaedia of Islam*, 3rd ed., https://referenceworks.brill.com/display/entries/EI3O/COM-40738.xml and cited sources.

19. For the history and doctrine of the Noqtavi movement, see Abbas Amanat, "The Nuqtavi Movement of Mahmud Pasikhani and His Persian Cycle of Mystical Materialism," in *Apocalyptic Islam and Iranian Shi'ism* (London: I. B. Tauris, 2009), 73–90 and cited sources (formerly published in *Essays in Mediaeval Isma'ili History and Thought*, ed. F. Daftary [Cambridge: Cambridge University Press, 1996], 281–98). For Noqtavism in Mughal India, see Abbas Amanat, "Nuqtavi Messianic Agnostics of Iran and the Shaping of the Doctrine of 'Universal Conciliation' (*sulh-i kull*) in Mughal India," in *Norm, Transgression and Identity in Islam: Diversity of Approaches and Interpretations / Norme, transgression et identité en Islam: Diversité d'approches et d'interprétations*, ed. Orkhan Mir-Kasimov (Leiden: Brill, 2014), 367–92.

20. For the Safavi order and its evolution, see Abbas Amanat, *Iran: A Modern History* (New Haven, CT: Yale University Press, 2017), chap. 1 and sources in "Further Readings." See also Saïd Amir Arjomand, *The Shadow of God and the Hidden Imam: Religion, Political Order, and Societal Change* (Chicago: University of Chicago Press, 1984); Walter Hinz, *Irans Aufstieg zum Nationalstaat im Fünfzehnten Jahrhundert* (Berlin: Walter de Gruyter, 1936); Michael Mazzaoui, *The Origins of the Ṣafawids: Shi'ism, Ṣufism, and the Gulat* (Wiesbaden: F. Steiner, 1972); and Jean Aubin, "L'avènement des Safavides reconsidéré (Études safavides III)," *Moyen Orient et Océan Indien* 5 (1988): 1–130; Kathryn Babayan, *Mystics, Monarchs and Messiahs: Cultural Landscape of Early Modern Iran* (Cambridge, MA: Harvard University Center for Middle Eastern Studies, 2003); Shahzad Bashir, "Shah Isma'il and the Qizilbash: Cannibalism in the Religious History of Early Safavid Iran," *History of Religion* 45 (2006): 234–56; Juan Cole, "Millenarianism in Modern Iran History," in *Imagining the End: Visions of Apocalypse from the Ancient Middle East to Modern America*, ed. Abbas Amanat and Magnus Bernhardsson (London: I. B. Tauris, 2002), 282–311. For Ṣafi al-Din Ardabili, see Fr. Babinger and R. M. Savory, "Ṣafī al-Din Audabīlī [sic]," *Encyclopaedia of Islam*, 2nd ed., https://referenceworks.brill.com/display/entries/EIEO/SIM-6446.xml.

21. For silk production and the trade of the Persian Gulf, see, for example, Rudi Matthee, *The Politics of Trade in Safavid Iran: Silk for Silver, 1600–1730* (Cambridge: Cambridge University Press, 1999) and Marcel Bazin and C. Bromberger, "Abrīšam ii. Trade and Production of Silk and Its Use in Crafts," *Encyclopaedia Iranica*, I/3, 229–47, https://iranicaonline.org/articles/abrisam-silk-index#pt2.

22. For Russian conquest of Circassia, see Vladimir Hamed-Troyansky, *Empire of Refugees: North Caucasian Muslims and the Late Ottoman State* (Stanford, CA: Stanford University Press, 2024).

23. See Vladimir Bobrovnikov and Irina Babich, eds., *Severnyi Kavkaz v sostave Rossiiskoi imperii* (Moscow: Novoe literaturnoe obozrenie, 2007); see also the foundational account of John F. Baddeley, *The Russian Conquest of the Caucasus* (London: Longmans, Green, 1908); P. G. Butkov, *Materialy dlĭa novoĭ istorii Kavkaza c–1722 po 1803 gody*, vols. 1–2 (St. Petersburg, 1869); for Russian co-optation of and shared interests with local elites during this period, see

Sean Pollock, "Empire by Invitation? Russian Empire-Building in the Caucasus in the Reign of Catherine II" (PhD diss., Harvard University, 2006).

24. On Cossacks of the Caspian steppes and their raids, see Shane O'Rourke, *The Cossacks* (Manchester: Manchester University Press, 2007) and Christoph Witzenrath, *Cossacks and the Russian Empire, 1598–1725: Manipulation, Rebellion and Expansion into Siberia* (London: Routledge, 2007).

25. For Gilan campaigns and earlier Russian expansion in the Caucasus, see Firuz Kazemzadeh, "Russian Penetration of the Caucasus," in *Russian Imperialism from Ivan the Great to the Revolution*, ed. T. Hunczak (New Brunswick: Rutgers University Press, 1974), 239–63. See also *Encyclopaedia Iranica* and Reza Rezazadeh Langaroudi, "Gilan vi. History in the 18th Century," *Encyclopaedia Iranica*, X/6, 642–45, https://iranicaonline.org/articles/gilan-vi and cited sources. For Volga Viking raids and trade expeditions, see Donald Frances Logan, *The Viking in History* (Abingdon: Routledge, 1992).

26. The southern fleet was in part built with lumber from the forests of Mazandaran, which was hauled across the Iranian plateau to Bushehr, while other vessels were purchased from Parsi shipbuilders in the port of Surat on the western coast of the Indian Ocean. Albeit ephemerally, Nader was able to reassert Iranian authority over Bahrain, recapture the strategic kingdom of Oman, and establish his hold on the entry points to the Arabian Sea and the Indian Ocean. For Nader's maritime ambitions, see Laurence Lockhart, *Nadir Shah: A Critical Study Based Mainly on Contemporary Sources* (London: Luzac, 1938), chap. 10, 105–11 and app. 1; Michael Axworthy, *The Sword of Persia: Nader Shah, from Tribal Warrior to Conquering Tyrant* (London: I. B. Tauris, 2006).

27. For shipbuilding projects under Nader, see Willem Floor, "The Iranian Navy in the [Persian] Gulf during the Eighteenth Century," *Iranian Studies* 20, no. 1 (1987): 31–53; and Ernest Tucker, *Nadir Shah's Quest for Legitimacy in Post-Safavid Iran* (Gainesville: University Press of Florida, 2006).

28. For a thorough examination of the Russian presence in the southern Caspian in the post-Safavid era and the aftermath of the peace with Nader Shah Afshar, see Kevin Gledhill, "The Caspian State: Regional Autonomy, International Trade, and the Rise of Qājār Iran, 1722–1797" (PhD diss., Yale University, 2020). For consequences of Safavid demise, see Laurence Lockhart, *The Fall of the Safavi Dynasty and the Afghan Occupation of Persia* (Cambridge: Cambridge University Press, 1958) and Rudi Matthee, *Persia in Crisis: Safavid Decline and the Fall of Isfahan* (London: I. B. Tauris, 2012). For the interregnum leading to the rise of the Qajars in the closing decades of the eighteenth century, see Amanat, *Iran*, 158–70 and cited sources in "Further Readings," 919–20.

29. For causes and consequences of two rounds of Russo-Persian Wars and its aftermath, see Muriel Atkin, *Russia and Iran, 1780–1828* (Minneapolis: University of Minnesota Press, 1980) and Maziar Behrooz, *Iran at War: Interaction with the Modern World and Struggle with Imperial Russia* (London: I. B. Tauris, 2023). See also Elton L. Daniel, "Golestan Treaty," *Encyclopaedia Iranica*, XI/1, 86–90, https://iranicaonline.org/articles/golestan-treaty and cited sources.

30. For Naser al-Din Shah's description, see his *Ruznāmeh-e Safar-e Farangestān*, ed. Moḥammad Ḥasan Khan Eʿtemād al-Salṭaneh (Tehran: Dār

al-Ṭebaʿ-e Dawlati, 1291/1874), 206–7, and English trans. by James Redhouse as *Diary of H.M. the Shah of Persia during his Tour through Europe in A.D. 1873* (London: J. Murray, 1874), 424–27.

31. For the Russian fishery concession, see, for example, Willem Floor and Mansoureh Ettehadieh, "Concessions ii. In the Qajar Period," *Encyclopaedia Iranica*, VI/2, 119–22, https://iranicaonline.org/articles/concessions#pt2 and cited sources. For Russian forestry concessions and the rivalry with Britain, see Saghar Sadeghian, "The Caspian Forests of Northern Iran during the Qajar and Pahlavi Periods: Deforestation, Regulation, and Reforestation," *Iranian Studies* 49, no. 6 (2016): 973–96. On the Karun River navigation concession, which led to the British Lynch Brothers' steamer navigation, see, for example, Shahbaz Shanavaz, "Karun River iii. The Opening of the Karun," *Encyclopaedia Iranica*, XV/6, 633–40, https://iranicaonline.org/articles/karun_3 and cited sources.

32. For Russian trade of the Caspian, see for example Marvin Entner, *Russo-Persian Commercial Relations, 1828–1914* (Gainesville: University of Florida Press, 1965); Charles Issawi, ed., *Economic History of Iran, 1800–1914* (Chicago: University of Chicago Press, 1971); and Abbas Amanat, ed., *Cities and Trade: Consul Abbott on the Society and Economy of Iran*, Oxford Oriental Institute Monographs (London: Ithaca Press, 1983).

33. For Iranian subjects in the Caucasus, see for example Touraj Atabaki, "Disgruntled Guests: Iranian Subaltern on the Margins of the Tsarist Empire," *International Review of Social History* 48, no. 3 (2003): 401–26; Hassan Hakimian, "Wage Labor and Migration: Persian Workers in Southern Russia, 1880–1914," *International Journal of Middle East Studies* 17, no. 4 (1985): 443–62.

34. On the rise and early development of the Bābi movement, see Abbas Amanat, *Resurrection and Renewal: The Making of the Babi Movement in Iran, 1844–1850* (Ithaca, NY: Cornell University Press, 1989) and cited sources. On the Ṭabarsi episode, aside from the above and the pioneering works by Edward Granville Browne, including his notes to *The New History (tarikh-i-jadid) of Mirza ʿAli Mohammad the Bab* (London: Cambridge University Press, 1893), see Siyamak Zabihi-Moghaddam, "The Babi-State Conflict at Shaykh Tabarsi," *Iranian Studies* 35, no. 1–3 (2002): 87–112. On the Caspian forests as a ground for resistance movements, see Saghar Sadeghian, "Caspian Forests as Political Setting: A Socioenvironmental Study of the Bābī Resistance at the Fort of Shaykh Ṭabarsi," in this volume. A closer study of the Ṭabarsi struggle, its social composition, and its apocalyptic dimension remains to be done.

35. For the events in this tumultuous period and the place of the Caucasian fighters, see Moritz Deutschmann, "Cultures of Statehood, Cultures of Revolution: Caucasian Revolutionaries in the Iranian Constitutional Movement 1906-1911," *Ab Imperio*, 2013, no. 2, 165–90; Cosroe Chaquèri, *The Russo-Caucasian Origins of the Iranian Left: Social Democracy in Modern Iran* (Richmond: Curzon, 2001); Janet Afary, *The Iranian Constitutional Revolution 1906–1911: Grassroots Democracy, Social Democracy & the Origins of Feminism* (New York: Columbia University Press, 1996); Kayhan A. Nejad, "From the Oilfield to the Battlefield: The Internationalization of Northern Iranian Revolution" (PhD diss., Yale University, 2021).

36. See Touraj Atabaki and Lana Ravandi-Fada'i, *Zhertvy Vremeni: Zhizn' i sud'ba iranskikh politicheskikh deĭateleĭ i trudovykh migrantov v mezhvoennyĭ period* (Moscow: IV RAN, 2020); Kayhan A. Nejad, "Provincial Revolution and Regional Anti-Colonialism: The Soviets in Iran, 1920–1921," *Slavic Review* 82, no. 2 (2023): 378–400. The gifted Azerbaijani intellectual Mohammad Amin Rasulzadeh represented another face of the Caucasian-Iranian symbiosis. His fate was nevertheless no less hazardous. After fleeing his homeland in 1908, Rasulzadeh joined the Iranian Constitutional Revolution and after 1908 served as the editor of *Irān-e Now*, the left-leaning flagship of Tehran newspapers. But upon his return to Baku and founding the Mosavat national democratic party, he was forced into exile, this time because of his critique of the Soviet annexation of the entire Caucasus. He lived an eventful life therefrom, first in Turkey, then under house arrest in Russia, and then as a peripatetic journalist in eastern Europe. In Germany he tried, unsuccessfully, to strike a deal with the Nazi leadership for creation of an independent Azerbaijan upon their conquest of the Caucasus. He died in Turkey in 1955, a disillusioned advocate of Pan-Turkism.

For generations, the aura of the Jangal revolutionaries and their affiliates captivated Iranians from all walks of life: nationalists of the postconstitutional period, the left (and especially the post-Tudeh guerilla organizations), the radical Islamists during 1979 revolution, and finally the propaganda machine of the Islamic Republic. This mythical construct, also popular with historians of modern Iran, at times obfuscated the reality of the Jangal and its romantic idealism. On the memory of the Jangal, see Janet Afary, "The Contentious Historiography of the Gilan Republic in Iran: A Critical Exploration," *Iranian Studies* 28, no. 1–2 (1995): 3–24; Kayhan A. Nejad, "Kuchek Khan Jangali," *Encyclopaedia Iranica Online* (forthcoming).

37. Kayhan A. Nejad, "To Break the Feudal Bonds: The Soviets, Reza Khan, and the Iranian Left, 1921–25." *Middle Eastern Studies* 57, no. 5 (2021): 758–76.

Part I

Early Expansion
Knowledge, Commerce, and Diplomacy in the Early Modern Caspian

CHAPTER 2

The Ottoman Empire and the Caspian Sea in the Sixteenth Century

Murat Yaşar

The Caspian Sea remained outside of Ottoman geostrategic and political calculations until the mid-sixteenth century when it became an essential element in Ottoman attempts to establish suzerainty over the Caucasus region in response to the rise of Muscovy and the weakness of the Safavid Empire. Ottoman policy in the empire's northern frontier zones, which included the Pontic-Caspian steppes and Caspian shores, converted to a more robust and active one as a result of the expansion of the Tsardom of Muscovy into the North Caucasus and the Caspian Sea as of 1552–56. Muscovite ambitions in this region forced the Ottoman Porte to take a more decisive stance and follow more of a vigorous strategy of territory- and subject-making in the North Caucasus, including Dagestan on the shores of the Caspian Sea. From then on, Ottoman designs over the Caspian Sea had three primary objectives: to establish a defined suzerainty over the North Caucasus borderland, to check the expansion of Muscovy, and to encircle the Safavid Empire, the principal rival of the Ottomans on their eastern frontier. In order to realize these objectives, the Porte implemented a policy of creating loyal vassals in the region ranging from the Black Sea to the Caspian Sea.

While external concerns, such as the rise of Muscovy and its activities in the North Caucasus borderland, were the main drivers of change in Ottoman northern policy, broader policy modifications at the Ottoman Porte did not happen in a vacuum or simply as a haphazard reaction to the developments in the north. Two influential sixteenth-century statesmen, Sokullu Mehmed Pasha and Özdemiroğlu Osman Pasha, both held the position of the grand vizier within the Ottoman imperial hierarchy and were the architects of this new and rigorous Ottoman policy and designs over the Caspian Sea after the ascension of Selim II (r. 1566–74) to the throne. These two pashas not only desired to turn the Caspian into another Ottoman-controlled sea, similar to the status of the Black Sea, but also followed effective strategies, while in power, to establish Ottoman control over the North Caucasus borderland. This region and the Caspian Sea were intrinsically connected to Ottoman plans to dominate their northern and eastern frontier zones put in motion by Sokullu Mehmed Pasha and continued by Özdemiroğlu Osman Pasha. By the end of the sixteenth century, the Ottoman Porte was on the verge of accomplishing its political and strategic objectives in both the North Caucasus and the Caspian Sea.

The first Ottoman military undertaking that was directly related to the Caspian and a turning point for the aforementioned change in Ottoman northern policy was the Astrakhan Campaign of 1569. The Ottoman Porte not only targeted the city of Astrakhan, which had been taken by the Tsardom of Muscovy in 1556, but also planned to put Ottoman ships for naval operations in the Caspian Sea. The Astrakhan Campaign was devised around the project of digging a canal between the Don and Volga Rivers to transport ships, siege weapons, supplies, and other materiel from the Ottoman cities of Kefe and Azak on the Black Sea shores to Astrakhan on the Caspian Sea. Contemporary Ottoman chroniclers state that Grand Vizier Sokullu Mehmed Pasha (in office, 1565–79) was always contemplating ways to conquer the whole of Iran proper. At this point, it should be remembered that the Safavids were the major imperial and ideological rivals of the Ottomans in the sixteenth-century Islamic world. Moreover, whereas Ottoman armies were victorious in their campaigns against the Safavids in the course of the sixteenth century, they were unable to retain and annex certain Safavid possessions in West Asia and the Caucasus, such as Shirvan and Tabriz. In many wars fought between the two powers since 1514, as soon as the main Ottoman army returned to their strongholds in Anatolia, the Safavids were able to come back and retake their core territories from the Ottomans. As such, Sokullu Mehmed Pasha was not only looking for ways to defeat the Safavid armies but also to permanently hold territories in the Caucasus and beyond. Accordingly, "some wise people" advised the grand vizier to dig a canal between the Don and Volga Rivers to be able to send naval ships from the Black Sea to the Caspian Sea.[1] In fact, when the Ottoman Imperial Council discussed the plans in 1568 for the Astrakhan Campaign, which was technically a campaign against the Tsardom of Muscovy, those officials who supported it at the Porte emphasized the value of Astrakhan as a gateway to the Caspian Sea for encircling the Safavid Empire.[2]

Moreover, letters from the Muslim khanates of Central Asia and local Tatars from the former khanates of Astrakhan and Kazan, conveying the message that they were unable to perform their pilgrimage duties now that Astrakhan was in the hands of the Russians, were a compelling reason for Ottoman Sultan Selim II to put his seal of approval on this campaign. Astrakhan was a crucial part of the Sunni Muslim pilgrimage route from Central Asia to Mecca, as the routes through Iran were not available to Sunni pilgrims. For this reason, the proponents of the Astrakhan Campaign stressed the role of the Ottoman sultan as the protector of the Sunni Muslims in the world to justify taking Astrakhan and bringing the Ottoman armies and ships to the Caspian Sea.[3]

At this point, Ottoman control and policies over the Black Sea in the sixteenth century may illuminate how the Ottoman policymakers perceived the idea of conquering Astrakhan and reaching the Caspian, as well as what it would have meant for Muscovy and the Safavid Empire, had the Ottomans been successful. Technically speaking, the Caspian Sea is an inland lake with an endorheic basin, whereas the Black Sea is an open body of water connected to the Mediterranean Sea through the Bosphorus Strait, the Sea of Marmara, and the Dardanelles Strait, around Gallipoli. However, in the early modern era, both the Caspian Sea and the Black Sea shared similarities in terms of the types of polities on their shores and the ease of control over these polities for an imperial power. Additionally, both the Caspian Sea and the Black Sea were at the intersection of various lucrative trade routes connecting Eurasia.

By the mid-sixteenth century, the Ottomans were able to establish complete control of the Black Sea, making it *mare nostrum*, with some centrifugal forces, such as the Cossacks, still threatening Ottoman control but not sovereignty. Ottoman domination over the Black Sea began with their conquest of Constantinople and Trebizond and the reduction of the Crimean Khanate to vassalage during the reign of Sultan Mehmed II (r. 1444–46, 1451–81). It reached its height during the reign of Süleyman I (r. 1520–66) with the annexations of Budjak and the surrounding coastal strips in eastern Europe in 1538. During this period, the Ottomans gradually annexed almost the entire shoreline of the Black Sea and governed these lands through their centrally appointed officials. The only exception to this was the North Caucasus coastline of the Black Sea where local Adyghe princes maintained their rule as vassals of the Ottoman sultan and/or the Crimean khan. The Porte benefited from this control in two significant ways that were economic and strategic. First, the Porte's domination and closure of the Black Sea to non-Ottoman shipping allowed the Ottomans to ensure the flow of wealth from the Black Sea shores to their capital, Istanbul, and other major cities in the Balkan Peninsula and in Anatolia.[4] The Ottoman preference for the native peoples or tribute-paying states engaging in shipping in the Black Sea also created a regional economy, providing the lands around the Black Sea an integral unity under Ottoman suzerainty, according to Halil İnalcık.[5] The ability to close the Black Sea to international trade at certain times provided the Ottoman Empire with a tool to prevent further increase in the prices of foodstuffs and other materials coming from the Black Sea region, as well.[6] Second, the Ottomans created a reliable safeguard on the passage between Anatolia and the Balkans to protect their capital against surprise attacks from the north.[7] John P. LeDonne compares the Ottoman Black Sea to a moat that offered the possibility of checking any expanding power on the northern shores before they approached the core areas of the empire.[8] While Ottoman control of the Black Sea protected the core territories of the Ottoman Empire from threats, it also required the Ottomans to establish their rule or some form of suzerainty in the north of the Black Sea, becoming a stepping stone for expansion.

Having achieved a high level of control over the Black Sea following their annexation of the Moldavian coastal zones in 1538,[9] the Ottomans in the 1560s could certainly appreciate the value of similar control over the Caspian Sea. Their first target, Astrakhan, functioned as a control and expansion point for the Caspian, just as Ottoman Kefe and Azak had done for the Black Sea. If the Ottomans were to annex Astrakhan as they had planned, they could have controlled the northern shores of the Caspian Sea and initiated their strategy of taking over the majority of its shores with their effective naval power. Considering that the Safavids did not excel in naval warfare and the Muscovites were busy fighting a war in Livonia, the Ottomans would undoubtedly have had the upper hand in the Caspian Sea. An Ottoman fleet in the Caspian would have given the Ottomans, who by now demonstrated the capability to build and use sea power effectively, a substantial strategic advantage. Such a fleet sailing from Astrakhan would have posed a grave threat to the Safavid Empire, not only in terms of its military value, but also as a bridge connecting the Porte with the Central Asian khanates, which sought Ottoman help several times in the second half of the sixteenth century against the Safavids or the Muscovites.

Similarly, the potential that the Muslim Central Asian Khanates of Khiva and Bukhara on the eastern part of the Caspian Sea presented to the Porte can be compared to the status of the Crimean Khanate in the north of the Black Sea within the Ottoman imperial system as a vassal. The Porte must have understood that these khanates and their rulers could be prospective clients and utilized in the same way that the Crimean Tatars were in numerous Ottoman campaigns in eastern Europe. Lastly, Ottoman control of the Caspian Sea also meant the control of its shipping and wealth, which could provide the Porte with a means of annexing and retaining the territories in the Caucasus and beyond. Certainly, Ottoman statesmen at the Porte appreciated the lucrative trade routes in the region and the revenues they produced.[10]

For these reasons, a campaign to wrest Astrakhan from Muscovy was approved and put in motion under the leadership of Grand Vizier Sokullu Mehmed Pasha. The Ottoman sources suggest that the Porte organized the Astrakhan Campaign to be small-scale, perhaps the size of an expeditionary campaign rather than a full-scale one.[11] However, the Astrakhan Campaign constitutes an unprecedented attempt for Ottoman campaigning strategies regarding its direction and the distance of the target from the supply lines and centers within the Ottoman Empire. The Porte had perfected its supply system on its eastern and western frontiers against the Safavids and Habsburgs, respectively, but this campaign to take a major city to the north of the Caspian Sea was the first major Ottoman undertaking on their northern frontier against the Tsardom of Muscovy, which the Ottomans considered to be a second-rate power. The major challenge for the Ottoman army was not confronting Muscovy, but obtaining and preparing the required provisions and transporting them, along with soldiers gathered from various parts of the empire, to Kefe/Azak and then to Astrakhan, a distance of nearly 1,500 kilometers (930 miles).

The distance and the direction of the campaign required the Ottoman Porte to use caution and limit the resources that could be spent on this venture. In this vein, one of the easiest ways to increase the number of soldiers was to recruit men from vassal chiefs and principalities on the way to Astrakhan, especially in the North Caucasus. Thus, in October 1568, the Porte wrote several letters to Circassian and Dagestani rulers.¹² The Porte instructed them to join the Ottoman/Crimean forces with their soldiers and serve the sultan. Besides, some Nogay chieftains, including even several from the Greater Nogay Horde, which was a client of the Muscovite tsar at that time, certain local chiefs in the North Caucasus, as well as Tatar nobles from Astrakhan and Kazan had already appealed to the Ottoman sultan for a campaign against the Muscovites and promised support.¹³ Accordingly, the Ottomans thought that their army would receive a substantial amount of help from these rulers on the route to Astrakhan. After the Porte issued the necessary orders to local governors, the Crimean khan, and local rulers of the North Caucasus regarding the transportation of the army and supplies, an Ottoman fleet carrying three thousand janissaries arrived in Azak on the north of the Black Sea in April 1569. In May of the same year, another Ottoman fleet with provincial cavalry, janissaries, and workers left for Azak. Eventually, in the summer of 1569, an Ottoman army, consisting of thirteen thousand to fifteen thousand troops, joined by the Crimean Tatar light cavalry of thirty thousand to fifty thousand led by Crimean Khan Devlet Girey, set out to capture Astrakhan.¹⁴ While Khan Devlet Girey was commanding the Crimean forces, the main Ottoman army was under the command of Kasım Pasha, who was Sokullu Mehmed Pasha's right-hand man in this campaign and the governor-general of Kefe.

The Ottoman-Crimean army first traveled to the area where the Don and Volga Rivers were closest in order to dig the proposed canal between the two rivers. However, after working on it for a while, Kasım Pasha decided that digging a canal to transport the ships was unfeasible. Taking into account the campaign season, he ordered the army to march to Astrakhan by land.¹⁵ In the process, though, they were unable to carry heavy siege weapons. The Ottoman army reached Astrakhan in September 1569. However, the month of September was already late in the campaign season, considering the colder climate of the northern Caspian Sea.¹⁶ While there were skirmishes between the Muscovite and Ottoman forces, a full siege of Astrakhan was not realized due to the lack of proper siege weapons. The unrest that arose among the Ottoman troops due to the rumors circulating in their camp that both Muscovites and Safavids were sending armies of relief made matters worse. These rumors, the lack of siege weapons, and the distance to the closest Ottoman centers fueled the boisterous protests of Ottoman soldiers who demanded to go back before the famously cold winter of this region began. Initially, Kasım Pasha planned to spend the winter outside of the new fortress of Astrakhan by repairing the old fortress that the Muscovites had abandoned when they took the city in 1556. In accordance with the plans drawn at the Porte, he wanted to restart the siege with fresh supplies in earnest in 1570. However, Ottoman troops made their discontent very clear and became extremely unruly, leaving the commander no choice but to retreat. Kasım Pasha began preparations to depart on September 26, 1569, and after a disastrous retreat reached Kefe through the North Caucasus, losing many troops and materiel en route.[17]

Rather than putting an end to Ottoman ambitions in the North Caucasus and the Caspian Sea, the failure of the Astrakhan Campaign, in fact, galvanized the newfound Ottoman interest in the region. Following this fiasco, the Porte seemed to appreciate the importance of the North Caucasus borderland and started an active policy of creating vassals in the area ranging from the Taman Peninsula to the Caspian Sea. Therefore, the Astrakhan Campaign was instrumental in changing Ottoman policymakers' perception of their northern frontier zones and the patterns of relationships in these areas. Meanwhile, the *shamkhāl*, the ruler of the Dagestani polity known as the Shamkhālate of Tarki and the primus inter pares ruler in Dagestan, accepted the sultan's sovereignty in 1569 by sending a letter with an envoy to Kasım Pasha. This most likely bolstered the agenda of Sokullu Mehmed Pasha and other Ottoman officials who promoted more active strategies in the North Caucasus and the Caspian Sea. In his letter, Shamkhāl Choban swore allegiance to the sultan and promised, "[he] will be a friend to friends of the sultan and enemy to enemies of the sultan."[18] The submission of the shamkhāl, even though it was rather nominal, was significant, as Dagestan was to be a cornerstone of the new Ottoman strategies over the North Caucasus and the Caspian Sea. Dagestan, with its coastal strip on the Caspian Sea, including the fortress of Derbent, a strategic passageway from the Safavid Empire to the North Caucasus, was a major strategic prize for the surrounding imperial powers. The most notable change regarding the Ottoman Porte's approach to the region was that after 1569, the Ottoman sultan began to solidify his presence and influence by directly corresponding with local rulers rather than through his vassal, the Crimean khan. Prior to the Astrakhan Campaign, the Porte left the affairs of the North Caucasus and Pontic-Caspian Steppe in the hands of the Crimean khans who considered themselves the legitimate rulers of these lands.[19] This active Ottoman presence and their ramped up subject- and territory-making strategies began to bear fruit in the region as of the 1570s, as the Porte was able to draw more local rulers to its side and assert its claims of sovereignty or suzerainty.

The Ottomans would find another opportunity to solidify their claims over the North Caucasus and the Caspian Sea during a later campaign against the Safavid Empire. When this large-scale imperial campaign began in 1578, the architect of the 1569 Astrakhan Campaign, Sokullu Mehmed Pasha, was still the grand vizier. We know that although the immediate objective of the 1578–90 war, from the Ottoman perspective, was to "save" the people of Shirvan and other Sunni peoples from the rule of the Shi'i Safavid dynasty, Sokullu Mehmed Pasha had more sophisticated plans in mind that encompassed the entire Caucasus, as well as the Caspian Sea. The details of the Ottoman-Safavid War of 1578–90 are beyond the scope of this chapter. For this reason, we will only examine below the aspects of this campaign related to the Caspian Sea and partially to the North Caucasus borderland.

As soon as the Ottoman-Safavid War started in 1578, the Porte's attempts at securing the North Caucasus borderland and winning over local rulers as clients intensified noticeably. In February 1578, the commander of the Ottoman armies, Lala Mustafa Pasha, sent letters from Istanbul to the local rulers in the North and South Caucasus, demanding their services. Among those who were asked to join the Ottoman army and serve the sultan in the campaign against the Safavids were Dagestani Shamkhāl Emir Mirza, Gazi Salih of Tabasaran (Tabarasan in Ottoman sources), and Tuchalav Mirza of the Avars.[20] As mentioned above, the shamkhāl was the most influential ruler in Dagestan. The Porte considered the shamkhāl a natural ally during this war not only because he and his people were Sunnis but also because he had already been assisting the Sunni leaders of Shirvan in overthrowing what they considered "Shi'i oppression," even though he was defeated by the Safavids previously.[21] He was also crucial, as the Ottomans knew, to the establishment of a permanent Ottoman presence in the Caucasus and the Caspian Sea. This presence would require the allegiance of the Dagestani rulers, especially the shamkhāl. From the perspective of the shamkhāl, Sunni Ottomans whose main centers of operation and core territories were far away from Dagestan were preferable to Shi'i Safavids who had annexed Shirvan in the South Caucasus and at one point controlled Derbent, posing a direct threat to the rest of Dagestan.

The efforts of the Porte and the timing of the campaign proved to be effective, as the Dagestani rulers decided to offer their allegiance to the Porte. In the summer of 1578, the shamkhāl sent an envoy to Lala Mustafa Pasha, the Ottoman commander in the field, to offer his submission to the Ottoman sultan. His envoy Hüseyin reached the Ottoman camp in Eastern Anatolia and presented to the Ottoman commander the shamkhāl's letter addressed to the sultan. In his letter, the shamkhāl praised Sultan Murad III (r. 1574–95) and stated that as the sultan demanded, his thirty thousand men were ready to fight against the Safavids.[22] Considering the status of the shamkhāl in Dagestan, his voluntary submission to the Porte as a vassal was a significant win for the Ottomans at this critical time. The Porte, especially its officials in the region, worked meticulously to cement this nominal tie and turn the shamkhālate into a proper Ottoman vassal on the Caspian shores. Ottoman historian Gelibolulu Mustafa Ali, who was familiar with the Ottoman plans over the Caucasus and the Caspian Sea and was with Lala Mustafa Pasha during the Safavid Campaign, counts the lands of shamkhāl in Dagestan among the conquests of the Porte.[23]

By September 1578, Ottoman armies were victorious over the Safavids and occupied a large chunk of the Caucasus stretching from Georgia to the Caspian Sea, including Shirvan. These lands were immediately annexed and turned into Ottoman administrative units of *sancak*s (provinces) and *eyalet*s (governor-generalships).[24] The formation of administrative districts and acquisition of allegiances from local rulers show that the Ottomans intended to stay in the region and make both the North and South Caucasus integral parts of their empire. As was the case with the previous campaigns against the Safavids, the actual challenge for the Ottoman Porte was not necessarily to invade the Safavid lands in the South Caucasus and West Asia, but to keep these occupied territories and fully integrate them into their imperial structure. When the campaign season was over in the same year, the main Ottoman army needed to return to their Anatolian strongholds. Since defending these territories against the soon-to-be-renewed attacks of the Safavid armies required major military installations and efforts, none of the high-ranking Ottoman commanders was willing to accept the position of the governor-general of the newly established *eyalet* of Shirvan, except Özdemiroğlu Osman Pasha. Özdemiroğlu Osman Pasha was a well-known governor and military commander who previously served in the Ottoman provincial system with distinction. For this reason, Lala Mustafa Pasha gladly appointed Özdemiroğlu Osman

Pasha as the governor-general of Shirvan and commander (*serdar*) of the Ottoman army that would stay in the Caucasus to defend the newly acquired territories, which was a demanding and almost impossible task.[25]

During this campaign, the Ottomans solidified their influence over the local rulers by using ideology, religion, and rewards. For example, the shamkhāl visited the camp of the Ottoman army in the north of Shirvan in October 1578 to personally submit to the Porte. Lala Mustafa Pasha rewarded this gesture with gifts and granted him the province of Şaburan in the new governor-generalship of Shirvan. Shirvan was divided into thirteen provinces after its annexation by the Ottoman Empire. Additionally, another Dagestani ruler, Tuchalav Burhaneddin of the Avars, received Ahtı, also a province of Shirvan.[26] Moreover, Tuchalav Burhaneddin, the Kaytak ruler (*usmi*), the Tabasaran ruler Gazi Salih, and the son of the Kaytak *usmi* sent their letters and submitted to the Ottoman sultan.[27] Seventeenth-century Ottoman traveler Evliya Çelebi writes that the Ottoman Porte gave several important fortresses to the shamkhāl and other Dagestani rulers to secure their loyalty, as the Ottoman commanders knew that without their support it would be challenging to defend and keep these lands.[28] In order to further strengthen the submission of the shamkhāl and other Dagestani rulers, Lala Mustafa Pasha arranged a marriage between Özdemiroğlu Osman Pasha, who was then the newly appointed governor-general of Shirvan, and a niece of the shamkhāl.[29] The bride was one of the daughters of Tuchalav Burhaneddin, who was the shamkhāl's brother. As can be seen, the Ottomans were then using all possible means of manipulation in Dagestan, establishing a network of loyal clients and vassals.

For this reason, after granting provinces in the South Caucasus to the shamkhāl and the Avar ruler, the Porte sent an imperial letter to the shamkhāl in January 1579. In this letter, the sultan praised him for his submission and instructed him to help the Ottoman soldiers who remained in Shirvan and other parts of the Caucasus. The sultan stressed that as long as the shamkhāl was loyal, he could expect more rewards from the Porte.[30] The Porte's strategies and objectives in Dagestan suited the general principles of Ottoman methods of conquest.[31] If the shamkhāl and other Shafi'i Muslim rulers of Dagestan were to become loyal vassals of the sultan, the Porte would be able to ensure a robust control over the North Caucasus borderland, both securing another supply route against the Safavids and checking the rising power of the Muscovites simultaneously. In this way, the North Caucasus polities, including those of the western and Kabardinian Circassians, who were less amenable to imperial control compared to the Dagestani polities, would be encircled by the Crimean Khanate in the west, the shamkhālate in the east, and the Ottoman *eyalet* of Shirvan as well as the vassal Georgian kingdoms in the south.

The shamkhāl indeed served the Ottomans in the region well. In late November 1578, the Crimean Tatar army sent to assist the Ottoman army was defeated in Shirvan by the Safavids, and their commander, Adil Girey, was captured.[32] The Ottoman army, which was in Shamakhi under the command of Özdemiroğlu Osman Pasha, decided to move to Derbent where defense against the Safavid troops was more likely to succeed due to the strong fortifications around the city. At that time, the shamkhāl was with Özdemiroğlu Osman Pasha. He accompanied and guided the Ottoman army as far as Derbent, advising and helping the Ottoman commander during the retreat from Shamakhi.[33]

Aside from being a strategic fortress for controlling passage along the coast, Derbent was situated at a perfect location for establishing a sphere of influence over Dagestan. It was a stone fortress located between the Principality of Tabasaran and the Usmiat of the Kaytaks. Özdemiroğlu Osman Pasha took advantage of this strategic fortress to secure Ottoman control of Dagestan. As we understand from chronicles written by eyewitnesses such as Gelibolulu Mustafa Ali, the shamkhāl and most other Dagestani rulers were generally cooperative and loyal to the Ottomans during the Ottoman-Safavid War of 1578-90.[34]

While in Derbent, Özdemiroğlu Osman Pasha found a similar-minded superior in the person of Grand Vizier Sokullu Mehmed Pasha. Both of them shared the same desire to realize one of the major Ottoman objectives in the region, which was to sail a powerful Ottoman navy on the Caspian Sea. A letter sent from Istanbul to Özdemiroğlu Osman Pasha in June 1579, when the Ottoman army secured its position in Derbent, clearly outlines the Ottoman designs over the Caspian Sea in the context of their northern policy. Sokullu Mehmed Pasha dispatched this letter as an answer to the letter of Özdemiroğlu Osman Pasha, then the governor-general and commander of the Ottoman forces in the Caucasus. It is one of the rare archival materials specifically related to and detailing Ottoman objectives in the Caspian Sea in the second half of the sixteenth century. Özdemiroğlu Osman Pasha explained in his initial letter to the Porte that Derbent, as a strategically positioned unique fortress, could be the naval base for a potential Ottoman fleet in the Caspian Sea. He explained that if the Porte were to build about twenty galleys equipped with proper weaponry, the Caspian Sea, its river network, and the surrounding lands would be easily conquered. In his response, Sokullu Mehmed Pasha agreed with Özdemiroğlu Osman Pasha, adding that Shirvan on the Caspian Sea in the South Caucasus was annexed so that the Porte would send an adequate number of naval ships to the region to acquire the lands and fortresses on its shores. However, the main obstacle that the Ottoman Porte needed to overcome was that of transporting the ships and equipment at a time when, as the letter stated, the Porte faced difficulty even sending supplies to the soldiers stationed in Tbilisi and Derbent due to the military activities of the Safavids.[35]

In fact, this was not the first time that the Ottomans intended to build ships in the region. In the summer of 1578, the Porte planned to construct several galliots (Ottoman: *kalite, kalyota*) in order to control the passageway between the Georgian Kingdom of Kakheti, which became an Ottoman governor-generalship granted to its king Alexander II, and Shirvan. The Ottomans deliberated about whether to place these smaller ships on the Kura River in the Caucasus. As a result, the Porte sent engineers and equipment to build such ships in 1578. However, as we come to understand from the letter, the commander of the Ottoman army then, Lala Mustafa Pasha, neglected the project, and the builders returned to the Porte. Perhaps also reflecting on his enmity with Lala Mustafa Pasha, Sokullu Mehmed Pasha stated in his letter that the failure of this particular project allowed the Safavids to attack the newly conquered lands in the Caucasus and to pose a constant threat to the Ottoman soldiers in the region.[36]

The grand vizier then proposed two possible means of putting Ottoman galleys in the Caspian Sea. One was to build them in Derbent or somewhere else in Dagestan with equipment and builders arriving from the Porte. For this reason, the grand vizier asked Özdemiroğlu Osman Pasha whether there were valonia oak trees and iron mines in the mountains of the Caucasus, as these were the raw materials needed for the construction of galley style ships at that time. The other possibility was to build them in Tbilisi in the South Caucasus. In this way, the grand vizier thought, some ships could be placed on the Kura River to protect the passageway between Kakheti and Shirvan, preventing the Safavid troops from attacking the Ottoman possessions, and others could reach Derbent on the Caspian Sea through the Kura River.[37]

While these plans and projects were in the making, Sokullu Mehmed Pasha, one of the architects of the new Ottoman northern policy, was assassinated in Istanbul in October 1579. The timing was unfortunate, but Özdemiroğlu Osman Pasha, through his activities in the Caucasus and the Caspian Sea, ensured the continuation of the active and effective Ottoman presence in the region, as envisioned by Sokullu Mehmed Pasha. By 1580, Özdemiroğlu Osman Pasha was successful in putting together a naval force in the Caspian Sea. This fleet became officially known as Bahr-i Kolzum Kapudanlığı, that is, the Admiralship of the Caspian Sea, when Özdemiroğlu Osman Pasha appointed the former governor of Azak, Mehmed Bey, as its first admiral and as governor-general of Derbent.[38] The Ottoman commanders in the Caucasus and statesmen at the Porte came to understand the significance and value of an Ottoman fleet sailing the Caspian Sea when the Safavids laid siege to Baku in 1581. During the siege, this famous city on the Caspian coast was reinforced by the Ottoman fleet carrying soldiers and gunpowder from Derbent to Baku without hindrance from the Safavids.[39] As expected, the reinforcements enabled the successful defense of the city. Unable to do anything about the Ottoman fleet in the Caspian Sea, the Safavids lifted their siege and left.

Following this event, the Porte informed Özdemiroğlu Osman Pasha that an adequate number of captains and workers to build more ships for the Caspian navy would be dispatched as soon as possible. As mentioned above, the Ottoman Porte entertained the idea of establishing an anti-Safavid and anti-Muscovite alliance with the Central Asian Khanates of Bukhara and Khiva following the intensification of its activities in the Caucasus. An Ottoman navy that could travel from the western shores of the Caspian Sea, then under the Ottoman rule, to its eastern shores, bypassing the Safavids in the south and the Muscovites in the north, would be able to establish a direct line of contact with the Central Asian Sunni Muslim polities. Accordingly, the Porte ordered Özdemiroğlu Osman Pasha to ensure the safety of an Ottoman envoy dispatched to Abdullah Khan of Bukhara in 1581 to relay to the khan that the Ottoman sultan would support his war effort against the Safavids. The sultan instructed Özdemiroğlu Osman Pasha to send the envoys via the Caspian Sea and report the details of their travels to the Porte.[40] The Porte was most likely considering the possibility of using the Caspian route for its contacts with the Central Asian Khanates, as it demanded a detailed report of the envoys' travel there and back.

The reports and activities of the Caspian navy must have made it clear to the Porte that having Ottoman ships in the Caspian Sea capable of controlling its shores was strategically important. Therefore, the

Porte continued its efforts to strengthen the already existing Caspian navy. The new admiral of the Caspian fleet, Admiral Ali, received an imperial letter in 1581. According to the letter, the Porte sent an order to ensure that the necessary equipment to construct more ships would arrive in Derbent safely from Kefe. Moreover, the Porte dispatched another imperial letter to the governor-general of Kefe, Cafer Pasha, instructing him to send the necessary equipment and materials for the construction of new ships from Kefe to Derbent without any delay.[41]

During this period, as the documents show, the Porte and the commanders in the field worked in harmony. Meanwhile, the Porte did not neglect the ongoing process of creating vassals in Dagestan. The sultan sent many more imperial letters and orders to the Dagestani rulers in this period. Most of these letters praised the local rulers for their submission and services to the Ottoman Porte, while instructing them to continue such services and expect more rewards in return. There are many orders for the shamkhāl and other Dagestani rulers in the 1580s regarding the security and safety of the North Caucasian supply route on which soldiers, messengers, and money traveled from Kefe to Derbent.[42] It is clear that in the 1580s, the Ottomans were able to establish a palpable sphere of influence over Dagestan with Derbent being an Ottoman governor-generalship.

While in the region, Özdemiroğlu Osman Pasha also encouraged trade in the Caspian Sea. Illustrating the effects of this policy, merchants from the Muscovy Company of England reached the Caspian traveling along the Volga River to Astrakhan. While in the Caspian Sea, the English merchants led by Robert Golding applied to the Ottoman governor of Baku for trading rights and safety of their goods in 1580. The Ottoman governor welcomed them and encouraged their presence in the region. Meanwhile, he informed Özdemiroğlu Osman Pasha about the English merchants and their request for an audience. Özdemiroğlu Osman Pasha allowed the merchants to travel to Derbent and met with them in person. He then approved their request to engage in commercial activities, including the purchase of large amounts of silk, in Dagestan and the Caspian Sea.[43] As can be seen, Özdemiroğlu Osman Pasha and his officials in the Caucasus sought to turn the region into a properly administered Ottoman territory and the Caspian Sea into another Black Sea under Ottoman control while encouraging economic and commercial life on its shores.

Özdemiroğlu Osman Pasha's foresight and successes did not go unnoticed by Ottoman Sultan Murad III. In 1583, the sultan decided to remove Crimean Khan Mehmed Girey II (r. 1577–84) for the latter's refusal to partake in the Ottoman campaigns against the Safavids. He ordered Özdemiroğlu Osman Pasha to travel to Kefe from Derbent in order to overthrow the Crimean khan on behalf of a more loyal candidate. Özdemiroğlu Osman Pasha succeeded in removing Mehmed Girey II and replacing him with Islam Girey (r. 1584–88), another member of the Girey dynasty, trusted by the Porte. After this successful mission, the sultan instructed him to travel to Istanbul, where a very pleased sultan granted him the post of grand vizier in 1584. Shortly after this significant promotion, Özdemiroğlu Osman Pasha was ordered to lead another army into the Safavid Empire, this time to take Tabriz, which he achieved in the same year of 1584. The following year, he died of natural causes.

Sokullu Mehmed Pasha and Özdemiroğlu Osman Pasha left in place an active and effective Ottoman policy in the Caucasus and the Caspian Sea. The Ottoman officials who took over their positions at the Porte as well as on the campaign field in the Caucasus continued these fruitful strategies in the 1580s. These policies brought the Ottomans their long-sought objectives of dealing a severe blow to the Safavids not just by defeating them on the battlefield but also by annexing a large portion of their lands in the Caucasus. The Ottoman-Safavid War ended with the Treaty of Istanbul signed in 1590, leaving the Caucasus under Ottoman suzerainty until 1603 when Shah ʿAbbas I (r. 1588–1629) of the Safavid Empire began another long war with the Ottoman Porte to retake the territories that had been lost.

Notes

1. İbrahim Peçevi, *Peçevi tarihi*, ed. Fahri Derin and Vahit Çabuk (Istanbul: Enderun, 1980), 1:468.
2. Gelibolulu Mustafa Ali ve Künhü'l-ahbar'ında II. Selim, III. Murat ve III. Mehmet devirleri, ed. Faris Çerçi (Kayseri: Erciyes Üniversitesi Yayınları, 2000), 2:6–7.
3. *Gelibolulu Mustafa Ali ve Künhü'l-ahbar'ında*, 2:6–8; Peçevi, *Peçevi tarihi*, 1:468–69.
4. Halil İnalcık, "The Question of the Closing of the Black Sea under the Ottomans," Αρχείον Πόντου 35 (1979): 74–110; Victor Ostapchuk, "The Human Landscape of the Ottoman Black Sea in the Face of the Cossack Naval Raids," *Oriente Moderno* 20 (2001): 23–95.
5. İnalcık, "The Question of the Closing of the Black Sea," 91–108.
6. İnalcık, "The Question of the Closing of the Black Sea," 75.
7. İnalcık, "The Question of the Closing of the Black Sea," 74–76.
8. John P. LeDonne, *The Grand Strategy of the Russian Empire, 1650–1831* (New York: Oxford University Press, 2004), 25.

9. Halil İnalcık, *Sources and Studies on the Ottoman Black Sea*, vol. 1, *The Customs Register of Caffa, 1487–1490* (Cambridge, MA: Harvard University Press, 1996), 110.

10. Halil İnalcık, "The Origin of the Ottoman-Russian Rivalry and the Don-Volga Canal (1569)," *Annales del'Universite d'Ankara* 1 (1947): 69.

11. For the military details of the campaign, see Murat Yaşar, "North Caucasus between the Ottoman Empire and the Tsardom of Muscovy: The Beginnings, 1552–1570," *Iran & the Caucasus* 20 (2016): 105–25.

12. Cumhurbaşkanlığı Devlet Arşivleri Başkanlığı, Osmanlı Arşivi, Mühimme Defteri (Turkish Presidency State Archives, Department of Ottoman Archives, Register of Important Affairs—henceforth MD) 7, no. 2246.

13. MD 7, no. 2723.

14. MD 7, no. 2757; Yaşar, "North Caucasus between the Ottoman Empire and the Tsardom of Muscovy," 116.

15. *Gelibolulu Mustafa Ali ve Künhü'l-ahbar'ında*, 2:7-9; Peçevi, *Peçevi tarihi*, 1:469-70. İnalcık, "Origin of the Ottoman-Russian Rivalry," 79–80; Akdes Nimet Kurat, *Türkiye ve İdil boyu* (Ankara: Türk Tarih Kurumu, 1966), 18; Akdes Nimet Kurat, "The Turkish Expedition to Astrakhan in 1569 and the Problem of the Don-Volga Canal," *Slavonic and East European Review* 40 (1961): 17.

16. Report of Kasım Pasha to the Porte on the Astrakhan Campaign (1569) published in French by Tayyib Gökbilgin, "L'expédition ottomane contre Astrakhan en 1569," *Cahiers du Monde russe et soviétique* 11, no. 1 (1970): 118–23. For a facsimile of the original document, see Alexandre Bennigsen et al., *Le Khanat de Crimée dans les Archives de Musée du Palais de Topkapı* (Paris: Mouton, 1978), 135–38.

17. Report of Simon Maltsev (1569) in P. A. Sadikov, "Pokhod Tatar i Turok na Astrakhan' v 1569," *Istoricheskie zapiski* 22 (1947): 153–64, and Kurat, *Türkiye ve İdil boyu*, appendices 6–7.

18. Report of Kasım Pasha to the Porte on the Astrakhan Campaign (1569), Bennigsen et al., *Le Khanat de Crimée*, 136–37.

19. For details, see Murat Yaşar and Chong Jin Oh, "The Ottoman Empire and the Crimean Khanate in the North Caucasus: A Case Study of the Ottoman-Crimean Relations in the Mid-Sixteenth Century," *Turkish Historical Review* 9 (2018): 86–103.

20. Gelibolulu Mustafa ʿÂli, *Nusret-nâme*, ed. Mustafa Eravcı (Ankara: Türk Tarih Kurumu, 2014), 163–64; Fahrettin Kırzıoğlu, *Osmanlıların Kafkas ellerini fethi (1451–1590)* (Ankara: Sevinç Matbaası, 1976), 305–6.

21. MD 6, no. 1186. The Porte sent a letter in May 1565 to Kasım Mirza of Shirvan who requested Ottoman help to overthrow Safavid rule. The letter stated, however, that there was peace between the Ottomans and Safavids. Kasım Mirza was advised to seek assistance from the shamkhāl, who was his relative.

22. Gelibolulu Mustafa ʿÂli, *Nusret-nâme*, 65.

23. Gelibolulu Mustafa ʿÂli, *Nusret-nâme*, 62–70.

24. Gelibolulu Mustafa ʿÂli, *Nusret-nâme*, 151–60.

25. Gelibolulu Mustafa ʿÂli, *Nusret-nâme*, 147–48.

26. Gelibolulu Mustafa 'Âli, *Nusret-nâme*, 147–48.
27. Gelibolulu Mustafa 'Âli, *Nusret-nâme*, 163–64.
28. Evliya Çelebi, *Evliya Çelebi seyahatnamesi*, vol. 7, ed. Yücel Dağlı, Seyit Ali Kahraman, and Robert Dankof (Istanbul: Yapı Kredi Yayınları, 2003), 298, 301.
29. *Tarih-i Osman Paşa*, ed. Yunus Zeyrek (Ankara: Kültür Bakanlığı Yayınları, 2001), 44. Mustafa Ali notes, "After a while, his [Tuchalav's] daughter was given to Vizier Osman Pasha and it was considered suitable to have one voice and one direction with the rulers of Dagestan." *Gelibolulu Mustafa Ali ve Künhü'l-ahbar'ında*, 2:306–7.
30. MD 32, no. 504. The letter reads, "You have been obedient, honest, and loyal to our exalted Porte.... May you be proud.... It is ordered that when [the order] arrives you should remain firm and unwavering in your loyalty and be on the same terms with our victorious soldiers stationed in these regions and, in case of an attack by the ill-fated *Kızılbaş* [Safavids], you should assist and support them [our soldiers]."
31. Halil İnalcık, "Ottoman Methods of Conquest," *Studia Islamica* 2 (1954): 103–29.
32. MD 32, no. 457.
33. *Tarih-i Osman Paşa*, 39.
34. *Tarih-i Osman Paşa*, 40–52.
35. MD 38, no. 380; Safvet, "Hazar denizinde Osmanlı sancağı," *Tarih-i Osmani Encümeni Mecmuası* 3 (1912): 860–61.
36. MD 38, no. 380; Safvet, "Hazar denizinde Osmanlı sancağı," 860–61.
37. MD 38, no. 380; Safvet, "Hazar denizinde Osmanlı sancağı," 860–61.
38. Kırzıoğlu, *Osmanlıların Kafkas ellerini fethi*, 333, 387.
39. MD 44, no. 36.
40. MD 44, no. 132.
41. Safvet, "Hazar denizinde Osmanlı sancağı," 861.
42. For example, MD 42, no. 382; MD 44, no. 87 and 122, no. 182, no. 190; and MD 51, no. 10.
43. *Early Voyages and Travels to Russia and Persia by Anthony Jenkinson and Other Englishmen*, vol. 2, ed. E. Delmar Morgan and C. H. Coote (London: Haklyut Society, 1886), 452–59.

CHAPTER 3

Papering Over a Diplomatic Gulf
Bureaucracy and Translation between Early Modern Central Asian and Muscovite Courts

Ulfat Abdurasulov

In April 1673 a certain Pahlavān Qoli Bek (Ruzumov), an envoy sent to Moscow by the Khivan ruler Anusha Khan (r. 1663-86), presented himself at the Posol'skiĭ Prikaz (Foreign Chancellery) and submitted a petition addressed to the Muscovite ruler Tsar Alexei Mikhaĭlovich (r. 1645-76). The submission of petitions (*chelobitnaĭa*) to the Romanov dynasts was a common practice among diplomatic personnel of the time. By means of a written appeal, foreign emissaries sought to solve the problems that they encountered in Muscovy.[1] The petition of Pahlavān Qoli was hardly unusual in terms of content: the Khivan envoy was requesting compensation from the Russian treasury for goods and commodities stolen from the mission en route by rebellious groups of Don Cossacks led by the ataman Sten'ka Razin.[2]

What is interesting for our purposes are the linguistic features of the document. Pahlavān Qoli's appeal to the Muscovite autocrat was

---

This chapter originates from the paper delivered at the conference "The Caspian in the History of Early Modern and Modern Eurasia," Yale University, March 29-31, 2019. The author wishes to thank Kevin Gledhill, Paolo Sartori, James Pickett, and Thomas Welsford for their valuable comments on earlier drafts. Research for this chapter has been made possible by the Austrian Science Fund (FWF Start Project—Y 704) and Petra Kappert Fellowship at the Universität Hamburg.

written in Persian (*farsovskim pis'mom*),³ while the response that the Muscovite foreign chancellery drafted on the tsar's behalf was written not in either Russian or Persian, as one might expect, but rather in Turkic, or, as it was identified in the Posol'skiĭ Prikaz's paperwork, in "Tatar script" (*tatarskim pis'mom*).⁴ The Khivan envoy's ambassadorial log (*posol'skaĭa kniga*) indicates that the reply in question was drafted by a translator (*perevodchik*) of the Muscovite foreign office named Abdul Baĭtsyn (aka Abdul Baĭtsyn Belĭalov), a person of Tatar origin born in the town of Kasimov,⁵ who was responsible for dealing specifically with Turkic communications throughout his career in office (1653-78).⁶

Examples such as this are ubiquitous in the history of diplomatic liaisons between the Central Asian principalities of Bukhara and Khiva and Muscovite Russia.⁷ The response to Pahlavān Qoli Bek's appeal is indicative of how the Muscovite authorities generally dealt with the various petitions submitted by Central Asian envoys and other members of their diplomatic retinues. When, for instance, in 1642 Kuzāy Nughāy, this time an envoy of Bukharan ruler Nadr Moḥammad Khan (r. 1642-45), submitted a petition to Tsar Mikhail Feodorovich (r. 1613-45), the main part of his appeal was written in Persian;⁸ the response that Posol'skiĭ Prikaz drafted on the tsar's behalf, by contrast, was written in Turkic.⁹

Russian diplomatic correspondence to the rulers of Bukhara and Khiva often followed a similar model. Over the course of the seventeenth century the letters that the Central Asian rulers sent off to Moscow more often than not were written in Persian. In their written response to these letters, however, the Muscovite authorities drafted replies in two versions, one in Russian (*russkim pis'mom*) and the other in Turkic (*tatarskim pis'mom*). In December 1690, for instance, the Khivan ambassador ʿAbdurraḥim Bek (Azhizov) delivered a message in Persian from Ārang Khan (r. 1689-95) to the coruling Muscovite Tsars Ivan V Alekseevich (r. 1682-96) and Peter I Alekseevich (r. 1682-1725).¹⁰ The Russian autocrats' letter of reply, however, was compiled in Russian, and the translated authorized version was composed in Turkic.¹¹ It seems, furthermore, that both the Russian and Turkic copies had equal status, for both were affixed with "the great royal seal." In a similar manner, Muscovite diplomacy favored Turkic in replying to the letters of other Central Asian rulers, whether from Bukhara or Balkh.¹² Perhaps even more surprisingly, this dynamic can be observed not only with the Central Asian principalities, but also in diplomatic communications with

Safavid Iran and Mughal India (both of which were predominantly Persophone courts).

The question thus presents itself: What was the rationale behind such linguistic inconsistency? Why, in diplomatic correspondence with the Central Asian rulers and diplomats of the time, was Muscovite diplomacy conducted in Turkic, even when fielding communications and enquiries that had originally been written in Persian?

In what follows, I explore the documentary practices of the Posol'skiĭ Prikaz of Muscovy, looking at how they dealt with diplomatic correspondence, mostly royal missives and petitions from Central Asian diplomats. I would like to further consider the multiplicity of the definitions of terms specifying the linguistic features of Central Asia in use in the nomenclature of Muscovite diplomacy. Although Muscovite Russia, Khiva, and Bukhara loom large in this study, they were part of a diplomatic culture integrating the Caspian littoral, the steppe zone, and beyond.[13]

The materials under consideration here lead to broader thematic implications. In his recent groundbreaking study of the Persian-speaking world, Nile Green further extended the conceptual scope of the term "Persianate" (a neologism originally coined by Marshall Hodgson) by bringing to the fore a concept of Persographia, which understands written Persian as a medium of written communication across the region stretching from the Balkans to Bengal.[14] To make better sense of the Persianate cosmopolis he emphasized the idea of "frontiers" as a means to concentrate on the relationship of Persian to other languages at "the spatial edges, social limits, and linguistic breaking points of Persian usage."[15]

In line with Green's agenda, this present chapter considers languages of diplomatic exchange between Muscovite Russia and Central Asia in the early modern era to highlight the diplomatic implications of language choice. Throughout all these exchanges, Persian was an important language of diplomatic interaction, but it was not the only language of exchange, a fact that allows me to assess the nature of Persian's constant negotiations with Turkic and Russian languages within the diplomatic register. In doing so, I hope to be able to show that the Muscovite diplomatic bureaucracy conceptualized the territories to the south, from the Polish-Lithuanian Commonwealth to the Central Asian principalities and, perhaps, further to India, as a frontier not of the Persephone world but of the

Turkic one,¹⁶ whereby Turkic vernaculars were considered the paramount linguistic medium in the diplomatic communication across that vast territory.

The Posol'skiĭ Prikaz: Paperwork and Language Taxonomy

In February 1673, a certain Maksim Matveev, a native of Vladimir in Muscovy and former musketeer (*strelets*) of the Russian Crown, was released after years spent in slavery in Khiva and Bukhara. Upon his arrival in Moscow, Matveev was subjected to interrogation at the Posol'skiĭ Prikaz. This office was one of the key governmental agencies of pre-Petrine Russia, which throughout the seventeenth century was in charge of receiving foreign embassies and dispatching Russian diplomats abroad.¹⁷ During the period we are discussing, the Muscovite foreign chancellery functioned as the locus of all diplomatic exchanges: this institution was where all diplomatic correspondence took place, whether incoming or outgoing, and where relevant information was centralized, produced, copied, and preserved.¹⁸ The Posol'skiĭ Prikaz became particularly prominent in the latter half of the seventeenth century.¹⁹ It was then that the office came to be headed by the leading statesmen of Muscovite Russia, carrying the rank of boyar, which is to say members of the upper stratum that surrounded the throne of the tsar.²⁰ The prominent heads (sing.: *nachal'nik*) of the Posol'skiĭ Prikaz, Afanasiĭ Ordin-Nashchokin (in office, 1667–71), Artamon Matveev (1671–78), and Vasiliĭ Golitsyn (1682–89), were bestowed with the honorific title of "keeper of the regal great seal and [overseer] of the state's diplomatic affairs."²¹ As such, the holders of this diplomatic office enjoyed an authority second only to the tsar in the administration and played decisive roles in shaping the course of Romanov foreign policy during this period.²² It is also worth mentioning that the remit of the Posol'skiĭ Prikaz was not confined solely to supervising diplomatic relations. The chancellery's jurisdiction extended to regulation of Muscovy's international trade relations, oversight of foreign subjects living within the realm, governance of the newly conquered western and southern frontier regions, and overseeing the redemption of Russian subjects (*polonīaniki*) who had been kept in captivity in other states, mostly in Central Asia and Crimea.²³ To this end, Maksim Matveev's questioning was part and parcel of the routine procedure followed by the foreign chancellery in almost every case of the release of the

Muscovite subjects from slavery. The undersecretary (*pod'iachiĭ*) of the Posol'skiĭ Prikaz, who had been in charge of taking minutes of Matveev's interrogation, left inter alia the following entry:

> And he, Maksimka [Matveev], while being held in captivity in Bukharan lands, managed to learn foreign languages [namely], Turkic (*Turskiĭ*), Tatar (*Tatarskiĭ*), Persian (*Persidskiĭ*), Bukharan (*Bukharskiĭ*), and Khivan (*Khivinskiĭ*).[24]

The observation may look striking, attesting as it does to the multiplicity of the definitions that were in use in the nomenclature of Muscovite diplomacy while describing Central Asia's linguistic landscape. Other evidence is equally suggestive. Amid seventeenth-century Muscovite diplomatic texts, one may come across other similar indications, also implemented by Muscovite clerks, in both colloquial and formal usage, that similarly differentiate the various languages and writing styles of Central Asia. This was the case especially on those occasions when Muscovite diplomatic clerks attempted to define the language of Central Asian diplomatic letters and ambassadorial petitions. One also encounters such terms as "Persian language" or "Persian script" (*farsovskiĭ iazyk*; *farsovskoe pis'mo*), "Tatar language" or "script" (*tatarskiĭ iazyk*; *tatarskoe pis'mo*), Turkic language (*turkskiĭ iazyk*), "Khivan" or "Urgenchi language" (*knivinskiĭ / iurgenskĭ iazyk*), and so on. These broad varieties of speech merit perhaps further clarification.

The term *farsovskiĭ* presents no obvious difficulty and presumably relates to Persian (also known by its endonym *fārsi*). Throughout the early modern period, Persian, Eurasia's greatest lingua franca of the times, as Nile Green has put it,[25] figured extensively in administrative and diplomatic communications produced across a vast area extending all the way from Bengal to the Balkans, and Central Asia was an integral part of this "Persianate" cosmopolis. It comes as little surprise, then, that many of the diplomatic letters addressed by Central Asian rulers to Muscovy or elsewhere were compiled in Persian.[26] This was true not only of letters from Bukhara or Balkh, where, as is known, Persian was the paramount language of chancellery and belles-lettres,[27] but also in Khorezm (Arab. *Khwārazm*), where it has often been assumed that "the literary language was predominantly, if not exclusively, Turkic."[28] Indeed, as we shall see, the letters that were conveyed to Moscow by Khorezmian (Khivan) ambassadors over the seventeenth century often were written in Persian.[29]

However, Persian was not the only language of diplomatic correspondence between Central Asia and Muscovy. Other materials of the Posol'skiĭ Prikaz provide clear evidence that diplomatic communications in both Bukhara and Khiva with Muscovite Russia were composed also in Turkic.[30] Furthermore, on some occasions in the seventeenth century diplomatic emissaries from Khiva or Bukhara presented the Russian authorities with multiple letters from their patrons, some of which were written in Persian and others in Central Asian (Eastern) Turkic, aka Chaghatay.[31] In the terminology of the Muscovite Posol'skiĭ Prikaz, the Chaghatay texts from Central Asia were predominantly designated as "Tatar" or "Tatar script" (*tatarskiĭ*; *tatarskoe pis'mo*).[32] Interestingly, though, this "Tatar" designation was applied not only to Chaghatay documents from Central Asia, but also to diplomatic texts from the Crimean Khanate, the Nogai Horde,[33] or even the Ottoman Empire.[34] It seems that use of the term "Tatar" in reference to various Turkic vernaculars and dialects had a long-established tradition in Muscovite diplomatic practice.[35] One of the earliest known archival inventories of the record repository of the Russian treasury (conventionally labeled as the "Tsars' Archive"), composed reportedly in the last quarter of the sixteenth century, designates the language of the diplomatic letters of the Crimean khans to the Muscovite rulers exclusively as being in Tatar (*tatarskoe pis'mo*), whereas the Turkic translation of the distinct surah of the Qur'an that reportedly was used by the sixteenth-century Muscovite diplomats for accepting oaths of allegiance from the Crimean and Noghay nobility was referred to as the "Tatar Qur'an" (*Kuran Tatarskiĭ*).[36] This and other evidence allows us safely to surmise that the designation "Tatar" functioned within the taxonomy of the Posol'skiĭ Prikaz as a kind of umbrella term to denote regional variations of Turkic vernacular that were used in a vast territory, from the Black Sea region to Kashghar.[37]

In addition to the terms "Tatar" and "Persian," Muscovite clerks refer also to the "Khivan" or "Urgenchi" language (*khivinskiĭ / iurgenskiĭ iazyk*), and to "Bukharan" (*bukharskiĭ*). One may assume that such designations served to convey the specific features of dialects from these respective regions of Central Asia. Yet trying to follow explicit logic and patterns of this Muscovite taxonomy is ultimately a fruitless enterprise. These variations in terminology may be attributed to the inconsistency with which clerks in Muscovy categorized languages. As some scholars have pointed out, one of the salient features of the Muscovite bureaucracy was the lack of stable codification for specific terminology.[38]

Dusmamat Kulmamatov, who has previously addressed the issue of the languages used in diplomatic communication between Muscovite and Central Asian courts, has justly pointed out that more often than not the languages were defined not by the self-designation of native speakers, but rather on an ad hoc basis, whether due to geographic or confessional attributes.[39]

Diplomatic texts provide a host of other interesting details about the languages of diplomatic exchange. As noted above, more often than not the letters that the Central Asian rulers of the time sent off to Moscow were written in Persian. By way of a written response to these letters, however, the Muscovite authorities drafted replies in two versions, one in Russian and the other in Turkic. In November 1683, for instance, the Khivan ambassador ʿAbdurraḥim Bek (Abreimbek) Asvebekov delivered Anusha Khan's message in Persian to the coruling juvenile heirs to the Russian throne, Tsars Ivan V and Peter I.[40] Reliance upon precedent seems, in the meanwhile, to have played a key role in bureaucratic practice and in the decision-making process of pre-Petrine Russia. Whatever sort of diplomatic decision needed to be made, whether determining the language of the tsar's letter to the foreign ruler, or the quantity and value of gifts to be sent, or setting the size of the per diem allowance for embassy members, and so on, Muscovite bureaucracy generally tended to follow precedent set by previous cases. It was perhaps for this reason that the clerks of the Posol'skiĭ Prikaz, on the occasion of drafting the reply letter to the Khivan ruler, issued a memorandum with references to earlier precedents, together with a request to their superiors for further instructions with regard to what language they should use for the tsar's reply:

> In previous years, during the reign of the [late] Great Sovereign, Tsar, and Grand Duke, of blessed memory Feodor Alekseevich, [namely] in [7]187 [from Earth's creation = 1679],[41] the Great Sovereign's royal letters to the Khans of Khiva were written in Tatar script.
>
> Now the Khivan khan's envoy Abreimbek has been [in Moscow on a diplomatic mission] to the Great Sovereigns [Tsars Ivan V and Peter I]. By the royal edict of the Great Sovereigns, it has been ordered to give a release to the Khivan envoy [and send him back] from Moscow to his Khan. [It has been also ordered] that the Tsars' Majesties' letter [of reply] should be sent along with him [the envoy], whereby to give reply to the issues raised by the Khan in his letter to the Great Sovereigns.

And now, concerning the languages in which the Great Sovereigns' letter to the Khivan khan should be written—whether in Russian or in Tatar script—what would be the will of the Great Sovereigns, Tsars, and Grand Dukes, the Autocrats of all Russia... Ioann Alekseevich and Peter Alekseevich?[42]

As we learn further from the ambassadorial log relating to the Khivan envoy's mission, the tsars' letter was finally entrusted to ʿAbdurraḥim Bek in May 1684. The entry left by the diplomatic clerks also provides some clues about the language choice of the tsars' missive:

> [The letter] is written in the courtyard of the reigning great city of Moscow, on the 3rd of May 7192 from Earth's creation [May 13, 1684]. The white letter of the Great Sovereigns [of Russia] is written on a sheet of Alexandrian paper, of the middle size,[43] in Russian (*Russkim pis'mom*). And the names and titles of the Great Sovereigns until [the word] "Moscovian" are written in gold.... [Whereas] only the name of the [Khivan Anusha] Khan is written in gold [and not his titles]. [The letter] is penned by the undersecretary (*pod'iachii*) of the Posol'skiĭ prikaz Ivan Favorov. [The letter] is sealed with the royal great seal.... To this regal letter is attached the copy in Turkic (*Tatarskim pis'mom*), written by the translator Suleyman Tolkachov.[44]

On certain occasions the letter from the Muscovite rulers to their Central Asian counterpart was dispatched in Turkic even without the supplementation of the Russian copy. For instance, in February 1671 Mollā Farrokh, an envoy of the Bukharan ruler ʿAbd al-ʿAziz Khan, during the farewell audience with the Russian autocrat, was entrusted with a letter to his patron. The original letter, as we learn from the ambassadorial log of the embassy, "was written in Tatar on a folio of Alexandrian paper of middle size" and was sealed with the "great royal seal."[45]

In 1695 the Posol'skiĭ Prikaz drafted three letters on behalf of Tsars Peter I and Ivan V to the rulers of Khiva, Bukhara, and Balkh on the occasion of a diplomatic mission by the Muscovite envoy, a merchant named Semën Malen'kiĭ (Malenkov), to the court of Shah Aurangzeb in India. In their missives the Russian autocrats requested that their Central Asian counterparts ensure safe passage for the Russian mission, which would be passing through their territories. All of these texts were compiled in Turkic and affixed with the great royal seal.[46]

Despite being drafted and sealed, these letters were never sent to their addressees, for the Russian government eventually chose another itinerary for Semën Malen'kiĭ's mission, namely through the Safavid realm, through Isfahan to Bandar Abbas and thence by sea to the port of Surat and on to the Mughal imperial centers.[47] In view of this revised itinerary, a new letter to the Safavid ruler Shah Solṭān Ḥosayn (r. 1694–1722) was compiled whereby the Muscovite authorities requested the safe passage of their diplomatic emissaries, this time through the Safavid realms. As previously in the case of the Central Asian rulers, the tsars' missive to the Safavid shah was also drafted in Turkic.[48] More surprisingly perhaps, the same language choice might be observed on the reply missive that Shah Solṭān Ḥosayn forwarded to Peter I, whereby he let the latter know about the safe passage of the Muscovite mission through Safavid territory.[49] This proved not to be a unique case, and similar examples may be found throughout the history of Russian-Safavid diplomatic communication in the early modern period.[50] Even the authors of *TSarskiĭ tituliārnik*, the most prestigious and illustrious of the pre-Petrine-era manuals on diplomatic correspondence as well as a compendium on the titles of the foreign dynasts, compiled by the Muscovite diplomatic chancellery in 1672, define the language of written diplomatic communication of the Muscovite rulers with Safavids in the following way:

> And the Great Sovereigns, Tsars, and Great *Kniāze*s of Russia have been in [diplomatic] exchange with Persian Shahs. And the Great Sovereigns' letters to them [the shahs] have been written in Tatar script on Alexandrian paper of large or middle size.[51]

It seems that Russian diplomatic correspondence to the Mughal emperors followed a similar language choice. Thus, for instance, when in 1646 the Russian couriers (*gontsy*) Nikita Syroezhin and Vasiliĭ Tushkanov took letters from Tsar Alexei Mikhaĭlovich to the court of Shah Jahan they were written in two copies, Russian and Turkic. "Two royal missives were compiled; the first was written in Russian on large Alexandrian paper . . . , the second one written in Tatar [also] on large Alexandrian paper . . . and both are stamped by the large [royal] seal," so we read in the records of the Posol'skiĭ Prikaz.[52]

In 1675 Muhammad Ῑusuf Kasymov, yet another Muscovite envoy, brought communications to Shah Aurangzeb. The tsar's missives were composed in three copies: Russian, Turkic (Tatar), and Latin.[53] All of them had an equivalent status as all three were written "on the large folio of Alexandrian paper" and stamped "with the same large [royal] seal."⁵⁴ In the instruction (*nakaz*) given to Kasymov on behalf of the Russian tsar, it was stipulated that Tatar and Latin copies of the tsar's letter were sent just "in case there is no one in India able to translate Russian script, and the [Tatar and Latin] letters should be given for [the purpose of the] genuine understanding of the tsar's missive."⁵⁵

As for Semën Malen'kiĭ, in 1694 he finally reached Mughal India and was received at Aurangzeb's military camp in the city of Burhanpur.⁵⁶ There he was granted a royal *farmān* on behalf of Aurangzeb, which conferred upon him the privilege of being able to trade freely within the Mughal realm.⁵⁷ Apart from the fact that Malen'kiĭ was the first Russian envoy who managed (after repeated attempts on the part of the Muscovite crown) to reach the Mughal court, no less striking was the fact that Aurangzeb's *farmān* entrusted to Malen'kiĭ was written in Turkic, and seemed to be the only known royal document in that language issued by the Mughal court.⁵⁸ One may only guess why the Mughal court would have issued an edict that was meant to be addressed to the city and the provincial governors of the Mughal realm in Turkic, rather than in Persian. It is particularly surprising given that even the lower levels of Mughal administration were more accustomed to dealing with Persian-language documents than ones in Turkic.⁵⁹ Moreover some wordings employed in the text of the *farmān* barely featured in the Mughal chancellery lexicon and were hardly understandable to the local audience of the realm.⁶⁰ But the matter perhaps becomes more understandable if we consider the linguistic expectations of the Muscovite court. Before their dispatch to the Mughal court, the Russian diplomats were instructed by Muscovite authorities that after arriving at their destination they should request that "the Shah [Aurangzeb] is to send his missive letters to the Great Sovereign [of Russia] in Turkic or in Latin."⁶¹ It has long been recognized that one of the metrics for gauging the efficiency of a Muscovite diplomatic mission abroad was the ability of the envoy to obtain a written reply from his host.⁶² The Muscovite authorities seemed to be adamant while demanding their emissaries make progress on that issue.⁶³ On previous occasions, Shah Aurangzeb had refused any contacts with the Muscovite court, arguing that no relations between the two courts had existed up until then, and that there was thus no need to initiate them now.⁶⁴ With this in mind one may conjecture that the *farmān* was needed for the Muscovite envoy first and foremost as a written proof of successful fulfilment of his diplomatic mission after his return to Moscow. It is also safe to assume that the role played by Muscovite Turkophone scribes, who according to Malen'kiĭ's ambassadorial log accompanied him on the journey, was instrumental in drafting the text of the charter. It seems that the choice of language was a matter of direct significance for the Russian envoy.

Turkic Dragomans of the Posol'skiĭ Prikaz

In order to make sense of the prevalence of Turkic over Persian in Muscovite diplomatic paperwork, it is perhaps worth addressing the specifics and practices of the Posol'skiĭ Prikaz. Long experience of communicating with Turkic chancelleries in the Ottoman Empire, the Crimean Khanate, and elsewhere, and of dealing with Turkic-speaking groups of Siberia and the Volga basin meant that there were many people in the foreign chancellery with the requisite experience to draft Turkic-language documents.[65] M. Moiseev has emphasized that Turkophone scribes of the Posol'skiĭ Prikaz played a major role in establishing standards of Turkic translation of tropes and formulae from Russian.[66] Another key fact to recall is the aforementioned reliance on previous precedents in Muscovite bureaucracy and the diplomatic chancellery. This was particularly noticeable in the case of rendering Russian royal titulature in diplomatic documents. It was a consistent priority for Moscow authorities when drafting diplomatic texts to ensure that foreign-language renderings of the tsar's name and titles should be accurate, and errors could be costly. A certain Grigory Kotoshkhin, one of the clerks of the Posol'skiĭ Prikaz, was subjected to corporal punishment for omitting a single word while rendering the tsar's lengthy titulature in one diplomatic text.[67] It comes as little surprise, therefore, that when composing responses to a Central Asian ambassador's petitions or drafting the missive letters to the Central Asian rulers it was considerably easier for the diplomatic clerks to utilize well-established Turkic-language formulas and templates than to trespass into the dimly understood quicksand of literary Persian. Such practices appear in turn to have influenced Central Asian diplomatic conventions: among the materials of the Posol'skiĭ Prikaz, one finds many petitions by Central Asian ambassadors that are compiled bilingually, with the main body of the communication in Persian, but the opening address, specifying the Russian autocrat's name and title, in Turkic.[68] This happened because on some occasions such petitions had been compiled with the assistance of Muscovite clerks, whereby the petitioner, whether the ambassador himself or his representative, referred to ready-made Turkic templates for rendering the Russian autocrat's titulature.

The demographic makeup of the Posol'skiĭ Prikaz's personnel similarly helps to explain the prevalence of Turkic in Muscovite diplomacy. According to some estimates, as many as half of all the foreign chancellery's dragomans (*tolmachi*, i.e., interpreters) in the later half the seventeenth century were Turkic-language specialists.[69] Andrey Beliakov in his recent comprehensive study provides detailed prosopographic information on the translating personnel of the Posol'skiĭ Prikaz. His statistical analyses not only clearly support the argument that the Turkic-language translators and dragomans constituted the largest body of the Posol'skiĭ Prikaz's translating personnel, but also illustrates that the number of Turkophone dragomans (even excluding those personnel who dealt with Ottoman Turkic) by far outnumbered those responsible for oral translation of Persian. For instance, for much of the seventeenth century the number of Turkic dragomans employed contemporaneously with the diplomatic office numbered from twenty-four to thirty-four, whereas the number of Persian-language dragomans at the same period of time never exceeded six.[70] A similar ratio may be observed on the number of Turkic and Persian translators (*perevodchiki*) of the Posol'skiĭ Prikaz. In the seventeenth century the number of Turkic-language translators was several times higher than those of Persian.[71] It does not come as a surprise, therefore, that the Muscovite bureaucracy from time to time encountered complications in dealing with Persian-language diplomatic materials. In 1675, shortly before the dispatch of the envoy to the court of Shah Aurangzeb, the Posol'skiĭ Prikaz managed to obtain, with the assistance of Indian merchants, written templates for rendering the Mughal emperor's name and titulature. However, while scrutinizing these texts the translators had to admit that as "the name of the Indian Shah is written in Persian words (*slovami farsofskimi*), . . . they are not able to translate those words from Persian to Slavonic [Russian]."[72]

A similar case occurred in 1693, when diplomatic letters supposedly written in Persian (*persidskie pis'ma*) had been delivered to Moscow, whereupon at the order of the Russian autocrat they were handed over to the diplomatic chancellery for the purpose of translation. While in the Posol'skiĭ Prikaz, however, the texts in question were handed over not to the Persian-language experts, as one might expect, but rather to the "Tatar language translators."⁷³ After having considered the texts, the Muscovite diplomatic translators came to the following conclusion: "those letters are [written] in Persian (*farsovskogo īazyka*) and because they do not know that Persian [dialect?] they are not able to translate them."⁷⁴

It may seem surprising that the Persian documents were handed over to translators who specialized in "Tatar" texts, rather than to Persian specialists. One might have expected the Muscovite foreign office to have at its disposal a number of personnel competent to work in Persian, especially bearing in mind Muscovy's long-standing and dynamic diplomatic contacts with Safavid Iran. Yet the evidence intimated above provides conclusive evidence about the Turkic-centric inclination of Muscovite diplomacy in dealing with the Islamic world to the south.⁷⁵

On Networks and Dragomans

The provenance of the translating staff of the Muscovite diplomatic agency is also salient, especially for those individuals who were involved in diplomacy with the Central Asian principalities. The translating personnel of the office consisted of translators (*perevodchiki*) and interpreters (*tolmachi*). It is worth mentioning that though in practice both offices had competency in providing translation services, Muscovite administrative nomenclature stipulated a clear-cut division between them. Thus, the former, who occupied a higher position in the diplomatic hierarchy, were responsible for providing translations of written texts, while the latter were mainly in charge of oral interpretation.⁷⁶ This hierarchy was also reflected in the two offices' respective modes of operation. The translators' duties assumed a standing (continual) location at the chancellery, whereas the interpreters were permanent participants in Muscovite diplomatic missions abroad and were actively recruited as bailiffs (*pristav*), that is to say, as officials charged with accompanying foreign diplomats during their sojourn within Muscovy.⁷⁷

The translating personnel who dealt with the Turkic languages were generally recruited from among Muscovy's various groups of Tatar subjects, particularly from Romanov, Kazan, Kasimov, and other towns in the Volga basin.⁷⁸ We also encounter a number of individuals, both dragomans and translators, who originated from Central Asia. One such figure was a man named Peter Khivinets. From the Posol'skiĭ Prikaz's personnel records, we learn that Peter was born in "the lands of

Khiva" but left his homeland "seeking the holy Orthodox Christian faith" and was granted status as a subject of the Russian tsar.[79] His linguistic skills were evidently appreciated in Russia: in 1677, a royal edict identified him as being "at the disposal of the State Posol'skiĭ Prikaz as an interpreter (*tolmach*) of Persian and Khivan languages."[80] As we further learn from personnel records, in 1683 and 1685 Peter Khivinets was included in diplomatic missions sent off to Crimea and Safavid Iran in the same capacity of dragoman.[81]

One thing that was common to many of these translators and interpreters was that they had some connection to Astrakhan, where there existed an extensive Central Asian mercantile diaspora. For much of the seventeenth century, the city of Astrakhan had served as the principal focal point for diplomatic communication with Central Asia; it was there that newly arrived emissaries sought authorization to proceed on to Moscow. Astrakhan's Bukharan inn (*Bukharskiĭ gostinnyĭ dvor*) was particularly important here, both as a marketplace and as an enclave for Central Asian émigré and mercantile groups.[82] We know, for example, that the Posol'skiĭ Prikaz's translators and interpreters were often sent to Astrakhan for the purpose of improving their skills in the Turkic and Persian languages.[83] We learn from other materials that this training took place at the Bukharan inn, where "one could find many people from Qizilbash, Bukhara, and Urgench who are skilled in the languages and grammars."[84] Thus, for instance, in 1649 a certain Poluekht Zverev, an ambassadorial clerk of the Posol'skiĭ Prikaz, was sent from Moscow to Astrakhan for the purpose of "learning the Tatar language and grammar" (*dliā naucheniia Tatarskogo iazyku i gramote*).[85] There, according to his own testament, he was trained by someone called Davlat Moḥammad Abiz (aka Devlet Abyz Melikov), a translator at the Astrakhan provincial administration and resident of the Bukharan inn who was of Khorezmian origin (*urgenchanin*).[86]

The Bukharan enclave in Astrakhan was not only a training venue, but also an environment for recruiting translators and dragomans for both the central Posol'skiĭ Prikaz and its various local branch offices. For instance, in 1649 the Astrakhan authorities turned their eyes to the residents of the *gostinnyĭ dvor* for a new interpreter for the local administration office. Three nominees from the residents of the inn, each of them "skilled in Tatar grammar," were then summoned to the office of provincial administration and subjected to language tests.[87]

It can be safely assumed that interpreters and translators were part of the broader commercial networks operating in the space between

Bukhara, Khiva, Astrakhan, and Moscow, and were associated with and closely integrated into them. The story of Davlat Moḥammad Abiz (Melikov), offers an illustrative example in this regard. We learn about this story from a petition by a certain Sutur Kidekov, known as an "Indian trading man," to Tsar Alexei Mikhaïlovich in February 1647. In his plea, Kidekov complained about various complications caused by the local administration with regard to Indian merchants who had just arrived in Astrakhan.[88] His particular displeasure had been caused by the group of interpreters (*tolmachi*) and, above all, by Davlat Moḥammad Abiz, the one of Urgenchi origin and the resident of the Bukharan inn, who worked as translator in the Astrakhan provincial administration. Sutur noted that Davlat Moḥammad exercised such influence over Astrakhani affairs that people were "less frightened of boyars and the Astrakhan governor (*voevoda*) than of Davlat Abiz." The entrepreneur further requested that the Moscow authorities remove the translator from Astrakhan as quickly as possible.[89]

Shortly after, yet another petition on behalf of another group of Indian merchants was submitted to the tsar, accusing the translator of various abuses. According to the appellants, Davlat Abiz was little more than a fraudster. They claimed that, by drawing on his contacts in the Astrakhan administration, Davlat Abiz was able to issue counterfeit deeds attesting to alleged debts (*zaemnye dolgovye obīazatel'stva*) supposedly incurred by newly arrived Indian merchants, and to recruit fictitious witnesses who, if cases came to trial, could testify on his behalf, thereby forcing the hapless Indians to meet their nonexistent obligations by means of "larger payoffs."[90]

The course of further events reveals a more complex picture. The authorities in Moscow, being extremely eager to entice Indian merchants to Astrakhan, resolved to address the Indians' complaint. Very soon, an edict was issued on behalf of Tsar Alexei Mikhaïlovich. The Astrakhan authorities were instructed to expel Davlat Abiz forthwith to the city of Kazan, along with his family members. But the translator evidently enjoyed the support of influential patrons from among the Astrakhan administration, who were ready to go so far as to sabotage the personal edict of the Russian autocrat. Upon receipt of the tsar's edict, in January 1649, the Astrakhan authorities dispatched to Moscow a written report. In this document, they argued that expelling Davlat Abiz from Astrakhan would be a rash move, given that "no other translators could be found in Astrakhan or elsewhere, except for Davlat." Davlat Abiz's backers also set about collecting testimonies in his support, including from high officials and the notables of Astrakhan, and the representatives of Russian and foreign mercantile groups. According to the Astrakhan officials' estimation, more than two thousand people attested to the Khorezmian translator's innocence.[91]

We learn from the document of personnel records that with the passage of time Davlat Moḥammad Abiz was moved to Moscow and promoted to the position of translator in the Posol'skiĭ Prikaz.[92] He appears to have occupied this position until 1683.[93] Even when in Moscow, Davlat Abiz did not cease contact with his networks in Astrakhan and Central Asia; quite on the contrary, he was able to maintain close liaisons with certain individuals who traveled between Bukhara, Khiva, Moscow, and Astrakhan.[94]

One way of making sense of this episode is by casting it as a reflection of the rivalry that evidently existed between various networks and commercial groups in Astrakhan. It would be an oversimplification, however, to see this rivalry simply as an intercommunal tension between Indian and Central Asia commercial factions. When demanding that Davlat Moḥammad be removed from office, the Indian complainants requested that he be replaced by somebody else from among the residents of the same Bukharan enclave, and even went so far as to suggest potential nominees.[95] Furthermore, Sutur's hostility to the Urgenchi Davlat Abiz did not prevent him from maintaining close commercial contacts with other Khorezmians, those from among the entourage of Khivan ruler Abu al-Ghāzī Khan (r. 1644–63).[96] Evidently, the dynamics at play here were complicated, reflecting a tapestry of interconnected interests: Bukharan, Khivan, and Indian commercial groups, Astrakhani administrators and nobles, and representatives of Muscovy's central authority.

It seems that dragomans and translators were the principal actors in this dynamic, liminal space. In this context, the work of Nathalie Rothman is perhaps instructive. In a seminal study, Rothman examines the role of dragomans in Venetian-Ottoman relations in the early modern period. She characterizes these figures as "trans-imperial subjects," that is, actors who "straddled and helped broker political, religious, and linguistic boundaries" between early modern state formations. She further argues that the role of dragomans was not confined to transmitting information across disinterested channels, but "rather [they] articulated diplomatic knowledge."[97] We still know very little about the capacity of such intermediaries in the region of Central Eurasia; furthermore, our understanding of how diplomatic knowledge was generated and preserved in this environment and how diplomatic genres were codified remains highly limited. But the story of Davlat Abiz reveals the importance of translators both as diplomatic intermediaries and as cultural brokers simultaneously traversing and reifying political, cultural, and linguistic boundaries between Muscovite Russia and Central Asia throughout the early modern period.

As a final observation, I should like to return to the question of the language employed in diplomatic communications between Muscovite Russia and Central Asian khanates over the seventeenth century. As outlined above, the material at our disposal provides conclusive evidence that Muscovite diplomacy was Turkic-centric, even when it was dealing with Central Asian diplomats who at the time generally preferred to operate in the acrolect of literary Persian. As a number of scholars have observed, however, starting in the eighteenth century the Central Asian khanates, and particularly Khorezm and Bukhara, began increasingly to use Turkic themselves as a medium for diplomatic communication with Russia.[98] This shift, which evidently was in line with the expectations of Russian authorities, suggests that Russia's preference for Turkic may have contributed to the broader vernacularization of the language. It might seem logical that the Moscow authorities' insistence on drafting diplomatic texts in Turkic had an impact on Central Asian diplomatic practices, at least when interacting with Russia. The evidence for a causal relationship in this regard remains suggestive rather than definitive but certainly offers one possible explanation for the demonstrable shift that occurred in diplomatic and linguistic practices at this juncture in Eurasian history.

Notes

1. See, for instance D. V. Liseĭtsev, *Posol'skiĭ prikaz v epokhu Smuty* (Moscow: Institut Rossiĭskoĭ Istorii RAN: 2003), 36.

2. Nauchno-istoricheskiĭ arkhiv Sankt-Peterburgskogo Instituta Istorii RAN (*NIASPII RAN*), f. 113, op. 1, d. 94 (*Posol'skie knigi snosheniĭ Rossii s Khivoi͡u*), ll. 40 ob–42 ob. On the circumstances of Pahlavān Qoli's life in city of Astrakhan under the atamans' authority, see Ulfat Abdurasulov, "Making Sense of Central Asia in Pre-Petrine Russia," *Journal of the Economic and Social History of the Orient* 63 (2020): 607–9.

3. NIASPII RAN, f. 113, op. 1, d. 94, l. 40ob.

4. NIASPII RAN, f. 113, op. 1, d. 94, ll. 42ob–43ob.

5. NIASPII RAN, f. 113, op. 1, d. 94, l. 43ob. Kasimov is a city in Russia, in the middle course of the Oka River. In the seventeenth century Kasimov was a

center of the Khanate of Qasim, a Tatar khanate, which in 1452–1681 was regarded as a vassal state, controlled by the rulers of Muscovite Russia. Until the eighteenth century the city of Kasimov was one of a few places wherefrom the greater part of the Tatar clerks and scribes were employed by the Russian chancelleries. See Dariusz Kołodzieczyk, *The Crimean Khanate and Poland-Lithuania: International Diplomacy on the European Periphery (15th–18th Century)* (Leiden: Brill, 2011), 22, 224.

6. A. V. Beliakov, *Sluzhashchie Posol'skogo prikaza 1645–1682 gg.* (St. Petersburg: Nestor-Istoriia, 2017), 101, 283. The bureaucratic system of pre-Petrine Russia elaborated a rather sophisticated set of chancellery practices, which we find preserved in the form of ambassadorial logs (*posol'skie knigi*). What makes these *posol'skie knigi* so particularly valuable is the fact that each of them generally constitutes an integral single set of documents, pertaining to the visit of a particular foreign mission to Muscovy. That is to say, one may find in the logs information regarding the entirety of an ambassador's visit, starting with notifications regarding his arrival at the Muscovite border, and proceeding then to record his itinerary thence to the capital, the protocol of his audiences with the Russian ruler, and the details of negotiations as well as originals and translations of the correspondence between the two monarchs. See N. M. Rogozhin, *Posol'skie knigi Rossii kontsa XV–nachala XVII vv.* (Moscow: Institut Rossiiskoĭ Istorii, 1994).

7. In the current chapter the terms "Bukhara" and "Khiva" are used as synonyms of the two Central Asian principalities of the time, the Khanate of Bukhara and the Khanate of Khiva respectively. The names "Khanate of Khiva" and "Khanate of Bukhara" were adopted in the eighteenth century from European (mostly Russian) literature for the state formations located in the interfluve of the Amu Darya and Syr Darya Rivers (the former) as well as on the territory of the Khorezmian oases (the latter). In seventeenth-century Muscovite diplomatic texts, the Khanate of Khiva was usually identified as "Iurgenskie zemli" or "Khivinskie zemli," i.e., "lands of Urgench" or "lands of Khiva," in reference to the Khanate's two main cities, whereas the "Khanate of Bukhara" was referred as "lands of Bukhara" ("Bukharskie zemli").

8. Petition of Kuzāy Nughāy to Mikhail Feodorovich, RGADA, f. 109, op. 1, 1644 g., d. 1, l. 107.

9. RGADA, f. 109, op. 1, 1644 g., d. 1, l. 107ob.

10. NIASPII RAN, f. 113, op. 1, d. 94, ll. 168–169ob. ʻAbdurraḥim Bek (Azhizov) was envoy of Ārang Khan to Moscow in 1689–91; see NIASPII RAN, f. 113, op. 1, d. 94, ll. 142ob–144. From 1682 through 1696 the Russian Tsardom was ruled by the half brothers Peter I and Ivan V. Until 1689 they had been ruling jointly under the informal regency of their elder sister, Sophia Alekseevna (r. 1682–89). In 1689 Peter I's court supporters managed to deprive Sophia of the regency, and Peter I ruled in his own right as co-tsar with his half brother. At the death of Ivan V in 1696 Peter I became the only ruler of Russia. See Richard S. Wortman, *Scenarios of Power: Myth and Ceremony in Russian Monarchy from Peter the Great to the Abdication of Nicholas II* (Princeton, NJ: Princeton University Press, 2006), 18–20.

CHAPTER 3

11. NIASPII RAN, f. 113, op. 1, d. 94, ll. 220ob–222; on similar cases, see also A. Samoĭlovich et al., eds., *Materialy po istorii Uzbekskoĭ, Tadzhikskoĭ i Turkmenskoĭ SSR. Chast' 1: Torgovlia s Moskovskim gosudarstvom i mezhdunarodnoe polozhenie Sredneĭ Azii v XVI–XVII vv.* (Leningrad: Izdatel'stvo AN SSSR, 1932) (henceforth *MIUTT*), 182–84 (doc. 62), 232–34 (doc. 94), 258–60 (doc. 110).

12. Samoĭlovich et al., *MIUTT*, 180–82 (doc. 62), 260–62 (doc. 111); NIASPII RAN, f. 113, op. 1, d. 93 (*Posol'skie knigi snoshenii Rossii s Bukharoiu*), ll. 25–25ob.

13. There were two main routes that had been adopted in the mid-seventeenth century as the main lines of passage for people and commodities between Muscovy and Central Asia. One such route, the so-called *Khivan route*, ran from the city of Astrakhan southeastward through Yaĭtsk (Gur'ev) at the mouth of the Yaĭk (Ural) River, and reached the Ust-Urt plateau. Thence it skirted the Aral Sea littoral from the northwest and reached the Khorezmian oases. Of no less importance was the Transcaspian maritime route that connected Astrakhan with the region of Mangyshlak. It was there that the terrestrial stretch of the route across Mangyshlak and Ust-Urt connected to the northwestern limits of the Khorezm; see A. N. Chuloshnikov, "Torgovlia Moskovskogo gosudarstva s Sredneĭ Azieĭ v XVI-XVII vekakh," in Samoĭlovich et al., *MIUTT*, 73–76; Audrey Burton, *The Bukharans: A Dynastic, Diplomatic and Commercial History, 1550–1702* (New York: St. Martin's Press, 1997), 391–99. Moreover, a Bukharan envoy who arrived at Tobol'sk in Siberia was not allowed to proceed further to Moscow in 1622. The Muscovite authorities recommended to the Bukharan ruler, on that occasion, that thenceforth his ambassadors to Moscow should be dispatched via Astrakhan, and not Siberia; see Samoĭlovich et al., *MIUTT*, 137–38 (doc. 30).

14. Marshall G. S. Hodgson, *The Venture of Islam: The Expansion of Islam in the Middle Periods*, vol. 2 (Chicago: University of Chicago Press, 1974), 293–94. Nile Green, "Introduction: The Frontiers of the Persianate World (ca. 800-1900)," in *The Persianate World: The Frontiers of a Eurasian Lingua Franca*, ed. Nile Green (Oakland: California University Press, 2019), 4–5.

15. Green, "Introduction," 8. On the cosmopolis paradigm, see Sheldon Pollock, *The Language of the Gods in the World of Men: Sanskrit, Culture, and Power in Pre-modern India* (Berkeley: University of California Press, 2006), 10.

16. I am grateful to Kevin Gledhill for sharing this observation during our conversation on the margins of the conference "The Caspian in the History of Early Modern and Modern Eurasia" (Yale University, March 29–31, 2019).

17. S. A. Belokurov, *O posol'skom prikaze* (Moscow, 1906); N. M. Rogozhin, *Posol'skiĭ prikaz-kolybel' rossiiskoĭ diplomatii* (Moscow: Mezhdunarodnye otnosheniia, 2003).

18. Rogozhin, *Posol'skie knigi Rossii kontsa XV–nachala XVII vv.*; Rogozhin, *Posol'skiĭ prikaz-kolybel' rossiiskoĭ diplomatii*, 14–25.

19. According to Marshall Poe, the chancellery of the Posol'skiĭ Prikaz was among the largest, best-funded, and most powerful and honorable of all the administrative bodies in seventeenth-century Muscovy; see his "The Muscovite State and Its Personnel," in *Cambridge History of Russia*, vol. 1, *From Early Rus to 1689*, ed. Maureen Perrie (Cambridge: Cambridge University Press, 2003), 457.

20. Belokurov, *O posol'skom prikaze*, 42. According to government edicts of the 1670s and 1680s only the upper ranks of the royal council (*Boyar Duma*),

invariably a boyar or an *okol'nichiĭ*, could have their name listed in the heading of chancellery documents; see Peter B. Brown, "Bureaucratic Administration in Seventeenth-Century Russia," in *Modernizing Muscovy: Reform and Social Change in Seventeenth Century Russia*, ed. Jarmo Kotilaine and Marshall Poe (London: Routledge Curzon, 2005), 73.

21. "TSarstvennye bol'shie pechati i gosudarstvennykh posol'skikh del oberegatel'"; see Belokurov, *O posol'skom prikaze*, 43.

22. N. M. Rogozhin, *U gosudarevykh del byt' ukazano* (Moscow: RAGS, 2002), 39; S. K. Bogoi͡avlenskiĭ, *Moskovskiĭ prikaznyĭ apparat i deloproizvodstvo v XVI–XVII vekakh* (Moscow: I͡azyki slavi͡anskoĭ kul'tury, 2006), 382.

23. Grigory Kotoshikhin, *O Rossii v tsarstvovanie Aleksii͡a Mikhaĭlovicha* (St. Petersburg: Izdanie Arkheograficheskoĭ Komissii, 1884); Brown, "Bureaucratic Administration in Seventeenth-Century Russia," 64.

24. NIASPII RAN, f. 113, op. 1, d. 94, l. 36.

25. Green, "Introduction," 2.

26. See, for instance, Samoĭlovich et al., *MIUTT*, letters of the rulers of Khorezm, 155–56 (doc. 44), 164–65 (doc. 49), 168 (doc. 53), 173–74 (doc. 57); Bukhara, 184–85 (doc. 64); Balkh, 152–53 (doc. 41), 229–31 (doc. 91).

27. James Pickett, *Polymaths of Islam: Power and Networks of Knowledge in Central Asia* (Ithaca, NY: Cornell University Press, 2020), 29–40; Paolo Sartori has recently argued that the Bukharan literati continued to write in Persian even over the colonial period well through Bolshevik revolution; see his "From the Demotic to the Literary: The Ascendance of the Vernacular Turkic in Central Asia (Eighteenth-Nineteenth Centuries)," *Eurasian Studies* 18 (2020): 218.

28. Yuri Bregel, "Introduction," in Shīr Muḥammad Mīrāb Mūnis and Muḥammad Riżā Āgahī, *Firdaws al-iqbāl: History of Khorezm*, ed. Yuri Bregel (Leiden: Brill, 1988), 1; see also Marc Toutant, "De-Persifying Court Culture: The Khanate of Khiva's Translation Program," in Green, *The Persianate World*, 244. Devin DeWeese has recently argued that before the nineteenth century "Khwarazm [was] the only part of Central Asia for which we can claim some sort of parity between Persian and Turkic"; see his "Persian and Turkic from Kazan and Tobolsk: Literary Frontiers in Muslim Inner Asia," in Green, *The Persianate World*, 136.

29. This was the case of Anusha Khan's letters delivered to Moscow in 1673 and 1681 respectively (see NIASPII RAN, f. 113, op. 1, d. 94, ll. 29ob–30; ll. 86ob–87ob), as well as one of Ārang Khan in 1891 (NIASPII RAN, f. 113, op. 1, d. 94, ll. 168–69ob).

30. Samoĭlovich et al., *MIUTT*, 146–48 (doc. 36), 154–55 (doc. 43), 174–76 (doc. 58).

31. Samoĭlovich et al., *MIUTT*, 138–39 (doc. 31), 155–56 (docs. 44–45).

32. On rare instances of employment of the term Turkic (*turskiĭ*) in Muscovite diplomatic texts, see NIASPII RAN, f. 113, op. 1, d. 94, ll. 203–203ob; NIASPII RAN, f. 113, op. 1, d. 93, l. 46.

33. See, for instance, D. A. Mustafina and V. V. Trepalov, eds., *Posol'skie knigi po svi͡azi͡am Rossii s Nogaĭskoĭ Ordoĭ, 1551–1561 gg.* (Kazan: Tatarskoe Knizhnoe Izdatel'stvo, 2006); A. V. Vinogradov et al., eds., *Posol'ska͡ia kniga po svi͡azi͡am Moskovskogo gosudarstva s Krymom, 1567–1572* (Moscow: Russkie Viti͡azi, 2016).

34. Barbara Kellner-Heinkele, "St. Petersburg and the Steppe People: Diplomatic Correspondences of the 18th Century from the Arkhiv Vneshnej Politiki Rossijskoj Imperii in Moscow," in *Proceedings of the 38th Permanent International Altaistic Conference (PIAC). Kawasaki, Japan August 7–12, 1995*, ed. Giovanni Stary (Wiesbaden: Harrassowitz Verlag, 1995), 225.

35. See M. A. Usmanov, "O dokumentakh russko-vostochnoĭ perepiski na tiurkskikh iazykakh v XV–XVIII vv. i ikh istochnikovedcheskom znachenii," in *Vostochnoe istoricheskoe istochnikovedenie i spetsial'nye istoricheskie distsipliny*, vol. 2 (Moscow: Nauka, 1994), 126–29.

36. A. A. Zimin, *Gosudarstvennyĭ arkhiv Rossii XVI stoletiĭa: Opyt rekonstruktsii* (Moscow: Institut Istorii AN SSSR, 1978), 93.

37. See further Usmanov, "O dokumentakh russko-vostochnoĭ perepiski na tiurkskikh iazykakh," 123–38; D. S. Kulmamatov, "Offitsial'nye pis'mennye iazyki Sredneĭ Azii i dvuiazychnye bukharskie chelobitnye XVII v.," *Oʻzbekistonda xorijiy tillar* 21, no. 2 (2018): 29–35.

38. A. V. Malov, "Trinadtsataia posol'skaia kniga v deloproizvodstve Posol'skogo prikaza: sostav, struktura, formirovanie," in Vinogradov, *Posol'skaia kniga po sviaziam Moskovskogo gosudarstva s Krymom*, 23.

39. Kulmamatov, "Offitsial'nye pis'mennye iazyki Sredneĭ Azii."

40. The 1682–84 mission of ʿAbdurraḥim Asvebekov had been initially dispatched by Anusha Khan to Tsar Feodor III Alekseevich (1676–82). In fact, however, Tsar Feodor had already passed away in May 1682, before the Khivan envoy's arrival, and the envoy was therefore received by Feodor III's successors, the double tsars Ivan V Alekseevich and Peter I Alekseevich; on this embassy, see NIASPII RAN, f. 113, op. 1, d. 94, ll. 68–132.

41. On the Byzantine calendar, a modified version of the Julian calendar, that had been in use in Muscovite Russia before 1700, see Charles Ellis, "Russian Calendar (988–1917)," in *The Literary Encyclopedia*, vol. 2.2.1.00, *Slavic and Russian Writing and Culture: Old, Medieval and Tsarist, 700–1917*, first published September 25, 2008, https://www.litencyc.com/php/stopics.php?rec=true&UID=5547.

42. NIASPII RAN, f. 113, op. 1, d. 94, ll. 101–101ob.

43. Alexandrian paper is a type of high-quality paper imported to Russia, reportedly from the eastern Mediterranean. It is on this type of paper of standardized size ("large" or "middle" sheet) during the seventeenth century that most of the Muscovite tsars' letters to the courts of foreign rulers were written; see N. B. Kardanova, "Paleograficheskoe oformlenie tsarskikh poslaniĭ k dozham Venetsii," *Izvestiia Volgogradskogo gosudarstvennogo pedagogicheskogo universiteta* 3 (2012): 53–54.

44. NIASPII RAN, f. 113, op. 1, d. 94, ll. 103–103ob.

45. NIASPII RAN, f. 113, op. 1, d. 93, ll. 25–25ob.

46. RGADA, f. 106, op. 2, d. 7; f. 109, op. 2, d. 18.

47. For a detailed description of Malenkiĭ's voyage to India, see V. A. Ulianitskiĭ, *Snosheniia Rossii s Sredneĭ Azieiu i Indeiu v XVI–XVII vv. Po dokumentam Moskovskogo Glavnogo Arkhiva Ministerstva Inostrannykh Del* (Moscow: Universitetskaia Tipografiia, 1889), 56; K. A. Antonova et al., eds., *Russko-indiĭskie*

otnosheniia v XVII v. Sbornik dokumentov (Moscow: Izdatel'stvo Vostochnoĭ Literatury, 1958), 371-73 (doc. 258).

48. RGADA, f. 77, op. 2, d. 75. For the facsimile and edition as well as Russian translation of Shah Solṭān Ḥosayn's letter, see Antonova et al., *Russko-indiĭskie otnosheniia v XVII v.*, 365-68 (doc. 255).

49. RGADA, f. 77, op. 2, d. 76; For the facsimile and edition of the text, see Antonova et al., *Russko-indiĭskie otnosheniia v XVII v.*, 365-68 (doc. 255). Ferenc Peter Csirkés in his recent study has shown that Turkic was an integral part of the Safavid court, and also, "to moderate extent," was used in diplomacy and royal correspondence; see his "'Chaghatay Oration, Ottoman Eloquence, Qizilbash Rhetoric': Turkic Literature in Ṣafavid Persia" (PhD thesis, University of Chicago, 2016), 292-95.

50. Vasily Bartol'd, for instance argued that "Tatar" "for a certain while" had been a paramount language of the diplomatic communication between the Muscovite and Safavid courts; see his "Istoriia izucheniia Vostoka v Evrope i Rossii," in V. V. Bartol'd, *Sochineniia*, vol. 9 (Moscow: Nauka, 1977), 374. Nikolay Veselovsky, an editor and publisher of a set of early modern diplomatic texts on Russian-Safavid relations, stated that the Moscow tsars' letters to the Safavid rulers "were compiled either way, in Persian, or in Tatar"; see his *Pamiatniki diplomaticheskikh i torgovykh snoshenii Moskovskoĭ Rusi s Persieĭ*, vol. 2, *TSarstvovanie Borisa Godunova, Vasiliia Shuĭskogo i nachalo tsarstvovaniia Mikhaila Feodorovicha* (St. Petersburg: Tovarishchestvo Parovoĭ Skoropechatni Iablonskiĭ i Perott, 1890-1898), i. According to P. P. Bushev, the first known letter written "in Tatar" delivered to the Safavid ruler on behalf of the Russian ruler, dates back to 1588; see his *Istoriia posol'stv i diplomaticheskikh otnoshenii Russkogo i Iranskogo gosudarstv v 1586-1612 gg. (po russkim arkhivam)* (Moscow: Nauka, 1975), 82.

51. *TSarskiĭ tituliarnik: Bol'shaia gosudareva kniga ili Koren' rossiiskikh gosudareĭ*, St Petersburg, Russian National Library, inv. no OP Erm. 440, fol. 208.

52. NIASPII RAN, f. 113, op. 1, d. 93, ll. 194ob-195.

53. Both the facsimile and the edition of the tsar's letters to Aurangzeb in Turkic are available in Antonova et al., *Russko-indiĭskie otnosheniia v XVII v.*, 205-9 (doc. 114).

54. See NIASPII RAN, f. 113, op. 1, d. 93, ll. 195, 229ob.

55. NIASPII RAN, f. 113, op. 1, d. 93, ll. 226.

56. N. B. Baĭkova, *Rol' Sredneĭ Azii v russko-indiĭskikh torgovykh sviaziakh (pervaia polovina XVI–vtoraia polovina XVIII v.)* (Tashkent: Nauka, 1964), 73-74.

57. RGADA, f. 56, op. 2, 1696 g., d. 5. For the facsimile of the *farmān* as well as the Russian translation, see Antonova et al., *Russko-indiĭskie otnosheniia v XVII v.*, 369-70 (doc. 256).

58. N. M. Gol'dberg, "Predislovie," in Antonova et al., *Russko-indiĭskie otnosheniia v XVII v.*, 18-19.

59. Muzaffar Alam, "The Pursuit of Persian: Language in Mughal Politics," *Modern Asian Studies* 32, no. 2 (1998): 317-49.

60. That is not, of course, to entirely dismiss the presence of Turkic in the Mughal courtly and administrative usage. A recent study by Benedek Peri has

made a compelling case for the ubiquity of Turkic in the court as well as in the governance of Mughal India throughout the early modern period; see his "Turkish Language and Literature in Medieval and Early Modern India," in *Turks in the Indian Subcontinent, Central and West Asia: The Turkish Presence in the Islamic World*, ed. Ismail K. Poonawala (Oxford: Oxford University Press, 2017), 227-62.

61. Dmitriĭ Kobenko, *Nakaz TSarii͡a Alekseĭa Mikhaĭlovicha Makhmetu Ĭusupu Kasymovu, poslannomu v 1675 godu k Velikomu Mogolu Aurenzebu* (St. Petersburg: Tipografii͡a V. Kirshbauma, 1884), 8.

62. I͡a. M. Rogozhin, "Dela Posol'skie," in *"Oko vseĭ velikoĭ Rosii": Ob istorii russkoĭ diplomaticheskoĭ sluzhby XVI—XVII vekov*, ed. E. V. Chistĭakova et al. (Moscow: Mezhdunarodnye otnosheniĭa, 1989), 26.

63. See, for instance, the Muscovite authorities' instructions (*nakaz*) given to the envoys: Vasiliĭ Daudov to Bukhara (NIASPII RAN, f. 113, op. 1, d. 93, ll. 222ob-223), Moḥammad Ĭusuf Kasymov to Mughal India (NIASPII RAN, f. 113, op. 1, d. 93, l. 228 ob.); see also Boris Pazukhin's report of his diplomatic mission to Bukhara in A. N. Truvorov, ed., "Nakaz Pazukhinym, poslannym v Bukharu, Balkh i Ĭurgench, 1669," *Russkai͡a istoricheskai͡a biblioteka* 15 (1894): 55.

64. "Translation of the letter of the Padishah Aurangzeb to the governor of Kabul Mukarram Khan (2 March 1676)," in Antonova et al., *Russko-indiĭskie otnosheniĭa v XVII v.*, 222 (doc. 128); on Muscovite endeavors to get in touch with the Mughal court, see Ulfat Abdurasulov, "A Passage to India: Rhetoric and Diplomacy between Muscovy and Central Asia in the Seventeenth Century," *Itinerario* 44, no. 3 (2020): 502-27.

65. See Usmanov, "O dokumentakh russko-vostochnoĭ perepiski na ti͡urkskikh ĭazykakh," 128; Liseĭtsev, *Posol'skiĭ prikaz v epokhu Smuty*, 34-35.

66. M. B. Moiseev, "Teneshevy-Baksheevy: Sem'ĭa perevodchikov i tolmacheĭ vtoroĭ poloviny XVI v.," in *Perevodchiki i perevody v Rossii kontsa XVI–nachala XVIII stoletiĭa*, ed. A.V. Beli͡akov et al. (Moscow: Institut Rossiĭskoĭ Istorii RAN, 2019), 84.

67. K. A. Aver'ianov, "Russkaĭa diplomatiĭa i kontrrazvedka v XVII veke," in *Rossiĭskai͡a diplomatii͡a: Istoriĭa i sovremennost'*, ed. I. S. Ivanov et al. (Moscow: Rosspen, 2001), 114. Avis Bohlen further argues that "to omit one of the long string of titles commonly used by the Tsars was therefore a grave insult"; see her "Changes in Russian Diplomacy under Peter the Great," *Cahiers du Monde russe et soviétique* 7, no. 3 (1966): 344.

68. See for instance, the petition of Khivan envoy Pāyanda Bek, 1666, RGADA, f. 138, op. 1, 1666 g., d. 1, l. 91; On the bilingual petitions of the Central Asian envoys at the Muscovite court, also see Kulmamatov, "Offitsial'nye pis'mennye ĭazyki Sredneĭ Azii."

69. See Rogozhin, *U gosudarevykh del byt' ukazano*, 33.

70. Beli͡akov, *Sluzhashchie Posol'skogo prikaza*, 150-52 (table 7).

71. Beli͡akov, *Sluzhashchie Posol'skogo prikaza*, 113-15 (table 5).

72. NIASPII RAN, f. 113, op. 1, d. 93, ll. 203-203ob.

73. RGADA, f. 138, op. 1, 1700 g., d. 20, l. 1

74. RGADA, f. 138, op. 1, 1700 g., d. 20, l. 2.
75. According to Michael Khodarkovsky, even the translations of diplomatic texts from Kalmyk into Russian and vice versa were made through the medium of Turkic language: "First, the documents were translated into Tatar and then into Kalmyk or Russian"; see his *Where Two Worlds Met: The Russian State and the Kalmyk Nomads, 1600–1771* (Ithaca, NY: Cornell University Press, 1992), 63–64; see also Dariusz Kołodzieczyk, "Tibet in the Crimea? Polish Embassy to the Kalmyks of 1653 and a Project of Anti-Muslim Alliance," *Acta Poloniae Historica* 114 (2016): 244–45.
76. *Ocherk istorii Ministerstva inostrannykh del: 1802–1902* (St. Petersburg: Tovarishchestvo R. Golike i A. Vil'borg, 1902), 22.
77. Rogozhin, *U gosudarevykh del byt' ukazano*, 32; *Ocherk istorii Ministerstva inostrannykh del*, 22.
78. Usmanov, "O dokumentakh russko-vostochnoĭ perepiski na tiurkskikh iazykakh," 129–30; Beliakov, *Sluzhaschchie Posol'skogo prikaza*, 100–101, 143.
79. RGADA, f. 138, op. 1, 1677 g., d. 1, l. 4.
80. RGADA, f. 138, op. 1, 1692 g., d. 10, l. 126.
81. RGADA, f. 138, op. 1, 1692 g., d. 10, l. 126.
82. Burton, *The Bukharans*, 460, 492.
83. Belokurov, *O posol'skom prikaze*, 55; N. G. Savich, "Iz istorii russko-nemetskikh kul'turnykh sviazeĭ v XII v. (Nemetsko-russkiĭ slovar'-razgovornik G. Nevenburga 1629 g.)," *Istoricheskie zapiski* 102 (1978): 250.
84. RGADA, f. 138, op. 1, 1642 g, d. 4, l. 1; see also Do'smamat Qulmamatov, "XVI–XVII asrlarda Moskva elchilik devoni sharq tarjimonlari va tilmochlari maktabining shakllanishi tarixi haqida," *O'zbekistonda xorijiy tillar* 13, no. 5 (2016): 126 (in Uzbek). "Qizilbash" (or "Qizilbash lands") was a designation commonly used in seventeenth-century Russia with regard to Safavid Iran. On rather rarer occasion one may encounter in the Muscovite diplomatic texts a designation "Shah's realm" (*Shakhova oblast'*), which had the same meaning.
85. RGADA, f. 138, op. 1, 1649 g., d. 13, l. 6.
86. RGADA, f. 138, op. 1, 1649 g., d. 13, l. 99 ob. On this individual, see below.
87. Antonova et al., *Russko-indiĭskie otnosheniia v XVII v.*, 89–91 (doc. 38).
88. On the activity of the Indian entrepreneurs in seventeenth-century Astrakhan as well as on Sutur Kidekov, see Scott C. Levi, *The Indian Diaspora in Central Asia and Its Trade, 1550–1900* (Leiden: Brill, 2002), 227–32.
89. Antonova et al., *Russko-indiĭskie otnosheniia v XVII v.*, 82–85 (doc. 33).
90. Antonova et al., *Russko-indiĭskie otnosheniia v XVII v.*, 89–91 (doc. 38).
91. Antonova et al., *Russko-indiĭskie otnosheniia v XVII v.*, 89–91 (doc. 38).
92. RGADA, f. 138, op. 1, 1649 g., d. 1, ll. 57–59.
93. Beliakov, *Sluzhaschchie Posol'skogo prikaza*, 316.
94. RGADA, f. 138, op. 1, 1649 g., d. 1, l. 58.
95. Antonova et al., *Russko-indiĭskie otnosheniia v XVII v.*, 89–91 (doc. 38).
96. Antonova et al., *Russko-indiĭskie otnosheniia v XVII v.*, 131–33 (doc. 59).
97. Nathalie Rothman, "Interpreting Dragomans: Boundaries and Crossings in the Early Modern Mediterranean," *Comparative Studies in Society and*

History 51, no. 4 (2009): 771–800; see also her *Brokering Empire: Trans-Imperial Subjects between Venice and Istanbul* (Ithaca, NY: Cornell University Press, 2012).

98. See Sartori, "From the Demotic to the Literary," 231–34; Sartori has also justly stated that "the ascendance of Chaghatay in Khorezm was concomitant to similar processes of Turkic vernacularization in [the broader region of] Central Eurasia" and, hence, should not be considered as an "isolated phenomenon" (219).

CHAPTER 4

Armenians and Russian Interests in the Caspian Sea, 1660–1795
George Bournoutian

The Caspian Sea until the seventh century was part of the Iranian world. By the sixteenth century, successive Arab, Seljuq, Mongol, and Turcoman invasions had not only Islamized a large part of the region surrounding the sea but had also changed its ethnic composition. The inhabitants of its western shores, predominantly Turco-Tatars who spoke Turkish dialects,[1] were divided into nomadic and sedentary groups, with a good number of the latter adopting the Twelver Shi'ism branch of Islam. The Iranian and Kurdish inhabitants had, for the most part, embraced Shi'ism, although a good number of Kurds were Yazidi and a small number of Iranians and Armenians had retained their Zoroastrian and Christian faith. The Armenians, meanwhile, had lost their kingdom in the mid-eleventh century and had no secular rulers in their historic homeland. Their Muslim overlords, therefore, had to deal with Armenian religious leaders as the representatives of their people. Thus, both the Safavid shahs and the Ottoman sultans viewed the supreme patriarch, or Catholicos, who resided at the Holy See of Echmiadzin, as the *khalifeh*, or caliph, of the Armenian people.[2]

During the same centuries, the Russian princes who had been subjugated by the Mongols had managed to establish a power base in Moscow. Ivan III (r. 1462–1505), known as the Great, established Moscow's

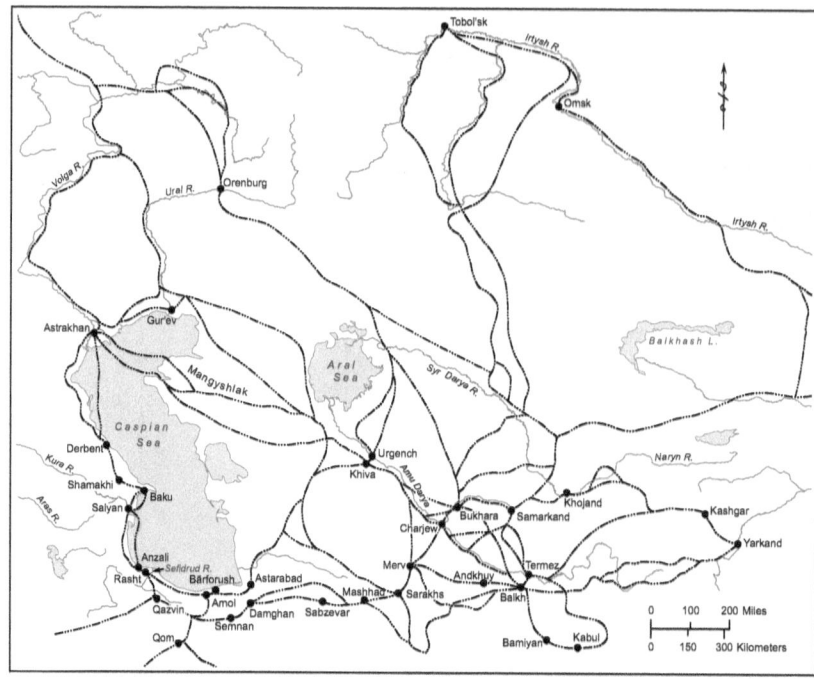

FIGURE 4.1. Trade routes of Central Asia in the seventeenth–eighteenth centuries. Adapted by Gordie Thompson, Castle Time Mapping, from the map in Yuri Bregel, *An Historical Atlas of Central Asia* (Leiden: Brill, 2003), 69. Used by permission of the estate of Yuri Bregel.

supremacy by annexing the neighboring principalities of Novgorod and Tver and by putting an end to Moscow's payment of tribute to the Mongols. Half a century later, Ivan IV (r. 1533-84), known as the Terrible, was officially crowned as tsar in 1547. In 1552, Ivan overthrew the Tatar dynasty of Kazan, and by capturing Astrakhan in 1556, he not only made the Volga a Russian river but, in essence, also opened the door for future Russian penetration into the Caspian Sea.[3]

The first Russian fort near the Caspian Sea was Terki (Terskiĭ Gorodok) erected near the northern bank of the Terek River in 1567. Soon after, Moscow's ascendency enabled a group of Cossacks, under the leadership of Andreĭ Shadrin, to establish the fort of Endereĭ (Andreevo) between the Terek and Sulaq (Russian: Sulak) Rivers. A century later, Cossacks had settled along a line that stretched from the northern banks of the Terek River, which served as the unofficial southern border of Russia.[4] According to one scholar, the Cossacks were "an excellent political weapon, mobile cavalry—restless, warlike and adventurous—at once bandits and colonists, who could be repudiated or who could be brought to obey."[5]

Meanwhile, throughout the sixteenth century, the South Caucasus, which formed one of the informal borders between Safavid Iran and the Ottoman Empire, was the scene of numerous battles between the two rivals. The Ottomans, with their superior firepower, periodically invaded and controlled the region. The military imbalance began to shift during the reign of Shah ʿAbbas I (r. 1587-1629). The shah organized new cavalry and artillery units and, in 1604-5, drove the Ottomans out of the South Caucasus.[6] It was during that campaign that the shah laid waste to the Iran-Ottoman frontier, situated in historical eastern Armenia,[7] by deporting an estimated 250,000 Armenians from the Yerevan-Nakhchevan regions to Iran.

The Armenian residents of Julfa, a prosperous town located at the banks of the Aras River, were not spared. The shah, who was aware of their wealth accumulated through exporting silk to Europe, ordered that the entire town of two thousand households be relocated in three days' time to Iran.[8] In the winter of 1605 he settled the Julfans across the river from his capital, Isfahan. The shah's benign policy toward the resettled Julfans bore fruit, and the new town became an Armenian enclave under royal protection known as New Julfa. The main item of trade was raw silk, which, in 1619, had become a royal monopoly.[9]

Shah ʿAbbas's efforts to establish a strong state were so successful that ten years after his death, the Ottomans had no choice but to end the century-long conflict and make peace with Shah Safi (r. 1629-42). The Treaty of Zohāb (May 17, 1639), which lasted for over eight decades,[10] recognized Iranian suzerainty over historical eastern Armenia, eastern Georgia (Kartli-Kakheti), the entire region of the southeastern Caucasus, and Dagestan. Historical western Armenia, western Georgia, and Mesopotamia remained under Ottoman control. Following the Zohāb treaty, the Armenian merchants from New Julfa, who could now transport their goods through the Ottoman lands instead of the Persian Gulf, established a global trading network of *commenda* agents between Asia and Europe.[11] One of the routes went from Tabriz to Bursa or Smyrna;[12] another took silk from Gilan and Shirvan to Bursa, via Tiflis, Kars, Erzurum, Sivas, Tokat, and Angora (Ankara). The most frequently used route was through Baghdad and the Levant traversing through Aleppo.[13]

By the third quarter of the seventeenth century, however, the Armenian merchants sought a shorter, safer, and less expensive route to

Europe. Political instability in Istanbul, raids by brigands in the interior of Anatolia, North African pirates in the Mediterranean, forty-day quarantines in the domains of Venice, as well as long distances and high expenses had reduced their profits.[14] The nonbelligerent agreement between Tsar Alexei (r. 1645–76) and Shah ʿAbbas II (r. 1642–66) created a perfect opportunity to explore a shorter and cheaper route.[15] The Julfan merchants, a number of whom had settled earlier in Astrakhan,[16] now sought to use the Volga as a channel to transport their silk to Europe. It is safe to conclude, therefore, that the Armenian merchants were responsible for Russia's interest in the Caspian Sea as a conduit for trade with the East and its future efforts to take control of that sea.

Between August 1659 and March 1660, representatives of the Julfan merchants, hoping to obtain transit rights for their merchandise, arrived in Astrakhan and Moscow with various offerings, including the famed "Diamond Throne" for Tsar Alexei.[17] Several years later, on May 31, 1667, the Julfa merchants succeeded in obtaining a trade convention that had long evaded the English and Dutch traders;[18] mainly they acquired the sole right to transport silk via the Caspian Sea to Astrakhan and Moscow. From there they could take their goods to Archangel'sk (via Yaroslavl) or to the Swedish port of Narva (via Tver and Novgorod). An abridged English translation of the agreement reads:

> From the summer of the year 7175 from the Creation [1667], the said Armenian merchants are permitted to bring silk and other merchandise to Astrakhan. The said merchandise will be weighed, recorded and shall be taxed according to this agreement. From goods in transit the Armenians shall pay ten *dengi* [five kopeks][19] per pood[20] of fine raw silk, worth twenty rubles a pood and the same amount for low quality raw silk, worth sixteen rubles per pood. All other items will be taxed ten *dengi* for each ruble worth of merchandise. Whatever is sold at Astrakhan shall be taxed ten *dengi* per ruble. The cost of transport to Moscow shall be one ruble per pood of merchandise. If the said merchants are short of cash, they can pay with one-twentieth part of the merchandise instead. Upon arriving in Moscow, the Armenian merchants shall pay a duty of ten *dengi* per ruble of merchandise they wish to carry on to Europe. For goods imported from Europe to Persia, the merchants shall pay two *altyn* [six kopeks][21] and two *dengi* for each ruble worth of merchandise. The Armenian merchants may purchase Russian merchandise and take it duty-free to Europe or

Persia. The said merchants can carry one hundred poods of provisions duty-free for the journey. They can also carry five vedro[22] of vodka per person duty-free. The customs officers in Astrakhan are instructed to facilitate the moving of the merchandise and are to act swiftly and honestly with the Armenian merchants.[23]

Although the Armenians had promised to transport four thousand bales of raw silk, the volume ended up being far less.[24] There were several reasons for this. Immediately after the trade convention, Moscow had to face the four-year-long uprising by Sten'ka Razin, which hampered the movement of goods.[25] The main obstacles that remained, even after Razin's execution, were the type of vessels used on the Caspian. They could not survive storms, and this resulted in damage or loss of merchandise. Moreover, the lack of a suitable harbor in Astrakhan and a Russian port on the Baltic,[26] coupled with occasional pirate attacks from the eastern shores of the Caspian, reduced the trade. The freezing of the Volga in winter, the heavy cost of transporting the goods to Moscow, and extortion and carelessness on the part of Russian officials along the route also discouraged the Armenians from transporting their wares via Russia.[27]

In February 1673, following continued Russian threats to cancel the silk trade convention, the Armenian merchants signed a new agreement. Their representatives took an oath on the Holy Bible promising that thereafter they would transport all their silk via Russia, provided that the Russians would deduct their transport losses from the duty agreed in the 1667 treaty and would safeguard the route from Astrakhan to Moscow. They also promised not to sell the silk to foreigners in Iran or Turkey, nor would they transport it to Europe through the Ottoman Empire.[28] Despite such promises, the bulk of Iranian silk and Indian cloth seems to have continued to be transported over the more familiar land route, via Aleppo and Smyrna, to Europe.[29]

Russian interest in the Caspian Sea assumed a more serious character during the reign of Peter I (r. 1682-1725). A number of Russian scholars have observed correctly that Peter realized the fact that Russian expansion westward was limited due to the strategic and economic interests of European powers.[30] Expansion into Asia, however, was not only possible, but would also make Russia a Eurasian empire.[31] This powerful state would serve as a cultural, diplomatic, and economic channel between Central Asia, China, India, Iran, and the rest of Europe.

Astrakhan on the Caspian-Volga and St. Petersburg on the Baltic would serve as the main conduits for such exchanges.

Dissatisfied with the volume of trade via Astrakhan,[32] Peter planned to make it the central terminus of a new silk road. The route would once again go through Central Asia. Caravans from China would travel, via Samarqand, Bukhara, and Khiva, to the Caspian coast. From there the merchandise would be transported to Astrakhan, while goods from India and Iran would arrive at Astrakhan through the Caspian Sea. Having insufficient information about the Caspian coastline, Peter sought to obtain reliable navigation charts.[33] Since his officials had little firsthand knowledge of the region, Peter sought information from non-Russians who were familiar with Iran and the South Caucasus and knew the local languages. One such individual was Israyel Ori, who, in 1701, had arrived in Moscow asking the Russian ruler to liberate Armenia from Muslim tyranny.[34] Peter, whose envoy to Iran had, in 1698, been rebuffed for not observing the proper protocol,[35] had just started his Great Northern War against Sweden. He therefore convinced Ori that after the conclusion of that war he would carry out Ori's plan.[36]

In June 1707, in order to gain further intelligence about Iran and the Caspian Sea, as well as to assure the commitment of the Armenians in Iran and the South Caucasus, Peter sent Ori as his envoy to Isfahan. Ori, together with fifty men, traveled to Isfahan via Astrakhan, Shamakhi, Qarabagh, and Tabriz. After meeting with various Armenian *meliks* in the South Caucasus,[37] Ori arrived in Isfahan in 1708. The Iranian officials did not trust him, and the Catholic missionaries and European merchants feared that Ori's mission was to increase Russian influence in the capital.[38] In the end, Ori, realizing the futility of his mission, used his position to enrich himself and some of his companions by importing a great quantity of merchandise to Iran without paying any duty, as well exporting Iranian goods duty-free to Astrakhan.[39] Ori died upon his return to Astrakhan in 1711 and was buried at the new Armenian church in that city.[40] His work was continued by his companion, a priest named Minas, who, in 1716, was named as the prelate of the Armenians in Russia by Catholicos Esayi Hasan-Jalalean (1701–28) of the Holy See at Gandzasar in Qarabagh, who continued to supply the Russians with information on Iran and the Caspian littoral.[41]

Since most Iranian silk continued to be transported via the Ottoman Empire, despite the promises of the Armenian merchants, Peter decided to divert the bulk of the silk trade through Russia by negotiating a Russo-Iranian trade agreement that would bypass the Armenians and would assure the transport of silk by Russian merchants to Europe, via the Caspian Sea, Astrakhan, and the Volga River. To achieve his plan, Peter sent an official embassy headed by Artemiĭ Volynskiĭ to the shah's court in 1715.[42] The following passages from his detailed instructions to Volynskiĭ are a clear indication of Peter's plan for the future:

> On your route to the shah's domain by land and sea you shall record all the stations, towns, and settlements. Which large rivers empty into the Caspian Sea? *To what locations can one sail from that sea? Is there a river from India that empties into that sea?* Does the shah possess any armed vessels or merchant ships on the sea? Are there any fortresses along the coastline, *especially in Gilan? What mountains or impassable places separate Gilan from other provinces along the Caspian?* Keep a confidential journal without attracting the attention of the Persians.
>
> You must try to conclude a new trade agreement that will assure the safety of our merchants, as well as facilitate and increase their trade with Persia (this agreement must be separate from our agreement made with the Armenians of Persia, a copy of which is enclosed). Is there any way that our merchants can trade with India using Persian routes? What goods are in demand in India? Russian merchants should be permitted to trade freely in Persia and to purchase any goods, especially raw silk from Gilan, in order to transport it to Russia without any obstacles. Try to convince the shah and his close advisors to order the Armenian merchants from [New] Julfa to transport all their raw silk via Russia. The route is shorter and will bring great financial rewards for the shah. The Armenian merchants of Julfa had promised Tsar Alexei Mikhaĭlovich to transport the silk via Russia; instead they continue to take it on camels via the long route through Turkey. *See if you can persuade* [bribe] *the shah's close advisors to abandon this route. Is it possible to impede this trade? Where and how?*
>
> Gather information on the Armenians in Iran. Are they numerous? Where do they live? Are any of their notables or merchants supporters of Russia? Behave kindly toward them and find out if there are any other Christians living there.
>
> *The piers of Nizavoĭ* [Niāzābād] *and Derbent are very small and shallow. Boats have to be dragged on the sand. Many vessels are thus left anchored ashore and perish. His Majesty the shah should permit us to seek a better location, which is safe from weather conditions and where we can establish a trading post.*[43]

Volynskiĭ reached Isfahan on March 25, 1717. It took many months to convince the court officials that Russia had no intention of invading Iran and to draft the articles of a trade agreement. On August 10, 1717, Volynskiĭ and the shah's main minister, Fatḥ-ʿAli Khan Daghestāni, signed a treaty containing ten articles:

1. Russian merchants would not be subjected to ill treatment or attacks.
2. Russian merchants were free to transport merchandise to Nizavoĭ (Niāzābād) or other locations.
3. Russian merchants would not be detained or delayed in any manner, and their bales would not be opened by covetous officials.
4. Russian merchants could freely sell their goods in Nizavoĭ, Shamakhi, or anywhere else they wished.
5. Russian merchants would not be hindered in renting camels or horses, and local officials in Nizavoĭ and Shamakhi would provide two guards for every ten camels in order to safeguard the said merchants from bandits.
6. Local *beglarbegs*, judges, and officials would not confiscate any goods or purchase them cheaper and would not take *kharāj* or any other sort of contribution.
7. The said merchants would be compensated for the value of merchandise stolen by bandits.
8. Russian merchants, like the Armenians, could buy as much silk as they wished in Shirvan or Gilan.
9. Since Russian merchants "have experienced nothing but losses" thanks to the Iranian-Armenian translators, a Russian official (consul) living in Shamakhi will facilitate the transactions between Russian merchants and Iranian officials.
10. Russian merchants will pay the same tariff as the Armenians for each bale of silk.[44]

On April 2, 1720, Volynskiĭ was named the governor of Astrakhan. He was instructed to keep Peter informed of the internal conditions in Iran and to gather additional information on the Caspian coastline. Reports on the Afghan rebellion and the arrival of the Ottoman envoy in Isfahan may have prompted Peter to wind down his Baltic campaign, rest his troops, and resupply the army and navy with the necessary ammunition, vessels, and provisions for his Caspian expedition, which he planned in 1723.⁴⁵ An unexpected event, however, gave Peter the excuse to act sooner. On August 15, 1721, that is, one month prior to the final treaty with Sweden, the Sunnis in Shirvan, long oppressed by the Shi'is, received aid from a Dagestani chief and laid siege to Shamakhi.⁴⁶ On September 9, the Sunnis, encouraged by the events in Iran, opened the gates, and the invaders massacred thousands of Shi'is and seized a great deal of goods belonging to Russian merchants. After that, the rebels placed themselves under the protection of the Ottoman sultan.

Volynskiĭ urged Peter to start his campaign in the summer of 1722; otherwise, he added, the Afghan rebels or the Ottomans could seize Gilan and the entire Caspian littoral. He also assured Peter that since the shah was preoccupied with the Afghans, an army of some twenty thousand would be enough to invade Iran. They would be joined by troops sent by King Vakhtang VI of Kartli and the men gathered by the Armenian *meliks*.⁴⁷ The Caspian Flotilla, composed of 285 ships, thirty-five of which were hospital and cargo vessels, was to transport a fifty-thousand-man army from Astrakhan.⁴⁸

Peter left Moscow on May 24, 1722, and reached Astrakhan on June 30. That same day, Peter issued a manifesto in Persian, Turkish, and the local Turkic dialect, prepared by Dmitriĭ Cantemir,⁴⁹ that justified his upcoming campaign. The manifesto stated that rebels had taken the city of Shamakhi, had killed and wounded Russian citizens, and had stolen four million rubles worth of goods. Since the Iranian government, due to its weakness, was unable to carry out its obligations under the treaty of 1717 and could not make up for the financial loss, the Russian State itself would answer this insult and punish the rebels. The manifesto stated that Russian troops were not at war with Iran, but had come with the sole purpose of maintaining order and safe trading conditions.⁵⁰

On July 13, Peter dispatched Boris Turkistanov to Tiflis, informing Vakhtang of his imminent arrival on the shores of Iran and instructing him to attack the Lezgis in Jar.⁵¹ Minas Vardapet who had accompanied Peter, together with fourteen Armenian volunteers, sent a message to Catholicos Esayi to meet Peter with the Armenian army in Shamkhor.⁵²

Peter reached Derbent on September 3 and was welcomed by the *nā'eb* of Derbent, Emām-Qoli Beg, who handed him the keys to the city. On the night of September 4–5, thirteen cargo ships arrived from Astrakhan and had anchored by Derbent, when a great storm broke up the vessels and left the army with only a month of supplies. Although some sources claim that an Ottoman envoy arrived and threatened Peter with war, it was the loss of provisions, the sickness among his troops, and the attacks by the Dagestani tribesmen that convinced Peter to return home.⁵³ It is clear that the Russians did not possess the necessary vessels and had miscalculated the difficulty of the terrain, as well as the climate and the hostility of the mountain tribesmen, which continued to haunt the Russian efforts to gain complete control of the western and eastern Caspian coasts for a long time.⁵⁴

After the fall of Isfahan, the Russians feared that the Afghans would advance to Gilan. Since the *vazir* of Rasht had written to Volynskiĭ asking for aid, Peter, prior to his departure from Astrakhan, had ordered a naval squadron to sail to Anzali. The Russian fleet went around the Absheron Peninsula and explored the channels by which the Kura River flowed into the Caspian, near Salyan. After that, the fleet sailed to Anzali and arrived at the mouth of the Pir-e Bāzār River in mid-December. Although the *ḥākem* of Gilan now refused to allow the Russians to disembark they ignored his request, left two companies in Pir-e Bāzār, marched to Rasht, and camped at a large stone caravanserai. The *ḥākems* of Gaskar (Ziābar), Astara, and Gilan gathered a large force of inexperienced peasants without firearms and attacked the caravanserai and the two companies at Pir-e Bāzār on March 29, 1723. They were routed by the better-trained Russian troops who had superior firepower.

Peter did not forget Baku, which had the only suitable harbor on the western shore of the Caspian. On July 1, 1723, three Russian naval squadrons sailed from Astrakhan for the bay of Baku. On July 18, the Russians reached Baku. When the governor refused them to allow them to disembark, the Russians opened fire from the two gunships, while their battalions went ashore. The troops disembarked, and the artillery ships faced the town. After a four-day bombardment, the city fell on August 5. The Russians left garrisons in two large stone caravanserais. After that, the Russians sent men to explore the Kur River and occupied Salyan.

The fall of Baku enabled the Russians to extend their control of Tabasaran and Kiura and reach the border of Shirvan at the Samur River. After his arrival in St. Petersburg, the Iranian envoy, Esmā'il Beg signed the Russo-Iranian Treaty (never ratified in Iran) by which Iran agreed to give up the regions of Derbent and Baku and the provinces of Gilan, Mazandaran, and Astarabad (the last two not occupied by Russia) in exchange for Russian aid in removing the Afghans. Moreover, Russia and Iran would consider each other's enemies as their own.⁵⁵

By the fall of 1723, the Russians had, therefore, succeeded in securing the western and southern coasts of the Caspian Sea. The Russian move into the Caspian littoral, the news of her treaty with Tahmasb II, as well as her contacts with King Vakhtang and the Armenians in Qarabagh, had alarmed the Ottomans. Taking advantage of the chaos in Iran and the rivalry among the princes in Georgia, the Ottomans attacked Kartli, placed their own puppet ruler in Tiflis, laid siege to Yerevan,[56] took Ganjeh, Sheki, and parts of Qarabagh, and reached Shirvan. The Ottoman objective was to reach Shamakhi in order to stop the Russian advance into the South Caucasus. The two belligerents almost went to war against one another but, after mediation by the French, agreed, in 1724, to divide the region. The Treaty of Constantinople (June 24, 1724) partitioned the South Caucasus between the two invaders.[57] Peter's health and his fear of provoking the Ottomans to cancel the treaty halted further Russian moves. Instead, they concentrated on defending the narrow Caspian coastline under their control.

In the meantime, having received Peter's messages, Vakhtang attacked the Lezgis and arrived in Shamkhor, where his troops, together with Armenian volunteers from Qarabagh, waited for the Russian arrival at Shamakhi.[58] Peter's departure and his subsequent treaty with the Ottomans, however, left the Georgians and the Armenians at the mercy of the local Muslim chiefs. Peter encouraged some of them to settle in Gilan. Vakhtang, together with some of his noblemen, as well as a number of Armenian leaders, fled to Russia in 1724, where they later formed their own ethnic squadrons within the Russian army.[59]

Thus, Peter, who had promised to free the Armenians and Georgians from Muslim rule, abandoned them both. The Ottomans took over regions with large Christian populations, while Russia ended up with areas inhabited mainly by Muslims. The fact is that Peter had never relied on the Armeno-Georgian promises and their exaggerated claims of military support, which he called "the customary audacious nature of these people."[60] His ultimate aim was not to annex the South Caucasus or to free its Christian population, but to gain control of the Caspian coastline with the sole purpose of expanding Russian trade in Asia and to keep the Ottomans from the region; a goal that he had accomplished by the treaties he had signed with both the Iranians and the Ottomans.

Peter's immediate successors, Catherine I (r. 1725-27) and Peter II (r. 1727-30), generally ignored the South Caucasus. Catherine, who was under the sway of her advisors, decided to reduce military expenditures, while Peter II abandoned the navy and ignored the affairs of state. The

Russian garrisons in Derbent, Baku, and Rasht were left without much logistical support and continued to suffer great losses from various illnesses, which forced Empress Anna to relinquish the Russian gains along the Caspian littoral in her Treaties of Rasht and Ganjeh (1732 and 1735) with the future Iranian ruler, Nader.

The reign of Catherine the Great saw a revival of Russia's contacts with both the Armenians and Georgians. Several individual Armenians once more sought to obtain Russian aid to free their land from Muslim rule. The first among them was Joseph (Hovsep) Emin. Emin was born in Iran, but had moved to India and then to England, where he had befriended Edmund Burke and, thanks to the sponsorship of the Duke of Northumberland, had been admitted to the Royal Military Academy in Woolwich. After serving as a volunteer in the war against France, Joseph traveled to Echmiadzin in 1759, via the historical Armenian lands in the Ottoman Empire. His plan was to form an Armeno-Georgian coalition against their Muslim overlords. The new Catholicos at Echmiadzin, Hakob of Shamakhi (1759-63), was agreeable to the plan and, in the summer of 1760, not only approached Teymuraz II and Erekle II of Georgia,[61] but also sent a letter to Empress Elizabeth asking her to help the Christians of the South Caucasus.[62] The Georgian and Russian monarchs, however, who were occupied with domestic issues, as well as foreign conflicts, did not respond. Having achieved little, Emin returned to London in 1761. He did not give up hope, however, and, following Ori's example, he decided to make direct contact with Russia. On September 1, 1761, he wrote a letter to Alexander Golitsyn, the Russian ambassador to England, asking him to give him a letter of introduction to Russian officials in St. Petersburg.[63] Golitsyn sent a French translation of Emin's letter (which was written in English) to the Russian chancellor, Mikhaïl Vorontsov.[64] In 1763, Emin, together with a group of Armenian volunteers from the Caucasus, arrived in Tiflis. Neither Erekle II, nor the new Catholicos at Echmiadzin, Simeon of Yerevan (1763-80), wished to upset the arrangements in the South Caucasus established by Karim Khan Zand. They also did not dare to incite the Ottomans or rupture their own relations with the neighboring khans without a concrete guarantee and the full support of a Russian army;[65] Emin's project thus ended in failure.[66]

In 1766, the decline of the Holy See of Gandzasar, which had occurred due to the conflict between the *meliks* and Ebrāhim Khan of Qarabagh, prompted Catholicos Simeon of Echmiadzin to petition Catherine to recognize Echmiadzin as the sole representative of the Armenians in

Russia and the South Caucasus. Two years later Catherine issued a decree by which Echmiadzin regained its authority.[67] On November 12, 1770, she issued another decree that permitted the Armenians to build churches in Moscow and St. Petersburg.[68] Catherine's benevolent policy toward the Armenians in Russia enabled a number of Russian Armenian merchants, some of whom had left Iran or had settled in Astrakhan, to attain a substantial degree of economic and political power. The most important of these were the Lazarev family of Moscow, who manufactured silk (in addition to being jewelers), Moses Sarafov, a merchant from Astrakhan, and the Shahamirean family of Madras.[69]

Russian expansion in the direction of the Kuban River and Crimea, as well as its involvement in the affairs of Moldavia, triggered the Russo-Ottoman War of 1768-74. In 1778, Catherine relocated the Armenian community of that region to a new settlement along the Don River, which was named New Nakhichevan (now part of Rostov-on-Don) in order to undermine the economy of Ottoman-controlled Crimea. Her war with the Ottomans and her move to establish ties with Georgia encouraged the Catholicos at Echmiadzin, Simeon of Yerevan, to appoint Archbishop Iosif Argutinskiĭ (Hovsep Arghutean), a scion of the Russian princely family Argutinskiĭ-Dolgorukiĭ, as the prelate of the Armenians living in Russia. Argutinskiĭ befriended Grigoriĭ Potemkin and, in 1780, together with Ivan Lazarev, participated in a meeting organized by Potemkin concerning Russian policy regarding the Armenians and other Christians in the South Caucasus. Together, they envisioned a Russian-Armenian Christian enclave.[70]

In 1782, Argutinskiĭ participated in the negotiations for the 1783 Russo-Georgian treaty. Learning of the Russo-Georgian talks, the five *meliks* of Qarabagh, Catholicos Hovhannes X Hasan-Jalalean of Gandzasar,[71] as well as Armenian leaders in Ganjeh and Shams al-Din, informed Pavel Potemkin and Archbishop Argutinskiĭ that if the Russians marched into Qarabagh, the Armenians would supply them with wheat, barley, millet, spelt, beans, fruit, beasts of burden, and armed men. They added that they had fed Nader's three-hundred-thousand-man army for three years without any problem. They promised to have thirty thousand armed men ready to join the Russian campaign.[72] Such exaggerated promises prompted Grigoriĭ Potemkin to write the following letter to Empress Catherine:

> I have ordered General Pavel Potemkin to gain the cooperation of Ebrahim Khan of Shushi.[73] At the appropriate time, his province, populated by Armenians, will be ruled by the Armenians and

will start the revival of Christian rule in Asia. Such is the promise I have given the meliks of Qarabagh in the name of Your Majesty.[74]

Catherine's pro-expansionist advisors, led by Grigoriĭ Potemkin, continued to remind her that Iran was in the midst of a struggle among various rival tribal leaders and could not respond militarily to a Russian advance into the South Caucasus. They added that a small Russian force would be sufficient to gain access to that region. Catherine, who was aware of the huge Russian casualties during and following Peter's campaign, as well as the reactions of the Ottomans to a Russian move into the region, at first hesitated to get involved in the squabbles among the khanates. She was, however, interested in using Christians, especially Armenians, to foster trade with Iran and India, which coincided with Potemkin's efforts to encourage the settlement of Crimean Armenians in Russia.[75]

In 1778, following the Irano-Ottoman discord over Basra and negotiations (1775–77),[76] Potemkin finally managed to convince Catherine to construct new ships for the Caspian Flotilla. After Karim Khan's death in 1779, Potemkin, in January 1780, once he had received assurances of substantial logistical aid from King Erekle II and the Armenians in Qarabagh, ordered General Suvorov to go to Astrakhan and to retake the Caspian littoral. Although by April Suvorov was in Astrakhan and was ready to start his campaign, the political situation in Europe halted the plan.[77]

Following the completion of the Georgian Military Road and the Treaty of Georgievsk (1783),[78] and especially after the Russo-Ottoman War of 1787–92, Potemkin put Argutinskiĭ in charge of the resettlement of Turkish Armenians in the city of Grigoriopol.[79] Argutinskiĭ had an audience with Empress Catherine and was responsible for the construction of the Armenian cathedral in New Nakhichevan.[80] Taking advantage of the Russo-Georgian treaty and assisted by Potemkin, Argutinskiĭ, who had been assured by the *meliks* of Qarabagh of logistical support, drafted a proposal for an Armeno-Russian treaty that would restore an Armenian kingdom under Russian protection. Russia would send six thousand men, while the Armenians would bear all the expenses.

Catherine the Great's main interest, however, was to establish trade depots in Gilan and Mazandaran and not to start a war with Iran.[81] Āqā Moḥammad Khan's sacking of Tiflis in 1795 gave her the excuse to issue a war manifesto, which echoed that of Peter. It was printed at the Armenian press in Astrakhan, the only such press that possessed such fonts. Her death and the Russian withdrawal, the second time in that century, once again left the Armenians and Georgians to their own fate.[82] It was only after Russia annexed eastern Georgia (1801) and made Tiflis the Russian headquarters of the Caucasus that, in order to protect that center, Emperor Alexander I ordered yet another Russian incursion into the South Caucasus, in order to supply Tiflis with men and provisions via the Caspian Sea.[83]

Notes

1. Contemporary Russian sources refer to them as "Tatars" or "Muslims." After 1918, they and their spoken dialect were identified as *Azeri* and the Caspian littoral from the Samur River to Astara became part of Azerbaijan. The educated among them continued to use the Perso-Arabic script until the second decade of the twentieth century, when the Soviets devised a new Latino-Cyrillic alphabet for them.

2. For examples of the former, see Shah Tahmasb's decree in Matenadaran Archives, folder 1a, doc. 12; see also Shah ʿAbbas's decrees, Matenadaran Archives, folder 1a, docs. 34, 37, 39; Shah Safi's decree in Matenadaran Archives, folder 1a, doc. 49; Shah ʿAbbas II's decree in Matenadaran Archives, folder 1a, doc. 68. For a list of Ottoman decrees, see Simeon of Erevan, *Jambr*, trans. G. Bournoutian (Costa Mesa: Mazda, 2009), 373–91. The Ottomans had established the *millet* system for their non-Muslim subjects. For details, see B. Ye'or, *The Dhimmi: Jews and Christians under Islam* (Rutherford: Farleigh Dickinson University Press, 1985).

3. For details, see V. O. Kluchevsky, *A History of Russia*, vol. 2 (New York, 1912).

4. In the second half of the eighteenth century, the line was called the "Caucasian Line," also referred to as "the Line" or the "Caucasus Defensive Line."

5. W. E. D. Allen, *A History of the Georgian People from the Beginning Down to the Russian Conquest in the Nineteenth Century* (London, 1932), 164. Although the rise of Muscovy prompted the Christian Orthodox Georgians to seek aid from Russia, the two Russian expeditionary armies were decimated by the warlike mountain tribes of Dagestan. After that Russia, for several decades, did not venture south of the Terek River, Allen, *History of the Georgian People*, 140.

6. Shah ʿAbbas's campaigns of 1604–7 are detailed by a number of primary sources, including *Afżal al-tavārikh*, whose author, Fażli Beg Khuzāni Esfahāni, was an eyewitness to ʿAbbas's campaigns in the South Caucasus. The third part of his work has been recently edited by K. Ghereghlou and published as *A Chronicle of the Reign of Shah Abbas*, 2 vols. (Cambridge: Gibb Memorial Trust, 2015). For more contemporary sources in Persian, see Eskandar Beg Torkmān (Monshi), *Tārikh-e ʿalam ārā-ye ʿAbbāsi*, 2 vols. (Tehran: Amir Kabir, 2003).

7. The historical Armenian kingdom was terminated in the eleventh century, and except for a number of significant Armenian-populated clusters located in the South Caucasus and eastern Asia Minor, the Armenians had become a minority in their historical homeland.

8. Aṛakʿel of Tabriz, *Book of History*, trans. G. Bournoutian (Costa Mesa: Mazda, 2010), 71–79.

9. According to Fażli Beg, Shah ʿAbbas, in the year 1028 AH (1619), sent an order to the *vazirs* and *kalāntars* of Gilan, Shirvan, Ganjeh, Qarabagh, Nakhchevan, as well as the governors of Tabriz and Ardabil, that forbade anyone from buying or selling silk. The bulk of the silk was to be sold to the group led by Khoja Safar and Khoja Nazar of New Julfa. See Khuzāni Esfahāni, *Chronicle*, 2:782.

10. The agreement is also called the Treaty of Zohāb or Qasr-e Shirin. For the complete text, see J. C. Hurewitz, *Diplomacy in the Near and Middle East: A Documentary Record*, vol. 1 (Princeton, NJ: Van Nostrand, 1956), 21–23.

11. For the most comprehensive and accurate account of this trade network, which was operated by Armenian roving or sedentary agents, see Sebouh Aslanian, *From the Indian Ocean to the Mediterranean: The Global Trade Networks of Armenian Merchants from New Julfa* (Berkeley: University of California Press, 2011).

12. The journal of an Armenian merchant from Agulis (in Nakhchevan) describes the route in detail. His caravan, containing silk from Isfahan, Kashan, and Tabriz, went through Yerevan, Erzurum, Tokat, Amasya, Çorum, Kayseri, Afyon (Afyonkarahisar) to Smyrna. After that, the wares were taken by ship to Venice and from there by land to Amsterdam. The return journey from Amsterdam to Smyrna was by sea. It went through Cadiz, Malaga, Alicante, and Livorno. See Zakʿaria of Agulis, *The Journal of Zakʿaria of Agulis*, trans. G. Bournoutian (Costa Mesa: Mazda, 2003), maps 1–5.

13. R. Matthee, *The Politics of Trade in Safavid Iran: Silk for Silver, 1600–1730* (Cambridge: Cambridge University Press, 1999), maps 2, 3, and 5.

14. For an eyewitness account of such incidents see Zakʿaria of Agulis, *Journal*, 43, 57, 60.

15. When in 1651, the Russians had tried to expand south of the Terek River by building a new fort, Iranian troops destroyed it and in 1653 forced the tsar to make peace: Matthee, *The Politics of Trade*, 169. An Armenian primary source Zakʿaria describes the administrative policy of Shah ʿAbbas II over parts of the South Caucasus, see *The Chronicle of Zakʿaria of Kʿanakʿer*, trans. George Bournoutian (Costa Mesa: Mazda, 2004).

16. A wooden Armenian church was erected there in 1630.

17. The said gifts had arrived in Astrakhan on August 7, 1659. They included fifteen flasks of Shiraz wine, three flagons of aromatic vodka, four flagons of rose-flavored vodka, a bottle of orange-flavored vodka, eastern perfumes, Indian sugared ginger, and other exotic fruits, as well as a painting of the Last Supper. The throne, together with precious rings, a silver brazier, and a silver box, was presented in Moscow on March 28, 1660. The total value of the throne and precious metals was 22,943 rubles, 6 *altyn* (18 kopeks), and 3 *dengi* (1.5 kopeks). The document detailing the items, located at RGADA, f. 100, o. 1, d. b, ll. 1–57, is reproduced in V. A. Parsamian, ed., *Armiano-russkie otnosheniia v XVII veke* (Yerevan: Izd. Akademii Nauk Armiamskoĭ SSR, 1953), 21–34 (doc. 5). For a partial English translation, see G. Bournoutian, ed., *Armenians and*

Russia, 1626–1796: A Documentary Record (Costa Mesa: Mazda, 2001), 9–11 (doc. 5). The throne is presently on display at the Armory Museum in the Kremlin.

18. Although between 1618 and 1626 Shah 'Abbas had received three Russian embassies with trade proposals, no concrete agreement had emerged. For the English and Dutch efforts, see Ronald Ferrier, "Trade from the Mid-14th Century to the End of the Safavid Period," in *The Cambridge History of Iran*, vol. 6, *The Timurid and Safavid Periods*, ed. Peter Jackson and Laurence Lockhart (Cambridge: Cambridge University Press, 1986), 459–65.

19. Since one Moscow ruble equaled two hundred *dengi*, the duty was only 5 percent per pood.

20. A pood equaled thirty-six pounds.

21. An *altyn* was worth three kopeks.

22. A vedro measured twenty-one pints.

23. The multifolio agreement, located in RGADA, f. 100, o. 1, dd. 1-4, ll. 1-35, can be found in Parsamīan, *Armīano-russkie otnoshenīia v XVII veke*, 44-64 (doc. 10); partial English translation in Bournoutian, *Armenians and Russia*, 15-17 (doc. 10). The route is illustrated in Matthee, *The Politics of Trade*, map 4.

24. Each bale weighed just over two hundred pounds. Estimates of the amount of silk produced in Iran varied widely; see Matthee, *The Politics of Trade*, 39–43. There is no information on the exact volume of silk brought by the Armenians. A document dated 1684 states that a group of merchants imported 4,083 lbs. of raw silk, RGADA, f. 100, o. 1, d. 9, ll. 1-2. Another document, dated 1685, has 6,978 lbs., RGADA, f. 100, o. 1, d. 3 ll. 27-29. Yet another document, dated 1687, records 3,810 lbs., RGADA, f. 100, o. 1, d. 1, l. 1.

25. Razin's movement started as an episode of unrest against the nobility and the loss of the traditional freedoms of the Cossacks. It soon attracted some twenty thousand soldiers and townspeople. The rebels sailed along the Volga down the western, southern, and eastern coast of the Caspian Sea, attacking various settlements. His capture and pillage of Tsaritsyn, Astrakhan, Saratov, and Samara forced the tsar to send a large army, who routed the rebels in October 1670. That defeat and the anathema issued by the patriarch of Moscow turned many of his followers against him. He was captured and sent to Moscow and was executed in June 1671. For further details, see P. Avrich, *Russian Rebels, 1600–1800* (London: Norton, 1972).

26. Since the port of Narva, until 1704, remained under Swedish control, the Armenians had to pay additional duties to the Swedes.

27. The fifty-foot-long row boats used to transport the goods from Astrakhan to Moscow took 131 days to reach Moscow (going upriver) and 89 days from Moscow (going downriver). Therefore, some goods were either transported by water to Kazan, Nizhny-Novgorod, and Yaroslavl from where they would continue by land to Moscow, or from Nizhny-Novgorod they were transferred to the Oka River to Vladimir, from where they were hauled on land to Moscow. M. A. Polievktov, *Ėkonomicheskoe i politicheskoe razvitie Moskovskogo gosudarstva XVII v. na Kavkaze* (Tiflis: Akademiīa Nauk Gruzinskoĭ SSR, 1932), 16–19.

28. RGADA, f. 100, o. 1, d. 3, ll. 11–12.

29. Aslanian, *From the Indian Ocean to the Mediterranean*, 67-70.

30. The most interesting study is by Oleg A. Nikonov, *Iran vo vneshnopoliticheskoĭ strategii Rossiĭskoĭ Imperii v XVIII v.* (Vladimir: Vladimir University Press, 2009).

31. He was the first Russian ruler to assume the title of emperor.

32. He was especially disappointed by the volume of silk carried by the Iranian Armenians to Astrakhan, which was far below the 1673 agreement.

33. Early efforts beginning in 1699 had resulted in little information. After his victory at Poltava (1709) Peter gave orders to chart the Caspian coastline. Although a number of such charts were produced, they contained errors.

34. Ori was a member of a group of Armenians, led by Catholicos Hakob of New Julfa, who planned to seek European aid against the Muslims. When Hakob died in Constantinople in 1680, Ori continued the journey alone. Although he received some assurances from European princes, after his return the new Catholicos at Echmiadzin, Nahapet, who owed his post to the shah, refused to deal with Ori. After that, Ori gained the support of some Qarabaghi *meliks*, who petitioned Peter to liberate them from Muslim rule; see G. A. Ezov', *Snosheniĭa Petra Velikago s armĭanskim narodom* (St. Petersburg: Imperatorskaĭa Akademiĭa Nauk, 1898), 9-27 (docs. 5-8).

35. P. P. Bushev, *Posol'stvo Artemiĭa Volynskogo v Iran v 1715-1718 gg.* (Moscow: Izd. Nauka, glavnaĭa redaktsiĭa vostochnoĭ literatury, 1978), 101, 120-21.

36. Ezov', *Snosheniĭa Petra Velikago*, 73-75, 110-11 (docs. 35, 36, 59).

37. The *meliks* of Qarabagh were autonomous petty princes who controlled five mountainous districts, known as *khamseh*. They had armed followers, had helped Shah 'Abbas in his war with the Ottomans, and were rewarded by various decrees; see Matenadaran Archives, folder 2a, docs. 25a., 26, 27, 28; National Archives of Armenia, f. 59, d. 1, l. 1.

38. Laurence Lockhart, *The Fall of the Safavi Dynasty and the Afghan Occupation of Persia* (Cambridge: Cambridge University Press, 1958), 63-65.

39. T. Krusinski, *The History of the Late Revolutions of Persia*, vol. 1 (London: J. Pemberton, 1733), 173-75. For a complete list of the merchandise, including silk, cotton goods, carpets, cloth, veils, shawls, muslin, and sashes, see Bournoutian, *Armenians and Russia*, 67-72 (doc. 69). Ori had also purchased twenty horses for Peter, which he brought to Astrakhan. Bournoutian, *Armenians and Russia*, 73 (doc. 70).

40. The trade with Russia, albeit slow, had brought a good number of Armenians to Astrakhan.

41. After Esayi's appointment, the rift between the two holy sees assumed a more serious character. Minas, who had the ear of the Russians, convinced Peter and his immediate successors to view Gandzasar as the sole representatives of the Armenians in Russia and the South Caucasus. Since until the reign of Catherine the Great, the Catholicoi at Echmiadzin were under the control of Iran or the Ottoman Empire, Gandzasar and its prelates continued to have the ear of Russian officials. For more details, see G. Bournoutian, "The Armenian Church and Czarist Russia," in *Between Paris and Fresno: Armenian Studies in Honor of Dickran Kouymjian* (Costa Mesa: Mazda, 2008), 431-36.

42. The account of his mission is based solely on two primary sources: Bushev, who includes relevant passages from Volynskiĭ's *Journal* located at RGADA, and the travel account of a Scottish physician, John Bell of Antermony, a member of the mission; see his *Travels from St. Petersburgh in Russia to Various Parts of Asia*, vol. 1 (Edinburgh: W. Creech, 1788).

43. Bushev, *Posol'stvo Artemiia Volynskogo v Iran*, 24-30. The italics indicate text underlined in Peter's own hand.

44. The complete text of the treaty in Russian is in *PSZ*, vol. 5, no. 3097.

45. P. G. Butkov, *Materialy dlia novoĭ istorii Kavkaza s 1722 po 1804*, vol. 1 (St. Petersburg: Imperatorskaia Akademiia Nauk, 1869), 9.

46. V. P. Lystsov, *Persidskiĭ pokhod Petra I, 1722-1723* (Moscow: Izd. Moskovskogo Universiteta, 1951), 113-15. Russia ended the war with Sweden with the Treaty of Nystad signed on September 10, 1721.

47. During his imprisonment in Isfahan, Vakhtang, who had refused to apostatize, had met Volynskiĭ and had requested Peter's aid. His treatment by Shah Solṭān Ḥosayn was later responsible for his refusal to aid the Safavids against the Afghans.

48. The earlier sources on Peter's campaign include Peter Henry Bruce, who accompanied Peter on his campaign and who left his impressions in book 7 of his *Memoirs* (London, 1782), Butkov, *Materialy dlia novoĭ istorii Kavkaza*, Lockhart, *Fall of the Safavi Dynasty*, and Lystsov, *Persidskiĭ pokhod Petra I*. The best and most recent source, based on numerous archival documents located at the RGADA, is I. V. Kurukin's *Persidskiĭ pokhod Petra Velikogo: Nizavoĭ korpus na beregakh Kaspiia (1722-1735)* (Moscow: Kvadriga, 2010). A. Stoyanov has made use of these in a chapter of his doctoral dissertation titled "Russia Marches South: Army Reform and Battlefield Performance in Russia's Southern Campaigns, 1695-1739" (Leiden University, 2017).

49. Dimitriĭ Cantemir was a Moldavian *hospodar*, whose father was a Crimean Tatar in the service of the Ottomans in Moldavia. He spent many years in Constantinople where he learned Greek, Turkish, and a number of other languages. In 1710, he turned against the Ottomans and joined Peter the Great, who made him a prince.

50. See F. I. Soĭmonov, *Opisanie Kaspiĭskogo moria i chinennykh na onom rossiĭskikh zavoevanie, iako chast' istorii Gosudaria Imperatora Petra Velikago* (St. Petersburg: Imperatorskaia Akademiia Nauk, 1763), 58-63. The English translation from a German version of the text is in Julius von Klaproth, *Travels in the Caucasus and Georgia Performed in the Years 1807 and 1808* (London, 1814), 194-96.

51. RGADA, f. 110, d. 110, o. 15, ll. 485-487. Turkistanov was a Georgian named Tukestanishvili, who was a colonel in the Russian army.

52. See Kat'oghikos Esayi Hasan Jalaleants', *A Brief History of the Aghuank` Region (Patmut`iwn Hamarot Aghuanits` Erkri): A History of Karabagh and Ganje from 1702-1723*, trans. George A. Bournoutian (Costa Mesa: Mazda, 2009), 64. The Russianized names of the Armenian volunteers, which include that of Petros Sarkis di Gilanents, are in AVPRI, f. 77, Russia's Relations with Persia (1722), reproduced in A. [H]. N. Khachatrian, ed. *Armianskoe voĭsko v XVIII veke* (Yerevan: Akademiia Nauk Armianskoĭ SSR, 1968), doc. 1.

53. Bruce, *Memoirs*, 343. Some sources note that one-third of his troops had perished.

54. The Russian state achieved control over this area with the final surrender of Shamil in 1859.

55. The treaty was signed in St. Petersburg on September 23, 1723. The text is in T. I͡uzefovich, ed., *Dogovory Rossii s" Vostokom": Politicheskie i torgovye* (St. Petersburg: Baksta, 1869), 185–89. For the English translation, see Bournoutian, *Armenians and Russia*, 115–16 (doc. 119). The treaty was never ratified in Iran. Tahmasb II refused to accept it, and Esmāʿil Beg had to flee to Astrakhan where he died two decades later. Despite this fact, Russia occupied much of Mazandaran.

56. The most detailed Armenian account of the Ottoman invasion and takeover of Yerevan is in Abraham of Yerevan's *History of the Wars, 1721–1738*, trans. G. Bournoutian (Costa Mesa: Mazda, 1999), 17–35. For an Ottoman account of the conquest, see Salahşur Khaseh Kemani Mustafa Ağa, *Revan Fathnamasi* (Istanbul: Boğazici University, 1970).

57. G. Noradounghian, *Recueil d'actes internationaux de l'Empire Ottoman*, vol. 1 (Paris, 1897), 233–36. Also see A. Tsutsiev, *Atlas of the Ethno-Political History of the Caucasus* (New Haven, CT: Yale University Press, 2014), map 2.

58. Catholicos Esayi Hasan-Jalaleants', who soon joined Vakhtang with the Armenian volunteers from Qarabagh, has left an eyewitness account of the aspirations of the combined army, *A Brief History*, 68–69. Esayi's claim of ten thousand Armenian volunteers was probably exaggerated.

59. Following the Russo-Ottoman Treaty of 1724, Vakhtang, together with his queen, two sons, and 1,186 members of Georgian nobility and clergy, crossed into Russia. See J. Foran, "The Long Fall of the Safavid Dynasty: Moving beyond the Standard Views," *International Journal of Middle East Studies* 24, no. 2 (1992): 294–96; Lockhart, *Fall of the Safavi Dynasty*, 117–19. A number of Armenian leaders also fled to Russia where they formed Armenian squadrons in the Russian army; see Bournoutian, *Armenians and Russia*, 154, 157–58, 160–62, 187–88 (docs. 175, 180, 183, 186, 220–23).

60. Sergeĭ M. Solov'ev, *Istoria Rossii*, vol. 18 (Moscow, 1868), 38. See also note 61, above.

61. During that time Teymuraz had gone to St. Petersburg to gain Russian support for eastern Georgia. He died in January 1762, and Erekle II became the ruler of the united Kartli-Kakheti.

62. Matenadaran Archives, folder 243, doc. 18; Russian translation in V. K. Voskani͡an, ed., *Armi͡ano-Russkie otnosheniia vo vtorom tritsatiletii XVIII veka*, vol. 3 (Yerevan: Akademii͡a Nauk Armi͡anskoĭ SSR, 1978), doc. 228.

63. RGADA, f. 1263, o. 1, d. 8177, ll. 1–2.

64. The Russian translation is in M. G. Nersisi͡an, ed., *Armi͡ano-russkie otnosheniia v XVIII veke*, vol. 4 (Yerevan: Akademii͡a Nauk Armi͡anskoĭ SSR, 1990), 39 (doc. 8).

65. Erekle's relations with the khans of Qarabagh and Yerevan fluctuated between friendship and enmity.

66. Nersisi͡an, *Armi͡ano-russkie otnosheniia v XVIII veke*, docs. 11–19, 25. In 1770, Emin returned to Calcutta, via Iran, and died there in 1808. His memoires, published in London in 1792, were revised by his great-great-granddaughter, Amy

Apcar, and published in Calcutta in 1918 under the title *Life and Adventures of Joseph Emin, 1726–1809, Written by Himself* (Calcutta: Baptist Mission Press, 1918).

67. Matenadaran Archives, folder 2, doc. 6, fols. 79-84, and folder 3, doc. 7a, fols. 1-3 and 5-6. See also G. A. Ezov', *Nachalo snoshenii Echmiadzinskago patriarshago prestola s russkim pravitelstvom* (Tiflis: Martirosyants, 1901).

68. *PSZ*, vol. 19, no. 13525.

69. *PSZ*, vol. 16, no. 11937; vol. 18, no. 13384; vol. 19, no. 13464. See also Bournoutian, *Armenians and Russia*, 234, 249 (docs. 275, 292-93).

70. Born in Georgia in 1743, Argutinskiĭ became a bishop in 1769 and, in 1773, was appointed as Echmiadzin's prelate in Russia. In 1778 he also became the spiritual leader of the Armenians of Crimea and, in 1780, led the Armenian emigration from the Crimea to Russia. In 1789, he established the first Armenian press in Russia in Astrakhan; see Leo, *Hovsep katoghikos Arghutean* (Tiflis: Rotinants, 1902); G. Aghaneants, ed., *Diwan hayots patmutean*, vol. 9.1 (Tiflis: Sharadze, 1911); S. Glinka, ed., *Sobranie aktov otnoshīashchikhsīa k obozrnīiu istorii armīanskogo naroda*, vol. 2 (Moscow: Lazarian, 1838), 69-70.

71. After being informed that the Armenian leaders had contacted Russia, Ebrāhim Khan killed the Catholicos in 1786. Although the khan placed his own puppet as Catholicos, the Armenians did not recognize him, and the see was left without a leader until 1794. In 1781 Ebrāhim Khan had also killed Melik Isaiah of Dizak.

72. RGADA, f. 15, o. 1, d. 149, ll. 190-191; f. 23, o. 1, d. 13, III/1, l. 142. Partial English translations in Bournoutian, *Armenians and Russia*, 284-86 (docs. 335-36). Once again, the Armenians had, most probably, exaggerated the number of troops; see note 61, above.

73. The Russians did not refer to Ebrāhim as the khan of Qarabagh, only of Shushi. They viewed the Armenian *meliks* as autonomous rulers of their domains in Qarabagh.

74. Rossiĭskiĭ Gosudarstvennyĭ Voenno-Istoricheskiĭ Arkhiv (hereafter RGVIA), f. 52, o. 2, d. 32, l. 1 (dated May 31, 1783).

75. See her decree (September 25, 1763) permitting Moses Sarafov to start silk production in Astrakhan, as well as her decree (January 13, 1765) permitting the Armenians to have their own court and observe their own laws there. Although such a court had been established in 1747, Empress Elizabeth's russification policy had halted its function. The Armenian law code of Astrakhan has been examined in F. G. Poghosyan's *Datastanagirk Astrakhani Hayots* (Yerevan: Akademiīa Nauk Armīanskoĭ SSR, 1967). See also the report of the Russian consul in Anzali, Ilīa Igumov, to the governor of Astrakhan, Nikita Beketov, in AVPRI, f. 77, o. 5, d. 10, l. 85.

76. John R. Perry, *Karim Khan Zand: A History of Iran, 1747–1779* (Chicago: University of Chicago Press, 1979), 254-55.

77. For the well-researched details, see Sean Pollock, "Empire by Invitation? Russian Empire-Building in the Caucasus in the Reign of Catherine II" (PhD diss, Harvard University, 2006), 199-239.

78. Following the treaty, the Armenian prelate in Russia, Iosif Argutinskiĭ joined Grigoriĭ Potemkin's plan to expand southward. The Armenians in the South Caucasus once again promised financial and military aid.

79. Glinka, *Sobranie aktov otnoshīashchikhsīa*, 3:331–32; *PSZ*, vol. 23, nos. 17246, 17260.

80. Glinka, *Sobranie aktov otnoshīashchikhsīa*, 3:335.

81. Catherine had sent Count Marko Voĭnovich to establish a Russian trade depot to connect Astrakhan with Iran, India, Central Asia, and Tibet. When the latter fortified the depot, Āqā Moḥammad Khan Qajar seized the Russians and released them only after they agreed to dismantle the forts and leave the region.

82. For a recent study, see Pollock, "Empire by Invitation?"

83. George Bournoutian, *From the Kur to the Aras: A Military History of Russia's Move into the South Caucasus and the First Russo-Iranian War, 1801–1813* (Leiden: Brill, 2020).

CHAPTER 5

Astrakhan and the Caspian Sea in Russia's Early Modern Political Geography

Guido Hausmann

This chapter aims at analyzing how visual representations, above all printed maps, were produced at the intersection of three interconnected historical processes. It focuses on particular actors and places their actions in historical contexts, but also on the geographical representation of the Caspian Sea itself.

A first important strand is that Russia's presence at the northern shore of the Caspian Sea was initially part of the larger process of Russia's state or imperial expansion to the east and southeast in the middle of the sixteenth century. Key events in making Russia an empire included the conquest of Kazan in 1552 and of Astrakhan in 1556. Indeed, Russia subjugated the power structures and territories of these khanates, which had never been part of it before, with populations of largely non-Orthodox, Muslim faith.[1] But if empire is defined as a certain kind of statehood and, in particular, as a process of empire building implying territorial expansion and the administrative management of difference, it might be more appropriate to regard the entire time period from the mid-sixteenth to the eighteenth century as such a process.[2] During this time imperial Russia's presence in the

---

I am grateful to Jörn Happel and Marietta Kausch for their suggestions and support in writing the chapter.

newly acquired areas along the Volga River was restricted to its construction and possession of a few newly established settlements along the river with some military and administrative personnel. They were fortresses of sorts with adjunct trading populations. The large steppe areas between these "towns" were inhabited by indigenous nomadic peoples such as the Nogai and, since the seventeenth century, by the Kalmyks.[3] After the fall of the Chinggisid Empire in the fifteenth century the nomads had built loose political structures on the steppe. Muscovite Russia's governing elites considered the areas of the nomads as largely unpopulated. At the mouth of the Volga, Moscow established the new town of Astrakhan, next to the former settlement that had been the medieval capital of the khanate. A brief though dramatic political shift occurred in 1722–23, when after the conclusion of a peace treaty with Sweden (1721), Russia turned its face toward Asia and conquered territories on the western shore of the Caspian Sea (Gilan, Derbent, Baku) and in the northern parts of Iran with its important silk-producing centers.[4]

A second important strand was international trade. The trade in raw silk from Iran and Central Asia to northwestern Europe transformed Russia economically during the seventeenth century into a transit country, with the Volga River as the key transport route and Astrakhan on the northern shore of the Caspian Sea as a trading center of growing domestic and international importance. The so-called Volga route served as an alternative northern route for international commerce during times of political and military insecurities in Iran and the Ottoman Empire.[5]

Since the Middle Ages, inter-Asian trade had moved from land to sea. In early modern times, Britain and the Netherlands traded with Asia also by sea via the Indian Ocean and Persian Gulf, whereas Russia was largely engaged in overland trade and "the means of communication between Russia and Asia by land remained practically unchanged. Speed, cheapness and tonnage" were the advantages of seaborne or oceanic trade.[6] The number of commodities exported from Russia to Asia was limited, and travel accounts of the late sixteenth century speak of Astrakhan's trade as quite poor. Nevertheless, Muscovite Russia abolished western European trading companies, such as the English Muscovy Company, and permitted merchants from Iran to use Russia (via Archangel'sk, which was established in 1584 on the White Sea) as a transit route for its Asian-European commerce, in particular with the silk-producing regions in northern Iran (Gilan, Mazandaran, Shirvan, and Qarabagh).[7]

This changed considerably in the last third of the seventeenth century after Russia had consolidated its relations with Sweden (1661) and Poland-Lithuania (1667) as a result of a shift in its fiscal policy. Regulations from 1667, 1673, and 1676 allowed Armenian merchants from Iran (above all from New Julfa, Isfahan) to use Russia as a transit trade route for its silk trade toward northern and western European ports, mainly Amsterdam.[8] Moscow's merchants were only rarely engaged in the re-export of Iranian goods through Archangel'sk or Novgorod toward northern and western Europe, and western European merchants remained banned from the transit trade. Indian merchants from Iran were similarly banned; they were only allowed to trade silk in Astrakhan, but not in Moscow. However, Russia did not succeed in monopolizing the trading route, and as a transit country for the silk trade it remained of secondary importance (5 percent of the silk export from Iran at the beginning of the eighteenth century passed through Russia). Tsar Peter I made a new effort to attract the silk trade from Iran to northwestern Europe toward Russia and to monopolize it, but again without major success, and by 1718 he lifted the privileges for the Armenian merchants from Julfa.[9] The picture, however, improved from the 1730s to the 1750s, when up to 20 percent, sometimes even up to 40 percent (in the 1740s) of the raw silk exported from Iran to western Europe was traded through Russia.[10]

With its multireligious and multiethnic population, and particularly its important merchant colony from India as well as its Armenian merchants, Astrakhan transformed during this time into a new hub. Tsar Peter I imagined Astrakhan in the early eighteenth century as an important international transit point that should attract much of the trade from other parts of the Caspian coast to it. It was to become Russia's window to the East or to Asia, as the newly created city of St. Petersburg had become Russia's window to Europe on the Baltic Sea.[11] This policy goal, however, could not be achieved in the long run.

The third major trend, the rise of the western European sciences and in particular of geography and cartography, was closely linked to Russia's state- or empire-building process in the eighteenth century. A smaller stratum of people with awareness of the western European sciences did exist in Russia before the eighteenth century. A sign of growing interest was the establishment of the first scholarly institutions in Kyiv and Moscow. A distinction between geographic knowledge and the rise of geography as an academic or scientific field was yet to be made. However, in general it can be argued that it was the accelerated state-building process under Peter I that created the demand for institutional knowledge bases and stimulated the support for acquiring knowledge in such fields. Key landmarks in this development were the founding of specialized schools for mathematics and navigation at the beginning of the eighteenth century, the foundation of imperial Russia's Academy of Sciences in 1724, and the founding of Russia's first university in Moscow in 1755.[12] In the 1730s and 1740s, large expeditions with clearly defined tasks were sent to Siberia and the Far East to explore Russia's border regions and its natural wealth. Visual representations of the Volga and the Caspian Sea, in particular printed maps, before the eighteenth century were of western European origin, but they were known in Russia as well and even produced in close relationship with Russian or other local populations. So far, I have not come across Russian-made visual representations of the Caspian Sea or of the non-Russian population of the Russian Empire, like the Nogai or peoples of Kalmyk origin.

This chapter makes three general arguments with regard to the mapping of the Caspian Sea in early modern Russia. First is that the mapping of the Caspian Sea was closely related to the discovery and actual use of the Volga for expansion, trade, and transportation.[13] No mapping of the Caspian Sea was possible without the Volga, which empties into the Caspian Sea and nurtured the interest in its size, its location, and in adjacent rivers, which also empty into the Caspian Sea and could be of use for further trade connections. Second is that mapmaking about the Caspian Sea started with general maps, which became more detailed and precise in the course of several decades from the late seventeenth to the mid-eighteenth century. It is even possible to speak of a process of differentiation from the more general maps toward the production of more detailed maps on parts of the Caspian Sea. One further argument is that the mapmaking of the Caspian Sea was considered by the Academy of Sciences overall less important in comparison with other border regions of Russia and that fewer maps of the Caspian Sea were produced and printed in Russia than of other border regions such as Siberia and the Russian north (the White Sea), as well as the northwest (the Baltic Sea). It is against this background that the geographical exploration and the cartography of Astrakhan and the Caspian Sea has to be analyzed.

The Caspian Sea in the Eyes of European Travelers and Mapmakers

There are a few maps of the Volga and the northern part of the Caspian Sea from the sixteenth and seventeenth centuries that are well known to most historians of Russia but that are nevertheless worth recalling, because they fortify my basic arguments. In the course of the sixteenth century, western European travel accounts agreed on the fact that the Volga emptied into the Caspian Sea, whereas throughout medieval times up to the early sixteenth century, many descriptions stated that it emptied into the Black Sea. Until the seventeenth century, very few western Europeans actually traveled on the Volga. The Englishman Anthony Jenkinson (1530–1611) of the English Muscovy Company was a rare exception with his travel on the Volga to Astrakhan in the 1560s and with his map of Russia.[14]

The astronomer, mathematician, philologist, and librarian Adam Olearius (1599–1671) traveled several times in the 1630s as a secretary of a Holstein-Gottorpian embassy through Russia and down the Volga

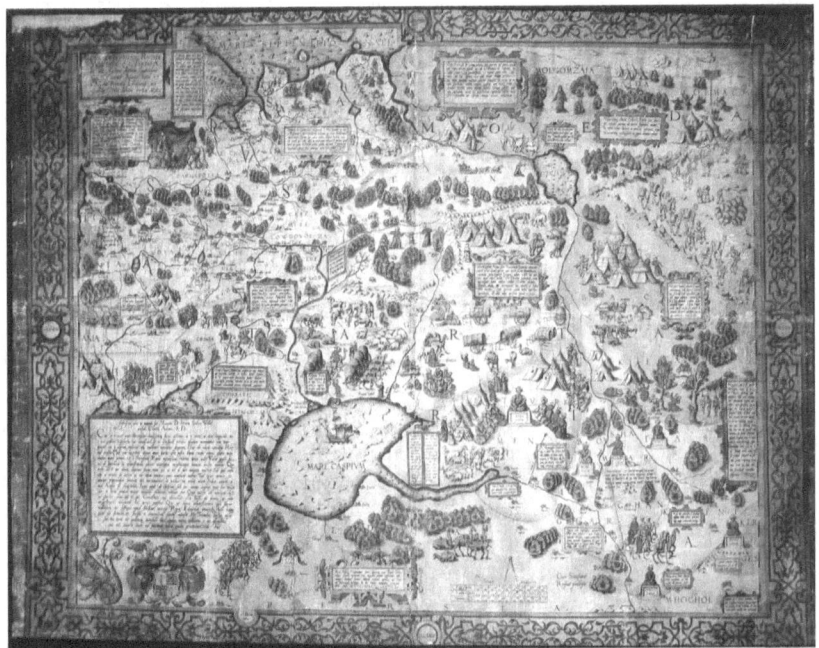

FIGURE 5.1. Anthony Jenkinson's map of Muscovy, 1562 *Nova absolvtaqve Rvssiae, Moscoviae & Tartariae*. Wrocław University Library Cartographic Collection.

FIGURE 5.2. Abraham Ortelius's copy of the Jenkinson map, published in his atlas, *Theatrum Orbis Terrarum* (1570). Wrocław University Library Cartographic Collection.

FIGURE 5.3. Adam Olearius, *Accurata delineatio Nobilissmi toti Europae Fluminis Wolgae olim RHA dictae per Adamum Olearium* (1663). David Rumsey Map Collection.

from the trading center Nizhny Novgorod to Astrakhan and further on to Iran, to explore the advantages and disadvantages of this trading route for the European-Asian trade. He published a travel account (first edition in 1647, second edition in 1656) and added to the second edition a map of the Volga on an inserted page, which became a landmark map for all western European travelers up to the middle of the eighteenth century.[15] This map was highly regarded by the educated elite in Moscow.[16] Not least and without any more detailed explanation, Olearius marked the Volga and the Caspian Sea as a border between Europe and Asia ("und taten durch Gottes gnädige Hilfe aus Europa (als den ersten Teil der Welt) gleichsam den ersten Schritt nach Asien, den Astrachan' liegt jenseits des Wolga-stroms, welcher Europa von Asien scheidet"), a statement that found in the course of the seventeenth and eighteenth centuries a number of followers in western Europe as well as in Russia, for example, by the Russian statesman Vasiliĭ Nikitich Tatishchev (1686–1750), who served as governor of Astrakhan in 1741–44.[17]

In the late seventeenth century, there was increased evidence in travel accounts of Astrakhan as a flourishing trading center with goods such as silk, fruits, fish, and salt.[18] A good example is the account of the Dutch traveler Johann Janszoon Struys, who sailed in the 1670s down the Volga to Astrakhan and published a travel account after his return to Amsterdam.[19] At the same time two new accounts enriched the knowledge of the Volga and Astrakhan in western Europe. In 1692, Amsterdam mayor Nicolaas Witsen (1641–1717) published an account on "Noord- and Oost-Tartarye." Two years earlier, he published a part of a diary of his journey through Russia in the 1660s, including a map of the northern and eastern part of Asia and Europe.[20]

FIGURE 5.4. Pierre Duval, *Carte du voyage de Perse et du Dagesthan, les années 1636, 1637 et 1638 selon la relation d'Olearius* (1677). Bibliothèque nationale de France, département Cartes et plans, GE DD-2987 (6734).

Figure 5.5. Gerardus Mercator, *Europa*, in *Atlas Minor Gerardi Mercatoris à I.Hondio plurimis æneis tabulis auctus atque illustratus* (1607).

Figure 5.6. Nicolas Witsen, *Tartaria, sive Magni Chami Imperium* . . . (1670). David Rumsey Map Collection.

FIGURE 5.7. Detail from Witsen's 1670 map, *Tartaria, sive Magni Chami Imperium*. . . . David Rumsey Map Collection.

FIGURE 5.8. Engelbert Kaempfer, "Two Perspectives of Astrakhan" (ca. 1683). © British Library Board, used by permission.

Witsen stood in close contact with the Westphalian physician and natural scientist Engelbert Kaempfer (1651–1716; the two exchanged letters) who is best known for his journey in 1683 as secretary of the Swedish envoy Ludvig Fabritius through Russia toward Iran, India, and Japan. With the travel account of Adam Olearius from 1656 in hand, he produced detailed drawings, an itinerary, and a diary of his journey down the Volga to Inner Asia, which remained unpublished until the nineteenth century. A more recent new edition shows two drawings of Astrakhan, which is typical for his visual depictions. His handwriting is so illegible that it is almost impossible to track down the meaning, but obviously he visited the Tatar neighborhood and the fish market of the town, which impressed him.[21]

Imperial Russia's Cartographic Exploration of the Caspian Sea in the Eighteenth Century

The geographer and historian Mark Bassin has stated that in the seventeenth century, maps in Russia were still "fragmentary and primitive."[22] We can assume that a basic geographic knowledge of the Caspian Sea existed around 1700, but nothing more. The reason was simply that foreign travelers were not so much interested in the Caspian Sea itself but perceived it more as a transit space. It is less easy to explain why the geography of the Caspian Sea was not of greater interest for Russia and the Russians. The major reason must have been that Russia's merchants were not trading overseas but instead relied on non-Russians to carry goods to and from Iran. Also, the Muscovite state was primarily interested in securing the open steppe frontier north of the Caspian Sea and not in political expansion south of the Caspian Sea. It is quite clear that Russia made increased efforts to secure its southern frontier since the last third of the seventeenth century. Evidence of this focus on securing the frontier can be found in agreements that secured the loyalty of the Don Cossacks to the tsar, and also of the Kalmyk people north of Astrakhan. Russia progressively moved its southern fortified lines further to the south to complete the Tsaritsyn fortification line in 1718, as Michael Khodarkovsky has shown.[23]

By 1700, even the northern coast of the Caspian Sea, which had been Russia's border since 1556, still was geographically unexplored.[24] The same holds true for its western coast to the mouth of the Terek, which also belonged to Russia, whereas the entire southern and southwestern coast were part of Safavid Iran.[25] The geographic exploration of the

Caspian Sea in the next twenty-five years was closely related to the ups and downs of the political and military interests of Peter I in the region. At around 1700 Peter I was primarily interested in Azov and the Black Sea (geographically explored by Cornelis Cruys). But at the same time, he also gave the order to explore the Caspian Sea and its coast. On that occasion, a first map was made in 1704 by a captain Eremej Meier, which, however, was lost or at least has not been discovered yet.[26] Meier himself lost his life during an uprising in Astrakhan in 1705. Then Peter's interest switched during the war with Sweden to the Baltic Sea region and toward a water connection between the upper Volga and the new capital St. Petersburg.[27] In the mid-1710s the Caspian Sea regained increased attention from Peter I.[28] Already in 1709 and in 1713, the captain of the Astrakhan port, the Frenchman Jean-Christophe Rentel, was ordered to explore the western coast of the Caspian Sea and to search for a suitable location for a port. As far as we know, Rentel did not produce a map.[29] In 1715, Tsar Peter I sent envoys to the shah to improve the economic and political relations with Iran.[30] In the same year, he ordered Prince Aleksandr Bekovich-Cherkasskiĭ and Aleksandr Kozhin to chart the Caspian Sea, in particular its eastern coastline. In 1719-20 he ordered the officers Karl van Verden (Werden?, ?-1731) and Fëdor I. Soĭmonov (1682-1769) to chart its western coastline. The latter two completed their work by 1720, when a map was printed bearing the names of Karl van Verden and Fëdor I. Soĭmonov.[31] Peter sent the map to the French Academy of Sciences, which had elected him as a member in 1717. It earned much praise from the French geographer Guillaume de Lisle (1688-1768), among others, who added in a publication in 1720 the following comment to his description of the Caspian Sea: "It is known that the Caspian Sea is not connected to any ocean and has remained, because of this fact, poorly researched. . . . Recently the tsar has given attention to it, and we have received new information about the Caspian Sea."[32] The newly acquired geographic knowledge of the Caspian Sea was used a few years later in the new atlas of the world of Johann Baptist Homann in Nuremberg (1725).[33]

The picture changed by 1720. Whereas in the centuries before geographic knowledge and technological skills were based in western Europe and spread from there to Russia, with Russians being involved as consultants at most, after 1720 the knowledge transfer changed its direction and the centers of knowledge production shifted toward Russia. Three points can highlight this shift. First, Peter I ordered the establishment of specialized schools in Moscow for the education of surveyors

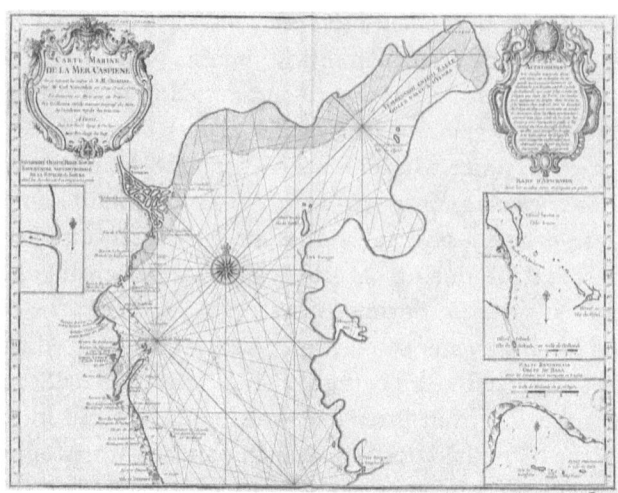

FIGURE 5.9. Carl Vanverden (Karl van Verden), *Carte marine de la Mer Caspiene levee Suivant les ordres de S.M. Czariene Par Mr Carl Vanverden en 1719, 1720, 1721 & Coste de Perse sur la mer Caspiene et oartie de celles de tartarie* (1721). Bibliothèque nationale de France, département Cartes et plans, GE BB 565 (14, 13).

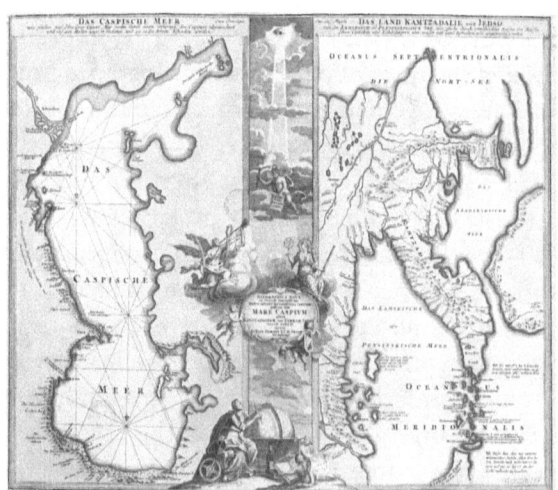

FIGURE 5.10. Io. Bapt. Homann, *Geographica nova ex oriente gratiosissima, duabus tabulis specialissimis contenta quarum una Mare Caspium, altera Kamtzadaliam seu Terram Jedso curiose exhibit* (1724). Bibliothèque nationale de France, département Cartes et plans, CPL GE DD-2987 (7409).

and geodesists with teaching staff from western Europe after his return from a western European grand tour at the end of the seventeenth century (including the 1701 foundation of the Moscow Mathematical and Navigational School and the 1715 foundation of the Naval Academy in St. Petersburg).[34] Second, by 1715 the school(s) had successfully trained a new cohort of geographers with the necessary mathematical and technical skills. The best known and most important geographer of the Caspian Sea was certainly the officer and (later) governor Fëdor I. Soĭmonov, who in 1719, together with Karl van Verden, was ordered to explore the lower Volga and the western and southern coastline of the Caspian Sea, to produce accounts on the navigation along the shores of the sea, and to study weather and wind conditions. Soĭmonov became famous as the first Russian to successfully publish a printed map of the Caspian Sea in 1720, followed by the first atlas of the sea in 1731.[35] In fact, the latter was the result of a joint effort by Aleksandr Bekovich-Cherkasskiĭ, Aleksandr Kozhin, Karl van Verden, and Fëdor I. Soĭmonov.

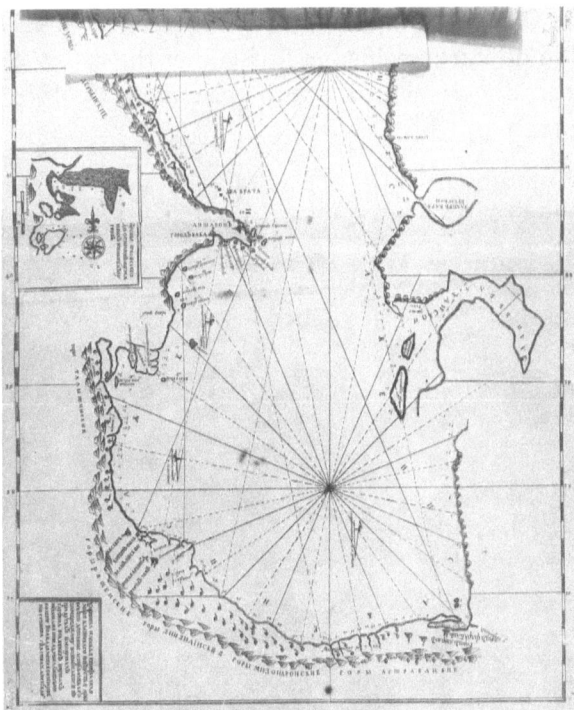

FIGURE 5.11. Fëdor I. Soĭmonov, map of the southern half of the Caspian Sea from his *Атлас Каспийского моря* [Atlas of the Caspian Sea] (1731).

A third point concerns the new knowledge of the Caspian Sea. When Peter I ordered the exploration of the Caspian Sea in 1715, Prince Bekovich-Cherkasskiĭ began to study its eastern shore in more detail. He founded two fortresses, presumably to secure the trade route to Khiva. He was then asked "to send people to find out about the route to Yarkand and India via the Amu-Darya and Syr-Darya rivers."[36] In 1714 Peter was told by the Turkmen Khoja Nefes from the peninsula of Mangyshlak that in earlier times the Amu-Darya had emptied into the Caspian Sea. The existence of the widespread myth about an old estuary of the Amu-Darya, which connected the Caspian Sea with India, was even testified by a German map from the sixteenth century.[37] Tsar Peter I wanted to verify this information, and in 1714 he ordered the detailed exploration of the eastern coastline of the Caspian Sea under the leadership of Prince Aleksandr Bekovich-Cherkasskiĭ. Attacks by Turkmens, who settled along the eastern coast, threatened the success of the expedition. Bekovich-Cherkasskiĭ, however, managed to verify the information and produced a map of the Caspian Sea, which was discovered by historians only in 1951. He also covered the southern coast of the Caspian Sea.[38] He lost his life in 1717 in an expedition to Khiva, and doubts remained in Russia over the nature of the Amu-Darya connection (was there a mouth of a river or a gulf connecting it to the Caspian?).

FIGURE 5.12 Sebastian Münster, *Tabula orientalis regionis, Asiae scilicet extremas complectens terras et regna* [map of Asia], from his *Cosmographey oder beschreibung aller Länder* . . . (1574). Universität-Bibliothek Heidelberg, https://doi.org/10.11588/diglit.55538#1153.

The new knowledge about the Caspian Sea must have been of some relevance for the Persian campaign of Peter I in 1722-23, which started after the conclusion of the peace treaty with Sweden in 1721. The trigger was domestic uprisings in Iran, and Peter revived his idea of Russia as the principal transit route for Iranian silk to Europe and Astrakhan as the hub of this endeavor. Soĭmonov commanded Russia's fleet from Astrakhan to the southern shore of the Caspian Sea during Peter's Persian campaign and produced drawings and maps of the sea. These have been discovered and published recently, showing the town of Derbent with the Caspian Sea, the mouth of the River Kura flowing into the sea, and the conquest of Baku.[39] The conquest of Baku, Derbent, and the northern Iranian territories was only short-lived, as the military campaign ended without success and the Russian army had to withdraw quickly to the north.[40]

Soĭmonov's atlas of the Caspian Sea, which was published a few years later in 1731, can be regarded as a joint effort of the state and a new generation of geographers. In 1725, Peter I ordered Soĭmonov to reexamine the map of 1720, partially for political reasons, because some fortifications, ports, and mouths of rivers on the southern shore were not noted on the 1720 map.[41]

The first maps of the Caspian Sea produced in Russia were thus the result of political interest, which was closely related to military-strategic and economic concerns. With their focus on scientifically accurate depiction of coastlines, Russia's new maps produced in the early eighteenth century shed a different light on the Caspian Sea than the maps of the sixteenth and seventeenth centuries.[42]

If we take the mapping of the Caspian Sea as part of a more general effort begun in the time of Peter I,[43] aimed at collecting detailed geographical knowledge of the country, then we can take as its final point the first general map of the Russian Empire in 1745.[44] The map was completed by the Geographic Department of the Academy of Sciences, founded only a few years earlier, in 1739. The Caspian Sea is depicted here by the first generation of geodesists and geographers from Peter's time, their successors of the 1730s,[45] as well as by foreign experts in the service of the Russian state, as the southeastern border of the empire.

During the second half of the eighteenth century, other types of cartography developed in Russia as well, including military topographic maps or battle maps for the College of War. In regard to the Caspian Sea, Russia's expansion to the Kazakh Steppe and Central Asia certainly

FIGURE 5.13. Detail from *Mappa Generalis Totius Imperii Russici* [map of the Russian Empire], commissioned by the Academy of Sciences, St. Petersburg (1745). David Rumsey Map Collection.

played a role. The Caspian Sea itself became less central to Russia's trade and strategic priorities than to the territories east and northeast of it, in particular Orenburg, but the Caspian-borne trade and expansion toward the Caucasus and Iran remained.[46] Administrative reforms and land surveying also fostered the making of new kinds of maps.

Two different maps of (parts of) the Caspian Sea from the time of Catherine II (1762–96) can demonstrate the process of new differentiation in cartography in Russia. The maps also testify to the continuous cartographic interest in the peripheries of the empire. From the 1760s on a new interest emerged in hydrography, including the Caspian Sea. The hand-drawn map compiled by Ivan Popov (the year of the map is unknown) shows the northeastern coast of the Caspian Sea and its connection to Khiva and Orenburg.[47] The map demonstrates the progress in precision that cartography had made in Russia in the course of the eighteenth century.

The second map was made by Riga physician Johann A. Güldenstädt (1745–81). Güldenstädt had participated in an expedition to Astrakhan and the Caucasus in the 1770s, and his notes were published postmortem in the year 1783 by the scholar Peter Simon Pallas.[48] Although a natural scientist by profession, with an interest in botany and related topics, he was also an explorer by nature, attracted by little-known territories in the Caucasus. His map testifies to the heightened standards of detailed depiction in Russian cartography in the second half of the eighteenth century. This shift becomes very clear if one compares his map with the first maps of the Caspian Sea at the beginning of the century. It does not seem that the production of this map was linked to political or military matters, as the ones by Soĭmonov. It is worth noting, however, that Russia fought wars at the time, particularly at its southern frontier and particularly against the Ottoman Empire in 1768-74.

This case study of early modern Russian cartography of the Caspian Sea verifies the general assumption that cartography and mapmaking

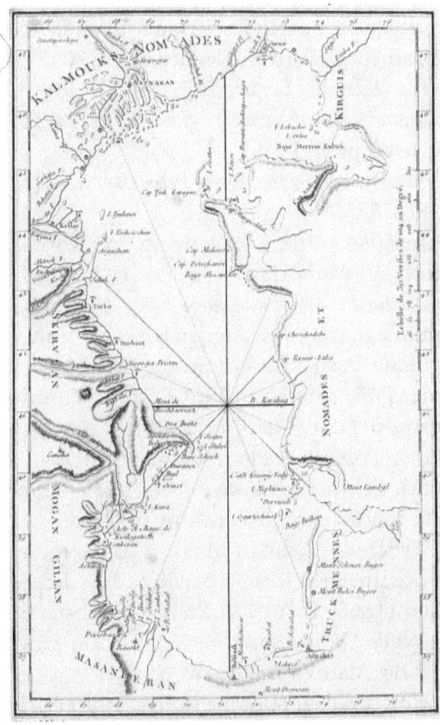

FIGURE 5.14. *Carte de la mer caspienne* [map of the Caspian Sea], *dressée en 7.bre 1776 d'après les dernieres observations par D. Guldenstaedt; gravé par P. F. Tardieu* (1783). Universitätsbibliothek Bern, https://doi.org/10.3931/e-rara-31295.

were historically closely linked with early modern state building, and in particular with territorial interests and claims. It is therefore probably a practice from above, linked to the interests and needs of the state, like Russia. However, my chapter also demonstrates that early modern mapmaking, as the early modern sciences in general, cannot be analyzed in the framework of the "nation" or the state alone. Cartography, as other sciences as well, was international, and its actors/agents were transnational actors. However, in early modern Russia the dynamics of cartography and mapmaking were limited to cultural exchange within Europe. In this regard an important shift occurred in Russia during the period under consideration, that is, during the reign of Peter I and the decades after his death.

Notes

1. Valerie A. Kivelson and Ronald G. Suny, *Russia's Empires* (Oxford: Oxford University Press, 2017), 61–64; Andreas Kappeler, *Russland als Vielvölkerreich: Entstehung, Geschichte, Zerfall* (Munich: Beck Verlag, 1992), 29–31.

2. For an even longer time period, see Nancy Shields Kollmann, *The Russian Empire 1450–1801* (Oxford: Oxford University Press, 2017), 55–57.

3. Kollmann, *The Russian Empire*, 67, 70–71; for more detail, see L. Liubomirov, *O zaselenii Astrakhanskoĭ gubernii v XVIII veke* (Astrakhan: Astrakhanskiĭ gubernskiĭ plan, 1926).

4. Lindsey Hughes, *Russia in the Age of Peter the Great* (New Haven, CT: Yale University Press, 1998), 57–59.

5. See David Christian, "Silk Roads or Steppe Roads? The Silk Road in World History," *Journal of World History* 11, no. 1 (2000): 1–26; on Astrakhan: N. M. Ushakov, ed., *Istoriia Astrakhanskogo kraia* (Astrakhan: Izdatel'stvo Astrakhanskogo gosudarstvennogo pedagogicheskogo universiteta, 2000), particularly 165–289; Elena Vasil'evna Gusarova, *Astrakhanskie nakhodki: Istoriia, arkitektura, gradostroitel'stvo Astrakhani XVI–XVIII vv. Po dokumentam iz sobranii Peterburga* (St. Petersburg: Nestor-Istoriia, 2009).

6. See A. M. Petrov, "Foreign Trade of Russia and Britain with Asia in the Seventeenth to Nineteenth Centuries," *Modern Asian Studies* 21, no. 4 (1987): 628–29.

7. The year 1632 was an exception in this regard.

8. See Stefan Troebst, "Isfahan-Moskau-Amsterdam: Zur Entstehungsgeschichte des moskauischen Transitprivilegs für die Armenische Handelskompanie in Persien (1666–1676)," in Stefan Troebst, *Zwischen Arktis, Adria und Armenien: Das östliche Europa und seine Ränder. Aufsätze, Essays und Vorträge 1983–2016* (Cologne: Boehlau Verlag, 2017), 35–69.

9. Wolfgang Sartor, "Der armenische Rohseidenhandel im 17. und 18. Jahrhundert: Die Russland-Route," in *Armenier im östlichen Europa: Eine Anthologie*, ed. Tamara Ganjalyan, Bálint Kovács, and Stefan Troebst (Vienna: Boehlau Verlag, 2018), 266.

10. Sartor, "Der armenische Rohseidenhandel," 266-68.

11. Andreas Renner, "Peter der Grosse und Russlands Fenster nach Asien," *Historische Zeitschrift* 306, no. 1 (2018): 71-96, https://doi.org/10.1515/hzhz-2018-0003.

12. General context in Loren R. Graham, *Science in Russia and the Soviet Union: A Short History* (Cambridge: Cambridge University Press, 1993), 16-27; James Cracraft, *The Revolution of Peter the Great* (Cambridge, MA: Harvard University Press, 2003), 40-46.

13. Guido Hausmann, *Mütterchen Wolga: Ein Fluss als Erinnerungsort vom 16. bis ins frühe 20. Jahrhundert* (Frankfurt: Campus, 2009).

14. See Lloyd E. Berry and Robert O. Crummey, eds., *Rude and Barbarous Kingdom: Russia in the Accounts of Sixteenth-Century English Voyagers* (Madison: University of Wisconsin Press, 1968); Hausmann, *Mütterchen Wolga*, 207-8.

15. Adam Olearius, *Vermehrte Newe Beschreibung der Muscowitischen und Persischen Reyse* (Schleswig, 1656), facsimile reprint, ed. Dieter Lohmeier (Tübingen: Niemeyer, 1971). Other travelers to Iran via the Volga were George Tectander (1581?-1614) and Peer Peerson (1570-1622); see Hausmann, *Mütterchen Wolga*, 196-97, 213-15; Nancy S. Kollmann, "Tracking the Travels of Adam Olearius," in *Word and Image in Russian History: Essays in Honor of Gary Marker*, ed. Maria Di Salvo, Daniel H. Kaiser, and Valerie A. Kivelson (Boston: Academic Studies Press, 2015), 133-46, https://doi.org/10.2307/j.ctt1zxsht1.15, for the contemporary translations of his travel account.

16. *Nova et accurata Wolgae fluminis, olim Rha dicti delineatio auctore Adamo Oleario* (Amsterdam, 1666); *Deianiia Petra Velikago, mudrago preobrazitelia Rossii i sobranyia iz dostovernykh istochnikov i raspolozhenyia po godam*, vol. 2 (Moscow, 1788), 181.

17. Mark Bassin, "Russia between Europe and Asia: The Ideological Construction of Geographical Space," *Slavic Review* 50, no. 1 (1991): 6.

18. Ushakov, *Istoriia Astrakhanskogo kraia*, 190-204.

19. Johann Jansz. Straußen, *Sehr schwere / widerwertige und Denckwürdige Reysen* ... (Amsterdam, 1678), 100-103; regarding Straußen, see Aleksandr Morozov, "Parusnyĭ master Ian Streĭs i ego puteshestvie," in *Ia. Ia. Streĭs: Tri puteshestviia.* (Riazan: Aleksandriia, 2006), 31-52; Kees Boterbloem, *The Fiction and Reality of Jan Struys: A Seventeenth-Century Dutch Globetrotter* (New York: Palgrave Macmillan, 2008).

20. See Nicolaas Vitsen, *Puteshestvie v Moskoviiu, 1664-1665: Dnevnik*, trans. V. G. Trisman (St. Petersburg, 1996); Anatoli N. Kirpichnikov, *Rossiia XVII veka v risunkakh i opisaniiakh gollandskogo puteshestvennika Nikolasa Vitsena* (St. Petersburg, 1995); Igor Wladimiroff, "Andries Vitsen and Nikolaas Witsen, Tsar Peter's Dutch Connection," in *Around Peter the Great: Three Centuries of Russian-Dutch Relations*, ed. Carel Horstmeier et al. (Groningen: INOS, 1997), 5-23.

21. Engelbert Kaempfer, *Rußlandtagebuch 1683*, ed. Michael Schippan (Munich: Iudicium Verlag, 2003); see also the edition of his letters: Engelbert Kaempfer, *Kritische Ausgabe in Einzelbänden*, ed. Detlef Haberland, vol. 2: *Briefe 1683-1715* (Munich: Iudicium, 2001), 149.

22. Bassin, "Russia between Europe and Asia," 7; Cracraft, *The Revolution*, 95-96; Valerie Kivelson, *Cartographies of Tsardom: The Land and Its Meanings in Seventeenth-Century Russia* (Ithaca, NY: Cornell University Press, 2006) on real-estate maps or drawings.

23. See Michael Khodarkovsky, *Where Two Worlds Met: The Russian State and the Kalmyk Nomads, 1600–1771* (Ithaca, NY: Cornell University Press, 1992), 163.

24. See Vladimir G. Goncharov, *F.I. Soĭmonov—pervyĭ russkiĭ gidrograf* (Moscow: Gosudarstvennoe Izdatel'stvo Geograficheskoĭ Literatury, 1954), 7.

25. See E. A. Kniazhetskaia, "Petr I—organizator issledovanii Kaspiĭskogo moria," in *Voprosy geografii Petrovskogo vremeni*, ed. M. I. Belova (Leningrad, 1975), 24. This work is the most detailed and convincing general description of the geographical exploration of the Caspian Sea I have found.

26. Kniazhetskaia, "Petr I," 25.

27. Guido Hausmann, "Die Unterwerfung der Natur als imperiale Veranstaltung: Bau und Eröffnung des Ladoga-Kanals in Russland im frühen 18. Jahrhundert," *Frühneuzeit-Info*, no. 2 (2008): 59–72.

28. Aleksey V. Postnikov, "The Russian Navy as Chartmaker in the Eighteenth Century," *Imago mundi* 52 (2000): 79–95. Olearius, *Vermehrte Newe Beschreibung*, 193.

29. Kniazhetskaia, "Petr I," 25.

30. P. P. Bushev, *Posol'stvo Artemiia Volynskogo v Iran v 1715–1718 gg. (po russkim arkhivam)* (Moscow: Izd. Nauka, Glavnaia Redaktsiia Vostochnoĭ Literatury, 1978).

31. A detailed account of the expedition of Verden and Soĭmonov can be found in *Zhizneopisaniia pervykh Rossiĭskikh admiralov ili opyt istorii Rossiĭskago flota* (St. Petersburg, 1831), chap. 2, 117: "In May 1720 von Verden and Soĭmonov left with their ships to the mouth of the Kura, and they continued to chart the western and southern shores of the Caspian Sea. They did not explore the eastern coastline, but the itinerary of Soĭmonov testifies that they approached it to determine the depth of the sea"; see also K. K. Giul', *Kaspiĭskoe More* (Baku: Azerbaĭdzhanskoe Gosudarstvennoe Izdatel'stvo Neftianoĭ i Nauchno-Technicheskoĭ Literatury, 1956), 18–19; see also the recent study on Karl van Verden in Gusarova, *Astrakhanskie nakhodki*, 236–52.

32. K. I. Shafranovskiĭ and E. A. Kniazhetskaia, "Karty Kaspiĭskogo i Aral'skogo more, sostavlennye v rezul'tate ėkspeditsii Aleksandra Bekovicha-Cherkasskogo 1715 g.," *Izvestiia Vsesoiuznogo Geograficheskogo Obshchestva*, no. 6 (1952): 541.

33. Postnikov, "The Russian Navy," 81; Johann Baptist Homann, Atlas Major, vol. 47, map 19, *Geographica nova ex oriente gratiosissima, duabus tabulis specialissimis contenta quarum una Mare Caspium, altera Kantzadalium seu Terram Jedso curiose exhibit*. Bibliothèque nationale de France, département Cartes et plans, CPL GE DD2987 (7409).

34. A. V. Postnikov, *Russia in Maps: A History of the Geographical Study and Cartography of the Country* (Moscow: Nash Dom, 1996), 36.

35. Fedor I. Soĭmonov, *Opisanie Kaspiĭskogo moria ot ust'ia reki Volgi, ot protoka Iarkovskago, do ust'ia reki Astrabatskoĭ, polozhenie zapadnogo i vostochnago beregov*,

glubiny, grunty, i vidy znatnykh gor (O.O., 1783); Leonid A. Gol'denberg, *Kartozhanin-Sibirskiĭ gubernator: Zhizn' i trudy F.I. Soĭmonova* (Magadan: Magadanskoe Knizhnoe Izdatel'stvo, 1979); Sergei F. Fel', *Kartografiia Rossii XVIII veka* (Moscow: Izdatel'stvo Geodezicheskoĭ Literatury, 1960); K. I. Shafranovskiĭ, "Rukopisnye karty Kaspiĭskogo moria F.I. Soimonova," in *Geograficheskiĭ sbornik*, vol. 3: *Istoriia geograficheskikh znanii i geograficheskikh otkrytii* (Moscow: Izdatel'stvo Akademii Nauk SSSR, 1954), 105, 107; Lev S. Berg, "Pervye russkie karty Kaspiĭskogo moria (s sviazi s voprosam ob urovne ego v XVII i XVIII vekakh)," *Izvestiia Akademii Nauk SSSR, Seriia geograficheskaia i geofizicheskaia* 3 (1940): 159–78; Karl von Baer, *Peters des Grossen Verdienste um die Erweiterung der geographischen Kenntnisse* (St. Petersburg, 1872).

36. Khodarkovsky, *Where Two Worlds Met*, 158.

37. Sebastian Münster, *Die Länder Asie nah ihrer gelegenheit biß in India werden in dieser Tafel verzeichnet* (1540).

38. See E. A. Kniazhetskaia, *Sud'ba odnoĭ karty* (Moscow, 1964), map inserted between pp. 74 and 75.

39. See I. V. Kurukin, *Persidskiĭ pokhod Petra Velikogo: Nizavoĭ korpus na beregakh Kaspiia (1722–1735)* (Moscow: Kvadriga, 2010), inserted drawings.

40. After the end of the campaign, trading relations improved immediately; see Sartor, "Der armenische Rohseidenhandel," 263.

41. See Shafranovskiĭ, "Rukopisnye karty Kaspiĭskogo moria F. I. Soimonova," 101.

42. For a broader perspective on the mapping of coastlines and navigation in the eighteenth century, see Paul Carter, "Dark with Excess of Bright: Mapping the Coastlines of Knowledge," in *Mappings*, ed. Denis Cosgrove (London: Reaction Books, 1999), 125–47.

43. See the chapter on sovereign maps and charts in the General Rules of 1720, in Postnikov, *Russia in Maps*, 36: "Every ministry should compile at the right time general and particular maps or charts that depict the boundaries, rivers, towns, places, churches, villages, forests and so on in order that ministries correct information about the State and its provinces."

44. *General Map of the Russian Empire, Compiled to the Best of His Abilities by Ivan Kirilov, Ober-secretary to the Governing Senate* (St. Petersburg, 1745).

45. For example, Ivan K. Kirilov (1695–1737), a secretary of the imperial Senate, published a map of the western shore of the Caspian Sea in the 1730s; see Postnikov, *Russia in Maps*, 43.

46. Postnikov, *Russia in Maps*, 50.

47. Ivan Popov, "Drawing compiled from collected information on Khiva by the director of Orenburg customs Velichko," in Postnikov, *Russia in Maps*, 56.

48. See Peter S. Pallas, ed., *Reisen durch Russland und im Caucasischen Gebürge* (St. Petersburg, 1787); see also the biography by Iuliia Kopelevich, *Iogan Anton Gil'denshted* (St. Petersburg, 1997).

Chapter 6

Nader Shah and the Caspian
A Sea too Far

Ernest Tucker

Nader Shah, like most military chiefs in Iran and Central Asia over many centuries, became a commander by showing his martial skills in leading land cavalry forces. Like many of his predecessors, he had limited real experience with substantial bodies of water, much less any awareness of the strategic and tactical use of naval forces. His origins in the foothills of the northwestern borders of Khorasan shaped his military and political outlook in a context far from any coastline.

Nevertheless, despite his humble origins in a distant corner of Iran quite remote from the sea, he gradually developed a strategic vision for creating an enormous empire designed to rival that of his model: the Turko-Mongol steppe conqueror Timur.[1] Such a vision eventually included expansion into territories on the shores of major lakes, seas, and oceans. Closest of these to Nader's homeland in northwestern Khorasan was the Caspian Sea.

By Nader's time, numerous cities along the western and southern Caspian coasts had long since developed into important entrepôts of overland trade, well established for centuries. Major commercial avenues linked east and west from Central Asia via Khorasan through such towns as Astrakhan, Derbent, and Astarabad (modern Gorgan).[2] By the 1720s and 1730s, the volume of trade carried on the Caspian and along its shores by Russian, Central Asian, Indian, Persian, and Armenian merchants made this route an important and growing part of the overland and riverine commercial systems linking Europe and Asia that had expanded enormously over the previous century across the growing Russian Empire.[3]

Human and geographical barriers lay between Nader's homeland of Khorasan and this expanding area of maritime merchant activity. Quite in contrast to its bustling western shoreline, the Caspian's sparse eastern coasts led into the Karakum desert. These shores also formed the maritime frontiers of nomadic Turkmen groups, most notably the Yomut and Tekke. One of their main sources of income was plunder from constant raids on caravans traveling the overland routes through Khorasan from Central Asia and beyond. They extended their techniques into the maritime arena as well, carrying out similar such raids using special types of boats to intercept traffic across the Caspian and even using such vessels to stage raids on Caspian coastal towns over many years.[4]

Nader's own identity as a member of the Qizilbash Turkoman Afshārs gave him membership in a group originally settled in northern Khorasan to defend Safavid territory against the constant raids of these Turkmen marauders.[5] His deep immersion in the final period of the continuous struggle to define the dimensions of Safavid control through endless cavalry clashes on the empire's northeastern frontiers shaped Nader's early military formation. He learned to be a warrior in early eighteenth-century Khorasan, where the reach of central Safavid authority had begun to weaken as dynastic politics became more absorbed by the politics and drama of the central court in Isfahan.

This left important provinces like Khorasan as contested areas for local warlords like Nader to assert increasingly greater claims to autonomy and status. At first, this battle space did not really include the Caspian Sea for a warrior so focused on land-based conflicts in his native area. Nader's horizons dramatically expanded, however, within a few years as his power and standing grew. The Caspian eventually became a part of Nader's strategic map: a key geographical feature to be exploited, if possible, as part of his larger programs of conquest.

His firsthand exposure to it through military campaigns in the Caucasus and in relations with the Russians on issues concerning it resulted in the signing of the Iranian-Russian treaties of 1732 and 1735 under his aegis (although before he formally took the throne as Iran's sovereign in 1736). By the 1740s, he had begun to see the importance of augmenting his land units with naval forces both on the Caspian Sea in the north and on the Persian Gulf and Indian Ocean in the south. In ways that paralleled his first forays into naval activity in the Persian Gulf and on the Indian Ocean, Nader hired an English merchant mariner, John Elton, to build him a fleet using materials from the forests of Gilan and Mazandaran.

Although he began this project too late in his career and with too few resources to have any real impact on his plans to maintain and expand his conquests, Nader Shah came to focus many of his final military campaigns on the northern frontiers of Iran, of which the Caspian Sea formed an integral part. Nader's difficulties with it are reminiscent of all the problems encountered by successful Eurasian land conquerors in guiding and managing maritime and naval actions.[6] Although evidence suggests that he wrestled with the strategic significance of maritime activities and certainly had some grasp of the commercial potential of its waterborne trade, the Caspian remained ultimately a "sea too far" for him, but his attempts to establish Iran's military presence there have not been forgotten by the modern Iranian navy.

Nader, despite his innovative use of military techniques, plans, and equipment, ultimately lacked the knowledge and resources to be able to exploit the military and economic possibilities of this important body of water. Nader's relationship with the Caspian reveals a clash between his strategic vision on the one hand, and his lack of necessary means, infrastructure, and leadership skills to implement his dreams on the other. An analysis of this clash, a situation similar to problems in other aspects of his reign, may shed light on this brief but pivotal part of Iran's eighteenth-century transition between the Safavid and Qajar eras that Nader's reign helped define.

The Caspian Sea and Nader at the Turn of the Eighteenth Century

Obstacles for any empire to establish enduring political control over the Caspian Sea for any length of time before the eighteenth century had proven extremely formidable, given the range of militarily capable and extremely autonomous groups of people living all around it. By the beginning of the eighteenth century, the Russians had been able to secure firm control over the trading city of Astrakhan and the northern Caspian region through their gradual push farther east and south down the Volga River and by strengthening their trade networks with Central Asia.

A century and a half earlier, Russia had confronted numerous difficulties in establishing this control, particular during the first major Ottoman-Russian conflict of 1568-70 that culminated with the Russians establishing permanent authority over Astrakhan. This set the stage for Tsar Peter I "the Great" (r. 1682-1725) eventually to flex Russia's muscles in the region, with the goal, as much as anything, to bolster the Caspian's role in east-west trade networks now given a new destination with the creation of Russia's new capital at St. Petersburg on the Baltic.

The sudden and tumultuous collapse in Iran of the Safavid dynasty under the onslaught of invading Afghans in the early 1720s enabled Peter's successful invasion and occupation of the southern Caspian coast. His new "Caspian Flotilla," the first "brown-water" (nonoceanic) fleet of the tsar's navy, greatly aided in campaigns to assert Russian dominance over regions near and far on the shores of the Caspian Sea that had hitherto remained under Safavid suzerainty for a long time.[7] This pioneering Russian naval force of several hundred vessels, commanded by one of the first Russians given the official rank of "admiral," Fëdor Apraksin, became established in the 1710s with its headquarters in the northern Russian Caspian port of Astrakhan. This new force gave Russia a major boost in its ability to project power in the region.[8] Its ships ferried heavy military equipment such as artillery on the Caspian in the brief Russo-Persian War of 1722-23. This conflict resulted in the Russian occupation of the shores of the southern Caspian littoral for the next decade.

Russian victory after this encounter proved to be the high-water mark of Peter I's activities in this region, since he passed away in early 1725, only a little over a year after the Treaty of St. Petersburg, an agreement to end this conflict negotiated by Russia and Iran in the fall of 1723, was signed. Although this treaty secured Russia's ostensible territorial control of the southern Caspian coastline, Iran's new Safavid ruler, Shah Tahmasb II, never ratified it. Tahmasb himself was already plunging into a series of military encounters to defend his right to claim the Iranian throne, a struggle that defined the rest of his time in power and saw Nader's swift rise to prominence as Tahmasb's main field commander.

After this victory and the demise of Tsar Peter I soon afterward, Russian focus soon shifted to the promotion of trade along the Caspian and establishing mercantile networks overseen by Russian consuls and agents in such coastal towns as Rasht and Derbent. Although Russian troops suffered substantial losses from disease and faced many difficulties in maintaining Russia's authority over the south Caspian littoral, the volume of trade through and around the Caspian remained constant, continuing to increase steadily in this era despite the unsettled political situation.

Notwithstanding upheavals set off in the region upon the fall of Safavid control, merchants continued to move goods through the Caspian region via trade networks of various nationalities, particularly those of the Armenians. Armenian traders had been long established in New Julfa, the town created for them in 1606 by Shah ʿAbbas I across the river from the Safavid capital city of Isfahan. One key route from there went north along the Caspian to the port city of Astrakhan, also home by this time to a thriving colony of Armenian merchants.[9]

Nader's later realization of the Caspian's importance, as evidenced particularly by the 1735 Treaty of Ganjeh, was still a little while in the future. At the time of the Russian advances along the Caspian littoral in the 1720s in the context of the burgeoning commercial scene that continued to grow and flourish there, Nader was far more focused on securing his own power base in his home territory of Khorasan. The process of proving himself the most important military commander for Shah Tahmasb II soon dragged him into bitter rivalry with Fatḥ-ʿAli Khan Qajar. Nader's power struggle with Fatḥ-ʿAli Khan in the fall of 1726 to assert dominance over Safavid military forces certainly brought the Caspian region into focus for him as never before.

The southern Caspian coastline, in the aftermath of the fall of Isfahan, remained dominated by the Qajar tribe, whose headquarters had long been in and around Astarabad, only a short distance from its waters. Over his whole career, Nader had both rivalries and key allegiances with important Qajar leaders, which meant that their home territory near the Caspian kept drawing his attention back there even as he pursued plans of conquest beyond this region. The Qajars, like all the important Qizilbash groups under the Safavids, had numerous factions and subgroups, which variously supported and opposed Nader as he amassed power.[10]

After Fatḥ-ʿAli Khan Qajar was put to death on charges of treason against Tahmasb, Fatḥ-ʿAli Khan's son Moḥammad Ḥasan Khan Qajar fled north to take refuge with the Yomut Turkmen on the Caspian's eastern shore. Although Nader eventually secured the grudging allegiance of other Qajars left in Astarabad, he marked his brutal displacement of Fatḥ-ʿAli Khan as the main commander for the Safavid forces by taking the name Tahmasb Qoli ("servant of Tahmasb") immediately afterward, perhaps to display his own loyalty to the Safavids as prominently and quickly as possible. As noted, the prominence of Mazandaran and Astarabad in the rise of the Qajars and their proximity to the Caspian brought the region rapidly into much sharper focus for him as he secured his own status as the principal Safavid military commander.[11]

Although Nader's main concern as he assumed the leadership of Safavid forces now shifted to the pursuit of the Afghans, strategic concerns near and around the Caspian region continued to shape his actions. Nader still had to suppress revolts of various Kurdish factions in northern Khorasan, who were aided by Turkmen from the region east of the Caspian, while he also confronted intrigues stirred up against him by Tahmasb II in Gilan and Mazandaran on the sea's southern shoreline. Nader waged a brief campaign in Mazandaran during the summer of 1728 to secure local rulers' allegiance to him there.[12] His activities in that region also prompted him to send messages to the Russians demanding the return to Iran of Gilan and other Caspian territories ceded to them in the unratified 1723 Treaty of St. Petersburg mentioned above.

By the end of the 1720s, the Russians were ready to negotiate with anyone who could successfully claim authority over the south Caspian region. Their approach to the region had shifted from any drive to establish formal territorial control over it to safeguarding it as a trade route: a key part of their expanding commercial networks reaching toward the east. This evolution is reflected in the text of a treaty they tried to conclude at Rasht in February 1729 with Moḥammad Saydal Khan, a representative of Ashraf, the final Hotaki Ghilzāi Afghan ruler of Iran. This document focused (like its predecessor Treaty of St. Petersburg) on securing the free flow of commerce between Russia and Iran. Like its successor agreements that were actually implemented and ratified, the Treaties of Rasht and Ganjeh (see below), it committed the Russians to return territories taken by Peter I in the early 1720s as well as creating a framework for tariffs, consuls, and trade harkening back to earlier Russo-Persian agreements. While this agreement quickly became a dead letter after Nader drove the Afghans out of Iran entirely later that year, its text still clearly situates it in the succession of such agreements going back at least to the Russo-Iranian Treaty of 1717 signed between Tsar Peter I and Safavid Shah Solṭān Ḥosayn.[13]

After first subduing the Abdāli Afghans at Herat in the spring of 1729 and then ending Hotaki Ghilzāi Afghan rule in Iran through his victory at the Battle of Mehmāndust in the fall of that year, Nader's military focus shifted in the early 1730s to confronting the Ottomans. His goal was to expel them from Safavid domains they had taken in the 1720s. Just as he was getting started in this task, a sudden new revolt staged by the Abdālis in Herat compelled Nader to rush eastward again. Nader's absence allowed Shah Tahmasb to wage his own disastrous offensive against the Ottomans that he lost badly, resulting in very unfavorable peace terms with them.

The Treaties of Rasht and Ganjeh

This sequence of events also coincided with another round of Russian peace overtures focused on the Caspian region, resulting in the Treaty of Rasht, finally concluded in February 1732 after a prolonged period of negotiation that had begun in October 1730.[14] This successful agreement restored to Iran all the territories ceded to Russia in the conflict of the early 1720s. Even more importantly, it offered a clear set of rules to govern commerce and trade between Russia and Iran, protecting the free flow of merchants on both sides. The treaty presented a framework for collecting customs duties and tariffs as well as specifying a means for resolving claims of damage, injury, and theft.[15] It was to be enforced by "agents or consuls in . . . cities where they may deem fit [to send them], and every respect commensurate with their duties will be shown them."[16] The trade provisions of this treaty were to remain in force over the next several decades, despite continuous eruptions of conflict and upheaval that engulfed Iran over the second half of the eighteenth century following Nader's demise.

The particular context of the 1732 Rasht Treaty shows that Russia and the Caspian were still not quite as central to Nader's strategic focus as they would become. Unlike in 1735, Nader did not sign the 1732 agreement, which was negotiated for Iran by an official described in the Russian text as "Mirza Moḥammad Ebrāhim Moṣṭafa Sarkār-e Khāsseh."[17] The phrasing of royal titles in the text of the treaty parallels the usage of earlier Russo-Persian agreements, with continuous paired references to Tsarina Anna as "Her Imperial Majesty" and to Tahmasb II as "His Majesty the Shah."[18] Although Nader was probably not directly associated with this treaty and the negotiations that led to it, it shaped the 1735 Treaty of Ganjeh that he did sign and negotiate (see below). Despite Nader's absorption with the task of removing the Ottomans at that time though, it seems probable that Russia's activities on the Caspian, particularly its use of naval forces, was beginning to make an impression on Nader as his campaigns drew him closer and more frequently to its shores.[19]

In 1732, Nader did remain much more occupied with managing the problems created by Tahmasb's catastrophic defeat by the Ottomans. This disaster precipitated Tahmasb's complete removal from power by Nader, allowing Nader to conduct a successful subsequent campaign in Ottoman Iraq now as regent to Tahmasb's infant son, enthroned as Shah 'Abbas III. After this new round of military action, Nader quickly secured a truce with the local Ottoman commander in Iraq, Ahmad Pasha. The central Ottoman government, though, delayed in responding to Nader's demand for the conclusion of a comprehensive peace agreement and the return of all Iranian territories taken earlier.

To prod them (and also perhaps to get the Russians' attention), Nader had Tahmasb Khan Jalāyir, one of his main commanders, attack Sorkhāi Khan I of Ghazi-Qumuq, a key Ottoman vassal leader in the Caucasus near the Caspian, in the fall of 1734.[20] This brought the Caspian region back into focus for Nader's activities. Sorkhāi Khan fled, so Nader occupied Shamakhi and threatened Russia with war if it did not leave Baku and Derbent, representing his moves to the Russian ambassador as necessary to get the Ottomans to leave places they had earlier agreed to surrender to him. Nader pursued a series of conflicts in this region that culminated with his defeat of a large Ottoman army at the Battle of Baghavard (Yeghevard in modern Armenia) in June 1735, followed soon thereafter by the surrender of the Ottoman fortress at Ganjeh, after he had besieged it for a period of time. As this siege was going on there, he and the Russian envoy, Prince Sergeĭ Golitsyn, signed a new treaty in March 1735 that essentially restored to Iran all of its territory Russia had occupied in the 1720s, as long as Nader agreed to be their staunch ally against the Ottomans.[21] Although political authority and lines of allegiance between various local rulers in the Caucasus and the larger empires around them remained unclear in the wake of Nader's campaign, the Russians now formally acknowledged the complete return of the southern Caspian coast to Iranian sovereignty.

This agreement was signed about one year before Nader's full assumption of royal authority as Nader Shah, but the way Nader and Iran are described in its text provided strong foreshadowing that this change was about to happen. The treaty text omits any reference to the nominal Iranian monarch, still then the infant figurehead 'Abbas III. Instead, its paired references to the two sides simply mentioned the "Iranian State" and "Russian Empire." The two sides' representatives were described as

Sergeĭ Golitsyn, acting on behalf of Tsarina Anna, "Her Imperial Majesty of All the Russias," and Nader himself, mentioned in the text in the first person as "I" without any statements about any putative Iranian monarch or higher authority at all.[22]

The introduction to the treaty offers a brief apologia for Nader as Iran's savior, observing:

> The Lord God Almighty . . . did not withhold his merciful spirit at all from the inhabitants of the Iranian State, but installed me as his servant. I went out with . . . many troops from the capital city of Khorasan province . . . to eliminate the rebels . . . [and] by God's mercy, with my care, the city of Isfahan and other provinces [of Iran] were cleansed of their enemies.[23]

The 1732 and 1735 treaties agreed on most basic substantive points, to the extent that sections 4 and 5 of the Treaty of Ganjeh explicitly affirmed that their terms and framework closely adhered to the rules established by the Treaty of Rasht. The most striking difference between these two documents appears in the latter agreement's explicit references to Nader's role in saving Iran and the implicit legitimacy and authority as a political figure that this provided him.

Nader's Treaty of Ganjeh with the Russians, together with the Ottomans' growing willingness to begin negotiating a lasting peace treaty with him, helped create the conditions that allowed Nader to take the throne as Nader Shah in the spring of 1736 at a special ceremony on the Moghan plain, only about 150 kilometers due west of the Caspian shoreline. Russia's military focus now could shift away from policing this area to resolving political issues in other parts of its empire as well as confronting the Ottoman Empire militarily north of the Black Sea.

In any clash with the Ottomans, Iran loomed as a more and more useful partner for Russia, given Nader's own anti-Ottoman military agendas and plans. This Russian desire to cultivate Nader as an ally against the Ottomans secured the role of the Caspian for the next few years as a relatively neutral military zone between Russia and Iran, by establishing clearer frontiers between the two empires and ending any overt hostilities between them.

More importantly, these accords also set the stage for the continued commercial flourishing of the Caspian region despite the military and political shifts there. Both Russo-Persian agreements of the 1730s discussed commercial and mercantile issues in some depth, a reflection of how, despite the end of formal Russian control and withdrawal of its forces from the southern Caspian coast, the Caspian's economic importance had still continued to grow over the previous few years. The end of Russian occupation also marked a shift in emphasis from military to commercial approaches in revising Peter the Great's strategic concepts of how to expand and strengthen economic ties to Iran and the Caspian.

Such a vision had helped shape Russia's policies since Tsar Peter I concluded a treaty with Safavid Iran in 1717 that was in part designed to promote trade.[24] Peter the Great's successors maintained his support for gaining easier access to silk from Gilan and Mazandaran, a commodity for which demand was rapidly increasing across Europe. In addition, the Russians generally continued to promote alternatives to conventional main trans-Asian trade links that either went overland through Ottoman territory or farther south via the maritime route of the Indian Ocean—they merely shifted to a more commercial strategy to promote their goals.

One indication of this underlying continuity of Russian economic policy in this region was the continued vitality of Caspian trade after 1736, particularly as evidenced by the volume of goods carried by Armenian merchant networks during the late 1730s and early 1740s.[25] Despite political and military turbulence, the role of the Caspian as a key nexus of commerce continued as Russia gradually began to expand into Central Asia over the next few years. Nader's own strategic vision for the Caspian though, as it finally emerged, came to concentrate much more on its military role. He paid much less attention than the Russians to its economic and mercantile dimensions, reflecting the focus on military conquest and activities that always provided the framework for his actions and policies.

The Caspian in the Era of Nader Shah

Nader's first actions as monarch reveal this emphasis on the military role of the Caspian. Having secured his place on the throne as Iran's new monarch with his coronation ceremony at Moghan in early 1736 and retaken lands conquered by Russia and the Ottomans in the 1720s, Nader now set out to finish his campaigns against the Hotaki Ghilzāi Afghans by subduing their home city of Qandahar. After achieving this, he set off toward India, ostensibly in pursuit of Afghan fugitives, but with the real intention of possibly defeating the Mughals and conquering their Indian empire, which he did at the Battle of Karnal near Delhi in February 1739.

All these campaigns took him far away from the Caspian, which he had put under the authority of his brother Ebrāhim. In the fall of 1738, Ebrāhim died fighting Lezgi tribesmen in the Caucasus, with whom he had renewed hostilities partly in an attempt to emulate military successes Nader's son Reżā-Qoli Mirza had recently achieved in Central Asia. During his absence in India, Nader had made Reżā-Qoli his viceroy in Mashhad and Khorasan, where Reżā-Qoli set about building his own power base after subduing Ilbārs II, the khan of Khwarazm.

It was during this period that two merchant mariners working for the British Russia Company, John Elton and Mungo Graeme, came to Gilan and Astarabad to explore the possibilities of establishing a trade route for the company across the Caspian from Russia via Iran through to Central Asia. After some negotiation, Reżā-Qoli granted them trading privileges, perhaps in order to promote some commercial alternative to his own royal merchant in Isfahan, who had recently become perceived as having too much power over Iran's export/import markets.[26]

By the spring of 1740, word came that Nader was on his way back from India. Although Reżā-Qoli came to Afghanistan to meet him, Nader was enraged to hear that the former Safavid Shah Tahmasb II had died in Reżā-Qoli's custody. Nader immediately replaced Reżā-Qoli as viceroy with his second son, Naṣrollah Mirza, and he took Reżā-Qoli with him on an expedition to subdue the rulers of Central Asia.

The Caspian and Nader's Emerging Plans for Khorasan

Upon returning to Khorasan from successful military expeditions to Central Asia and India, Nader began to pay attention to the idea of reimaging his home territory, envisioning Mashhad and its environs as the center of his empire. Many actions he took at the end of his reign in connection with it seem linked to a desire to refocus his realm there. These included the creation of a kind of memorial to his achievements at his mountain fortress of Kalāt-e Naderi. Other aspects of this new focus appeared through the attention he paid to the shrine of Imam Reżā in Mashhad, along with his reported attempt to settle a community of Armenians in a quarter of Mashhad to be called New Nakhjevān in imitation of the Safavids' New Julfa Armenian quarter in Isfahan.[27]

For Nader, the Caspian Sea now became more obviously associated with the goal of recentering his domains in Khorasan. It was the closest maritime gateway to this area, and with its proximity to an expanding Russian Empire, this region became a potential arena for Nader's power projection more than ever before. As eighteenth-century British merchant Jonas Hanway pointed out:

> Nadir Shah had for some time formed a design of building ships on the Caspian; to this he was induced not only by the unsettled state of his country, but also by a particular inclination of conquering the Lezgi Tatars [sic].... He saw... it would be impossible to support an army in that quarter without... provisions, which must necessarily be brought to him by sea.... The Turkmen Tatars [sic] on the eastern coast had by frequent incursions excited the Shah's resentment; but their sandy and inhospitable country could be... [attacked] only by water.[28]

The Caspian Sea lay strategically between two groups of Nader's long-standing foes: rebellious tribes of the Caucasus to its west and various groups of Turkmen to its east. By the 1740s, Nader came to appreciate the potential for using the Caspian to support his land-based military actions against these two important enemies.

Nader's first foray into naval activities had taken place in the Persian Gulf in the 1730s. He appointed Moḥammad Laṭif Khan as his commander there to coordinate the naval components of Nader's military activities along Iran's southern coast.[29] Laṭif did this first by acquiring British and other European trading ships at ports there and later arranging for ships to be built in India and brought to Iran. Laṭif Khan's success unfortunately aroused the jealousy of Nader's army commander in the Persian Gulf region, Moḥammad-Taqi Khan Shirāzi, who eventually had Laṭif Khan poisoned.[30] Shirāzi, though, only dabbled in naval affairs, since his main focus, like Nader's, remained on land-based military activities.

John Elton: Captain Jamal Beg of Nader's Caspian Fleet

In parallel to such activities in the Persian Gulf and on the Indian Ocean, Nader had employed the Caspian Sea for ancillary military operations in the 1730s as well by hiring foreign ships (in this case, mostly Russian vessels) to transport supplies to his forces there and even sometimes ferry troops during his offensives against rulers in the Caucasus. It was even reported that he appointed Moḥammad Ḥosayn Khan (presumably referring to a leader of the Yokhāribāsh Qajar faction then serving as his governor of Mazandaran) as a naval commander on the Caspian in 1738.[31] Jonas Hanway, a merchant sent by the British Russia

Company to help scout out the region for trade opportunities in the 1740s, noted that Mashhad was an easy journey from Astarabad and the Caspian coast. He foresaw the possibility of creating a substantial English trading presence in Mashhad as it became more and more established as the eventual center of Nader's domains.³²

From Hanway's perspective, the major foreign companies trading with Iran operating in the south on the Persian Gulf and Indian Ocean, the British and Dutch East India Companies, had virtually abandoned their business relationships with the old Iranian capital city of Isfahan by 1743. "The trade which it formerly enjoyed, is transplanted to, and centers in Mashhad, which is at too great a distance from the Persian Gulf or the Eastern [Indian] Ocean."³³ To contrast with this, Hanway painted a very rosy picture of how, "in particular, the commodiousness of the roads between Mashhad, Gilan, and the northern provinces of Persia will enable the [British] Russia Company to import raw silk much cheaper than . . . merchants [trading through the Ottoman Empire]."³⁴

There is little evidence that Nader ever focused on such trade issues so directly. By the 1740s, however, he had begun to think more strategically about the Caspian.³⁵ This was a propitious time for the monarch to meet John Elton. Elton, the British Russia Company agent who had made the trade agreement with Reżā-Qoli Khan mentioned above, was an experienced English mariner who had already spent a number of years in the Caspian region assessing the feasibility of creating an English-run Caspian trade network linking Russia and Iran.

Among his other tasks, Jonas Hanway had been sent out by the Russia Company to check up on Elton. He found out that Elton had entered Nader's service and received the name Jamal Beg to become an Iranian admiral and organize an effort to build ships for an Iranian fleet on the Caspian.³⁶ It seems very likely that Peter the Great's creation of the Caspian squadron and the Russian naval activities there in the previous decades provided inspiration for Nader in carrying this out.

Despite Nader's enthusiasm for naval construction on the Caspian and Elton's skill and experience as a mariner, neither he nor Nader had any real expertise at all in the process of or needs for shipbuilding. Elton "met with great difficulties, the timber being knotty, and the roads to the shipyard hardly passable."³⁷ Such problems notwithstanding, this project marked the period of Nader's greatest strategic focus on the Caspian Sea.

In June 1743, he ordered Elton to survey its southeastern coast.³⁸ Nader was clearly planning to create a fort and station a garrison in it on the east Caspian coast at the Balkan Gulf to keep watch on the Turkmen there. Elton produced a series of Caspian coastal maps eventually published in England that became standards of the region's cartography for their time.[39] The shipbuilding project, coming late in Nader's reign, had an oppressive impact in the area. Local peasants had to donate labor as well as materials. Many of them were forced to abandon rice cultivation and silk production, their main sources of income, when made to carry out Nader's wishes. Elton had to dredge in harbors for sunken anchors dropped by Russian and other merchant ships.[40] In spite of the considerable obstacles he faced, Elton managed by 1745 to assemble a small squadron of vessels that featured two eighteen-gun frigates.[41]

The Russians, with their own goals of expanding influence over the Caspian, grew more and more hostile to Elton's activities over several years. Elton's inspiration to build ships for Nader had its roots in his partnership with another English seafarer, Thomas Woodroofe, with whom he published the maps mentioned above. Elton and Woodroofe earlier had arranged to have a ship built at Kazan designed to be used by British merchants on the Caspian.

When they employed it to bring rice from the south Caspian port of Anzali to the port of Derbent for Nader's army camped there in 1742, this enraged the Russians, who hired thugs to go and beat up Woodroofe. Although Elton hung on in the region for the next five years until Nader's assassination, his shipbuilding activities no doubt rapidly became severely curtailed by the general lack of funds available from Nader's treasury and the rising turmoil at the end of the monarch's reign, so he shut down his operations completely upon Nader's death. When Elton himself was killed in 1751 during the chaotic period following Nader's demise, this terminated official Iranian naval activities on the Caspian for a long period. To ensure this, Russians soon destroyed the remaining Iranian ships and naval supplies from Nader's fleet that they found at a port near Rasht.

The End of Nader's Reign in the Caspian Region

The end of Nader's plans for the Caspian, as part of his larger concept of establishing the new center of his empire in Mashhad, seems also linked to the brutal revolt against Nader launched in early 1744 by the Āshāqabāsh faction of the Qajars. Moḥammad Ḥasan Khan Qajar (father of Āqā Moḥammad Khan, subsequently considered the founder of the Qajar dynasty) now led this group and joined with the Yomut Turkmen against the Yokhāribāsh Qajars. Some leaders of the Yokhāribāsh Qajars had been more or less allied with Nader for some time, so Astarabad became the scene for some ruthless score settling between these factions. It was this clash that resulted infamously in towers of skulls being erected (as reported by Hanway), but this is a measure of the degree to which Nader's grand schemes and ideas had collapsed, given the terrible divisions that this showdown revealed.

In the wake of this civil war, soon followed by Nader's own demise, the south Caspian region reverted to its earlier status as a refuge for the Qajars as they secured power over an Iran divided after Nader's sudden end. Their gradual creation of a new polity in Iran paralleled Russia's steady expansion of control over the entire region east and north of the Caspian through the next century.

The Caspian itself remains an area of contest between several powers today, and the Iranian navy still traces the origins of its Northern Fleet to the squadron created by Nader Shah. The complexities of Nader's relationships there with the Russians and others suggests it might be very fruitful and informative to think about parallels between struggles on the Caspian then and now. Although this sort of comparison must now factor in such questions as the impact of competition for control of natural resources like natural gas and oil, the intricate mix of cultural, religious, military, and economic confrontation and cooperation that continues today around the Caspian somehow recalls in certain ways the situation there nearly three centuries ago.

Notes

1. For discussion of this idea, see Ernest Tucker, *Nadir Shah's Quest for Legitimacy in Post-Safavid Iran* (Gainesville: University of Florida Press, 2006) and Michael Axworthy, *The Sword of Persia: Nader Shah, from Tribal Warrior to Conquering Tyrant* (London: I. B. Tauris, 2006).

2. For comprehensive discussion of the Transcaspian trade that developed and flourished during the sixteenth century between Russia and Safavid Iran, see Rudi Matthee, "Anti-Ottoman Politics and Transit Rights: The Seventeenth-Century Trade in Silk between Safavid Iran and Muscovy," *Cahiers du Monde russe* 35, no. 4 (1994): 739–61.

3. For discussion of the growing importance of Caspian trade in the first half of the eighteenth century, see N. G. Kukanova, *Torgovo-ėkonomicheskie otnosheniia Rossii i Irana v period pozdnego feodalizma* (Saransk: Izdatel'stvo Mordovskogo Universiteta, 1994); and Kevin Gledhill, "The Caspian State: Regional Autonomy, International Trade, and the Rise of Qājār Iran, 1722–1797" (PhD diss., Yale University, 2020), 142–83.

4. See Xavier de Planhol, "Caspian Sea, i. Geography" in *Encyclopaedia Iranica*, V/1, 48–50, https://www.iranicaonline.org/articles/caspian-sea-i, and Guive Mirfendereski, "Caspian Sea, ii. Diplomatic History in Modern Times," in *Encyclopaedia Iranica Online*, https://www.iranicaonline.org/articles/caspian-sea-ii-diplomatic-history-in-modern-times.

5. Note the use here of the phrase "Qizilbash Turkoman" to describe the Shi'i Turkic tribesmen who formed the backbone of Safavid military power, among whom Nader's Afshārs were a key group. This is in specific contrast with the independent, primarily Sunni Turkmen groups such as the Yomut who populated the steppes between the Caspian and Oxus, preserving various degrees of independence from the larger powers around them (i.e., the Safavid, Uzbek, Russian, and Mughal polities) through the nineteenth century.

6. For discussion of such complexities in the case of the Mongols, see David O. Morgan, "The Mongols and the Eastern Mediterranean," *Mediterranean Historical Review* 4, no. 1 (1989): 198–211.

7. Igor Zonn, Aleksey Kosarev, Michael Glantz, and Andrey Kostianoy, *The Caspian Sea Encyclopedia* (Berlin: Springer, 2014), 372.

8. Laurence Lockhart, *The Fall of the Safavid Dynasty and the Afghan Occupation of Persia* (Cambridge: Cambridge University Press, 1958), 178.

9. For discussion of the trade connections forged by Armenian merchants between New Julfa and Astrakhan, see Sebouh Aslanian, *From the Indian Ocean to the Mediterranean: The Global Trade Networks of Armenian Merchants from New Julfa* (Berkeley: University of California Press, 2011); and Edmund Herzig, "The Armenian Merchants of New Julfa, Isfahan: A Study in Pre-modern Asian Trade" (PhD diss., University of Oxford, 1991).

10. For discussion of the rise of the Qajars, see Gledhill, "The Caspian State," 1–87.

11. Laurence Lockhart, *Nadir Shah: A Critical Study Based Mainly on Contemporary Sources* (London: Luzac, 1938), 26, and Lockhart, *Fall of the Safavi Dynasty*, 310.

12. Mirzā Mahdi Khān Astarābādi, *Tārikh-e Jahāngoshā-ye Nāderi*, ed. 'Abdallāh Anvār (Tehran: Kiyānush, 1377/1998), 84.

13. For the Russian text of this treaty, see T. Iuzefovich, ed., *Dogovory Rossii s" Vostokom": Politicheskie i torgovye* (St. Petersburg: Baksta, 1869), 189–93.

14. Lockhart, *Nadir Shah*, 58.

15. Iuzefovich, *Dogovory*, 197–99.

16. J. C. Hurewitz, *Diplomacy in the Near and Middle East: A Documentary Record* (Princeton, NJ: Van Nostrand, 1956), 47.

17. Iuzefovich, *Dogovory*, 195.

18. Iuzefovich, *Dogovory*, 199.

19. The main chronicle of Nader's reign, the *Tārikh-e Jahāngoshā* of Mirzā Moḥammad Mahdi Khan Astarābādi, makes a point of describing the Russians' use of ships in this campaign. (Astarābādi, *Tārikh-e Jahāngoshā-ye Nāderi*, 17). It is notable, though, that this is virtually the only reference in this major Persian work on Nader Shah to naval activities on the Caspian.

20. Lockhart, *Nadir Shah*, 83.

21. Axworthy, *Sword of Persia*, 153–54.

22. I͡uzefovich, *Dogovory*, 203.

23. I͡uzefovich, *Dogovory*, 202-3.

24. For discussion of this agreement, see Goodarz Rashtiani, "Iranian-Russian Relations in the Eighteenth Century," in *Crisis, Collapse, Militarism & Civil War: The History and Historiography of 18th Century Iran*, ed. Michael Axworthy (Oxford: Oxford University Press, 2018), 163-82.

25. For discussion of the central role Armenian traders continued to play on the Caspian between 1736 and 1744, see N. G. Kukanova, *Ocherki po istorii Russko-iranskikh torgovykh otnoshenii v XVII–pervoĭ polovine XIX veka: Po materialam russkikh arkhivov* (Saransk: Mordovskoe knizhnoe izdatel'stvo, 1977).

26. Lockhart, *Nadir Shah*, 175.

27. For discussion of these plans, see Sussan Babaie, "Nader Shah, the Delhi Loot, and the 18th-Century Exotics of Empire," in Axworthy, *Crisis, Collapse, Militarism & Civil War*, 215-34; and Tanburi Arutin Efendi, *Tahmas Kulu Han'ın Tevarihi*, ed. by Esat Uras (Ankara: Türk Tarih Kurumu Basımevi, 1942), 36.

28. Jonas Hanway, *An Historical Account of the British Trade over the Caspian Sea* (London: Dodsley, 1753), 1:161.

29. Not much is known about Moḥammad Laṭif, except that he once was described by a Dutch agent as "an ingenuous man, who has learnt too much about European customs at Istanbul." Willem Floor, "The Iranian Navy in the Gulf during the Eighteenth Century," *Iranian Studies* 20, no. 1 (1987): 39n38.

30. Michael Axworthy, "Nader Shah and Persian Naval Expansion in the Persian Gulf, 1700-1747," *Journal of the Royal Asiatic Society* 21, no. 1 (2011): 34-37.

31. Floor, "The Iranian Navy," 53.

32. Hanway, *Historical Account*, 1:35-36.

33. Hanway, *Historical Account*, 1:39.

34. Hanway, *Historical Account*, 1:40. For a comprehensive study of the British Russia Company and the activities of Hanway and Elton at this time, see Matthew P. Romaniello, *Enterprising Empires: Russia and Britain in Eighteenth-Century Eurasia* (Cambridge: Cambridge University Press, 2019).

35. It is noteworthy that Nader's main contemporary Persian chroniclers (Moḥammad Kāẓem Marvi and Mahdi Khan Astarābādi) make almost no mention at all of the Caspian, especially given that Jonas Hanway describes how Mahdi Khan himself at one point was given authority as "admiral" over the Caspian by Nader. See Hanway, *Historical Account*, 1:282-83.

36. Hanway, *Historical Account*, 1:70.

37. Hanway, *Historical Account*, 1:121.

38. Hanway, *Historical Account*, 1:130.

39. For a good example of one of these, see John Elton and Thomas Woodroofe, "A Plain Chart of the Caspian Sea" (1745), SOAS University of London, © 2016, https://digital.soas.ac.uk/LOAC000204/00001/citation.

40. Hanway, *Historical Account*, 1:162.

41. Axworthy, *Sword of Persia*, 236. Frère Bazin, "Mémoires sur les dernières années du règne de Thamas-Koulikan," in *Lettres édifiantes et curieuses, écrites des missions etrangères*, vol. 4, *Mémoires du Levant* (Toulouse: Noel-Etienne Sens, 1810), 254.

CHAPTER 7

Follow the Armenians
British Plans for the Caspian in the Eighteenth Century
Matthew P. Romaniello

From its first arrival in the sixteenth century, the British Russia Company hoped to exploit Moscow's location to access the Silk Roads in hopes of importing Iranian, Indian, and Chinese goods. In 1558, only one year after the company charter was first signed, one of its merchants, Anthony Jenkinson, reached Astrakhan on the north shore of Caspian Sea to observe Russia's trade with Asia, in hopes of finding an opportunity for the company to exploit.[1] It would take nearly two centuries, but Jenkinson and the Russia Company's aspirations were realized in the Anglo-Russian Commercial Treaty of 1734, when the company received permission from the Russian government to carry on a trade with Iran through Russia.[2]

Onslow Burnish was a secretary of the Russia Company working in the factory in St. Petersburg in the 1730s. Before working for the Russia Company, he had been a secretary of the East India Company, which informed his observations on the potential trade with Iran. Russia's grant of access to Iran created an auspicious window, as the East India Company had been expelled from Isfahan in 1735. When the first Russia Company merchants reached the northern Iranian city of Rasht in 1739, they were the only Western merchants in the city.[3] There were hurdles before the new trade could be established on a permanent footing. The Russian government had authorized the company's access in the 1734 treaty, but Britain's Parliament had not yet altered the Acts of Navigation to allow the company to import goods from Iran to Britain. Iranian exports were the exclusive monopoly of the East India Company, with a small caveat allowing the British Levant Company to purchase Iranian silk if it was available in Ottoman markets. The expulsion of the East India Company from Iran and the disruption of the Iran-Ottoman trade did nothing to alter British laws. Therefore, Burnish's expert opinion on the Iran trade was one of the most valuable tools available for the Russia Company to persuade Parliament to adjust the Acts of Navigation. As part of his efforts, Burnish submitted a memo to the British foreign secretary in 1740, explicitly calling for "English merchants to follow the Example of the Armenians, & enter upon a profitable Trade which they hitherto overlooked or neglected" by allowing the company to exploit its Caspian access and assume control of Iran's silk exports.[4]

For a British merchant to instruct his government that his colleagues needed to follow the trade established by Armenian merchants operating between Iran and Russia is a unique moment in British commercial history. To further suggest that the East India Company's trade with Iran was a failure and only the Russia Company could hope to reclaim that trade is perhaps more surprising. Earlier studies might have suggested overland Eurasian trade declined in the eighteenth century, but in the 1740s a group of British merchants proclaimed overland commerce held more potential than the overseas trade currently managed by the East India Company.[5] It was a short window, because the Russian government would revoke its permission to travel to Astrakhan within a decade, but the arguments offered in the 1740s to pressure the British government to reestablish Britain's unique trade with Iran through Russia would persist for decades to follow.

Two Plans for the Caspian

The Anglo-Russian Commercial Treaty of 1734 provided the Russia Company access to "Persia" for trade; Persia in the context of the treaty was the Iranian territory under the control of Nader Shah. It was not inserted in the treaty because of Britain's negotiating success, but rather the clause was included by the Russian government to support its ongoing efforts to develop its trade with Iran. At the end of Peter the Great's Caucasian campaign (1722–23), Russia gained possession of Gilan, Shirvan, and Astarabad (modern Gorgan). Russia returned

Astarabad and Gilan to Iran in the Treaty of Rasht (1732) and the remaining territory in the Treaty of Ganjeh three years later.[6] In exchange for conceding its territorial claims, Russia signed favorable trade terms with the new Iranian government under Nader Shah's leadership. As historian A. I. Iukht has argued, Russia's most profitable port in the 1730s was Astrakhan, taking in customs duties collected on goods imported from Iran and the Caucasus. Astrakhan would hold this position until the end of the Seven Years' War in 1763 created a peace-inspired trade boom in the Baltic.[7] The Anglo-Russian Commercial Treaty's Iran concession brought more merchants into the Caspian trade, and therefore potentially increased Russia's revenues from import/export duties.

Before 1734, British merchants in Russia were not allowed to travel south or east from Moscow. Gaining Russia's permission to travel southeast along the Volga River to Astrakhan and beyond did not immediately allow an overland Britain-Iran trade, because physical access to Iran was only one of the issues facing the merchants. Parliament passed a series of Navigation Acts between 1660 and 1696 that regulated its global commerce; this system was monitored by a special office created for this purpose, the Board of Trade and Plantations. Under the acts, the East India Company held the exclusive monopoly on the Iran trade. It was the only company to hold legal permission to import goods from Iran. There was a small exception made for the Levant Company that held a monopoly over trade with the Ottoman Empire. If Iranian silk was exported into the Ottoman Empire, the Levant Company could purchase that silk in Ottoman ports, but the Levant merchants were not allowed to negotiate any formal relationship with Iran. When the Russian government legalized British access to Iran, the Russia Company did not hold the legal right to import any goods from Iran to Britain without a parliamentary act to change the terms of the Acts of Navigation.

The British negotiators involved in the discussions that became the treaty in 1734 understood the Iran concession was a legal complication. The negotiators wrote with concern to the foreign secretary in London, explaining that Britain's Russia-Iran trade "may intrench on the act of Navigation & may perhaps alarm the East India Company, ... but in our humble opinion we think the thing cannot be attended by any consequences that can in the least prejudice Trade."[8] Once the treaty was signed, including the Iran clause, the Russia Company dedicated its efforts to persuade Parliament of the necessity of legalizing this trade, despite immediate objections from both the East India and

Levant Companies, who correctly understood their own commercial interests were threatened. The fact that this debate played out in London, and not in Isfahan, Rasht, or even Astrakhan, reflected the British style of global trade, which focused solely on its interests. The British expectation of its merchants' ability to control global markets was limitless. One of the British negotiators even claimed that the Russia Company would displace not only the East India Company but also the Russians from the Caspian trade, reporting that "tho' the Russ made a very advantageous Treaty of Commerce with Persia, about three years ago, yet as they understand little or nothing of foreign Trade, they reap no advantage by it."[9] Considering British merchants had not seen Astrakhan since the sixteenth century, they were hardly reliable observers about Russia's ongoing success with its Iran trade, nor did the British understand that they were being used by the Russian government to support its own successful venture.

Information about the Caspian trade was a necessity for the company to convince Parliament to support its potential Iranian exports. For its fact-finding efforts, the company turned toward John Elton as a local expert. Elton entered Russian service in 1736, when he joined Ivan Kirilov's cartographic expedition to Orenburg, developing a new quadrant and recording a lunar eclipse in Ufa that allowed him to determine the longitude of the city. His success on the Orenburg mission allowed him to lead another expedition to map the depths of the Caspian Sea. By 1739, Elton left Russian service to undertake the Russia Company's exploratory mission to Rasht. For the company, Elton was an excellent choice as both a British merchant and Russia's leading expert on navigating the Caspian Sea.[10]

Elton documented his mission to Iran in detail in hopes of providing Parliament with sufficient evidence of the viability of trading with Iran through Russia. Not all of his information was encouraging. In Astrakhan, Elton arranged to join a company of Armenians traveling to Rasht in three weeks, using his time in the city to investigate the state of the trade among Astrakhan's silk merchants. The news was not good, as the unsettled nature of Iran during its civil war had led to new restrictions on trade. "They say that hitherto, the Persian Trade from Astrakhan was open and free, & foreign merchants importing goods into Persia, might carry them to what Market they liked best, & dispose of them to whom they pleased; but that this Year, all Goods that arrive at Reshd [Rasht], are obliged to be there sold, and that the Shach, thro his own Merchants is become the sole Buyer. . . . Also that the Shach had Engrossed all the Raw Silk to himself, so that those who would buy silk must buy it of his Merchants, and not of the Persian Boors as formerly."[11] Nor was there good news about other Asian trade opportunities, as the Iranian conflict had interfered with Bukhara's trade as well. Elton discovered that it was no longer possible to reach Bukhara through Iran, preventing him from further exploring Central Asian and Chinese goods that might be purchased there.[12] Elton's remark is one of the first indications that the British hoped to exploit access to Astrakhan and Rasht as a way of buying a broad range of Asian commodities. While none would be legal to import to Britain under the current terms of the Acts of Navigation, Elton believed that once the company received the right to import silk from Iran, permission could be extended to other desirable goods.

It was not only the current restrictions on trade that concerned Elton. All of the ships traveling on the Caspian Sea were owned by Russian merchants, but they were used by the Armenian merchants traveling to Derbent, Baku, and Rasht. Elton argued that Russian interest in this transit was limited to supplying the Russian army along the Caspian coast, leading him to conclude that Russian merchants "do not trouble themselves with foreign Trade." Furthermore, Elton pointed out that the Russians were not good sailors nor had adequate ships. As a result, the Caspian trade was "wholly in the hands of the Armenians and Indians."[13] Elton's final assessment was that this created an opportunity for the British, as Russian disinterest in the trade left a gap in the market, and British-constructed vessels would provide future merchants a considerable advantage in transportation.[14]

In Rasht, Elton negotiated with the Iranian government for a treaty to allow the Russia Company to operate and investigated the market to detail Britain's potential profits. Much of his report focused on the activities of Armenian merchants, whom he believed were actively working against British interests. He reported that the Armenians had in fact been responsible for expelling the East India Company's merchants from Isfahan. According to his unnamed informant, the Armenians had protested to Nader Shah that while the British had "free trade" in Iran, the Armenians did not have that privilege in Britain. While the company's agent had attempted to provide "satisfaction" to the shah, the shah was not satisfied, ordering the agent "forthwith to leave Ispahan. Others say that the Shach sent & demanded a sum of money for the Agent, which he refused to give him alledging the Persian Treasury was much indebted to the Company."[15] This was important for Elton, as he suggested if the East India Company had been effective in responding to these claims, the British would be in a far better position in Iran. After all, the recent failures to export silk "must be intirely owing to the neglect or mismanagement of the East India Company's servants." As a result, "the Hollanders" currently controlled the market, which was a defeat for "the Honour of Our Nation" in Elton's estimation.[16]

The conclusion of Elton's investigation of the current state of commerce was that the Russia Company could restore British trade in Iran, while the East India Company could not. It was necessary to establish a good relationship with Nader Shah, in order to circumvent the ongoing plots of the Armenians and, implicitly, their Dutch trading partners. Elton was positive this could be accomplished. Once it had, he saw greater opportunities. He believed a permanent presence in northern Iran would facilitate a new trade between the British and the Bukharans. According to Elton, it was well known that the Bukharans had a great demand for "European commodities," which could be supplied "by way of Persia; from Siberia the Russ can't cross the Step to Bucharia. . . . Neither can the Bucharians be supply'd by way of the East Indies, as they lay so far Inland."[17] In fact, Elton suggested this might be the most profitable part of the British trade in Iran. It is not clear, however, whether Elton truly believed that the only safe route to Bukhara was through northern Iran, or if his concern was bypassing Russia's restriction on British trade inside the empire. Had the Bukharan plan come to fruition, the Russia Company would have circumvented both Russia's trade with the Bukharans as well as the East India Company's. As Elton concluded, "the British Merchants can't fail but to enter the Persian Trade with a certain View of very considerable Profits."[18]

While Elton's optimism could have made a positive impression on Parliament, not all of the merchants in the Russia Company were as convinced about their potential success. This group was led by Onslow Burnish, former secretary of the East India Company now working for the Russia Company. In a lengthy response to Elton's report, also submitted to Parliament, Burnish raised questions about Elton's reliability, because he found it unlikely that Elton would "be able to obtain such Priviledges as he shews us from the Regent of the Kingdom," when the British, Dutch, and French East India companies failed to do so without significant expenses.[19]

Elton's suspect accomplishments aside, Burnish was equally positive about Britain's potential benefits from its new trade. Burnish outlined the current political situation in Iran to demonstrate that the commercial hub would remain in Rasht and not return to Isfahan, therefore the East India Company would not be able to return to its factory in the former capital. According to Burnish, "if it be Politck in the Sophy to desire to establish a new Intercourse with Europe, which can only take place by way of the Caspian and Volga, Reason of State will still be more forcible to induce the Court of Petersburgh to concur in the same Design."[20] As proof of Russia's support for Britain's efforts, Burnish noted that the government had "already given them leave to build a Ship in her own Dock at Casan [Kazan'], for the Navigation of the Caspian Sea, & when the Benefits which must naturally flow from this Commerce to the Russ Nation come once to be felt, it cannot be doubted that the Court of Petersburgh will grant all the Safe Guards & Privileges which the Merchants may think necessary for the Prosecution of it."[21]

These new ships that Russia allowed the British to build became a key part of Burnish's arguments about the financial benefits for Britain for placing the Iran trade in the Russia Company's hands. "It is self evident, that nothing can promote the Interest of England more than a Trade which will increase the Export of our Woollen, & reduce the Price of our Silken Manufactures."[22] The Russia Company could purchase silk in Iran, transport it across the Caspian and up the Volga River on British ships, and then move the goods onto company ships in the Baltic. The East India Company, meanwhile, first had to negotiate access to Iran, and then had to travel the remarkable distance through the Indian Ocean, around the Cape of Good Hope, which required negotiations with the Dutch, and eventually reach Britain. In Burnish's calculation, Russia Company commodities from Gilan would reach London costing "17 pcent" less for "a Bale of the finest silk" and "25 pcent" less for "the coarsest sort of Silk." The savings was a result of the lower cost of "the Transport of Goods," which also benefitted the export of British wool to Iran.[23]

Both Elton and Burnish shared a common goal—the adjustment of the Acts of Navigation—but offered different arguments. Elton offered a grander vision of the Russia Company dominating not only the Iran trade but also Central Asia through its new access to the region by way of Bukhara. Having traveled to Rasht, Elton also drew attention to the key role of the Armenian merchant community along the entire trade route. While Burnish even suggested that the British follow in the footsteps of the Armenians, he never believed their presence was an obstacle to trade as did Elton.[24] Burnish articulated a more concrete plan to suggest the Iran trade would be more economical in the company's hands, focusing on the lower costs for imports and increased value of exports. In either case, without the support of Parliament, the company's aspirations were only that.

Operating on the Caspian

Legalizing the new trade would not be accomplished in Russia or Iran, but rather in London. In October 1740, the Russia Company's petition for the right to trade in Iran was officially read at the Board of Trade and Plantations in preparation for the parliamentary debate. It was a sizeable file, containing two memorials from Elton, the manuscript copy of his journal, Burnish's assessment, and a summary of the entire proposal and its benefits from the foreign secretary.[25] The board endorsed the petition, passing the entire file to the king for his approval on November 11, 1740. The board emphasized Elton's proposal to supply Iran and "the Countrys adjacent with all Sorts of Woolleen Goods to a far greater degree & at much easier Tare than they are now vended there." The board was fully confident in the project, concluding "that the great & many advantages that will accrue to his Kingdom by so cheap & easy a Conveyance of the Manufactures therefore in this Channel of Trade appeared to them so manifest, That they humbly conceived this Proposal deserved the utmost attention & encouragement."[26]

The Russia Company also made a direct appeal to the House of Commons for the necessary change to the law before the end of November. After a delay to hear objections raised by the Levant and East India Companies, the hearing was finally held in Parliament on December 18, 1740, with the Russia Company offering a concise plea for supporting its new concession. The export of wool to Iran was important for the country, and the ongoing war with Spain prevented regular transportation to the Ottoman Empire. As a result, the company warned that the silk trade was currently dominated by Armenian merchants on behalf of their Dutch partners.[27] Elton's suggestion of launching a new trade with Bukhara and Central Asia was not raised, but the company reiterated Burnish's idea that the Russia Company could successfully prevent the Dutch from reentering the Iranian market.[28] After months of debate, the company was granted permission to export from Iran through Russia to London on June 24, 1741, the first adjustment to the Acts of Navigation in decades.[29] Shortly after receiving official notice, the Russia Company advanced £30,000 to its St. Petersburg office to establish a new factory in Rasht.[30] The Anglo-Russian Commercial Treaty extended this privilege to the Russia Company in 1734, but it took seven years to legalize the trade, suggesting the British government was at least as much of an obstacle as the Russians were to a new business operating on the Caspian Sea.

With the Iran trade legalized and its first factory built in Rasht, the Russia Company had seemingly accomplished its goals following the 1734 treaty. However, starting the trade only inspired new hopes for further concessions from the Russian government to improve their position. In the spring of 1742, the company formally requested the support of Britain's ambassador to Russia to seek to lower their transit duties along the Volga, as well as reach an agreement with the Russian government that no duties be paid until they reached the Baltic ports. This objection was primarily the result of high tariffs at Astrakhan, which the company claimed were not imposed on the Armenian merchants involved in the Iran trade. Furthermore, the company requested Russian permission to export "Lead, Tin, or Pewter" to Iran, as Iran continued to be supplied with those products by British merchants in the Levant Company through the Ottoman Empire rather than by the Russia Company, because of Russia's prohibition on the potential weapons trade.[31]

The company's London office made further requests to the British crown to support its trade the following year. In October 1743, for example, it informed the government that the trade was an immediate success, "Exporting considerable Quantities of our Woollen Goods, & other Manufactures, and Importing Raw Silk for Employing our Looms at home." However, Iran was dangerous as the governor of Gilan was forcing payment of taxes by "Terrors & Threats of hanging up by the Heals and drubbing" the British factors in the region. The company petitioned the king that the "Trade in the Persian dominions must be exposed to great Loss, and utter Ruin, unless they, their Factors, & Effects, can be secured from the Violence of such despotick Governors." Therefore "your Majestys Subjects Adventurers in this New Trade" requested a direct appeal from the king to Nader Shah for protection.[32]

The optimism of the London office was not matched by their colleagues in Russia. In the summer of 1742, reports were arriving in St. Petersburg that Elton had entered Iranian service and was constructing a new European-styled navy for the shah on the Caspian, a direct threat to Russia's control over the sea.[33] In addition, Elton was accused of smuggling metalwork into Iran, for which the company had only just requested permission that had not yet been granted. Knowing that the government could revoke its permission to allow the Iran trade, the company office in St. Petersburg dispatched Jonas Hanway to Iran in the fall to investigate. When Hanway returned to Astrakhan in the fall of 1743, his report confirmed the company's worst fears. Elton was engaged in constructing ships for the shah, but the shah had arranged for shipbuilders to be brought in from Gujarat. Hanway observed that the project itself seemed unlikely to begin, as the "apparent want of material and Workmen" made it impracticable, therefore there was no "great occasion for umbrage to those Concerned." Hanway offered few thoughts on the other accusations, as he believed it was "evident" that Elton was not a smuggler, but rather that these false rumors "have been industriously spread by the Armenians or other Enemies of the British Company, purposely calculated for some pernicious Design, or the advancement of their interest in opposition to that said Company."[34]

Hanway's warning did little to alter the requests of the company office in London, but the Russian government was actively investigating Elton's activities in Iran. On January 17, 1744, the foreign secretary notified the current British ambassador to Russia, James O'Hara, Baron Tyrawley, that the Russian ambassador to Britain, Prince Shcherbatov, had "made lately some Complaints against the Conduct of Mr. Elton."[35] The secretary instructed O'Hara to investigate Elton's conduct in Russia, not yet knowing that this had been done the previous year, but the nature of the Russia Company's London office's defense to the secretary suggested otherwise.[36] According to the company's explanation, the beginning of the dispute was that the Russian consul in Rasht, Semën Arapov, notified Elton that the company's ships on the Caspian were required to follow the same regulations for transportation as the Russian ships; in other words, the ships could only leave Iran with Arapov's permission. Elton rejected this interpretation, departing Iran when he chose, which sparked a longer list of complaints to the Russian government. Elton reported that Arapov inspired a mutiny among Elton's Russian crew, "in So much that he and the other English under him were frequently in danger of their lives and distress'd both on board and at home." Furthermore, Elton was accused of "carrying on a Clandestine Trade" in "Pewter, Tin, and Sailcloth," which, the company argued, Elton could trade as part of the "Sundry Goods" allowed in the Iran trade.[37]

The company's defense was disingenuous. The metalwork included items that the Russian government specifically declared contraband in the Anglo-Russian Commerce Treaty. The Russian government again denied the request of the company to trade these items in 1742. However, the company suggested that the previous agreements had not expressly banned these items, and it was not possible for them to know the Iranians intended to turn the metal to weapons or use the sailcloth for sailing. This led to the final and "most enormous Crime laid to his Charge," of having agreed to construct a navy for the shah on the Caspian.[38] This act was the main objection of the Russian ambassador, but the company offered Hanway's rationale that "as a matter of Fact known to us, that long before Mr Elton ever was in Persia, Shah Nadir intended to have some Vessels on the Caspian." Indeed, they suggested, this was proven by the simple fact that the shah hired, and could always hire more, Gujarati shipbuilders.[39] Elton was unnecessary if Iran wanted a Caspian fleet.

When the company office in St. Petersburg received word of Shcherbatov's complaints in April, it immediately defended Elton's conduct, offering that "the moment they are persuaded that Mr. Elton is guilty of the Accusations laid to his Charge, [they] will withdraw their Commissions from him, . . . and oblige him to leave Persia. Yet as we have had the strongest assurances from himself and persons sent expressly to Persia to enquire into his Conduct, & the merit of the Complaints made against him, that he had been greatly misrepresented by Mr. Arapoff."[40]

The British protests were not assisted by Russia's own success with its Iran trade or the general decline in Anglo-Russian relations in the 1740s. Russia's Senate issued a new decree on the Caspian trade in the spring of 1744, compiling the laws over the previous decade to lay out a set of "best practices" for Astrakhan's role and the responsibilities of the city's "Customs Magistrate" in monitoring the activities of the Armenians, Bukharans, Indians, Iranians (lit. men from Gilan, *Gilianskiĭ*), and Agryzhans.[41] According to the Senate decree, no merchant could be allowed to exit or enter the city without paying appropriate customs, and all were regulated under local laws.[42] In July 1744, the Senate passed a new law regulating the export of gold and silver from Astrakhan to Iran, which required further merchant inspections to enforce.[43] The British hopes of easing tariffs and facilitating faster transit through Astrakhan were unlikely to receive a friendly hearing from the Russian government when these requests contradicted Russia's own commercial regulations.

Without new concessions to improve the Iran trade, the Russia Company was in need of a dramatic gesture to improve its current position.

Observing that the Russian government "threw Obstacles in the way of Our Commerce to Persia without having regard to the Treaty aforementioned," they cashiered Elton in hopes of assuaging Russian criticisms. By 1745, the company "turn'd him out of their service, and took all possible pains to get him out of Persia by offering him a Considerable Pension, and their Interests to procure him a Suitable Employment in England."[44] While the company considered this an act of good faith, the Russian government moved to end British access to Iran, banning the trade in 1747.

The end of the Iran trade was not well received by the Russia Company. In a petition sent to the British crown, the company accused the Russian government of punitive and unjust actions. While Elton had been "disapproved of, and discouraged by all Your Majesty's Subjects in that Trade," the Russians "avenged on the whole Body, and made use of [Elton's conduct] as a handle to put a Stop to this Commerce, thro' Russia to Persia, & an excuse for treating Your Majestys Subjects very Ill, on many occasions."[45] In other words, it was unfair that the Russian government was punishing the company for the fact that Elton had enlisted in Nader Shah's service and had begun constructing a navy on the Caspian for him.[46] These claims were supported by a list of incidents demonstrating the unfair reaction of the Senate, which "revers'd all the Decrees, which were granted in favour of the British Trade." The boats constructed by Elton in Kazan' for the Caspian trade "were forced by the Russia Government, to Sell them to Russ Merchants" in Astrakhan "at a very great Loss." Furthermore, the merchants accused the new Russian resident in Rasht, Fëdor Lvovich Cherkasov, of inciting the treasurer at Rasht, Aga Hasan, to plunder the British factory. The merchants estimated their losses between £70,000 and £80,000 in 1748. Despite the accusations, the company expected the Russian government to support its return to Iran, as well as the support of the Russian resident in making restitution claims against the Iranian government.[47] With this request following Russia's removal of Britain's access to Iran by at least a year, it was quite easy for the Russians to ignore this petition. Britain's window on the Caspian ended nearly as soon as it began.

Protesting to the British crown in 1748 was far from the last attempt made by the Russia Company to reestablish its position on the Caspian. However, the company remained divided on the best approach. Some merchants like Hanway argued for a complete return to Iran as if the expulsion had not occurred, but others suggested an alternate path.[48]

Martin Kuychkan Mierop, one of the most active British merchants in the Iran trade, recommended the company abandon any operations in Iran and instead request the right to establish a new "House of Trade or Factory" in Astrakhan. This would leave the risks of the Iran trade in the hands of the Armenians and provide the opportunity for purchasing goods from Central Asia and India in Astrakhan as well. Mierop had spent nine years in Iran and three more in Astrakhan for the company; no other member of the company had his years of experience with the Caspian trade. Based on his intimate knowledge, his plan was quite detailed, naming the ships, captains, and merchants in Iran who could support this effort.[49] Mierop's suggestion, however, fell on deaf ears, as the British were unwilling to concede any business to its competitors. In 1740, the company may have viewed the East India and Levant Companies, as well as the Dutch and French, as its competition. A decade later, however, it was clear the trade between Astrakhan and Iran was dominated by the Armenians, and the British had no better solution than conceding the Caspian Sea to them.

The Russia Company received permission to trade in Iran through Russia in 1734, investigated the trade in 1739, and, because of Elton's activities on behalf of the Iranian government, faced Russian enquiries in 1744, only to lose it permanently in 1747. Having pursued the trade since the 1550s, its short opportunity was only an aberration in the relationship between Britain, Russia, and Iran. Onslow Burnish may have advised the British crown of the benefits of having the Russia Company follow the Armenians into the Caspian, but reality had fallen far short of his optimistic projections. Burnish's admiration for Armenian merchants was also exceptional, as his fellow British merchants consistently blamed Armenian merchants for interfering in their commerce by actively conspiring with Russian or Iranian authorities to expel the British from Iran. Following the Armenians was no longer as much an aspiration as it was a necessary concession.

Notes

1. For this early period, see R. W. Ferrier, "The Terms and Conditions under which English Trade Was Transacted with Safavid Persia," *Bulletin of the School of Oriental and African Studies* 49, no. 1 (1986): 50–53.

2. Matthew P. Romaniello, *Enterprising Empires: Russia and Britain in Eighteenth-Century Eurasia* (Cambridge: Cambridge University Press, 2019), 112–24.

3. The British only noted the absence of Dutch or French merchants. The activities of Russian or Armenian merchants, for example, was generally

discounted despite their presence. See Kevin Gledhill, "The Caspian State: Regional Autonomy, International Trade, and the Rise of Qājār Iran, 1722–1797" (PhD diss., Yale University, 2020), 162–82 and 205–15.

4. The National Archives, Kew, Richmond Surrey (hereafter TNA), SP 36/53, fols. 10–24, "Onslow Burnish to Lord Harrington," October 6, 1740; quote on 12v.

5. For a discussion of the "decline" theory, see Scott C. Levi, *The Bukharan Crisis: A Connected History of 18th-Century Central Asia* (Pittsburgh: University of Pittsburgh Press, 2020), 120–72.

6. Gledhill, "The Caspian State," 144–52.

7. A. I. I͡ukht, "Uchastie rossiĭskogo kupechestva v torgovle Rossii s Zakavkaz'em i Iranom v 1725–1750, gg.," in *Torgovli͡a i predprinimatel'stvo v feodal'noĭ Rossii*, ed. L. A. Timoshina and I. A. Tikhoni͡uk (Moscow: Arkheograficheskiĭ tsentr, 1994), 230–51.

8. TNA, SP 91/15, fols. 135–36, "Forbes and Rondeau to Harrington," April 13, 1734.

9. TNA, SP 91/20, fols. 6–10, "Rondeau to Walpole," July 24, 1736; quote on 8v.

10. Romaniello, *Enterprising Empires*, 106–7, 132–42.

11. TNA, CO 388/41, "Captain Elton's Journey to Persia, Anno 1739," fol. 12.

12. TNA, CO 388/41, "Captain Elton," fol. 13.

13. TNA, CO 388/41, "Captain Elton," fol. 16.

14. TNA, CO 388/41, "Captain Elton," fol. 67.

15. TNA, CO 388/41, "Captain Elton," fol. 49.

16. TNA, CO 388/41, "Captain Elton," fol. 53.

17. TNA, CO 388/41, "Captain Elton," fols. 55–56.

18. TNA, CO 388/41, "Captain Elton," fol. 59.

19. TNA, SP 36/53, fols. 10–24, "Onslow Burnish to Lord Harrington," October 6, 1740; quote on 17r.

20. TNA, SP 36/53, "Burnish to Harrington," fol. 18r.

21. TNA, SP 36/53, "Burnish to Harrington," fol. 18v.

22. TNA, SP 36/53, "Burnish to Harrington," fol. 19r.

23. TNA, SP 36/53, "Burnish to Harrington," fol. 19v.

24. The Armenian role has been well studied, including N. G. Kukanova, *Ocherki po istorii Russko-iranskikh torgovykh otnoshenii v XVII–pervoĭ polovine XIX veka: Po materialam russkikh arkhivov* (Saransk: Mordovskoe knizhnoe izdatel'stvo, 1977); and A. I. I͡ukht, "Russko-Armianskai͡a kompanii͡a 'Persidskogo torga' v seredine XVIII veka," *Patma-banasirakan handes* 2:3 (1983): 224–39.

25. TNA, CO 388/40, Aa. 25, "A Paper put into the hand of Mr. Finch, at Petersburg, in July 1740, containing a Project for Opening a Trade by the British Merchants in Russia, to those Parts of Persia, adjacent to the Southern Parts of the Caspian Sea"; TNA, CO 388/40, Aa. 26, "Another Paper from Capt. Elton upon the Same Subject as the foregoing"; the foreign secretary's summary is TNA, CO 388/40, Aa. 24, "Newcastle to the Lords Commissioners."

26. British Library, Add. MS 14035, fols. 41–44, "Bladen, Plumer, Brudenell, Croft to the King," November 11, 1740; quotes on 41r and 42r.

27. The Armenian-Dutch economic connection running through Russia was established early in the seventeenth century; the Russia Company frequently invoked apprehensions about this connection to mobilize government action. On the history of the Armenian-Dutch relationship, see Inna Lubimenko, "The Struggle of the Dutch with the English for the Russian Market in the Seventeenth Century," *Transactions of the Royal Historical Society*, 4th ser., 7 (1924): 27-51. As part of the negotiations for the necessary adjustment of the Acts of Navigation, the Armenian-Dutch alliance was frequently mentioned. In addition to the material mentioned in note 24, also see TNA, SP 91/28, fol. 177, "Reasons for appointing a Consul General in Russian with the Power to appoint Vice Consuls at Riga, Archangel, Muscow, Saratoff, & Astracan," August 5/16, 1741, art. 5.

28. TNA, SP 36/53, fols. 23-26, "A Memorial relating to the Scheme, for opening a trade to Persia Thro' Russia," [1741]; quote on 25r.

29. "Abstract of the Bill for opening Trade To and From Persia, thro' Russia," in *The History and Proceedings of the House of Commons from the Restoration to the Present Time*, vol. 12 (London: Richard Chamber, 1742), 262-65.

30. National Records of Scotland, Edinburgh, GD 24/1/454/1/15, "Graeme to Stirling," September 12, 1741.

31. TNA, SP 91/29, fols. 210-11, "Copy of a Petition presented by the Russia Company," July 30, 1742. Russia's ban on these products predated the British involvement in this trade, at least to 1717, nearly two decades before the British arrived in Astrakhan. See RGADA, f. 276, op. 1, d. 618, ll. 3-3ob. Thanks for Kevin Gledhill for this citation.

32. TNA, SP 36/62, part 2, fol. 33r-v, "Petition of the Russian Company trading to Persia," October 25, 1743.

33. On Nader Shah's navy, see Laurence Lockhart, "The Navy of Nadir Shah," *Proceedings of the Iran Society* 1 (1938): 3-18; Willem Floor, "The Iranian Navy in the Gulf during the Eighteenth Century," *Iranian Studies* 20, no. 1 (1987): 31-53; and Michael Axworthy, "Nader Shah and Persian Naval Expansion in the Persian Gulf, 1700-1747," *Journal of the Royal Asiatic Society* 21, no. 1 (2011): 31-39.

34. TNA, SP 91/36, fols. 25-26, "Letter from Hanway," November 7, 1743.

35. TNA, SP 91/36, fol. 19, "Carteret to O'Hara," January 17, 1744.

36. TNA, SP 91/36, fols. 21-24, "Russia Company to Carteret," [January 1744].

37. TNA, SP 91/36, "Russia Company to Carteret," fol. 22r.

38. TNA, SP 91/36, "Russia Company to Carteret," fol. 22v.

39. TNA, SP 91/36, "Russia Company to Carteret," fol. 23r.

40. TNA, SP 91/36, fols. 158-60, "Persian Merchants to O'Hara," April 6, 1744; quote on 158r-v.

41. On the Agryzhan community, see Scott C. Levi, *The Indian Diaspora in Central Asia and Its Trade, 1550–1900* (Leiden: Brill, 2002), 122-23.

42. *PSZ*, vol. 12, no. 8919, 77-78, April 13, 1744.

43. *PSZ*, vol. 12, no. 8991, 169-70, July 13, 1744.

44. TNA, SP 36/111, fols. 244–46, "The Humble Petition of the British Merchants, trading thro' Russia to Persia," [1750]; quote on 244 r–v.

45. TNA, SP 36/111, "The Humble Petition," fols. 244v–245v.

46. Lockhart, "The Navy of Nadir Shah," 14–18.

47. TNA, SP 36/111, "The Humble Petition," fols. 244v–245v.

48. Hanway laid out his arguments in his *Historical Account of the British Trade over the Caspian Sea*, 4 vols. (London: Dodsley, 1753).

49. TNA, CO 388/50, fols. 99–100, "Martin Kuyckan Mierop about the Persia Trade," December 21, 1762; quote on 99v.

Part II

Ascendency and Annexation

Empire-building, State-formation, and the Transition to the Modern

CHAPTER 8

"Under the Pretense of Trade, They Drew Maps"

Qajar Views of Russia and Russian Mapmaking in the Caspian in the Eighteenth Century

Kevin Gledhill

On December 15/26, 1781, Russian naval officers based at Gorāduvin in eastern Mazandaran were invited to a gathering near Galugāh by forces loyal to Āqā Moḥammad Khan Qajar, the founder of the Qajar Dynasty in Iran. The Russians, under the command of a Montenegrin naval officer, Captain Marko Voĭnovich, had arrived nearly five months earlier to establish a trading outpost with the approval of Āqā Moḥammad. Now, they accepted an invitation from Ḥāji Moḥammad Āqā 'Emrānlu to attend observances of 'Ashura in remembrance of the martyrdom of Imam Ḥosayn, his family, and supporters, which occurred in 61/680.[1]

The invitation was a trap. One member of the expedition, Karl von Hablitz, a native of Königsburg, left an account of the episode.[2] He claimed that Āqā Moḥammad gave secret instructions to local headmen to establish friendly relations with Voĭnovich and "at some opportune moment, try to seize him as a prisoner and compel him to demolish the

---

This chapter emerged from a project supported by the Title VIII Combined Research and Language Training Program, which is funded by the U.S. State Department, Title VIII Program for Research and Training on Eastern Europe and Eurasia (Independent States of the Former Soviet Union) and administered by American Councils for International Education: ACTR/ACCELS. The opinions expressed herein are the author's own and do not necessarily express the views of either the U.S. Department of State or American Councils.

settlement started [by the Russian expedition] on the shore of the Bay of Astarabad."³ Von Hablitz interpreted this betrayal as an example of the Iranian character, saying that the Qajar ruler "availed himself of common Persian means, that is, perfidy," to detain the officers.⁴ In this regard, he mirrors the often-used trope of "eastern venality," observed by Muriel Atkin in Russian consuls' writings from eighteenth-century Gilan and Shirvan.⁵ Despite his doubts about the invitation, Voĭnovich gathered his officers and went to the village of the official who invited him, Ḥāji Moḥammad Āqā. The Russian officers never arrived. Instead, members of the retinue found themselves "surrounded by an armed mob of people and held under guard." Qajar officials arrived, informed them of their khan's orders, and demanded the destruction of their settlement.⁶

Qajar accounts differ in both their tone and their explanation of the causes of the arrest, but the fact of this ambush is beyond dispute. The mid-nineteenth-century chronicler Reża-Qoli Khan Hedāyat identifies Ḥāji Moḥammad Āqā 'Emrānlu as the commander who executed the plan, stating that he "unrolled the spread of mirth with wine, such that the heads of that party were warmed without shame by people-scattering drunkenness. Ḥāji Moḥammad Āqā carried out the capture and jailing and shackling of Kerāfes [from *Graf*, or Count, Khan, i.e., Voĭnovich]. The Astarabadis took him and his companions, clapped them in chains, and took them before the Shahzādeh [the future Fatḥ-'Ali Shah]."⁷

The decision to arrest Voĭnovich and his men and to expel the Russians from their recently established factory at Gorāduvin marked a sudden reversal of Qajar policies toward Russia. It is made all the more puzzling by the return of the Russian Caspian Flotilla under Captain Nikita Baskakov in late 1782 and his warm reception by Āqā Moḥammad. By April 1783, the Qajar khan granted the Russians the right to trade and settle on the same plot of land they had occupied under Voĭnovich. He wrote to Baskakov, "Concerning the transit of merchants and granting to them of Gorāduvin . . . I have shown them beneficence and mercy and ordered all local landholders to endeavor in the tasks of assistance and satisfaction of that which is requested to construct their settlement" in order to conduct commerce there.⁸ In December 1782, Āqā Moḥammad ordered Armenian and Iranian merchants to leave other ports and operate only out of Gorāduvin. He also invested the equivalent of twenty thousand rubles with a company of merchants to trade there on his behalf.⁹ So what caused the break between the two sides in 1781?

Several possible answers may be found for this question. An early Qajar account cites the oppression of the people of Mazandaran by the Russians, who "coerced the people of low means of the villages and rural places of Ashraf to sow their grains and supply the herds they desired."[10]

Equally significantly, Qajar sources complain of Russian treachery and a military threat to Astarabad. This danger was made possible by advance planning and the preparation of maps. In numerous chronicles produced for the Qajar court, the Russian presence in the region and commercial activity are characterized as mere pretense, covering more sinister motives of conquest. Voĭnovich, who in these sources is always known as Kerāfes Khan, had claimed an interest only in trade, while he requested land on which to conduct this business. He appealed to Fatḥ-ʿAli Khan, "the world-protector, who by delegation of his glorious uncle held authority in Mazandaran, [saying] that a piece of land would suffice ... so in that district they may construct buildings."[11]

Moḥammad-Taqi Sāru'i, who wrote the official history of Āqā Moḥammad with the patronage of Fatḥ-ʿAli Shah, expressed his suspicion of Russian motives bluntly. He notes that a group of Russians had come to Rasht late in the reign of Karim Khan Zand (d. 1193/1779), traveling east from there to the major centers of Mazandaran. "In every place, they made observations of the roads, farms, conditions, occurrences, residences, pastures, mountains, and plains of that region. They created plans of the cities and images of the wild beasts and birds on the pages [of their journals] and illustrated reports."[12] Sāru'i calls special attention to Russian officials' geographic research, presumably including the expeditions of Samuel Gottlieb Gmelin for the Academy of Sciences in the 1770s and Voĭnovich's own mapmaking in the Bay of Astarabad in 1781. Sāru'i drew a clear line between these activities and a clandestine plan of conquest. He wrote, "Their goal was the acquisition of intelligence and the conquest of the domain" (gharaż-e ishān ḥosul-e baladiyyat va taskhir-e mamlakat bud).[13] Qajar court writers understood the proposal of a commercial establishment and mutual exchange as disingenuous: a trick designed to lower the defenses of their commanders and allow Russian officers to carry out the work of intelligence gathering, including cartography. The studies they conducted would lay the foundation for an assault on Astarabad.

This narrative allows new reflection on how Qajar officials regarded the Russian Empire and its motives in the Caspian Sea during the post-Safavid era. Some scholars have written about Iranian views of Russia during this period. Rudi Matthee has noted the Voĭnovich expedition as one of a series of increasing contacts in the second half of the eighteenth century. These encounters included Russian cultivation of alliances with the rulers of Talesh and protectorate negotiations with Hedāyat-Allah Khan of Gilan in the 1770s and 1780s.[14] Matthee notes the growing complexity in Iranian elite views of Russia in the eighteenth and nineteenth centuries. On the one hand, Iranian princes and bureaucrats took the rapid expansion and reorganization of the Russian state that began with Peter I and continued under Catherine II as a model to replicate in Iran. On the other hand, Russian expansionism brought Iranian military defeat and the cession of territory in the Caucasus by 1828, creating a sense of threat, loss, and humiliation.[15] Like most works on the subject, Matthee's focus falls more on the writings of the period after 1804 and the outbreak of war in the Caucasus. Maryam Ekhtiar notes a similar mix of fear and urgency for reform based on the Russian model. These two attitudes were interconnected and drew on one another. Ekhtiar ultimately finds a greater degree of self-confidence in confronting Russia in the eighteenth century than in the Qajar period. Catherine the Great was a particular subject of fascination as a female ruler with wide renown in Iran.[16] In both of these works, analysis of Qajar writings about Russia begins in the reign of Fatḥ-'Ali Shah or with the reform projects of 'Abbās Mirza. Maziar Behrooz saw the Voĭnovich expedition of 1781 as the first serious contact the Qajars had with Russia. While the Qajars expelled the Russians from Mazandaran, their low opinion of this northern neighbor only changed to one of grudging respect and reform-minded emulation as Russian power became more apparent over time.[17] A chronological gap emerges in the literature between works that examine mutual perceptions across the Caspian in the Safavid period and under Nader Shah and those that identify the greater sense of threat and respect in the Qajar era.[18]

This chapter seeks to address this gap and to find continuities between the eighteenth century, when political authority in the southern Caspian fragmented and Russian initiatives in the region intensified, and the nineteenth-century polarization of the region between Russia and the Qajar monarchy that had emerged from the Caspian shores.

The decision to arrest Voĭnovich and his squadron drew on a set of long-developing notions about the Russian Empire formed along the coasts of the Caspian Sea in the eighteenth century. These perceptions were forged by diplomatic missions and cartographic surveys of the 1710s, which laid the groundwork for the invasion and military control of the southern shores of the Caspian by Peter I after the collapse of the Safavid Empire. With the loss of territory to Russia and St. Petersburg's separate peace with the Ottomans, a narrative of Russian treachery and aggression emerged in the Persian-language histories of the period. Confrontation with Russian forces in Gilan produced a sense of betrayal and of the unlimited ambition of the Petrine state for expansion. The subsequent occupation of Shirvan, Dagestan, and Gilan and competition for control of the Caspian littoral only deepened this impression, which spread from court-sponsored writing into Safavid-revivalist histories created outside the centers of military and political power. The occupation depended on the production of intelligence and maps, and their creation began even before 1722.

However, for aspiring rulers of the Iranian north, including the Qajars of Astarabad, relations with Russia also held out the possibility of revenue through overseas trade in a time of economic collapse elsewhere in Iran. This trade sometimes brought iron, coins, and weapons (despite St. Petersburg's attempts to prohibit their export). All of these goods were needed in the multisided conflicts of post-Safavid Iran. The Qajars engaged with Russian diplomats to promote trade beginning in the 1750s. By the 1780s and 1790s, Āqā Moḥammad pursued a coherent policy toward Russia in the Caspian Sea, holding that the Romanovs' only legitimate interests there were commercial, while he forcefully opposed the construction of fortifications or the production of intelligence, including mapmaking. These prohibited activities were understood as prerequisites to conquest. As a result, the fortified factory built by Voĭnovich was destroyed, while Baskakov was welcomed back and trade resumed within a year.

Qajar perceptions of Russia were the product of a Caspian world increasingly linked together by imperial expansion and commercial networks that grew over the course of the eighteenth century. Mapmaking and the placement of artillery on shore heightened the Qajar perception of threat, invoking memories of the 1720s. Despite this, Āqā Moḥammad Khan hoped to maintain access to Russian goods and divert the revenues of trade away from ports held by rival rulers. At this early stage, these two competing understandings of the Russian Empire that formed in the Caspian forced the Qajars to seek a difficult balance between confrontation and concessions in dealing with the naval squadrons that arrived from the north.

Narratives of Treachery and the Appeal of Trade, 1722–1779

In July 1722, Peter the Great arrived at Astrakhan in the Volga Delta. From there, he planned to launch an invasion of northern Iran, using overland routes through the Caucasus and by sea over the Caspian.

He commissioned a manifesto to be drafted by Dmitriĭ Cantemir, who had entered his service from Ottoman Wallachia. Cantemir engaged in polemical works regarding the Ottomans and Islam and used his expertise in Middle Eastern languages in his work as a printer on behalf of the Russian state.[19] In the manifesto, the emperor listed his casus belli, citing raids against Shamakhi in Shirvan, where Russian subjects lost over four million rubles in goods and currency to rebels from the North Caucasus. Having still "not been given satisfaction, the emperor therefore resolved to punish the insurgents and prevent disrespect to the shah's authority."[20]

While the campaign was justified by the need for punitive action against the Lezgis for these attacks, Peter also claimed to act on behalf of the Safavids themselves. He assured Tahmasb II, the Safavid claimant then seeking refuge in the north from Ghilzāi Afghan forces in Isfahan, that no harm would come to any of his subjects or their homes and that officers had strict orders to punish abuses by their soldiers.[21] The 1722 campaign was framed, therefore, as defense of Russian subjects trading in Iran under the terms of a 1718 treaty with Shah Solṭān Ḥosayn; but it was also presented as an effort to restore legitimate Safavid authority in the Caucasus and along the Caspian coast.

Peter's army occupied the major towns between Derbent and eastern Gilan by the following summer. A treaty was signed with representatives of Tahmasb at St. Petersburg on September 12/23, 1723. Under its terms, the shah recognized permanent Russian sovereignty over the Caspian shores, extending as far east as Astarabad, and he pledged to provide horses, camels, bread, meat, and salt for the upkeep of Russian troops at fixed prices.[22] These concessions were justified by the friendship between the two monarchies and Russian commitment to Safavid restoration elsewhere in Iran. Peter's intervention was presented as a necessity only because Shah Solṭān Ḥosayn (r. 1694–1722), the last recognized Safavid ruler and father of Tahmasb, had been "unable to enforce justice for this disturbance [the raids at Shamakhi]"; however, Russian forces aimed only to "aid against rebels and enemies and to protect his [Tahmasb's] Persian throne" and would collaborate with the Iranian claimant to place all other provinces under the "peaceful possession of the Persian state."[23]

Despite this rhetoric, Peter's court began preparations for Russian expansion over the Caspian Sea before 1722. Numerous historians have noted that Peter's interest in expanding contacts with Iran grew in the 1710s, driven by the tsar's desire to exclude the Ottomans from the region, to gain greater control over the silk trade to western Europe, and to secure the steppes between the Caucasus and the Crimean Khanate.[24] As victory over Sweden in the Great Northern War (1701-21) became certain, Peter accelerated outreach to Iran in order to create a stable commercial avenue through Russia via the Caspian-Volga-Baltic route. This project began in 1715 with the dispatch of Artemiĭ Volynskiĭ on a mission to Isfahan to negotiate a permanent commercial treaty with Shah Solṭān Ḥosayn.[25] Volynskiĭ spent the next three years traveling and negotiating with the shah's court, reaching an agreement in July 1717 (ratified in St. Petersburg the following year) that expedited the travel of Russian merchants into Iran, ensured them of security on the roads to and from Shamakhi, guaranteed their freedom to move without exceptional road tolls, and allowed them to buy and sell silk independently of official representatives of the shah in Gilan and Shirvan.[26]

Peter also ordered Volynskiĭ to collect military and political intelligence, and the ambassador included recommendations to the tsar with implications for later military campaigns in the Caspian. I. V. Kurukin has noted the strategic considerations in Volynskiĭ's instructions. Peter ordered his emissary to cultivate local Christian populations as commercial partners, to advocate for an anti-Ottoman alliance, and to examine the geography of the region for its commercial and military infrastructure.[27] Volynskiĭ reported on the "weakness" of Safavid power in the north and the possibilities to project Russian power there, even if he identified the independence of the Shamkhālate of Tarki in Dagestan and that region's geography as obstacles to expansion. He anticipated chaos within Iran, and his dispatches depict a state of "disorder" in the Safavid domains. He assured the tsar of the nonmilitary character of Gilan's people and the ease of victory there.[28] By the time of the 1722 campaign, Volynskiĭ had been installed as the first governor of the new Astrakhan Governorate at the northern edge of the Caspian. From there, he handled the organization, shipbuilding, and other logistics for the campaign into Iran in preparation for Peter's arrival.[29]

In order to better advance the strategic and economic goals of the Russian court, Peter authorized a series of expeditions to study, explore, and map the Caspian and surrounding lands, beginning in 1715. As Kurukin has noted, these missions were the most that could be achieved while the war with Sweden continued, but they were part of a larger project to access Asian markets through Iran to India that included the organization of a trading company and military planning.[30]

Mapmaking and geographic writing on the Caspian provided a foundation of knowledge that would enable the expansion of Russian power in the 1720s. As Guido Hausmann argues in his chapter in this volume, mapmaking was a project of the Russian state, drawing on numerous sources of expertise as part of its efforts to expand its political and commercial reach to the south and east.[31] Fëdor Soĭmonov, who participated in two expeditions under Captain-Lieutenant Karl van Verden to map and describe the Caspian in 1719 and 1720, clearly connected the production of geographic knowledge to Russian expansion. He noted Volynskiĭ's concerns over the need to secure Russia's southern frontiers around the Caspian, adding that this was "not possible, due to a lack of knowledge of the routes and harbors and shores." He also judged the missions valuable to merchants, who had previously traveled across the Caspian "in darkness."[32] In command of one of five ships that were built for the mission at Kazan and Astrakhan, Soĭmonov set out as part of a larger expedition that included 150 marine troops assigned from the Astrakhan garrison in the spring of 1719. As they sailed down the western shore of the Caspian Sea, the seas and coastline were "recorded on a map in detail by Captain von Verden"; Soĭmonov praised his commander's work for its precise scientific charting of the path from the entrance to the Volga to Gilan.[33] His account of the two journeys included episodes of encounter with local elites, the dangers of the sea with its few natural protected harbors (other than Baku and Astarabad) and powerful storms, and topographic descriptions of lands surrounding the sea.[34] To the east, the 1714–17 missions led by Aleksandr Bekovich-Cherkasskiĭ to Khiva ended in massacres at the hands of Shir Ghāzi Khan of Khorezm, thwarting a Russian effort to control commercial routes into Central Asia and through it to India. Despite this failure for the Russian court, the missions provided some of the first detailed maps of the eastern shores of the Caspian, accumulating knowledge on which later expansion projects might build.[35]

By 1724, Russian troops under Mikhaĭl Matiushkin had occupied Gilan and diplomats secured the recognition of Russian rule there by treaty with Tahmasb II, marking a sharp increase in Russian engagement with the Caspian and control over it. Kurukin notes that the 1723 St. Petersburg Treaty came at little immediate cost to the Russian Empire and provided a legal justification for its domination of the region. As a result, Russian officers built new networks of relations with local ruling and economic elites.[36]

Mapmaking became a significant tool of administration under Matiushkin. In 1726, his headquarters produced maps that are now preserved in the Russian State Military-Historical Archive. This collection includes Matiushkin's "Map of Some Parts of the Persian State, which consists of Gilan, Gaskar, Kutum [eastern Gilan], and Astara Provinces."[37] This map takes on the perspective of Russian officials arriving from the north, placing the Alborz Mountains at the top of the map, with the Caspian at its bottom. While lacking the technical precision of the maps executed by Voĭnovich in the 1780s, it focuses on salient features needed to occupy and control the province, with rivers and mountains shown to divide the region fully from the rest of Iran. No roads or passages to the south appear, marking the separation of the Caspian coast from the interior (a reality in law since the 1723 treaty). The map is defined by its focus on water. It is centered around the lagoon at Anzali, with each river and stream running inland, connecting it to the key towns of the interior of Gilan. This is one of a series of maps produced for Matiushkin during the 1720s. Other maps included the major roads through the mountains, converging on urban centers like Rasht, Qazvin, and Ardabil, as well as river mouths up the coast in Talesh.[38]

With the rise of Nader Shah and the growing difficulty of maintaining the occupation, the Russian state secured a second treaty at Rasht in 1732, exchanging control of strategically valuable territory for tariff-free trading rights and a permanent diplomatic presence. As a result, Russia succeeded in developing an economic infrastructure and its consular service in the Caspian through the rest of the eighteenth century.[39]

Iranian Views of Russians in the Caspian

In the nearly sixty years between the fall of the Safavids and the arrest of Voĭnovich, two separate understandings about Russia took hold along the Caspian coast of Iran. First, official Afsharid chroniclers, as well as non-court-affiliated historians who longed for Safavid restoration, interpreted the occupation of the 1720s as a betrayal that demonstrated the fundamental untrustworthiness of the Russian Empire, which sought to conquer Iranian land. By the 1780s, the Qajars interpreted mapmaking as a tool of this project, a reasonable conclusion based on the connection between conquest and cartography during the occupation. Second, the Qajars and others came to see Russians as a source of wealth in a time of economic collapse south of the Alborz. They welcomed economic relations across the Caspian Sea, while simultaneously maintaining earlier suspicions of direct Russian power.

The June 1724 Treaty of Constantinople between Russia and the Ottoman Empire shifted the ground underneath Tahmasb II. Ernest Tucker has noted the incentives that the Porte had to make peace, which brought a measure of stability in the eastern borderlands and allowed them to consolidate territorial gains in the South Caucasus and Azerbaijan.[40] Less than a year before this, Tahmasb had recognized the loss of the Caspian shores in exchange for "aid against rebels and enemies" and the protection of his claim to the throne in Isfahan. Both sides had pledged themselves to act together "against the rebels and do all possible to drive them out and leave the shah in peaceful possession of the Persian state."[41] From the Safavid perspective, the agreement made at Constantinople revealed the insincerity of Russian commitments to reestablish their legitimate authority in Iran.

By Rabi'i al-Awwal 1137 (November–December 1724), Tahmasb responded to this apparent betrayal with an appeal to the leading figures of Gilan to rise up and expel the Russians. He ordered forces be raised in Gaskar, Astara, Dashtvand, and other locations in Talesh, and for them to march on Rasht in order to "defeat and remove the enemies."[42] The sense of betrayal underlying this decision is obvious from the work of Mahdi Khan Astarābādi, writing with the patronage of Nader Shah. According to his account, Tahmasb had sent his embassy to St. Petersburg to ask for help during the Ottoman and Afghan invasions. In response, the Russians sent their ships to Rasht, where they built a fortress just outside the city. But "all of Dār al-Marz [the Caspian provinces] between Niāzābād [in Dagestan] up to Astarabad" had been ceded in exchange for aid in restoring Safavid rule. Instead, the Russians "extended the hand of conquest, claimed the right to rule and assigned [control of Gilan] to their great commander with ten thousand men." As a result, the shah rallied the local landholders who attempted to drive them out, attacking the Russians in Rasht from two sides.[43] The Russians, Astarābādi wrote, saw off this challenge and spent two years in complete control of the region. During that time, they ruled and took the revenues of the provincial *divān* for themselves. In 1726, they faced a rebellion led by a *qalandar* dervish in the east of Gilan, which also failed to dislodge the occupying armies.[44]

"UNDER THE PRETENSE OF TRADE, THEY DREW MAPS"

This episode marks the origin of the first narrative informing Āqā Moḥammad Khan in 1781: one of Russian aggression and desire to conquer Iran. For Astarābādi, Peter's promises of alliance and support gave him a pretense to introduce armies into Iran, occupying its territory and seizing revenues. This narrative passed from Astarābādi into the history of Mirza Moḥammad Khalil Marʿashi, a grandson of Mir Sayyid Moḥammad Marʿashi, the former supervisor of the tomb of Imam Reżā. Mir Sayyid Moḥammad briefly ruled in Mashhad as Soleymān II Safavi in 1749.[45] According to Mirza Moḥammad Khalil, "a company of Rus came by sea to Tabarestān with the goal of conquering Gilan."[46] This episode appears in the text as one of several invasions and defeats for Tahmasb before his appointment of Nader to take command of his armies. Rather than recounting the full details of the Russian invasion, Mirza Moḥammad Khalil cited Astarābādi, transmitting the narrative of Russian aggression and duplicitousness into his own work and directing the reader to the original account.[47]

It is easy to imagine how this idea of Russia reached the Qajars of Astarabad. According to Solṭān Ḥāshem Mirza, the son of Soleymān II and uncle of Mirza Moḥammad Khalil, the Qajars were close allies and supporters of the Marʿashi project of Safavid restoration. Moḥammad Ḥasan Khan, the father of Āqā Moḥammad who challenged Karim Khan Zand for control of northern and western Iran in the 1750s, had earlier served as a commander and official of the Marʿashi-Safavid court at Mashhad.[48] The official Afsharid versions of the Russian presence in Iran would also have been available in Mashhad and clearly entered the thinking of some of the Marʿashis themselves. Furthermore, the first Qajar court chronicler, Moḥammad-Taqi Sāruʾi, had been an assistant of Mahdi Khan Astarābādi and drew on his style in composing his own history, called *Tārikh-e Moḥammadi*, from 1797.[49] Across northern Iran, the major factions aspiring to rule inherited a sense of Russian betrayal in the occupation and the Treaty of Constantinople that recognized Ottoman claims in the west and northwest.

If Iranian rulers in the north regarded Russia as fundamentally expansionist, they nonetheless found value in the commercial networks that formed around the Russian consulate in Gilan (first at Rasht and reestablished in Anzali in 1750). A. I. Îukht has examined the volume of trade at Astrakhan in the second half of the eighteenth century. While he notes a sharp drop in trade after Nader Shah's assassination in 1747 and again during the Zand-Qajar-Afghan conflict of the 1750s, the volume of exchange across the Caspian spiked in the 1770s and 1780s. In

1787, just one year after Āqā Moḥammad finally captured Gilan and consolidated his hold on the southern shore of the sea, customs office receipts at Astrakhan reached 1.34 million rubles.⁵⁰

While many products were exchanged in the Caspian, silk exports from Gilan and Shirvan represented the largest share. In April 1777, Consul Grigoriĭ Merk reported to the College of Commerce (the forerunner of the Ministry of Commerce, created by Peter I) that silk production had risen rapidly during the relative stability of the Zand period (in Gilan, from 1759 to 1779). Whereas Iran had produced only thirty thousand *man* of silk in the 1740s during the British Russia Company's presence in Gilan, it now produced one hundred thousand according to the consul.⁵¹ These numbers are hard to verify and may represent the tendency, observed by Matthew Romaniello, for merchants and diplomats to shape political decisions at home (in this case, in St. Petersburg) by rhetorical strategies. These framings included overstating the potential of the trade in the Caspian.⁵² However, Merk's estimate matches that of Khoja Sarkis, a former Zand customs agent in Rasht who informed the British East India Company on the trade of the Caspian coast in 1767.⁵³ By the mid-1780s, thirty thousand poods (541.7 tons or 83,338 *man*) of silk reached Astrakhan every year.⁵⁴ This quantity nearly equals Willem Floor's estimate of about six hundred tons produced annually at the height of the Safavid silk trade and exceeds estimates of the output of the late Safavid period considerably.⁵⁵ In a period of economic collapse across the Iranian plateau, geographic protections of the Alborz Mountains and dense forests, as well as demand for Iranian goods in Russia, produced a rare island of prosperity in Gilan. As a result, Samuel Gottlieb Gmelin estimated the annual income of Gilan's autonomous ruler at two million rubles in the early 1770s.⁵⁶

The Qajars had periodic contacts with the consulate and merchants in Gilan, dating back to at least the 1750s. After Moḥammad Ḥasan Khan first captured the region in 1752, he apparently confiscated goods from Russian merchants and diplomats to fund further campaigns. A legal dispute in St. Petersburg between Iranian-born Armenian merchant Luka Shirvanov and his commercial agent revealed that diamonds purchased on Shirvanov's account were seized by Moḥammad Ḥasan around that time. According to the agent, the Qajar commander had taken two diamonds worth five thousand rubles after making demands to turn them over at the consulate. The Qajar *sardār* never compensated him for these goods.⁵⁷ In spite of this episode, trade continued between Rasht and the southeastern Caspian, and these contacts could produce further tensions between Consul Peter Chekalevskiĭ and Moḥammad Ḥasan Khan. A 1755 edict to the consulate from the College of Commerce prohibited merchants from traveling to Astarabad. This decision came in response to a dispute with a factor working on behalf of Moḥammad Ḥasan Khan.[58]

Despite these confrontations, contacts continued and Russian interest in the southeastern Caspian grew through the 1770s. By September 1771, Gmelin recommended the creation of a factory in Mazandaran. He wrote with optimism about the potential for trade in cotton and silk, as well as the suitability of the region to support a settlement with rice cultivation. Critically, he found goods from India in Mazandarani markets at low prices, holding out the promise for Asian transit trades to the Volga.[59] The thriving silk markets of Gilan and sporadic contacts between Russians there and the southeastern Caspian created a powerful enticement for the Russian court, the Astrakhan-based trading houses, and the Qajars to expand relations.

Āqā Moḥammad Khan encountered Voĭnovich's expedition early in his rise to power. After his father's defeat in 1758, Āqā Moḥammad spent a brief period among the Yomut Turkmens, before going to Shiraz as Karim Khan's hostage in the early 1760s. On the vakil's death in 1779, he escaped to the Caspian coast and began to consolidate his hold on the Qajar lands around Astarabad, fighting a series of campaigns against his half brothers. By 1785, he had defeated them and held off a Zand siege of Astarabad, emerging suddenly as the predominant power in Iran and advancing on Isfahan and Gilan.[60] His precarious hold on the region and frequent military challenges required him to find new sources of revenue. This necessity may help to explain his initially warm reception of the squadron.

However, Āqā Moḥammad Khan defined a limited legitimate sphere of Russian interest in Iran. His views become clear from a later document in which he demanded the submission of Erekle II of Kartli-Kakhetia (eastern Georgia) and rejected Tiflis's (Tbilisi's) status as a vassal monarchy of the tsars under the 1783 Treaty of Georgievsk. Āqā Moḥammad sent this letter in either 1795 or 1796, around the time of his campaign against Erekle and infamous sack of Tiflis. After this campaign, he took the throne as shah on the Moghān steppe. Castigating the Georgian king for his treaty with Russia, he stated that Russians had long traded with Iran but that their "affairs are only in merchant trade."[61] He refused to recognize any territorial claims or the separation of eastern Georgia from the Guarded Domains of Iran. Under this framing, the Russian Empire was not to be excluded entirely from the Caucasus and Caspian shores, as its value as a commercial partner remained significant. But he sought to narrow the scope of the Russian presence to a purely economic one. He intended to sever St. Petersburg's ties to its partners among ruling elites of the Caucasus and Caspian, and he asserted his own territorial claim over all of the former Safavid Empire.

These two impressions of Russia as a valuable trading partner and an expansionist foe hiding behind legitimate interests were forged in the eighteenth-century Caspian world. Each of these considerations structured Qajar responses to the Voĭnovich expedition and its mapmaking and fortress building along the coast.

The Voĭnovich Expedition and Its Expulsion

Russian interest in the southeastern corner of the Caspian Sea grew rapidly in the 1770s, driven by the potential of a factory there to serve as a commercial entrepôt between Astrakhan, Central Asia, Iran, and India. A Yomut mission to St. Petersburg helped to drive this interest, as did further expansion of commercial fishing, seal hunting, and oil trades.[62] Von Hablitz makes clear the opportunity perceived by Catherine, Grigoriĭ Potemkin, and other key figures in the Russian capital, who saw a vacuum opened by the western European powers' engagement in the American War of Independence that might allow Russia to gain a predominant share of South Asian goods flowing into Europe.[63]

Efforts to access the southeastern Caspian were to be led by military officers and began with geographic research. By 1777, Potemkin requested an imperial edict to authorize a naval expedition to the eastern shore and survey the pasture lands of the Kyrgyz (Kazakh) nomads, hoping to improve commercial routes to the Uzbek khanates via Mangyshlak.[64] The following year, Potemkin placed General Aleksandr Suvorov in command of the construction of a flotilla at Kazan and Astrakhan.[65] Voĭnovich (presumably known to Suvorov from his service in the Mediterranean during the Russo-Ottoman War of 1768–74) received the command of this squadron, reporting directly to Potemkin. His orders required him to protect Russian merchants along the western coast of the Caspian, while maintaining secrecy as he proceeded to Astarabad to set up the factory.[66]

Voĭnovich carried out extensive research of the geography of the eastern Caspian, before settling on Ashraf (now Behshahr) as his intended location for settlement. While acknowledging the economic potential of seal hunting and petroleum at Ogurja Island, he decided against building there due to flooding, its sandy soil that is not suited to agriculture, and the risk of Turkmen raiding by sea.[67] He ultimately selected Ashraf for the safe harbors in the Bay of Astarabad and links to commercial routes into Khorasan and Central Iran. He also expressed excitement at resources there that would support a large settlement with rice, fruits, and mulberry trees. This settlement would allow for the production of raw silk.[68] While requests for the cession of Ashraf were refused, it was eventually permitted at Gorāduvin, further east along the coast, near Galugāh. Construction there began in the autumn of 1781 and included an infirmary, storehouses, barracks, residences for merchants, a pier, baths, a bakery, and other buildings at this site.[69] While waiting for Āqā Moḥammad's approval, the officers of the Caspian Flotilla produced a series of maps of the Bay of Astarabad.[70]

The construction of a fortified base at Gorāduvin and the production of maps activated Qajar suspicions of Russian expansionism. Just as Astarābādi commented on Russian fortification near Rasht as a provocation and sign of Peter's intentions to seize Gilan, Qajar historians noted similar building projects near Astarabad. According to later Qajar chronicler Moḥammad Ḥasan Khan, ʿEtemād al-Saltaneh, the khan ordered the squadron's arrest and destruction of the fortress when Voĭnovich had cannons brought on shore from the ships. These posed a danger to the people of Astarabad itself, should the Russians march against the city with artillery.[71] Karl von Hablitz attributed their arrest to the "envy of the other Persian khans . . . they convinced him [Āqā Moḥammad] that Russia's goal was [something] other than the establishment of trade and that they had readied an army there for the conquest of Persia."[72] Such suspicions had clearly spread widely through the region and would have gained credence with the creation of artillery batteries at Gorāduvin. As early as the late 1790s, Sāruʾi wrote his account in which the squadron used trade as a pretense, masking a desire for intelligence gathering and conquest, beginning with the mapping and description of the region.[73] The arrest of the squadron in December 1781 reflects the prevailing attitude toward Russian military officers and diplomats across northern Iran at that time, drawing on the memory of Peter's Iranian Campaign of the 1720s.

The arrests, however, did not mark a complete rejection of Russian trade and contacts. Āqā Moḥammad selected an ambassador to travel to St. Petersburg: "for the extension of firm unity and removal of hostilities from both sides . . . he sent him to the Pādshāh of Rus [Catherine II]."[74] Voïnovich found himself in a standoff with the Qajar ruler until his departure in April 1782, but agreed to take this emissary to the Russian capital to preserve the trust of other leading figures of the region. He hoped to maintain useful ties built before December 1781 in the event of Āqā Moḥammad's downfall.[75] While this mission failed (receiving no audience at the Russian court), continued contacts took place with Baskakov's arrival in October of that year.

In welcoming Baskakov back to Gorāduvin, Āqā Moḥammad sought to redirect the Caspian trade away from rivals and to the southeastern corner of the sea. In December, he ordered his officials to offer full logistical support to the Russians, in exchange for their pressure on merchants to cut off activities at other ports outside of Qajar control. To promote the project, he invested the equivalent of twenty thousand rubles, with merchants trading on his behalf with the Russians in Mazandaran.[76] The first merchant ships to arrive brought a wide variety of goods, including canvas, broadcloth, brocades, cast-iron cauldrons, sewing needles, candies, scissors, alcoholic drinks, and wool fabrics. They also included military supplies, the sale of which into Iran was ordinarily restricted by the Russian court. These included firearms with shot, daggers, swords, and iron.[77] Against the backdrop of multisided conflict among the Qajars and against Zand and Göklen Turkmen rivals, these supplies offered a lifeline to Āqā Moḥammad as he sought to assert his authority in the north.

In summary, Qajar perceptions of Russia drew on more than a half century of contacts dating to the immediate aftermath of Safavid collapse and to the expansion of Transcaspian trade in the post–Nader Shah period. Two distinct views of the Russian Empire coexisted at the time: one of veiled expansionism advanced through the study and mapping of Iranian lands, and another of a legitimate Russian commercial presence that served the needs of would-be rulers who controlled the southern Caspian's few available ports. Āqā Moḥammad Khan sought to define a limited sphere of Russian activity that was purely commercial and useful to his own project of consolidating control over the former Safavid lands. By eliminating rival ports, he hoped to monopolize the revenues of the Caspian trade under his appointed commercial agents, providing a firm material basis for his emerging polity. These contacts, therefore, could be instrumentalized to serve Qajar ambitions, while removing the dangers posed by mapmaking and fortified trading posts.

"UNDER THE PRETENSE OF TRADE, THEY DREW MAPS"   185

This episode reveals significant features of the Caspian world and Iran in the late eighteenth century. The relative prosperity of the Caspian coast provided the material means for expansion for the autonomous rulers north of the Alborz and in the South Caucasus. But this was a competitive environment, in which the Qajars were one of numerous factions seeking to attract trade to ports under their control at the expense of rivals. These interests incentivized a balancing act in relations with Russia, made evident in Āqā Moḥammad's sudden reversals between welcoming invitation to and reprisals against the Russian naval presence in Mazandaran.

Notes

1. One officer of the Russian Flotilla described the "celebration" as occurring on "December 15, a day of remembrance in honor of one considered a prophet." While this phrasing reveals a profoundly limited understanding of Shiʿism, ʿAshura (Muḥarram 10) did fall on December 15, 1781, according to the Julian calendar (then in use in Russia), and December 26 according to the Gregorian. See Lt. Rading, "O proisshestviiakh sluchivshikhsia pri osnovaniĭ Russkago seleniia na beregu Astrabadskago zaliva v 1781 godu," in Zhurnal" Ministerstva Vnutrennikh Del," ed. P. B. Butkov (St. Petersburg, 1839), 21.

2. Von Hablitz (1752–1821) was a naturalist who wrote a geographical text on Crimea after his time in Iran. He first traveled to Iran with fellow German (from Tübingen) botanist Samuel Gottlieb Gmelin in his two trips for the Russian Academy of Sciences from 1771 to 1774. Willem Floor has provided a short biographic note on von Hablitz, who wrote under the name Karl Ivanovich Gablits, as a footnote in his translation of Gmelin's travel account. See Samuel Gottlieb Gmelin, *Travels through Northern Persia, 1770–1774*, trans. Willem Floor (Washington: Mage, 2007), xxi.

3. [Karl Ivanovich Gablits], *Istoricheskiĭ zhurnal byvshikh v 1781 i 1782 godakh na Kaspiĭskom more Rossiiskoĭ èskadry pod komandoiu flota kapitana vtorago ranga Grafa Voĭnovicha* (Moscow: Tipografiia S. Selivanovskogo, 1809), xvii.

4. [Gablits], *Istoricheskiĭ zhurnal byvshikh*, xvii.

5. Muriel Atkin, *Russia and Iran, 1780–1828* (Minneapolis: University of Minnesota Press, 1980), 44.

6. [Gablits], *Istoricheskiĭ zhurnal byvshikh*, xvii–xviii.

7. Reżā-Qoli Khān Hedāyat, *Tārikh-e Rowżat al-Ṣafā-ye Nāṣeri*, vol. 9, part 1, ed. Jamshid Kiānfar (Tehran: Esāṭir, 1380/2002-3), 7267.

8. Rossiĭskiĭ Gosudarstvennyĭ Voenno-Istoricheskiĭ Arkhiv, (hereafter RGVIA), f. 52, o. 1/194, d. 288, ll. 7–7ob.

9. RGVIA, f. 52, o. 1/194, d. 288, ll. 5–5ob; Baskakov gave the same figure in a letter to Astrakhan Governor Mikhaĭl Zhukov: RGADA, f. 23, o. 1, d. 13, ch. 3, l. 118.

10. BL, Add. MS 27243, Moḥammad Fatḥ-Allāh b. Moḥammad-Taqi Sāruʾi, *Tārikh-e Moḥammadi*, 1222/1807, fol. 73r.

11. Hedāyat, *Tārikh-e Rowżat al-Ṣafā-ye Nāṣeri*, j. 9, b. 1, 7266.
12. BL, Add. MS 27243, fols. 72r–v.
13. BL, Add. MS 27243, fol. 72v.
14. Rudi Matthee, "Facing a Rude and Barbarous Neighbor: Iranian Perceptions of Russia and Russians from the Safavids to the Qajars," in *Iran Facing Others: Identity Boundaries in a Historical Perspective*, ed. Abbas Amanat and Farzin Vejdani (New York: Palgrave Macmillan, 2012), 102–3.
15. Matthee, "Facing a Rude and Barbarous Neighbor," 103–8.
16. Maryam Ekhtiar, "An Encounter with the Russian Czar: The Image of Peter the Great in Early Qajar Historical Writings," *Iranian Studies* 29, no. 1–2 (1996): 57–70.
17. Maziar Behrooz, "From Confidence to Apprehension: Early Iranian Interaction with Russia," in *Iranian-Russian Encounters: Empires and Revolutions since 1800*, ed. Stephanie Cronin (New York: Routledge, 2013), 50.
18. For the earlier period, we may include Matthee's characterization of Safavid-era views of Russians as an uncivilized people compared to other Europeans and lacking in diplomatic etiquette. See Rudi Matthee, "Between Aloofness and Fascination: Safavid Views of the West," in "Historiography and Representation in Safavid and Afsharid Iran," special issue, *Iranian Studies* 31, no. 2 (1998): 233–34. More recently, Goodarz Rashtiani has argued for a pattern of gradual Russian encroachment on Iranian sovereignty in the second half of the century, representing a shift from imperial competition and confrontation with Iran in the Caspian in the time of Nader. See Goodarz Rashtiani, "Iranian-Russian Relations in the Eighteenth Century," in *Crisis, Collapse, Militarism & Civil War: The History and Historiography of 18th Century Iran*, ed. Michael Axworthy (Oxford: Oxford University Press, 2018), 163–82. Rashtiani largely focuses on the period to 1747 and on concrete objectives of states and their confrontations, rather than the image of Russia in the southern Caspian. Oleg Nikonov gives some attention to the value Iranian elites found in partnerships with Russia, with autonomous khans in the north cultivating ties with the Anzali consulate in competition with one another for commercial and strategic advantage. See Oleg A. Nikonov, *Iran vo vneshnepoliticheskoĭ strategii Rossiĭskoĭ Imperii v XVIII v.* (Vladimir: Vladimir University Press, 2009), 328. Most of this work considers imperial strategy and the methods by which Russian diplomatic, commercial, and naval presence took root in the Caspian and northern Iran over the eighteenth century. For the Qajar era itself, Abbas Amanat has argued that the transition in views of Russia in Iran is embodied in some writings of Mirza Abu al-Qāsem Farāhāni Qā'em Maqām, who moved from a confrontational position toward Russia to one of accommodation, while contrasting Russian action and imperial power to the perceived weakness and ineffectiveness of the Qajars. See Abbas Amanat, "'Russian Intrusion into the Guarded Domain': Reflections of a Qajar Statesman on European Expansion," *Journal of the American Oriental Society* 113, no. 1 (1993): 35–56.
19. David Schimmelpennick van der Oye, *Russian Orientalism: Asia in the Russian Mind from Peter the Great to the Emigration* (New Haven, CT: Yale University Press, 2010), 38–42. Cantemir's role in composing the 1722 manifesto

is mentioned in F. I. Soĭmonov, *Opisanie Kaspiĭskago morii̇a i chinenykh na onom rossiĭkikh zavoevaniĭ, ii̇ako chast' istorii Gosudarii̇a Imperatora Petra Velikago* (St. Petersburg: Imperatorskaii̇a Akademii̇a Nauk, 1763), 58.

20. Soĭmonov, *Opisanie Kaspiĭskago*, 60.
21. Soĭmonov, *Opisanie Kaspiĭskago*, 60-61.
22. T. İuzefovich, ed., *Dogovory Rossii s" Vostokom": Politicheskie i torgovye* (St. Petersburg: Baksta, 1869), 187-88.
23. İuzefovich, *Dogovory*, 186-87. The notion of continuity in relations between the Russian Empire and "Persian State" became a feature of Russian relations with all Iranian rulers of the eighteenth century. This idea was reinforced by the normative influence of the Treaties of Rasht (1732) and Ganjeh (1735). Russian diplomats and merchants valued this fictitious continuity because of trading privileges in the treaties; the Qajars for the same reason and because of their own claims to a legitimate Safavid succession. In 1781, this led Āqā Moḥammad Khan to reject Voĭnovich's request to build his trading settlement at Ashraf, given its connection to ʿAbbas I and its significance to the project of Safavid restorationism under Qajar leadership. See Kevin Gledhill, "The 'Persian State' and the Safavid Inheritance: Views from the Caspian, 1722-1781," in *The Idea of Iran*, vol. 11, *Transition to a New World Order*, ed. Charles Melville (London: Bloomsbury, 2022), 57-79.
24. P. P. Bushev cites all of these reasons for Peter's decision to send a mission seeking a commercial treaty to Iran in 1715, which he viewed as part of a wider effort to build knowledge of the region and diplomatic ties to Iran and Central Asia. See P. P. Bushev, *Posol'stvo Artemii̇a Volynskogo v Iran v 1715–1718 gg. (po russkim arkhivam)* (Moscow: Izd. Nauka, glavnaii̇a redaktsii̇a vostochnoĭ literatury, 1978), 9-11. Nikonov addresses the economic motives of the court in St. Petersburg, which sought greater engagement with Europe and benefits of integrating its economy to it by connecting the Volga-Caspian route to the Baltic Sea. The Caspian also held out the promise of manufacturing growth in the eighteenth century with the import of raw fabrics. See Nikonov, *Iran vo vneshnepoliticheskoĭ*, 14-17.
25. Bushev, *Posol'stvo Artemii̇a Volynskogo v Iran*, 7. Volynskiĭ traced his roots to an old princely family and rose in status through the patronage of Vice-Chancellor P. P. Shafirov, with whom he was captured by Ottoman forces during the 1711 Pruth Campaign and later returned to Russia. See Bushev, *Posol'stvo Artemii̇a Volynskogo v Iran*, 15.
26. N. G. Kukanova, *Torgovo-ėkonomicheskie otnoshenii̇a Rossii i Irana v period pozdnego feodalizma* (Saransk: Izd. Mordovskogo universiteta, 1993), 23.
27. I. V. Kurukin, *Persidskiĭ pokhod Petra Velikovo: Nizovoĭ Korpus na beregakh Kaspii̇a* (Moscow: Kvadriga, 2010), 31-33.
28. Kurukin, *Persidskiĭ pokhod Petra Velikovo*, 35-38.
29. V. V. Kulakov, *Astrakhan' v persidskoĭ politike Rossii v pervoĭ polovine XVIII veka* (Astrakhan: Astrakhanskiĭ universitet, 2012), 17-21.
30. Kurukin, *Persidskiĭ pokhod Petra Velikovo*, 40-41.
31. See chapter 5 of this volume, Guido Hausmann, "Astrakhan and the Caspian Sea in Russia's Early Modern Political Geography."

32. Soĭmonov, *Opisanie Kaspiĭskago*, 32.
33. Soĭmonov, *Opisanie Kaspiĭskago*, 33-35.
34. Soĭmonov, *Opisanie Kaspiĭskago*, 30-54.
35. See René Létoille, "Les expeditions de Bekovitch-Tcherkassy (1714-1717) en Turkestan et le début de l'infiltration russe en Asie Centrale," in *Boukhara-la-Noble*, Cahiers d'Asie Centrale 5-6 (Tashkent: Cahiers d'Asie Centrale, 1998), 259-84.
36. Kurukin, *Persidskiĭ pokhod Petra Velikovo*, 112-13.
37. RGVIA, f. 446, o. 1, d. 111.
38. RGVIA, f. 446, o. 1, d. 112.
39. Nikonov, *Iran vo vneshnepoliticheskoĭ*, 171.
40. For more on Ottoman efforts to stabilize this frontier and fears over increasing conflicts as a consequence of Afghan rule, see Ernest Tucker, *Nadir Shah's Quest for Legitimacy in Post-Safavid Iran* (Gainesville: University Press of Florida, 2006), 24-27.
41. Iuzefovich, *Dogovory*, 186-87.
42. "Farmān by Shāh Tahmāsp II," in Bert Fragner, "Ardabil zwischen Sultan und Schah: Zehen urkunden Schah Tahmāsps II," *Turcica* 6 (1975): 189.
43. Mirzā Mahdi Khān Astarābādi, *Tārikh-e Jahāngoshā-ye Nāderi*, ed. ʿAbdallah Anvār (Tehran: Chāp-e Bahman, 1341/1962-63), 17.
44. Astarābādi, *Tārikh-e Jahāngoshā-ye Nāderi*, 17.
45. This work was one of two produced by members of the Marʿashi family, recounting their lineage and the events of Soleymān's rule. Ernest Tucker has grouped these into the category of openly Safavid revivalist historical works, a subgenre of history writing in the eighteenth century, with "nostalgic retrospectives" on the fallen dynasty. See Ernest Tucker, "Persian Historiography in the 18th and Early 19th Century," in *Persian Historiography*, ed. Charles Melville, vol. 10 of *A History of Persian Literature*, ed. Ehsan Yarshater (New York: I. B. Tauris, 2012), 269-70.
46. Mirzā Mohammad Khalil Marʿashi, *Mojmaʿ al-Tavārikh, dar Tārikh-e Enqerāż-e Ṣafavieh va Vaqāieʿ-e Baʿad*, ed. ʿAbbās Eqbāl (Tehran: Ketābkhāneh-e Sanāʾi-e Ketābkhāneh-e Ṭahvari, 1362/1984-85), 74.
47. Marʿashi, *Mojmaʿ al-Tavārikh*, 74.
48. He held the title of *Eshik-Āqāsi-Bāshi*. See Solṭān Hāshem Mirzā, *Zabur-e Āl-e Dāvud: Sharh-e erṭebāt-e Marʿashi bā selāṭin-e Ṣafavieh*, ed. ʿAbd al-Ḥosayn Navāi (Tehran: Mirās̱-e Maktub, 1379/2001-2), 109. Nominally, this office referred to the keeper of the gate into the interior household of the Safavid shahs, though in practice the officeholder typically controlled access to the shah, managed bureaucrats, and oversaw public court ceremonies. These responsibilities made its holder one of the key figures of the Safavid court. See Roger M. Savory, "Ešīk-Āqāsī-Bāšī," in *Encyclopaedia Iranica*, VIII/6, 600-601, https://iranicaonline.org/articles/esik-aqasi-basi. Gholām Reżā Zargarinezhād has noted that later Qajar writers did not mention Mohammad Hasan Khān's role at the court of Soleymān II, cleaning up the transition from Safavid to Qajar rule by eliminating this episode and introducing him in the context of resistance to Durrani Afghan invasion. See Gholām Reżā Zargarinezhād, *Tārikh-e*

Irān dar Dowreh-ye Qājārieh, ʿAṣr-e Āqā Moḥammad Khān (Tehran: Sāzmān-e Moṭālaʿeh va Tadvin-e Kotob-e ʿolum-e ensāni-e Dāneshgāhā, 1395/2017–18), 180.

49. Abbas Amanat, "Legend, Legitimacy, and Making a National Narrative in the Historiography of Qajar Iran (1785–1925)," in Melville, *Persian Historiography*, 297.

50. A. I. I͡ukht, "Torgovli͡a Rossii so stranami vostoka vo vtoroĭ polovine XVIII v. i armi͡anskoe kupechestvo," *Istoriko-filologicheskiĭ zhurnal Akademii Nauka Armi͡anskoĭ SSR*, no. 2 (1981): 87.

51. RGADA, f. 276, o. 1, d. 647, l. 36.

52. See Matthew P. Romaniello, *Enterprising Empires: Russia and Britain in Eighteenth-Century Eurasia* (Cambridge: Cambridge University Press, 2019).

53. BL, IOR/R/15/1/1, fol. 67r.

54. Mikhaïl Dmitrievich Chulkov, *Istoricheskoe opisanie rossiĭskoĭ komertsii pri vsekh portakh i granitsakh*, vol. 2, pt. 2 (Moscow: Universitetskai͡a tipografii͡a, 1785), 459.

55. Willem Floor, *The Persian Textile Industry in Historical Perspective, 1500–1925* (Paris: Societé de l'Histoire de l'Orient, L'Harmattan, 1999), 14. It is worth noting that Floor's statistics are based on only partial data drawn from the records of European trading companies. Without more complete records of exports to Russia and the Ottoman Empire as well as domestic uses, we cannot reach a precise figure of silk production and trades in the Safavid period.

56. Gmelin, *Travels through Northern Persia*, 98. For an overall picture of Iran's economic condition in the eighteenth century, its continuing shortages of currency, and the impacts of post-Safavid conflicts, see Willem Floor, "The Persian Economy in the Eighteenth Century: A Dismal Record," in Axworthy, *Crisis, Collapse, Militarism & Civil War*, 125–50.

57. V. K. Voskani͡an, Dzh. O. Galusti͡an, and V. M. Martirosi͡an, eds., *Armi͡ano-russkie otnosheniī͡a vo vtorom tridtsatiletii XVIII veka: Sbornik dokumentov*, vol. 3 (Yervan: Izd. Akademii͡a Nauk Armi͡anskoĭ SSR, 1978), 309.

58. RGADA, f. 276, o. 1, d. 619, l. 10.

59. Gmelin, *Travels through Northern Persia*, 245.

60. For a more complete account of his military campaigns, see Gavin Hambly, "Āghā Muḥammad Khān and the Establishment of the Qājār Dynasty," in *Cambridge History of Iran*, vol. 7, *From Nader Shah to the Islamic Republic*, ed. Peter Avery, Gavin Hambly, and Charles Melville (Cambridge: Cambridge University, 1991), 104–43. Hambly acknowledges the often-emphasized violence of Āqā Moḥammad's campaigns but sees him as someone driven by a political vision of a unified state within Iran and a key figure in the country's modern history.

61. A. N. Artizov, ed., *Iz istorii rossiĭsko-gruzinskikh otnosheniĭ k 230-letii͡u zaklī͡uchenii͡a Georgievskogo traktata: Sbornik dokumentov* (Moscow: Drevlekhranilishche, 2014), 599.

62. Kh. A. Ataev, *Torgovo-ėkonomicheskie svi͡azi Irana s Rossieĭ v XVIII–XIX vv.* (Moscow: Nauka, 1991), 76.

63. [Gablits], *Istoricheskiĭ zhurnal byvshikh*, v.

64. Nikonov, *Iran vo vneshnepoliticheskoĭ*, 267.

65. Rading, "O proisshestviiakh sluchivshikhsia," 10.
66. Rading, "O proisshestviiakh sluchivshikhsia," 38; [Gablits], *Istoricheskiĭ zhurnal byvshikh*, vi.
67. RGVIA, f. 52, o. 1/194, d. 244, ll. 27–27ob.
68. RGVIA, f. 52, o. 1/194, d. 244, ll. 28ob, 30.
69. Rading, "O proisshestviiakh sluchivshikhsia," 41; [Gablits], *Istoricheskiĭ zhurnal byvshikh*, xiv.
70. These are now held in the Russian State Military-Historical Archive. See RGVIA, f. 446, o. 1, dd. 330–34.
71. Moḥammad Ḥasan Khān, *Tārikh-e Mont'aẓam Nāṣeri*, vol. 3 (Boston: Harvard University, 1990), 39.
72. [Gablits], *Istoricheskiĭ zhurnal byvshikh*, xv.
73. BL, Add. MS 27243, fols. 72r–v.
74. BL, Add. MS 27243, fol. 73v.
75. Rading, "O proisshestviiakh sluchivshikhsia," 45.
76. RGVIA, f. 52, o. 1/194, d. 288, ll. 5–5ob; RGADA, f. 23, o. 1, d. 13, ch. 3, ll. 118, 122.
77. RGVIA, f. 52, o. 1/194, d. 268, ll. 27–27ob.

CHAPTER 9

Caspian Forests as Political Setting
A Socioenvironmental Study of the Bābi Resistance at the Fort of Shaykh Ṭabarsi

Saghar Sadeghian

In 1844, Sayyed 'Ali Moḥammad, known as the Bāb (gate), established the Bābi faith in Shiraz, Iran. Delivering a messianic and revolutionary message for Iranian society, and claiming to be the twelfth hidden Imam of Shi'ism, the Bāb was arrested and imprisoned several times before his eventual execution in Tabriz in July 1850.[1]

In 1848, when the Bāb was imprisoned in Chehriq, a citadel in the Iranian province of West Azerbaijan, some of his followers resolved to liberate him. Molla Ḥosayn Boshruyeh, the Bāb's first disciple, led these followers, who launched their expedition from Mashhad. Before embarking for Azerbaijan, however, the Bābis planned to liberate another prominent Bābi who was imprisoned in Sari, Molla Moḥammad 'Ali Bārforushi, also known as Qoddus. Molla Ḥosayn and 202 other followers left for Mazandaran on July 21, 1848 (Sha'ban 19, 1264). From Mashhad, this party passed through Nayshābur, Sabzevār, Mazinān, Biyārjomand, Mayāmay, Armiyān, Shahrud, Deh Molla, Āstāneh, Chashmeh 'Ali, Firuz Kuh, Savād Kuh, Urim, Shirgāh, and some smaller

---

My gratitude goes to Abbas Amanat, Kevin Gledhill, and Kayhan Nejad for giving me the opportunity to be a part of this book. I am also grateful to William Duvall for his comments and suggestions on the earlier draft of this chapter.

villages before arriving at Bārforush, by which time their ranks had swelled to 315 members.[2]

Moḥammad Shah died on September 5, 1848 (Shawwal 6, 1264). Three days later, Naser al-Din Mirza, then the governor of Azerbaijan, received the news of his father's death. Although he declared himself the new shah on the thirteenth of September, he had to overcome many obstacles during the first two months of his reign.[3] When Naser al-Din Mirza left for the capital, new governors were appointed to Azerbaijan. The Bābis had to evaluate the situation and gather intelligence on the next governor before embarking for Azerbaijan, as the potential for unrest remained in Azerbaijan, Tehran, or even the entire country following the shah's death. In Bārforush, the Bābis anticipated hearing news and information about developments in Tehran, and intended to draw on the city's economic resources, thus resolving to regroup there before mobilizing to liberate the Bāb.[4]

The Bābis arrived at Bārforush on September 11, 1848.[5] Already having been attacked several times on their way through Mazandaran, the Bābis soon realized that the authorities in Mazandaran were similarly hostile to their presence. Trapped in the caravanserai in Sabzeh Maydān of Bārforush, Molla Ḥosayn and his followers accepted an offer by 'Abbās Qoli Khan Lārijāni, the governor of Bārforush, to be escorted outside the town and through the forest. The escorts, however, abandoned the Bābi band in the forest. After a series of violent confrontations, the Bābis eventually traveled to Afrā, a village about twelve kilometers (two farsakh) from Bārforush, before finally arriving at Shaykh-e Ṭabarsi's shrine in Afrā on September 21, 1848.[6] Anticipating yet more attacks, the Bābis prepared defenses, as Molla Ḥosayn ordered his followers to fortify the shrine and strengthen the walls. The Bābis also succeeded in rescuing and relocating Qoddus from Sari, where he had been imprisoned, to the Ṭabarsi shrine.[7] The estimated number of the Bābis at the fort was reported as anywhere between three hundred and two thousand.[8]

The Bābis engaged in several small skirmishes while staying in the fortress, but more serious battles began five months later, when Naser al-Din Shah ordered the governor of the province to put an end to the unrest.[9] Since the local troops could not defeat the Bābis, the national military took action. Mahdi Qoli Mirza, a Qajar prince, was designated governor of Mazandaran and sent with cannons to the region to fulfill the mission, commanding anywhere from 600 to 3,500 troops.[10] 'Abbās Qoli Khan Lārijāni accompanied the new army as well.[11] From this moment, the Ṭabarsi movement emerged as an issue of national importance that commanded the shah's attention. At a certain point, the number of troops, including those from Mazandaran, was reported as roughly twelve thousand.[12] Although possibly exaggerated, this was an astronomical number, a sign of how serious the resistance had become to the central government. Tactically, and due to the location of the unrest, the government troops could not penetrate the fortress easily. Most of the battles were held outside of the fortress, when some of the Bābis would emerge to attack the government troops. In one of the attacks on February 2, 1849 (Rabiʿ al-Awwal 9, 1265), ʿAbbās Qoli Khan shot and killed Molla Ḥosayn. On the same day, forty other followers were killed.[13]

During the next phase of fighting, the military surrounded the fort, firing upon it with cannons, and gunning down any who attempted to flee. At this point, while the Bābis were suffering from hunger, Mahdi Qoli Mirza sent notes to the dispersed Bābis, signing and sealing the Qur'an as an assurance that he would afford all of them amnesty if they ceased fighting and abandoned the fort. Despite Qoddus's warning, the Bābis accepted the offer perforce. The troops disarmed the Bābis, killed many, and sold others as slaves, while a few escaped.[14] They sent Qoddus with two other Bābis to Bārforush, where one of the clerics of Bārforush, Saʿid al-ʿOlama', led a mob that attacked Qoddus, removed his clothes and turban, chained him, and steered him through the market and streets, where the people cursed and spit on him before beating him to death and burning his body in a fire.[15] Qoddus's death on May 16, 1849 (Jamadi al-Thani 23, 1265) marks the end of the Ṭabarsi uprising.[16]

The Battle of Fort Ṭabarsi can be interpreted by applying Hobsbawm's theorization of the "Primitive Rebel," which he defines as "banditry of the Robin Hood type, rural secret societies, various peasant revolutionary movements of the labour religious sects and the use of ritual in early labour and revolutionary organizations."[17] Hobsbawm argues that "the 'career' of a bandit almost always begins with some incident, which is not in itself grave, but drives him into outlawry."[18] Charges against a person instead of their crime, false accusations or testimony, errors in judgement or unjust verdicts, could all create a rebel. The rebels were normally honored and supported by the local residents, who considered them to be victims who fought "against the oppression of the state."[19] The Bābis were sent to the forest to be abandoned and were attacked several times before launching their resistance. Thus, the unjust behavior of the local authorities arguably made them into outlaws.[20] This is not the only instance of Hobsbawm's theory one may apply to the Bābis. It is worthwhile, therefore, to review the socioeconomic dynamic of the region before analyzing the event in relation to its physical environment.

Bārforush

Bārforush (also Bālforush, today Bābol) and its vicinity, including ʿAli Ābād (Shahi, today Qāʾem Shahr), served as the space for the events at the Fort of Ṭabarsi. This location gave specific sociopolitical attributes to the story. Located in the south of the Caspian Sea, Bārforush has long been one of the major cities of Mazandaran Province in Iran. First known as Bārforush Deh ("the village where loads are sold"), it was once a stopping point for ship cargos to be exchanged between Mashhad-e Sar (today Bābolsar) and Ḥāji Tarkhān (Astrakhan). Driven by merchant immigration, Bārforush gradually grew into a town with a population of ten thousand to twenty thousand in the 1850s–1860s.[21]

Economy

Although only a second-class trade town, Bārforush was an international crossroads for Iran. The trade directed through Bārforush would move on both sea and land, directing goods both domestically throughout Iran and internationally. Merchants from as far as Isfahan and Kashan would bring their goods to Bārforush to trade them via the Caspian Sea in the Caucasus and Russia.[22]

Considering the amount of goods and money exchanged in Bārforush, the presence of other countries, and the extent of the regions interconnected through the city, Bārforush's prominence in the power dynamic of nineteenth-century northern Iran is evident. Bārforush represented one-sixth of Iranian export income, and thus played a major role in the national economy. This would draw the attention of some other countries, including Russia, as news spread more rapidly to and from Bārforush. Given the town's economic and political importance, one may understand why ʿAbbās Qoli Khan, the governor, tried to negotiate and convince the Bābis to leave Bārforush with his own escorts.[23] Out in the forests, the Bābis could be abandoned, and thus more easily "silenced."

Demography, Religious Diversity, and Networks of Power

In the mid-1950s, Mirza Ebrāhim reported that Bārforush had six Emāmzādeh (descendants of the Shi'a Imams) shrines, forty-eight tekkiyeh (places to demonstrate and mourn for the martyrdom of the third Shi'ite Imam, Ḥosayn), twelve mosques, six schools, and fourteen public baths.[24] James Baillie Fraser (1783–1856) reported about twenty-three schools (madraseh) in the 1820s, with many religious studies students, "learned men," and merchants.[25] Considering the population of the town (ten thousand to twenty thousand), Bārforush had a relatively large number of schools per capita.

Religious diversity characterized nineteenth-century Mazandaran, including Bārforush, as Sufism had become popular in the region with new converts from Shi'ism.[26] Rabino reported that, although majority Shi'a, some Kurdish 'Ali-Allahis resided in Mazandaran.[27] He also wrote about the "countless" Sayyeds, especially descendants of Imam Reżā (the eighth Imam), in Mazandaran.[28] Bārforush had thirty-five quarters (Maḥalleh). With a history of more than three hundred years, the Jewish quarter (Yahud Maḥalleh, which later became Kalimi Maḥalleh) had fifty houses, about 350 Jews, two synagogues, and a school. The Jews of Bārforush derived most of their income from selling alcoholic beverages and textiles.[29] Although a relatively diverse city, Bārforush was not necessarily welcoming to all populations. In 1866 a number of Jews were massacred, and many more were forcibly converted.[30]

Religious and social divisions and tensions manifested in Bārforush and contributed to the intensity and longevity of the local Bābi uprising. At the time of the Ṭabarsi siege, the population of the city was fractious and disunified. As Abbas Amanat argues, such tensions had already existed in Bārforush prior to the Ṭabarsi unrest. "The chief actors—the nonconformist millenarian, the forces of established 'ulama supported by the state, the factional urban division, the conflicting economic interests—are all present."[31] That tension reached its peak with the Ṭabarsi movement. Apart from divides between Muslim and non-Muslim or Iranian and foreigner, Bārforush was divided along sectarian Ḥaydari-Ne'mati divisions, which later morphed into Shaykhi-Oṣuli divisions.[32] Merchant-landowner divisions also marked Bārforush, splitting the 'olama'. Molla Moḥammad Ḥamzeh Shari'atmadār, supporter of peasants and petit landowners, commanded more support among the Ne'mati quarter; Sa'id al-'Olama' garnered the support of the city's wealthier classes. Qoddus, one of the key actors in the Ṭabarsi movement, was also drawn into this sectarian factionalism. While Qoddus and Shariʿatmadār were Shaykhi, Saʿid al-ʿOlama' was affiliated with Oṣulis.

In 1845, prior to the Ṭabarsi movement, Qoddus had already been well known in Bārforush, as his criticism of the ʿolama"s behavior enraged Saʿid al-ʿOlama', leading the Oṣulis to condemn Qoddus. Some clerics of the town incited the Bārforush population against Qoddus.[33] This rivalry provides one potential explanation for Saʿid al-ʿOlama"s murder of Qoddus after the Bābis were forced from the Fort of Ṭabarsi. It also potentially explains why the high-ranking merchants in Bārforush, supporters of Saʿid al-ʿOlama', were not involved in the event. At the same time, Shariʿatmadār supported the Bābis and gifted them food and supplies when they were in the caravanserai of Bārforush.[34]

The administration of Mazandaran was in the hands of the governor general, who would appoint all the governors of different districts, mostly on a hereditary basis.[35] ʿAbbās Qoli Khan Lārijāni (Savād Kuhi), a prominent landowner in Mazandaran with his own army, was the governor of Bārforush and ʿAli Ābād at the time of the Ṭabarsi battle.[36] Impelled by the sectarian divisions in Bārforush, ʿAbbās Qoli Khan, a great merchant and landowner, sided with Saʿid al-ʿOlama', and thus chose to confront the Bābis, push them out of Bārforush, and fight them in the Fort of Ṭabarsi.

Environment, the Brutal Enemy

The dense, impassable Caspian forests have played host to several episodes of political resistance in Iranian history. As James Scott argues, forests are a peripheral, ungoverned surrounding of the state, representing a challenge and a threat as the home of fugitive and mobile populations. These ungoverned landscapes and their people are "fiscally sterile."[37] Those who take shelter in the forests find it "convenient to raid the settlements of sedentary farming communities subjects [sic] to the state."[38] Geographically difficult terrain such as mountains, marshland, forests, and deserts—known as "shatter zones"—are the first destination for the refugees from state power, "joining others outside the state's reach."[39] The Alborz Mountains, with an altitude of three thousand to four thousand meters and covered with dense Caspian forests, were just such a refuge zone for guerilas. Among the most recent examples of this are the Jangal Movement (1914–21) and the Tudeh

Party militancy, led by the Cherik-hā-ye Fadā'i-ye Khalq-e Irān (Iranian People's Fadā'i Guerrillas, est. 1971).

Although the political, economic, and religious dynamics of Bārforush and Mazandaran at the time of the Ṭabarsi unrest were important, the role of the environment is unusually prominent. Several attempts by 'Abbās Qoli Khan Lārijāni and Mahdi Qoli Mirza, who commanded troops numbering four hundred to two thousand, failed to defeat the Bābis for eight months, in large part because of the regional environment.[40] At the time, after only three miles, the road from Sari to Bārforush would "plunge into deep forest." Bārforush was itself situated in a dense forest with residents "scattered amongst the trees."[41] Fraser indicates:

> I never saw a place of which it was so difficult to acquire an idea from ocular observation. The whole town being built in and surrounded by a forest of high trees . . . , the buildings are indeed so screened and separated by foliage, that except when passing through the bazars, a stranger would never suspect that he was in the midst of a populous city.[42]

Hidden living quarters were connected with some pathways, which could not be easily found by nonlocal visitors.[43] Fraser explains, "No one in his senses would be mad enough to attempt to penetrate it [jungle]; but a guide will show you a 'hole in the wall,' a crevice, a thing like a rabbit-run through which he introduces you to a pathway at first scarcely perceptible, winding like a snake through the bushes, but which increases in size as you get on."[44]

The Caspian forests were impassable. This was acknowledged by many travelers to the region, including Naser al-Din Shah, who was lost in the dense woods several times during his journey to the north. In one of his travelogues, he explains that "this forest is so broad, big, and unlimited that anyone, no matter how savvy and intelligent they are, if they do not know [the region], will disappear without a trace. No one will hear from them anymore."[45] The shah observed that the ground of the forest was all covered by red flowers and grass, there was no soil to mark the footprints, and the trees were all the same height, not taller or shorter so that one could use them as signposts, especially when foggy or dark.[46]

There was no established road through the forest, as dense, thorny bushes and tree roots covered the ground, rendering them unnavigable even for horses. The pathways, if they existed, were narrow and coated in sticky mud. The high elevation also posed an obstacle to navigation, as most of the route to the Fortress of Shaykh Ṭabarsi alternated between high mountains and low valleys. The rivers, like the River Bābol, were too deep and rapid-moving to transverse, except during the summer months.[47] Writing about 'Ali Ābād and Bārforush, Naser al-Din Shah commented that "there is a road from 'Ali Ābād to Bārforush that passes by Shaykh Ṭabarsi Fortress. This was a good, nonmuddy road. Those who passed through it, praised it. Since we did not know that road, we went via the regular road."[48] It is interesting to note that the shah avoided a visit to the vicinity of the fort. To Fraser, 'Ali Ābād was "a very miserable village" with "no view of Balfroosh [Bārforush] to be obtained; for on approaching that town, you only see a dense forest."[49] The road to Mashhad-e Sar also brought travelers through the forest and was very difficult to pass. Although only sixteen kilometers long (2.5 farsakh), it would take a day to cross when it was raining.[50]

A century earlier, Jonas Hanway, a British merchant who traveled to the region in 1749–50, described Mazandaran:

> This province also abounds in water, of which many streams issue from the springs in the mountains. . . . They tell a story of an inhabitant of the low-lands who, when asked the length of the province, answered, "tool [ṭul] up to the waist," the word tool [ṭul] in Persic signifies length; but, in the dialect of the province, mud.[51]

In the mid-nineteenth century, irrigating watercourses divided the areas used for rice cultivation, rendering them impassable for horses, and sometimes even killing those who attempted to cross.[52] Fraser describes the road "sunk in many places considerably lower than the level of the surrounding country, . . . so that we sometimes rode for miles in water up to the saddle-girths, not knowing whether the next step might plunge us overhead in some deep hole."[53] These were the conditions in good weather, and presumably worse during the winter with heavy rain or snow. Fraser accurately observed in 1833:

> I never saw, nor can I imagine, a stronger or more impracticable country, in a military point of view, than these provinces. Roads—that is, made roads—there are none [except the old almost disappeared one, constructed by Shah 'Abbās, which could not be found without a guide]. And, even when found, it would be useless for military purposes, from the numerous breaks and gaps in its course, and from the impenetrable jungle which surrounds it on all sides, and affords cover for all sorts of ambuscades and surprises.[54]

One should consider that the national troops would have needed to take the roads similar to those described by Fraser and Naser al-Din Shah. Then, one can imagine the challenges facing the military en route to Ṭabarsi Fortress: swamps, marshes, quicksand, reed fields, bramble, high mountains with snow (even in September), heavy rain, and floods.[55]

The troops faced further challenges upon their arrival at the Ṭabarsi Fort. First, at the time of the Ṭabarsi battle, Iran relied on imported muskets, cannons, howitzers, and fabricated matchlocks, which do not function well when wet.[56] Considering the regular heavy rain or occasional snows in Mazandaran, these firearms were not very effective.[57] The unrest unfolded mostly during fall and winter, seasons of heavy rain and snow. On one occasion, heavy snowfall remained on the ground for seventeen days.[58] Zavvāreh'i recounts an occasion when Molla Ḥosayn and some other Bābis went outside the fort to attack government troops encamped in a trench amid light rain. The soldiers ran away, but the commander stayed, attempting repeatedly to discharge the gun, but to no avail. Then two Bābis tried to attack him with their swords, but they lost their swords. They then attempted to shoot a flintlock pistol, but the pistol did not have a flint. With no other recourse, they jumped on him and hammered his head with the pistol handle.[59]

Both the Bābi rebels and the government soldiers faced great difficulties fighting in the Mazandaran climate. Without appropriate weaponry, neither side was able to organize major offensives, and thus the battle unfolded with long intervals between moments of combat. Furthermore, the majority of combatants from both sides were not from the region, and were not used to the very humid, wet, and cold climate of Mazandaran. The combatants confronted sickness, body malfunction, or constant fatigue that slowed or even prevented any sustained combat. Third, many of the Bābis in the fort were not able to fight, because the majority were 'olama' who had spent their entire lives in studying and reading. Only about one-third (110 out of 313) of the Bābis in the fort agreed to fight.[60] Fourth, the troops needed food and supplies, something difficult to get from villagers who were not necessarily happy with the governors' act of bringing war to their region. Finding food and supplies was also a challenge for the Bābis, as will be addressed later in this chapter.

The shrine of Ṭabarsi was brick with wood and a ceramic roof. There was a small mosque attached to the building. The shrine building was surrounded by short fences, and all around this land, there were dense forests and farmlands.[61] E. G. Browne, who visited the site in September

1888, describes it as "a flat, grassy enclosure surrounded by a hedge, and containing, besides the buildings of the shrine and another building at the gateway, . . . nothing but two or three orange trees and a few rude graves covered with flat stones, the last resting-places, perhaps, of some of the Bábí defenders."[62] The resistance took place in a shrine, an unsuitable defensive position for the rebels. However, the Bābis strengthened the walls and dug a ditch around the shrine to keep the enemy away. According to Zaʿim al-Dawleh Tabrizi, when Molla Ḥosayn arrived at the Ṭabarsi shrine, he found it suitable for his goal, especially as the site was sufficiently endowed with water and fruit trees. Molla Ḥosayn first built an octagon fortress with eight tall towers, and then built strong shelters from large trees on top of each tower. In the walls of the shelters, they created holes for spotting the attackers and shooting them. The Bābis then dug a ditch around the fortress, thirty-four feet (ten zarʿ) wide and thirty-four feet deep. The Bābis piled the soil from the ditch between the wall and the ditch. Tabrizi also gives details about trenches, several deep wells, and sharp spears installed in the holes.[63] Similarly, Zavvāreh'i writes about the ditch, the fortification, towers, and walls. He also reports that the Bābis dug a well for water, built a bath in the site, and made two gates on the eastern and western sides of the shrine.[64] Sotudeh writes that the fortress had an underground tunnel connecting the fortress to a village in the vicinity, Dizehvā, from which a person called Jabbar would bring the Bābis food and supplies.[65] (There is no sign of such construction in the site now, nor was there when Browne visited it.) Tabrizi explains that once the unrest had ended, Mahdi Qoli Mirza visited the site in disbelief that Molla Ḥosayn could have established such a fortress at the site without military training or knowledge of geometry. He then collected the goods in the fortress and distributed them among the military and villagers.[66]

It merits mention that some major leaders of the battle were from the region and were familiar with the region and its unique climatic and geographical features. This foreknowledge played an important role in the Bābis' survival, as the Bābis initially arrived in the region with no guide and little experience in the region. Once in the shrine, some Bābi leaders from Mazandaran visited or joined the resistance and helped them survive. Mirza Ḥosayn ʿAli Nuri, Baháʾuʾlláh, who had lived in the city of Nur in Mazandaran, boasted connections with and knowledge about the region. When Baháʾuʾlláh visited the Bābis in the shrine, he advised them on techniques to strengthen their position in the fortress.

Qoddus, upon his liberation and union with the Bābis at the shrine, ordered them to dig a ditch around the fortress.[67] Qoddus was from Bārforush and the son of a ricegrower. As a child, he would collect firewood in the forests, imbuing him with knowledge of the climate, forests, and means of resistance and survival.[68] As such, Bahá'u'lláh and Qoddus rather than Molla Ḥosayn made the greatest contributions to the construction of fortifications. Once again, the situation in the Fort of Ṭabarsi is comparable with Hobsbawm's three "sections" of a "village anarchist movement": the "village population" who hosted the rebels; Qoddus, Bahá'u'lláh, and Sharīʿatmadār as the "local preachers" and "leaders"; and Molla Ḥosayn and the Bābis, with national profiles, as the "outsiders and external influences."[69]

As for the food and supplies, the Bābis had access to some resources before their complete encirclement in the fort. In the mid-nineteenth century, it was not unusual for Iranians to have and carry guns with them, as villagers supplied their own firearms when summoned to serve in the military.[70] Council Abbott reported about Astarabad in 1848 that "most of the villagers in this insecure country possess matchlocks."[71] Mazandarani writes that before leaving Mashhad toward Mazandaran, Molla Ḥosayn received a sword and a horse as gifts and "all the other disciples also had weapons with them."[72] In addition to firearms, the Bābis were able to procure food from the nearby forests before taking shelter in the shrine, as the region abounded with fruit trees, including pomegranate and common medlar, and also sheltered animals including the common pheasant, little bustard, and hawks.[73] Moreover, the Bābis bought food and supplies when they were in the caravanserai of Bārforush.[74] Tabrizi writes that, once in the shrine, Molla Ḥosayn sent his followers to different villages and towns to buy sheep, chicken, eggs, fish, cereals, grass for animals, and other supplies. The exact means of procurement of these foodstuffs, however, are unclear. Some sources say they bought the supplies. Others say that they ransacked the villages. Finally, some say that Molla Ḥosayn told the Bābis to first attempt to buy the food, and if the villagers refused to sell, then to ransack their stores.[75]

Despite the antagonism of the Bārforush clerics and the preexisting animosity among some Bābis and the 'olamā', the public perceived the Bābi rebels to be victims of the government, and thus lent their support, or at least sympathies. The Bābis successfully recruited some local residents and received visitors from the vicinity who presented them with gifts or sold them goods such as warm clothing, sugar, and tea.[76]

The villages in the vicinity were mostly owned by Bārforush merchants, sayyeds, and royal families.[77] Some had connections with the Bābis and supported them. One example is Naẓar ʿAli Khan, a convert, whose village was attacked by the Bābis because they had confused it with Qādi Kalā (Qādi Kolā), another village whose residents had attacked the Bābis. The Bābis attacked Naẓar ʿAli's village, killed some residents, including (mistakenly) even Naẓar ʿAli's mother. Despite this, Naẓar ʿAli visited Molla Ḥosayn in the fortress and gifted the Bābis rice, a horse, and four hundred sheep. Molla Ḥosayn ordered the Bābis to allow the sheep to graze around the fortress, and to consume their milk.[78]

In the last phase of the battle, the military surrounded the fortress and started shooting whomever emerged. The Bābis endured great hardship and slowly began to disperse and give up. During the battle, especially in the last phase, after Molla Ḥosayn was killed and the Bābis were trapped in the fortress, the Bābis began consuming the dead horses of the battlefield, including even Molla Ḥosayn's prized steed. Desperate for sustenance, the Bābis even burned, crushed, and swallowed the horses' bones and skins with warm water. In the final stages of the fighting, they were forced to eat the leather from shoes, sword covers, bags, and saddles. Finally, they managed to survive on dried grass or only water.[79] Only thanks to the constant precipitation of Mazandaran did they maintain a supply of water.

The environment—the deep forests, the condition of the roads, and the climate—presented difficulties for both sets of combatants. Initially, the Bābis could continue the battle so long as they maintained ties with the villages and outer forest to obtain their food and supplies. Their hardships began in earnest when they were cut off and surrounded in the fort, thus forcing them to negotiate with the governor. The local and national troops, on the other hand, faced difficulties even reaching the battlefield, where they then faced the additional challenge of waging war amid constant rain or snow. The troops also needed food and supplies, which they had to procure from the villages in the vicinity or Bārforush as well. It was easy neither to provide for such a large number of soldiers, nor to carry the supplies to the battlefield. Thus, despite the government's apparent military advantages, the governor was also ready to negotiate an end to the siege.

One cannot study the Battle of Fort Ṭabarsi without considering the role of the Caspian littoral in shaping, prolonging, and finally ending the surrounding events. Even given the importance of economic and social factors, Mazandaran's unique environment was the foremost cause of the battle's long duration. Like other antistate actors Hobsbawm described in *Primitive Rebels*, the Bābis were attacked and pushed to the shrine. Although the state denounced the Bābis as criminals, the residents dismissed the accusations and provided them aid. Considering the support of both the local village population and the Bābis throughout Iran, the Ṭabarsi resistance exemplifies Hobsbawm's "village anarchist movement." James Scott's theory is also applicable when considering how unreachable spots such as forests created a space of resistance, as the Mazandaran humidity, constant rain and snow, and unnavigable pathways extended the duration of the siege.

Notes

1. D. M. MacEion, "Bāb, 'Alī Moḥammad Šīrāzī," *Encyclopaedia Iranica*, III/3, 278–84, https://www.iranicaonline.org/articles/bab-ali-mohammad-sirazi.

2. If questioned by authorities, the liberators were to claim that they were traveling to the shrine cities of Najaf and Karbala ('Atabāt). Noṣratollāh Moḥammad Ḥosayni, *Ḥażrat-e Bāb* (Ontario: Mo'asseseh-ye Maṭbu'āt-e Bahā'i, 1995), 411, 432–33; Abbas Amanat, *Iran: A Modern History* (New Haven, CT: Yale University Press, 2017), 243; Nabil Zarandi, *The Dawn-Breakers*, trans. Shoghi Effendi (Wilmette, IL: U.S. Baha'i Publishing Trust, 1932), 324–25; Asadollāh Fāżel Māzandarāni, *Tārikh-e Ẓohur al-Ḥaqq*, vol. 2, https://www.academia.edu/42358413/Tarikh_Zuhur_Al_Haqq_Volume_2_ظوهرالحق_جلد_2, 257–59; Sayyed Ḥosyn Mahjur Zavvāreh'i Ṭabāṭabā'i, *Vaqāye'/Tārikh-e Mimiyeh*, Persian MS (authored ca. 1849), Ann Arbor, University of Michigan British Manuscript Project 749(4), #1, 10–17-19, 24.

3. For more details, see Abbas Amanat, *Pivot of the Universe* (Los Angeles: University of California Press, 1997), 89–100.

4. Māzandarāni, *Ẓohur al-Ḥaqq*, 265–67.

5. Māzandarāni, *Ẓohur al-Ḥaqq*, 269–70; Zavvāreh'i, *Mimiyeh*, 25; Siyamak Zabihi-Moghaddam, "The Babi-State Conflict at Shaykh Tabarsi," *Iranian Studies* 35, no. 1-3 (2002): 96. Māzandarāni writes that the Bābis arrived at Bārforush on a Friday, Dhu al-Qa'deh 10, which will be sometime around October. Based on the chronology other sources introduce, Zabihi-Moghaddam's date is more reasonable.

6. Mirza Ebrāhim (last name unknown), *Safarnāmeh-ye Astarābād va Māzandarān va Gilān*, ed. Mas'ud Golzāri (Tehran: Entesharāt-e Bonyād-e Farhang-e Irān, 1977), 125; Zavvāreh'i, *Mimiyeh*, 27, 33; Zabihi-Moghaddam, "The Babi-State Conflict," 96.

7. Zarandi, *The Dawn-Breakers*, 351–54, 357–58, 368–75; Moḥammad Ḥosayni, *Ḥażrat-e Bāb*, 432; Moḥammad 'Ali Malek Khosravi, *Eqlim-e Nur* (Tehran: Mo'asseseh-ye Maṭbu'āt-e 'Amri, 1958), 50–54.

8. See Siyamak Zabihi-Moghaddam, *Vāqe'eh-ye Qal'eh-ye Shaykh Ṭabarsi* (Darmstadt: Mo'asseseh-ye 'Aṣr-e Jadid, 2002), 24, 81–82.

9. Zavvāreh'i, *Mimiyeh*, 48–49.
10. Mirza Ebrāhim reports 3,500: Ebrāhim, *Safarnāmeh-ye Astarābād*, 128. Smith and Momen report 600; see Peter Smith and Moojan Momen, "Martyrs, Babi," *Encyclopaedia Iranica Online*, https://www.iranicaonline.org/articles/martyrs-babi-babi.
11. Manuchehr Sotudeh, *Az Āstārā tā Astārabād*, 4th ed., vol. 4 (Tehran: Nashr-e Āgāh, 1996), 367–68.
12. Zabihi-Moghaddam, *Vāqeʿeh-ye Qalʿeh-ye Shaykh Ṭabarsi*, 28.
13. Zavvāreh'i, *Mimiyeh*, 57–61; Zarandi, *The Dawn-Breakers*, 380–82.
14. Zavvāreh'i, *Mimiyeh*, 68–90; Zarandi, *The Dawn-Breakers*, 399–414.
15. Sotudeh, *Āstārā tā Astārabād*, 368. A similar narrative is given by Tabrizi: Moḥammad Mahdi Zaʿim al-Dawleh Tabrizi, *Meftāḥ-e Bāb al-Abvāb yā Tārikh-e Bāb va Bahāʾ*, trans. to Persian by Hasan Farid Golpāyegāni (Isfahan: Markaz-e Taḥqiqāt-e Rāyāneh'i-ye Qāʾemiyeh, n.d.), 140–49.
16. Zarandi, *The Dawn-Breakers*, 415. Dates contradict in different sources. Zavvāreh'i writes that Qoddus's death was on the fourteenth of Nowruz (April 3) whereas Zarandi gives a later date. Based on Sotudeh, the event took place between September 1848 (Dhu al-Qaʿdeh 1264) and October 1849 (early Shawwal 1265) (Sotudeh, *Āstārā tā Astārabād*, 368). Zabihi-Moghaddam gives the dates September 1848 to May 1849 (Zabihi-Moghaddam, "The Babi-State Conflict," 96).
17. E. J. Hobsbawm, *Primitive Rebels* (New York: W. W. Norton, 1959), 1.
18. Hobsbawm, *Primitive Rebels*, 16.
19. Hobsbawm, *Primitive Rebels*, 16.
20. Hobsbawm, *Primitive Rebels*, 84.
21. Sotudeh, *Āstārā tā Astārabād*, 177; James B. Fraser, *Travels and Adventures in the Persian Provinces* (London: Longman, Rees, Orme, Brown, and Green, 1826), 85; Charles Philip Issawi, *The Economic History of Iran, 1800–1914* (Chicago: University of Chicago Press, 1971), 28; Alexandre Bohler, *Safarnāmeh-ye Bohler*, ed. ʿAli Akbar Khodāparast (Tehran: Enteshārāt-e Ṭus, 1977), 33.
22. James Baillie Fraser, *An Historical and Descriptive Account of Persia* (Edinburgh: Oliver & Boyd, Tweeddale Court; London: Simpkin & Marshall, 1834), 291–92; Issawi, *The Economic History of Iran*, 31–32, 130, 278. For more details, see Consul Abbott, *Cities & Trade: Consul Abbott on the Economy and Society of Iran 1847–1866*, ed. Abbas Amanat (London: Ithaca Press, 1983), 11, 31–33.
23. Zavvāreh'i, *Mimiyeh*, 33.
24. Ebrāhim, *Safarnāmeh-ye Astārābād*, 118; Bohler, *Safarnāmeh*, 33; Sotudeh, *Āstārā tā Astārabād*, 180.
25. Fraser, *Travels and Adventures*, 85.
26. Fraser, *Travels and Adventures*, 91–92. Fraser compares their practices and their mysterious circles with the ones of freemasons.
27. H. L. Rabino, *Mazandaran and Astarabad* (London: Luzac, 1928), 14.
28. Rabino, *Mazandaran*, 11.
29. Ebrāhim, *Safarnāmeh-ye Astārābād*, 117–18; Bohler, *Safarnāmeh*, 33; Sotudeh, *Āstārā tā Astārabād*, 179–80.
30. Issawi, *The Economic History of Iran*, 31–32.

31. Abbas Amanat, *Resurrection and Renewal: The Making of the Babi Movement in Iran, 1844–1850* (Ithaca, NY: Cornell University Press, 1989), 186.
32. For some information about these divisions, see John R. Perry, "Ḥaydari and Neʿmati," *Encyclopaedia Iranica*, XII/2, 70-73. For more information about Shaykhi/Oṣuli, see Todd Lawson, "Exegesis iv. In Akbari and Post-Safavid Esoteric Shiʿism," *Encyclopaedia Iranica*, IX/2, 123-25, https://www.iranicaonline.org/articles/exegesis-iv.
33. Amanat, *Resurrection and Renewal*, 182-86.
34. Māzandarāni, *Ẓohur al-Ḥaqq*, 286.
35. Rabino, *Mazandaran*, 14-15.
36. Naser al-Din Shah Qajar, *Ruznāmeh-ye Safar-e Māzandarān* (Tehran: Entesharāt-e Farhang-e Irān Zamin, 1977), 239, 247.
37. James C. Scott, *The Art of Not Being Governed* (New Haven, CT: Yale University Press, 2009), 6.
38. Scott, *The Art of Not Being Governed*, 6.
39. Scott, *The Art of Not Being Governed*, 6-7.
40. Ebrāhim, *Safarnāmeh-ye Astarābād*, 127-29.
41. Fraser, *Travels and Adventures*, 80.
42. Fraser, *Travels and Adventures*, 83-84.
43. James B. Fraser, *A Winter's Journey (Tâtar), from Constantinople to Tehran* (London: R. Bentley, 1838), 468-72.
44. Fraser, *A Winter's Journey*, 470-71; Rabino, *Mazandaran*, 8-9 (Rabino's book refers to page 48; it is 468.)
45. Qajar, *Safar-e Māzandarān*, 35-36.
46. Qajar, *Safar-e Māzandarān*, 39-41.
47. Qajar, *Safar-e Māzandarān*, 60-80, 124; Bohler, *Safarnāmeh*, 36.
48. Qajar, *Safar-e Māzandarān*, 229.
49. Fraser, *Travels and Adventures*, 80.
50. Bohler, *Safarnāmeh*, 35.
51. Jonas Hanway, *An Historical Account of the British Trade over the Caspian Sea*, vol. 1 (London: Dodsley, 1753), 284. Mirza Ebrāhim mentions that there were no dense forests around Bārforush. This contradicts other sources: Ebrāhim, *Safarnāmeh-ye Astarābād*, 115.
52. Rabino, *Mazandaran*, 8; Fraser, *Travels and Adventures*, 80.
53. Fraser, *Travels and Adventures*, 80.
54. Fraser, *A Winter's Journey*, 468.
55. Rabino, *Mazandaran*, 4.
56. Rudi Matthee, "Firearms i. History," *Encyclopaedia Iranica*, IX/6, 619-28, https://iranicaonline.org/articles/firearms-i-history.
57. In some countries, like the United States, people would place a "cow's knee," a piece of leather covered by grease or wax, to protect the flintlock. There is not enough evidence to know if Iranians were using such covers.
58. Zarandi, *The Dawn-Breakers*, 361; Zavvāreh'i, *Mimiyeh*, 49.
59. Zavvāreh'i, *Mimiyeh*, 43-44.
60. ʿAbbās ʿAbdu'l-Bahá, *Maqāleh-ye Shakhsi Sayyāḥ* (Germany: Mo'asseseh-ye Maṭbuʿāt-e ʿAmri, n.d.), 20.

61. Māzandarānī, *Ẓohur al-Ḥaqq*, 293.

62. E. G. Browne, *A Year amongst the Persians* (London: Black, 1893), 565. What Sotudeh writes seems more likely: "There is no sign of the graves of the Bābis who were killed and buried in the area. Even Molla Ḥosayn's exact grave is not known. He asked his followers to bury him with clothes and gun in a hidden spot so that the Muslims could not find and exhume his body." Sotudeh, *Āstārā tā Astārabād*, 369.

63. Tabrizi, *Meftāḥ-e Bāb*, 141.

64. Zavvāreh'i, *Mimiyeh*, 44–46.

65. Tabrizi, *Meftāḥ-e Bāb*, 142; Sotudeh, *Āstārā tā Astārabād*, 368–69.

66. Tabrizi, *Meftāḥ-e Bāb*, 148. See also Zarandi, *The Dawn-Breakers*, 357–58; Māzandarānī, *Ẓohur al-Ḥaqq*, 293–94. De Gobineau describes the fortification very similarly to Tabrizi. He might have used the same source. Arthur comte de Gobineau, *Les religions et les philosophies dans l'Asie centrale* (Paris: Didier et cie, 1866), 189–90. Shoghi Effendi gives the translation of Gobineau's passage in a footnote of *The Dawn-Breakers*, 357–58.

67. Zarandi, *The Dawn-Breaker*, 349, 357–58. Zavvāreh'i, *Mimiyeh*, 45–46.

68. Amanat, *Resurrection and Renewal*, 181, 187; Ḥāji Mirza Jāni Kāshāni, *Noqtat al-Kāf* (Leiden: Brill, 1910), 199.

69. Hobsbawm, *Primitive Rebels*, 84.

70. Abbott, *Cities & Trade*, 19.

71. Abbott, *Cities & Trade*, 19.

72. Māzandarānī, *Ẓohur al-Ḥaqq*, 257.

73. See, for example, Qajar, *Safar-e Māzandarān*, 137, 147.

74. Zavvāreh'i, *Mimiyeh*, 45.

75. Sotudeh, *Āstārā tā Astārabād*, 368–69; Tabrizi, *Meftāḥ-e Bāb*, 141–42; Ebrāhim, *Safarnāmeh-ye Astarābād*, 126–27.

76. Hobsbawm, *Primitive Rebels*, 84; Zavvāreh'i, *Mimiyeh*, 45; Māzandarānī, *Ẓohur al-Ḥaqq*, 286.

77. Qajar, *Safar-e Māzandarān*, 230–31.

78. Māzandarānī, *Ẓohur al-Ḥaqq*, 294–95; Zavvāreh'i, *Mimiyeh*, 38–39. It is important to note that the first phase of Bābi settlement in the shrine was relatively calm and peaceful, allowing them to fortify the site and even allow their animals free range to graze outside its walls. Considering the number of the people in the fort, however, the sheep must have been great in number. Otherwise, the Bābis would have quickly consumed the milk and eventually the meat.

79. Zarandi, *The Dawn-Breaker*, 394–95; Māzandarānī, *Ẓohur al-Ḥaqq*, 348–49.

CHAPTER 10

The Custom of Customs
Licit and Illicit Crossings in the Caspian Sea, 1864–1917
Rustin Zarkar

In July 1838, a new Russian ship sailed into the harbor near Bibiheybat, off the coast of Baku in the Caspian Sea. The ship, named the *Martha*, was assigned to the Baku Customs Department for the purpose of patrolling the western coast of the Caspian Sea. The department was established just two decades earlier to inspect caravans crossing the Iranian-Russian border in the South Caucasus, and now the officials, who had no previous experience working on the water, were responsible for sailing over four hundred miles to check merchant ships and circumvent smugglers of undeclared and prohibited goods.[1]

By 1842, the *Martha* was in poor condition, with damage to both its starboard and portside, a rotting cargo hold, and massive leakage from the hull.[2] When the minister of finance asked the governor of Transcaucasia whether funds should be used to repair the *Martha*, the governor wrote that there had only been seven reported instances of smuggling in the region during the ship's active service, and that he believed the costs of repairing and maintaining the ship would be more than the amount lost through circumvented tariffs.[3] Consequently, the *Martha* was sold at public auction in 1844 to recuperate some of the department's financial losses.[4]

CHAPTER 10

Within fifty years of the *Martha* incident, however, the volume and type of smuggling in the Caspian Sea had drastically changed. On December 11, 1896, the head of the Baku Customs Department, R. Danilovich, wrote a secret report to the Petrovsk Customs Department (present-day Makhachkala, Dagestan) that rose significant alarm. Baku officials discovered thirty-eight individual cases of gunrunning in just under three months. They intercepted 327 Berdan rifles, 129 revolvers, and hundreds of thousands of ammunition cartridges, which were packed in boxes, trunks, and barrels hidden on ships sailing from Baku and Petrovsk. The officials surmised that the dangerous cargo was headed to Astrakhan, up the Volga River to Nizhny Novgorod, and finally to Moscow.[5] How did the Caspian transform from a seemingly quiet border zone to a hotbed of smuggling and banditry? How were smugglers able to move so much illicit material under the eyes of the Customs Department and in what ways did the tsarist bureaucracy attempt to control these threats to internal and regional stability?

From 1809 until the 1880s, the primary objective of the customs staff in the Caspian region was to ensure a protectionist economic policy that would encourage Russian manufactured exports in Asia. High tariffs for non-Russian subjects, prohibitions of certain items, and demands for luxury items such as silk and tea engendered an informal market conducted through maritime smuggling. In response, the Customs Departments familiarized themselves with the geography of the area, identified potential smuggling sites, and established friendly relations with local elites. By the end of the nineteenth century, however, new transportation technologies facilitated and regularized movement for people in the region from all walks of life, and radical ideas about the state of society led to bouts of unrest and political violence. Customs Departments that were trained to monitor maritime trade in the Caspian were now forced to reckon with new forms of contraband in Baku, Petrovsk, Krasnovodsk, and Astrakhan: firearms, subversive literature, and dangerous revolutionaries.

Using customs documents housed at Central State Archive of the Republic of Dagestan in Makhachkala and the Russian State Historical Archive in Saint Petersburg, this chapter highlights the institutional history of the tsarist Transcaucasian and Transcaspian Customs Departments in their attempts to prevent smuggling in and around the Caspian.[6] By examining the customs documents, one can identify various sources of bureaucratic anxiety and the challenges of day-to-day governance, which are seemingly overlooked in the narrative of tsarist state centralization in the Caspian region. The documents elucidate the rough and porous nature of Russian governance in the sea and how smugglers exploited these deficiencies over the course of the nineteenth and early twentieth centuries. The Russian state adapted to the new flow of contraband, but only incompletely and ineffectively.

Historical Context: Russian Customs Policy and State Formation

While tariffs, duty collection, and trade prohibitions have a long history in Russia and Eurasia, customs as a bureaucratic institution emerge out of larger processes of modern state formation.[7] According to anthropologist Brenda Chalfin, customs authority is a key component of statehood and depends on a "professional and publicly employed bureaucracy" and "the capacity of the state to seek revenue via means that are codified, legitimate, and enforceable."[8] Customs regimes territorialize space by demarking border zones and advance the state's economic and security interests within those zones by regulating human mobility and the circulation of material goods.[9] In tsarist Russia, the development of a modern and bureaucratic customs administration developed unevenly across its imperial frontiers.

Historically, customs regimes functioned differently in the Caspian region than in Russia's European borderlands. Before the 1650s, trade in Muscovy was an arduous and complicated endeavor. In addition to an extensive customs code, there were over seventy different internal customs zones that put tremendous financial strain on any merchant moving goods through different parts of the tsardom.[10] After dissatisfied Muscovite merchants protested both the complex system as well as the power and privileges afforded to foreign traders, the Commercial Code of 1653 (*Torgovy ustav*) was introduced. This charter abolished some extraneous internal customs duties, adopted uniform weights and measures, and established a tariff of 6 percent for non-Russian subjects operating outside the port of Arkhangelsk.[11] Protectionist policies were later extended in the New Commercial Code of 1667 (*Novotorgovyĭ ustav*). In the new charter, the ports of Arkhangelsk and Astrakhan were designated as special border towns beyond which foreign merchants needed special permission to conduct business.[12] Moreover, traders were subjected to increased inspections at ports, restrictions on where they could establish offices and residences, new quality controls, higher tariffs (21 percent versus the standard 5 percent for Russian merchants), as well as prohibitions on carrying certain items like precious metals and tobacco.[13]

These restrictions, however, were not applied equally to all foreigners, but heavily differentiated between European and Asian merchants. Europeans, who entered Muscovy from the port of Arkhangelsk on the White Sea, carried manufactured goods that were cheaper than locally produced items. Trade from Asia, on the other hand, was conducted through the port of Astrakhan on the Caspian Sea, and merchants from Iran, India, and Central Asia were encouraged as they primarily carried raw materials (cattle, cotton, raw leather, wool, and fruits) or luxury items (tea and silk), which were seen as less of a threat to the fledgling Russian manufacturing industry.

With the establishment of the Russian Empire under Tsar Peter I (r. 1682-1725), these mercantilist policies were expanded through several key trade statutes, laying the foundations for a modern customs administration in the Caspian region and across the empire at large. Peter I established the Commerce College, which created new customs offices that solely specialized in foreign trade. These offices were found at European border crossings and were staffed with full-time civil servants who received specific instructions and materials such as books, ledgers, and forms from the Russian Academy of Sciences.[14] The expansion of the customs service also coincided with new tariffs in 1724 that further increased duties for foreign merchants carrying luxury goods and prohibited European traders from transiting Russian territory in order to reach Asian markets (in an attempt to create a Russian monopoly).[15] This policy led to a deluge of contraband smuggling into Russia, and antismuggling procedures were implemented, such as the construction of border outposts and checkpoints, the creation of new stamps and letterheads for preventing document forgeries, and exacting harsh punishment for carrying contraband, including confiscation of goods, heavy fines, forced labor sentences, and even exile.[16]

This division between European and Asian customs regimes became more pronounced in the latter half of the eighteenth century. In 1755, Empress Elizaveta Petrovna (r. 1741-62) introduced a new customs charter, which attempted to strengthen the customs service in order to combat smuggling in Europe. Instead of lowering tariffs to discourage smuggling on the Polish border, customs patrols (*tamozhennyĭ ob"ezdchikov*) were formed, and new maritime inspection procedures were introduced for the Baltic Sea trade. This customs patrol continued to expand under the reign of Catherine II (r. 1762–96), as it was standardized into a full-time customs border guard in 1782.[17]

While customs policy in Europe was increasingly becoming regularized in the eighteenth century, Asian customs policy was much more ad hoc. As Russian armies gradually pushed southward in an attempt to pacify the steppe lands north of the Caspian Sea, customs districts were placed at major frontier forts like Kizilyar (1735) and Orenburg (1734) to monitor trade caravans and establish working relationships with local rulers for the purpose of securing safe passage for merchants. Consequently, customs houses in Asia such as Kizilyar, Astrakhan, and Orenburg gradually developed different customs rules and regulations in comparison to the European frontier, as they were able to determine their own tariffs on a case-by-case basis.

These negotiations with local rulers often resulted in much lower customs duties. For example, in March 1760, two Kizilyar customs officials wrote to the local commander in order to determine who is subject to the tariffs dictated by the 1755 decree described above. In the letter, the customs officials Zolner Tarumov and Pavel Sekachev state that the new rules have caused much anger and dissatisfaction among the Kabardian and Nogai people who cannot afford the high customs tax. They requested that the "petty trade" (*melkaĩa torgovlĩa*) of mountain and steppe peoples should not be subject to the same tariffs as the long-distance silk merchants.[18] The extension of duty-free trade for local merchants residing on the Caspian frontier seems to be common policy for much of the late eighteenth century, as evidenced by a 1765 statute that formally relieved Kabardians and Kumyks from paying duty fees.[19]

The imperial Russian customs system developed unevenly in different geographic areas. On the borderlands with Europe, Russian economic interests dictated a protectionist policy that would prevent high-quality European goods from outcompeting local-produced Russian ones. This policy inadvertently led to a boom in smuggling, which was met with antitrafficking measures that led to the bureaucratization of the Customs Department and securitization of the border. On the Caspian frontier, however, the customs regime relied heavily on local elites to facilitate the safety of long-distance trade and the viability of a market for Russian-made goods abroad. Consequently, the intense inspections, customs collection, and border surveillance that were introduced in Europe were either curtailed or not fully implemented in the Caucasus and Central Asia during the eighteenth century.

Establishing the Transcaucasian Customs Department (1809–1870)

Imperial Russian customs regimes regulating the flow of Asian goods entered a new period during the Russo-Persian Wars (1803-28). With territorial gains in the South Caucasus and its demonstration of naval supremacy in the Caspian Sea, the Russian customs service (governed from Tbilisi and Astrakhan) opened new customs offices in Tbilisi (1803) and Baku (1807), as well as smaller customs outposts across the newly acquired territory, such as at Derbent, Salyan, and Shirvan.[20] These offices were staffed with just a handful of personnel, with anywhere from six to fifteen people responsible for inspecting caravans, bookkeeping, and managing relationships with the local populace.[21] With such a fast-paced development of new customs institutions, dramatic steps were taken in order to better monitor and streamline the rules for Asian trade. In 1811, the Customs Department was officially transferred to the newly established Ministry of Finance, and it decided that a new series of laws and regulations were needed on Russia's southern frontier.[22]

On May 30, 1817, the new customs charter on "Asian Trade" was passed, which created a standardized "Asian tariff" across the southern frontier, the purpose of which was to remove excessive tariffs on raw materials from Iran, Central Asia, and China, while also creating incentives for the export of Russian industrial goods.[23] A year later, on January 1, 1818, a new law reorganized the customs areas into three divisions: Astrakhan (which included Baku), Orenburg (including the Siberian forts of Tobolsk and Tomsk), and Georgia (which included parts of the former Yerevan Khanate). Moreover, the 1818 law outlined the regulations for how merchants should register at customs outposts, the steps customs staff should take to place goods in (and release them from) quarantine, how vessels should load and unload their cargo once they arrive or leave port, as well as which goods are prohibited from being imported.[24] The 1817 and 1818 statutes were the first attempt for the Russian Empire to bring about the customs practices tested on the European border to the Caspian region.

Over subsequent decades, the customs policy in the Asian frontier region could be characterized by three main political and economic objectives: firstly, to promote a lucrative economic environment for Russian industry in Asia (a policy that, as described above, had dated back to the middle of the eighteenth century); secondly, to prohibit European goods from crossing the border into the South Caucasus; and finally, to placate foreign Persian, Central Asian, and Caucasian merchants with relatively low tariffs in order to prevent smuggling of contraband and to foster a positive image of the Russian Empire.[25] However these strategies produced mixed results and often contradicted one another.

For example, while the 1817 and 1818 tariffs (as well as the Treaty of Turkmenchay in 1828) attempted to decrease gratuitous tariffs on Persian, Caucasian, and Central Asian merchants, the disparity between Russian and non-Russian subjects (1 percent vs. 5 percent) incentivized a segment of the merchant community to avoid paying duties, either through declaring Russian subjecthood or by trafficking goods.[26] Moreover, the new 1831 tariff, which banned the import of all European goods traveling to Russian ports and prohibited the export of Russian weapons, shipping supplies, and copper coins, forced a large pool of items (roughly more than three hundred) into the informal market and were consequently smuggled across the border and through the ports of Baku and Astrakhan. Furthermore, three costly wars in the late 1820s forced the Customs Department to raise certain duties in order to refill state coffers, which once again led to a rise in smuggling throughout the 1830s and 1840s and a sharp decrease in customs revenue.[27]

To combat this chronic smuggling issue, the Astrakhan and Transcaucasian customs districts removed certain prohibitions on trade goods, reinforced the border guards and expanded their operations, and began maritime patrols. P. Chernushevich, the author of *Sluzhba v mirnoe vremia* (Service in peacetime), a history of the border guard corps published in 1900, wrote that the customs staff and border guards expanded their surveillance operations from the 1830s to the 1850s. They surveyed the Caspian coast near Astara and Lenkoran, demarcating estuaries that could possibly harbor smugglers and provide secret routes for trafficking. According to the Baku customs officials, one of the most high-frequency maritime routes started on the Iranian side of the city of Astara, where smugglers would load contraband onto small vessels. They would quickly sail to Kizil Agach Bay (roughly fifty kilometers north of Lenkoran), where they would either continue sailing upriver (if the winds were favorable) or hire pack animals to reach the town of Salyan and later Shamakhi.[28] For goods destined for Baku, ships originating from Iran were unloaded near the village of Pirsaat, where they were then to follow the coastal road until they reach the Absheron Peninsula.

To close down these smuggling routes, the Baku Customs Department sent additional border guard attachments to Salyan and the Pirsaat valley, but some officials advocated for intercepting smugglers on the sea rather than waiting until they unloaded on shore. In 1857, after documenting the major maritime lines used by smugglers, the border guard corps petitioned the Ministry of Finance for funds to construct naval vessels that would cruise along the Caspian coast and protect merchant shipping.[29] Additionally, the chief of the Transcaucasian Customs Department wrote to the governor of Transcaucasia to request that the Caspian Flotilla reintroduce maritime patrols in order to stop smugglers who had taken up positions on islands off the coast of Baku.[30] However, both of these requests were denied. Citing financial costs, the Caucasian commander-in-chief stated that naval policing had not successfully prevented smuggling, and therefore it should not be seriously considered.

Without a maritime antismuggling strategy, trafficking continued unabated for another decade. The Baku customs district raised the issue once again when smuggling cases could no longer be ignored, and they finally received a vessel in December 1869; however, the customs district was responsible for all costs related to its construction, planning, and maintenance.[31] These cases fueled the general grievances of the Baku district customs staff that they were constantly underfunded and understaffed in comparison to their European counterparts. It was not until 1879 that new customs regulations attempted to raise the Transcaucasian Customs Department to the same standards as on the European frontier (in terms of manpower and resources per square kilometer), though its implementation was only moderately successful.

Over the first three quarters of the nineteenth century, the customs operating in the Caspian region gradually transformed from a small contingent of far-flung customs outposts into four distinct districts equipped with full-time personnel, border guards, quarantine warehouses, and even ships for surveillance (in the case of Baku and Astrakhan districts). With the standardization of the Customs Departments along European lines, the Baku, Transcaucasian, and Astrakhan customs services were able to conduct their duties more efficiently. However, the expansion of the customs service in the Caspian also correlated with a rise of smuggling not just within the region, but also across all borders of the Russian Empire. According to historian E. V. Ereshko, from 1849 to 1885, there were 154,501 documented cases of smuggling, worth an amount of roughly 3,900,000 rubles.[32] While the majority of these cases were economic in nature, the last quarter of the nineteenth century witnessed the rise of politically sensitive contraband: prohibited items that were categorized as a threat to state security, such as weapons and subversive literature.

The same processes of state formation that aimed to strengthen the customs in the Caspian Sea were partially responsible for the evolving nature of smuggling in the middle and the late nineteenth century. In an attempt to consolidate political control in the Caspian basin, to facilitate foreign and domestic trade, and to fill the state treasury with duties, the imperial Russian state encouraged the building of private shipping either through local merchant ship-owners in Baku and Astrakhan, as well as large Russian-owned private firms such as the Kavkaz i Merkuriĭ steamship company (founded in 1849). Coupled with the establishment of other major transportation infrastructure projects in the region, such as the Transcaucasian railway (1865–83) and the Transcaspian railway (1879–1901), the Caspian region became increasingly interconnected, allowing goods, people, and postage to traverse the sea at unprecedented rates.

During this transformative period, the Baku customs staff adopted new strategies to counteract smuggling, which in turn led to new tactics being developed by smugglers. For much of the nineteenth century, smugglers attempted to avoid paying customs duties by traveling in secluded areas and circumventing customs outposts at the border. Consequently, a new method of border control was implemented, in which customs guards were organized into two separate lines. In the first line, sentries monitored the border on foot, while the second line consisted of mounted patrolmen who would intercept any smugglers who managed to evade detection by any means necessary—including violence; beyond the second line, the responsibility for apprehension of smugglers was transferred to the police department, allowing the customs agents to focus solely on the border zones.[33]

As a result, smugglers attempted to pass their contraband through the customs inspections undetected. On May 5, 1898, the head of the Baku Customs Department wrote that firing at smugglers at Astara had indeed discouraged them from crossing the border openly; the traffickers were now more likely to conceal their goods in the hopes that the inspectors might overlook them.[34] Using boxes and barrels with double bottoms, smugglers hid high-duty items such as tea, tobacco, and textiles in secret compartments. In other instances, they would hide such items among a large quantity of low-tariff goods like cotton fabric, nuts, and fresh fruit.[35] For example, in 1894, a merchant on the Iranian-Caucasus border attempted to smuggle rolls of silk by wrapping them with several inches of lower-duty cotton print. When confronted by the customs agents, the merchant asked for forgiveness and stated that he was unfamiliar with the complicated Russian tariff regulations.[36]

In order to preempt claims of ignorance, several legal statutes were amended to allow the Customs Department to punish perpetrators regardless of intent. In the 1885 Criminal and Correctional Penal Code and the Customs Charter of 1892, punishment for smuggling—heavy fines, confiscation, or imprisonment—would be imposed irrespective of the culprit's awareness of such activity.[37] Such legislation increased the cooperation between the Customs Department and the police, particularly when smugglers would refuse to pay their fines.[38]

As an industrial and economic center, Baku simultaneously became a major site for the international labor movement and the rising intelligentsia in Iran, the Caucasus, Central Asia, and Anatolia. The increased mobility highlighted above corresponded with a greater exchange of ideas and the emergence of new social and political movements, such as constitutionalism, nationalism, and social democracy. With the formation of radical circles calling for the end of absolutist rule across the region, revolutionaries took advantage of Caspian smuggling routes to circulate much-needed weapons, supplies, and propaganda for their clandestine activities. During this period, the Caucasus became an epicenter for political violence, and the Baku Customs Department worked diligently to combat the flow of political contraband from Iran and the Ottoman Empire.[39]

The conflict between the Ottoman state and Armenian nationalists became a major driver for the trafficking of political contraband. As early as 1895, the Baku customs staff stated that groups such as the Armenian Revolutionary Party (Dashnaktsutyun) smuggled weapons into eastern Anatolia.[40] As a result, the Baku Customs Department ordered its staff to thoroughly search all Armenians entering the Russian Empire, even those arriving from Iran.[41] While the Hamidian massacres (1894-96) instigated the flow of weapons, it had reached its zenith during the 1905 Russian Revolution and the Iranian Constitutional Revolution (1905-11). The conflict led to an increased demand for weaponry, and guns flowed in many directions: Russian revolutionaries received English- and German-made weapons from across the Polish border, while Persian and Armenian revolutionaries used merchant ships and tankers to deliver both foreign and Russian-made guns between Baku, Lenkoran, and Anzali.[42] Explosives were also moved through this illicit network, and on February 28, 1908, Ḥaydar Khan 'Amu-Oghlu Tāriverdi's Russian-made bombs were used in an unsuccessful assassination attempt against Moḥammad 'Ali Shah.[43] The Baku Customs Department increased security at each Caspian port and even levied additional fines and sentences on gunrunners, but these measures were not enough to impede the gun trade.[44]

The political events of the early 1900s demonstrated to the customs staff that the department was unable to stop the movement of undesirables in and out of the empire. The Baku Customs Department and the local police attempted to monitor mobility through a strict passport regime and the issuance of "wanted" circulars of known revolutionaries, criminals, and deportees, but this system was constantly undermined by bribes, forgeries, and operational constraints.[45] For example, after the 1903 Baku riots, the Russian Ministry of Foreign Affairs requested that the Iranian government stop issuing passports to Persian subjects en route to Baku; nevertheless, this did not deter many from crossing the border, and in fact it resulted in a loss of revenue for the Russian consulates in Iran that collected fees for passport registration.[46] The Baku customs staff resigned itself to the reality that if someone were adamant about crossing the border, they would eventually do so.[47]

Establishing a Customs Regime in the Transcaspian Borderlands (1894–1914)

The Transcaucasian Customs Department faced insurmountable challenges in controlling the flow of goods and people from Ottoman and Iranian lands, resulting in a seemingly constant evaluation and reevaluation of tactics, strategies, and norms over the course of the nineteenth century. Its counterpart on the eastern side of the Caspian littoral, the Transcaspian Customs Department, had similar growing pains, albeit they were condensed to a period of a decade as opposed to a century. Like the Baku and Petrovsk customs documents, reports from the Transcaspian Customs Department highlight the various sources of bureaucratic anxiety and the challenges of day-to-day governance as the advent of Russian rule established new legal systems, security apparatuses, and economic institutions that more formally regulated movement across the changing political and geographic frontier—smoothing out the "rough edges" between Iran and tsarist Central Asia.[48]

Throughout the nineteenth century, Russian armed divisions gradually made a southward push from the steppe, building fortification lines and bringing the khanates of Bukhara (1868), Kokand (1868), and Khiva (1873) under Russian suzerainty; the Karakum Desert and the Kopet Dag Mountains were the only areas in Central Asia not under direct or indirect Russian control.[49] In preparation for the Skobelev expedition to subjugate the Tekke Turkmens of the Akhal Oasis in 1880 and 1881, the tsarist military apparatus began planning the construction of the railway that would help maintain a consistent flow of supplies and equipment for the armed forces.[50] Other objectives included linking the major urban centers (such as Ashgabat, Marv, Charjew, Bukhara, Samarkand, and Tashkent) and cotton-producing regions of Central Asia to the Caspian Coast, facilitating trade with the Indian subcontinent, and "conquering the markets" of northern Iran.[51]

Constructed mostly by Turkmen and Persian laborers, the railroad had reached the cities of Ashgabat by November 1885 and Marv by February 1886, dramatically improving the speed and volume of trade to and from the cities in Iran and Afghanistan.[52] By 1889, the railway had already proven to be financially profitable, moving over 2,579,000 rubles of goods (which is approximately $34 million today). Collection responsibilities were originally given to tsarist garrisons. The first customs house was built at Uzun Ada in 1889, and collectors were also stationed along railway stops further inland.[53] By June 1894, all customs responsibilities were transferred from the Ministry of War to the Ministry of Finance, and the Transcaspian Customs Department was founded.[54]

According to the British Vice-Consul Ringler Thomson in Mashhad in May 1895, the staff of the Customs Department was brought from other parts of the empire and consisted of the head of customs, "2 brigadiers, 2 senior orderly officers, 9 stations chiefs, 2 doctors, 9 dressers, 21 border guards, and 2 transportable orthodox churches with a chaplain and chanter"; 298 mounted men and 472 Turkmen tribal warriors also provided additional supervision of convoys.[55] Customs houses were built in the major urban centers along railroads mentioned earlier, as well as in smaller outposts near the border areas such as in Dushak, Serakhs, and Chikishlyar.

As soon as the department was operational in February 1895, the officials clearly realized that they were facing insurmountable challenges. The opening of the customs houses and the dispatching of border guards funneled the flow of goods—which had previously been dispersed all across the unregulated border—to specific roads and urban centers. This increase in traffic put additional stress on the small number of customs agents who already had difficulty inspecting two hundred to three hundred camel caravans that could stretch for more than two to four kilometers.[56] Consequently, certain outposts like those in Ashgabat and Dushak scrambled to conduct their operations in a timely manner while others such as Yoloten were left completely idle with almost no declarations over the course of a year.[57]

Additionally, the customs houses were located hundreds of kilometers from one another, making communication among the station chiefs and the allocation of resources incredibly difficult. With the vast expanse between customs houses and outposts (particularly with those located away from the railroad), it was nearly impossible for the head of the department to examine the various sites and determine the status of the customs houses.[58] The department was forced to request additional revenue and staff from the Ministry of Finance, but until those resources arrived, the agents were forced to make do by traveling to different customs houses, working long hours, doubling up on responsibilities, and relying more on the local population to carry out convoy inspection and man border outposts.[59]

The customs agents often complained about their plight to the head of the department. Letters were written describing food shortages and lack of water and medical supplies; many station chiefs exclaimed that the conditions they faced were akin to some form of punishment or exile.[60] These physical and psychological stresses greatly decreased the productivity of the customs houses. The agents reported that they were constantly sick and frequently requested leave so they could return to their families. Unfortunately, the majority of these requests were declined, as the Customs Department did not have enough money to cover their travel allowances or that of replacement staff.[61]

When the agents were healthy enough to carry out their responsibilities, they realized that it was quite challenging to convey the social practice of customs to the local population. According to the customs director, there was a stark contrast between the way trade was carried out in the western borderlands in Central Europe and what they encountered in Transcaspia. On Russia's western border, all European merchants carry detailed papers stating their identity, the types and number of products they carry, as well as affidavits from other customs houses along the trade route. Persian and Afghan merchants, however, often did not carry passports, were unfamiliar with the latest customs tariffs, and could barely speak or read enough Russian to understand the details of the stamps issued to them.[62] As a result, many disputes occurred between the Customs Department, border guards, and foreign merchants.

Initially, border guards and customs agents strictly enforced the new regimes of paper, confiscating any products that had not been declared once inside Transcaspian territory. For example, in one instance in August 1895, a Persian merchant who had bought goods in Marv was arrested in Tesh-Kepri for not carrying papers; he was then sent to Takhte-Bazar where he was fined, forced to show receipts for the goods he carried, and then interrogated about his identity before being released.[63] In another instance, a Saryk Turkmen merchant who was unable to speak Russian or Persian was forced to travel more than fifty kilometers to the nearest customs house to obtain a certificate to authorize his trade.[64] These cases of arrests and heavy fines caused much anxiety among the merchants, and for a time, it discouraged traders from declaring goods and even prevented many of them from entering the Transcaspian oblast entirely.

Concerned about the reduction in trade, the head of customs wrote to the Ministry of Finance that the department must be more accommodating and flexible toward the local traders, until they are able to familiarize themselves with the customs rules. In order to facilitate this, the department relaxed the inspections at interior offices further from the border. Additionally, they ordered several Turkmen *jigit* to accompany each caravan convoy and provide the merchants with security and translation.[65] The employment of these warriors, however, created a new set of troubles for the department.

In the department reports for the Ministry of Finance, there were multiple complaints from Persian merchants concerning their treatment at the hands of the Turkmen *jigit*. With the establishment of the Iranian-Turkmen border convention of 1881, various Turkmens found themselves in the service of the Russian military. The Persian inhabitants of Khorasan and the Turkmen tribes, however, previously had an antagonistic relationship, as Turkmen raiders often encroached upon cities such as Mashhad, Quchan, and Astarabad in search of slaves, cattle, and agricultural products.[66] The Customs Department cites that Persian merchants often expressed distrust toward their convoy guards due to this history, and tensions also arose due to sectarian differences (with Persians adhering to Twelver Shi'ism and Turkmen following the Sunni tradition).[67]

In Takhte-Bazar, it was documented that three *jigit* named Darya Kula, Sagat, and Muhammad Juma were witnessed attacking a Khivan merchant with their swords, and then proceeded to whip two Afghan heralds outside of the town.[68] This event, along with others like it, stirred a debate among the agents about the usage of Turkmen troops for military purposes, as well as what legal avenues were available for addressing unsanctioned violence against merchants and trade. However, the Customs Department was apprehensive about completely abolishing Turkmen-led convoys, since the *jigit* served as a form of indigenous authority to build trust with the tribal populations and prevent them from returning to raiding.[69] It was finally decided that the Customs Department would continue using Turkmen for caravan convoys and border control, but the *jigit* were to be supervised by at least three Russian soldiers to prevent any perceived wrongdoing.[70]

As discussed earlier, the nascent border regime generated a new set of political and economic conditions for merchants, who tried to either adhere to, manipulate, or outright circumvent the new restrictions put in place. Over the course of the 1890s, the customs reports describe increasing numbers of Persian and Afghan merchants receiving the appropriate documentation for the importation of goods to Transcaspia, through registering for passports from their respective countries, utilizing personal bookkeeping, and even entering the Russian merchant guild system in order to bring goods further into the empire. As Persian and Afghan merchants became more established in the region, they soon began using official channels to petition the Customs Department to expand the list of goods allowed through the checkpoints, such as pistachios, gemstones, gold, and textiles.[71]

While many merchants observed the new customs regulations, the department's lack of staff and the desolate terrain made it incredibly easy for merchants to engage in smuggling. Along the mountain ranges to the south, Persian and Afghan merchants made use of less-traveled mountain passes to avoid the eyes of the border guards. Near the Caspian coastline, Yomut Turkmens from the Persian side of the border would sail shallow draft boats up the coast and bring tea, opium, and agricultural goods past the customs houses in Hasan Quli and Chikishlyar.[72] And even along the designated trade routes, merchants were able to creatively hide contraband such as green tea, opium, and gunpowder in the caravan. For example, an 1896 customs report states that smugglers often stuffed items under their saddle pillows, or hid them in carts filled with construction materials and women's clothing.[73]

Merchants of the Russian Empire were also guilty of engaging in unauthorized practices, like taking advantage of the Customs Department's issuance of excise taxes on Russian exports such as sugar, matches, kerosene, and textiles. Excise taxes (or a state-sanctioned financial reimbursement for specific exports) were often employed to offset transportation and storage costs. They also encouraged domestic merchants to keep their prices competitive in foreign markets. Frequently, Russian, Armenian, and Azerbaijani merchants would head to a customs house, collect their reimbursement, and rather than continuing to Persian and Afghan cities, immediately sneak back into Russian territory to sell their goods at higher prices. Another scheme described in the reports mentioned several merchants filling sugar bags with sand only to make a profit off of excise taxes. Throughout the 1890s, customs agents became increasingly aware of these tactics, but it was clear nothing could be done to curb smuggling. Even punitive measures could not be taken against smugglers, since these actions could potentially discourage law-abiding merchants and incense the local population.[74]

Through the examination of documents produced by the Transcaspian and Transcaucasian Customs Departments, this chapter traces the development of a new border regime that shaped economic and social relations of peoples across the Caspian region. At the beginning of the nineteenth century, tsarist customs policy toward the Caspian region was not formally defined, and less attention and fewer resources were given to monitoring movement in comparison to the European borderlands. Within a hundred years, however, Russian officials had determined that contraband fueled economic and political instability and sought to develop new strategies to circumscribe smuggling, albeit with limited success.

Tsarist customs agents were woefully overworked and lacked adequate supplies to accomplish the seemingly impossible task of monitoring the newly established border between Iran, Afghanistan, and the Ottoman Empire. Customs documents elucidate sources of bureaucratic anxiety and the challenges of day-to-day governance to tsarist statecraft and territoriality—anxieties that are seemingly overlooked in the discourse on Russian state centralization and the steady expansion of colonial administration in Central Asia and the Caucasus. Further research on the subject must take into account the various economic regimes on the other side of the border, particularly the Iranian and Afghan customs regimes that were also going through a period of transformation and standardization.

Notes

1. "April 23, No. 365," in P. Chernushevich, *Sluzhba v mirnoe vremīa* (Saint Petersburg, 1900), 189.
2. "October 29, 1842, No. 15832," in Chernushevich, *Sluzhba v mirnoe vremīa*, 191.
3. "June 23, 1843, No. 673," in Chernushevich, *Sluzhba v mirnoe vremīa*, 193.
4. "February 11, 1844, No. 335, Transcaucasian Customs District to the Department of Foreign Trade," in Chernushevich, *Sluzhba v mirnoe vremīa*, 192.
5. Tsentral'nyĭ gosudarstvennyĭ arkhiv Respubliki Dagestan (Central State Archive of the Republic of Dagestan) (hereafter TsGARD), f. 13, o. 1, d. 48, no. 38.
6. Over the last decade, several Russian-language dissertations have explored the history of customs regimes and foreign trade in Caspian Sea ports. This scholarship, however, tends to focus on economic goods and does not describe other forms of contraband as I have listed above. Moreover, these studies tend to focus on one city or customs district at a time, as opposed to a comprehensive customs regime in the Caspian region. Refer to Ėliza Musatovna Ozdamirova. "Vostochnoe kupechestvo v Russko-Aziatskoĭ torgovle cherez Astrakhan v pervoĭ polovine XIX veka" (PhD diss., Chechen State University, 2016); Aĭnura Mamed Gizi Mamedova, "Torgovo-tamozhennaīa politka tsarizma," v severom Azerbaĭdzhane v pervoĭ polovine XIX veka" (PhD diss., Baku State University, 2013); Bakhtiër Abdikhakimovich Alimdzhanov, "Ėkonomicheskaīa politika Rossiĭskoĭ imperii v Turkestanskom general-gubernatorstve (vtoraīa polovina XIX-nachalo XX VV)" (PhD diss., St. Petersburg State University, 2016).
7. The premodern history of customs in Russia was discussed in Konstantin Nikolaevich Lodyzhenskiĭ's *Istoriīa Russkogo tamozhennogo tarifa* [The history of the Russian customs tariff] (St. Petersburg: V. C. Balasheva, 1886).
8. Brenda Chalfin, "Global Customs Regimes and the Traffic in Sovereignty," *Current Anthropology* 47, no. 2 (2006): 247.
9. Pierre Lapradelle, *La frontière: Etude de droit international* (Paris: Les Editions Internationales, 1928).
10. For a detailed account of Russian customs bookkeeping in the seventeenth century and its gradual transformation during the 1700s, refer to V. G. Balkovaīa, "Organizatsiīa tamozhennogo deloproizvodstva v Rossiĭskoĭ imperii v XVIII veke," *Vestnik saratovskoĭ gosudarstvennoĭ īuridicheskoĭ akademii*, no. 5 (2012): 11–17.
11. *Polnoe sobranie zakonov Rossiĭskoĭ imperii, to i: c 1649 do 1675*, ed. Nikolai Pavlovich (St. Petersburg: Vtorogo otdeleniīa sobstvennoĭ ego imperatorskogo velichestva kantseliarii, 1830), vol. 1, 302.
12. Valentina Piliaeva, *Istoriīa tamozhennogo dela i tamozhennoĭ politiki Rossii* (Moscow: Litres, 2017), 136–37.
13. A. A. Timofeeva, *Istoriīa predprinimatel'stva v Rossii: uchebnoe posobie* (Moscow: Flinta, 2011); Lodyzhenskiĭ, *Istoriīa Russkogo tamozhennogo tarifa*, 33; *Polnoe sobranie zakonov Rossiĭskoĭ imperii*, 408.

14. Balkovaĭa, "Organizatsiĭa tamozhennogo deloproizvodstva v Rossiĭskoĭ imperii," 16.

15. Lodyzhenskiĭ, *Istoriĭa Russkogo tamozhennogo tarifa*, 34.

16. Lodyzhenskiĭ, *Istoriĭa Russkogo tamozhennogo tarifa*, 70–71.

17. "On issuing a general tariff for all ports and border customs offices of the Russian Empire, except Astrakhan, Orenburg, and Siberia, September 27, 1782," in O. I. Chistĭakov and T. E. Novitzkaĭa, *Zakaonodatel'stvo Ekaterini II*, vol. 2 (Moscow: Izd. ĭuridicheskaĭa literatura, 2001), 791.

18. "Report of the Kizilyar frontier customs to Kizilyar commandant I.L. Frauendorf," TsGARD, f. 379, o. 1, d. 468.

19. "Order of the Office of the Kizilyar commandant of the Kizilyar border customs to release Kabardians and Kumyks from duty fees, in accordance with the decree [of 1765]," TsGARD, f. 379, o. 1, d. 790, 59.

20. Mamedova, "Torgovo-tamozhennaĭa politka t͡sarizma," 34.

21. P. Y. Taran and B. V. Zmerzly, "Establishment and Activity of Customs Offices in Siberia, Far East and Middle East from the Second Half of the XVIII Century to Beginning of the XIX Century," *Uchenie zapiski tavricheskogo natsional'nogo universiteta im. V. I. Vernadskogo, seriĭa ĭuridicheskie nauka* 26, no. 2-1 (2013): 132.

22. *Vneshniaĭa politika Rosii (XIX–nachale XX vv.) dokumenti Rossiĭskogo MIDa*, vol. 7 (Moscow, 1970), 22.

23. According to the new tariffs, Russian-made exports would have a flat rate 1 percent duty on all goods, while there was a system of escalating duties for imports based on the degree of processing. E. A. Solonchenko, "Aziatskiĭ tarif i tamozhenii ustav 1817g. i popitki ikh peresmotra v pervoĭ polovine XIX V," *Vestnik OGU* 16, no. 35 (2013): 570–72.

24. *Polnoe sobranie zakonov Rossiĭskoĭ imperii c 1649*, ed. M. Speranskiĭ, vol. 35 (Moscow, 1830), 328–42.

25. V. Vitchevskiĭ, *Torgovaĭa, tamozhennaĭa i promyshlennaĭa politika Rossii co vremen Petra Velikogo do nashikh dnei* (St. Petersburg, 1909), 362.

26. *Polnoe sobranie zakonov Rossiĭskoĭ imperii c 1649*, "June 3rd, 1831, No. 4621 and 4622," vtoroe sobranie, vol. 6, 151.

27. Mamedova, "Torgovo-tamozhennaĭa politka t͡sarizma," 92.

28. Chernushevich, *Sluzhba v mirnoe vremĭa*, 231.

29. Chernushevich, *Sluzhba v mirnoe vremĭa*, 210.

30. Chernushevich, *Sluzhba v mirnoe vremĭa*, 210.

31. Chernushevich, *Sluzhba v mirnoe vremĭa*, 211.

32. These figures do not include cases from the Prussian-Russian border. E. V. Ereshko, "Rossiĭskoe zakonodatel'stvo kontsa XIX–nachala XX v.v. bor'be c kontrabandoĭ," *Istoricheskaĭa i sotsial'no-obrazovatel'naĭa misl'*, no. 3 (2011): 113.

33. Ereshko, "Rossiĭskoe zakonodatel'stvo kontsa XIX–nachala XX," 114.

34. TsGARD, f. 20, o. 1, d. 31, no. 24.

35. It was also common for merchants to label European goods as Persian- or Ottoman-made in order to avoid the prohibition. TsGARD, f. 13, o. 1, d. 1, no. 2.

36. TsGARD, f. 13, o. 1, d. 1, no. 1.

37. *Ulozhenie o nakazaniiakh ugolovnykh i ispravitel'nykh 1885 g.* (St. Petersburg, 1904), 757-58.
38. TsGARD, f. 20, o. 1, d. 31, no. 1.
39. For a description of the political groups operating the Caucasus at the turn of nineteenth century, refer to Anna Geifman, *Thou Shalt Kill: Revolutionary Terrorism in Russia, 1894–1917* (Princeton, NJ: Princeton University Press, 1993).
40. TsGARD, f. 13, o. 1, d. 48, no. 38.
41. TsGARD, f. 15, o. 1, d. 48, no. 24.
42. TsGARD, f. 13, o. 1, d. 66, no. 26.
43. According to tsarist customs officials, a shipment of bombs similar to the ones used in the February 28 attack was also discovered in Anzali. TsGARD, f. 20, o. 1, d. 4, no. 8.
44. TsGARD, f. 20, o. 1, d. 39, no. 15.
45. TsGARD, f. 20, o. 1, d. 31, no. 31.
46. TsGARD, f. 20, o. 1, d. 39, no. 40.
47. TsGARD, f. 20, o. 1, d. 66, no. 47.
48. In their seminal article "Toward a Comparative History of Borderlands," Baud and Schendel highlight the life cycle of a borderland and explain the processes in which a state consolidates territory. Within this schematic timeline, our period in focus (1894-1914) could be categorized as an *adolescent borderland*, "where economic and social relations are already beginning to be confined by the existence of a new border regime, yet old networks have not yet disintegrated and still form powerful links across the border." Michiel Baud and Willem Van Schendel, "Toward a Comparative History of Borderlands," *Journal of World History* 8, no. 2 (1997): 214–15.
49. Adrienne Edgar, *Tribal Nation: The Making of Soviet Turkmenistan* (Princeton, NJ: Princeton University Press, 2006), 30.
50. Alex Marshall, *The Russian General Staff and Asia, 1800–1917* (London: Routledge, 2014), 3-5.
51. Rossiĭskiĭ Gosudarstvennyĭ Istoricheskiĭ Arkhiv (Russian State Historical Archive) (hereafter RGIA), f. 21. o. 7, d. 741, no. 302.
52. V. N. Fursov and V. N. Testov, "Vozvedenie i funktsionirovanie transkaspiĭskoĭ magistrali v 80-x-nachale 90-x gg. XIX V," *Nauch'ie vedomosti BelGU ser. istoriia, politologiia. ėkonomika, informatika* 15, no. 27 (2013): 113–18.
53. "Arrangements for Collection of Customs Duties in the Transcaspian Region," *Board of Trade Journal*, July–December 1889, 625-26.
54. *Diplomatic and Consular Reports, Annual Series*, "No. 1607, Persia: Report on the Trade and Commerce of Khorasan for the Financial Year 1894-95" (London: H. M. Stationery Office, 1895), 1–5.
55. *Diplomatic and Consular Reports*, 3–5.
56. RGIA, f. 21, o. 7, d. 743, no. 143.
57. RGIA, f. 21, o. 7, d. 741, nos. 111–12.
58. RGIA, f. 21, o. 1, d. 330, no. 612.
59. RGIA, f. 21, o. 7, d. 743, no. 146.
60. RGIA, f. 21, o. 7. d. 741, nos. 1–20; RGIA, f. 21, o. 7, d. 743, no. 186.
61. RGIA, f. 21. o. 1, d. 743, no. 186.

62. RGIA, f. 21, o. 1, d. 331, no. 86.
63. RGIA, f. 1278, o. 7, d. 315, nos. 53–55.
64. RGIA, f. 1278, o. 7, d. 315, no. 62.
65. RGIA, f. 21, o. 1, d. 409, no. 82.
66. Moritz Deutschmann, *Iran and Russian Imperialism: The Ideal Anarchists, 1800–1914* (New York: Routledge, 2016), 67.
67. RGIA, f. 1278, o. 7, d. 315, no. 80.
68. RGIA, f. 1278, o. 7, d. 315, no. 68.
69. RGIA, f. 1278, o. 7, d. 315, no. 68.
70. RGIA, f. 21, o. 1, d. 409, no. 82.
71. RGIA, f. 21, o. 1, d. 409, no. 143.
72. RGIA, f. 21, o. 1, d. 329, no. 3.
73. RGIA, f. 21, o. 1, d. 329, no. 3.
74. RGIA, f. 21, o. 1, d. 329, no. 3.

CHAPTER 11

The Transcaspian Railroad in the Works of Nikolaĭ Karazin, 1842-1908

Elena Andreeva

Located on the border between Asia and Europe, the Caspian Sea and surrounding areas have long played a role as a crucible of cultures, which have clashed and fused there since antiquity. Prime among these is Russia, whose contacts with Iran possibly date to the ninth century.[1] Russia's conquests and domination, starting in the time of Peter the Great (r. 1682-1725) and escalating in modern times, played a prominent role in the history of the Caspian area. Russia's expansion into the Caucasus in the first half of the nineteenth century, and into Central Asia in the second half of the same century, opened a new era in the history of the Caspian region— the era of heavy Russian presence. The Caspian region thus figured prominently in the works of Nikolaĭ Karazin (1842-1908), who was a talented and popular Russian painter, writer, journalist, book illustrator, war correspondent, traveler, and ethnographer. At the same time, he was a soldier who participated in the Russian military campaigns in Central Asia—and later in its exploration—during the second half of the nineteenth century. This chapter examines his artistic images of the Transcaspian railroad and his understanding of the role the railroad played in incorporating the region east of the Caspian (Transcaspia) into the Russian Empire.

CHAPTER 11

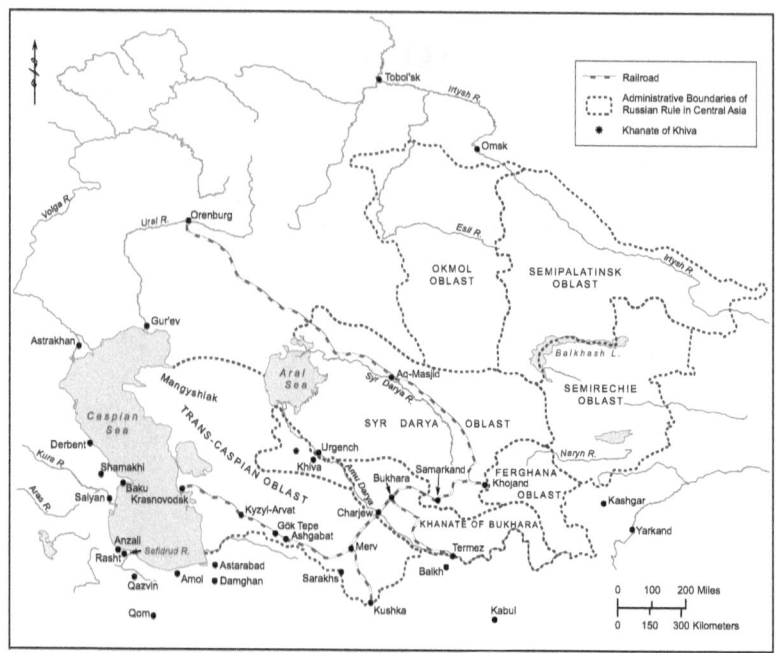

FIGURE 11.1. Western Turkestan under Russian rule, end of the nineteenth and beginning of the twentieth centuries. Adapted by Gordie Thompson, Castle Time Mapping, from the map in Yuri Bregel, *An Historical Atlas of Central Asia* (Leiden: Brill, 2003), 91. Used by permission of the estate of Yuri Bregel.

Russia's expansion into Central Asia occupied an important place in Russia's political and cultural life in the second half of the nineteenth century. The Russians "were anxious to obtain a secure frontier on the steppe, which would maintain imperial prestige and prevent the disruption of trade routes by the Kazakhs."[2] Their attempt to find a stable and "natural" frontier was also motivated by desire to "garrison their troops and safely defend their soldiers and their subjects."[3] At the same time, Russian policies in Asia were directly connected with those in western Europe. By the middle of the nineteenth century, Russia's internal weakness resulted in its falling more and more behind western Europe in technological and military developments. Diplomatic failures in Europe were followed by a humiliating defeat in the Crimean War (1853-56). Russia's international prestige in Europe (which had been significant after the defeat of Napoleonic France) plummeted, and its role in European politics was dramatically reduced. As a result, Russia's policies toward Central Asia and the Far East, as well as its aggressive policy in Iran, gained in significance. To compensate for the blow to the prestige of the ruling elite, including the military leaders, Russia tried to catch up with its European rivals by imperialist expansion into Central and East Asia.

Russian military operations against the Central Asian khanates began in 1864, with Tashkent falling in 1865. In July 1867, General Konstantin Petrovich von Kaufman was appointed the governor-general of Turkestan, a newly formed unit. It was under Kaufman's command that Nikolaĭ Karazin participated in the 1868 military campaigns against the forces of Bukhara. Kaufman would become Karazin's hero and patron for several decades to come. In 1873, Russian troops led by Kaufman captured Khiva, followed by the annexation of huge territories to Russia.[4] After several military campaigns, Kokand was annexed to Russia in February 1876.[5] Transcaspia, populated mainly by Turkmens, was next to fall to the Russians. The city of Krasnovodsk, which had been established on the eastern shore of the Caspian Sea in 1869, became the main base for the operations. Russian advances led to resentment among the Turkmens, whose raids were now followed by Russian punitive expeditions.

Karazin spent a total of more than ten years in Turkestan, and his extensive experience of Central Asia and his lifelong passion for the area and its peoples illuminated his visual and literary works. Mainly unknown to the modern Western public,[6] he was the winner of multiple credits and awards during his lifetime and an immensely popular and prolific artist. He created around four thousand drawings and watercolors, around one hundred paintings, and illustrated dozens of books.[7] A complete collection of his literary works, ranging from novels to short stories, essays and travelogues, consists of twenty-five volumes. In the era when Central Asia was experienced by Russians firsthand and incorporated into mainstream Russian culture as its internal Orient, Karazin was among the very first artists who introduced Central Asia to the general Russian public, providing a prism through which they looked at Russia's new frontier society. During this period of time, the routine use of photography for purposes other than portraits was still in its infancy.[8] Hence Karazin's keen eye for observation, passion for details, and extraordinarily skilled and vivid images—and the combination of different media he employs—provide rich ethnographic, geographic, and topographic details in an easily digestible form.

Karazin's art, filtered through the lens of a benevolent participant in the Russian imperial conquest and colonization, aspired to offer a realistic reflection of Central Asia, but was simultaneously very much a part of several colonial projects of his time. His art about Turkestan clearly demonstrates the "dynamic exchange" between individual writers and the processes of empire building, with culture serving as a theatre or even a battleground for "various political and ideological causes."[9] Since Russia proper was closely connected to its non-Russian territories, Russians were strongly affected by the territories they ruled,[10] and it was mainly the relationship to the southern and eastern margins of the empire that formed the "Russian national identity as expressed in literature."[11] As Russians aspired to prove their Europeanness to themselves and their west European counterparts, the conquest of Central Asia and construction of the Transcaspian Railroad there were to serve as a symbol of Russia's success as a colonial empire bringing technological progress and the light of civilization to the previously barbaric areas. To Russians and western Europeans, the railroad in the nineteenth century was a powerful symbol of technological progress, colonial power, and the superiority of the West.[12]

The idea of constructing a railroad in Transcaspia first emerged after the failed campaign under General Mikhaïl Pavlovich Lomakin against the Turkmens in 1879; the newly appointed General Mikhaïl Dmitrievich Skobelev "made construction of a railroad from the Caspian to the borders of the oasis conditio sine qua non" in order to assist the military advance and secure supplies.[13] In his detailed article dedicated to the railroad and his trip along it in 1888, Lord G. Curzon explains that since one of the main causes of failure in the earlier campaigns had been "the scarcity and sacrifice of transport animals [camels]," it was suggested to Skobelev to build a "light line of railway from his base on the Caspian."[14] General Mikhaïl Nikolaevich Annenkov, who had much experience in military transport in the Turkish war, was summoned by Skobelev "and recommended the use of 100 miles of steel rails." A special railway battalion was recruited in Russia, with the unskilled labor performed by Iranian and Turkmen workers; and though Skobelev at first looked at the railroad project as only an accessory means of transport, "yet the work was steadily and efficaciously persevered with by Annenkoff and his battalion." As a result, on January 24, 1881, Skobelev "carried the Turkoman fortress of Gök Tepe by storm, and drowned all further resistance in blood."[15] As the railroad construction went on, so did the conquest of the rest of Transcaspia. A few days after the fall of Gök Tepe, a force under Colonel A. N. Kuropatkin captured Ashkhabad. In May 1881, Transcaspia was declared an *oblast'* of the empire. The capture of Merv in 1884 and the annexation of Kushka taken from Afghanistan in 1885 almost erupted into open warfare with Great Britain, but the Pamir Treaty of 1885 between the two empires stopped further Russian advances in this direction and settled the Afghan boundaries.[16] The Transcaspian area was initially under the rule of the Caucasian administration, but in 1897 was added to Turkestan.[17]

The railroad was initially called the Transcaspian Military Railroad since military and strategic priorities defined the railroad construction in the first place: instead of building a direct connection across an easy steppe from Orenburg to Tashkent, the first line started from the shores of the Caspian across extremely hostile desert, so that sea water and naphtha had to be sprayed on the sand to turn it into a steady trackbed. The initial line was built quickly, reaching Kyzyl-Arvat, Ashkhabad, and Merv, with a branch connecting a barren oasis of Kushka on the Afghan border; none of those places had any commercial significance. Only in 1888 did the Transcaspian railroad reach Samarkand; it reached Tashkent by the end of the century. The Orenburg-Tashkent railroad opened in 1906.[18] The line was on a five-foot gauge, with the rails of steel laid upon wooden sleepers. The line was a single one everywhere except at the stations where sidings or triangles were laid for an engine to reverse.[19] It was built incredibly fast—its first section, twenty-six kilometers long, was built in ten days. Trains running on the just finished railroad sections transported rails, sleepers, and other materials, including water. As new sections of the railroad and new stations were being opened, officers and privates from the engineering battalions were assigned positions there.[20] Similar to the military administration set up in Turkestan, the railroad also had the "strikingly military *personnel*," with the bulk of the staff, including engine drivers, station masters, guards, conductors, ticket collectors, pointsmen, and telegraph and post office clerks, composed of soldiers and officers. Civilians were employed mainly as engineers and architects.[21] Karazin sketched an Iranian railroad guard: alert and serious, he is standing next to the railroad tracks.[22]

The idea of constructing a railroad in the newly conquered areas was by no means limited to Transcaspia. It would open a new era of communication between the metropole and the new colonies. Kaufman, trained as a military engineer, had recognized the significance of a railway connection between the metropole and Tashkent for both military security and economic integration from the earliest days of his administration. Already in 1879, Nikolaĭ Karazin had returned to Central Asia as part of a scholarly expedition, known as "Samarskaĭa uchënaĭa ėkspeditsiĭa"

(Samara Scholarly Expedition), charged with exploring the basin of the Amu-Darya and potential directions for the future railroad. As the expedition explored the Karakum and Kyzylkum Deserts, they found that the deserts, especially in the Aral area, were not impenetrable but were rather rich with flora and water, and therefore were suitable for railroad construction. Assigned the duties of the expedition secretary, Karazin was charged with studying the everyday life of the local population and writing a detailed description of the expedition's journey. At the beginning of his description, he explains the significance of a railroad: "God willing, in the nearest future [with this railroad] we shall reliably connect our rich, vast, politically and economically important new acquisitions in Central Asia to the border of Europe, Orenburg."[23]

Karazin's pride in the railroad was far from unique: his contemporaries saw it as an important sign of Russia's advancement as a "civilized" empire on a par with her western European competitors, mainly the British. According A. I. Rodzevich, a correspondent of the newspaper *Russkie Vedomosti* and an agent of the Severnoe Telegrafnoe Agentstvo (Northern Telegraph Agency) in Transcaspia, who dedicated a book to the railroad, "all our abovementioned acquisitions [Central Asia, Persia, Afghanistan, and India] would not have had such a significance if the combination of the accomplishments of bayonets-bullets and elaborate diplomacy in the remote East were not crowned with the iron crown of the Transcaspian railroad."[24] According to another book, also about the railroad, by another journalist and writer, Ivan Vatslik, "Construction of the Transcaspian railroad by the hands of Russian warriors weaves a new leaf into the laurels bestowed upon our army.... By construction of this railroad General Annenkov opened the most remote corners of the inhabited world to civilization."[25] Even Lord Curzon, the future British viceroy of India and no friend to the Russians, concludes his report on the railroad in the following way:

> In conclusion, I think I may add that no one here grudges Russia the advantages, political, military, or commercial ... provided she uses them fairly, and in interest of peace; on the contrary, we may join in congratulating her and General Annenkoff upon the successful execution of what ought, in sagacious hands, to become a powerful instrument of civilization, and an agent for the public good.[26]

Prior to the Russian conquest and construction of the railroad, the eastern shore of the Caspian Sea was considered dangerous: Turkmen nomads played a paramount role in the slave trade—as raiders, merchants, and slave owners.[27] In a number of his works, Karazin provides examples of brutal attacks, enslavement, and suffering. Parties of Turkmens both traded with the Russians arriving from Astrakhan on boats and captured them when possible. For example, a story and a drawing entitled *Dobycha s berega* (Loot from the shore) narrates such a catastrophic episode, when the whole Russian fishing boat crew were captured, and their boat looted and burned.

According to the man telling his story, the son of the boat's owner, he and his comrades suffered terribly on their march through the sands; out of thirteen men, seven died on the way, the rest were sold separately in Chimbaĭ. They were never to meet again. His father died in slavery; his wife Maria who had been with him on the boat "got herself employed as a wife of a mullah near Khiva and produced a number of dark kids." The man himself grew old in slavery, endured beatings and other hardships, and was finally freed when the Russians conquered Khiva (1873). The concluding paragraph of the essay proclaims: "only now, when the Russian troops have occupied this region, when in Mangyshlak and

FIGURE 11.2. Nikolaĭ Karazin, *Dobycha s berega*, 1876. *Niva* 16 (1876): 275.

Krasnovodsk permanent fortifications have been built, in order to guard the peace in dead Ust'-I̐urt, we can hope that such episodes will happen less and less often, and possibly will stop altogether; that the steppe wind and the green sea wave will cover with sand and wash away the last traces of the bloody deeds of the desert knights."[28] Additionally, political stability and improved transportation brought by the Russian conquest opened Turkestan to Russian settlers. Driven by land shortages, uncertain harvests in the north, and the hope of finding fertile, welcoming lands, settlers took the land route south from Orenburg—in the 1890s, the Transcaspian railroad opened a safer, but more costly, route.[29] The local people would refer to the railroads as *shaĭtanlyk* (devil's tricks/devildom), according to the artist, which would not prevent them from taking advantage of the benefits they offered.[30]

Nikolaĭ Karazin was invited as a guest to the opening of the railroad in 1888. He traveled along it and reflected its history in a travelogue titled "Na puti v Indii̐u" (On the way to India) and the beautiful large-sized watercolor album *Zakaspii̐skai̐a zheleznai̐a doroga* (The Transcaspian railroad).[31] His travelogue's title refers to India because the artist proceeded to travel to India after his trip along the Transcaspian railroad and also, as he explains, "because the new railroad constitutes one of the most important and difficult links of this way, by history itself meant for closeness and spiritual renewal of two worlds—European culture and the main culture of the ancient Orient."[32] This was the artist's last trip to his beloved Turkestan. In 1888, the entire journey of nine hundred miles from the Caspian to Samarkand without a break would take seventy-two hours. There were sixty-one stations in all, "varying from substantial structures in brick and stone to dingy wooden shanties half buried in the sand."[33] The "rolling stock" consisted of 100 to 150 locomotives and from 1,500 to 2,000 wagons. Passenger traffic, "of purely secondary consideration," did not offer first-class carriages, but "a limited number of excellent second-class carriages," with the cost of a second-class ticket from the Caspian to Samarkand being 38 rubles or 3.16 British pounds. Along some segments of the railroad, a speed of thirty to forty miles per hour could be attained, though the average speed to be expected was around twelve to fifteen miles per hour.[34]

The cover of Nikolaĭ Karazin's watercolor album summarizes his message about the Transcaspian railroad: it is a highly decorative combination of easily recognizable symbols.[35] In the center, we see a steam engine with smoke coming out of its pipe, with the name of the new railroad and the date of its opening inscribed on it. On the engine rests a two-headed eagle, alert and looking around, with the imperial crown suspended in the blue sky above both his crowned heads. The engine is also decorated with Russian military flags and banners and is guarded by two "white shirts" (Russian soldiers), who are assisted by a local man with a rifle. In front of the steam engine, three local men are deeply engaged in studying a large book and are surrounded by "Oriental" paraphernalia: a water pipe, a traditional tea set, and a water jug. In the very front, rich "Oriental" fruits are displayed, including melons and grapes. A tiger with bare teeth but with a somewhat scared expression on his severe snout is looking on such an innovation from the reeds in the foreground. In the back, a ship is battling waves on the Caspian. It is hard to miss the message of the impressive Russian achievements in this old land that has its own merits to contribute: the scholarly wisdom of its people and the richness of its nature.

Both the album and the travelogue incorporate several paintings or drawings of different shape and size into larger panoramas—the style popular during Karazin's time that also seems to portend later eclectic forms, such as newsreels, TV, or social media. A steaming train makes its way surrounded by landscape, human dwellings, and figures of men and animals. Some buildings look European, including newly built train stations, and even fountains, while many others look local, including mosques, mud huts, and ruins. In the album, the artist used the exquisite combination of sand-yellow and sky-blue colors for the background with columns of smoke and steam, dark or light grey, clearly symbolizing technological progress. On one page, for example, a crowd of excited horsemen in colorful robes is surrounding a steam engine decorated with brightly colored banners.

"Na puti v Indiiu" is one of three travelogues authored by Karazin; his travelogues combined new modes of travel writing: imperial ethnography and the rise of the natural sciences that had originated in the eighteenth century.[36] The travelogue is a combination of four letters and drawings; many of these images later appeared in the watercolor album. The travelogue includes seven full pages of drawings, and there are also separate images accompanying the text. Though the black-and-white prints do not have the benefit of subtle watercolors, the masterful contrast of black, white, and grey produces pictures impressive in a different way. They also benefit from the accompanying detailed descriptions by the artist.

The artist proudly reports on his trip from Astrakhan to Samarkand, as he follows the progression of boats and the train, supplying information about the area, its flora and fauna, its people and history, especially the history of the Russian conquest. In a coincidence, he arrived in Astrakhan on a Volga steamboat named *Konstantin Kaufman* after his patron. From the Volga Delta, the passengers had to take a smaller boat to deliver them to the "nine feet" depth off the Caspian shore—the minimal depth required for seagoing ships. At the "nine feet," Karazin explains, one finds a whole "floating city, bustling with energy and feverish activities." Every ship company has its own allocated space, with huge barges anchored here. Karazin and his travel companions used "the biggest and richest [Russian] company in the East ... Kavkaz i Merkuriĭ." At the "nine feet" floating dock, they moved to a "colossal two-piped" ship *Imperator Aleksandr III*, which Iranian porters were loading with cargo. Karazin includes drawings of their boat approaching the "nine feet" and the Iranian porters, one of whom is carrying a concert piano on his back, an episode that impressed him immensely and that he mentioned in his description. He also included a drawing of the ship *Aleksandr III*, a vessel with a large wheel, two masts, and two pipes.[37] According to the author, the Caspian is a "very restless sea"—its rolling is much worse than the ocean's due to its relative shallowness and short waves. Open shores allow steppe winds to blow through and turn into dangerous sea storms.[38] They proceeded south to Petrovsk (modern Makhachkala), a city "dozing in expectation of railroad construction that will connect it to Vladikavkaz." After passing Derbent where they were unable to dock because of a strong wind, they sailed around the Absheron Peninsula and arrived in Baku.[39]

The narrative is illustrated with a view of Petrovsk from the sea, with several sailboats anchored by the shore, of the Absheron lighthouse also seen from the sea, and a small but vivid drawing of sailboats on the Caspian.[40] In Baku the travelers stayed for a day during which they were able to explore the "White City" with residential houses, shops, and markets, and the "Black City," the industrial part, "which quickly creates millionaires and equally quickly turns millionaires into poor beggars." They visited Balakhan (Balaxanı), located twelve versts away from Baku, where oil was extracted to be then processed in the "Black City." The author laments how much oil is being wasted, soaking the ground, spilling into the sea, and forming malodorous ponds on its shores: "this is predatory, obtuse, fidgety, lacking any calculations, and often senseless, inexcusable robbery with a pogrom of nature's gifts, which ... will in its time punish the predators with complete depletion of the resources."[41] This emotional outpouring sadly sounds rather modern

FIGURE 11.3. Nikolaĭ Karazin, *Vidy goroda Baku*, in "Na puti v Indiiu," 1888. *Niva* 37 (1888): 917.

today. The artist includes detailed drawings of Baku's busy docks and the oil drills in Balakhan.[42] After loading a huge cargo of sugar destined for Bukhara, *Aleksandr III* sailed off east toward the Uzun-Ada Bay, "the starting point of the new Transcaspian railroad, which has connected by rails the capital of Peter the Great with the ancient capital of great Tamerlane."[43] Karazin's album includes two paintings of large ships on the Caspian, one at daytime, another at night.[44] Uzun-Ada Bay with a broad sea bar in the center is pictured on an almost identical watercolor and a drawing: its docks are not very busy, most of the houses on the sand are of Russian style, with only several tents visible, and with a building that looks like a small domed church.[45] The line of the railroad starts here, though we cannot see the very beginning of it since the bar turns and has a hill. There are several railroad branches that stretch directly to the docks.

Nikolaĭ Karazin pictures the railroad as transforming the life of the area: the plain, "gloomy, swarming with robberies" in the past, now looks "comfortable and cultured," with "the smoke of well-being and

FIGURE 11.4. Nikolaĭ Karazin, *Uzun Ada*, in "Na puti v Indiiu," 1888. *Niva* 38 (1888): 940.

peace" rising from Turkmen felt tents. "Turkmens transition from their free predatory life to peaceful agriculture," the wheel "replacing the primitive way of transportation on pack animals"; all lead to cheerful prosperity.[46]

The collision of the old and the new constitutes one of the main themes of both the drawings and the paintings. This collision does not necessarily imply the exclusion of the old, but rather points toward the old yielding to the new. On one page of the watercolor album, several camels scatter away fearfully from the unfamiliar sight of the train, while others watch uncomprehendingly. Several travelogue drawings also picture camels and sheep next to trains.[47] Similar drawings contrasting camels and trains appeared in other works by the artist. For example, a drawing titled *Konkurenty* (Rivals) appeared in *Niva* in 1890. It was published with the following explanation:

> The scene observed by our talented correspondent can be often seen in our Asian steppes since the construction of the Transcaspian railroad. A half-unloaded caravan of camels is resting on both sides of the tracks; the camels and their guide are looking blankly at the approaching steam engine, whistling and puffing menacingly, as it pulls such a huge load behind it, that it puts even the biggest caravans out of competition. Two eagles soar in the transparent air of the desert, as if foreshadowing the approaching disappearance of the primitive trade relationship.[48]

According to a modern scholar, this popular drawing was likened to a propaganda poster glorifying the victory of technology over nature.[49]

Advantages of railroad bridges over boats is also demonstrated in Karazin's images. His train crossed three bridges on its way: across the Tejend, across the Murghab at Merv, and the longest one across the Amu-Darya at Charjew. The bridge over the Amu-Darya, whose bed "is constantly shifting and the channel has a tendency to move to the east," was built in four sections. It was constructed initially of wood, upon more than three thousand piles, driven together in clusters of five into the bed of the stream. Lord Curzon also reported that the level of the rails was about thirty feet above low and about five feet above high water. It took Curzon's train traveling in 1888 fifteen minutes to slowly cross the bridge. About two kilometers long, the bridge was constructed in 103 days.[50]

In his watercolor and on the drawing, Karazin shows the long line of the bridge over the vast stretch of water in the center, with a train crossing it: "On the long, elegant wooden bridge, thrown as a light thread over the four-*versta* river spreads, one train after another, wagons are stretching, loaded with various construction materials."[51] In the foreground, docked boats are pictured, including two brand new steamboats, *Tsar* and *Tsaritsa* (Tsarina), meant for sailing up the river to Kerki and even Kelif, and down the river to Petro-Aleksandrovsk.[52] In the watercolor, a rowing boat is also seen crossing the river, while in the drawing, it is a steamboat. In the painting, the dark line of the railroad separates the light blue of the sky and of the water and produces an impression of a horizontal axis of the painting. The drawing, however, seems to be dominated by the smokestacks from the train and the steamboats. The travelogue also includes a drawing of another bridge, over the Murghab river at Merv: the scale of the river and the bridge is much smaller.[53]

There are also several distinctive-looking "water trains" pictures by the artist: they deliver water from the springs in the Kopet Dag Mountains in wooden containers loaded on train platforms.[54] "Proximity of the mountains, located no more than eight versts from the railroad, provides railroad stations with excellent water flowing in the pipes under pressure. Most stations have fountains that spray water pretty high, with reservoirs around them," explains Karazin.[55] In his travelogue, he included images of the mountains and the train running in a narrow pass between mountain ridges on both sides.[56]

Similar to most Westerners experiencing the Orient, Karazin pictured Russian domination as the only remedy for the contemporary state of decay and backwardness of Central Asia as a place of bygone glory. Picturesque ruins appear in many of Karazin's works, including the watercolor album and the travelogue dedicated to the Transcaspian railroad. While his description of Ashkhabad is accompanied by the image of the ancient ruins of Anau, an old mosque "with exquisite majolica arabesques on its façade,"[57] the description of Merv includes a referral to the ruins of ancient Merv, Bairam-Ali, with the signs of rich and elaborate irrigation. On a drawing, immediately behind the dark ruin of Bairam-Ali, a cheerfully running train with a light cloud of steam can be seen.[58] "A train, speeding past these silent ruins, witnessing pages of the remote history of the Orient, presents a fantastic picture, especially at night," points out Karazin.[59] The "most amazing ruin" for him is the Sultan Sanjar mosque—its image is included in the travelogue and the album.[60] Its silhouetted ruin looks picturesque against a dramatically lit evening sky, and next to it, on a contrasting painting in light blue, yellow, and green colors, a train is steaming its way toward the viewer. A painting of another ruin, most likely of a citadel, is also placed next to a painting of a modern train station with smoke rising from a tall pipe.[61]

One interesting subject pictured by Karazin in the album, as well as in some other works, is *burlaki*, or rope pullers, on the Amu-Darya. In one of the album paintings, four skinny native men with muscular limbs, wearing hats and tattered shirts barely reaching their knees, are pulling at ropes as they walk on the shore next to the river.[62] Silhouettes of three or four other men are seen in the boat; two of them are pushing with poles. The drawing brings to mind the famous painting by Il'ia Repin, *Burlaki na Volge* (Barge Haulers on the Volga), depicting a large group of exhausted men in rugged clothes pulling a relatively large boat on another great river. Those local men who help to move boats up the river are also referred to as *kaikchi* (from *kaik* or *qāʾeq*, boat in Persian). The traditional role of the *kaikchi* was also being modernized by the railroad, according to the artist: men who can be described as "railroad *burlaki*" appear on a small watercolor. Four men are sitting on a small open handcar on two wheels: two in the front looking forward are most likely a Russian soldier and an officer. Two other men sitting behind them are looking back, at those who are pushing the car and toward the viewers. They are most likely local men and perhaps would take their turn pushing the car. The car is being pushed by two local men in similar red robes and high furry hats. They are leaning against the car as they are running on the rails. The car must be moving at a reasonable speed—the red flag on the car is flying in the corresponding direction.

Karazin describes several stations on his way, among them Kyzyl-Arvat, the main administrative station of the new road, with first-class workshops and the railroad manager residence: "the streets of the town are mostly paved, lighted at night with lanterns, and next to the station—even with electricity. Houses are very beautiful, carefully surrounded with gardens, [there are] superb Russian and native markets, where you can purchase everything necessary for life, a military club, infirmaries, and primary schools; and all that in some five-six years was generated by the cultured energy (*kul'turnaĩa energiia*), as if by a magic wand."[63] The accompanying drawing, similar to those in the railroad album, shows modern buildings next to the tracks, smoking tall pipes, and a Turkmen with his sheep.[64]

The artist then gives a fascinating and accurate description of the Bakharden underground lake located about one hundred kilometers west from Ashkhabad: "This underground realm of darkness and quiet presents a fantastic picture full of charming beauty, only disturbed by the repulsive squeak of multiple bats and their soundless flight."[65] This lake is depicted on several drawings,[66] and on one of the watercolors in the album: a dramatic black square in the center of the page, with several figures dimly lighted by the red flame of a torch. The traveler then proceeds to the Gök-Tepe station, where "the old Turkmen fort, the center of the Teke tribe, is standing—huge, square, surrounded by mud walls, half-washed away by rain, witness to the heroic defense of the Turkmen, who eventually were unable to resist the courage of the

FIGURE 11.5. Nikolaĭ Karazin, *Kyzyl-Arvat*, in "Na puti v Indiiu," *Niva* 38 (1888): 941.

FIGURE 11.6. Nikolaĭ Karazin, *Bokhardemskoe podzemnoe ozero*, *Niva* 39 (1888): 964.

attackers." Here the author, while referring to the storming of Gök-Tepe by Skobelev in 1881, demonstrates his ability to empathize with the defeated enemy, though he immediately notices "the gravemounds of our fallen heroes" next to the walls still carrying marks of the horrendous explosion and holes from artillery shells.[67] The message to the readers is that suffering on both sides is clearly lamentable, but the outcome is the benevolent transformation of the region from which the local people are benefiting as well.

Several stations later, the train arrives in Ashkhabad, the capital of the Transcaspian area and the main base of the Transcaspian army. Karazin's drawing presents the part of the city adjacent to the train station.[68] The author praises Ashkhabad's new buildings, workshops, fountains, pools, a church, and gardens as they all attest to its prosperity, but a monument to the fallen artillerists reminds the readers about the price of that prosperity. Marketplaces are bustling with business, and Armenians, Tatars, and Persians mainly trading here now, while in the past "they would not dare to even get close"—apparently because of the threat of the Turkmen raids.⁶⁹ In the album, the page dedicated to Ashkhabad includes paintings of the same part of the town, a Russian church, two military monuments including the one to the artillerists, and a colorful market scene. The next thriving city where the train stops is Merv, famed for its fertile soil, its abundance of water, and its position as an essential caravan trade center. Now all those treasures have been put to a proper use, according to the author:

> Currently the city (Russian Merv) is located on both banks of the Murgab River: on the right bank—the railroad and commercial section, on the left—administrative and military ones. The city has grown in three years—and has grown amazingly! When you look at these clean buildings, attractively hiding in the gardens, these markets bustling with life, trains going back and forth, cabmen, signs of shops and stores, you completely forget that very recently only half wild tents of barbarians were to be found here, and the lawlessness of knife and gallows was the only ruler.⁷⁰

The Russian Merv on the picture includes several European buildings and a tent next to the river, with a train approaching the bridge over it.⁷¹ The last town Karazin describes in this travelogue is the oasis of Charjew, the "Central Asian Chicago," with the temporary residence of the head of construction. The author talks excitedly about "boiling life" there, with crowds of workers and soldiers busy with construction, with hundreds of train cars moving loads of construction materials for the section of the railroad toward Samarkand. Similar to the other previously described town-stations, there are already new military barracks, a market, a social club, a restaurant, and even a "hotel" with numbered tents for visitors. Fresh water, an abundance of shade, and agricultural produce in Charjew "make life tolerable and comfortable even for small budgets, therefore family elements among the newcomers are encouraged and [therefore] dominant." Nikolaï Karazin concludes the last article about his railroad trip with a hymn to Russian rule and Kaufman's role in it: "in Kara-Kurgan, the train enters our domain again, ours since the Bukhara campaign of 1868 and the conquest of Samarkand by Konstantin Petrovich Kaufman, who has not survived till this time, for whom God did not mean to enjoy the results of his benevolent administrative activities."⁷²

Notes

1. P. P. Bushev, *Istoriia posol'stv i diplomaticheskikh otnoshenii Russkogo i Iranskogo gosudarstv v 1586–1612 gg. (po russkim arkhivam)* (Moscow: Nauka, 1976), 29–30.
2. A. S. Morrison, *Russian Rule in Samarkand, 1868–1910: A Comparison with British India* (Oxford: Oxford University Press, 2008), 30.
3. Scott C. Levi, *The Rise and Fall of Khoqand, 1709–1876* (Pittsburgh: University of Pittsburgh Press, 2017), 216.
4. Yuri Bregel, "The Russian Conquest of Central Asia and the First Decades of Russian Rule," section II of "Central Asia vii. In the 18th-19th Centuries," *Encyclopaedia Iranica*, V/2, 193–205, https://iranicaonline.org/articles/central-asia-vii.
5. Richard A. Pierce, *Russian Central Asia 1867–1917: A Study in Colonial Rule* (Berkeley: University of California Press, 1960), 34–37.
6. Two of his novels and an essay have been translated into English: *Dvunogii volk*, trans. by Boris Lanin as *The Two-legged Wolf: A Romance* (University of California Libraries, 1894); *Na dalekikh okrainakh*, trans. by Anthony W. Sariti as *In the Distant Confines* (Authorhouse, 2007); "N. Karazin. Camp on the Amu Daria," trans. by Elena Andreeva and Mark Woodcock, *Metamorphosis*, Spring 2010. See the detailed bibliography on Karazin in Elena Andreeva, *Russian Central Asia in the Works of Nikolai Karazin (1842–1908)—Ambivalent Triumph* (Cham: Springer, 2021).
7. E. V. Nogaevskaia, "Nikolai Nikolaevich Karazin, 1842-1908," in *Russkoe iskusstvo: Ocherki o zhizni i tvorchestve khudozhnikov. Vtoraia polovina deviatnadtsatogo veka II*, ed. A. I. Leonov (Moscow: Iskusstvo, 1971), 358.
8. Margaret Dikovitskaia, "Central Asia in Early Photographs: Russian Colonial Attitudes and Visual Culture," in "Empire, Islam and Politics in Central Asia," ed. Uyama Tomohiko, special issue, *Slavic Eurasian Studies* 14 (2007): 104–5.
9. Edward Said, *Orientalism* (New York: Vintage Books, 1979), 14–15, 23–24, quoted in Susan Layton, *Russian Literature and Empire: Conquest of the Caucasus from Pushkin to Tolstoy* (Cambridge: Cambridge University Press, 1994), 9, xiii.
10. Willard Sunderland, "Shop Signs, Monuments, Souvenirs: Views of the Empire in Everyday Life," in *Picturing Russia: Explorations in Visual Culture*, ed. Valerie A. Kivelson and Joan Neuberger (New Haven, CT: Yale University Press, 2008), 104.
11. Katya Hokanson, *Writing at Russia's Border* (Toronto: University of Toronto Press, 2008), 13.
12. Daniel Brower, *Turkestan and the Fate of the Russian Empire* (London: Routledge Curzon, 2003), 79–81; Jeff Sahadeo, *Russian Colonial Society in Tashkent, 1865–1923* (Bloomington: Indiana University Press, 2010), 120.
13. I. Ia. Vatslik, *Zakaspiiskaia zheleznaia doroga: Eia znachenie i budushchnost'* (St. Petersburg: Parovaia Skoropechatnaia Iablonskii i Perrot, 1888), 8–9.
14. G. Curzon, "The Transcaspian Railway. By the Hon. G. Curzon, M. P.," *Proceedings of the Royal Geographical Society and Monthly Record of Geography, New Monthly Series* 11, no. 5 (May 1889): 275.

15. Curzon, "The Transcaspian Railway," 275, 277.
16. Pierce, *Russian Central Asia*, 37–42; David MacKenzie, "The Conquest and Administration of Turkestan, 1860–85," in *Russian Colonial Expansion to 1917*, ed. Michael Rywkin (London: Mansell Publishing, 1988), 226.
17. Andreas Kappeler, *The Russian Empire: A Multiethnic History*, trans. by Alfred Clayton (Harlow: Longman, 2001), 197.
18. Morrison, *Russian Rule in Samarkand*, 34–35.
19. Curzon, "The Transcaspian Railway," 276–77.
20. V. A. Prishchepova, *Illiustrativnye kollektsii po narodam Tsentral'noĭ Azii vtoroĭ poloviny XIX–nachala XX veka v sobraniiakh Kunstkamery* (St. Petersburg: Nauka, 2011), 363–64.
21. Curzon, "The Transcaspian Railway," 280.
22. *Niva* 39 (1888): 964.
23. Nikolaĭ Karazin, "Samarskaia uchënaia ekspeditsiia," *Vsemirnaia illiustratsiia* 576 (1880): 75.
24. A. I. Rodzevich, *Ocherki postroĭki Zakaspĭskoĭ voennoĭ zheleznoĭ dorogi i eia znacheniia dlia russko-sredneaziatskoĭ promyshlennosti i torgovli* (St. Petersburg: Parovaia tipografiia Muller i Bogel'man, 1891), 3.
25. Vatslik, *Zakaspĭskaia zheleznaia doroga*, 11.
26. Curzon, "The Transcaspian Railway," 293.
27. Jeff Eden, *Slavery and Empire in Central Asia* (Cambridge: Cambridge University Press, 2018), 6.
28. *Niva* 16 (1876): 277.
29. Brower, *Turkestan and the Fate of the Russian Empire*, 131.
30. *Niva* 49 (1885): 1198. Along with *utun-kaik* (fiery boat), those technological innovations were gradually becoming more and more appealing to the Muslims of Central Asia, who started to travel to Mecca for pilgrimage from Samarkand to Orenburg, Nizhny Novgorod, Moscow, and Odessa.
31. This album is kept at the State Museum of Oriental Art in Moscow, but its cover and six of its pages have been published in P. Wageman and Inessa Kouteinikova, eds., *Russia's Unknown Orient: Orientalist Paintings 1850–1920* (Groningen: Groninger Museum, 2010), 56–59.
32. *Niva* 37 (1888): 916.
33. Curzon, "The Transcaspian Railway," 280.
34. Curzon, "The Transcaspian Railway," 280, 278.
35. Wageman and Kouteinikova, *Russia's Unknown Orient*, 56.
36. Nile Green, "Introduction: Writing Travel, and the Global History in Central Asia," in *Writing Travel in Central Asian History*, ed. Nile Green (Bloomington: Indiana University Press, 2014), 18; Yuri Slezkine, "Naturalists versus Nations: Eighteenth-Century Russian Scholars Confront Ethnic Diversity," in *Russia's Orient: Imperial Borderlands and Peoples, 1700–1917*, ed. Daniel R. Brower and Edward J. Lazzerini (Bloomington: Indiana University Press, 1997), 27–57.
37. *Niva* 37 (1888): 918.
38. *Niva* 37 (1888): 916–18.
39. *Niva* 37 (1888): 918–19.
40. *Niva* 37 (1888): 920.
41. *Niva* 37 (1888): 919.

42. *Niva* 37 (1888): 917.
43. *Niva* 37 (1888): 919.
44. Wageman and Kouteinikova, *Russia's Unknown Orient*, 57.
45. Wageman and Kouteinikova, *Russia's Unknown Orient*, 57; *Niva* 38 (1888): 940.
46. N. N. Karazin, "Na puti v Indiĩu," *Niva* 38 (1888): 943.
47. *Niva* 38 (1888): 940, 941; *Niva* 40 (1888): 988.
48. *Niva* 29 (1890): 740, 746. Another image of a camel with a resting traveler and an approaching train can be found in Karazin's travelogue "Na puti v Indiĩu," *Niva* 40 (1888): 988.
49. Prishchepova, *Illiustrativnye kollektsii*, 365.
50. Curzon, "The Transcaspian Railway," 278, 287. According to Prishchepova, in 124 days. See Prishchepova, *Illiustrativnye kollektsii*, 365. In 1901, it was replaced by an iron bridge: March 2, 2016, https://mytashkent.uz/2016/03/02/115-let-mostu-cherez-amudaryu-u-chardzhou/.
51. Wageman and Kouteinikova, *Russia's Unknown Orient*, 59; *Niva* 40 (1888): 990. One *versta* equals 0.67 miles.
52. *Niva* 40 (1888): 990.
53. *Niva* 39 (1888): 965.
54. Wageman and Kouteinikova, *Russia's Unknown Orient*, 58; *Niva* 38 (1888): 940.
55. *Niva* 38 (1888): 943.
56. *Niva* 38 (1888): 940.
57. *Niva* 39 (1888): 965, 967.
58. *Niva* 40 (1888): 988.
59. Karazin, "Na puti v Indiĩu," *Niva* 40 (1888): 990.
60. *Niva* 39 (1888): 965, and Wageman and Kouteinikova, *Russia's Unknown Orient*, 58, respectively.
61. Wageman and Kouteinikova, *Russia's Unknown Orient*, 58.
62. Wageman and Kouteinikova, *Russia's Unknown Orient*, 59.
63. Karazin, "Na puti v Indiĩu," *Niva* 38 (1888): 943.
64. Karazin, "Na puti v Indiĩu," *Niva* 38 (1888): 941.
65. Karazin, "Na puti v Indiĩu," *Niva* 39 (1888): 967.
66. Karazin, "Na puti v Indiĩu," *Niva* 39 (1888): 964.
67. Karazin, "Na puti v Indiĩu," *Niva* 39 (1888): 967.
68. Karazin, "Na puti v Indiĩu," *Niva* 39 (1888): 965.
69. Karazin, "Na puti v Indiĩu," *Niva* 39 (1888): 967.
70. Karazin, "Na puti v Indiĩu," *Niva* 39 (1888): 967.
71. Karazin, "Na puti v Indiĩu," *Niva* 39 (1888): 965.
72. Karazin, "Na puti v Indiĩu," *Niva* 40 (1888): 990.

CHAPTER 12

Border Crossings
Iranian Artists in Tsarist Russia and Georgia
Layla S. Diba

                              Recent studies of Russo-Iranian relations in the nineteenth and twentieth centuries have called for a rethinking of the topic beyond the diplomatic, economic, and military spheres, to include cultural history and other disciplines. Scholars have also emphasized the need for more in-depth research on the nature and extent of the interaction between the two nations.[1] This book on the Caspian region seems an appropriate context for discussing the role of tsarist Russia and the Caucasus Viceroyalty (present-day Georgia) as a little-known locus for Iranian modernity in the arts.

    The question of Russian influence first arose in the course of my research on royal Persian paintings of the Qajar era and modern Iranian art. These investigations revealed hitherto unsuspected interactions between Iranians and Russians in art training and suggested that further research on the role of Russian academic art in the development of Iranian modernism would prove fruitful.[2]

    This chapter is a revised and expanded version of a paper presented in November 2014 at The Ohio State University's Russo-Persian Workshop "Winning and Losing the Great Game: Literature, Art, and Diplomacy between Russia and Iran." The final product greatly benefited from the scholarly discussions of the participants and from the research of Ehsan Siahpoush, Melanie Gibson, and Haideh Sahim and the editorial assistance of Melis Cokuslu.

CHAPTER 12

FIGURE 12.1. ʿAbbās Rassām Arzhangi (1892–1975), *Still Life with Melons, Peaches and a Spoon*. Iran, dated Shamsi AH 1297 / AD 1918. Oil on canvas. 11 x 26.8 inches (28 x 68 centimeters unframed). Signed "Rassām Arangi 1297." Museum of Islamic Art, Doha, Qatar. 82.2011

The role of Russian academic training in art has received little attention from historians of Iranian art compared to that of the leading exponent of European-style painting, Moḥammad Ghāffari Kamāl al-Molk. Ghāffari had first been trained at the Iranian court academy located at the Dār al-Fonun School and later in Florence and Paris. In 1911, he founded his own School of Fine Arts, the Madraseh Ṣanāye'-e Mostaẓrafeh that he directed until 1927. The school became the principal known site of art education prior to World War II, and Ghāffari was subsequently hailed as the father of Iranian modernism.[3]

This chapter will argue that other Iranian artists of the era sought another modernism in Russia at the Academy of St. Petersburg, in Tiflis, and in Moscow.[4] Comparisons of the work of Ghāffari as well as of Mirza ʿAli Akbar Mozayyan al-Dowleh (another court painter and teacher at the Dār al-Fonun, who graduated in 1867 from the Academie des Beaux Arts in Paris) with that of one artist who traveled to Russia at the same time, ʿAbbās Rassām Arzhangi, shows a comparable level of skill and supports our contention of Russian artistic influence.[5]

The First Wave of Iranian Artists: The Early Nineteenth Century

Perso-Russian cultural relations actually date back to the early nineteenth century, when Iran and Russia fought two wars over Azerbaijan and the Caucasus (1804–13 and 1826–28). An unsigned monumental battle painting, dateable 1804–10, formerly located in the Golestān

Palace, is probably the work of Mirza Bābā, one of the Tehran court's leading painters. The composition shows Fatḥ-'Ali Shah at the left directing the troops. However, the Iranian armies were in fact led by Crown Prince 'Abbās Mirza (1799-1833), governor of Azerbaijan, whose seat was in Tabriz. Another painting dated 1815-16 is the work of Allahverdi Afshār, 'Abbās Mirza's principal court painter.[6] The work is executed in an accomplished style of academic realism, revealing the skill of Tabriz artists in the use of depth and modeling considerably earlier in the nineteenth century than previously thought, and perhaps earlier than in Tehran, a theme to which we will return.[7] The painting points to the role of Tabriz as a conduit to Russian-style modernity.

Prince 'Abbās Mirza was known as a reformer with a firm belief in European education as the key to modernization. His goal was primarily to modernize the Iranian army, although students were sent abroad to acquire skills ranging from medicine to, as we shall see, art training. Two groups of Iranians were sent by him to England: one in 1811, the other in 1815. All but one returned to Iran in 1819. In the 1820s, he sent an additional four students abroad including a certain Mirza Ja'far Tabrizi to Moscow in 1822-23 to study "printing."[8]

In 1991, D. Safarilieva first revealed the presence of an artist by the name of Ja'far Moḥammad in early nineteenth-century Russia. According to the author, Ja'far arrived in St. Petersburg from England in 1822 and attended the St. Petersburg Academy of Fine Arts. He graduated with honors in 1824.[9] The article was based on Russian archives and on a surviving work by the artist in the academy, where it hung for many years along with other royal portraits. Ja'far was awarded the silver medal for his portrait in watercolor of 'Abbās Mirza.

The portrait, when compared to that of Allahverdi and other court artists of the era, is very skilled indeed, as Safarilieva recognized in her discussion of the combination of Western and traditional styles in the work.[10]

However, this article did not come to the attention of Iranologists until Adel Adamova's pioneering 1998 essay on Perso-Russian diplomatic and artistic relations.[11] In discussing the same portrait of 'Abbās Mirza, she cites yet another primary source, an 1825 article from a St. Petersburg newspaper that reveals that the artist was sent by 'Abbās Mirza because of his precocious skill. Apparently, he successfully copied English prints at the age of fifteen and by 1817 had executed a remarkable painting of a Russian diplomatic mission headed by General

FIGURE 12.2. Moḥammad Jaʿfar (d. 1826). Portrait of ʿAbbās Mirza, 1824. Watercolor. Museum of the Academy of Arts, St. Petersburg. Image courtesy of Firuza Melville.

Ermolov.[12] The article gives his age as twenty-four and states he was the son of a certain Tabriz court official by the name of "Mir Alisyer."[13]

Many other details of his visit are revealed in these lively archival documents: how his hosts' respect for the Iranian student and their concern for his social and religious needs led them to consult with Iranian Armenian merchants in Russia, the financial assistance accorded to him, and the social interaction between the Iranian artist and his hosts. Jaʿfar Moḥammad also followed exactly the same curriculum as the other students and produced studies of nudes drawn from life and copies of Russian portraits. Unfortunately, this very talented artist died in 1826 of tuberculosis.[14]

Additionally, a second artist's stay in Georgia has recently been recorded. It appears that the aforementioned Allahverdi Afshār was sent to Tiflis by ʿAbbās Mirza in 1821 to study lithographic printing and returned to Tabriz with a complete set of lithographic equipment. The skill of the 1816 painting suggests this may not have been his first visit abroad.[15]

Allahverdi is a relatively well-known figure in the annals of Iranian painting, as he came from the Afshār tribe of Orumieh, which contributed a number of important artists to the field in the eighteenth and nineteenth centuries. However, Jaʿfar Moḥammad is thus far unrecorded in Persian sources. The Russian sources state that Jaʿfar Moḥammad arrived from England in 1822. This might suggest he be identified with one of the students in England, Mirza Jaʿfar Ṭabib, who studied medicine. Dennis Wright and Nile Green, however, assert that, along with the other students, he was put on a boat in 1819 going back to Tabriz via Constantinople.[16] The biographies and achievements of the students who returned to Iran are well known.[17] It seems more likely that Jaʿfar Moḥammad be identified with Mirza Jaʿfar Tabrizi, one of the third group of students, sent to Moscow to study printing in 1822. Could "printing" be lithographic printing, as was the case in Tiflis, and did Mirza Jaʿfar then continue on to St. Petersburg?[18] Future research in the histories of Tabriz and poetic anthologies may reveal more information on these artists.

The dates of Jaʿfar Moḥammad's and Allahverdi's visits fall between two other much better-known episodes in the cultural encounters between Iranians and the West in this era: on the one hand, the stay of Iranian students in England and, on the other hand, the mission of Prince Khosrow Mirza Qajar to Russia in 1829 in expiation for the murder of the Russian poet and diplomat Alexander Griboedov.[19] The aforementioned documents record how ʿAbbās Mirza took advantage of the lull in hostilities between the First and Second Russo-Persian Wars to advance his modernization agenda. They also date the first art education contacts between Russia and Iran as early as the 1820s, the same time as contacts with England and nearly thirty years before Iranian students were sent to France.

The Second Wave of Iranian Artists: The Late Nineteenth and Early Twentieth Centuries

Subsequent episodes did not occur until the early twentieth century, when tsarist Russia was in decline and on the brink of revolution, and Iran was in constitutional ferment. Artists from two artistic dynasties—both from Tabriz—came to Tiflis to study. The question is whether they came to study art or revolution. As Marina Alexidze has noted, Tiflis was the closest portal to European culture and arts, but it had also been a center for Iranian political refugees, Persian-language printing, and anticlerical intellectuals since the early nineteenth century. Thus, the city offered a very congenial cultural atmosphere for the Tabrizi artists.[20] Until 1917, Tiflis was also the center of the Caucasus Viceroyalty that stretched from the Caspian to the Black Sea. Iago Gocheleishvili draws an evocative portrait of the city as cosmopolitan, multiconfessional, and trilingual (Georgian, Persian, and Arabic).[21] Baku was another city that drew Iranian immigrants, but they were either peasants or laborers in the oil fields, sometimes in the hundreds of thousands. While political ideas as well as arms and revolutionary activists spread from Baku to northern Iran, cultural transmission would predominate in Tiflis in both the sphere of art training as well as print culture.[22]

According to Persian sources, Āqā Ebrāhim, court painter to Moẓaffar al-Din Shah, visited Russia in the 1890s.[23] His two sons, Mir Ḥosayn (1881–1963) and ʿAbbās Rassām (1892–1975), who later adopted the surname Arzhangi, traveled to Tiflis in 1903 and stayed until 1908.[24] At some later point they went to Moscow. By 1914, the outbreak of World War I caused them to return to Iran. Thus, they appear to have spent a total of eleven years in Russia. We should note that all dates cited here are approximate and based on Iranian family sources, websites, and accounts of friends and admirers. The sometimes anecdotal and subjective nature of the evidence is due to the fact that these artists were not official Tehran court artists, so they were largely excluded from the canonical narrative of Iranian modernism. Also, we must take into account a certain level of self-censorship and misrepresentation by the artists themselves, particularly in relation to their Russian connections during the Reżā Shah period.

The principal reason why these artists went to Tiflis instead of St. Petersburg was that while Tehran turned to France and western Europe in its search for modernity, Tabriz (which was the second city of Iran and the seat of the crown prince) had become the principal conduit for Russian modernity as filtered through the southern Caucasus and its principal cities, Tiflis and Baku.

Their decision may also have been influenced by Tiflis's proximity or to financial issues, since they were not sent by the court and their costs were no longer paid for by the Russian or Iranian governments, as was the case with Moḥammad Jaʿfar and Allahverdi Afshār or perhaps even in the case of Āqā Ebrāhim. Furthermore, instruction in European-style easel painting and sculpture were available at the Tiflis Academy of Art and Sculpture and Secondary School of Painting and Sculpture. The academy had existed since the 1860s, and the secondary school was established subsequently. A photograph of the academy in 1884 by Dmitriĭ Ermakov provides visual confirmation for the exterior appearance of the building. The interior of the academy is magnificently decorated in the Qajar style of a quality comparable to the Golestān Palace Museum. As Marina Alexidze has discussed, numerous buildings were decorated by Iranian craftsmen during this era and stand as testaments to the close cultural and artistic ties between Iran and Georgia.[25]

Additionally, they may have selected Tiflis due to the presence in Tabriz of an Armenian-Georgian painter originally from Tiflis but trained in St. Petersburg, by the name of Akop Ovnatanian. He was an accomplished portrait painter who after 1870 and until his death in the 1880s painted official portraits of Naser al-Din Shah and Moẓaffar al-Din Shah.[26] He may have known Mirza Āqā Ebrāhim and discussed educational opportunities in Tiflis with him.

Finally, they were likely seeking refuge from the unsettled conditions in Tabriz and hoped to establish contact with the Russian and Iranian émigré intelligentsia: certainly, the dates of their stay coincide with the Russian Revolution of 1905, when the southern Caucasus was a hotbed of agitation. As the revolutionary icon Rosa Luxemburg has famously written, "the area was aflame" with radical movements and ideas.[27] More recently Houri Berberian has successfully argued that the southern Caucasus was a pivotal site for the transmission of revolutionary ideas, through the telegraph, road and railroad systems, and the press across the Russian, Iranian, and Ottoman imperial boundaries.[28]

Their sojourn in Tiflis has recently been studied by Grigol Beradze who has identified a number of watercolors by the younger of the two brothers, ʿAbbās Rassām Arzhangi, dated circa 1903-8, 1910-12, and 1932 in the collections of the National Museum of Georgia.[29]

The earlier works correspond with the brothers' stay in Russia and perhaps date their move to Moscow to 1912. The style corresponds to the realistic portrayal of genre subjects popular in early twentieth-century Russia and Iran, primarily intended for the tourist trade. The works are related to various forms of popular art, including painting produced for coffeehouses and political cartoons, to photography, and to illustrated books.[30] Although we do not have detailed evidence of the brothers' academic curriculum in Tiflis and Moscow such as we had for Jaʿfar Moḥammad, the painting of a still life by ʿAbbās Rassām Arzhangi, dated 1918, that is, after his return to Iran in 1914, reveals the technical expertise the brothers must have acquired.

FIGURE 12.3. ʿAbbās Rassām Arzhangi, *Vendor of Crockery*. Tiflis (?). Circa 1903–8 (?). Watercolor. Shalva Amiranashvili Museum of Fine Arts (Georgian National Museum), No. sxm/ag 146. Image courtesy of Grigol Beradze and Irina Koshoridze.

Unfortunately, it is still unclear what their studies in Moscow were and the location of their training. There *was* a Moscow school of painting founded in 1865 that is thought to have been more democratic than its St. Petersburg counterpart and taught a style described as "Russian nationalist realism."[31] The rules of admission may have been less strict or its approach more congenial to painters of their generation. No other early works of the brothers have come to light.

After his return to Tabriz, Mir Ḥosayn Mosavvar Arzhangi established a school of painting in 1918. Although little is known of its activities and influence, or if it taught academic as well as traditional painting in watercolor and other crafts, as was the case with the madreseh in Tehran—which was, at least in part, its model—we may conjecture that the technical style taught there was based on Russian painting as taught in Tiflis and, later, in Moscow and that the still life by ʿAbbās is thus far the main surviving evidence of Russian influence on the brothers' practice.

A closer look at ʿAbbās Rassām Arzhangi's later career shows that, in addition to his academic style, he continued to work in the traditional mode of Persian manuscript illustration, which shows little evolution from the early works in Georgia.[32] After ʿAbbās Rassām Arzhangi returned to Iran in 1914, he continued his career for the next half century in Tabriz and Tehran, where he worked prolifically in a variety of styles and independently of government patronage. ʿAbbās Arzhangi was also a political cartoonist early in his career and a children's book illustrator, wrote art criticism, and illustrated classics of Persian literature.[33] Mir Ḥosayn appears to have worked primarily as a carpet designer. Let us recall both brothers were active well into the 1960s and 1970s, yet their work reflected nothing of the modernist styles being experimented with in postwar Iran, particularly cubism. The brothers certainly did not introduce European or Russian avant-garde painting to prewar Iran but produced tourist art and carpet designs typical for their generation.

Another artist who traveled to Tiflis was Ḥosayn Ṭāherzādeh Behzād (1887–1962) (not to be confused with Ḥosayn Behzād).[34] Ṭāherzādeh Behzād was born in Tabriz in 1887. His father was a government official and cleric. He was one of five brothers and was especially close to his younger brother Karim who would become one of Iran's leading architects during the Pahlavi era. According to Karim, Ḥosayn was trained as a painter in the Tiflis and Istanbul academies.[35] At an early age he was also politically active. Ḥosayn was appointed to a local *anjoman* (powerful electoral council) and became involved with the Tabriz liberation movement.[36]

Having attracted the attention of the government, he was forced to flee to Tiflis and for three years studied at the academy, that is, from circa 1904–7. However, this was also a period in which the intellectual freedom in Tiflis inspired him to channel his talent and political ambitions into the illustrated press. During this time, he was jailed with other leading constitutionalists in Tiflis and was threatened with return to Tehran and certain death, only to be saved by the abdication of Moḥammad ʿAli Shah. He returned to Tabriz and received permission to travel to Istanbul to further his studies around 1908.[37]

Although information on Ḥosayn's early works and career is still sketchy, his stay in Tiflis appears to have coincided with that of ʿAbbās Rassām and perhaps Mir Ḥosayn, and they must have frequented the same circle of émigrés. An undated watercolor painting of a crockery vendor signed by him now in the Saʿadābād collection may be the only visual evidence of the academic training he acquired during this time.

FIGURE 12.4. Ḥosayn Ṭāherzādeh Behzād, *Vendor of Crockery*. Signed Ḥosayn Ṭāherzādeh Behzād with tughra. Tiflis (?). Circa 1905–8 (?). Watercolor, 30 x 40 cm. Saʿadābād Museum of Fine Arts, Tehran.
Source: Neʿmatollāh Keikāvusi, *Promenade in the Picture Gallery: An Album of Iranian and European Paintings from the Sadābād Museum of Fine Arts, Tehrān* (Tehran: Negar Books, 1992), 57, fig. 9.

Evidence of his activities as an illustrator for constitutional newspapers is much more plentiful.[38] His role as an agent of cultural and political change is clearly connected to his brother Karim. Karim was particularly active in the constitutional movement, as he himself has described in a history of the uprisings of Tabriz in the constitutional era that he published in 1954. Between 1907 and 1911, Tabriz was the site of the struggle between nationalist, Russian, and royalist forces and the constitutionalists, which ended with the siege and occupation of Tabriz by Russian troops in 1908. After the defeat of the constitutionalist forces, Karim fled Tabriz for Istanbul along with many other reformers, as well as Ḥosayn.[39]

The day-to-day siege of the city was first recounted by E. G. Browne in his "Chronology of the Persian Revolution," appended to his seminal 1914 work, *The Press and Poetry of Modern Persia*.[40] This episode has recently

FIGURE 12.5. *Mollā Nāṣr al-Din*, no. 25. "With only a mullah or only a khan, one cannot create a constitution. But put a khan and a mullah together and you've already got yourself a constitutional body." Tiflis, ca. 1906/1907. Cartoon, polychrome image.
Source: *Slavs and Tatars Presents Molla Nasreddin: The Magazine that Would've Could've Should've* (Zurich: JRP Ringier, 2011), 147.

been revisited and vividly described by James Clark, including the shifting loyalties of the Tabrizis in their struggle for survival. Clark mentions the influence of local newspapers in stirring up resistance. According to Clark, the Russian commander was very aware of their impact.[41]

Print culture was an important development during this period, as evidenced by Browne's study of the constitutional press, which, as the author states on the title page, was entirely based on a manuscript of a local interlocutor, Mirza Moḥammad 'Ali Khan "Tarbiyat" of Tabriz.[42] Anticolonial and anticlerical imagery illustrated the texts of lithographed newspapers. Certainly, artists played a role in the nationalist movement, and the cartoons they made were highly critical of Moḥammad 'Ali Shah and foreign imperial intervention in Iranian affairs.

This was a perilous occupation, as evidenced by the fact that both artists signed their works with pseudonyms, in the case of 'Abbās

Rassām, "'Abbās al-Ḥosayni," and in the case of Ḥosayn Ṭāherzādeh Behzād, "Binich" (*binesh*, wisdom), signatures that will eventually help to identify a corpus of their works. Their illustrations were a form of visual resistance to imperialism.[43] We should note that their message was as immediate or perhaps more so than that of the texts, since the papers were read to illiterate audiences in coffeehouses where the illustrations played a significant role in conveying political messages.

According to Karim, Ḥosayn provided illustrations for the newspapers *Mollā Nāṣr al-Din*, *Ḥashārāt al-Arż*, *Āzarbāijān*, and *Shaidā*. This has recently been supported by the editor 'Abd al-Ḥosayn Nāhidi Āzar in his introduction to a facsimile publication of *Āzarbāijān*.[44] *Mollā Nāṣr al-Din* was published primarily in Tiflis from 1906 to 1931 and was considered the most influential paper of its time. It was celebrated not only for its political daring but for the sophisticated satirical polychrome illustrations.[45] The artists collaborative Slavs and Tatars have studied the paper closely and have stated that the illustrations were the work of three artists: Oskar Ivanovich Schmerling (1862–1938), director of the Tiflis School of Drawing and Sculpture, Joseph Rotter, and 'Aẓim 'Aẓimzādeh.[46]

It seems probable that Ḥosayn was a student of Schmerling and could also have joined him at *Mollā Nāṣr al-Din* as an apprentice, although none of the illustrations appear to be signed by him. This theory can be supported by the technical, formal, and thematic similarities between the illustrations of *Mollā Nāṣr al-Din* and those assigned to Ḥosayn in *Ḥashārāt al-Arż* and *Āzarbāijān*.

The latter were published in 1907–8 in Tabriz, that is, subsequent to the beginnings of *Mollā Nāṣr al-Din*. Technically, the Tabriz illustrations were executed in polychrome as was the case with *Mollā Nāṣr al-Din*, which argues that their illustrator must have been trained at the Tiflis paper. Stylistic similarities include the figural style, certain iconographic preferences such as trees and tree trunks, and the figure of a wise, aged interlocutor paired with a *Mollā Nāṣr al-Din*-like figure.[47]

The production of these illustrations appears to coincide with Ḥosayn's stay in Tiflis and the Tiflis penal system or may be dated before his incarceration. Alternatively, he may have been able to return to Tabriz. Whatever the case may be, given the close contacts between the Tiflis and Tabriz revolutionary circles and the fluidity of geographical boundaries, Ḥosayn's drawings could have been easily smuggled back to Tabriz.[48]

BORDER CROSSINGS 259

FIGURE 12.6. *Ḥashārāt al-Arż*, no. 12. "The Myrmidons of the ex-Shah Moḥammad ʿAli attend and report on a Constitutional Meeting." Tabriz, June 3, 1908. Lithographed cartoon, originally polychrome image.
Source: Edward G. Browne, *The Press and Poetry of Modern Persia* (Cambridge: Cambridge University Press, 1914), 76.

By 1911 both brothers had made their way to Istanbul. The final evidence for the attribution of these cartoons to Ḥosayn is a handful of cartoons by Ḥosayn published in 1911 in the Istanbul paper *Shaidā*, which exhibit remarkable similarities with the earlier unsigned illustrations. Four of the cartoons are signed H. T. Tabrizi and three, Binich. The first cartoon, signed Binich and depicting a Russian commander delivering an ultimatum to a constitutionalist leader, was published by Browne and identified as the work of Ḥosayn.[49] It was not until 1954 that his brother Karim illustrated and described a second cartoon signed "Binich" as the work of Behzād, thus confirming Browne's identification.

The cartoon vividly depicts a key moment in the politics of the era. In 1911, the American advisor Morgan Shuster was called upon by the

FIGURE 12.7. *Ruznāmeh-ye Āzarbāijān*, no. 19. Cartoon of a street-fight (?), caption illegible. Tabriz, AH 1325 / AD 1907. Lithographed cartoon, originally polychrome image.
Source: 'Abd al-Ḥosayn Nāhidi Āzar, ed., *Ruznāmeh-ye Āzarbāijān, 1324, 1906: Nakhostin Ruznāmeh-ye Fokāhi va Tanz-e Tasviri dar Irān* (Tabriz: Nashr-e Akhtar, 2015), 149.

Iranian government to reform Iranian finances, a move that greatly threatened British and Russian interests. He stayed in Iran from May to December 1911, the approximate date of this cartoon.

Ḥosayn stayed in Istanbul until 1917, when he graduated with a degree in art and his brother with a degree in architecture and engineering. These were formative years for his style when a form of academic realism was current in the Ottoman capital and yet artists were still trained in the craft tradition. We know Ḥosayn practiced calligraphy and made drawings for carpets as well as teaching.

After 1917, Ḥosayn and Karim traveled to Berlin where they associated with a group of émigré Iranian intellectuals and publishers. He did not return to Iran until 1925, at the invitation of an emissary of Reżā Shah. He was by then known as a highly skilled calligrapher, graphic artist, painter, and carpet designer. When he returned to Iran, not only did he restructure the National Academy established by Kamāl al-Molk,

FIGURE 12.8. Ḥosayn Ṭāherzādeh Behzād signing as "Binich" (wisdom). *Shaidā*, no. 5. "Russia presents her second ultimatum to Persia. In the background are seven others." Istanbul, Muharram 2, 1330 (December 25, 1911). Cartoon.
Source: Cambridge University Library, NPR.a.16

but he became Reżā Shah's chief court painter, responsible for the great murals in a Pahlavi realist national style in the royal palaces and a formative influence in the creation of a pseudo-modern Safavid style. Ḥosayn may have renewed contacts with some of his colleagues from his student days in Tiflis: Ḥosayn's watercolor of *A Vendor of Crockery* (Fig. 12.4 herein) is very similar to a 1932 version of the same theme by Arzhangi in the Tiflis Museum. The works may be evidence of a renewed collaboration.

Although Ḥosayn was clearly a radical early in his life, ʿAbbās Rassām Arzhangi's politics are less clear. He never received the patronage of the Pahlavi court, which may be an indication where his sympathies lay. How do we explain Ḥosayn's shifting allegiances? Did he recant his beliefs and become a royalist? Or should we identify him as a nationalist in exile who wanted to return to his homeland and help rebuild it? His brother Karim, who also returned to Iran and became one of Reżā

FIGURE 12.9. Ḥosayn Ṭāherzādeh Behzād signing as "Binich" (wisdom). *Shaidā*, no. 3. "The American Envoy Morgan Shuster attacked by Russia and Great Britain." Istanbul, Dhū al-Ḥijjah 1, 1329 (November 23, 1911). Cartoon.
Source: Cambridge University Library, NPR.a.16.

Shah's chief architects, explained in his history of Tabriz that when he and his brother were in Berlin they vowed to return to Iran and elevate the fine arts, painting and architecture, to the level of European art.[50] This version of history is, however, complicated by Ḥosayn's relationship with an illustrious Azerbaijani carpet designer and educator, Laṭif Karimov (1906–91), who spent his childhood and youth in Iran. In the 1920s, he worked with Ḥosayn in Tehran in setting up a silk production atelier. However, he was also involved in trying to organize the Mashhad textile workers' unions, an activity that led the Iranian authorities to deport him back to Azerbaijan. Again, the reading of the events of this complex era demands great awareness of its ambiguities and seeming contradictions. As Matin-Asgari has discussed, the political ideologies of Iran's first generation of intellectuals evolved over time: Hassan Taqizadeh, for instance, became a strong proponent of modernization under Reżā Shah and may serve as a model for Ḥosayn's later conversion.[51] Wherever the truth lies, Ḥosayn's role as an agent of change has been erased from the narratives of Iranian modernism, and even under the Islamic Republic his complete biography could not be published.[52]

In conclusion, this chapter has shown the usefulness of the following avenues of research for the rethinking of Russo-Iranian cultural contacts: the education of Iranian students abroad in the Qajar and early constitutionalist periods; the importance of Tabriz and Tiflis as mediators between Persian and Russian culture and modernity; and the genealogical approach to Iranian art emphasizing histories of families of artists.

We may end with some cautious and preliminary conclusions. Taking this long historical view has allowed us to recognize how early in the nineteenth century Iranians from Tabriz turned to Russia in their search for modernization, as seen through the episodes of Moḥammad Jaʿfar and Allahverdi Afshār. It also emphasized that concurrent with Perso-Russian political and military rivalries, a certain level of collaboration and mutual respect existed between Iranians and Russians of the professional classes. The later nineteenth-century artists were truly "transnational" both politically and artistically, and their story reflects the political culture and artistic climate of Tabriz and the southern Caucasus in the constitutional era.

The influence of Russian painting per se, which ranged from realism and impressionism and postimpressionism to abstraction, appears to have played a conservative or superficial role in the formation of Iranian modern art. As we have shown, on their return, the Arzhangi brothers continued to work in an early twentieth-century style well into the 1930s and beyond, and Behzād was the principal architect of the early modern realist Pahlavi style.[53] However, compared to their contemporary Kamāl-al-Molk—whose career has been extensively studied and whose corpus of hundreds of works has been preserved in the Golestān Museum—Mir Ḥosayn Arzhangi and his brother ʿAbbās Rassām have received little recognition for their role in the history of modern Iranian art, a recognition perhaps denied them because of their political beliefs. The same may be said for Ḥosayn Ṭāherzādeh Behzād and his better-known contemporary Ḥosayn Behzād.

One area where we may certainly discern the role of the southern Caucasus in the transmission of artistic styles, political ideologies, and technology is in print culture, where avant-garde artists and intellectuals of varying social backgrounds and nationalities worked together. During the constitutional era, Iranian bazaar artists collaborated with academic painters such as Ḥosayn Ṭāherzādeh Behzād and ʿAbbās Rassām Arzhangi. This blending of high and low culture would prove to be a significant aspect of Iranian modernism and perhaps a distant legacy of the interaction with Russian revolutionary culture and politics as played out in the Caspian region.[54]

Notes

1. Stephanie Cronin, "Introduction," in *Iranian-Russian Encounters: Empires and Revolutions since 1800*, ed. Stephanie Cronin (London: Routledge, 2013), 1.

2. We should note at the outset an imbalance between the primary sources for the early nineteenth-century examples, which are in Russian with one single Persian source; see Marina Alexidze, "Persians in Georgia (1801-1921)," *Journal of Persianate Studies* 1, no. 2 (2008): 254-60 (citing a 2000 Georgian article), reprinted in Marina Alexidze, *Georgia and the Muslim East in the Nineteenth Century: Studies in the History of Culture, Religion and Life* (Tbilisi: Ilia State University: George Tsereteli Institute of Oriental Studies, 2011), 29. The later nineteenth- / early twentieth-century episodes are thus far based exclusively on Persian sources. This state of the field reflects challenges discussed by the historian Stephanie Cronin in the area of language and negative cultural attitudes toward Russia. See Cronin, "Introduction," 1-2. The question of Russia as a source for Iranian modernity and the critical role of Azerbaijan is discussed in depth by Afshin Matin-Asgari, "The Impact of Imperial Russia and the Soviet Union on Qajar and Pahlavi Iran", in Cronin, *Iranian-Russian Encounters*, 12, 19, and 22-23. Already in 1996, the historian Janet Afary in her groundbreaking study *The Iranian Constitutional Revolution, 1906-1911: Grassroots Democracy, Social Democracy, and the Origins of Feminism* (New York: Columbia University Press, 1996), 341, asked why the multiethnicity and multi-ideological nature of the

Constitutional Revolution was erased from the historical narrative during the Pahlavi era.

3. See Layla Diba with Ahmad Ashraf, "Kamal-al-Molk, Mohammad Ḡaffari," *Encyclopaedia Iranica*, XV/4, 417–33, https://iranicaonline.org/articles/kamal-al-molk-mohammad-gaffari.

4. For a study of another neglected teacher and painter of the era, see Aydin Aghdashloo, "A Short Introduction to the Works of Asghar Petgar and His Time," *Shargh*, May 11, 2011, 15. See also Bahram Ahmadi, *L'enseignement universitaire de la peinture en Iran: Problèmes et Influences* (Saarbrücken: Press Académiques Francophones, Akademikerverlag, 2012), 187; and Layla Diba, "The Formation of Modern Iranian Art: From Kamal al Molk to Zenderoudi," in *Iran Modern*, ed. Fereshteh Daftari and Layla Diba (New York: Asia Society Museum, 2013), 45–48.

5. Mirzā ʿAli Akbar Mozayyan al-Dowleh, *Still Life*, AH 1325 / AD 1907-8, Christie's "Art of the Islamic and Indian Worlds," sale 7843, lot 159, closed April 13, 2010, http://www.christies.com/lotfinder/paintings/still-life-signed-mozayen-al-dowleh-qajar-5303064-details.aspx.

6. Signed Allahverdi Afshār, *Crown Prince Abbas Mirza and Court Officials*, Iran, dated AH 1231 / AD 1815-16, oil on canvas, 59 7/8 x 73 1/4 in. (152 x 186 cm), State Hermitage Museum, St. Petersburg, VR-1115, in Layla Diba, ed., *Royal Persian Paintings: The Qajar Epoch, 1785–1925* (New York: Brooklyn Museum of Art in association with I. B. Tauris, 1998), 199.

7. Adel Adamova, "Art and Diplomacy: Qajar Paintings at the State Hermitage Museum," in Diba, *Royal Persian Paintings*, 66–75.

8. The number of students varies from six to seven. See M. Minovi, "Avvalin Kāravān-e Ma'refat," *Yaghmā*, no. 62 (1953): 181–85. Monica Ringer, *Education, Religion, and the Discourse of Cultural Reform in Qajar Iran* (Costa Mesa: Mazda, 2001), 28–29. It is unclear if by "printing" is meant a printing press or a lithographic press. Nile Green maintains the Mirza Ṣāleh was the first to learn *chāp-e sangi* in 1829: *The Love of Strangers: What Six Muslim Students Learned in Jane Austen's London* (Princeton, NJ: Princeton University Press, 2015), 310, although new evidence presented herein suggests otherwise. See also Shiva Balaghi, "Political Culture in the Iranian Revolution of 1906 and the Cartoons of Kashkul," in *Political Cartoons in the Middle East*, ed. Fatma Müge Göçek (Princeton, NJ: Princeton University Press, 1998), 62–63.

9. D. Safaralieva, "Iranskiĭ uchënik Akademii" [An Iranian student of the academy], *Khudozhnik*, no. 8 (1991): 56–58. My thanks to Firuza Melville for translating this article.

10. Safaralieva, "Iranskiĭ uchënik Akademii," 56–58.

11. Adamova, "Art and Diplomacy," 66–75. According to Firuza Melville the painting of ʿAbbās Mirza is missing and only known from photographic sources.

12. Alekseĭ Petrovich Ermolov (1777–1861) was commander-in-chief of Russian forces in the Caucasus and later governor of Georgia. The painting may be dated sometime between his arrival in 1817 and Jaʿfar Moḥammad's departure for Russia in 1822.

13. This is the original transliteration. Adel Adamova prefers "'Ali-ye Sayyar." The text may also be read Mihr 'Ali Shir. At this time, we have no further information on this individual.

14. Safaralieva, "Iranskiĭ uchënik Akademii," 56–58, and Firuza I. Melville, "Khosrow Mirza's Mission to St. Petersburg in 1829," in Cronin, *Iranian-Russian Encounters*, 72.

15. Nugzar Ter-Oganov, "Two Iranian Authors, Majd Os-Saltananeh and Yahya Dowlatabadi, on Tblisi," in *Typological Researches*, vol. 4 (Tbilisi: Georgian Academy of Sciences, 2000), 408, cited in Alexidze "Persians in Georgia." For Allahverdi, see Olimpiada P. Shcheglova, "Lithography i. In Persia," *Encyclopaedia Iranica Online*, http://www.iranicaonline.org/articles/lithography-i-in-persia.

16. Denis Wright, *The Persians amongst the English: Episodes in Anglo-Persian History* (London: I. B. Tauris, 1985), 80, and Green, *The Love of Strangers*, 313–14.

17. Minovi, "Avallin Kāravān-e Maʿrefat," 181–85, and Green, *The Love of Strangers*, 305–17.

18. A further complication is the student's name: the archives refer to him as Jaʿfar Moḥammad, yet he signed his work Moḥammad Jaʿfar and the 1825 article refers to him as such. The inversion of names was probably not an infrequent occurrence.

19. See Melville, "Khosrow Mirza's Mission to St. Petersburg," 69–93, for the most recent survey of the evidence and especially 70–71 on Iranian perspectives of Russia not just as a colonial power but also as a symbol of modernity.

20. Alexidze, "Persians in Georgia," 254–60, and Alexidze, *Georgia and the Muslim East*, 29.

21. Iago Gocheleishvili, "Georgian Sources on the Iranian Constitutional Revolution, 1905–1911: Sergo Gamdlishvili's Memoirs of the Gilan Resistance," in Cronin, *Iranian-Russian Encounters*, 223n4.

22. Gocheleishvili, "Georgian Sources," 207–13. See also Kayhan Nejad, "From the Oilfield to the Battlefield: Transcaucasian Labor and Iranian Constitutionalism, 1904–11," virtual lecture, April 16, 2021, Iran Colloquium, Yale University.

23. "Arjangi Family History," accessed January 30, 2012, http://arjangi.org/rassam.

24. The adoption of this surname refers to *Arzhang*, the illustrated book of Māni, the legendary founder of Persian painting and Manichaeism. It was the highest compliment that could be awarded to an artist.

25. For further information on the history of the academy and its building and for the date of the Ermakov photograph, see "Tbilisi State Academy of Arts," Wikipedia, last edited July 8, 2024, https://en.wikipedia.org/wiki/Tbilisi_State_Academy_of_Arts. See Alexidze, *Georgia and the Muslim East*, 22–23.

26. Diba, *Royal Persian Paintings*, 245–46 and references therein.

27. Rosa Luxemburg, chap. 3, "Development of the Mass Strike Movement in Russia," from *The Mass Strike, the Political Party and the Trade Unions* (1906), Rosa Luxemburg Internet Archive, 1999, https://www.marxists.org/archive/luxemburg/1906/mass-strike/ch03.htm.

28. Houri Berberian, *Roving Revolutionaries: Armenians and the Connected Revolutions in the Russian, Iranian, and Ottoman Worlds* (Oakland: University of California Press, 2019), 82–83, 95.

29. Grigol Beradze, "Looking Back and Ahead: An Insight into Iranian Influence in the Caucasus," paper presented at the Conference of the G. Tsereteli Institute of Oriental Studies of the Ilia State University, Tbilisi, October 1–2, 2014. My thanks to Drs. Irina Koshoridze and Grigol Beradze for sharing this unpublished paper with me.

30. See Corien J. M. Vuurman and L.A. Fereydoun Barjesteh van Waalwijk van Doorn (Khosrovani), "Vividly Painted Watercolours: Artistic Purchases from Persian Bazaars," *Journal of the International Qajar Studies Association* 12–13 (2013): 53–141, and Diba, *Royal Persian Paintings*, 276–77 for coffeehouse paintings, 281 for cartoons, 262 for photography.

31. "Moscow School of Painting, Sculpture and Architecture," Wikipedia, last edited October 24, 2024, https://en.wikipedia.org/wiki/Moscow_School_of_Painting,_Sculpture_and_Architecture.

32. ʿAbbās Rassām Arzhangi (signed Sayyed Rassām), *A Girl Lying Down on the Carpet, with an Open Book and Qalyan*, AH 1330 / AD 1912, paper, cardboard, opaque watercolors, 24 x 34 cm, Shalva Amiranashvili Museum of Fine Arts (Georgian National Museum), inv. no. sxm/ag 341; and ʿAbbās Rassām Arzhangi (signed Rassām Arzhangi), *Woman Playing Tombak*, AH 1351 / AD 1932, unknown location. Images courtesy of Grigol Beradze and Irina Koshoridze.

33. See Beradze, "Looking Back and Ahead"; Ahmadi, *L'enseignement universitaire de la peinture en Iran*, 188, and unpublished research of Ehsan Siahpoush and the author.

34. The following account is from Diba, "The Formation of Modern Iranian Art," 48–49, and Layla S. Diba, "The Making of a Modern Iranian Artist: Hossain Taherzadeh Behzad and the Illustrated Constitutional Press," unpublished paper delivered at the International Congress of Iranian Studies, Vienna, 2016, the subject of a forthcoming publication.

35. It is also possible that Ḥosayn may have attended a language academy. I thank George Bournoutian for this suggestion, personal communication, November 2014.

36. See Afary, *The Iranian Constitutional Revolution*, on the *anjoman* and Tabriz in particular, 71–81.

37. Karim Ṭāherzādeh Behzād, *Qiyām-e Āẕarbāijān dar Enqelāb-e Mashrutiat-e Irān* (Tehran: Eqbāl, 1334/1954), 429.

38. Rassām Arzhangi's activities—while more limited—will be discussed in Diba forthcoming (see note 34 above).

39. Ṭāherzādeh Behzād, *Qiyām-e Āẕarbāijān*, 27–29.

40. E. G. Browne, *The Press and Poetry of Modern Persia* (Cambridge: Cambridge University Press, 1914; repr. 1983), 310–36.

41. James D. Clark, "Constitutionalists and Cossacks: The Constitutional Movement and Russian Intervention in Tabriz, 1907–11," *Iranian Studies* 39, no. 2 (2006): 217.

42. Browne, *The Press and Poetry of Modern Persia*, ix.

43. Balaghi, "Political Culture in the Iranian Revolution," 62–63.

44. Ṭāherzādeh Behzād, *Qiyām-e Āẕarbāijān*, 429, and ʿAbd al-Ḥosayn Nāhidi Āẕar, ed., *Ruznāmeh-ye Āẕarbāijān, 1324, 1906: Nakhostin Ruznāmeh-ye Fokāhi va Tanz-e Tasviri dar Irān* (Tabriz: Nashr-e Akhtar, 2015).

45. Afary, *The Iranian Constitutional Revolution*, has discussed the paper, the ethnic Iranian origins of its editors, and its influence on *Āẕarbāijān* and other Iranian newspapers, 119–21. For the most recent comprehensive study of *Mollā Nāṣr al-Din*, see Janet Afary and Kamran Afary, *Mollā Nasreddin: The Making of a Modern Trickster (1906–1911)* (Edinburgh: Edinburgh University Press, 2022). For the original periodicals, see *Mollā Nasreddin (1906–1931)*, vol. 1, *1906–1907* (Baku: Azerbaijan Academy of Sciences, 1988); *Mollā Nasreddin (1906–1931)*, vol. 2, *1908–1909* (Baku: Azerbaijan Dovlet Neshriyyat, 2002); *Mollā Nasreddin (1906–1931)*, vol. 3, *1909–1910* (Baku: Çinar-Çap Neshriyyati, 2005).

46. *Slavs and Tatars Presents Molla Nasreddin: The Magazine that Would've Could've Should've* (Zurich: JRP Ringier, 2011), 4.

47. For examples of trees and tree trunks, and of the figure of a wise, aged interlocutor paired with a *Mollā Nāṣr al-Din*-like figure, see Āẕar, *Ruznāmeh-ye Āẕarbāijān*, 148, 15, and 163, respectively. I wish to thank Melanie Gibson for drawing my attention to the source.

48. Gocheleishvili, "Georgian Sources," 207–9 and notes.

49. Browne, *The Press and Poetry of Modern Persia*, 112–13.

50. Quoted in Bijan Shafei, Sohrab Soroushiani, and Victor Daniel, *Karim Taherzadeh Behzad Architecture: Architecture of Changing Times in Iran* (Tehran: Did Publications, 2004), 14–15n1.

51. Matin-Asgari, "The Impact of Imperial Russia," 22.

52. This description is based on numerous sources and original research for a forthcoming monograph. See note 34, above.

53. Beradze, "Looking Back and Ahead" has a more positive opinion of the Arzhangis' role.

54. Diba, "The Formation of Modern Iranian Art," 48–49.

Part III

Resistance to Supremacy

Contesting Imperial and State Control on the Southern Caspian Littoral

CHAPTER 13

In the Glocal Crossfire
Russia, Britain, and the Caspian, 1916–1919
Denis V. Volkov

The hostilities of the Great War, which also engulfed the entire Middle East shortly after the start of the war in Europe, devastated Iran in all the major existential dimensions—political, economic, and social. Iran's internal state had already been deplorable, owing to the century-long British-Russian stand-off in Iran, the recent Constitutional Revolution (1905-11), and nationalist unrest, as well as the presence of Russian military forces in Iran's northwest. As a scholar of Iran has written: "At no time since the civil wars of the eighteenth century had Iran faced a darker political moment than the period between 1915 and 1921. War and occupation coincided with the eclipse of nationalist hopes and the rise of secessionist movements. The rippling effects of the Bolshevik Revolution and Iran's ill-fated 1919 treaty with Britain further complicated the quagmire."[1] However, it should also be noted that armed hostilities between some of the main WWI adversaries had begun on Iran's soil several months before the assassination of

---

The author expresses his profound gratitude to the editors of this volume—Abbas Amanat, Kayhan Nejad, and Kevin Gledhill—for their insightful comments, and to all the organizers of the conference "The Caspian in the History of Early Modern and Modern Eurasia" that took place in March 2019 at the Yale MacMillan Center. Support from the Basic Research Program of the National Research University Higher School of Economics (HSE University) is gratefully acknowledged.

Archduke Franz Ferdinand. It was precisely the border areas inhabited by Kurds in west and northwest Iran where local combat groups, usually guided by Ottoman military officer-instructors, began their frequent attacks on Russian forces, starting from late winter 1914. These areas would later be designated the Persian Front of WWI.[2]

The events that unfolded during these years were deeply rooted in the entanglements of the so-called Great Game, which itself was heavily influenced by the protracted developments of the "Eastern Question." The empirical history of the British, French, and Russian presence in the Persianate world during the nineteenth and early twentieth centuries—political, military, or economic—has been fairly well studied by scholars such as Kazemzadeh, Keddie, Geyer, Vucinich, Ivanov, and Kulagina.[3] Later, benefiting from newly accessible archival collections and the productive application of postmodernist theories, others shed light from new angles on many shadowy lacunae and offered entirely new perspectives. Among many others, it is worth mentioning Aliev, Atabaki, Amanat, Cronin, Matthee, Richard, Bast, Chaquèri, and Andreeva.[4]

A separate body of secondary sources could be considered as nearly primary ones for the study of the history of the Caspian: the firsthand written evidence authored by the decision-making participants of the kaleidoscopic set of events that took place between 1915 and 1921 in northern Iran, Transcaucasia, and Transcaspia. In addition to empirical factual material, they provide us with what researchers seldom find in archival collections containing reports related to foreign policy and intelligence activities in the region, as well as correspondence between ministries and other state bodies. These, in turn, reveal the motives of the main decision-makers and the spirit of the time as perceived by these individuals. In terms of the British presence, the published writings of British military officers and political representatives are of foremost importance, since in all senses Britain was the only prevailing force in this region in this period after filling the vacuum left by Russia's withdrawal. First and foremost, it was Major General Lionel C. Dunsterville (1865-1946) who, due to the strategic spending of huge sums of money to secure his dashing military advance from Mesopotamia via northwest Iran to Baku, played a crucial role in the establishment of the Caucasian Caspian Alliance Government (1918-19).[5] Next in importance is an acknowledged historian of Iran, Brigadier-General Sir Percy M. Sykes (1867-1945), who raised the South Persia Rifles and was instrumental in helping the Russians protect Isfahan against Bakhtiari tribes during the war.[6] He left Iran only at the very end of

1918, and shortly later coauthored his memoirs, *Through the Deserts and Oases of Central Asia*, with his sister Ella Constance Sykes (1863–1939), herself an expert on Iran.[7] One should also mention Sir Arnold T. Wilson (1884–1940), civil commissioner for Mesopotamia in 1918–20, a staunch opponent of Arab autonomy and nationalism. It is noteworthy that he was one of the authors of the Iranian-Ottoman boundary and shared hardships and deprivations during the 1,200-mile eight-month journey of the Quadripartite Boundary Commission in 1913–14 together with Vladimir Minorsky (1877–1966), then his Russian counterpart. This very Minorsky later became one of the founders and foreign minister of the Caucasian Caspian Alliance Government.[8]

Another subordinate of Sir Percy Cox (1864–1937) to leave invaluable firsthand written evidence was Cecil J. Edmonds (1889–1979), an energetic actor and political officer for the region who also served in the Norperforce and was involved in the 1921 coup, as argued by Richard.[9] Finally, this hall of fame could be crowned with the writings of Lieutenant-Colonel Frederick M. Bailey (1882–1967), and Political and Intelligence Officer Reginald Teague-Jones (1889–1988). The former acted in Russian Turkestan (1918–20) and even ended up as a Bolshevik Cheka employee leading the hunt for himself—"a British rogue spy."[10] The latter, a Russianist, assisted in the establishment of the Caucasian Caspian Alliance Government that had overturned the Bolshevik rule in Transcaspia and was later stigmatized in the Soviet Union for decades as a British officer who had ordered the execution of the 26 Baku Commissars.[11] After his withdrawal from Turkestan, Teague-Jones had to live the rest of his life under the pseudonym of Ronald Sinclair out of fear of Bolshevik retribution, only making his secret diaries available for publication shortly before his death in 1988.[12] Therefore, given the professional agency of this extremely colorful mixture of British orientalists and Russianists, and their sometimes decisive involvement in the events and developments in question, it is difficult to overestimate the historiographical value of their eyewitness writings, which "often provide much of the meat to the skeleton constituted by official political reports and documents."[13]

As mentioned by Bast, such individuals "occupied a rather particular position within the framework of Britain's war-time and post-war intervention in Persia. . . . [They] operated at the nexus of warfare and diplomacy. Thus, [their accounts allow] for unique insights into how British military activities and British diplomatic measures, which were often conducted in far from perfect harmony with one another, played out on the ground in interaction with Iranian interlocutors as well as with representatives of other intervening powers, be they friends or foes."[14] Among these friends were Russians who did not accept the Bolshevik coup and fought against any manifestation of Bolshevism on Iran's territory, in the Caucasus, and in Central Asia. Their eyewitness evidence also constitutes another vast body of invaluable sources on the period, albeit modest in numbers and in quality of presentation due to the consequent hardships and perturbations of life in exile.[15] Some revealing material can be found in the memoirs of General Anton Denikin (1872–1947) as well as in the writings of the chief-commander of the Russian Expeditionary Forces in Iran (1915–18), Cavalry General Nikolay Baratov (1865–1932), namely *Persidskiĭ front Pervoĭ mirovoĭ* (The Persian Front of WWI).[16] It was precisely the remains of Baratov's forces who, lavishly paid by the British and under the command of the would-be head of the Caucasian Caspian Alliance Government, then merely Lieutenant-Colonel Lazar' Bicherakhov (1882–1952), constituted the main combat force of the Dunsterforce on their way from west Iran to Baku.[17] Another central figure of the developments on the Persian Front was the legendary Cossack Lieutenant-General Andrei Shkuro (1887–1947), who left his very telling *Zapiski belogo partizana* (Notes of a White Guerrilla Warrior).[18] In his storied career, Shkuro developed the guerrilla tactics among Russian forces both in the Western and Persian Fronts of WWI. He later served as the most successful commanding officer of the White Voluntary Army, earning the honor of Knight of the British Order of the Bath.

A separate body of revealing autobiographical documents, including those related to the region and the period of 1918–19, can be found in the State Archive of the Russian Federation under the title "Maria Wrangel Collection." After the poisoning of General Pyotr Wrangel (1878–1928) in Paris by Bolsheviks, his wife Maria took possession of the archive of the Russian All-Military Union, which he had formerly headed. She continued corresponding with emigrant Russian military officers and collecting their writings.[19] In all the above writings, in addition to a very detailed description of military hostilities and Russian troops' interaction with Iranians, one can find how Russian senior officers established and fared in their relations with their Entente allies. In particular, they shed new light on Russian engagement with the British, and particularly with General Dunsterville—topics that are still absent from international scholarship on the period.

However, it is noteworthy that English-language scholarship has addressed Britain's involvement in the Caspian, specifically during 1918-19, at a certain length by now. As soon as British archives started to open and the autobiographical life-writing of some of the most secret participants in the events became available in the second half of the twentieth century, researchers offered their updated analyses.[20] Research on the topic was later furthered by significantly more comprehensive and balanced works by scholars such as Kelly, Richard, and Ter Minassian.[21] Recently, there have appeared a very small number of Russian-language works by researchers such as Genis, Ter-Oganov, Bezugol'nyĭ, and Shishov, with a rather variable quality of analysis based on declassified archival documents pertinent to the Russian side of the topic.[22] Notwithstanding their interventions, Russian-language material has mainly not been integrated into international scholarship, just as Russian-language firsthand evidence on Russians' activities in the Caspian in the period 1918-19 remains seriously under-studied.

This chapter aims to undertake the first steps in tackling the above lapse, and to problematize the issue of the appearance and activities of the Caucasian Caspian Alliance Government, which became feasible only due to the confluence of political, military, and economic factors of global and local importance. In this sense, the Caspian represented a totally unique case. In addition to British and French forces, in winter 1918, there were still a few dozen thousands of Russian military forces remaining on Iranian soil, out of the seventy thousand to ninety thousand deployed in Iran's west and northwest during the earlier years of WWI.[23] These forces were rapidly diminishing in number, partially because of considerable desertion but mainly due to the official withdrawal launched in early 1918 by General Baratov. By this point, the remaining Russian forces were poorly financed and anticipated only further suspense after returning to their country, now marked by its lack of central power and stability. Unsurprisingly, many soldiers and officers thus opted to stay in Iran as mercenaries in the British service, further tempting their military fates and becoming part of the strategic plans to defend British India against the contemplated German and Ottoman advance through the Caucasus and Central Asia. Of course, it should be noted that this cooperation was neither officially nor in spirit of a mercenary nature, since the financial support was part of the Alliance treaty. As such, these were the relations of equals, contributing different elements to the joint war effort.[24]

As argued by Kelly, "During the first three years of the war, the British government had relied on the imperfect Anglo-Russian cordon sanitaire, which stretched from Egypt through southern Palestine, Mesopotamia, Persia and Afghanistan, to defend British India."[25] The February 1917 Revolution and, particularly, the October 1917 Bolshevik coup fostered the chaos of disobedience in the rank and file of the Russian military exhausted by the war, destroying its combat readiness and inducing the British to deal with an entirely different strategic setting. The line "along the Central Asiatic or Transcaspian Railway, which linked Batoum—via Baku, the Caspian Sea, Krasnovodsk and Askabad—to Merv, Bokhara and/or Tashkent,"[26] suddenly became extremely vulnerable in the face of the Central Powers' imminent-seeming offensive. Even if Germany and the Ottomans' assault on India would ultimately not be undertaken because of multiple logistical hurdles, their advance into the Caucasus and Central Asia could have secured them huge amounts of raw material, including wood, cotton, and, most importantly, oil.[27] Therefore, as concisely stressed by Major-General Dunsterville ex post facto in 1921, "obviously something had to be done."[28] Looking forward, we should note that the British succeeded, not so much in preventing Germans and Ottomans from penetrating into the Caucasus, but indisputably in securing the most important raw materials. This was achieved due to the employment of Lieutenant-Colonel Bicherakhov's Cossacks, and his establishment of the Caucasian Caspian Alliance Government.

The equilibrium that had so carefully been put together by the allied efforts, and that had looked reasonably firm along the line from Mesopotamia and all the way through the Caucasus to Transcaspia, collapsed in the blink of an eye due to the October 1917 coup and the Bolsheviks' declaration of the unilateral withdrawal of Russia from the war.[29] According to the firsthand evidence, the British supreme command considered it impossible to find new troops to fill the vast gap. As such, the command initially determined to send selected officers and NCOs to Tiflis in order to organize a combat unit consisting of locals and form a line of resistance against the Turks, as well as to hire the most combat-ready remainders of Baratov's forces in Iran to prevent the collapse of the Persian Front.[30] However, the first part of the plan failed, as Dunsterville's mission was unable to reach Tiflis.[31] Therefore, all military, financial, and political efforts on the site were concentrated on the formation of a strategic line from northwest Persia to the Caspian Sea. The main military force of this line originated from the three hundred men remaining from the once one-thousand-strong guerrilla detachment commanded by Lieutenant-Colonel Lazar' Bicherakhov, one of Baratov's best officers.[32]

It should be noted that the commander-in-chief of the British forces in Mesopotamia, Lieutenant-General William Marshall (1865–1939), became acquainted with Bicherakhov before Dunsterville arrived in Baghdad on January 18, 1918. In August 1917, adapting the well-proven guerrilla tactics established in 1916 by then-Cossack Captain Shkuro, Bicherakhov formed an extended detachment of thirty officers and one thousand Cossack cavalry equipped with machine guns, artillery, and transport vehicles. This was meant for operations against Turkish and Kurdish units in the enemy rear. In October 1917, the detachment successfully ambushed and captured a brigade of 2,500 Persian gendarmes with Swedish, German, and Turkish officer-instructors on the River Diyala in the vicinity of Qaṣr-e Shīrīn. The detachment then delivered the prisoners to the British, who granted Bicherakhov's soldiers military honors and an allowance. Bicherakhov's detachment then fought alongside the British near Qezel-Rabbāṭ and Qareh-Tappeh until a temporary lull set in, during which time his Cossacks found no outings more adventurous than regular tourist visits to the fabled city of Baghdad.[33]

Bicherakhov's successful October 25, 1917, operation became the last episode of WWI in which the Russian army took prisoners of war on all fronts. As early as November 28, 1917, after the issuance of the Bolsheviks' first decrees and the unilaterally proclaimed truce with the Germans, Bicherakhov sent a telegram to Baratov, asserting: "I have decided: 1) to remain at the front; 2) to continue fighting; 3) not to participate in the truce; 4) to consider all negotiations treacherous.... This is my decision and only I will answer for it to Russia." Baratov's resolution on the telegram stated: "Well done, Bicherakhov!"[34] So was the decision of several hundred other Cossacks who shortly after, beginning in early February 1918, joined Bicherakhov during his recruiting campaign in Iran, lavishly sponsored by Dunsterville. When on February 3, 1918, Dunsterville met Bicherakhov for the first time, he noted that Bicherakhov's detachment had dwindled to only three hundred Cossacks.[35] With only this small initial contingent, Bicherakhov and Dunsterville built the army of thirty thousand of the Caucasian Caspian Alliance Government by autumn 1918.[36]

Bicherakhov's personal biography is also of note. Bicherakhov, famed for shouting at and ostentatiously refusing to shake the hand of Lord

George Curzon (1859–1925) during their meeting in London in 1919 (of which more is said later in this chapter), was born on November 15, 1882, into the family of an Ossetian officer who served in the tsar's convoy in St Petersburg.[37] Bicherakhov spent his childhood in Tsarskoe Selo (the residence town of the Russian imperial family), playing with his peers from the tsar's family. He received his military education in the same prestigious Moscow military school (Alekseevskoe voennoe uchilishche) as the famous military orientologist Lieutenant-General Andrei Snesarev (1865–1937). It is curious that Bicherakhov served among Russian troops occupying north and west Iran before WWI and in an action against hostile Kurds, being severely wounded in 1911.[38] Having become a war invalid, he retired from military service and returned to Russia. However, at the outset of the First World War, he hurried to join Baratov's Expeditionary Corps, and it was only in June 1917 that he was entrusted to form a guerrilla detachment from the best Cossacks of the whole corps by Baratov.[39]

As mentioned above, Britain considered the Caspian to be of supreme importance both in terms of the defense of India and in terms of establishing control over the territories abandoned by Russia's imperial power that were rich in oil (the eastern Caucasus) and cotton (Central Asia).[40] In this context, in addition to Baku, specific attention was to be paid to "the permanent occupation of Krasnovodsk" (modern Türkmenbaşy, a port on the eastern side of the Caspian Sea—a gate to Central Asia), as was stipulated in the telegram received from the War Ministry by Dunsterville.[41] After Dunsterville's unsuccessful attempt to reach Tiflis via Anzali, which was "infested by the Jangalis and Russian revolutionary soldiers,"[42] and due to the severe shortage of British troops, the choice fell upon Russian volunteers from Baratov's corps. They were recommended to Dunsterville by General Marshall as combat-capable, disciplined, and utterly loyal to their beloved commander, Lieutenant-Colonel Bicherakhov, "a truly heroic figure," as later described by Dunsterville.[43] It became clear that the money allocated to be spent for Georgians, Armenians, and Russians in the Caucasus would be spent here, in Kermanshah and Hamedan. By that time, Bicherakhov's detachment ceased receiving an allowance from the corps, which was hastily withdrawing from Iranian territory.[44] Therefore, it happened that the parties found each other "for their mutual benefit,"[45] putting together their symbolic and material capital.

The military match did not necessarily lead to the successful fusion of cultures, though. As a literary digression herein, it is worth noting that even not every Russian officer was happy with the internal lifestyle of the Russian garrison in Iran established by Baratov, let alone the British. He possessed certain peculiarities in his behavior that, in the context of the time, were attributed to his descending from the military nobility of Caucasian origin by some and would cause criticism. The former private tutor to Ahmad Shah, Staff-Captain Konstantin Smirnov (1877–1938), who served at Baratov's headquarters in 1915-16, was highly critical about Baratov's strategical and tactical skills as a commander as well as about his habit of frequent and protracted drinking parties.[46] According to Dunsterville's diaries, the author once experienced cultural shock from Baratov's behavior:

> Such an appalling lunch with the Russian officers—General Baratov made a long speech and I replied in a short one, thinking it was all over. But he made 11 more. He toasted us, the British Army, our wives and families, our regiments, the Baghdad Army, the capture of Baghdad, the Union of the Churches, General Maude, General Marshall and many others, 1.30 to 5.30. My brain was rotted with platitudes, and my interior disturbed with endless food and drink. I was very cautious with the latter, but just sipped some very poor and sour Persian wine. Then Gen. Baratov and I kissed each other, and we were free at last—a whole day wasted.[47]

According to the agreement finally signed on March 26, 1918, Bicherakhov undertook not to leave his positions in Iran until they were filled by British troops, to coordinate all his military activities with the British command, and to prioritize fighting against Kuchek Khan's forces. The latter was necessary to clear the way to the Caspian Sea, making eventual provisions for joint operations in the Caucasus. On the other side, the British guaranteed the payment of factual expenses. Due to Bicherakhov's insistence, the agreement specifically stressed the exclusion of any mercenary element to their relationships.[48] In fact, being impressed by each other's character, Dunsterville and Bicherakhov developed very warm relations from the outset. General Marshall even once commented that "Dunsterville had obviously been under Bicherakhov's great influence."[49]

The amount of funding, however, was truly impressive. The first installment amounted to one million Iranian *qeran*s, which at the time was equivalent to roughly thirty thousand pounds.[50] For the purpose of comparison, one could mention a squabble that took place in the second half of 1919 between Sir Percy Cox, Earl Curzon, and the British treasury regarding exactly the same sum, which constituted Britain's share of the total of 160,000 tumans' monthly funding of the entire Persian Cossack Division.[51] However, there was one peculiar element underlying the whole financial side of this seemingly costly enterprise and making it far from a heavy burden for British taxpayers. For the entire year of 1918, Bicherakhov's forces' expenditures amounted to ten million *qeran*s, but also to thirty-five times more in rubles (one ruble was roughly five *qeran*s at the time). On average, Bicherakhov's Cossacks' monthly allowance was nine million rubles.[52] Where did all this money come from? As evidenced in the memoirs of one of Bicherakhov's officers quoting his British counterpart: "Certainly from Basrah."[53] Suffering from a severe shortage of cash, the Supreme Government of Russia's North Region, which was controlled by the Whites, thus applied to Britain in early summer 1918 with a request to print five hundred million imperial Russian rubles. With Petrograd and Moscow in the hands of the Bolsheviks, London printed imperial banknotes (*nikolaevki*) on a regular basis for the White armies, which were much more widely accepted throughout 1918 on the territory of the former Russian Empire than various other denominations, including *kerenki*.[54] Therefore, presumably, in the interests of the alliance and the expediting of the matter, the British directly used imperial rubles as their own means of payment, since as soon as Bicherakhov's troops left Iran, their expenses were paid only in the newly printed imperial *nikolaevki*.[55] Both in Iran and in the Caucasus, payments were fully made immediately as required. All this, multiplied by the military prowess of Bicherakhov's still not-numerous forces and his skillful command, allowed for a rapid advance of the joint British-Russian force through northwest Iran and their eventual arrival in Baku.

Nevertheless, Bicherakhov's high price was questioned more than once by the War Office, and Dunsterville invariably exclaimed that, in addition to Bicherakhov's financial scrupulosity, Bicherakhov's military and organizational skills were worth every penny spent.[56] Already decorated with the British orders C.B. (Companions of the Order of the Bath) and D.S.O. (Distinguished Service Order) by that time, Bicherakhov continued to prove his prowess. On March 28, 1918, he took Qazvin shortly before the Jangalis were about to do so. If the Jangalis had succeeded, Tehran would have raised their colors and the whole enterprise would have failed, as noted by Dunsterville.[57] Consequently, as hardly expected even by Dunsterville himself,[58] Bicherakhov succeeded in defeating the Jangalis at the Manjil bridge, which was well fortified and where the Jangalis had several-times superiority in numbers. The defeat by Bicherakhov (with insignificant casualties among his Cossacks) was so disappointing and crucial for the Jangalis that, as stated later by Ehsān-Allah Khan Dustdār, they lost their morale. Many returned home, and the revolutionary *Ettehād-e Eslām* committee "was about to dismiss the troops and to abandon all guerrilla activities."[59]

Shortly after, Bicherakhov arrived in Anzali, where he undertook to evacuate Baratov's Expeditionary Corps. However, an external hazard in the form of the Turks' advance toward Baku was imminent. The so-called Baku Commune was frantically looking for additional military force but, most importantly, for professional military commanders. This became another peculiar development of the period, when the strategic and tactical interests of outwardly opposed forces coincided. In this case, all three of the main actors of the region—the British, the Bolsheviks, and the Whites—were ready to make every effort to prevent the Ottomans from taking Baku. This led Bicherakhov to take a critical step that ruined his potentially remarkable career in the White Army. After certain negotiations, and after making clear to the Bolsheviks that he was determined to keep out of politics, Bicherakhov accepted the command of Baku's defense from the Bolsheviks for the sake of preserving his country's territorial integrity and fighting against foreign aggression. In fact, while disagreeing with the Bolsheviks' ideology and being sponsored by the British, he officially became a high-ranking Red Army commander licensed by the British. As he wrote: "At first, I just wanted to safely take my forces and the corps' possessions to the North Caucasus, but then decided to help everybody who was against the Germano-Turks."[60]

However, having occupied positions between Baku and the advancing Turkish troops in July 1918, Bicherakhov did not receive the significant reinforcement promised by both the Bolsheviks and the British. Moreover, to Bicherakhov's dismay, the Baku Bolsheviks, supported by the fiercely anti-British central Soviet government, entered into negotiations with the Germans. For their part, the Germans promised to preserve Bolshevik power in Baku in case of its voluntary surrender and the ousting of the British. The Bolsheviks even primarily undertook to secure oil reservoirs from destruction and to supply Baku oil to the Germans and Turks, as well as to hand over Bicherakhov's Cossacks and the insignificant British force to the Germans in case of their advance on Baku.[61] On realizing all the consequences that would ensue from a betrayal so unthinkable for all ancien régime officers, Bicherakhov once and for all completely reconfigured his attitude toward the Bolsheviks and withdrew his forces to Derbent in Dagestan, from where he was destined to open a new chapter in his tumultuous but short-lived career as a military commander-in-chief, and now a statesman.

Only a few days after Bicherakhov's withdrawal from the positions, on August 1, 1918, the Baku Bolsheviks were overthrown by what could be considered the progenitor of the Caucasian Caspian Alliance Government, the so-called Central-Caspian Dictatorship and its Provisional Executive Committee of the Soviet, a rather inclusive political conglomeration embracing socialist revolutionaries, Mensheviks, and Armenian Dashnaks. They immediately organized an effective defensive line for Baku, applied to the British for aid, and appointed Bicherakhov commander-in-chief of the Caucasus, including all land troops and Caspian naval forces. Shortly before this, the socialist revolutionaries and Mensheviks, not without the help of Major-General Wilfrid Malleson stationed in Mashhad, succeeded in their uprising against the Bolsheviks on the opposite side of the Caspian Sea, in Askhabad (modern Ashgabat). Thus, the Transcaspian Provisional Government was established and immediately proposed to unite all their material and human resources as well as political power with their confederates in the Caucasus.[62] So, after Bicherakhov's men ousted the Bolsheviks from Derbent and reached the River Terek, the emerging power controlled vast territories including the north and east Caucasus, west and north Iran (Bicherakhov maintained strong communications with the Persian Cossack Division and the Russian ancien régime Legation), the Caspian Sea, and Transcaspia. A figure with indisputable authority was needed to head this new imposing body, which was to be called the Caucasian Caspian Alliance Government. With his impressive capital, both symbolic and material, who could have been a more unifying figure for all local patriotic anti-Bolshevik elements in the Caspian than the now full Colonel Lazar Bicherakhov?

It appears that after his disastrous experience of working with the Bolsheviks, Bicherakhov came to the conclusion that they were no less the enemies of his motherland than the "Germano-Turks" who wanted the disintegration of his country. His rather simplistic and orientalist opposition to pan-Islamism and the demonstrative apolitical status of a professional military man were no longer able to respond to the tasks of the moment. His new status of a land-gatherer (*sobiratel' zemel'*) was incompatible with his political illiteracy, as acknowledged by Bicherakhov himself.[63] Here, the acting head of the Russian Legation, Vladimir

Minorsky, turned out to be very instrumental for Bicherakhov. Bicherakhov coordinated all steps with political implications in 1918 with the Russian Legation in Iran. Having authored the Caucasian Caspian Alliance Government constituent charter, Minorsky received the post of minister for external relations (foreign affairs), but was the godfather to the whole enterprise of the alliance. He constantly commuted between Tehran, Ashkhabad, and Baku, and guided Bicherakhov in all political affairs.[64] It is noteworthy that among other stipulations, the government charter defined its main principles as "restoration of Russia's statehood and reunification of the divided regions of the Russian Democratic Republic, continuation of the struggle against German-Turkish aggression and the establishment of order and legality on the fundamentals that existed before October 25, 1917."[65] Headed by Bicherakhov, the government proclaimed its ultimate goal, after the cleansing of Russia from the "Bolshevik disease," as the hand-over of power to the All-Russia Constituent Assembly to decide the further destiny of Russia. The Bolsheviks were associated with terror, exploitation of international enmity, and conciliation with the external enemy. As conceived by Minorsky, his cooperation with Bicherakhov throughout all 1918 and early 1919 was to "support the Russian Cause" (*Russkoe delo*) during the civil war.[66]

The Armistice of Mudros (October 30, 1918) and the withdrawal of Ottoman troops introduced fundamental changes to the region. The British no longer needed Bicherakhov's stronghold to stand in the way of Ottomans' potential advance toward Caspian and Central Asian resources. Now British forces were controlling these resources themselves, and the focus switched to the struggle against the Bolsheviks. This also included the mounting support of local nationalism and the establishment of independent states in the Caucasus, which in the eyes of individuals such as Bicherakhov and Minorsky, who aspired the restoration of Russia's pre-WWI borders, represented sheer separatism. As such, they no longer fit into British plans.[67] In addition, by late 1918, the Voluntary Army under the command of General Denikin had been carrying out successful operations against the Bolsheviks in the south and had reached the territory controlled by Major-General Bicherakhov's thirty-thousand-strong forces,[68] which now were to be incorporated into Denikin's army. Ironically enough, the Baku episode undeservedly turned out to be destructive for the military careers of both Dunsterville and Bicherakhov. The British supreme command considered the former's activities to protect Baku unsuccessful and recalled him. The short-sighted Denikin could not forgive the latter's brief cooperation with the Bolsheviks and did not offer him a post in the Voluntary Army, compelling him to resign on January 14, 1919. After merging with Denikin's army, many of Bicherakhov's officers and soldiers were stripped of their ranks and the combat awards conferred by Bicherakhov. In their negotiations with Denikin, the British also insisted on the dismissal of the Caucasian Caspian Alliance Government, which they claimed to conflict with their plans for the establishment of independent states in the Caucasus.[69]

The British forced Bicherakhov's withdrawal from the scene—similar to Minorsky's later removal from Iran by Sir Percy Cox[70]—in a rather sophisticated manner. After his resignation, Bicherakhov was given the rank of British army general and was invited to London with his closest senior officers. According to their memoirs, Bicherakhov was to be introduced to King George V, who was going to award him the title of lord and the Order of the Garter. Most importantly, Bicherakhov was told that the War Office was waiting for him to agree plans for further actions against the Bolsheviks.[71] There is no evidence that the meeting with the king took place, nor is Bicherakhov's surname mentioned on the list of the Knights of the Garter.[72] Meanwhile, Bicherakhov and his officers indeed lived in London in a luxurious hotel for quite a while as the guests of the king. However, Bicherakhov's numerous energetic efforts to get in touch with the War Office remained in vain. Finally, after spending much effort, with the help of the Russian ambassador and Sir Samuel Hoare (1880–1959), the former MI-6 head in Petrograd and future secretary of state for air, a meeting with Lord George Curzon was arranged. At the meeting, Bicherakhov realized that not only was he no longer of relevance and that no one even intended to discuss his plans against the Bolsheviks, but also that the British were refusing to pay the delayed remunerations to his wounded Cossacks and the families of the killed. This had been agreed with General Marshall in Mesopotamia and paid by Dunsterville on a routine basis when he was in command, but had remained outstanding after his dismissal. This was too far from Bicherakhov's occidentalized notion of "the English gentlemen." He felt even more offended by Curzon's consolatory offer "to do something for the general only." Therefore, Bicherakhov openly accused the British of not keeping their word and abruptly finished the meeting, outwardly demonstrating his contempt and refusing to pay due respect to Curzon.

The next day, Bicherakhov and his headquarters were notified that they had ceased to be the guests of the king.[73]

The eventual outcome of Bicherakhov's incredible activities in Mesopotamia, Iran, and the Caucasus deeply impacted him. As he depicted it in one of his letters to Denikin: "At first, due to contingency I had a detachment, then I accidentally gathered an army, then a fleet joined me by accident. The same simple contingency will wash everything away from my hands and I will remain without a single soldier."[74] The fact that Bicherakhov had suffered the full unexpected debacle not on the battleground from the enemy but from the allies and his own compatriots (the White Army) remained incomprehensible and no less than a betrayal for him. After all, Bicherakhov had continued fighting the external enemy after the Western Front collapsed and had founded an organized anti-Bolshevik movement in the Caspian, amassing an army of thirty thousand, in comparison with Denikin's force of slightly more than forty thousand. He never returned to Russia and eventually settled in France, working as a cook in a small restaurant owned by one of his fellow Ossetian countrymen. He did not write his memoirs and never shared his memories with those of his brothers-in-arms who did.[75]

Being unversed in political affairs, Bicherakhov, of course, was far from able to properly analyze this "contingency," which in fact was a confluence of multiple political, military, economic, and even cultural factors of global and local character. All of these factors, in turn, were cemented by Bicherakhov's own charisma, military prowess, nobleness, and discursive perceptions of *Russkoe delo*. Once again, as the most crucial region of the broader Persianate world, the Caspian found itself in the crossfire of the WWI participants' interests due to its strategic importance as an economic and cultural hub with great political and military potential. Bicherakhov's case came to be only one part of a much bigger picture that still remains to be properly understood. What appears clear enough is that none of the three main parties were able to formulate long-term strategies in such circumstances. The anti-Bolshevik forces were not united and did not follow any joint cause. Both the Bolsheviks and the British intermittently recruited interim travel companions and abandoned them according to momentary political expediency, as in the case of the Bolsheviks with the Jangalis and the Iranian left; in the multiple cases of the British withdrawal of support from individual actors of *Russkoe delo*, Caucasian nationalists, and the White movement; and, finally, in the British settlement of terms with the Bolsheviks.

Notes

1. Abbas Amanat, *Iran: A Modern History* (New Haven, CT: Yale University Press, 2017), 390.

2. Aleksandr Shishov, *Persidskiĭ front (1909–1918)* (Moscow: Izdatel'skiĭ dom Veche, 2010), 4–5. See Denis V. Volkov, *Russia's Turn to Persia: Orientalism in Diplomacy and Intelligence* (Cambridge: Cambridge University Press, 2018), 111, 115, 133. Nugzar Ter-Oganov, "A Russian Officer's Letters on Russian and British Activities in Iran during World War I," in *Russians in Iran: Diplomacy and Power in the Qajar Era and Beyond*, ed. Rudi Matthee and Elena Andreeva (London: I. B. Tauris, 2018), 173–85. See also Oliver Bast, *Les Allemands en Perse pendant la Première Guerre mondiale: D'après les sources diplomatiques françaises* (Paris: Peeters, 1997); Bast, *La Perse et la Grande Guerre: Etudes réunies et présentées* (Tehran: Inst. Français de Recherche en Iran, 2002); Touraj Atabaki, ed., *Iran and the First World War: Battleground of the Great Powers* (London: I. B. Tauris, 2006).

3. Firuz Kazemzadeh, *Russia and Britain in Persia, 1865–1914: A Study in Imperialism* (New Haven, CT: Yale University Press, 1968); Kazemzadeh, *The Struggle for Transcaucasia, 1917–1921* (New York: Philosophical Library, 1951); Nikki Keddie, *Qajar Iran and the Rise of Reza Khan* (Costa Mesa, CA: Mazda, 1999); Wayne S. Vucinich, ed., *Russia and Asia: Essays on the Influence of Russia on the Asian Peoples* (Stanford, CA: Hoover Institution Press, 1972); Dietrich Geyer, *Russian Imperialism: The Interaction of Domestic and Foreign Policy, 1860–1914* (Oxford: Berg, 1987); Mikhail Sergeevich Ivanov and Viacheslav Zaĭtsev, eds., *Novaia istoriia Irana* (Moscow: Nauka, 1988); Liudmila Kulagina, *Rossiia i Iran (XIX—nachalo XX veka)* (Moscow: Kliuch-S, 2010).

4. See Saleh Mamedogly Aliev, *Istoriia Irana: XX vek* (Moscow: Kraft+IV RAN, 2004); Atabaki, *Iran and the First World War*; Atabaki, *Beyond Essentialism: Who Writes Whose Past in the Middle East and Central Asia?* (Amsterdam: Aksant Academic Publishers, 2012); Abbas Amanat and Assef Ashraf, eds., *The Persianate World: Rethinking a Shared Sphere* (Leiden: Brill, 2019); Amanat, *Iran*; Stephanie Cronin, ed., *Iranian-Russian Encounters: Empires and Revolutions since 1800* (London: Routledge, 2013); Cronin, *The Army and the Creation of the Pahlavi State in Iran, 1910–1926* (London: I. B. Tauris, 1997); Bast, *Les Allemands en Perse pendant la Première Guerre mondiale*; Bast, "The Council for International Propaganda and the Establishment of the Iranian Communist Party," in Atabaki, *Iran and the First World War*, 163–76; Bast, "Putting the Record Straight: Vosuq al-Dowleh's Foreign Policy in 1918/19," in *Men of Order: Authoritarian Modernization under Atatürk and Reza Shah*, ed. Touraj Atabaki and Erik J. Zürcher (London: I. B. Tauris, 2004), 260–81; Matthee and Andreeva, *Russians in Iran*; Cosroe Chaquèri, *The Soviet Socialist Republic of Iran, 1920–1921: Birth of the Trauma* (Pittsburgh: University of Pittsburgh Press, 1995); Elena Andreeva, *Russia and Iran in the Great Game: Travelogues and Orientalism* (New York: Routledge, 2007); Yann Richard and Willem M. Floor, *Iran: A Social and Political History since the Qajars* (Cambridge: Cambridge University Press, 2019); Nikki N. Keddie,

Roots of Revolution: An Interpretive History of Modern Iran (New Haven, CT: Yale University Press, 2006).

5. See Lionel Dunsterville, *The Adventures of Dunsterforce* (London: Edward Arnold, 1920); Dunsterville, *Stalky's Reminiscences* (London: Jonathan Cape, 1928); Dunsterville, *More Yarns by "Stalky"* (London: Stalky & Co., 1931). See also Lionel Dunsterville, "From Baghdad to the Caspian, 1918," *Geographical Journal* 57, no. 3 (1921): 153-64.

6. The South Persia Rifles were a military force that at its peak consisted of eight thousand local tribal and sedentary recruits commanded by British officers, acting from 1916 to 1921 in the Iranian provinces of Fars, Isfahan, and Kerman. For more detail, see Floreeda Safiri, "South Persia Rifles," *Encyclopaedia Iranica Online*, https://www.iranicaonline.org/articles/south-persia-rifles-militia.

7. See Percy M. Sykes and Ella C. Sykes, *Through Deserts and Oases of Central Asia* (London: Macmillan, 1920); Percy Sykes and Lionel Dunsterville, "From Baghdad to the Caspian in 1918: Discussion," *Geographical Journal* 57, no. 3 (1921): 164-66. On Sykes's activities, see also Antony Winn, *Persia in the Great Game: Sir Percy Sykes, Explorer, Consul, Soldier, Spy* (London: John Murrey, 2004). Also see Denis Wright, "Sykes, Percy Molesworth," *Encyclopaedia Iranica Online*, https://www.iranicaonline.org/articles/sykes-percy.

8. See Arnold Wilson, *Loyalties: Mesopotamia, 1914-1917. A Personal and Historical Record* (London: Oxford University Press, 1930); Wilson, *Mesopotamia, 1917-1920: A Clash of Loyalties. A Personal and Historical Record* (London: Oxford University Press, 1931). On Wilson's cooperation with Minorsky, see Denis V. Volkov, "Vladimir Minorsky (1877-1966) and the Iran-Iraq War (1980-8)," in Matthee and Andreeva, *Russians in Iran*, 188-216, and Arnold Wilson, A. C. Wratislaw, and Percy Sykes, "The Demarcation of the Turco-Persian Boundary in 1913-1914: Discussion," *Geographical Journal* 66, no. 3 (1925): 237-42.

9. Cecil J. Edmonds, *East and West of Zagros: Travel, War and Politics in Persia and Iraq, 1913-1921*, ed. Yann Richard (Leiden: Brill, 2010), xiv. See Cecil J. Edmonds, *Kurds, Turks and Arabs: Politics, Travel and Research in North-Eastern Iraq, 1919-1925* (London: Oxford University Press, 1957). Edmonds's *East and West of Zagros* was prepared with devotion for publication by another scholar of Iran, Yann Richard, with a remarkable introduction. Also see Oliver Bast, "Cecil John Edmonds. East and West of Zagros: Travel, War and Politics in Persia and Iraq, 1913-1921," *Abstracta Iranica*, 34-35-36 (2017), https://doi.org/10.4000/abstractairanica.48458. On the Norperforce, see Denis Wright, "Ironside, William Edmund," *Encyclopaedia Iranica Online*, https://iranicaonline.org/articles/ironside-william-edmund.

10. See Frederick M. Bailey, "A Visit to Bokhara in 1919," *Geographical Journal* 57, no. 2 (1921): 75-87. Also see Frederick M. Bailey, *Mission to Tashkent* (London: J. Cape, 1946). On Bailey's activities, see also Peter Hopkirk, *Setting the East Ablaze: Lenin's Dream of an Empire in Asia* (London: Kodansha International, 1984). See also Arthur Swinson, *Beyond the Frontiers: The Biography of Colonel F.M. Bailey, Explorer and Special Agent* (London: Hutchinson of London, 1971).

11. These were elevated to the status of sacred innocent victims by Soviet propaganda until the collapse of the USSR.

12. See Reginald Teague-Jones, *The Spy Who Disappeared: Diary of a Secret Mission to Russian Central Asia in 1918* (London: Gollancz, 1990); see the very informative introduction by Peter Hopkirk therein. Also see Taline Ter Minassian, "Some Fresh News about the 26 Commissars: Reginald Teague-Jones and the Transcaspian Episode," *Asian Affairs* 45, no. 1 (2014): 65-78. In the article, Ter Minassian questions the Soviet version and studies "how the legend grew and why the involvement of an agent of British Imperialism fitted a propaganda need." Also see an exhaustive study on Teague-Jones's persona in Taline Ter Minassian and Tom Rees, *Most Secret Agent of Empire: Reginald Teague-Jones, Master Spy of the Great Game* (London: Hurst, 2014).

13. Willem Floor, "Edmonds C. J., *East and West of Zagros: Travel, War and Politics in Persia and Iraq 1913–1921*, ed. with intro. by Yann Richard [review]," *Bulletin critique des Annales islamologiques* 23 (2013), https://www.ifao.egnet.net/bcai/28/58.

14. Bast, "Cecil John Edmonds."

15. See Touraj Atabaki and Denis V. Volkov, "Flying away from the Bolshevik Winter: Soviet Refugees across the Southern Borders (1917-30)," *Journal of Refugee Studies* 34, no. 2 (2001): 1900-1922.

16. See Anton Denikin, *Ocherki Russkoĭ smuty* (Paris: J. Povolozky & Co. Editeurs, 1921). See Hoover Institution Archives, Collection 81131, N. N. Baratov papers.

17. See Alekseĭ Bezugol'nyĭ, *General Bicherakhov i ego Kavkazskai͡a armii͡a* (Moscow: Tsentrpoligraf, 2011).

18. See Andreĭ Shkuro, *Zapiski belogo partizana* (Buenos Aires: Seiatel', 1961). Shkuro's hatred toward the Bolsheviks was so lasting and burning that in 1944 he secured himself an appointment as head of the Cossack Reserve Troops at the SS General Headquarters. Having been extradited to the Soviets by the British at the end of WWII, he was hanged in 1947 on Stalin's orders after protracted torture.

19. In this huge collection, see, for example, documents related to Iran: Gosudarstvennyĭ Arkhiv Rossiĭskoĭ Federat͡sii (hereafter GARF), f. 10003, op. 12, k. 46.

20. For example, see L. P. Morris, "British Secret Missions in Turkestan, 1918-19," *Journal of Contemporary History* 12, no. 2 (1977): 363-79. Also see Hopkirk, *Setting the East Ablaze*; Hopkirk, *On Secret Service East of Constantinople: The Plot to Bring down the British Empire* (Oxford: Oxford University Press, 1994); Hopkirk, *The Great Game: On Secret Service in High Asia* (London: Kodansha, 1994). Also see Ter Minassian and Rees, *Most Secret Agent of Empire*.

21. See Sean Kelly, "How Far West? Lord Curzon's Transcaucasian (Mis)Adventure and the Defence of British India, 1918-23," *International History Review* 35, no. 2 (2013): 274-93. See also Yann Richard, "Foreword," in Edmonds, *East and West of Zagros*, xi-xviii. See also Ter Minassian, "Some Fresh News about the 26 Commissars."

22. See Vladimir Genis, *Krasnaia Persiia: Bol'sheviki v Giliane, 1920–1921. Dokumental'naia khronika* (Moscow: MNPI, 2000); Genis, *Vitse—Konsul Vvedenskii* (Moscow: MYSL', 2003). See also Nugzar Ter-Oganov, *Persidskaia kazach'ia brigada, 1879–1921 gg.* (Moscow: IV RAN, 2012); Ter-Oganov, "A Russian Officer's Letters." See also Bezugol'nyĭ, *General Bicherakhov*. See also Shishov, *Persidskiĭ front*.

23. See Atabaki and Volkov, "Flying Away from the Bolshevik Winter," 0000.

24. See Dunsterville, *The Adventures of Dunsterforce*, 77–78.

25. Kelly, "How Far West?," 275.

26. Kelly, "How Far West?," 275.

27. Kelly, "How Far West?," 275–76.

28. Dunsterville, "From Baghdad to the Caspian, 1918," 153.

29. See the documents of the collection *Mirnye peregovory v Brest-Litovske s 9(22) dekabria 1917 g. po 3(16) marta 1918 g.*, vol. 1 (Moscow, 1920). See also Peter Holquist, *Making War, Forging Revolution: Russia's Continuum of Crisis, 1914–1921* (Cambridge, MA: Harvard University Press, 2002). See also Sheila Fitzpatrick, *The Russian Revolution* (Oxford: Oxford University Press, 2008).

30. See Dunsterville, *The Adventures of Dunsterforce*, 4–6.

31. See the notes for the days February 16–20, 1918, in Lionel Dunsterville, *The Diaries of General Lionel Dunsterville, 1911–1922*, The World War I Document Archive, accessed September 10, 2020), http://www.gwpda.org/Dunsterville/Dunsterville_1918.html. See also Dunsterville, *The Adventures of Dunsterforce*, 23.

32. See Dunsterville, "From Baghdad to the Caspian, 1918," 153–54.

33. See Bezugol'nyĭ, *General Bicherakhov*, 28–29. See Dunsterville, "From Baghdad to the Caspian, 1918," 154.

34. Bezugol'nyĭ, *General Bicherakhov*, 31.

35. See Dunsterville, *Diaries*.

36. RGVA, f. 39779, op. 2, d. 35, l. 8.

37. As was put in 1920 by Dunsterville, quite in the orientalist spirit of the time: "an Ossietin Cossack, one of those semi-wild tribes that are typical of the North Caucasus" (Dunsterville, *The Adventures of Dunsterforce*, 21). It is noteworthy that by WWI there were four hundred generals in the Russian army, and 25 percent of them were of Ossetian origin: Fedor Kireev, "Osetinskiĭ fenomen v istorii Terskogo kazach'ego voĭska," *Dar'ial* 5 (2003): 270–84. For the Curzon episode, see Bezugol'nyĭ, *General Bicherakhov*, 249–51.

38. He was lamed, had a wound through his lung, and a maimed left hand.

39. See RGVA, f. 39779, op. 2, d. 20, ll. 21–28; d. 24, l. 222. See also Bezugol'nyĭ, *General Bicherakhov*, 23–26.

40. The National Archives (hereafter TNA), CAB 27/24, Eastern Committee, 13th Meeting, Minutes, June 11, 1918. See also Sergei Lavrov, "Politika Anglii na Kavkaze i v Sredneĭ Azii v 1917-1921 gg.," *Voprosy istorii* 5 (1979): 81.

41. RGASPI, f. 71, op. 35, d. 282, ll. 82–83.

42. At the time, Dunsterville had twelve officers, two clerks, forty-one cars with drivers, and one armored vehicle (Dunsterville, *The Adventures of Dunsterforce*, 16, 27).

43. See Dunsterville, "From Baghdad to the Caspian, 1918," 159. See also Dunsterville, *The Adventures of Dunsterforce*, 21-22.
44. See Bezugol'nyĭ, *General Bicherakhov*, 40.
45. Dunsterville, "From Baghdad to the Caspian, 1918," 159.
46. See Nugzar Ter-Oganov, "Letters from Officer/Orientalist K.N. Smirnov from the Caucasian Front as a Source for the Study of the Military/Political Situation in Turkey and Iran in 1914-1917," Voennyĭ sbornik 6, no. 4 (2014): 213.
47. See Dunsterville, *Diaries*, February 12th, 1918
48. See Dunsterville, *The Adventures of Dunsterforce*, 77-78.
49. RGASPI, f. 71, op. 35, d. 282, l. 5.
50. See Dunsterville, *The Adventures of Dunsterforce*, 156.
51. TNA, FO 248/1262 (Persia, Cossack Division Payment, b) Disposal of Russian Officers), 165164/W/34 (Cox to Foreign Office and to the Treasury).
52. See Bezugol'nyĭ, *General Bicherakhov*, 46.
53. Nikolai Lishin, *Na Kaspiĭskom more: God Beloĭ bor'by* (Prague: Morskoĭ zhurnal, 1938), 32.
54. The banknotes printed after the February revolution under Kerensky's Provisional Government. See Bezugol'nyĭ, *General Bicherakhov*, 47-48.
55. See Lishin, *Na Kaspiĭskom more*, 31.
56. See Dunsterville, *The Adventures of Dunsterforce*, 122.
57. Dunsterville, *The Adventures of Dunsterforce*, 121.
58. See Dunsterville, *Diaries*, April 14, 1918.
59. See Rudolf Abikh, "Natsional'noe i revoliutsionnoe dvizhenie v Persii v 1917-1919 gg. (Vospominaniĭa Ėhsan Ully-Khana)," *Novyĭ Vostok* 26-27 (1929): 134.
60. Bezugol'nyĭ, *General Bicherakhov*, 75.
61. RGVA, f. 39779, op. 2, d. 34, l. 12. See also Bezugol'nyĭ, *General Bicherakhov*, 85-86. See also Dunsterville, *The Adventures of Dunsterforce*, 196, 198-99.
62. Dunsterville, *The Adventures of Dunsterforce*, 89-91, 93-94.
63. See Bezugol'nyĭ, *General Bicherakhov*, 96.
64. GARF, f. 200, op. 1, d. 376, ll. 17, 54 (Minorsky's cables to the head of the All-Russia Provisional Government). See also Bezugol'nyĭ, *General Bicherakhov*, 143-44.
65. RGVA, f. 39779, op. 2, d. 51, ll. 8, 8ob.
66. RGVA, f. 39779, op. 2, d. 51, l. 9a.
67. AVPRI, f. 134 (Minorsky collection), op. 1, d. 212, ll. 1-5. See also TNA, FO 248/1262 (Russian Officials, 1919), l. 8 (Cox to FO, 13.01.1919). GARF, f. 446, op. 2, d. 56, ll. 137, 137ob (Intelligence report to Denikin, September 13, 1919).
68. In October 1918, Minorsky also negotiated with the All-Russia Provisional Government (headquartering in Ufa and then in Omsk) the official acknowledgement of the Caucasian Caspian Alliance Government and delivered Bicherakhov the new rank of major-general, bestowed on behalf of the supreme command of the White forces in Omsk (GARF, f. 200, op. 1, d. 378 [Minorsky's correspondence with the General Headquarters]; f. 200, op. 1, d. 376, l. 17, 54).

69. See Bezugol'nyĭ, *General Bicherakhov*, 231–35.

70. TNA, FO 248/1262 (Russian Officials, 1919), l. 67 (Cox to FO on Minorsky, September 15, 1919); WO 106/55/26 (Persia, Section 1), l. 86584 (Cox to Curzon on Minorsky, September 3, 1919). See also AVPRI, f. 134 (Minorsky collection), op. 1, d. 212, ll. 1–5. See also TNA, FO 248/1262 (Russian Officials, 1919), l. 8 (Cox to FO, January 13, 1919).

71. See Bezugol'nyĭ, *General Bicherakhov*, 238.

72. "List of the Knights of the Garter," *Heraldica*, accessed September 10, 2021), https://www.heraldica.org/topics/orders/garterlist.htm.

73. See Bezugol'nyĭ, *General Bicherakhov*, 249–51.

74. RGVA, f. 39779, op. 2, d. 39, l. 8.

75. See Bezugol'nyĭ, *General Bicherakhov*, 12, 252.

CHAPTER 14

The Jangal Movement and Regional Revolutionaries in Northern Iran, 1914–1921

Kayhan A. Nejad

On May 18, 1920, Soviet representatives landed in Anzali and, alongside the leadership of the Jangal Movement of Gilan (1914–20), founded the Soviet Socialist Republic of Iran (SSRI, 1920–21). While providing a critical lifeline to the Jangalis, the establishment of the SSRI spelled the end of the ideological flexibility that characterized their movement, which had forged ties with the Bolsheviks in Baku and other revolutionary actors throughout northern Iran, Central Asia, and the South Caucasus. These movements, variously rooted in the ideas of democratic socialism, national liberation, pan-Islamism, and even pan-Turkism, posed a broad-reaching challenge to both British imperialism and Bolshevism through the late stages of the Russian Civil War (1917–22). The Jangalis' emergence in this space of political and ideological contestation raises questions on the directions and interrelations of their movement: Where did the Jangalis fit among the revolutionary movements of the Iranian north, and did their movement reflect unique potential for an alliance with Russian socialists?

Some scholars have evaluated revolution in northern Iran in terms of its broader geopolitical significance, centering the diplomatic and strategic functions of the SSRI for the foreign actors involved. Primarily, historians have probed Moscow's withdrawal of support for the SSRI, centralizing debates between a cautious majority of early Soviet leadership and a small cadre of maximalist revolutionaries in the Caucasus.[1] In her study of early Soviet Azerbaijan, for example, Sara Brinegar probes state economic interests, arguing that the Russian Soviet Federative Socialist Republic allowed the Azerbaijan Soviet Socialist Republic's expansion into the Iranian north to safeguard the flow of Baku oil.[2] Relatedly, the work of Denis V. Volkov has demonstrated that British alliances with the anti-Bolshevik White Russian movement in the Iranian north and the South Caucasus were shifting and contingent.[3] In so doing, Volkov has complicated the work of historians such as Stephen Blank, who centered Soviet fears of British countermeasures in explaining the Red withdrawal from the Iranian north.[4]

This emphasis on early Soviet policy debates may distance the SSRI from the contiguity of northern Iranian revolutionary movements from which it emerged. In her work on revolutionary challenges to the late Qajar and early Pahlavi states, however, Stephanie Cronin has examined the revolutionary movements that developed on the Jangalis' eastern and western flanks, including in Khorasan and Iranian Azerbaijan.[5] Pezhmann Dailami has also probed the Jangalis' early links with regional Bolshevik movements to argue that the Jangalis espoused leftist beliefs despite their alliance with the Central Powers during the First World War.[6] The emergence of these movements, while dissimilar, suggested a broad dissatisfaction with the state of Iran in the early twentieth century, and the search for alternatives rooted in Iranian and non-Iranian political cultures.

While reflective of the revolutionary currents flowing through northern Iran in the early twentieth century, the Jangal insurgency developed in its early years as a distinctly Iranian and Gilani movement. This chapter resituates the Jangal Movement in this non-Bolshevik tradition of northern Iranian revolutionary protest. In so doing, it argues that the Jangalis accorded ideologically with geographically contiguous protest movements in northern Iran rather than with Bolshevism prior to 1920. Moreover, it asks why, despite the ideological affinities between the Jangalis and other northern Iranian revolutionary movements, the Soviets identified Gilan rather than Iranian Azerbaijan or Khorasan as the most viable conduit for the socialization of Iran.

Revolution in the Iranian North

In the early twentieth century, South Caucasian revolutionaries came to the aid of their Iranian counterparts, providing materiel, manpower, and ideological backing against both the Qajar monarchy (1794–1925) and the Russian and British Empires. In 1905–6, Iranian and South Caucasian revolutionaries affiliated with the Baku Committee of the Russian Social Democratic Labor Party (Rossiĭskaia sotsial-demokraticheskaia rabochaia partiia, RSDRP) began crossing into northern Iran, establishing the Hidden Center (Markaz-e Ghaybi) in Tabriz and orchestrating acts of political violence throughout the Iranian north.[7] In tandem, RSDRP leaders began agitating among the Iranian and Russian Muslim wage laborers in the Baku oil industry following their formation of the Hümmət (Hemmat) Party in 1904.[8] Hümmət functioned not only to radicalize Baku labor, but also to link the city's revolutionary elements with socialist and socialist-leaning Iranian parties, namely the Ejtemā'iyyun-e 'Āmiyyun (Social Democrats) and its more moderate offshoot, the Ferqeh-ye Demokrāt (Democrats).[9]

The Baku radical tradition imprinted on the Second Constitutional Majles (parliament) of 1909–11, in which the Democrats emerged as the leading party.[10] Reflecting the early organizational efforts of Caucasian revolutionaries including Ḥaydar Khan 'Amu-Oghlu Tāriverdi (d. 1921), the Democrats adapted the socialist demands of the Baku Bolsheviks to a uniquely Iranian political context. As such, the Democrats proposed to secularize Iranian political institutions, promote the welfare of the rural poor, and protect Iranian sovereignty.[11] As the Constitutional Revolution entered its latter phases, initiated by the anticonstitutional coup of Moḥammad 'Ali Shah in Tehran (June 23, 1908) and the ensuing rebellion of the *Anjoman-e Āẕarbāyejān* (Anjoman of Azerbaijan) in the Iranian northwest, South Caucasian revolutionaries found a common cause with their Iranian counterparts.[12] Hundreds of Russian subjects thus crossed the Aras River into Iranian Azerbaijan, where they helped repel Qajar-aligned forces that had besieged Tabriz.[13] A second corps of revolutionaries traveled via the Caspian to Gilan, entering into an ideologically tenuous alliance with the forces of Moḥammad Vali Khan Tonekāboni (Sepahsālār) and establishing another center of resistance to the anticonstitutional coup.

Contemporary observers recognized the revolutionary links between the South Caucasus and northern Iran, including the presence of Russian subjects among the constitutionalists in Tabriz.[14] For a multitude of reasons, the Russian government relieved the siege of Tabriz in May 1909.[15] This episode, however, did not mark the end of Russian intervention in the Constitutional Revolution, but rather the start of a protracted occupation of the Iranian north. In December 1911, the Russian government moved decisively to end the Constitutional Revolution itself, issuing an ultimatum forcing the closure of the Second Majles, and expanding its occupying force across the Iranian north, including in the Gilani cities of Rasht and Anzali.[16]

The Russian military remained in northern Iran from 1911 through the First World War and Russian Civil War, during which time it grappled with revolutionary and antioccupation insurgencies. Despite the Russians' explicit anticonstitutional bent, as marked by the summary execution of dozens of constitutionalists in Tabriz in January 1912, some of the early resistance to Russian occupation stemmed from anticonstitutional factions. In the Iranian northwest, tribal elements began launching small-scale attacks on Russian soldiers within weeks of the closure of the Second Majles.[17] In the northeast, meanwhile, royalists occupied the shrine of Imam Reżā in Mashhad, signaling not an overt challenge to Russian occupation, but rather their independent political mobilization.[18] From the Russian perspective, however, these were only partially distinguishable. After a weeks-long standoff, Russian forces killed hundreds of the demonstrators. Further repressive measures by occupying Russian soldiers, including forcing Tabriz's nonparticipation in the 1914 elections to the Third Majles, brought only mixed success in suppressing Iranian resistance and political mobilization.[19]

At the outset of the First World War, Ottoman, imperial German, and Austrian agents intensified their efforts to unseat Russo-British control of Iran, cultivating alliances with the various Iranian rebellious movements that re-formed after the suppression of the Constitutional Revolution. Appearing as a counterweight to Britain and Russia, and having no obvious interests in annexation of Iranian territory, Germany secured the cooperation of much of the Iranian intelligentsia during the First World War, including many of the leading Democrats of the constitutional period. In addition to patronizing a Persian-language nationalist press in Berlin, German agents fomented anti-Entente insurgencies throughout Iran, most notably around Shiraz. Furthermore, the Germans helped establish a short-lived government-in-exile in 1915 in the cities of Qom and Kermanshah to counterbalance the intermittent Anglophilic cabinets in Tehran.[20]

Ottoman overtures to the Iranian public and intelligentsia were less effective, complicated by their territorial designs on the Iranian northwest, especially during the two Ottoman occupations of Tabriz in 1915 and 1918.²¹ The Ottoman government simultaneously disseminated pan-Turkic and pan-Islamic propaganda in Iranian Azerbaijan and the Iranian northeast, while focusing its propaganda in Tehran solely on the promotion of pan-Islamism.²² A temporal shift also marked Ottoman propaganda efforts, which trended away from pan-Islamic to pan-Turkic appeals after the Arab Revolt of 1916.²³

The records of the tsarist Ministry of Justice assert that German and Austrian agents, aided by a large contingent of German-speaking Russian citizens, forged ties with pan-Turkic and pan-Islamic organizations in Tashkent, Marv, and Ashgabat beginning in 1914.²⁴ Operating from the German consulate in Mashhad, at least sixteen of these agents purportedly established links with so-called Pan-Islamic Committees in Central Asia, which fomented rebellion against the Russian state with Ottoman financial support.²⁵ Notably, German and Ottoman agents worked not only with the native Turkic populations of these cities, but also with resident Persians, some of whom were manumitted slaves captured in Turkmen raids into the Iranian northeast over the previous decades. Together, they allegedly formed a revolutionary "Persian-Tatar Committee" (Persidsko-Tatarskiĭ Komitet), which may have sought to incite Central Asian public sentiment against the Russian state.²⁶

While Russian forces suppressed revolutionism in Central Asia and northern Iranian urban areas with some success, they had more difficulty asserting control on the southern Caspian littoral, where dense forest cover allowed the outmatched Iranian rebels to contend with the Entente's overwhelming military advantage. In 1911, four years prior to the emergence of the Jangal insurgency in Gilan, Amir Mo'ayyed Savādkuhi (d. 1932) most effectively exploited this tactical deficit, organizing a small-scale guerilla insurgency against Russian soldiers in Mazandaran.²⁷ Savādkuhi also built strategic alliances with Ottoman and Austrian agents, and with antitsarist Turkic rebels from Central Asia, establishing his own transnational links between revolutionary movements on the Caspian littoral. Distinguishing the Jangal Movement from Savādkuhi's revolt, however, was its ability to forward a coherent political alternative to Tehran, at least in its latter stages.

Both the February and October revolutions majorly reconfigured the Russian state relationship with the Jangalis, with important ramifications for the rest of Iran. As the bulk of Russian soldiers in Gilan were redeployed to the Caucasus in 1917, the Jangalis emerged from the forests to carry out famine relief efforts in the provincial capital of Rasht.[28] In so doing, the Jangalis reflected their movement's broader ambitions, and especially their commitment to social welfare. According to the movement's best-known firsthand chronicler, Ebrāhim Fakhrā'i (d. 1988), the Jangalis aspired primarily to ameliorate poverty, without regard to religious and ethnic divides.[29] Toward this end, in early 1920, the Jangali leadership drafted a program that codified this goal and their adherence to the principles of social democracy.[30]

From their movement's inception, the Jangalis needed to implement their program around the political impositions of stronger external actors. After years of Russian domination in the Iranian north, however, the October Revolution reduced the remaining Russian consulates to dependence on British financial support and the relegation of White Russian policy to British interests. After the first Bolshevik overtures to the Iranian government in early 1918, the existence of White Russian consulates also raised a dilemma for the Tehran government, which had to balance the interests of competing Russian diplomatic envoys before the outcome of the Civil War was decided.[31] While a contingent of Russian soldiers remained in northern Iran, the White consulates themselves faced a shortage of funds from their British backers, the prospect of capture by Bolshevik units, and the challenges of parrying socialist propaganda in Iran. Furthermore, as its military fortunes waned during the Russian Civil War, the White government was forced to contend with the wavering loyalties of the Iranian Cossack Brigade, and eventually the remnants of the Russian army on the southern Caspian littoral.[32]

As the Russian Civil War continued, the White Mission in Tehran and the White consulates across the Iranian north continued to gather and relay intelligence, but were increasingly unable to counter the Bolshevik presence in Iran. As their agents trickled into Gilan, Mazandaran, Qazvin, Khorasan, and Tehran, the Soviets announced the abrogation of tsarist-era concessions in the country and affirmed a commitment to Iranian sovereignty.[33] Almost simultaneously, Mirza Kuchek Khan established contacts with Soviet agents in Baku, courting their assistance even as he continued to cooperate with Ottoman, German, and Austrian officers.[34] Thus, for a brief moment in late 1917 and early 1918, some of the loosely linked anti-Entente movements appeared to have found a new and largely accommodative patron in the Bolsheviks, who initially reciprocated their overtures.

Even before the outbreak of the First World War and the Bolshevik ascendance, the tsarist Russian state faced difficulties policing its southern border.[35] These issues compounded in the second decade of the twentieth century, as the breakdown of central state authority allowed revolutionaries of different ideological stripes to coordinate and seek refuge across international borders, including in Gilan province. As argued by Dailami, the southern Caspian littoral's early receptiveness to the radical tradition of the 1908-9 Tabriz resistance stemmed in part from the clandestine movement of Georgian Bolsheviks to the region before 1915.[36] This trend continued into the First World War, as Russian and British documentary evidence attests also to the flight of escaped Ottoman prisoners to the Caspian littoral, where they were received by Mirza Kuchek Khan himself.[37] In parallel, Turkmen fleeing the repression of the 1916 revolt resettled along the southern Caspian, especially among Savādkuhi's forces in Mazandaran, even as refugees from this province were fleeing to Tehran.[38] While all these aforementioned trends usually developed under regional leadership, revolutionary and foreign agents traveled between them, reflecting and perhaps contributing to their shared anti-Entente orientation.

On its own, anti-Ententism was insufficient to build a cohesive revolutionary movement. Major ideological and ethnolinguistic differences marked the anti-Entente movements in northern Iran, especially in Iranian Azerbaijan and Khorasan. Most seriously, the second Ottoman occupation of Tabriz and failed pan-Turkic appeals to the city's population sparked a regionalist backlash among the Tabrizi Democrat leadership.[39] For their part, Hemmat and other Social Democrat-affiliated elements in Baku also drifted further from their revolutionary compatriots in Tabriz, advocating an internationalist vision of revolution that was less resonant not only in northern Iran, but also in Baku. There, much of the population was gravitating toward the nationalist Müsavat Party (Equality, 1912) and the consolidation of a national identity initially centering, but later hostile to the cultural, linguistic, and historic ties between Azerbaijan and Iran.[40] And, while the First World War provided a common enemy against which to coordinate their activities, Austrian and German instrumentalization of pan-Islamism proved insufficient to overcome the antagonisms between some Turkmen and Iranian communities in Central Asia. The Ottoman turn toward pan-Turkism further precluded Iranian-Turkmen cooperation in Central Asia, as various Turkmen revolutionary movements sought independence from both Russia and Iran as the First World War drew to a close.[41]

The Jangal Movement was not immune to the emergent fractures in these anti-Entente insurgencies. Although Mirza Kuchek Khan enjoyed broad public support by almost every account, contemporary White Russian observers reported, albeit not without reflecting their own anti-Jangali inclinations, that he faced some local backlash for his coordination with German and Ottoman officers.[42] More serious were the splits in the Jangalis' multinational alliance, which included Armenian, Georgian, Ottoman Turkish, Russian Muslim, German, and Austrian agents in addition to its core Gilani contingent. These splits emerged in an unfavorable moment. Only three years after its establishment in 1914, the Jangal Movement contended with a series of shocks that reconfigured political dynamics in Gilan: sequentially, the extension of the Russian Civil War to the Iranian north, the defeat of the Central Powers, and the military offensives of the future monarch, Reżā Khan (r. 1925–41). Together, these developments destabilized the Jangalis in Gilan, hastening the movement's collapse in 1920–21.

Revolutionism after the First World War

The defeat of the Central Powers did little to reverse Iranian political provincialization, or allow for the consolidation of central government control over the competing local and foreign interests on the Iranian borderlands. After the abrogation of the 1919 Anglo-Persian Agreement and the ensuing collapse of the government of Prime Minister Ḥasan Voṣuq al-Dawleh (d. 1951), various uprisings and political movements throughout the country competed with his short-lived successors for regional autonomy.[43] Some three thousand kilometers away, the Red Army defeated General Anton Denikin's advance on Moscow in November, moving toward victory in the Russian Civil War. Soon after, the Bolshevik capture of Baku (April 28, 1920) and push into Central Asia brought the Red Army to the Iranian border, most of which was controlled by autonomous and rebellious local actors including the Tabrizi Democrat Moḥammad Khiyabani (d. 1920) and the Kurdish tribal leader Semko Shekāk (d. 1930) in northwestern Iran, and the revolutionary Gendarme commander Moḥammad Taqi Khan Pesiyan (d. 1921) in the Iranian northeast.

Among a number of revolutionary leaders, Khiyabani played an outsized role in the history of Iranian-Russian socialism, as his movement emerged from the geographic heart of the 1908–9 Tabriz resistance. Over the course of the subsequent decade, the internationalist tradition of Tabriz partially fell away, as the Russian and Ottoman occupations turned many inhabitants away from foreign actors and ideological imports. Beyond this opposition to non-Iranian and even non-Azerbaijani influence, however, Khiyabani did not present a coherent ideological alternative to the government in Tehran, then led by Prime Minister Ḥasan Pirniyā Moshir al-Dawleh (d. 1935). Furthermore, despite ample evidence of Khiyabani's popular appeal in Tabriz, his movement failed to establish meaningful institutional roots in the city, leading to its rapid collapse in the face of the central government's offensive in September 1920.[44] Rather, Khiyabani commanded the attention of large crowds in the city center with rhetoric on order, constitutionalism, and Iranian territorial integrity.[45]

The Khiyabani uprising was an explicitly non-Bolshevik movement.[46] Even so, some of its followers displayed apparent enthusiasm for Bolshevism and adopted Bolshevik symbols in their public processions.[47] Furthermore, the Khiyabani movement developed on the border with Soviet Azerbaijan at a time when the Bolsheviks were rapidly expanding southward and courting even ideologically distant movements of national liberation. As late as May 1920, some elements of Soviet leadership were apparently still considering a push into Tabriz, hoping to capitalize on years of agitation among the public by socialists from Baku.[48] Despite all of this, the Weimar German consulate in Tabriz, rather than the Soviets, made the only serious effort to reorient the Khiyabani movement to socialism. Russian and British intelligence reports reveal that the former German consul to Shiraz and organizer of the wartime National Committee for the Defense of Iranian Independence (Komiteh-ye melli-ye ḥāfeẓin-e esteqlāl-e mamālek-e Irān), Kurt Wustrow, entered into an alliance with local Bolshevik elements in Tabriz, planning a coup to establish socialist control in the city.[49] Khiyabani reacted forcefully to the coup attempt, arresting Bolshevik agitators and delivering a number of public speeches warning against collaboration with any foreign actors. Nearly simultaneously, news arrived in Tabriz of the establishment of the SSRI, an ideologically distant and politically menacing alternative to the Khiyabani movement.[50] Bolshevism never again emerged as a meaningful force in the Khiyabani movement, but became a target of scorn and suspicion in Khiyabani's rhetoric.

Only a few weeks after the start of the Khiyabani uprising, Soviet forces entered Baku, overthrowing the short-lived Azerbaijan Democratic Republic (1918–20) and installing a Soviet government under the leadership of Nariman Narimanov (d. 1925). Foremostly, Nariman sought to secure the allegiances of the Baku hinterlands, which had theretofore resisted any attempt at Sovietization.[51] Even in Baku itself, Narimanov was forced to accommodate the former officers of the independent Azerbaijani state, some of whom realigned themselves with the new government despite their evident pan-Turkic sympathies. Soviet sources indicate that some of these same officers traveled to Tabriz and Rasht to cultivate alliances built on the principle of pan-Islamism with, respectively, the Khiyabani movement and the Jangal insurgency.[52] In so doing, these officers reflected a broader trend in the postwar Middle East, as the leadership of the Young Turks adapted their political activities to liberationist goals in a loose alliance with the Bolsheviks.[53] The actions of these officers, however, foretold a more general breakdown in the Bolshevik alliance with various national liberation movements in Muslim-majority territories and states, including in Russian Turkestan and Iran.[54]

The flight of the pan-Turkic officers to northern Iran indicates continuity in migration patterns from the late tsarist through the early Soviet period. While some Caucasian and Central Asian refugees traveled to Tehran and farther south, a majority seemingly settled in Iranian Azerbaijan, the Caspian littoral, and Khorasan, the very loci of northern Iranian revolutionary movements. From the west, the records of the Foreign Ministry of Azerbaijan—both before and after the Red Army invasion—evidence concern over Azerbaijani refugees fleeing interethnic violence in the South Caucasus, which coincided with the flight of Armenian refugees into Iran.[55] As the countryside of Iranian Azerbaijan was wracked by interethnic violence and massacres, the Caspian link to Anzali emerged as an alternative route for both Armenian and Azerbaijani refugees fleeing Baku.[56] In one sense, the flight of some refugees to Gilan rather than Iranian Azerbaijan mirrored the deterioration of the historic ties between Tabriz and the South Caucasus; excepting the uprising of 'Abol-Qāsem Lāhuti in January 1922, the defeat of the Khiyabani movement marked the effective end of the Tabriz revolutionary tradition that had developed in symbiosis with Baku from the establishment of the Markaz-e Ghaybi.[57]

The severing of the Baku-Tabriz revolutionary link left the Bolsheviks only the southern Caspian littoral and Iranian Khorasan as viable points of entry into Iran. Indeed, as argued by Dailami, some among Soviet leadership envisioned Turkestan rather than Baku as the most likely springboard for Iranian revolution.[58] In the summer of 1919,

Bolshevik agents transited from Turkestan to the Caspian city of Gorgan and even to Gilan itself, bolstering the Bolshevik presence in the province prior to the landing at Anzali.[59] On the eastern Soviet-Iranian border, however, popular hostility to the idea of socialism once again threatened the promise of revolution. Even after the 1917 Revolution, the flight of the Turkmen to northeastern Iran continued and even accelerated. And, while centuries-old ethnic and religious tensions continued to divide the Turkmen from their new Iranian hosts, White Russian consular reports and correspondences with the Iranian foreign ministry indicate that many of the fled Turkmen accepted offers of Iranian citizenship rather than returning to former tsarist territories then under Bolshevik control.[60] In Turkestan itself, the Turkmen population reacted forcefully to Soviet rule, avoiding conscription, staging acts of scattered violence, or fleeing across international borders.[61] The intelligence reports of the Russian Mission in Iran confirm the hostility of the Turkmen to Bolshevization, despite the existence of some small-scale Bolshevik-backed revolutionary societies in major Central Asian urban centers.[62] These societies, as well as the limited Bolshevik penetration of the government gendarmerie in Khorasan in the years prior to 1921, did not provide a sufficient base of support on which to build a presence in the Iranian northeast, despite Pesiyan's late appeals for Soviet aid against Tehran.[63]

As evidenced by the defeats of the Khiyabani and Pesiyan movements, the early Soviet leadership's designs did not translate to meaningful support for revolutionary movements, both socialist and nonsocialist, on the Soviet-Iranian land border. Despite their nonsupport for revolutionary movements in Iranian Azerbaijan and Khorasan, however, the Soviets moved decisively to introduce Bolshevism on the Caspian littoral. Several factors explain the emergence of the Caspian as the preferred conduit for the Bolshevization of Iran. First, as previously mentioned, the Soviet pivot toward the Caspian stemmed in part from the initiative of Mirza Kuchek Khan himself, who appealed to the Soviets in Azerbaijan for aid against the British even as local Democrats fortified Tabriz against Bolshevik penetration.[64] Second, the early Soviet leadership had immediate geopolitical and economic interests in Gilan. Even as the Soviets secured most of the territory of the former Russian Empire, a significant contingent of White Russian ground and naval forces remained in the southern Caspian in 1920. Furthermore, a number of White consulates remained in northern Iran, complicating

Soviet efforts to secure Iranian diplomatic recognition, especially under the premiership of Voṣuq.⁶⁵

Upon their initial landing, the Soviets clearly communicated their strategic interests in Gilan. Batyrbek Lokmanovich Abukov (d. 1938), one of the Soviet commanders, announced to a crowd of Anzali residents that the Soviets had arrived firstly to defeat Denikin's forces in the area, and only secondly to aid the effort against the British on the invitation of Mirza Kuchek Khan.⁶⁶ Furthermore, the first account of the landing in *Izvestiĭa* and other Soviet newspapers claimed that the Soviets had no interest in domestic Iranian political affairs and were simply looking to defeat the White fleet to safeguard the transit of oil from Baku to Soviet Russia.⁶⁷ Soon after the declaration of the SSRI, however, *Izvestiĭa* quickly reversed course, devoting front-page accounts to the heroism of Mirza Kuchek Khan and the Iranian Red Army, and lauding Iran as the newest front of the international revolution.⁶⁸

On their own, Soviet state interests are insufficient to explain the Anzali landing, as in 1920 the Soviets still harbored hopes of expanding their revolution westward and southward.⁶⁹ Rather, some Soviet revolutionaries, especially those belonging to the Caucasian Bureau (Kavbiuro) of the Russian Communist Party, identified the potential for adoption of socialist tenets in Gilan and selected the province as an ideal laboratory for the introduction of Bolshevism. The transmissibility of this project throughout the rest of Iran, however, was in question. Even prior to the landing at Anzali, early Soviet leaders understood that socialism had little mass purchase in Iran and was largely localized to the north and northwest.⁷⁰ Without fully acknowledging the appeal of non-Bolshevik movements of social and economic reform, the Soviet leadership highlighted the popularity of the Jangalis as an indicator of Gilan's receptiveness to Bolshevik revolution.⁷¹ This theory hinged on the rural element of the Jangal Movement, which both White and Soviet correspondences characterized as "peasant" (*krest'ânskoe*) and "agrarian" (*agrarnoe*).⁷² Such characterizations reflected the Caucasian Bolsheviks' familiarity with the region from the Lesser Autocracy, as the only nontribal rural uprisings of significance during the Constitutional Revolution developed along the southern Caspian littoral.⁷³

The unraveling of the Jangal-Communist alliance, which had already begun by July 1920, pushed the Jangal Movement into its first period without foreign alliances since its earliest months. In questioning the rupture in the Jangali-Communist alliance, it may be posited that the

Communists did not identify the ideological continuities between the Jangalis and other northern Iranian movements prior to the establishment of the SSRI, or alternatively, that they wished to co-opt the movement despite its ideological distance from Russian socialism. This second potentiality testifies to the difficulties of revolutionary propagation to any other province in the Iranian north. Indeed, by 1921, the Soviet leadership's widespread recognition of these difficulties motivated their pivot toward the ascendant premiership of Rez̤ā Khan and his modernizing project for the Iranian state.[74]

The story of the Caspian conduit is also one of Iranian political provincialization. Molded by the same ideological influences, constitutional-era origins, and great-power interests, the political trajectories of northern Iranian revolutionary movements nonetheless diverged after the First World War. While the exchange of persons and even revolutionary agents between these movements continued until 1921, there was little direct coordination between them. Rather, postconstitutional Iranian revolutionary movements developed with a remarkable degree of localization, allowing the Jangal Movement to reconcile their platform with the principles of Bolshevism. Nonetheless, the Jangal Movement retained its distinctly Iranian characteristics through the existence of the SSRI, as evidenced by the deterioration of relations between the Jangalis and Bolsheviks, and the largely autonomous political paths charted by the two groups after their union in the summer of 1920.[75]

The alliance between the Jangalis and Communists, while intended to negotiate the ideological distance between them, only underscored the divergent aims of their respective movements. Even so, given the Jangalis' flexible alliance-formation prior to 1920, their reorientation toward a Bolshevik-adjacent movement was itself notable. This was possible in a certain historical moment, one in which various revolutionary groups channeled their dissatisfaction with the existing political order in Iran with only a limited understanding of the ideological underpinnings of the revolutionary currents to their north. As revealed by the collapse of the SSRI, this may have been a strategic mistake. Evidently, despite their noncooperation, the rebellious movements of the Iranian north had more in common with each other than with any strain of Russian socialism.

Notes

1. See, for example, Cosroe Chaquèri, *The Soviet Socialist Republic of Iran, 1920–1921: Birth of the Trauma* (Pittsburgh: University of Pittsburgh Press, 1995).

2. Sara G. Brinegar, *Power and the Politics of Oil in the Soviet South Caucasus: Periphery Unbound, 1920–29* (London: Bloomsbury Publishing, 2024).

3. Denis V. Volkov, "In the Glocal Crossfire: Russia, Britain, and the Caspian, 1916–1919," in this volume.

4. Stephen Blank, "Soviet Politics and the Iranian Revolution of 1919–1921," *Cahiers du Monde russe et soviétique* 21, no. 2 (1980): 173–94.

5. Stephanie Cronin, *Soldiers, Shahs and Subalterns in Iran: Opposition, Protest and Revolt, 1921–1941* (New York: Palgrave Macmillan, 2014).

6. Pezhmann Dailami, "The Bolshevik Revolution and the Genesis of Communism in Iran, 1917–1920," *Central Asian Survey* 11, no. 3 (1992): 51–82; Pezhmann Dailami, "The Bolsheviks and the Jangali Revolutionary Movement, 1915–1920," *Cahiers du Monde russe et soviétique* 31, no. 1 (1990): 43–59.

7. See Ṣamad Sardāriniyā, *Naqsh-e Markaz-e Ghaybi-e Tabriz dar enqelāb-e Mashruṭiyat-e Irān* (Tehran: Akhtar, 2015/16).

8. Gosudarstvennyĭ Arkhiv Rossiĭskoĭ Federatsii (State Archive of the Russian Federation, hereafter GARF), f. 124, o. 45, d. 45 (3); GARF, f. 124, o. 45, d. 49.

9. Mansour Ettehadieh, "Constitutional Revolution v. Political Parties of the Constitutional Period," *Encyclopaedia Iranica*, VI/2, 199–202, https://iranicaonline.org/articles/constitutional-revolution-v.

10. See Mangol Bayat, *Iran's Experiment with Parliamentary Governance: The Second Majles, 1909–1911* (Syracuse: Syracuse University Press, 2020).

11. Ettehadieh, "Constitutional Revolution v."

12. See Vanessa Martin, "Constitutional Revolution ii. Events," *Encyclopaedia Iranica*, VI/2, 176–87, https://iranicaonline.org/articles/constitutional-revolution-ii.

13. Moritz Deutschmann, "Tabriz under Siege," in *Iran and Russian Imperialism: The Ideal Anarchists, 1800–1914* (New York: Routledge, 2016), 175–94.

14. On the presence of Russian subjects in Tabriz, see, for example, *Novoe Vremya*, no. 11897 (April 27, 1909): 3.

15. See James D. Clark, "Constitutionalists and Cossacks: The Constitutional Movement and Russian Intervention in Tabriz, 1907–11," *Iranian Studies* 39, no. 2 (2006): 199–225; see also Deutschmann, *Iran and Russian Imperialism*, 183–87.

16. Alisa Shablovskaia, "Russian Hubris in Iran: Diplomacy, Clientelism, and Intervention (1907–1912)," *Ab Imperio*, 2019, no. 1, 79–103.

17. *Iuzhnyĭ Kavkaz*, January 4, 1912, no. 70; January 8, 1912, no. 73, pp. 2–3; January 10, 1912, no. 74, p. 2; *Russkiĭ Kavkaz*, February 23, 1912, no. 110, p. 4.

18. On this episode, see Rudi Matthee, "Infidel Aggression: The Russian Assault on the Holy Shrine of Imam Reza, Mashhad, 1912," in *Russians in Iran: Diplomacy and Power in the Qajar Era and Beyond*, ed. Rudi Matthee and Elena Andreeva (London: I. B. Tauris, 2018), 137–70.

19. See Mansour Ettehadieh, "Constitutional Revolution iv. Aftermath," *Encyclopaedia Iranica*, VI/2, 193–99, https://iranicaonline.org/articles/constitutional-revolution-iv.

20. Oliver Bast, "Germany ix. Germans in Persia," *Encyclopaedia Iranica*, X/6, 567–72. https://iranicaonline.org/articles/germany-ix.

21. Touraj Atabaki, "Pan-Turkism and Iranian Nationalism," in *Iran and the First World War: Battleground of the Great Powers*, ed. Touraj Atabaki (London: I. B. Tauris, 2006), 121–36.

22. Atabaki, "Pan-Turkism"; Atabaki, "Going East: The Ottomans' Secret Service Activities in Iran," in Atabaki, *Iran and the First World War*, 29–42.

23. See Atabaki, "Going East."

24. GARF, f. 124, o. 57, d. 595.

25. GARF, f. 124, o. 52, d. 316.

26. GARF, f. 124, o. 52, d. 316.

27. See Mostafa Nuri, *Sardār Savādkuhi: Sargozasht-e Esmāʿil Khān Amir Moʾayyed Bāvand*)Tehran: Shirāzeh Ketab, 1397/2018-19).

28. Pezhmann Dailami, "Nationalism and Communism in Iran: The Case of Gilan, 1915–1921" (PhD diss., University of Manchester, 1994), 76–77.

29. Ebrāhim Fakhrāʾi, *Sardār-e Jangal* (Tehran: Jāvidān Publishers, 1997), 56.

30. Kayhan Nejad, "Provincial Revolution and Regional Anti-Colonialism: The Soviets in Iran, 1920–1921," *Slavic Review* 82, no. 2 (2023): 378–79.

31. Chaquèri, *Soviet Socialist Republic of Iran*, 145–46.

32. Raskolnikov to Trotsky (June 6, 1920) in M. A Persits, *Persidskiĭ front mirovoĭ revoliutsii: Dokumenty o Sovetskom vtorzhenii v Gilian (1920–1921)* (Moscow: Kvadriga, 2009), 56–59.

33. Chaquèri and Mikhail Volodarsky both argue that the abrogation of concessions was a partial ruse, as the Soviets sought new means to continue the tsarist-era Russian domination of Iran. See Chaquèri, *Soviet Socialist Republic of Iran*, 183–84; Mikhail Volodarsky, *The Soviet Union and Its Southern Neighbours: Iran and Afghanistan, 1917–1933* (Portland, OR: F. Cass, 1994), 49–52; Nejad argues that the abrogation reflected the Soviets' principled anti-imperialism. See Kayhan Nejad, "To Break the Feudal Bonds: The Soviets, Reza Khan, and the Iranian Left, 1921–1925," *Middle Eastern Studies* 57, no. 5 (2021): 771, n. 6.

34. Chaquèri, *Soviet Socialist Republic of Iran*, 110.

35. See Rustin Zarkar, "The Custom of Customs: Licit and Illicit Crossings in the Caspian Sea, 1864–1917," in this volume.

36. Dailami, "Nationalism and Communism," 49–50.

37. Dailami, "Nationalism and Communism," 51; see also GARF, f. 124, o. 69, d. 732.

38. Nuri, *Sardār Savādkuhi*, 205–11; see also, for example, GARF, f. 4712, o. 1, d. 41 (50); GARF, f. 4738, o. 2, d. 201 (79).

39. White Russian observations of the Tabriz Democrats' anti-Ottoman turn may be found in GARF, f. 4714, o. 1, d. 19 (85); Pezhmann Dailami also addresses this turn in his "Pan-Islamism and the Role of the Central Powers," in Atabaki, *Iran and the First World War*, 137–62.

40. Tadeusz Swietochowski, *Russian Azerbaijan, 1905–1920: The Shaping of National Identity in a Muslim Community* (London: Cambridge University Press, 2004), 73.

41. See Alisa Shablovskaia, "'The Persian Gate to Revolution': Bolshevik Networks and Post-WWI Transnationalism in Iran," in this volume.

42. GARF, f. 4714, o. 1, d. 19 (104).

43. This agreement was signed in 1919 between the Iranian government and the British, but abrogated in the face of strong international and domestic opposition. Some scholars now interpret the signing as evidence of Voṣuq's skillful negotiation of Iranian geopolitical weakness following the First World War. See Oliver Bast, "Putting the Record Straight: Vosuq al-Dowleh's Foreign Policy in 1918/19," in *Men of Order: Authoritarian Modernization under Ataturk and Reza Shah*, ed. Touraj Atabaki and Erik J. Zürcher (London: I. B. Tauris, 2017), 260–82.

44. Homa Katouzian, "The Revolt of Shaykh Muḥammad Khiyabani," *Iran* 37 (1999): 168–69.

45. Khiyabani, "Āẕarbāyejān āzādi-ye Irān rā ta'amin khāhad kard" (May 2, 1920), in Hādī Khosrawshāhī, *Nehżat-e Āzādestān va Shahīd Shaykh Moḥammad Khīyābānī* (Tehran: Markaz-e Asnād-e Enqelāb-e Eslāmī, 2011), 265–67; "Mā bāyad Irān rā āzād konim" (June 10, 1920), 347–49. As his movement developed, Khiyabani minimized the early separatist tendencies of some of his supporters, instead envisioning the expansion of his movement to Tehran. See Khiyabani, "In qiyām cheh mikhāhad?," June 2, 1920, 338–39.

46. Katouzian, "Revolt of Shaykh Muḥammad Khiyabani," 156–57.

47. GARF, f. 4738, o. 1, d. 124 (187).

48. Chaquèri, *Soviet Socialist Republic of Iran*, 156.

49. GARF, f. 4738, o. 1, d. 124 (187); see also Katouzian, "Revolt of Shaykh Muḥammad Khiyabani," 165–67; Bast, "Germany ix."

50. Chaquèri, *Soviet Socialist Republic of Iran*, 212, 465–66.

51. See Sara Brinegar, "The Oil Deal: Nariman Narimanov and the Sovietization of Azerbaijan," *Slavic Review* 76, no. 2 (2017): 372–94.

52. "Statements from the Record of the 15th Meeting of the Political Bureau of the Central Committee of the Russian Communist Party" (May 25, 1920), in Persits, *Persidskii front*, 38.

53. Alp Yenen, "Internationalism, Diplomacy and the Revolutionary Origins of the Middle East's 'Northern Tier,'" *Contemporary European History* 30, no. 4 (2021): 497–512.

54. The break between the Bolsheviks and the national-liberationists is evidenced by the case of Mirsaid Sultan-Galiev (d. 1940). See Terry Martin, "The Politics of National Communism, 1923 to 1930," in *The Affirmative Action Empire: Nations and Nationalisms in the Soviet Union, 1923–1939* (Ithaca, NY: Cornell University Press, 2001), 211–72; see also Jeremy Smith, "The Twelfth Party Congress and the Sultan-Galiev Affair," in *The Bolsheviks and the National Question, 1917–23* (New York: Palgrave Macmillan, 1999), 213–38.

55. GARF, f. 4738, o. 2, d. 201 (79–80, 86–87).

56. GARF, f. 4714, o. 1, d. 19 (85, 164, 172).

57. On the Lāhuti uprising, see Stephanie Cronin, "The Provincial Cities in Revolt (ii): Major Abulqasim Lahuti and the Tabriz Insurrection of 1922," in *Soldiers, Shahs and Subalterns in Iran: Opposition, Protest and Revolt, 1921–1941* (New York: Palgrave MacMillan, 2014), 101–27.

58. Dailami, "The Genesis of Communism," 72

59. Dailami, "Nationalism and Communism," 161.

60. GARF, f. 4712, o. 1, d. 41.
61. GARF, f. 4738, o. 1, d. 95.
62. GARF, f. 4712, o. 1, d. 41.
63. Cronin, *Soldiers, Shahs and Subalterns in Iran*, 112-13.
64. Nejad, "Provincial Revolution," 385.
65. Voṣuq al-Dawleh to the Commissar of International Affairs of the RSFSR (May 1920), in Persits, *Persidskiĭ front*, 42.
66. Report of Chilingar'ĩan (late July 1920), in Persits, *Persidskiĭ front*, 131.
67. *Izvestiĩa*, June 8, 1920, no. 132, p. 969; see also *Krasnaĩa Gazeta*, June 10, 1920, no. 125, p. 3.
68. See, for example, *Izvestiĩa*, June 16, 1920, no. 129, p. 976; *Izvestiĩa*, June 23, 1920, no. 135, p. 982.
69. Nejad, "Provincial Revolution."
70. L. M. Karakhan to Raskolnikov and Ordzhonikidze (May 30, 1920), in Persits, *Persidskiĭ front*, 40-41.
71. F. F. Raskolnikov to L. D. Trotsky (June 6, 1920), in Persits, *Persidskiĭ front*, 55; G. V. Chicherin, "Theses on the Question of the Actions of the Communists in the East" (June 14, 1920), in Persits, *Persidskiĭ front*, 66-67.
72. GARF, f. 4712, o. 1, d. 41; Chicherin, "Theses," in Persits, *Persidskiĭ front*, 66.
73. Janet Afary, "Peasant Rebellions of the Caspian Region during the Iranian Constitutional Revolution, 1906-1909," *International Journal of Middle East Studies* 23, no. 2 (1991): 137-61; see also Dailami, "Nationalism and Communism," 14.
74. Nejad, "To Break the Feudal Bonds."
75. Nejad, "Provincial Revolution."

CHAPTER 15

"The Persian Gate to Revolution"
Bolshevik Networks and Post-WWI
Transnationalism in Iran

Alisa Shablovskaia

Soviet authorities conceived the foundation of the Soviet Socialist Republic of Iran by joint Iranian-Soviet forces in May 1920, followed by the creation of the Iranian Communist Party (ICP), as some of the first regional undertakings on the path to world revolution, a promising first step toward the "liberation of the East" from British hegemony. However, the Irano-Soviet treaty of friendship, signed less than a year after the formation of the ICP, marked the death warrant of the Gilan Republic, as all Soviet diplomatic and material support to the republic was gradually drawn away. The reversal of the Bolshevik foreign policy line in the early 1920s has been largely perceived as a manifestation of Soviet "duality" and the betrayal of Eastern revolutionaries. Therefore, many historians adopted the "duality" perspective while stressing the Politburo's central role in the formulation of Soviet Eastern policy.[1] Not free of teleology, this narrative was explicitly Moscow-centered and downplayed the importance of the Caspian region as a conjunction of various anti-imperialist networks. Meanwhile, the activism of transnational revolutionaries partaking in the Soviet expansion to the East defined not only geographical vectors of Bolshevik policy but also its heterogeneous and hybrid nature. This chapter seeks to bring to the debate the Indian, Ottoman, and Azeri agencies that heavily impacted the early Soviet designs in Iran while benefiting from the inclusiveness of the early Bolshevik revolutionary project.[2]

The complex multicultural aspect of early Bolshevik networks was discarded by Soviet authorities themselves from the moment of their establishment. Though many members of the Bolshevik ruling elite started their careers as revolutionaries in the Caucasus and actively participated in the Iranian Constitutional Revolution (1905–11), the crystallization of the Soviet orientalist trope of the "backward East" during the Russian Civil War (1917–22) led to the perpetuation of the tsarist civilizing discourse in the Soviet historiography and literature on the Orient.[3] However, the Soviet official discourse did not reflect the scope of interactions between the Bolsheviks and Eastern anti-imperialist and revolutionary movements. With the gradual affirmation of the transnational historiographical perspective, different vectors inside Soviet foreign policy appeared as constituent parts of what Samuel J. Hirst qualified as a "transnational anti-imperialist moment."[4] Drawing on this already established approach, this chapter demonstrates how various anti-imperialist discourses and agendas were intertwined on the transnational level in the Iranian project of the Bolsheviks.[5] Largely inspired by the scholarship that puts emphasis on transnational and universalist trends in the early Bolshevik Eastern policy,[6] this chapter probes how Indian, Ottoman, and Azeri revolutionaries contributed to the formation of Soviet Iran policy. Starting with a brief episode of Indo-Soviet cooperation, reminiscent of the nineteenth-century Russian "fantastic" projects of the conquest of India, the chapter then focuses on the more lasting Turco-Soviet partnership—the legacy of World War I—and ends with a short appraisal of the Caspian regional nexus between Iran and Azerbaijan, which would significantly shape Russian policy in Iran during the century to come.

The hybridity of the early Soviet revolutionary stance and action in the Caspian region, and specifically in Iran, has long been overshadowed by the strategic imperatives of Soviet diplomacy. If the Cold War historiography of early Irano-Soviet entanglements stressed the continuities between tsarist imperialism and Soviet expansionism,[7] the reassessment of the Soviet patronage of anti-imperialist movements after 1991 highlighted their instrumentality in broader Soviet foreign and domestic policy designs.[8] The studies by Chaquèri and Genis demonstrated the significance of the Iranian revolution in the Soviet negotiations with the British government and the subsequent conclusion of the Soviet-British accord in 1921. Both Chaquèri and Genis affirmed the critical role of the Caucasus-based Bolsheviks in the alienation of the local Iranian insurgent forces, and emphasized the diplomatic pragmatism of Georgii Chicherin, who served as People's Commissar for Foreign Affairs in the Soviet government from 1918 to 1930. The recent work by Hasanli added a new domestic dimension to this already established narrative on the pragmatist Soviet diplomacy, uncovering the profound discrepancies between the agendas of Moscow and Baku-based authorities where Iran was to play an instrumental role. Though all the above-mentioned authors were drawing on rich collections of archival sources, they did not attempt to surpass the binary framework of geopolitical pragmatism versus Soviet revolutionary idealism.[9] As a result, the references to Bolshevik revolutionary internationalism in the intraparty correspondence were omitted or even approached, not without reason, as manifestations of early Soviet imperialism.[10]

Yet another strand of scholarship, focused on Soviet institutional history and the decision-making process, evolved simultaneously with the "pragmatism-idealism" controversy-oriented historiography. Through the critical analysis of multiple Bolshevik discourses, Blank depicted the inconsistencies of Soviet policy in Iran as a by-product of the "Lenin-Stalin" ideological rift: the uncertainties of the Bolsheviks over the role of Moscow in the development of non-Russian communist parties led, according to Blank, to the organizational disunity in the conduct of the Iranian revolution.[11] As soon as the Russian archives became accessible to a wide range of scholars, the internal tensions inside the Politburo, the uneasy relations between various Soviet institutions and agents, and the complexity of local revolutionary contexts all came to light. Consulting British and Soviet documents, Dailami and Bast questioned the causes of the Gilan Republic's collapse and examined the agency of local actors. Though they reached diametrically opposed conclusions,[12] these authors revealed the eclecticism of Soviet institutional structures and local networks from the Caucasus to Central Asia. Both Bast and Chaquèri grasped intuitively the multilayered transnational character of Soviet foreign and nationality policies, but narrowed the scope of their research down to the Irano-Soviet interactions and the paradiplomacy of southern Soviet Republics.

The Indian Nexus

After the failure of Bolshevik representatives to initiate diplomatic relations with the Iranian government, the new Russian authorities concentrated their efforts on propaganda. Bolshevik emissaries were present on Iranian territory since 1916–17 and, notably, during the ephemeral Baku Commune, but Moscow still afforded no strategic importance to Iranian revolutionary potential.[13] The establishment of Bolshevik headquarters in Tashkent in 1919 marked a new stage in the structural development of Bolshevik revolutionary transnationalism: intelligence collection, language courses, and ideological work were conducted from the Tashkent "military-industrial" base.[14] Tashkent became the center of revolutionary activism in the East, where ideas, political groups, and individuals were interacting, negotiating, and forming new hybrid structures, all while operating a series of tactical and ideological tools. Thus, the security preoccupations of the Bolsheviks, which focused on the weakening of the British rival in the frontier space, soon became intertwined with a broad range of other anti-imperialist movements that deployed pan-Islamic, pan-Turkic, and nationalist rhetoric. Though the popularity of pan-Islamic slogans, widely used by German-Ottoman propaganda, did not result directly in its integration into the Bolshevik populist stance, it began to play an important role in the early Bolshevik agenda through a complex process of cooperation with native revolutionaries and local elites.[15]

The Tashkent-based Indian revolutionaries were among the most important actors who shaped Bolshevik international policy in the region. Dating back to the beginning of the twentieth century, the history of transnational revolutionary militancy of Indian anti-imperialists was marked by their involvement with the Triple Alliance during World War I, as well as their considerable impact on the Chinese revolutionary movement.[16] The Indian dissenters first sought Russian support against the British when the self-proclaimed Indian Provisional Government (IPG) arrived in Kabul from Berlin with a German mission in 1915. Approached by Indian emissaries in 1916, the general-governor of Turkestan declined the Indian proposal to attack the British, but the Indians continued their exchanges with Russian revolutionaries from the Russian Social Democratic Labor Party (RSDLP) all through 1917.[17] When the Anglo-Russian wartime entente was ended by the separate peace agreement of Brest-Litovsk, the IPG renewed its attempts to win Russian support. In March 1919, the IPG established contact with Nikolai Bravin, former tsarist consul and the first Soviet envoy to Tehran, who was building the Bolshevik propaganda apparatus in Tashkent. These exchanges culminated in a personal meeting between Lenin and the foreign minister of the IPG, as well as in the creation of the Indian section in the Tashkent revolutionary center. The scope of activities of the Indian sections was not, however, limited to India alone; in the case of military intervention, the way from Tashkent to India went through Iran and Afghanistan, and the success of this intervention was highly contingent on the loyalties of the British sepoy soldiers in both India and Iran.

The pan-Islamist ambitions and personal connections of Indian revolutionaries offered Bolsheviks more political weight among the Muslims of the former Russian Empire, as well as enticing prospects of expansion in Iran and Afghanistan.[18] The key figure in the emergent Muslim-Bolshevik anti-imperialist movement was "professor" Mohammad Moulavi Barakatullah, who also drew one of the first designs for Bolshevik intervention in Iran.[19] Mohammad Barakatullah was a native of Bhopal State and had been pursuing revolutionary activities for several years in the United States, Japan, Egypt, and Turkey. A news agent for the emir of Afghanistan from 1909 to 1913, he later exercised duties as professor of Hindustani at Tokyo University. In November 1914 Barakatullah joined the Berlin "Indian Committee."[20] After his arrival in Kabul together with the German mission in 1915, Barakatullah became extremely influential in the court of the Afghan ruler Habibullah and befriended Prince Amanullah, the future emir. During his stay in Germany and Afghanistan Barakatullah was appointed foreign minister of the IPG in exile and declared his solidarity with the Indian Khilafat movement (1919-24).[21] While in Russia, after having joined the Bolshevik propaganda forces, Barakatullah conducted agitational work for the Soviets in Kazan, Ufa, Samara, Ashgabat, and Tashkent, and exercised influence on some religious scholars from Petrograd to Tashkent, with whom he published several fatwas. The core of Barakatullah's thesis was the compatibility and even complementarity between Islam and communism, as he explicitly stated in his article "Bolshevik Ideas and the Islamic Republic," published on April 14, 1919, in the Tashkent periodical *Ishtirokiun*. Barakatullah's Indian companions equally favored the marriage of Islam with politics: "Prince" Pratap, the president of the IPG, authored a book titled *Religion of Love*, and Abdul Rab Barg, another Indian leader, organized public meetings in Tashkent where he preached the democratic nature of Islam.[22]

The place of Iran in Barakatullah's international strategy was that of a central element in the chain-link fence of states preventing British incursion in the region. Moving between Kabul, Tashkent, and Moscow, he elaborated a detailed plan of fighting the British on the Ashgabat front via alliance-building with Central Asian popular leaders, Afghan Emir Amanullah, and the Iranian Democratic Party (IDP). Though his main attention was still directed at Afghanistan, Barakatullah was also counting on Neẓām al-Salṭaneh and Hassan Taqizadeh from the IDP, who were closely connected to the German-sponsored Iranian Provisional Government (Barakatullah was most probably personally acquainted with Taqizadeh since their joint work in Berlin).[23] As for the possibilities of Bolshevik intervention in Iran, according to Barakatullah, the possession of Mashhad was of key importance in the Bolshevik war with the British, as the Mashhad sanctuary was a powerful symbol for the whole Islamic world.[24]

Despite the early Bolshevik overtures to the new Afghan emir, whom they believed could become the symbol of Islamic unity in the struggle with British imperialism,[25] Moscow afforded little attention to Indian designs to drive the British out of the region with the aid of local Muslim leaders.[26] No specific funds were allocated to Barakatullah,[27] but his ideas continued to be present in the Bolshevik internal correspondence. For instance, in October 1920, David Gopner, a Moscow emissary in Turkestan, prepared a report on the reassessment of Indo-Iranian revolutionary potential: "While waiting for a more propitious situation in Afghanistan, the Indian revolutionary base must be without any delay transferred to Turkistan, where the military preparations should start with feverish intensity." Gopner elaborated the "corridor-like" (*koridornym putem*), or nationalist and "organic" (*organicheskim putem*), or peasant scenarios of revolutionary transfer to Iran, which were to have led to the occupation of the Persian Gulf by the "Red Muslim troops." He concluded at the end of his report that "after Persia and Arabistan are purged from the British and their minions, it will be India's turn."[28] The Indian revolutionaries in Tashkent, split between the pan-Islamist agenda of Barakatullah and purist communist doctrine of M. N. Roy,[29] were soon transferred to Moscow, while the Soviet support for the Khilafat movement quickly withered away.[30] Nevertheless, the legacy of the Indian anti-imperialist movement remained tangible in the Iranian policy of the Bolsheviks who continued to punctuate their anti-British propaganda with pan-Islamic notes throughout the 1920s.[31]

The Ottoman and Turkmen Nexus

Ottoman pan-Islamic and pan-Turkic propaganda during World War I heavily impacted the relations of the Bolsheviks to pan-Islamism and their use of the concept of jihad. Pan-Islamic and pan-Turkic propaganda, and local networks created during the first two decades of the twentieth century, proved to be conducive to the post–October 1917 revolutionary mobilization. South of the Russian border, the prewar rapprochement between the Ottomans and Indian Muslims laid the basis for the subsequent Indo-Ottoman cooperation under the auspices of the Bolsheviks.[32] In Turkestan, the Islamic heritage of the Jadid, the nascent Turkic revolutionary groups, and the well-known pan-Islamism of Sultan-Galiev were imbibed with the spirit of Ottoman pan-Turanism. Willing to fight the "second phase of war" after the empire's capitulation, many Ottoman officers and officials joined the Bolsheviks, the most noteworthy example being that of the Ottoman Triumvirate member Enver Pasha, who was influenced by pro-Russian moods in Germany as well as by Bolshevik alliance with the Turkish nationalists.[33] It is thus no surprise that former agents of Ottoman influence were interested in the spread of Bolshevik propaganda in Iran.

The key figure of the Ottoman-Bolshevik nexus in Iran was captain Mehmed Kazım Bey, an Ottoman officer who had been heading the Ottoman section of the Turco-German mission in Afghanistan in 1915. Kazım Bey arrived at Tashkent in 1919 together with Barakatullah and impressed the Soviet authorities with his "fantastic plan" to occupy Mashhad and ignite the revolutionary fever among the Iranians "weary of Indian pagans" from the British troops.[34] Kazım Bey intended to unite Soviet power and local military chiefs, notably from the Yomut Turkmen. Kazım Bey positioned himself as an ardent advocate of anti-imperialist struggle against the British and attempted to convince the Tashkent authorities of the readiness of the Afghans to join Bolsheviks in this endeavor.[35] Kazım Bey was charged by the Tashkent Bolsheviks with the conduct of Soviet propaganda among the Iranian Turkmen. Yet Kazım Bey's agitation in Iran promoted pan-Ottoman and pan-Turkic ideas much more than communism.

The Bolshevik headquarters on the southern Caspian littoral were situated on the island Āshurādeh, while two other cells were established in Kara Su and Astarabad (Gorgan). Besides propaganda among Turkmen tribal chiefs, Kazım Bey, accompanied by five representatives of the Republic of Turkistan, entered into contact with the governor of Astarabad, who turned out to be hostile to the Iranian government.[36] Joined by Nuri Pasha, the half brother of the former Ottoman War Minister Enver Pasha, Tashkent emissaries succeeded in winning the support of the Jafarbai tribe from the Yomut Turkmen.[37] Kazım Bey's revolutionary message (and serious material investments on the part of Tashkent Bolsheviks)[38] appealed both to Turkmen sentiment of alterity vis-à-vis the Qajars and that of affinity to the Ottoman Turks: he encouraged the Turkmen to seek independence from Tehran and join the Ottoman Empire. If they were to reject Ottoman rule, Kazım Bey maintained that the Turkmen could form an autonomous political entity similar to the "independent state of Azerbaijan."[39]

Encouraged by Kazım Bey and provided with material aid by the Bolsheviks, the Turkmen were effectively fighting the British and Iranian troops, but their engagement with the Bolsheviks remained ambiguous; communist ideas were never popular in the Turkmen steppe. However, Turkmen agency in the spread of revolutionary networks and Bolshevik influence cannot be denied. Contrary to the nationalist appeals of the German-Ottoman propaganda in Iran, the pro-Ottoman pan-Turkic discourse of Kazım Bey targeted the uneasy relations between the locals and the Tehran government, which imposed on the Turkmen numerous economic restrictions and heavy charges for smuggling.[40] Organized on the basis of primitive democracy where nomadism served also as an expression of Turkmen sovereignty,[41] the local Turkmen population did not associate Bolshevik propaganda with the nationalist perspective of self-determination, but perceived it as a catalyst to switch loyalties from the Qajars to the Ottoman Turks.[42] Nevertheless, the concentration of various anti-imperialist networks in the Turkmen steppe between 1918 and 1920 could not have left intact the political imagination of its inhabitants.

Notably, the close contacts of the Turkmen leaders with Nikolai Iomudskii, a former tsarist official in Turkestan of Turkmen origin, might have resulted in the growth of political awareness among the Turkmen. During his years of service in Turkestan, Iomudskii lodged reformist criticisms of the Russian imperial administration. After the Bolshevik coup of 1917, he first joined the White forces and then the Persian Cossack Brigade, which was then operating under British auspices. As a representative of the Cossack Brigade in the Turkmen steppe Iomudskii engaged in informal negotiations with the Turkmen tribal chiefs and finally escaped in 1920 to Soviet territory, where he began his political and academic career.[43] Iomudskii's views on empire, modernization, and progress might have seriously impacted the Iranian Turkmens' perception of the Bolsheviks.[44] In the early 1920s, Iranian internal dynamics, namely the harsh centralization policy and rise to power of Reżā Khan (Pahlavi), also strengthened the Turkmen attraction to Bolshevik

Russia. Yet the continuous link between the Iranian Turkmen and the Bolshevik border authorities, which was epitomized in the Turkmen rebellion of 1925,[45] also originated in local entanglements, where Russian imperial, Ottoman, Indian, and Turkmen trajectories intersected in the shared space of revolutionary contagion.

The Azeri Nexus

While Indian and Ottoman transnational actors joined the Bolsheviks sometime after 1917, the Azeri revolutionaries had maintained extremely close relations with the Bolshevik RSDLP since 1905. Therefore, it is problematic to separate their agency from that of the Bolshevik state authorities in the period after 1917. Yet the activities of the Azeri revolutionaries not only permitted the Irano-Soviet collaboration but also shaped what was later labeled as "Soviet" policy in Iran.[46] One of the most important Azeri Bolshevik figures embodying the transnational aspect of regional revolutionary solidarities was Nariman Narimanov. A member of the Azeri socio-democratic party Hümmət since 1905, Narimanov coordinated the participation of Hümmət in the Iranian constitutional movement and, from the time he joined the RSDLP in March 1917, assured the integration of his local and regional networks into the Bolshevik polity. An ardent proponent of secularism, and one of the foremost advocates of the Eastern revolutionary movement, Narimanov was sensitive to the question of Azeri leadership, tacitly opposing Moscow's grip over the revolutionary transfer to the East.

The collaboration between the Baku revolutionaries and the Iranian insurgents was not a linear uninterrupted process. Though the Baku Commune (1917–18) closely collaborated with the Iranian anti-imperialist guerrilla movement of Kuchek Khan,[47] the authorities of revolutionary Baku never consciously transferred the revolutionary nexus from Baku to Iran. Under the threat of Ottoman intervention, the late Baku Commune turned out to be dependent on British military support, and the commune's reliance on the Armenian Dashnaktsutiun stoked constant tensions between the Iranians and the Caucasian Bolsheviks. Furthermore, in contrast to the openly transnational orientation of the Tashkent policy, Baku, menaced by Turco-German forces, remained hostile to pro-German Iranian democrats, who were fighting in Tabriz with local Bolshevik groupings.[48] Thus, Iran still did not take part in the broader revolutionary project embodied in the Baku Commune, which was instead trying to divert the members of the

Iranian-Azeri Socio-Democratic Party (1917) from propaganda activities on Iranian territory.[49]

After the fall of the commune, by the end of 1919, the Iranian question was revived in the Narodnyĭ Komissariat Vnutrennikh Del (NKID, People's Commissariat of Internal Affairs) by Nariman Narimanov, a crucial member of Hummət, which came to be integrated into Adalat. The subsequent domination of the former Hummət contingent over the members of Adalat furnished the Azeris a certain legitimacy in their later claim of leadership in the Iranian question.[50] In 1919, Stalin invited Narimanov to lead the Eastern Department of the NKID, but his position together with the whole Eastern Department seemed to have been purely formal, if not symbolic. Narimanov's suggestions on the Eastern policy were mostly ignored by the NKID. In November 1919, when Afghanistan emerged as a potential ally of the Soviets in their anti-imperialist struggle against the British, Narimanov delivered Chicherin an ardent message stressing the revolutionary potential of the East. Narimanov's East appeared as a fertile ground for Bolshevik propaganda, as pan-Islamism had already lost its position: "Can Afghanistan, under the banner of pan-Islamism together with Turkey and other Muslim countries in alliance with Germany, harm our interests on the Turkestan front? What sort of pan-Islamism are we talking about when Azerbaijan at this moment, so decisive for her future, refused to support Dagestan? Bukhara refuses to support Afghanistan against England."[51]

Narimanov was also trying to justify Moscow's investment in Eastern policy by downplaying the counterrevolutionary threat emanating from native elites: "Will the counterrevolutions strike from the East? Ridiculous! We were not afraid of the counterrevolution from the West, with its tanks, but we are afraid of the Muslim East with its daggers."[52] Narimanov's Iranian policy was versed in the same anti-imperialist tone as the foreign policy designs formulated by Barakatullah and Kazım Bey: Iran must be integrated into a larger Eastern program of revolutionary transfer as soon as possible to reinforce the Soviet alliance with Afghanistan. Yet their pan-Islamist rhetoric was judged by Narimanov as unacceptable, and preference was given to consequential ideological work carried out by "reliable" communists.

Narimanov's vision of "reliable" communists did not exactly correspond to that of Chicherin, who feared the capricious tendencies of peripheral Bolshevik authorities in the foreign policy sphere. In order to put the Turkestan communists under central control, a special commission (Turkkomissia) was sent from Moscow to Tashkent,[53] and the same commission was charged by Chicherin with propaganda activities in the East, which seriously limited the room for maneuver for the Caucasian Bolsheviks.[54] Though the Turkkomissia soon charted an autonomous course vis-à-vis the NKID, it was conceived and maintained as a tool of control over transborder revolutionary dynamics through an alternative network independent from Baku. A parallel section of Adalat was created in Tashkent, and Avetis Solṭānzādeh (Mikaelian), a loyal Bolshevik with no background in the political activities of the region, was sent by the NKID in order to organize the Iranian revolutionary movement. Furthermore, the first Congress of the new Adalat was organized deliberately, under Moscow's guidance, in Tashkent and not in Baku as Narimanov planned.[55] The bifurcation of the nascent Iranian communism was a result of Moscow's conscious choice to opt for a top-down revolutionary transfer.

Despite Chicherin's attempts to restructure the Iranian revolutionary network, the new party turned out to be extremely weak and disorganized. By May 1920, the Department of International Propaganda of the Turkkomissia (Sovinterprop) began considering reorientation with the Leftist branch of the IDP, who "in contrast to Adalat, has a minimum programme." In addition, the party was subject to criticism by Turkkomissia, mostly for its lack of organization and its unreliable members.[56] However, Chicherin still preferred to entrust the Iranian revolutionary policy to an outsider such as Solṭānzādeh, and not to the protégé of Narimanov, Ḥaydar Khan, who was a veteran of the Iranian constitutional movement and the WWI guerrilla movement directed against the Allied forces. After the fall of Solṭānzādeh as party leader, Narimanov succeeded in placing Ḥaydar Khan at the head of the ICP and continued to support the Iranian insurgents even after the failure of the Gilan Republic, followed by Chicherin's veto.[57] It would be erroneous, however, to interpret Chicherin's policy as a victory for diplomatic pragmatism, as Chicherin's initial position on the Eastern question was closer to Narimanov than to Trotsky, who looked westward to Europe.[58] It was Narimanov's drive for autonomy and the scale of his personal network in the East that was at the heart of Chicherin's distrust. Finally, despite the centralizing ambition of the NKID in the early 1920s, Narimanov's involvement in the Iranian revolution had long-standing consequences in both the Soviet Iranian and domestic policy vis-à-vis the Republic of Azerbaijan.

The establishment of the Soviet Republic of Gilan and the creation of the Iranian Communist Party in June 1920 did not result from spontaneous decisions taken in Moscow, nor were they projects limited to Irano-Russian interactions. The extension of the Turkestan front to Iran was discussed by various regional actors, who were attracted by Bolshevik universalism and sought a powerful ally in their struggle with Great Britain. The ideological component of early Bolshevik anti-imperialism was extremely multifaceted, diverse, and most importantly inclusive (yet with its own considerable limits, of course): pan-Islamism, pan-Turkism, and transborder solidarity were not only evident in Bolshevik propaganda, but also shaped the course of the Bolshevik policy. In crystallizing the Bolshevik strategy in Iran, the agency of Indian, Ottoman, and Caucasian transnational actors was of crucial importance. Yet ideologies soon intermingled with personal and institutional loyalties, finally leading to the polarization of the debate around Soviet policy toward the East. Nevertheless, the regional importance of Iran as a junction of diverse transnational networks remained tangible for many decades both in Soviet foreign policy and in Iranian sociopolitical developments.

Notes

1. See for example Loren Goldner, "'Socialism in One Country' before Stalin, and the Origins of Reactionary 'Anti-Imperialism': The Case of Turkey, 1917-1925," *Critique* 38, no. 4 (2010): 631-61.

2. Here "agency" refers to the power of individuals and groups to alter the dominant (Soviet) revolutionary paradigm.

3. Michael Kemper, "Red Orientalism: Mikhail Pavlovich and Marxist Oriental Studies in Early Soviet Russia," in "A Muslim Interwar Soviet Union," special issue, *Die Welt des Islams* 50, no. 3-4 (2010): 445. On the continuity of the Russian orientalist tradition in the Soviet era, see Denis V. Volkov, *Russia's Turn to Persia: Orientalism in Diplomacy and Intelligence* (Cambridge: Cambridge University Press, 2019); Vera Tolz, *Russia's Own Orient: The Politics of Identity and Oriental Studies in the Late Imperial and Early Soviet Periods* (Oxford: Oxford University Press, 2011).

4. Samuel J. Hirst, "Transnational Anti-Imperialism and the National Forces: Soviet Diplomacy and Turkey, 1920-23," *Comparative Studies of South Asia, Africa and the Middle East* 33, no. 2 (2013): 214. See also Michael David-Fox, "The Implications of Transnationalism," *Kritika: Explorations in Russian and Eurasian History* 12, no. 4 (2011): 885.

5. The transnational approach is equally present in recent scholarship on Iranian history and society. Notably, Fariba Adelkhah cites the example of Ḥaydar Khan, one of the founders of the Iranian Communist Party, whose

complex trajectory defined the multicultural nature of the early Iranian communist movement. Fariba Adelkhah, *Les mille et une frontières de l'Iran: Quand les voyages forment la nation* (Paris: Karthala, 2012), 104.

6. The field of transnational history of early Soviet foreign policy was pioneered by Taline Ter Minassian with her fundamental work *Colporteurs du Komintern: L'Union Soviétique et les minorités au Moyen-Orient* (Paris: Presses de Sciences Po, 1997). For more recent examples of the transnational approach, see Ivan Sablin, *Governing Post-Imperial Siberia and Mongolia, 1911–1924* (London: Routledge, 2017); Hirst, "Transnational Anti-Imperialism and the National Forces."

7. See, for example, Mikhail Volodarsky, *The Soviet Union and Its Neighbours: Iran and Afghanistan, 1917–1933* (Portland, OR: F. Cass, 1994). For a larger chronological perspective of Russian imperialism in Iran, see Firuz Kazemzadeh, "Iranian Relations with Russia and the Soviet Union, to 1921," in *The Cambridge History of Iran*, vol. 7, *From Nader Shah to the Islamic Republic*, ed. Peter Avery, Gavin Hambly, and Charles Melville (Cambridge: Cambridge University Press, 1991), 314–49.

8. Cosroe Chaquèri, *The Soviet Socialist Republic of Iran, 1920–1921: Birth of the Trauma* (Pittsburgh: University of Pittsburgh Press, 1995); Vladimir Genis, *Krasnaia Persiia: Bol'sheviki v Giliane, 1920–1921. Dokumental'naia khronika* (Moscow: MNPI, 2000); Jamil Hasanli, *The Sovietization of Azerbaijan: The South Caucasus in the Triangle of Russia, Turkey, and Iran, 1920–1922* (Salt Lake City: University of Utah Press, 2019).

9. The old debate on pragmatism and idealism in Soviet foreign policy is resumed in Michael J. Carley, *A Hidden History of Early Soviet-Western Relations* (Lanham: Rowman & Littlefield, 2014), xi–xvi; Jon Jacobson, "Essay and Reflection: On the Historiography of Soviet Foreign Relations in the 1920s," *International History Review* 18, no. 2 (1996): 351.

10. See, for example, M. A. Persits, *Zastenchivaia interventsiia: O Sovetskom vtorzhenii v Iran* (Moscow: Muraveĭ-gaĭd, 1999). For a broader perspective on Soviet imperialism, see Dominic Lieven, "The Russian Empire and the Soviet Union as Imperial Polities," *Journal of Contemporary History* 30, no. 4 (1995): 607–36; Yuri Slezkine, "Imperialism as the Highest Stage of Socialism," *Russian Review* 59, no. 2 (2000): 227–34.

11. See Stephen Blank, "Soviet Politics and the Iranian Revolution of 1919–1921," *Cahiers du Monde russe et soviétique* 21, no. 2 (1980): 173–94. For a general analysis on the applicability of the term "Stalinism" to the history of the Comintern, see John McIlroy and Alan Campbell, "Bolshevism, Stalinism and the Comintern: A Historical Controversy Revisited," *Labor History* 60, no. 3 (2019): 165–92.

12. While Bast tries to ascribe some kind of autonomous Iranian agency in the formation of the ICP to Solṭānzādeh and portrays him as a victim of the interventionist policies by the "Caucasians," Dailami underscores the tactical blunders in Solṭānzādeh's policies and attributes the crucial role in the evolution of the ICP to Ḥaydar Khan 'Amu-Oghlu Tāriverdi. Pezhmann Dailami, "The Bolsheviks and the Jangali Revolutionary Movement, 1915–1920," *Cahiers*

du Monde russe et soviétique 31, no. 1 (1990): 43–59; Dailami, "The Bolshevik Revolution and the Genesis of Communism in Iran, 1917–1920," *Central Asian Survey* 11, no. 3 (1992): 51–82; Dailami, "The First Congress of Peoples of the East and the Iranian Soviet Republic of Gilan, 1920–21," in *Reformers and Revolutionaries in Modern Iran: New Perspectives on the Iranian Left*, ed. Stephanie Cronin (London: Routledge Curzon, 2004), 87–106; Oliver Bast, "The Council for International Propaganda and the Establishment of the Iranian Communist Party," in *Iran and the First World War: Battleground of the Great Powers*, ed. Touraj Atabaki (London: I. B. Tauris, 2006), 163–80. The polarization of the Gilan Republic historiography, as it appears through the comparison of Dailami's and Bast's works, was observed by Janet Afary already in 1995, when she warned against "populist histories," built on the heroic depiction of different protagonists of the Gilan revolution. Janet Afary, "The Contentious Historiography of the Gilan Republic in Iran: A Critical Exploration," *Iranian Studies* 28, no. 1–2 (1995): 3–24.

13. For the depiction of early Bolshevik activities among the Russian army and Iranian population, see Boris Shumiatskii, *Na postu sovetskoĭ diplomatii: Pervyĭ sovetskiĭ diplomat v Irane I. O. Kolomiitsev* (Moscow: IVR, 1960), 23; Viktor Shklovskii, *Sentimental'noe puteshestvie* (St. Petersburg: Azbuka-klassika, 2006; originally published 1921), 90–146.

14. Persits, *Zastenchivaia interventsiia*, 26.

15. See Ben Fowkes and Bülent Gökay, "Unholy Alliance: Muslims and Communists—An Introduction," *Journal of Communist Studies and Transition Politics* 25, no. 1 (2009): 1–31.

16. For the pan-Asianism of the Indian liberation movement and its impact on Chinese society, see Carolien Stolte and Harald Fisher-Tiné, "Imagining Asia in India: Nationalism and Internationalism (ca. 1905–1940)," *Comparative Studies in Society and History* 54, no. 1 (2012): 65–92; B. R. Deepak, "The Colonial Connections: Indian and Chinese Nationalists in Japan and China," *China Report* 48, no. 147 (2012): 147–70.

17. G. L. Dmitriev, *Indian Revolutionaries in Central Asia* (Delhi: Hope Greenwich Millenium Press, 2002), 33.

18. See K. Humayun Ansari, "Pan-Islam and the Making of the Early Indian Muslim Socialists," *Modern Asian Studies* 20, no. 3 (1986): 509–37. It is worth mention that Indian pan-Islam was opposed to the Arabic project of the reestablishment of the Arab caliphate, which found the lukewarm support of Great Britain during WWI. Conor Meleady, "Negotiating the Caliphate: British Responses to Pan-Islamic Appeals, 1914–1924," *Middle Eastern Studies* 52, no. 2 (2016): 188.

19. On Barakatullah's trajectory, see Iqbal Husain, "Barakatullah—a Half-Forgotten Revolutionary," *Proceedings of the Indian History Congress* 66 (2005–6): 1061–72; K. Humayun Ansari, "Maulana Barakatullah Bhopali's Transnationalism: Pan-Islamism, Colonialism, and Radical Politics," in *Transnational Islam in Interwar Europe: Muslim Activists and Thinkers*, ed. Götz Nordbruch and Umar Ryad (New York: Palgrave Macmillan, 2014), 181–210.

20. Frederick J. Moberly, *Operations in Persia: 1914–1919*, ed. Imperial War Museum (London: HMSO, 1987), 84.

21. The Khilafat movement was a political protest campaign launched by Muslims of British India to restore the caliph of the Ottoman Caliphate as an effective political authority.

22. It is worth mentioning that Lenin read *Religion of Love* but did not accept Pratap's theses. Dmitriev, *Indian Revolutionaries*, 48, 56, 63-64; Alexandre Andreyev, *Soviet Russia and Tibet: The Debacle of Secret Diplomacy, 1918-1930s* (Leiden: Brill, 2003), 96.

23. Hasan Taqizādeh, *Zendegi-ye ṭufāni: Khāṭerāt-e Sayyed Ḥasan Taqizādeh*, ed. Iraj Afshār (Tehran: Enteshārāt-e 'elmi, 1372/1993), 183; Mohammed Alsulami, "Iranian Journals in Berlin during the Interwar Period," in Nordbruch and Ryad, *Transnational Islam in Interwar Europe*, 159.

24. Barakatullah to the government of the Russian Soviet Federative Socialist Republic, "O zadachakh Afganskoĭ revoliutsii," April 22, 1919, in Iu. N. Tikhonov, ed., *Sovetskaiã Rossiĭ v bor'be za "Afganskiĭ Koridor" (1919-1925): Sbornik Dokumentov* (Moscow: Kvadriga, 2017), 31.

25. See Faridullah Bezhan, "Pan-Islamism in Afghanistan in the Early Twentieth Century: From Political Discourse to Government Policy, 1906-22," *Islam and Christian–Muslim Relations* 25, no 2 (2014): 193-210; Faiz Ahmed, *Afghanistan Rising: Islamic Law and Statecraft between the Ottoman and British Empires* (Cambridge, MA: Harvard University Press, 2017), 161-207.

26. Karakhan to Bogoiavlenskii, June 12, 1919, in Tikhonov, *Sovetskaiã Rossiĭ v bor'be*, 35.

27. Instead, it was M. N. Roy who received arms and funds to organize an uprising of Indian tribes on his arrival in Tashkent in September 1920. John P. Haithcox, *Communism and Nationalism in India: M. N. Roy and Comintern Policy, 1920-1939* (Princeton, NJ: Princeton University Press, 1971), 22.

28. Gopner to the Central Committee of the Bolshevik branch of the Russian Communist Party (TsK RKP[b]), "Our Current Tasks in Central Asia," October 18, 1920, in Tikhonov, *Sovetskaiã Rossiĭ v bor'be*, 138, 145.

29. K. Maitra, "Comintern, Roy and the Possibility of an Armed Revolution in India," *Proceedings of the Indian History Congress* 39, no. 2 (1978): 652-59; Sobhanlal D. Gupta, *Comintern and the Destiny of Communism in India, 1919-1943: Dialectics of Real and Possible History* (Kolkata: Seribaan, 2006), 82.

30. Telegram by Turkburo TsK RKP(b), RGASPI, f. 61, op. 2, d. 17, l. 8.

31. See, for example, V. V. Naumkin, "Nekotorye aspekty diplomaticheskogo sopernichestva Sovetskogo Soĭuza i Velikobritanii v Aravii v 1920-e gg," *Vostok*, no 2 (2018): 6-19.

32. See Syed Tanvir Wasti, "The Political Aspirations of Indian Muslims and the Ottoman Nexus," *Middle Eastern Studies* 42, no 5 (2006): 709-22. For the broader impact of Ottoman Turanism, see Sinan Levent, "Common Asianist Intellectual History in Turkey and Japan: Turanism," *Central Asian Survey* 35, no. 1 (2016): 121-35.

33. On Enver Pasha's contacts with the Soviets, see Şuhnaz Yilmaz, "An Ottoman Warrior Abroad: Enver Paşa as an Expatriate," *Middle Eastern Studies* 35, no. 4 (1999): 40-69; Azade-Ayse Rorlich, "Fellow Travelers: Enver Pasha and the Bolshevik Government 1918-1920," *Asian Affairs* 13, no 3 (1982): 288-96;

Salahi R. Sonyel, "Enver Pasha and the Basmaji Movement in Central Asia," *Middle Eastern Studies* 26, no. 1 (1990): 52-64. The proper motivation of such transnational actors as Enver Pasha should be located between transnational solidarity, nationalism, and geopolitics. For an analogous approach, see Michael Goebel, "Geopolitics, Transnational Solidarity or Diaspora Nationalism? The Global Career of M.N. Roy, 1915-1930," *European Review of History* 21, no. 4 (2014): 485-99.

34. Report by Bravin, March 24, 2019, in Tikhonov, *Sovetskaīa Rossiī v bor'be*, 28.

35. Report by Bravin.

36. Telegram by Golkin, July 1920, Service Historique de la Défense (hereafter SHD), 1KMI 87 (Brigade cosaque, Perse), reel 25.

37. Gadji Khan to Mashhad, February 8, 1920, SHD, 1KMI 87 (Brigade cosaque, Perse), reel 25.

38. Sergent Vysotskii to the chief of the Cossack brigade of Astarabad, SHD, 1KMI 87 (Brigade cosaque, Perse), reel 25.

39. Anonymous to Astarabad customs, September 2, 1919, SHD, 1KMI 87 (Brigade cosaque, Perse), reel 25.

40. Report by Sergeant Vysotskii, 1919, SHD, 1KMI 87 (Brigade cosaque, Perse), reel 25.

41. See William Irons, "Nomadism as a Political Adaptation: The Case of the Yomut Turkmen," in "Uses of Ethnohistory in Ethnographic Analysis," special issue, *American Ethnologist* 1, no 4 (1974): 635-58; Michael John Denison, "Why Do Sultanistic Regimes Arise and Persist? A Study of Government in the Republic of Turkmenistan, 1992-2006" (PhD diss., University of Leeds, 2006), 87.

42. The Russian patronage was of little attraction to the Iranian Turkmen. During the passage of the German mission across the Karakum Desert in 1915, most of the Turkmen tribes showed themselves hostile toward tsarist Russia, while there was still one Turkmen regiment, formed by Russian officers. Oskar von Niedermayer, *Unter der Glutsonne Irans: Kriegserlebnisse der deutschen Expedition nach Persien und Afganistan* (Dachau bei München: Einhorverlag, 1925), 200-201.

43. For the biography of Iomudskii, see Anton Iskhanov, "A.N. Samoilovich (1880-1938) i ego polevye informanty: Konstruirovanie Turkmenskoĭ kul'turnoĭ identichnosti" (PhD diss., Higher School of Economics, Moscow, 2021). For the administrative activities of Iomudskii as a member of the Turkestan Central Executive Committee, see Nikolai Alun Thomas, *Nomads and Soviet Rule: Central Asia under Lenin and Stalin* (London: I. B. Tauris, 2018), 90-91.

44. On Iomudskii's political thought in the prerevolutionary period, see Moritz Deutschmann, *Iran and Russian Imperialism: The Ideal Anarchists, 1800-1914* (New York: Routledge, 2016), 144-46.

45. See Robert Olson, "The Turkoman Rebellion in Eastern Iran, 1924-5: Its Consequences and the Soviet Reaction," *Die Welt des Islams* 31, no 2 (1991): 216-27.

46. On the role of the Azeri authorities in the Soviet Iranian policy in the 1920s, see Etienne Forestier-Peyrat, "Red Passage to Iran: The Baku Trade Fair

and the Unmaking of the Azerbaijani Borderland (1922-1930)," *Ab Imperio*, 2013, no. 4, 79-112. For the pre-WWII context, see Dzhamil' Gasanly, *Sovetskaiā politika po rasshireniiu iuzhnykh granits: Stalin i Azerbaĭdzhanskaiā karta v bor'be za zeft'' (1939-45)* (Moscow: ROSSPEN, 2017).

47. Kārgozār of Gilan to the Iranian Ministry of Foreign Affairs, May 27, 1918 (Sha'bān 16, 1336), in Kāveh Bayāt, ed., *Irān dar Jang-e Jahāni-ye Avval: Asnād-e vezārat-e dākheleh* (Tehran: Enteshārāt-e Sāzemān-e Asnād-e Melli-ye Irān, 1381/2002), 409-12; see also Dailami, "The Bolsheviks and the Jangali Revolutionary Movement."

48. Dailami, "The Bolshevik Revolution and the Genesis of Communism in Iran," 68.

49. Narimanov to Lenin, November 1, 1919, in Tikhonov, *Sovetskaiā Rossiĭ v bor'be*, 43.

50. Dailami, "First Congress of Peoples of the East," 93-94.

51. Narimanov to Lenin, November 1, 1919, in Tikhonov, *Sovetskaiā Rossiĭ v bor'be*, 43-44.

52. Narimanov to Lenin, November 1, 1919, in Tikhonov, *Sovetskaiā Rossiĭ v bor'be*, 43-44.

53. Report by Bravin, March 24, 1919, in Tikhonov, *Sovetskaiā Rossiĭ v bor'be*, 27-29.

54. The "Caucasians," who among others counted Stalin, Ordzhonikidze, and Narimanov, were far from being a monolithic political force. Stalin later alluded to the instrumental role of Narimanov in his Eastern policy. Tadeusz Swietochowski, *Russian Azerbaijan, 1905-1920: The Shaping of National Identity in a Muslim Community* (London: Cambridge University Press, 2004), 109.

55. Hasanli, *Sovietization of Azerbaijan*, 80.

56. "Protokol № 11 Zasedaniia biuro Soveta Internatsional'noĭ Propagandy na Vostoke," GARF, f. R5402, op. 1, d. 31, l. 11.

57. Gopner to Rothstein, November 4, 1921, RGASPI, f. 159, op. 2, d. 51, ll. 58-59.

58. For the Chicherin-Trotsky debate on Eastern policy, see Chicherin to Lenin, June 4, 1920, in Tikhonov, *Sovetskaiā Rossiĭ v bor'be*, 103-4.

CHAPTER 16

Pragmatic Elements of Early Soviet Policy toward Iran

Iurii Demin

The Caspian region has long been one of the centers of world politics and focal points of the great powers' struggle. The strategic importance of the region, including Iran as an integral part, was well understood both by the leadership of the Russian Empire and by the Bolsheviks who succeeded them. Though the Soviets initially rejected the political inheritance of their predecessor, they soon became actively involved in the power struggle in the region, using various methods, including those previously condemned, to achieve their goals. The main aim of this chapter is to characterize early Soviet policy toward Iran and to identify main objectives behind the decisions and the actions of the Soviet leadership in regional and international contexts.

In the last few decades, various authors have written on and discussed the nature of Soviet policy toward Iran, focusing differently on the factors that influenced its course and direction. Here, Soviet authors formed a separate group, as their positions were determined by the theoretical and ideological premises on the existence of an inextricable link between foreign policy and social system, and the class

---

This article is an output of a research project implemented as part of the Basic Research Program at the National Research University Higher School of Economics (HSE University).

characteristics of a certain state. Accordingly, the foreign policy of a "workers-and-peasants" Soviet state was contrasted with the foreign policy of imperialist powers.[1] Some researchers wrote within similar analytical frameworks but arrived at essentially opposite conclusions, associating Soviet foreign policy, particularly the intrusion in Iran (1920–21), mainly with a radical and an expansionist Bolshevik ideology.[2] A de-emphasis on ideology and heightened attention to the Bolsheviks' strategic and geopolitical interests is visible in scholarship of those studying the Soviet policy toward Iran in the context of great-power rivalry.[3]

The research proposed is based on the analysis of unpublished documents and demonstrates that an ideological component played a subordinate role and gave way to the mainly pragmatical approach of Moscow toward achievement of its goals in Iran. And here we regard as important to concretize our position with two statements:

1. It is important to differentiate between the early Bolsheviks, an antisystem party, and the later Bolsheviks, state managers forced to deal with issues of survival of the Soviet state within the existing system of international relations.
2. Soviet policy toward Iran cannot be examined outside of regional and international contexts. The regional context is important, as many acts of force by Moscow were influenced by its interests in the Caspian. The international situation (which, of course, could be perceived and interpreted in different ways) stimulated the Bolsheviks to adjust their policies toward Iran and influenced their actions, choice of means, and possible partners inside and outside of Iran.

Internal processes in Soviet Russia and characteristics of the Bolsheviks' regime had an impact on Soviet foreign policy. The Bolsheviks, having seized power in Russia, did not immediately and totally abandon their revolutionary ideals, as indicated, for example, by their attempt to organize an uprising in Germany in 1923. But the international situation around Soviet Russia stimulated the Bolshevik leadership to adapt its ideological attitudes and goals to the existing external conditions. There was a process that can be called "socialization of nonconformist states,"[4] or, in other words, the adaptation of the behavior of an element of the system of international relations to the existing successful practices in the system. In the context, we can mention H. Kapur and E.

Carr, who noted the limiting influence of the outside world on the actions of the Bolsheviks and the transformation of Soviet foreign policy toward greater prudence and pragmatism.[5]

The Soviet Intrusion into Gilan and the Soviet-Iranian Treaty of 1921

In accordance with our objective, we consider it necessary to analyze some key moments and directions of early Soviet policy toward Iran.

The first connections of the Bolsheviks with Iranian revolutionaries date back to the time of the Constitutional Revolution. But until the early 1920s, the East, including Iran, played a secondary role in the Bolsheviks' revolutionary strategy and practice. After the failure of postwar revolutionary outbreaks in Europe, the Bolsheviks began to pay more attention to the East. Hence some researchers see in the Soviet intervention in Gilan (1920) mainly a display of radical Bolshevik ideology and an attempt to "export" a revolution to the East.[6]

However, we cannot disregard the earlier Bolsheviks' failed efforts to establish diplomatic relations with Tehran, the British attempts to use Iran as a base for military intervention in Transcaucasia and Central Asia, as well as the conclusion of the Anglo-Persian Agreement (1919). These events could not but contribute to the radicalization of the Bolsheviks' attitude toward Tehran. It is also necessary to take into consideration the critical importance for Moscow of the oil fields in Baku, the vulnerability of which influenced its policy in the Caspian region.

Regardless of motivation, the Bolshevik leadership demonstrated sufficient prudence after the establishment of the Soviet republic in Gilan. Moscow did not recognize the republic officially while providing military support through Soviet Azerbaijan and beginning diplomatic negotiations with Tehran. Even if initial military success in Gilan may have given rise to the Bolsheviks' ambitions, as early as the fall of 1920, the Bolshevik leadership began to recognize the absence of real revolutionary prospects in Iran.[7] As a result, Moscow used the republic as a means of exerting political pressure on both Tehran and London.

There was no consensus among the Bolsheviks concerning a change in the political line toward Iran. Yet the leadership of Soviet Azerbaijan and the Caucasian Bureau were able to only partially sabotage Moscow's decisions by sending armaments and troops to Gilan after the conclusion of the Soviet-Iranian Treaty of 1921. The organized resistance to the new policy among the Iranian communists ended following the death of Ḥaydar Khan and the destruction of the republic. The directions of the Comintern were changed correspondingly.

Some authors criticized Moscow for an opportunistic policy toward the Jangal Movement.[8] However, the downfall of the republic and the defeat of the Jangalis were not merely a result of another opportunistic maneuver by the Bolsheviks, but in fact marked the completion of the initial period in the relationship between them and Iranian revolutionaries. The Bolsheviks, having emerged as a revolutionary party, actively supported revolutionaries in neighboring Iran. But, having won the Civil War and finding itself in a new political situation, the Bolshevik leadership chose to rethink its earlier viewpoints. Long-term state interests prevailed over doubtful revolutionary prospects. In that connection head of Soviet diplomacy G. V. Chicherin told G. K. Ordzhonikidze that the changed external political situation, the need for foreign loans and cooperation with "capital," required more flexible policy and the promotion of confidence to the Soviet state.[9]

The strategic interests of the Soviet state were reflected in the content of the Soviet-Iranian Treaty of 1921. The treaty was examined in detail, and its evaluations widely ranged from positive to extremely negative ones.[10] Inclusion of articles V and VI, which clearly restricted Iranian sovereignty, however, must be seen in the contemporary international context, the domestic circumstances of Iran (whose territory was still occupied by the British), and Moscow's determination to provide security for its southern borders. Later on, that determination was reflected in articles II, III, and IV of the Treaty of Warranties and Neutrality (1927).

The Soviet renunciation under the treaty of 1921 of the previous unequal treaties, agreements and conventions, loans and concessions, as well as the bequest of an expensive immovable property to Tehran were also designed, at least partly, to further the long-term political goals of Moscow. Thus, Chicherin informed the Politburo that the treaty would have been an excellent instrument of agitation in favor of Soviet Russia and against Great Britain.[11]

The treaty of 1921 provided Moscow with a legal channel to intervene in Iranian affairs in the case of emerging threats, real or farfetched, to its national security. Thus, in the 1920s Moscow actively used article XIII and to some extent article XIV to prevent "hostile" foreign capital from coming close to the Soviet southern borders.

The Soviet Policy toward Former Concessions in the North of Iran

One of the tools that tsarist Russia, along with Great Britain, used to strengthen its influence in Iran was the acquisition of concessions by private and state capital (telegraph lines, roads, the Anzali port, the Lianozov fishing concession, etc.). Soviet Russia, renouncing the former tsarist concessions in Iran under the treaty of 1921, in practice tried to maintain control over the use of the most important of them. It was done either through legal means (article XIII of the treaty obliging Tehran not to transfer the property received under the agreement to any third state or its citizens) or just by use of force. Of particular interest for the Bolsheviks were the fisheries: according to article XIV Tehran accepted to conclude a contract with Moscow concerning their future exploitation.

The history of the fishing concession began in 1873, when S. M. Lianozov received a shah's *farmān* granting him a monopoly right on fishing in the river estuary of the Iranian Caspian shore. World War I and the Civil War in Russia led to the bankruptcy of the Lianozovs' company and rescission of the concession by Tehran (1918). The Bolsheviks, after landing in Anzali (May 1920), nationalized the fisheries and put into operation the part of them that they physically controlled (Anzali and Ḥasan Kiyāde in Gilan province).[12] Moreover the Soviet representatives started negotiations with the government of the so-called Persian Republic (Gilan). The negotiations ended on November 12, 1920, by the conclusion of a draft treaty, according to which the republican government leased the Iranian Caspian coastal waters to Soviet Russia for thirty-five years.[13] However, the establishment of official Soviet-Iranian diplomatic relations made its implementation impossible.

As a result, in September 1921, Moscow gave mandates to negotiate the issue to the Soviet representatives in Tehran.[14] The negotiations were soon deadlocked because of a complete incongruence of the Soviet and Iranian positions. Whereas the Iranian government insisted upon the joint exploitation of the fisheries, Moscow sought sole exploitation in exchange for a certain percentage of the fisheries' net profit.[15] Attempts by the Soviet mission in Tehran to buy out the Lianozovs' company's shares were thwarted by Iranian officials.[16]

Tehran, considering the Bolsheviks' presence in the fisheries illegal and not coming to an agreement with them, in November 1922 resumed the concession of Lianozov's heirs by the decision of the arbitration court. In response, the Soviet diplomats were able to convince one of the heirs, Martin Lianozov, to go to the USSR and sell his rights and properties (in Anzali and Astara) to a Soviet joint-stock company, thus creating a legal cover for Soviet presence in the fisheries.[17] The legality of the deal was denied by Tehran, but in the existing international conditions legal casuistry gave way to the factor of power, and the Soviet side continued to exploit parts of the fisheries that it physically controlled. When in May 1924, the local military governor sent troops to the fisheries in Ḥasan Kiyāde, they were met by Soviet soldiers.[18] Tehran's plans to hand over fishing permits to individuals willing to pay more were neutralized either by Moscow's banning the purchase of fish and caviar from them or, if it concerned Soviet citizens, by not issuing licenses and visas.[19]

The Bolsheviks' persistence was explained not only by the economic prospects of the fisheries. Initially, the Soviet economic managers counted on the full recoupment of expenses for the operation of fisheries through the sale of black caviar alone.[20] However, such calculations were probably overstated. This exaggeration, along with the introduction of a self-financing system for the Soviet enterprises and organizations, led to a situation when at the turn of 1923-24 the Russian state agency for fisheries started to advocate for a temporary cessation of the fisheries' exploitation.[21] The opinion soon changed, but legal uncertainty and the self-financed system forced the fisheries administration to reduce activity. If in 1920-21 the fisheries produced 281,344 poods of fish (including 38,181 sturgeon) and 4,466 poods of caviar, in 1923-24 they produced only 35,000 poods of fish (only sturgeon) and 5,365 poods of caviar.[22]

A more important role in the fisheries issue, in our view, came on the initiative of the Revolutionary Military Council, which pointed out that the fisheries' loss would necessitate funding to strengthen the Soviet military presence in the Caspian Sea.[23] The Soviet diplomacy, apparently, took a similar position. Thus, in October 1926 K. K. Iurenev, a Soviet ambassador in Iran, wrote Chicherin that the possession of the fisheries enabled Moscow to control the Caspian southern shore and created a barrier to British expansion.[24]

The issue could be resolved only through diplomatic channels, and on October 7, 1924, a treaty was signed to establish a joint-stock Soviet-Iranian company for twenty-five years with equal shares in fixed capital, profits, and company management.[25] The treaty was ratified by the Politburo and adopted by the Council of People's Commissars but faced procrastination in the Majles.²⁶ After subsequent negotiations, stimulated by Soviet economic pressure, the agreement on the fisheries was signed on October 1, 1927. The agreement helped Moscow to maintain its positions in the southern Caspian until the fisheries were nationalized by Tehran (1953).

The same intensions of the Soviet government can be seen in its attitude toward the port of Anzali. After the Soviet troops' landing at Anzali, the port was placed under the authority of Soviet officials. The following demand of the republican government (June 27, 1920) to transfer management to Rasht was ignored.²⁷ After the fall of the republic and until 1927 the port was de facto controlled by Moscow despite article X of the treaty of 1921. In 1924, Shumiatskii even proposed the establishment of a joint Soviet-Iranian company to manage the port for twenty-five years.²⁸ On the basis of the proposal an outline agreement was developed that was approved by the Politburo in January 1925.²⁹ However, in this case Moscow did not possess any legal means to force Tehran to agree to a joint management of the port and by agreement of 1927 relinquished control of it to the Iranian government. In exchange, Tehran, inter alia, agreed to exclude foreign nationals from work in the port for twenty-five years.³⁰ That, along with the fisheries agreement, clearly displayed Moscow's desire to prevent the entry of a "hostile" power into the Caspian region.

Moscow applied a different tactic with the same goal in its approach to the northern oil concession. Let us recall that the oilfields in the south of Iran were under the control of the Anglo-Persian Oil Company. The company's rights were based on the D'Arcy Concession (1901) that covered the biggest part of Iran excluding five northern provinces: Azerbaijan, Astarabad (Gorgan), Gilan, Mazandaran, and Khorasan—the sphere of influence of the Russian Empire. The fall of the empire opened northern Iran for external actors, including the United States and Great Britain.

London based its demands on its purchase of shares of a Georgian nobleman, Khoshtariya (1919), who had a shah's *farmān* for oil exploitation in the north of Iran. At the same time, Tehran tried to use policy of attracting "a third power" to weaken British and Russian influence. As a result, Standard Oil was given the right to exploit oil in the five northern provinces for fifty years (November 1921).

At first, Soviet diplomats vehemently challenged Tehran's decision, referring to article XII of the treaty of 1921. But facing Tehran's determination, which pointed out the illegitimacy of Khoshtariya's concession (not approved by the Majles), and Iranian public opinion, Moscow decided to change its approach to the issue. That resulted in a decision to accept a concession to exploit the northern oil for any "neutral" foreign company. Standard Oil entered into agreement with the British, and the action discarded the possibility of any agreement with that company for Moscow.

The geographical factor and the underdevelopment of the Iranian transport infrastructure favored Moscow, allowing transportation of oil from the north of Iran through either the Soviet territory or the territories controlled by the British. Eventually, the Bolsheviks established contacts with the Sinclair company, which also decided to take part in the Iranian oil business and was not against cooperation with Moscow. As early as January 1922 the company signed an agreement with the Russians on the exploitation of oil in the north of Sakhalin. In July 1922, in Moscow, the head of the company, H. Sinclair, began negotiations concerning the establishment of a joint company for exploiting and selling Soviet oil.[31] Representatives of the company also discussed with the Soviet side the possibility of the transportation of oil from future north Iranian oil fields.[32] As a result, Soviet diplomats in Iran supported Sinclair by conducting corresponding negotiations with Iranian political figures.[33] Eventually, the treaty between the company and the Iranian government was signed in December 1923.

It should be noted that Moscow regarded its cooperation with Sinclair in the context of possible normalization of Soviet-American relationships. For that purpose, the Politburo requested G. L. Piatakov (the head of the Main Concession Committee) to inform Sinclair that a treaty on Soviet oil could be concluded only after establishment of "more normal" Soviet-American relationships.[34] Moscow demonstrated sufficient flexibility and readiness to allow large foreign capital to approach its southern borders in exchange for the prospect of improving the international situation of the USSR. At the same time, supporting Sinclair, Moscow left its hands free and officially continued to adhere to the position of not recognizing the right of Tehran to transfer former Russian concessions to foreigners.[35] Therefore, when the Bolsheviks learned about the agreement between Sinclair, whose positions were undermined by the Teapot Dome Scandal, and Standard Oil, they applied article XIII of the treaty.

Conducting negotiations with potential foreign partners, Moscow also decided to participate in the oil business in northern Iran. Through Khoshtariya's mediation, the Soviet diplomats obtained *farmāns* for mining operations in Semnan and Damghan in 1924.[36] After exploratory drilling, the joint-stock company Kevir-Khurian Limited was established (1926). The government of Iran and representatives of the Iranian ruling elite received part of the company's shares.

At the same time, the course on accelerated industrialization adopted in the USSR required a reduction in all secondary expenditures. In April 1926 the Politburo decided to keep down the Soviet expenses on the concession and later spoke in favor of attracting foreign capital.[37] Attempts to attract foreign partners were unsuccessful, and high costs, legal ambiguities around the territory, infrastructure, and terms of Soviet-Iranian participation in the company hindered its activities.[38] In such circumstances the continued existence of the company (until 1951) can be explained largely by political reasons.

Ideological attitudes played a secondary role in the Soviet concession policy giving way to the need to ensure strategic security of the Soviet state. The Bolsheviks not only tried to prevent the penetration of a "hostile" power to the north of Iran, but also sought to use Soviet transit potential to improve the international situation of the USSR. Similarly, Moscow used its trade opportunities in northern Iran both to ensure its security and to strengthen cooperation with German business (Soviet-German societies Rustranzit and Rusgertorg).

The Soviet Trade Policy toward Iran

By the beginning of the twentieth century, tsarist Russia had become Iran's main trading partner, using geographical factors and the country's underdeveloped transport infrastructure. Trade with Iran was promoted more by the efforts of the tsarist administration than by Russian businessmen themselves, especially since the weak Russian industry did not sufficiently saturate the domestic Russian market.[39] Using trade as a political tool was a characteristic feature of international relations in the period,[40] and the Bolsheviks, taking power in Russia, in many respects began to follow the established patterns.

The establishment of Soviet-Iranian diplomatic relations, as well as the adoption of the New Economic Policy in Soviet Russia (1921), paved the way for mutual trade development. However, even before those, the Bolsheviks began to perceive trade as an important tool of Soviet foreign policy. Thus, in December 1920, A. M. Lezhava, deputy commissar for foreign trade, stated that the political aim of the Soviet trade policy in the East was to prevent the establishment of foreign (i.e., Western) economic dominance there.⁴¹ But Soviet-Iranian trade relations soon ran into contradictions, caused primarily by the Soviet monopoly of foreign trade and Moscow's unwillingness to give Iran the right of free import transit through Soviet territory.

The question of a monopoly on foreign trade with the East, which provoked the merchants' protests there, revealed a contradiction in the positions of the Soviet diplomats and traders. Chicherin personally perceived the trade mainly as a tool for supporting the Eastern merchant class, bourgeoisie, seeing it as a potential rival to Western imperialism.⁴² As early as 1920, Soviet diplomacy began to call for the active use of Iranian merchants for the purposes of restoring the Soviet-Iranian trade (while the People's Commissariat for Trade and Industry considered the idea futile).⁴³ The top Soviet leadership initially appeared to be not ready to accept the position of diplomats. Thus, in September 1922, the Soviet diplomats' proposal to exclude the north of Iran from the scope of the monopoly was rejected by the Politburo.⁴⁴

However, the problem soon went beyond the trade relations themselves and harmed the Soviet interests in different Eastern countries. As a result, Moscow was forced to reconsider its position on Eastern trade. Already in 1922, a number of privileges for Asian merchants were introduced for the period of Baku's and Nizhny Novgorod's fairs. In November 1922 the Soviet diplomats put forward a declaration concerning Moscow's readiness to provide Iranian merchants with the right to export and import some goods, bypassing the Soviet monopoly on foreign trade.⁴⁵ In March 1923, the declaration was enacted by a directive of the Commissariat for Foreign Trade.

Another tool for attracting Iranian merchants (and their capital) was to be mixed-capital enterprises, a number of which were created by the Soviet initiative in 1923-24 (Rupeto, Persazneft, Persshelk, Sharq, Perskhlopok, Rusperssakhar, Bazzāz-e Irān va Rūs). The enterprises soon became important economic actors, and in the years 1924-25 about half of all bilateral trade went through them.⁴⁶

On the issue of import transit to Iran, Moscow also decided to modify its previous position. It should be noted that tsarist Russia used the closure of the transit of European goods through the Transcaucasus to strengthen Russian positions in the north Iranian market.⁴⁷ The Bolsheviks also did not grant Iran the right of import transit under the treaty of 1921 (while granting the right to neighboring Afghanistan). Later, however, they provided Tehran a limited import transit across Soviet territory. That was a well-thought-out step, especially since the

Soviet industry did not allow for the required range and quantity of goods to be supplied to the Iranian market.

Moreover, the Bolsheviks decided to use the opportunities of transit trade to fight the British domination of the northern Iranian market (which it received after the Russian Civil War), as well as to strengthen ties with German business. Thus, in April 1922 a cooperation agreement was signed with a Hamburg-based company, Robert Wenkhaus and Co., and the following spring a Russo-German trade and transit society was organized. To compensate for the weakness of Soviet industry, the Bolsheviks also used the resale of European goods to Iran or, as in the case of sugar, the purchase of foreign goods for the Soviet market in order to release a similar Soviet product for export. Sugar was one of the most liquid and profitable items of the Soviet export to Iran, but its production in the USSR was not sufficient for export. For that reason, the newly established mixed-capital enterprise Rusperssakhar was allowed to buy sugar abroad. Then, the imported sugar was to be sold in the USSR by Sakharotrest (the Sugar Trust of the USSR), which in exchange supplied Rusperssakhar with a Soviet sugar for export purposes.[48]

The combination of different approaches resulted in the increase of the Soviet-Iranian trade volume. But the methods of the Soviet economic bodies, companies, and mixed-capital enterprises elicited harsh criticism by Iranian merchants and officials. On the one hand, some Soviet economic actors used weak competition for some goods in the north Iranian market and set inflated prices for them. For example, the Oil Syndicate of the USSR put the price on kerosene for Turkey at around fifty kopeks per pood, and for Iran at one ruble seventy-five kopeks; the price on gasoline for Turkey was two rubles forty kopeks per pood, for Great Britain two rubles, and for Iran nine rubles seventy kopeks in the years 1922–23.[49] The introduction of a self-financing system for the Soviet enterprises and organizations influenced the prioritization of their own economic needs.

On the other hand, some of the Soviet-Iranian mixed-capital enterprises, bypassing the monopoly on foreign trade, became monopolies themselves (oil products, sugar, textiles). Moreover, the lion's share of the authorized capital stock of the enterprises (the Iranian portion) was concentrated in the hands of a small group of Iranian merchants. For example, Hāji Moʿin al Tojjār Būshehri, a prominent Tehran merchant, held half of Iranian merchants' stocks of Sharq and took part in other mixed-capital enterprises.[50]

One of the reasons for this situation was the aim of fighting British trade predominance in Iran, which in the situation of high prices of Soviet goods was achieved with the method of "leveling prices." According to this method, prices for some goods were reduced for facilitating their selling in the interior of Iran. The price reduction was compensated by the artificial increase of prices for the same goods in the areas closer to the Soviet borders. "Leveling prices" pushed the Soviet trade and economic bodies to cooperate with large merchants, with whom it was easier to agree on selling major consignments of the Soviet goods in exchange for their distribution in certain areas of Iran.

As a result, in the years 1924–25, in Moscow a dispute broke out over the foreign trade's methods between the People's Commissariat for Foreign Trade and the People's Commissariat for Foreign Affairs, where Chicherin generally took the upper hand: the mixed-capital enterprises and the Soviet economic bodies were obliged to work with a "wide range of middle and small merchants," some enterprises (for example, Ruspersakhar) were liquidated, and Iranian merchants were given the right to buy and export the Soviet goods (with some exceptions) freely.[51] Meanwhile the changes in the Soviet trade policy, which happened in 1926, left behind the discussion between the Soviet diplomats and traders.

Introduction of elements of free trade with Eastern countries contributed to an increase in the negative foreign trade balance of the USSR. And Moscow, adopting a strategy of forced industrialization, initiated review of its Eastern trade policy. As early as August 1926, the Politburo adopted as a temporary directive "a draft regulation on the trade policy with the countries of the East." The regulation, while pointing out the necessity of the promotion of the Eastern countries' economic development, clearly stipulated that the latter should be carried out in compliance with the commercial and monetary interests of the USSR. It was emphasized that the Soviet trade in the East should be based on a principle of balanced trade with a prospect of obtaining an active balance.[52]

The principle of balanced trade was reflected in the Soviet-Iranian commercial agreement of 1927 and dealt a heavy blow to the interests of Iranian merchants and government. A sharp increase of the Soviet share in Iranian import became an anticipated feature of its implementation. The principle indicated the changing purpose of Soviet trade policy in the East: the needs of accelerated economic development of the USSR, and not support of certain social groups or the fight against imperialism there, were taking precedence.

The Soviet Policy toward Antigovernmental and Separatist Movements in Iran

The ethnic, cultural, and geographic diversity of Iran, as well as the coexistence of different economic and social orders, made problematic the central authorities' efforts to keep control over the country. The problem became acute during periods of weakening central authority, as it was in the first two decades of the twentieth century. At the same time, as part of the modernization process, Iran was undergoing a paradigm shift in its governance aimed at unifying the country.[53]

The Bolsheviks, who at the turn of 1919-20 relied on supporting antigovernment movements in Iran, soon changed their policy in favor of the central government in the country. In line with the policy, Soviet diplomacy, in conjunction with the Comintern, aimed at strengthening the nationalist bourgeois movement in Iran. At the level of ideology, the new policy was supported by attitudes according to which the semi-colonial and underdeveloped country, also being in a state of feudal fragmentation, needed centralization for economic progress and independence. Moreover, the destruction of the republic in Gilan, removing the obstacle to the development of Soviet-Iranian relations, simultaneously deprived the Bolsheviks of an important lever of influence on the domestic political situation in Iran. As a result, in 1922-24 the Bolsheviks tried to create and strengthen the so-called National Bloc, which was to unite representatives of various political parties, groups, and social strata, including the bourgeoisie and landlords, and to establish a strong national government in Iran. And, after the fiasco of the enterprise, they turned to support Reżā Khan.[54]

However, there was no unity in the ranks of the Bolshevik leadership regarding Tehran's centralizing policy, especially concerning the situation of some ethnic minorities in Iran. The development and maintenance of a common position was complicated by several circumstances:

1. The centralization was accompanied by violence and abuse by the military and civil administration.
2. Some ethnic minorities were "divided" ones (living within the limits of more than one state).
3. The uprisings in the territories inhabited by some ethnic minorities occurred under autonomist and separatist slogans (Azeris [1920], Kurds [1918-22, 1926], Turkmen [1924-25]).
4. Some external players tried to use the uprisings for their own purposes.

And here, not only ideology and Moscow's strategic concerns, but also the particular interests and nationalist sentiments of the leadership of the Soviet Azerbaijan and Turkmenistan intertwined in the issue.

In the beginning of the twentieth century, Baku became one of the most important centers of revolutionary work in Iran. In 1920, the city became the seat of the Council of Propaganda and Action of the Peoples of the East, and Moscow's support for the republic in Gilan was carried out under the cover of Soviet Azerbaijan. It is not surprising that Baku tried to perform an independent role in Iran, actually opposing Moscow's decision to withdraw troops from Gilan (1921). Moreover, as Mustafa-Zade pointed out, the actions of the Baku leaders revealed their pan-Azerbaijani sentiments and hopes for the unification of Iranian and Soviet Azerbaijan.[55] There was information about the supply of weapons and money to individual leaders and tribes in Iranian Azerbaijan in the early 1920s, as well as about a committee in Baku whose goal was to unite Soviet and Iranian Azerbaijan.[56] But such incidents could only be of a limited nature and were not able to reverse the new line of Moscow's policy toward Iran.

The leadership of the newly created Soviet Turkmenistan also tried to take an independent position in relation to the Turkmen revolt in Iran (1924–25). In the autumn of 1924, Soviet and Turkmen party leaders, including the future head of the Turkmen SSR, K. S. Atabaev, suggested that the Central Committee of the Russian Communist Party (Bolsheviks) agree to the creation of a Young Turk Party in Iran. It was also proposed to achieve the granting of self-government by Tehran to Iranian Turkmens living in the area of Gorgan, or to change the Soviet-Iranian border there.[57] Faced with the dissent of Moscow, the leaders of Soviet Turkmenistan and even individual representatives of the Soviet authorities on the ground tried to help the rebels by themselves.[58] However, Moscow took a hard line, issuing respective directives and taking measures to strengthen the border. Moreover, support was provided to the Iranian government by the transportation of government troops and ammunition, and by the backing of the blockade of the rebels.[59]

The position of Moscow, in addition to the above-mentioned considerations, was also influenced by the conviction that antigovernment and separatist movements in Iran were supported by the British. It was considered that London inevitably, in order to maintain its influence, had to fight the centralizing activities of "bourgeois nationalists" in the East. Moreover, Moscow feared that potential territorial changes

Table 1. The Soviet press's coverage of the Kurdish uprisings and the prospects of a possible independent Kurdish state, 1921–30 (Pravda, Izvestiia)

YEAR	1921	1922	1923	1924	1925	1926	1927	1930
Number of publications	2	2	4	4	7	8	3	5
Positive coverage				1				
Neutral coverage	2	1	2		1	2		1
Negative coverage		1	2	3	6	6	3	4
By country								
Positive				Iraq				
Neutral	Turkey	Iran	Iran, Turkey		Iraq	Iran, Turkey		
Negative		Iraq	Iran, Iraq	Turkey, Iran, Iraq	Turkey, Iran	Turkey, Iran, Iraq	Iran, Iraq	Turkey

near the Soviet borders could pose a threat to the security of the USSR. Thus, the Eastern Secretariat of the Executive Committee of the Comintern, analyzing the Kurdish uprisings in 1930 in Turkey (in which some of the Iranian Kurds were also involved), recognized the desire of the "Kurdish nation" for independence. But, at the same time, the Comintern officials were concerned about the possible use of a Kurdish state by the British as a "counterrevolutionary springboard" near the Soviet borders.[60] Such concerns can be clearly seen in the coverage of the Kurdish uprisings and the prospects of a possible Kurdish state by the central Soviet press.[61]

Doubts about the expediency of supporting the Kurdish uprisings were shared on the ground. Thus, Shumiatskii thought that a Kurdish state could exist only under the protectorate of the Turks or the British.[62] A Comintern official under the alias "Mark" raised doubts about the political feasibility of supporting the Kurds, because it could bring the USSR into conflict with Iran, Turkey, and Great Britain.[63] As a result, the appeals of representatives of the rebellious Kurds of Turkey, Iraq, and Iran (1922, 1923, 1926) for help to Soviet diplomats were unsuccessful.[64] But while Moscow was wary of the Kurdish uprisings in neighboring countries, in Syria in 1926 the French Communist Party was directed to support the uprising of the Druze nomads on the basis of the right to self-determination.[65] The question of supporting antigovernment and separatist movements for Moscow remained primarily a question of political expediency.

The following "left turn" of the Comintern's strategy in 1927–29 influenced the assessment of the Reżā Shah regime. The Iranian communists were directed to overthrow the monarchy, establish a federal people's republic, and work among the toiling masses of "oppressed peoples" in Iran (the Arabs, the Kurds, the Turkmen, and others).[66] The changes were brought about for reasons of foreign policy (the war between the Kuomintang and the Chinese Communists, the severance of Soviet-British diplomatic relations) and the struggle inside the Bolshevik Party. The Bolsheviks also began to fear the possibility of close cooperation between Tehran and London. At the same time, the shah's position did not seem stable against the backdrop of the uprisings in Iran.

However, as in the years of the "Gilan revolution," Moscow took a twofold position. On the one hand, the Comintern instructed the Iranian communists to overthrow the Reżā Shah regime, but on the other, Moscow continued to develop diplomatic and economic relations with Iran. The Bolsheviks could not afford open actions that could lead to the rupture of diplomatic relations with Tehran. Thus, the Bolshevik leadership did not support Ehsān-Allah Khan Dustdār's repeated proposals (winter–summer of 1927) to send him and his associates to Iran to organize a revolution there.[67]

Therefore, in practice, the new guidelines were not able to change anything. The Iranian Communist Party remained a tiny, underground, urban organization and was unable to establish control over the uprisings that took place in the country. The shah's regime proved more stable and soon managed to establish control over the situation in Iran. Moreover, the security of the southern borders, a strategy of forced industrialization, and the building of socialism in one country demanded from Moscow the policy of status quo.

Early Soviet foreign policy demonstrates an example of the change in the nature of the foreign policy of initially "revolutionary" states and their "socialization" into the system of international relations. The necessity of state building and the survival of the Soviet state required the Bolsheviks to depart, at least in practice, from their original ideologized or idealistic declarations and appeals to the working masses (unless it was assumed that they were exclusively propagandistic in nature).

Similarly, there was a rejection of attempts to revolutionize Iran in favor of building bilateral relations and concluding treaties aimed, inter alia, at ensuring the security of the Soviet southern borders and securing the "neutral" status of the country.

The public rejection of the tsarist policy toward Iran in practice led to the use of certain established means and methods, including those previously condemned, to achieve the goals set. In particular, that can be seen in the use of power politics, trade, transit policy, concessions, or former concession rights to consolidate Soviet influence and prevent the penetration of "hostile" capital into the north of Iran.

The significance of the Caspian region for Moscow, especially the Baku oil fields, had a great influence on the line of Soviet policy toward Iran. The need to ensure security in the region, in particular, can be seen in Moscow's policy toward the former tsarist concessions in Iran, especially the northern oil concession, the fishing concession, and the port of Anzali. At the same time, Moscow was ready to allow limited access to the region by external players, as it did, for example, with regard to German and American businesses, in order to compensate for its own economic weakness, enfeeble British influence, and improve the international position of the USSR.

Driven by strategic interests, Soviet Russia, like its predecessor, was drawn into a new variation of the Great Game in the region. Iran, after the initial Soviet revolutionary experiments of 1920–21, de facto resumed its role as a kind of "buffer" between the two powers. Both the Bolsheviks and British diplomacy supported a strong central government there and helped Rezā Khan come to power. Moscow refused to support any movements in the region that spoke with separatist slogans, thereby demonstrating its reluctance to radical territorial changes. The situation changed in the mid-1940s, when Moscow, under the influence of the successful outcome of the Second World War and its disagreements with the Iranian government, in particular over the granting of an oil concession by Tehran to the Soviet Union, promoted the creation of the Kurdish and Azerbaijani autonomous entities in the zone of Soviet occupation in northwestern Iran.

As part of trade policy, Soviet diplomats tried to support the Iranian merchants, the "bazaar," considering them as an ally in the fight against Western imperialism, primarily British. However, attempts to combine the interests of the Iranian commercial bourgeoisie and Soviet trade and industry were not very successful, and in 1926–27, Moscow, by switching to the net balance principle, demonstrated the priority of its own economic goals.

The process of forming the Soviet state, the party apparatus, and factionalism in the ranks of the Bolsheviks also affected the course of early Soviet policy toward Iran, which demonstrates the clash of interests of various groups within the party and Soviet apparatus, between various government bodies, the union center, and national suburbs, which manifested itself during the Gilan revolution and, later, in particular, in Soviet-Iranian trade and Soviet policy toward the uprisings of certain ethnic minorities in Iran.

Ideology certainly played a role in early Soviet policy toward Iran. At the ideological level, the policy was supported by the attitudes according to which the underdeveloped, semi-independent country needed centralization, economic development, and the passage of a bourgeois stage of development. At the same time, the analysis of the Soviet concession and trade policy, as well as the positions of the Bolshevik leadership during the Gilan revolution and the subsequent course in relation to the Kurdish question demonstrate the priority of pragmatic attitudes and political expediency. The left turn in the Comintern's strategy that followed in 1927–29 also did not lead to any dramatic upheavals in Soviet-Iranian relations. State interests gradually obscured the revolutionary chimeras, and ideology gave way to the pragmatic interests of the emerging Soviet state.

Notes

1. See Semën L'vovich Agaev, *Iran v period politicheskogo krizisa, 1920–1925 gg.: Voprosy vneshneĭ politiki* (Moscow: Nauka, 1970), 41–42, 61–62, 135; Aleksandr Ivanovich Demin and Vladimir Vladimirovich Trubetskoĭ, "Vnutrennai͡a i vneshnai͡a politika monarkhii Pekhlevi v 1925–1928 gg.," in *Iran: Ocherki noveĭsheĭ istorii*, ed. Artëm Zavenovich Arabadzhi͡an (Moscow: Nauka, 1976), 37–39; Mikhail Sergeevich Ivanov, *Noveĭshai͡a istorii͡a Irana* (Moscow: Mysl', 1965), 27–28, 42–43.

2. See Nāṣer 'Aẓimi Dowbakhshari, *Revāyat-e now az jonbesh va enqelāb-e Jangal* (Tehran: Zharf, 1394/2015), 96–97, 121; Nasrollah Saifpour Fatemi, *Diplomatic History of Persia, 1917–1923: Anglo-Russian Power-Politics in Iran* (New York: Moore, 1952), 150–57, 191–97; Sergeĭ Vi͡acheslavovich Moshkin, *Revoli͡utsii͡a izvne: Istoriko-politologicheskie ocherki* (Ekaterinburg: Uro RAN, 1997), 24–46, 94–112; Moiseĭ Aronovich Persits, *Zastenchivai͡a interventsii͡a: O Sovetskom vtorzhenii v Iran, 1920–21 gg.* (Moscow: Airo-XX, 1996), 10–16.

3. See Zaven Artëmovich Arabadzhi͡an, *Iran: Protivostoi͡anie imperii͡am (1918–1941)* (Moscow: IV RAN, 1996), 51–71, 113–26; Mikhail I. Volodarsky, *Sovety i*

ikh iuzhnye sosedi Iran i Afganistan (1917–33 gg.) (London: Overseas Publications Interchange, 1985), 34–105; Nāser Jāhān Ārā, *Tārikh-e ravābeṭ-e tejāri-ye Irān va Showravi az enqelab-e oktobr tā soquṭ-e Reżā shāh* (Amol: Vāreshvā, 1390/2011), 44–52, 115–17; Iraj Zoghi, *Tārikh-e Ravābeṭ-e Siyāsi-ye 'Irān va Qodrathā-ye Bozorg, 1900–1925* (Tehran: Pazhang, 1368/1989), 366, 376–79, 384–85.

4. See Kenneth Waltz, *Theory of International Politics* (Reading, MA: Addison-Wesley, 1979), 127–28.

5. See Harish Kapur, *Soviet Russia and Asia 1917–1927: A Study of Soviet Policy towards Turkey, Iran and Afghanistan* (Geneva: Geneva Graduate Institute of International Studies, 1966), 14–15; Edward Carr, *The Russian Revolution: From Lenin to Stalin, 1917–1929* (New York: Free Press, 1979), 42–47.

6. See Persits, *Zastenchivaia interventsiia*, 10–16; Moshkin, *Revoliutsiia izvne*, 96–105; Fatemi, *Diplomatic History of Persia*, 155–57, 191–96, 255; Dowbakhshari, *Revāyat-e now az jonbesh va enqelāb-e Jangal*, 96–97.

7. See Vladimir Leonidovich Genis, *Krasnaia Persiia: Bol'sheviki v Giliane, 1920–21: Dokumental'naia khronika* (Moscow: MNPI, 2000), 253–61, 324–25; Vladimir Leonidovich Genis, "Krasnyĭ shantazh," *Rodina*, no. 5 (2001): 110–11.

8. See Moḥammad-'Ali Manshur-Gorgāni, *Siyāsat-e dōwlat-e Showravi dar Irān az 1296 tā 1306*, vol. 1 (Tehran: Maẓāheri, 1326/1947), 146; Shāpur Ravāsāni, *Nehżat-e Jangal: Zamine-hā-ye ejtemā'i* (Tehran: Daftar-e pazhuhesh-hā-ye farhangi, 1381/2002), 98–100.

9. Georgii Chicherin to Sergo Ordzhonikidze, Letter, November 29, 1921, RGASPI, F. 85, o. S/Persia, d. 38, pp. 15–15b.

10. See Moḥammad-'Ali Maḥmud, *Pazhuhesh dar tārikh-e diplomāsi-ye Irān* (Tehran: Mitrā, 1361/1982), 324; Ivanov, *Noveĭshaia istoriia Irana*, 42–44; Salekh Mamedogly Aliev, *Istoriia Irana: XX vek* (Moscow: Kraft+IV RAN, 2004), 130–31; Mokhammad Khasan Makhdiĭan, *Istoriia mezhdunarodnykh otnosheniĭ Irana i Rossii (XIX–nachalo XXI veka)* (Moscow: IV RAN, 2014), 52–53; 'Abdol-Reżā Hushang Mahdavi, *Siyāsat-e khāreji-ye Irān dar dōwrān-e Pahlavi* (Tehran: Nashr-e Alborz, 1374/1995), 11.

11. Georgii Chicherin to the Politburo, Note (copy), RGASPI, F. 159, o. 2, d. 51, p. 127.

12. A. Mnatsakinov, Memorandum of the chief accountant of "Persryba," RGAE, F. 9262, o. 1, d. 50, pp. 1–3.

13. Draft treaty (copy) on leasing of the Caspian shore, Arkhiv Vneshneĭ Politiki Rossiĭskoĭ Federatsii (Archive of Foreign Policy of the Russian Federation, hereafter AVPRF), F. 094, o. 5, file folder (hereafter f.f.) 105, d. 26, pp. 18–19; Nikolaĭ P. Briukhanov to the Small Council of People's Commissars, Note (copy), March 21, 1921, AVPRF, F. 094, o. 5, f.f. 105, d. 26, p. 16.

14. "The main points of the Russian-Persian relationships during the period from December 2/15, 1917 (Armistice in Brest-Litovsk) to December 1, 1921," Reference data (copy), AVPRF, F. 04, o. 18, f.f. 109, d. 50643, p. 16.

15. Theodore Rothstein to Georgii Chicherin, Telegram (copy), December 1, 1921, RGASPI, F. 5, o. 1, d. 2198, p. 96; Theodore Rothstein to Georgii Chicherin, Telegram (copy), December 4, 1921, RGASPI, F. 5, o. 1, d. 2198, p. 101.

16. Minutes of the Fisheries Commission, Shahrivar 16, 1302, Edāreh-ye Asnād va Tārikh-e Diplomāsi Vezārat-e Omur-e Khārejeh (Department of Documents and History of Diplomacy of the Ministry of Foreign Affairs, Iran, hereafter EATD), SH1302, c. 56, d. 4, p. 111.1.

17. Boris Shumiatskii, Report (copy) on concession policy in Persia, August 31, 1924, AVPRF, F. 04, f.f. 118, d. 50769, pp. 71-72; Boris Shumiatskii to the Ministry of Foreign Affairs of Iran, Note, February 17, 1924, EATD, SH1302, c. 56, d. 4, p. 155; Minutes of the Fisheries Commission, Shahrivar 16, 1302, EATD, SH1302, c. 56, d. 4, p. 111.1.

18. Boris Shumiatskii, "The Soviet-Persian affairs for May 1924," Reference data (copy), AVPRF, F. 028, o. 12, f.f. 32, d. 2, pp. 181-83.

19. Georgii Chicherin to Gurevich, copy to Moiseĭ Frumkin, Note (copy), September 18, 1925, AVPRF, F. 028, o. 10, f.f. 31, d. 9, p. 197; Georgii Chicherin to Georgiĭ Pĭatakov, copy to Moiseĭ Frumkin, Note (copy), April 3, 1925, AVPRF, F. 028, o. 10, f.f. 31, d. 9, pp. 60-61; Vlas Megrelivshvili to the Consul General of Persia in Tiflis, Note (copy), April 7, 1926, EATD, SH1305, c. 58, d. 1, pp. 57-57.1.

20. Brĭukhanov to the Small Council of People's Commissars, Note (copy), March 21, 1921, AVPRF, F. 094, o. 5, f.f. 105, d. 26, p. 16b.

21. Georgii Chicherin to Boris Shumiatskii, Letter (copy), January 17, 1924, AVPRF, F. 04, o. 18, f.f. 151, d. 586, p. 52.

22. Mnatsakinov, Memorandum of the chief accountant of "Persryba", 4-11. A pood is a unit of measurement equivalent to about sixteen kilograms.

23. Georgii Chicherin to Boris Shumiatskii, January 17, 1924, 52.

24. Konstantin Iurenev to Georgii Chicherin, Dispatch (copy), October 16, 1926, AVPRF, F. 04, o. 18, f.f. 127, d. 227, p. 6.

25. Garegin Apresov, "Soviet-Persian affairs for October 1924," Report (copy), November 17, 1924, AVPRF, F. 04, f.f. 118, d. 5071, pp. 10-15.

26. Minutes of the Politburo meeting N 32, October 30, 1924, RGASPI, F. 17, o. 163, d. 459, p. 19; Georgii Chicherin to Garegin Apresov, copy to Boris Shumiatskii, Note (copy), November 6, 1924, AVPRF, F. 04, o. 18, f.f. 119, d. 50778 (141), p. 66.

27. Bachkovskiĭ, "The condition of the Anzali port," Report (copy), August 5, 1920, GARF, F. R-5402, o. 1, f. 503, p. 1.

28. Boris Shumiatskii, "Soviet-Persian affairs for September 1924," Report (copy), AVPRF, F. 04, f.f. 118, d. 50770, pp. 88-89b.

29. Georgii Chicherin to the Politburo, copies to the members of the Board of the People's Comissariat of Foreign Affairs, Mikhail Frunze, Grigoriĭ Sokol'nikov, Georgiĭ Pĭatakov, Moiseĭ Frumkin, Andreĭ Lezhava, Note (copy), January 12, 1925, AVPRF, F. 028, o. 10, f.f. 31, d. 9, p. 6; Minutes (copy) of the Politburo meeting N 45, January 15, 1925, RGASPI, F. 17, o. 3, d. 485, p. 2.

30. See "The note exchange between the government of the USSR and the government of Persia concerning the Pahlavi port," October 1, 1927, in I. M. Gorokhov et al., eds., *Documenty vneshneĭ politiki SSSR*, vol. 10 (Moscow: Gospolitizdat, 1965), 428-34.

31. The report on the conversation of Georgiĭ Pi͡atakov with Harry Sinclair and Albert Fall, July 14, 1922, in G. N. Sevost'i͡anov et al., eds., *Rossii͡a i SSHA: Ėkonomicheskie otnoshenii͡a 1917–1933, sbornik dokumentov* (Moscow: Nauka, 1997), 58–60.

32. Shumi͡atskii, Report (copy) on concession policy in Persia, August 31, 1924, 85–90.

33. Boris Shumi͡atskii to Josef Stalin, Letter, April 24, 1925, RGASPI, F. 558, o. 11, d. 828, p. 21.

34. Minutes of the Politburo meeting N 17, July 16, 1923, RGASPI, F. 17, o. 163, d. 348, pp. 5–5b.

35. Georgii Chicherin to Aleksandr Minkin, copy to Moiseĭ Frumkin, Feliks Dzerzhinskiĭ, Georgiĭ Pi͡atakov, Note (copy), April 25, 1925, AVPRF, F. 04, o. 18, f.f. 140, d. 438, p. 14.

36. Boris Shumi͡atskii to Georgii Chicherin, Letter (copy), September 11, 1924, AVPRF, F. 04, f.f. 118, d. 50770, pp. 22–23.

37. Minutes of the Politburo meeting N 21, April 22, 1926, RGASPI, F. 17, o. 163, d. 558, p. 29; Minutes of the Politburo meeting N 61, October 14, 1926, RGASPI, F. 17, o. 163, d. 598, pp. 9–10.

38. Alekseĭ Kocheshkov, "Severoiranskai͡a neft': Iz istorii diplomaticheskikh batalii͡," in "Russian Oil in the XXI Century," special issue, *Mezhdunarodnai͡a zhizn'* 14 (2010): 149–60; Alekseĭ Chernykh to the Ministry of Foreign Affairs of Iran, Note, March 31, 1937, EATD, Shamsi 1316, c. 15, d. 1, pp. 14–19.

39. See Lev Sobotsinskiĭ, *Persii͡a: Statistiko-ėkonomicheskiĭ ocherk* (St. Petersburg: "Ėlektropech" I͡a. Krovitskogo, 1913), 161–65.

40. See Edward Carr, *The Twenty Years' Crisis, 1919–1939: An Introduction to the Study of International Relations* (London: Macmillan, 1946), 124–32.

41. Minutes (copy) of the meeting of the Council of Foreign Trade, December 9, 1920, RGASPI, F. 85, o. S/Persia, d. 51, p. 8.

42. Georgii Chicherin to Boris Shumi͡atskii, Letter (copy), February 7, 1924, AVPRF, F. 04, o. 18, f.f. 151, d. 586, p. 53.

43. Aron Sheĭnman to the deputy commissar for foreign affairs, Dispatch, June 9, 1920, AVPRF, F. 94, o. 4, f.f. 2, d. 7, p. 12.

44. Minutes of the Politburo meeting N 28, September 28, 1922, RGASPI, F. 17, o. 163, d. 297, p. 26.

45. "The main forms of the Russian-Persian relationships from November 1922 to April 1923," Report (copy), AVPRF, F. 04, o. 18, f.f. 112, d. 50691, p. 30.

46. See M. Granat, "Organizatsii͡a torgovli SSSR s Vostokom," in *Torgovli͡a SSSR s Vostokom (sbornik stateĭ i materialov)*, ed. V. Ksandrova et al. (Moscow: AO "Promizdat," 1927), 16.

47. See Li͡udmila Kulagina, *Rossii͡a i Iran (XIX—nachalo XX veka)* (Moscow: Kli͡uch-S, 2010), 101, 114–16; Sobotsinskiĭ, *Persii͡a*, 158–60.

48. Varlaam A. Avanesov to the Supreme Soviet of the National Economy, copy to Lezhava A. M., Note (copy), RGAE, F. 8102, o. 1, d. 15, p. 18.

49. Georgii Chicherin to Boris Shumi͡atskii, Note (copy), December 27, 1923, AVPRF, F. 028, o. 10, f.f. 31, d. 1, pp. 115–16.

PRAGMATIC ELEMENTS OF EARLY SOVIET POLICY   347

50. Konstantin Iurenev to Georgii Chicherin, Report (copy), February 8, 1926, AVPRF, F. 04, o. 18, f.f. 149, d. 567, p. 14.

51. Minutes of the Politburo meeting N 46, August 12, 1926, RGASPI, F. 17, o. 163, d. 583, pp. 18–19.

52. Minutes of the Politburo meeting N 46, August 12, 1926, pp. 14–16.

53. See Ervand Abrahamian, "Communism and Communalism in Iran: The Tudah and the Firqah-i Dimukrat," *International Journal of Middle East Studies* 1, no. 4 (1970): 292–96; Stephanie Cronin, "Re-interpreting Modern Iran: Tribe and State in the Twentieth Century," *Iranian Studies* 42, no. 3 (2009): 359–64; Patricia Higgins, "Minority-State Relations in Contemporary Iran," *Iranian Studies* 17, no. 1 (1984): 42–47; Michael Zirinsky, "Imperial Power and Dictatorship: Britain and the Rise of Reza Shah, 1921–1926," *International Journal of Middle East Studies* 24, no. 4 (1992): 647–48.

54. See Iurii A. Demin, "Sovetskaiā diplomatiiā i eë rol' v sozdanii i deiatel'nosti natsional'nogo bloka v Irane (1922–1924)," *Vestnik Volgogradskogo gosudarstvennogo universiteta. Seriiā 4, Istoriiā. Regionovedenie. Mezhdunarodnye otnosheniiā* 22, no. 4. (2017): 67–72, https://doi.org/10.15688/jvolsu4.2017.4.7.

55. See Rakhman Mustafa-Zade, *Dve respubliki: Azerbaĭdzhano-rossiĭskie otnosheniiā v 1918–1922* (Moscow: MIK, 2006), 288.

56. "Tribes of North-Eastern Azerbaijan," Report (copy), November 22, 1921, AVPRF, F. 94, o. 7a, f.f. 106, d. 1, p. 340; Moshaver al-Mamalek to Chicherin, Note (copy), October 16, 1923, AVPRF, F. 94, o. 7, f.f. 6, d. 2, p. 196–196b; Dispatch of the Iranian Consulate in Yerevan to the Ministry of Foreign Affairs of Iran, Āzar 14, 1305, in Mahmud Ṭāherahmadi, ed., *Asnād-e ravābeṭ-e Irān va Showravi dar dowreh-ye Reżā Shāh (1304–1318)* (Tehran: Sāzemān-e Asnād-e Melli-ye Irān, 1374/1995), 12–13.

57. Georgii Chicherin to Boris Shumiatskii, Note (copy), October 30, 1924, AVPRF, F. 04, o. 18, f.f. 119, d. 50778 (141), p. 65.

58. Bulletin of the Plenipotentiary representation of the USSR in Persia, June–July 1925, RGASPI, F. 495, o. 90, d. 116, p. 85; Report (copy) on events in Yomudistan, October 20, 1925, RGVA, F. 110, o. 7, d. 19, p. 11; Tkachinskiĭ (Kerim Gasanov) to Fëdor Petrov (Raskol'nikov), Report (copy), April 14, 1925, RGASPI, F. 495, o. 90, d. 109, pp. 9–12.

59. Ivan German to Otto Karklin, Matveĭ Berman, Letter (copy), September 1, 1924, RGVA, F. 110, o. 7, d. 50, pp. 2–3; Minutes of the Politburo meeting N 21, September 4, 1924, RGASPI, F. 17, o. 163, d. 448, p. 16; Minutes of the Politburo meeting N 64, May 21, 1925, RGASPI, F. 17, o. 163, d. 491, pp. 22–22b; Konstantin Iurenev to Georgii Chicherin, Dispatch (copy), AVPRF, F. 04, o. 18, f.f. 127, d. 226, pp. 18–18b.

60. Resolution on Turkey of the Eastern Secretariat of the Executive Committee of the Comintern (ES ECC), January 1931, RGASPI, F. 495, o. 154, d. 417a, pp. 9–10.

61. See "Vosstanie Kurdov," *Izvestiiā*, April 3, 1921, 2; "K vosstaniiu Kurdov," *Izvestiiā*, November 29, 1921, 1; "Persiiā (Vosstanie Kurdov)," *Izvestiiā*, June 18, 1922, 3; Sherif Monatov, "Kurdistan," *Izvestiiā*, December 16, 1922, 2; A. Sadovskiĭ, "Novyĭ Anglo-bufer–'nezavisimyĭ Kurdistan'," *Izvestiiā*, January

13, 1923, 2; G. Astakhov, "Po Anatolii (Putevye zametki)," *Izvestiia*, February 3, 1923, 3; "Raznoglasiia sredi Kurdov," *Pravda*, February 17, 1923, 2; "Neudachnye proiski Anglichan v Persii (novaia intriga)," *Izvestiia*, April 3, 1923, 2; Mikhail Sharonov (G.V. Chicherin), "Novye ėtapy mirovykh antagonizmov," *Pravda*, September 5, 1924, 2; Irandust, "Opiat' Mosul," *Izvestiia*, September 23, 1924, 1; "Smysl Angliĭskogo ul'timatuma Turtsii," *Izvestiia*, October 17, 1924, 1; "Mosul'skaia neft' i Angliĭskie nervy," *Izvestiia*, October 19, 1924, 3; "Proiski Angliĭskikh imperialistov v Kurdistane," *Izvestiia*, January 1, 1925, 1; "Kontrrevoliutsionnoe vosstanie v Turtsii,", "Ugroza kontrrevolyucii v Turtsii," *Izvestiia*, February 27, 1925, 1; "Kontrrevoliutsionnoe vosstanie v Turtsii, *Izvestiia*, March 3, 1925, 1; "Mezhdunarodnoe obozrenie (Vosstanie Kurdov v Turtsii i ego mezhdunarodnoe znachenie)," *Izvestiia*, March 3, 1925, 2; "Kontrrevoliutsionnoe vosstanie v Turtsii," *Izvestiia*, March 5, 1925, 2; Iust K. "Reaktsionnoe vosstanie v Turtsii (Ot nashego Angorskogo korrespondenta)," *Izvestiia*, April 18, 1925, 2; "Eshche ob Anglichanakh v Khorosane," *Izvestiia*, September 12, 1925, 2; S. Iavorskiĭ, "Mezhdunarodnaia nedelia," *Pravda*, April 4, 1926, 6; Irandust, "Kontrrevoliutsionnyĭ zagovor v Turtsii," *Pravda*, June 23, 1926, 2; "Bor'ba v Persii (Vosstanie Kurdov)," *Pravda*, August 15, 1926, 2; "Vosstanie Kurdov v Persii (Vo glave Kurdov angliĭskie ofitsery)," *Pravda*, September 9, 1926, 2; "Vosstanie Kurdov podderzhivaetsia Angliei," *Pravda*, September 11, 1926, 2; "Stolknovenie mezhdu Kurdami i Turetskimi voĭskami," *Pravda*, October 2, 1926, 2; "Raznye izvestiia," *Pravda*, October 8, 1926, 2; Konstantinov R. "Britanskie 'interesy' v Persii (K raskrytiiu zagovora na Reza-shakha)," *Izvestiia*, October 8, 1926, 2; S. Iavorskiĭ, "1926 god (Obzor mezhdunarodnoĭ zhizni)," *Pravda*, January 1, 1927, 5-6; Irandust, "Persiia na pereput'e," *Pravda*, March 16, 1927, 2; "Angliia—'drug narodov Vostoka' (Gnusnye vypady 'Deĭli Telegraf'—Istochnik Persidsko-Turetskogo konflikta)," *Pravda*, October 5, 1927, 2; "Lourens pod maskoĭ Kurda," *Pravda*, July 22, 1930, 1; "Zakulisnye vdokhnoviteli Kurdskogo vosstaniia," *Izvestiia*, August 13, 1930, 1; G. Gastov, "Politicheskoe razdvoenie Kemalizma," *Izvestiia*, August 19, 1930, 2; "K napadeniiam na Turetskuiu granitsu," *Izvestiia*, August 25, 1930, 2; "Kurdskiĭ miatezh na puti k likvidatsii," *Izvestiia*, September 11, 1930, 1.

62. Boris Shumiatskii to Georgii Chicherin, Letter (copy), RGASPI, F, 495, o. 90, d. 89, p. 1.

63. Mark to Fëdor Petrov, Letter, December 15, 1926, RGASPI, F. 495, o. 90, d. 129, pp. 15-16.

64. Mikhail Slavutskiĭ to Georgii Chicherin, Letter (copy), September 7, 1926, AVPRF, F. 04, o. 18, f.f. 127, d. 226, pp. 174-75; Manvel Gasratian, *Kurdy Turtsii v noveĭshee vremia* (Erevan: Aĭastan, 1990), 51-52; Mikhail Lazarev, *Kurdistan i Kurdskiĭ vopros (1923–1945)* (Moscow: Vostochnaia literatura, 2005), 36, 40-41.

65. "The situation in the North African colonies and in Syria and the tasks of the French Communist Party," Resolution (copy) adopted at the meeting of the Presidium of the Executive Committee of the Comintern, March 31, 1926, RGASPI, F. 495, o. 2, d. 67, pp. 116-18, 120-21.

66. "Resolution on the Persian question," of the ES ECC, October 10, 1927, RGASPI, F. 495, o. 90, d. 141, pp. 71-79; "Theses on the international and domestic situation of Persia," adopted by the Second Congress of the Iranian Communist Party (1927), RGASPI, F. 495, o. 90, d. 150, pp. 24, 26; Manifesto of the Iranian Communist Party to the workers of Persia, RGASPI, F. 495, o. 90, d. 154, pp. 42, 51-52.

67. See Ehsān-Allah Khan to the Third Communist International, Note (copy), February 22, 1927, RGASPI, F. 495, o. 90, d. 143, pp. 12-12b; Note (copy) to the Third International, Eastern Department, February 24, 1927, RGASPI, F. 495, o. 90, d. 143, p. 15; Ehsān-Allah Khan to Fëdor Petrov, Note, March 30, 1927, RGASPI, F. 495, o. 90, d. 143, p. 16; Ehsān-Allah Khan to Fëdor Petrov, Note, April 11, 1927, RGASPI, F. 495, o. 90, d. 143, pp. 18-18b; Ehsān-Allah Khan to Nikolaï Bukharin, copies to Josef Stalin, Sergo Ordzhonikidze, Note, July 12, 1927, RGASPI, F. 495, o. 90, d. 143, pp. 27-28.

Chapter 17

Maritime Horizons
The Caspian Sea in Soviet-Iranian Relations, 1930s–1980s
Etienne Forestier-Peyrat

As Europe was engulfed in the initial shockwaves of the Second World War in fall 1939, a naval school opened its doors to a first cohort of students in Baku, the capital of Soviet Azerbaijan. The decision to set up the institute had been taken earlier in March by Admiral N. Kuznetsov as part of a countrywide effort to strengthen Soviet naval training.[1] The Caspian had occupied a strategic position in the first years of the Soviet regime, in the context of the civil war and confrontation with Great Britain. In April 1920, Trotsky cabled an order to "clear the White fleet off the Caspian Sea at any cost," leading to a temporary intervention in northern Iran under the pretext of chasing General Anton Denikin's forces.[2] But two decades of relative absence of the Caspian area from major strategic concerns had followed; until the early 1930s, the relative openness of the Soviet-Iranian border led to a renewed intensity of circulations, human and material, that marked a prolongation of the transboundary dynamics that had shaped the tsarist Russian-Iranian borderlands since the nineteenth century, while adding a distinctively political dimension.[3]

The end of the 1930s marked a decisive change in this regard, as the Great Terror struck the region in 1937–38, with a series of brutal deportations of border populations and foreigners. The "Iranian Operation" was particularly brutal, leading thousands of people to be immediately expelled by Soviet security forces to Iran or Central Asia. Caspian ships served as the main transport for these deportees, as British diplomat Fitzroy Maclean discovered during a brief and unauthorized stay in the Lenkoran region, in Soviet Talesh.[4] The deportation of "Iranians" from the Soviet Caucasus and other populations from Turkmenistan in the East took place in a context where Režā Shah's sympathies for Nazi Germany were a source of growing worries in the USSR. Although material cooperation between Iran and the Nazis remained limited, this perceived proximity would lead, after the Nazi invasion of June 1941, to a joint British-Soviet occupation of Iran, despite the proclaimed neutrality of the country.[5]

The Caspian Sea was, however, not only metaphorically taken in the nets of man-made politics. It was also, as a body of water and ecosystem, more and more impacted by the effects of economic, agricultural, and industrial planning, stemming in particular from Stalin's developmental state, which simultaneously aimed at "taking possession of nature and society," as stated by Klaus Gestwa.[6] In the early 1930s, biologists and economists had warned about the potential impact of the great dams planned in the Volga area on the already diminishing level of the Caspian Sea and its fisheries. By blocking the upstream migrations of anadromous fishes, the dams indeed threatened what had been the most important domestic fisheries in tsarist Russia.[7] Scholarship on the Caspian sea from the 1930s to the 1980s should therefore not only look at the sea from a conventional international relations perspective, but try to understand how the very fabric of interstate relations in the region was reshaped by ideas of modernization and their impact, especially in a space where different conceptions of modernity encountered.[8] Economic and environmental concerns, in this closed maritime space, often outweighed seemingly strategic considerations in the 1950s-1970s.

Such scholarship can, indeed, contribute to this perspective by bringing a local viewpoint on what remains, as far as Soviet-Iranian relations are concerned, essentially perceived at a macrolevel. The Caspian region is one of the many border areas where the distinction between local politics and world politics was blurred during the Cold War years, as recent local histories and ethnographic researches demonstrate.[9] The particular nature of this blurring is, however, connected to the physical and environmental characteristics of the Caspian sea itself, trapped between the Caucasus and Central Asia. Some aspects of this impact were reconstructed, two decades ago, by Guive Mirfendereski's book, *A*

Diplomatic History of the Caspian Sea. In this book, Mirfendereski focused on the practical dimension of the Soviet-Iranian interaction in the Caspian with focuses on fisheries, borders, and military capacities.[10] It is indeed in the interplay of power politics and the effects of developmental programs on a closed sea that the original story of the Caspian sea in the second half of the twentieth century can be told.

Caspian Crossroads in the Second World War

Despite the signing of a new trade agreement in March 1940 between Iran and the USSR, the months that preceded the Nazi invasion of the Soviet Union were times of anxiety on both sides of the Caucasian border. The Caspian area, as the entire Caucasian and Central Asian borderlands, were explicitly put under heightened vigilance to prevent the crossing of spies or "saboteurs." Iran was increasingly perceived during the late 1930s as a German satellite, due to numerous trade agreements and the shah's well-known personal preference.[11] The temporary reversal of alliances brought about by the Molotov–Ribbentrop Pact did not put an end to these fears, but added a new threat from the south, as France and Great Britain drew plans to bomb the Caucasian oil industry in Batumi, Grozny, and Baku, the final of which was assigned to the Royal Air Force.[12] While never put into action due to French defeat in June 1940, the plans revealed the possibility of the Caspian Sea being taken again into direct military confrontation. After the launch of Operation Barbarossa, however, the main threat switched to the west and the Caspian Sea now became an evacuation route for industrial and oil equipment from the Caucasus to Central Asia, under the shells of the *Luftwaffe*.[13] Reconciling British and Soviet governments, the Nazi invasion indirectly resulted in a joint occupation of Iran on August 25, 1941.

Allied occupation of Iran brought about an intensive use of the country in the Soviet war effort. Over time, northern Iran and the Caspian region played three roles in this effort. First, Soviet troops immediately set out to confiscate German assets in the area as "trophies" shipped to the USSR.[14] While the Soviet invasion was mainly land-based, the Soviet fleet also occupied the port of Pahlavi (Anzali) and helped in the initial show of force.[15] Second, as Nazi forces moved ever further south- and eastward and Transcaucasia became de facto a "Soviet island," British and US shipments transited through Iran in what soon came to be known as the "Persian corridor." The corridor made use of the recently built Transiranian railway that ran from the Persian Gulf to Bandar-e Shah, on the eastern Caspian shore.[16] Although assessments vary, the then head of Iranian railways, Ḥosayn Nafisi, suggested more than five million tons transited through Iran until the end of the war.[17] This strategic importance of the Caspian ports accelerated measures to develop their infrastructures: investments were made in 1941 in Pahlavi and Nowshahr, and the Soviet government approved, on June 16, 1943, a new train of measures to modernize roads, railroads, and ports along the Caspian coast.[18]

Third, the Caspian region itself was used as an economic and agricultural hinterland. The exploitation of fisheries, a concession given to a Russian entrepreneur in the Qajar area and renegotiated in October 1927, was intensified during the war, and local fishermen were submitted to more and more restrictions in their daily activity, especially when Soviet military ships moored in Caspian ports.[19] Massive Soviet procurements of foodstuffs created tensions on the local market, a phenomenon accentuated by the reduction of Soviet exports of some staples, especially sugar. While pamphlets circulated anonymously and accused the Soviets of pillaging Iran, "rice riots" erupted in 1942 in the cities of Gilan and Mazandaran, leading the Red Army to establish tighter controls over trade and even announce grain shipments to Iran in spring 1943.[20] In some places, Iranian authorities tried to moderate the destruction of ecosystems resulting, for instance, from the mass felling of trees in Gilan and Gorgan.[21] While the presence of Soviet forces had initially been perceived as an opportunity for all discontents of Reżā Shah's reign, the strengthening grip Moscow exerted on the region raised concerns due to the recent experience of Bolshevik support for a Gilan Republic in 1920–21.[22]

The place of the Caspian region during the fateful years of 1945–46 has generally been overshadowed by the attention paid to the Azerbaijan and Kurdistan crisis.[23] While no separatist movement similar to the Azerbaijani Democratic Party (ADP) emerged in the Caspian region as such, similarities could be observed; the ADP made claims to parts of western Gilan, and the Caspian area was, above all, a major place of activism for the Tudeh Party, which established in some places parallel administrations under Soviet tutelage.[24] When Stalin approved in June 1945 the strengthening of Soviet economic and industrial interests in northern Iran, a military flotilla anchored in front of Anzali.[25] In order to consolidate the extent of Soviet prerogatives in the region, the Caspian fleet commander solicited in January 1946 a survey of existing treaties on navigation, fisheries, and borders between the USSR and Iran.[26]

A Sea of Confrontation

Soviet withdrawal and the collapse of Azerbaijan People's Government in December 1946 marked the height of tensions along the Soviet-Iranian border. Numerous border incidents were reported on both sides, especially after the United States and Iran signed on October 16, 1947, an agreement "relating to a military mission to Iran." Northern Iran and the Caspian area became natural places for US military advisers, and Soviet diplomacy repeatedly denounced the supposed militarization of the border area. Tensions culminated after an attempt was made on the shah's life on February 4, 1949, at the University of Tehran. While providing a pretext to ban the Tudeh Party, it also led to the closing of the Iranian consulate general in Baku and several Soviet consulates in northern Iran.[27]

While they can be perceived from the perspective of great-power confrontation, the early years of the Cold War also meant a break in the social and economic life of Caspian populations. During the Soviet occupation of northern Iran, many expellees of 1937–38 worked for Soviet authorities and hoped to regain their right to work in the Caucasus or Central Asia at the end of the war, to meet relatives left in the USSR, or to requalify for pensions. However, their hopes were largely dashed in the late 1940s, as testified by Soviet archives and private memoirs alike. People who tried to reenter Soviet borders were arrested and deported to the Gulag or, in the best cases, expelled to Iran.[28] Those who tried to return to Iran faced both Soviet repression and Iranian obvious reluctance to let this population in. For people coming from the Caspian region, an additional difficulty was presented by the sad state of the records office (*sabt-e ahvāl*), which did not allow for simple confirmation of their identity.[29]

The coming to power of Mossadegh and his attempts to nationalize oil production weakened the British position in Iran but did not produce a clear break in this general mood of antagonism. Moscow and the Tudeh Party were extremely cautious about steps that could play into the hands of Washington and would not necessarily increase Soviet influence in the country. As it related to the Caspian, a significant example of this was Mossadegh's policy of terminating Soviet concessions in the fisheries sector and turning them into a state monopoly in

January 1953, although the majority of the catches were still exported to the Soviet Union.³⁰ A leftover of the tsarist period, the fisheries had been renewed several times but had come under repeated criticism. In the late 1940s, Iranian authorities publicized several fact-finding missions that demonstrated the violation of labor legislation and operating rules in the fisheries.³¹ Obviously aimed at reducing Soviet influence over the local population, this pressure also represented a balancing act in the simultaneous fight against the British for Iranian oil.³²

Moments of appeasement and tensions—such as when Iran joined the Baghdad Pact in 1955—alternated in the 1950s, but the Caspian area itself was no longer at the center of diplomatic attention. The stage of open confrontation in the border area came to rest after the two countries signed a border agreement in May 1957. This was the final point of several years of border demarcation under the control, on the Iranian side, of general and senator-for-life Amān-Allāh Jahānbāni, a former comrade of Reżā Shah, trained in Russia as many aristocrats had been until the First World War.³³ The agreement laid the basis for a defusing of tensions across the region.

Détente and Rapprochement in a Closed Sea

The trends apace in the 1960s, especially economic globalization and interbloc cooperation, did not impact on the Caspian area, a closed sea, as strongly as they did on regions more open to international influences. Geographical constraints prevented it from becoming an international trade passage such as the Baltic and Black Seas, but navigation grew again as trade soared between Iran and the Soviet Union, as well as between Baku, Krasnovodsk, and Astrakhan, the three main Soviet ports. In 1971, following a specific Soviet-Iranian agreement a year earlier, bilateral sea trade reached 513,500 tons.³⁴ The export of Azerbaijani oil accounted for an important part of this freight, but the Caspian State Navigation Company (Kaspar) also developed connections to northern Europe and global markets through the Volga-Baltic canal.³⁵ While Azerbaijan represented a smaller share of oil production, the development of offshore gas exploitation in the early 1960s created huge expectations for the development of Baku.³⁶ Azerbaijani authorities were keen to support this growth and promote the international profile of their city. The city's Azizbekov Oil Institute was home to more than five hundred foreign students in the early 1970s, becoming an important training place for oil and gas workers.³⁷ Similarly,

Eastern European navies sent trainees to complete their education in Baku.[38]

The Caspian did not enjoy, as far as the Soviet Union was concerned, the numerous advantages that turned the Black Sea coasts into a socialist Riviera, an achievement Khrushchev could vaunt during a visit in a Bulgarian resort, in 1962.[39] The Soviet effort to develop seaside leisure infrastructures in the Caucasus definitely favored the Georgian Republic and its flagship resort areas in Ajara and Abkhazia.[40] By contrast, the attempts to create a similar tourism sector on the Absheron Peninsula, north of Baku, foundered on the lack of adequate infrastructure, as the environment of the steppe was less amenable than the green landscapes of the western Caucasus.[41] By contrast, the Caspian region was a renowned place for tourism on the Iranian shore, where the luxuriant forests and landscapes of Gilan and Mazandaran attracted the new Iranian bourgeoisie.

While the Caspian area had been home to royal summer palaces and hunting places since the Safavid dynasty, the 1950s brought the first stages of middle-class tourism to the region. Cities like Chalus, Nowshahr, Ramsar, and Namak Abrud were quickly transformed by the building of "high-rise apartments and hotels and gated tourist resorts." International architects took part in projects such as the Caspian Hyatt Hotel (1974) and foreign—especially US—influences were often translated, until the 1970s, with little concern for local traditions in architecture and for the environment.[42] Moḥammad Reżā Shah's support for tourism appeared as a combination of cultural modernization and economic targets that increased Iran's international visibility: In 1975, it was announced that the country aimed to attract one million foreign tourists and eight million domestic tourists by 1978, a considerable increase compared to the 360,000 foreign tourists who visited the country in 1974.[43]

The rapid development of cross-border activities created a growing milieu of political, administrative, and economic elites who played important roles in forms of regional rapprochement. Mikail Nazarov, head of the Trade and Finances Department of the Azerbaijani Central Committee in the 1970s, recalls how Azerbaijanis played key roles in promoting trade with Iran and placing Baku as the key Caspian hub. The state company for trade with the "East" (Vostokintorg) established a branch in Baku and multiplied contacts with traders in northern Iran.[44] The archives of the Soviet consulate in Rasht testify to similar efforts to bring closer Iranian elites and the USSR. In late summer 1970, a few weeks before the opening of a much-propagandized gas pipeline connecting Iran to the Soviet Union and, westward, European markets, the consulate suggested intensifying networking with top Iranian officials in Gilan.[45] The consul wanted to invite to Soviet Azerbaijan the governor general of Gilan, 'Ali Aşghar Ṭāheri, and the governor of Bandar Pahlavi.[46] Both of them had worked for the Interior Ministry and managed other provinces before coming to the Caspian region. Their attitude toward the Soviet Union was assessed as "loyal," but it was primarily their interest in the local development of Gilan that motivated their turn to the Soviet side.[47] In embracing a developmental agenda, Iranian elites in the Caspian region could resort once again to resources offered by their proximity to the Soviet Union.

Developmental States and Caspian Concerns

The development of cross-border trade did offer many opportunities for exchange, but it was, interestingly enough, also the unintended consequences of the developmental models on both sides of the borders that created incentives for cooperation. Soviet society and state structures were fully part, in the 1960s–1970s, of the global trend toward rising concern about the environmental impact of development.[48] The Caspian Sea itself had attracted even earlier attention due to the mystery of its falling sea level and loss of seventy-five thousand square kilometers. The Caspian's three-meter fall from 1929 to 1970 birthed several theories. Some attributed it to evaporation in the Turkmen Kara Bogaz lake, and a dam was built in 1980 to prevent Caspian waters pouring into the lake, without much success.[49] This specific concern combined with a more general awareness about the fragility of maritime ecosystems that could be found also in Eastern Europe in the Baltic and Black Seas.[50] As water pollution and coast erosion became prominent concerns, on September 23, 1968, the Soviet government adopted a decree, "On Measures to Prevent Pollution in the Caspian Sea," targeting in particular the practice of using exploding devices in the oil and gas industry and the disposal of contaminated water, which had reached five hundred thousand cubic meters a day by 1967, according to internal Soviet reports.[51]

Soviet measures against water pollution were directly connected to its impact on fisheries. This impact was amplified by the effect of gigantic dams on the Volga, a "must-have" of Cold War developmental ideology, East and West.[52] In 1971, Soviet fisheries accounted for

550,000 tons, against 6,300 for Iran. Centered around the Astrakhan region, Caspian fisheries represented 63.6 percent of all Russian fisheries in 1913, but only 19.3 percent in 1950 and 6.8 percent in 1970.[53] This was, essentially, the result of the growth of Soviet global fisheries, initiated in 1956 with a massive program of long-range shipbuilding, but a decline in actual figures was also noticeable.[54] As soon as 1962, measures were taken in the USSR to prevent the harvesting of sturgeons in open sea, as fear of a crisis in the caviar industry grew. A simultaneous concern appeared in Gilan, where fisheries, although more limited in volume, employed approximately ten thousand people, many of them temporary migrants coming from neighboring districts. In this sense, it hearkened back to the interwar period, when the fight against natural plagues such as locust invasions had been a cornerstone of Soviet cooperation with Tehran.[55]

On November 30, 1970, a major speech was made in the Iranian Senate by Jahanshah Saleh, a former minister of health and close friend of the shah, concerning pollution in the Caspian area.[56] Drawing international comparisons, Saleh suggested the Caspian could turn into a "dead sea" similar to Lake Erie, whose man-made eutrophication in the 1960s had led to catastrophic ecological effects and sparked a successful movement to reverse the trend.[57] This assessment was not isolated, since activists and officials like Eskandar Firuz simultaneously alerted public opinion and state authorities about the effects of chemical and industrial pollution.[58] But the arena was prestigious and the tone of the speech sinister enough to create a public debate closely monitored by Soviet diplomats.[59] This public debate had connecting points to some contested aspects of Soviet internal policies, as some Iranian columnists welcomed the idea of diverting Siberian rivers to maintain the falling level of the Caspian, a well-known play toy of some Soviet planners.[60]

The tone of the debate on Caspian pollution was, however, far from being an indictment of Soviet policies. Saleh actually noted in his November 1970 speech that joint action with the USSR was made easier by the context of détente. Taking up again and again the issue in the early 1970s, Saleh targeted the inaction of bureaucrats in the face of air and water pollution in the country. Quoting Soviet Academician Kasimov, Saleh approvingly noted the launch of Soviet actions to reduce pollution in the Volga Delta and Azerbaijan, and deployment of water purifying systems in the Volga, Kama, and Ural basins.[61] Indeed, the development of tourism, industry, and urban areas increased the ecological footprint of Iran in the region.[62] From 1946 to 1989, the wooded area in the Caspian region fell from 3.6 million to 1.9 million hectares.⁶³ Although attacking the administration, Saleh was not alone, as he often quoted the shah's support for environmental measures, as illustrated in the creation of the Organization for the Protection of Environment (Sāzemān-e Hefāzat-e Moḥiṭ-e Zist) in 1971. A trip to the Soviet Union in June 1972 by Iraj Vahidi, the minister of water and power, revealed the extent of similar issues across the Caspian sea in agriculture, energy, and environment, and cooperation translated into a series of agreements.⁶⁴ The importance of these local initiatives was demonstrated by the Iranian decision to host in the Caspian resort of Ramsar an international conference on the protection of wetlands, in January–February 1971, with direct echoes in the regional setting.⁶⁵

Revolution on the Sea in the 1980s

As recorded by Iran's first revolutionary ambassador, Mohammad Mokri, in his memoirs, the Islamic Revolution and its consequences significantly changed the context of Soviet-Iranian relations around the Caspian Sea in somehow contradictory directions. A professor in Kurdish studies and long-time exile in France, Mokri was fully part of the initial effort of the new regime to design a new foreign policy, under the motto "Neither East Nor West" (*Na Sharq, Na Gharb*).⁶⁶ During the first months of the revolutionary government, Mokri traveled several times to Baku and organized meetings with local Iranians, calling Muslims of the Soviet Union to solidarity. While the new government ostensibly broke with all vestiges of foreign domination, Mokri suggested a new legal settlement for the Caspian Sea in order to share equally its resources and ensure free navigation.⁶⁷ The annual Soviet-Iranian conference on Caspian navigation became the locus for Iranian claims. Simultaneously, though, tensions erupted around Iranian attempts to spread their influence among Muslims of the Soviet Union. Soviet authorities rejected requests to transfer an Iranian consulate from Leningrad to Central Asia. Iran retorted by closing the consulate in Leningrad in summer 1980 and demanded the reciprocal closure of the Soviet consulate in Rasht.⁶⁸ With less than two hundred Soviet citizens in Gilan, the Iranians argued, the consulate "was in a strategic location—near headquarters for the navy general staff, the Revolutionary Guards, and radio and television offices—and would surely be used for spying activities."⁶⁹ Tensions rose as Moscow refused to close the Rasht consulate. For Iran, this deterioration of relations on the Caspian littoral contributed to a regional isolation accelerated by war with Iraq after September 1980. Mokri himself advocated a place to intensify sea transit in order to compensate for the danger of land transit in Iranian Azerbaijan. This state of tensions lasted until the late 1980s, when the thaw in Iranian politics and the perestroika opened new opportunities for bilateral relations.

Notes

1. A. P. Kurochkin and V. T. Tatarenko, *Apsheronskiĭ meridian: Dokumental'naia povest'* (Baku: Azerbaĭdzhanskoe gosudarstvennoe izdatel'stvo, 1989), 5-8.

2. M. A. Persits, *Zastenchivaia interventsiia: O Sovetskom vtorzhenii v Iran i Bukharu v 1920-1921 gg.* (Moscow: Muraveĭ-gaĭd, 1999), 91; Vladimir L. Genis, "Les Bolcheviks au Guilan: La chute du gouvernement de Koutchek Khan (Juin-Juillet 1920)," *Cahiers du Monde russe* 40, no. 3 (1999): 459-96; Moḥammad 'Ali Kāzembiki, *Daryā-ye Khazar va qodrathā-ye bozorg: Imperiyālizm-e Britāniyā (1335-1338 h.q.)* (Tehran: Markaz-e asnād va tārikh-e diplomasi, 1384/2005).

3. Touraj Atabaki, "Incommodious Hosts, Invidious Guests: The Life and Times of Iranian Revolutionaries in the Soviet Union, 1921-1939," in *Reformers and Revolutionaries in Modern Iran: New Perspectives on the Iranian Left*, ed. Stephanie Cronin (London: Routledge Curzon, 2004), 147-64; Cosroe Chaquèri, *The Russo-Caucasian Origins of the Iranian Left: Social Democracy in Modern Iran* (Richmond: Curzon, 2001); Etienne Forestier-Peyrat, "Red Passage to Iran: The Baku Trade Fair and the Unmaking of the Azerbaijani Borderland (1922-1930)," *Ab Imperio*, 2013, no. 4, 79-112; Moḥammad Puraḥmad Jaktāji, ed., *Gilān-nāmeh: Majmu'-eh-ye maqālāt-e Gilānshenāsi*, vol. 3 (Rasht: Enteshārāt-e tā'ati, 1369/1990), 255-63.

4. Fitzroy MacLean, *Eastern Approaches* (London: Four Square Books, 1967), 33-34, and Terry Martin, "The Origins of Soviet Ethnic Cleansing," *Journal of Modern History* 70, no. 4 (1998): 813-61.

5. Rashid Khatib-Shahidi, *German Foreign Policy towards Iran before World War II: Political Relations, Economic Influence and the National Bank of Persia* (London: I. B. Tauris, 2013); Yair P. Hirschfeld, *Deutschland und Iran im Spielfeld der Mächte: Internationale Beziehungen unter Reza Schah, 1921-1941* (Dusseldorf: Droste Verlag, 1980).

6. Klaus Gestwa, "Das Besitzergreifen von Natur in Gesellschaft im Stalinismus: Enthusiastischer Umgestaltungswille und Katastrophischer Fortschritt," *Saeculum* 56, no. 1 (2005): 105-38; Stephen Brain, "The Great Plan for the Transformation of Nature," *Environmental History* 15, no. 4 (2010): 670-700.

7. Gregory Ferguson-Cradler, "Forecasting Fisheries: Prediction and the Planned Economy in the Interwar Soviet Union," *Cahiers du Monde russe* 58, no. 4 (2017): 615-38; George A. Taskin, "The Falling Level of the Caspian Sea in Relation to Soviet Economy," *Geographical Review* 44, no. 4 (1954): 516.

8. David C. Engerman et al., eds., *Staging Growth, Modernization, Development, and the Global Cold War* (Amherst: University of Massachusetts Press,

2003); Julia Obertreis, "Der 'Angriff auf die Wüste' in Zentralasien: Zur Umweltgeschichte der Sowjetunion," *Osteuropa*, no. 4–5 (2008): 37–56.

9. Heonik Kwon, *The Other Cold War* (New York: Columbia University Press, 2010), viii; Mostafā Nuri, *Ruzgār-e biqarāri-ye Māzandarān va Gorgān dar eshqāl-e Artesh-e Sorkh, 1320–1325* (Tehran: Sāzemān-e Asnād va Ketābkhāneh-ye Melli-e Jomhuri-ye Eslāmi, 1394/2015); Christian Bromberger, *Un autre Iran: Un anthropologue au Gilān* (Paris: Armand Colin, 2013); Etienne Peyrat, *Histoire du Caucase au XXe siècle* (Paris: Fayard, 2020).

10. Guive Mirfendereski, *A Diplomatic History of the Caspian Sea: Treaties, Diaries and Other Stories* (Basingstoke: Palgrave, 2001).

11. Antoine Fleury, *La Pénétration Allemande au Moyen-Orient 1919–1939: Le cas de la Turquie, de l'Iran et de l'Afghanistan* (Geneva: Institut Universitaire des Hautes Etudes Internationales; Leiden: Sijthoff, 1977), 258–61.

12. Patrick R. Osborn, *Operation Pike: Britain versus the Soviet Union, 1939–1941* (Westport: Greenwood Press, 2000); Sylvain Champonnois, "Les projets Franco-Britanniques de bombardement aérien de l'industrie pétrolière Soviétique du Caucase (1939-1940)," *Guerres mondiales et conflits contemporains* 1, no. 269 (2018): 33–55; René Girault, "Les relations Franco-Soviétiques après Septembre 1939," *Cahiers du Monde russe et soviétique* 17, no. 1 (1976): 27–42.

13. A. Igolkin, *Sovetskaiā neftianaiā politika v 1940–1950 godakh* (Moscow: Institut Rossiĭskoĭ Istorii, 2009), 57–58.

14. Letter of the Azerbaijani Commissariat of Health to the Azerbaijani Council of People's Commissars, September 27, 1941, ARDA, f. 411, op. 25, d. 170, l. 399.

15. Maḥmud Ṭāheraḥmadi, ed., *Tārikh-e ravābeṭ-e Irān va ettehād-e Jamāhir-e Showravi 1325–1345* (Tehran: Edāreh-ye asnād va tārikh-e diplomāsi, 1393/2014), 11.

16. Szczepan Lemańczyk, "The Transiranian Railway: History, Context, Consequences," *Middle Eastern Studies* 49, no. 2 (2013): 237–45; Robert W. Coakley, *The Persian Corridor as a Route for Aid to the USSR* (Washington, DC: Center of Military History, US Army, 1990).

17. Nuri, *Ruzgār*, 48.

18. Decision of the State Defense Committee, June 16, 1944, RGASPI, f. 644, op. 2, d. 180, ll. 101–4.

19. Note of the Soviet Embassy in Tehran to the Iranian MFA, July 16, 1943, in Minā Zahir Nejād Ershādi, ed., *Gozideh-ye asnād-e daryā-ye khazar va manāṭeq-e shomāli-e Irān dar Jang-e Jahāni-ye Dovvom* (Tehran: Daftar-e motāle'āt-e siyāsi va bayn-al-melali, 1375/1997), 291–92; Mirfendereski, *A Diplomatic History of the Caspian Sea*, 158–59.

20. Aleksandr Orishev, *Iranskiĭ uzel. skhvatka razvedok, 1936–1945 gg.* (Moscow: Vech, 2009), 211–14.

21. Nuri, *Ruzgār*, 46–47.

22. Janet Afary, "The Contentious Historiography of the Gilan Republic in Iran: A Critical Exploration," *Iranian Studies* 28, no. 1–2 (1995): 3–24.

23. Cəmil Həsənli, *İkinci Dünya Müharibəsi İllərində Azərbaycan Hərbi, Siyasi və Diplomatik Münasibətlərində (1939–1945)* (Baku: Yazıçı, 2015); Louise Fawcett, *Iran and the Cold War: The Azerbaijan Crisis of 1946* (Cambridge: Cambridge University Press, 1992).

24. Intelligence Summaries of the British Military Attaché, January 4, 1945, and August 14, 1945, in R. M. Burrell and Robert L. Jarman, eds., *Iran Political Diaries 1881–1965*, vol. 12, *1943–1945* (London: Archive Edition, 1997), 352 and 602.

25. Report of the French Embassy in Tehran, June 5, 1945, Archives du Ministère des Affaires étrangères (Paris), DAP, Asie, 1944–1955, Iran, 31.

26. Letter of the Soviet MFA to the Azerbaijani MFA, January 25, 1946, ARDA, f. 28, op. 4, d. 41, l. 2.

27. Ṭāheraḥmadi, *Tārikh-e ravābeṭ-e Irān*, 44.

28. Letter of the Azerbaijani Border Guard Directorate to the Azerbaijani MFA, July 6, 1946, ARDA, f. 28, op. 4, d. 34, l. 55.

29. Ḥosayn Aḥmadi, "Talāsh-e mohājerin-e nādem dar Showravi barā-ye bāzgasht beh Irān," *Moṭāleʾāt-e Āsiyā-ye markazi va Qafqāz*, no. 58 (1386/2007): 73–87.

30. Mirfendereski, *A Diplomatic History of the Caspian Sea*, 171.

31. Intelligence Summary of the British Military Attaché, August 6, 1947, in R. M. Burrell and Robert L. Jarman, eds., *Iran Political Diaries 1881–1965*, vol. 13, *1946–1951* (London: Archive Edition, 1997), 344.

32. Interview with Frederick W. Flott, former US diplomat, by Charles Stuart Kennedy, October 27, 1992, Association for Diplomatic Studies and Training Foreign Affairs Oral History Project, https://memory.loc.gov/service/mss/mfdip/2004/2004flo02/2004flo02.pdf.

33. Amanollāh Jahānbāni, *Marzhā-ye Irān va Showravi* (Tehran: Chāpkhāne-ye melli, 1336/1957), 88–89.

34. Report on the Foreign Relations of the Azerbaijani Soviet Socialist Republic, March 17, 1972, ARDA, f. 28, op. 11, d. 20, l. 19.

35. Müsəllim Həsənov, *Azərbaycanda Gəmiçilik: Sənədli Tarix* (Baku: Azərbaycan Xəzər Dəniz Gəmiçiliyi, 2018), 138–39.

36. Letter of the Azerbaijani Central Committee of the Communist Party to the Central Committee in Moscow, July 30, 1963, Rossiĭskiĭ Gosudarstvennyĭ Arkhiv Noveĭsheĭ Istorii, f. 5, op. 31, d. 223, ll. 112–13.

37. Leyla Sayfutdinova, "Mapping the Mobility of Azerbaijani Soviet Engineers," *Labor History* 59, no. 3 (2018): 316–30; letter of the Azerbaijani MFA to the permanent representation in Moscow, Spring 1972, ARDA, f. 28, op. 11, d. 20, l. 42.

38. "Ausbildung in Baku," *Marinekameradschaft KSS e.V. Rostock-Warnemünde Broschüre*, Part 4, 2015, available at https://www.freunde-von-kss.de/projekt-1159/1159-ausbildung-in-baku.

39. Johanna Conterio, "'Our Black Sea Coast': The Sovietization of the Black Sea Littoral under Khrushchev and the Problem of Overdevelopment," *Kritika: Explorations in Russian and Eurasian History* 19, no. 2 (2018): 327–61.

40. Christian Noack, "Coping with the Tourist: Planned and 'Wild' Mass Tourism on the Soviet Black Sea Coast," in *Turizm: The Russian and East European Tourist under Capitalism and Socialism*, ed. Anne E. Gorsuch and Diane P. Koenker (Ithaca, NY: Cornell University Press, 2006), 281–304.

41. Jörg Stadelbauer, "Der Fremdenverkehr in Sowjet-Kaukasien: Gesamtstaatliche Bedeutung, Räumliche Strukturen und Entwicklungsprobleme," *Zeitschrift für Wirtschaftsgeographie* 30, no. 1 (1986): 1–21.

42. Pamela Karimi, "Tourism and Urbanism in Iran: Top-Down and Ad-Hoc Developments in the Caspian Region," in *Routledge Handbook on Middle East Cities*, ed. Haim Yacobi and Mansour Nasara (London: Routledge, 2020), 177-95.

43. "Complexes Planned for Upsurge in Tourism," *Iran Economic News* 1, no. 2 (February 1975): 5; on tourism in Pahlavi Iran, see Roqayya Javādi, "Sāzmān-e Jahāngardi va Ta'asir-e ān bar Tos'e-ye Gardeshgari dar dowreh-ye Pahlavi-e dovvom," *Ganjineh-ye asnād* 23, no. 1 (Spring 1392/2013): 40-61.

44. Mikhail Nazarov, *Apparat i li͡udi: Zapiski o moem vremeni* (Baku: Apostrof, 2010), 100-102.

45. Per Högselius, *Red Gas: Russia and the Origins of European Energy Dependence* (Basingstoke: Palgrave Macmillan, 2013), 172.

46. Letter of the Azerbaijani MFA to the Azerbaijani Central Committee of the Communist Party, September 21, 1970, Azərbaycan Respublikası Prezidentinin İşlər İdarəsi Siyasi Sənədlər Arxivi, f. 1, op. 58, d. 191, ll. 2-4.

47. Personal note concerning the Governor General of Gilan, 'Ali Asghar Ṭāheri, undated (September 1970), ARDA, f. 28, op. 11, d. 19, l. 6.

48. Marc Elie and Carole Ferret, "Verte, la steppe? Agriculture et environnement en Asie Centrale," *Études rurales*, no. 200 (2017): 64-79.

49. Paul Josephson et al., *An Environmental History of Russia* (Cambridge: Cambridge University Press, 2013), 231.

50. Tuomas Räsänen and Simo Laakkonen, "Cold War and the Environment: The Role of Finland in International Environmental Politics in the Baltic Sea Region," *Ambio* 36, no. 2-3 (2007): 229-36.

51. Letter of the Deputy Minister of Oil Industry, S. Orudzhev, to the Deputy Minister of Water Resources, I. Borodavchenko, August 5, 1971, RGAE, f. 436, op. 2, d. 1475, l. 46.

52. Artemy M. Kalinovsky, *Laboratory of Socialist Development: Cold War Politics and Decolonization in Soviet Tajikistan* (Ithaca, NY: Cornell University Press, 2018); Christopher Sneddon, *Concrete Revolution: Large Dams, Cold War Geopolitics, and the US Bureau of Reclamation* (Chicago: University of Chicago Press, 2015).

53. François Carré, "Les Pêches en Mer Caspienne," *Annales de Géographie* 87, no. 479 (1978): 1-3.

54. Carmel Finley, *All the Boats on the Ocean: How Government Subsidies Led to Global Overfishing* (Chicago: University of Chicago Press, 2017), 92-93.

55. Etienne Forestier-Peyrat, "Fighting Locusts Together: Pest Control and the Birth of Soviet Development Aid, 1920-1939," *Global Environment* 7, no. 2 (2014): 536-71.

56. Speech of Senator Jahanshah Saleh in the Senate, Āzar 9, 1349 (November 30, 1970), reproduced in ARDA, f. 28, op. 11, d. 18, ll. 8-12.

57. Laurel Sefton MacDowell, *An Environmental History of Canada* (Vancouver: UBC Press, 2012), 192-95.

58. Eskandar Firuz, *Khāṭerāt-e Eskandar Firuz* (Bethesda: Ibex Publishers, 2012), 313-16.

59. "The Future of the Caspian Sea," *Kayhan*, Āzar 11, 1349 (December 2, 1970), reproduced in ARDA, f. 28, op. 11, d. 18, l. 15.

60. Marie-Hélène Mandrillon, "L'expertise d'etat, creuset de l'environnement en URSS," *Vingtième siècle: Revue d'histoire*, no. 113 (2012): 108 and 112.

61. Speech of Senator Jahanshah Saleh in the Senate, Ordibehesht 4, 1351 (April 24, 1972), *Mashruh-e mozākerāt-e Majles-e senā*, Sixth Legislature (Tehran: 1975).

62. Report of the Soviet Consulate in Rasht, July 1978, RGAE, f. 436, op. 2, d. 4076, ll. 16–19.

63. Saghar Sadeghian, "The Caspian Forests of Northern Iran during the Qajar and Pahlavi Periods: Deforestation, Regulation, and Reforestation," *Iranian Studies* 49, no. 6 (2016): 975.

64. Ṭāheraḥmadi, *Tārikh-e ravābeṭ-e Irān*, 151.

65. G. V. T. Matthews, *The Ramsar Convention on Wetlands: Its History and Development* (Gland: Ramsar Convention Bureau, 1993).

66. Mohammad Reza-Jalili, *Diplomatie islamique: Stratégie internationale du Khomeynisme* (Paris: Presses universitaires de France, 1989), 13.

67. Mohammad Mokri, *Les frontières du nord de l'Iran: Caucase, Asie Centrale* (Paris: Geuthner, 2004), 148–50.

68. "Konsulgari-e Showravi dar Rasht beh sarkonsulgari tabdil shod," *Enqelāb-e Eslāmi*, Shahrivar 1, 1359 (August 23, 1980), in Mohammad Mokri, *Na sharqi, na gharbi, Jomhuri-ye Eslāmi: Majmu'-eh-ye sokhanrānihā va akhbār-e montasher shodeh dar jarā'id darbāreh-ye ravābeṭ-e Irān* (Tehran: Mo'asaseh-ye enteshārāt-e Amir Kabir, 1362/1983–84), 410–11.

69. "Soviets Asked to Close Consulate Office in Rasht," *Tehran Times*, August 26, 1980, in Mokri, *Na sharqi, na gharbi, Jomhuri-ye Eslāmi*, 417.

Bibliography

"'Abbas Qoli Khan Sartip Lārijāni." *Bānk-e Eṭṭelāʿāt-e Rejāl*. Last updated September 13, 2013. http://rijaldb.com/fa/12244/لاریجانی+سرتیپ+خان+عباسقلی.
Abbott, Consul. *Cities & Trade: Consul Abbott on the Economy and Society of Iran 1847–1866*. Edited by Abbas Amanat. London: Ithaca Press, 1983.
ʿAbduʾl-Bahá, Abbas. *Maqāleh-ye Shakhsi Sayyāḥ*. Germany: Moʾasseseh-ye Maṭbuʿāt-e ʿAmri, n.d.
Abdurasulov, Ulfat. "Making Sense of Central Asia in Pre-Petrine Russia." *Journal of the Economic and Social History of the Orient* 63 (2020): 607–33.
Abdurasulov, Ulfat. "A Passage to India: Rhetoric and Diplomacy between Muscovy and Central Asia in the Seventeenth Century." *Itinerario* 44, no. 3 (2020): 502–27.
Abikh, Rudolf. "Natsional'noe i revoliutsionnoe dvizhenie v Persii v 1917–1919 gg. (Vospominaniia Ėhsan Ully-Khana)." *Novyĭ Vostok* 26–27 (1929): 125–61.
Abraham of Yerevan. *History of the Wars, 1721–1738*. Translated by G. Bournoutian. Costa Mesa: Mazda, 1999.
Abrahamian, Ervand. "Communism and Communalism in Iran: The Tudah and the Firqah-i Dimukrat." *International Journal of Middle East Studies* 1, no. 4 (1970): 291–316.
"Abstract of the Bill for opening Trade To and From Persia, thro' Russia." In *The History and Proceedings of the House of Commons from the Restoration to the Present Time*, 12:262–65. London: Richard Chamber, 1742.
Abulafia, David. *The Great Sea: A Human History of the Mediterranean*. Oxford: Oxford University Press, 2011.
Adamova, Adel. "Art and Diplomacy: Qajar Paintings at the State Hermitage Museum." In *Royal Persian Paintings: The Qajar Epoch, 1785–1925*, edited by Layla Diba, 66–75. New York: Brooklyn Museum of Art in association with I. B. Tauris Publishers, 1998.
Adams, Jan. "The US-Russian Face-off in the Caspian Basin." *Problems of Post-Communism* 47, no. 1 (2000): 49–58.
Adelkhah, Fariba. *Les mille et une frontières de l'Iran: Quand les voyages forment la nation*. Paris: Karthala, 2012.
Afary, Janet. "The Contentious Historiography of the Gilan Republic in Iran: A Critical Exploration." *Iranian Studies* 28, no. 1–2 (1995): 3–24.
Afary, Janet. *The Iranian Constitutional Revolution, 1906–1911: Grassroots Democracy, Social Democracy, and the Origins of Feminism*. New York: Columbia University Press, 1996.

Afary, Janet. "Peasant Rebellions of the Caspian Region during the Iranian Constitutional Revolution, 1906-1909." *International Journal of Middle East Studies* 23, no. 2 (1991): 137-61.

Afary, Janet, and Kamran Afary. *Mollā Nasreddin: The Making of a Modern Trickster (1906–1911)*. Edinburgh: Edinburgh University Press, 2022.

Ağa, Salahşur Khaseh Kemani Mustafa. *Revan Fathnamasi*. Istanbul: Boğazici University, 1970.

Agaev, Semën L'vovich. *Iran v period politicheskogo krizisa, 1920–1925 gg.: Voprosy vneshneĭ politiki*. Moscow: Nauka, 1970.

Aghaneants, G., ed. *Diwan hayots patmutean*. Vol. 9.1. Tiflis: Sharadze, 1911.

Aghdashloo, Aydin. "A Short Introduction to the Works of Asghar Petgar and His Time." *Shargh*, May 11, 2011, 15.

Ahmadi, Bahram. *L'enseignement universitaire de la peinture en Iran: Problèmes et Influences*. Saarbrücken: Press Académiques Francophones, Akademikerverlag, 2012.

Aḥmadi, Ḥosayn. "Talāsh-e mohājerin-e nādem dar Showravi barāye bāzgasht beh Irān," *Moṭāle'āt-e Āsiyā-ye markazi va Qafqāz*, no. 58 (1386/2007): 73-87.

Ahmed, Faiz. *Afghanistan Rising: Islamic Law and Statecraft between the Ottoman and British Empires*. Cambridge, MA: Harvard University Press, 2017.

Alam, Muzaffar. "The Pursuit of Persian: Language in Mughal Politics." *Modern Asian Studies* 32, no. 2 (1998): 317-49.

Alexidze, Marina. *Georgia and the Muslim East in the Nineteenth Century: Studies in the History of Culture, Religion and Life*. Tbilisi: Ilia State University: George Tsereteli Institute of Oriental Studies, 2011.

Alexidze, Marina. "Persians in Georgia (1801-1921)." *Journal of Persianate Studies* 1, no. 2 (2008): 254-60.

Aliev, Salekh Mamedogly. *Istoriia Irana: XX vek*. Moscow: Kraft+IV RAN, 2004.

Alimdzhanov, Bakhtiër Abdikhakimovich. "Ėkonomicheskaia politika Rossiĭskoĭ imperii v Turkestanskom general-gubernatorstve (vtoraia polovina XIX-nachalo XX VV)." PhD diss., Saint Petersburg State University, 2016.

Allen, W. E. D. *A History of the Georgian People from the Beginning Down to the Russian Conquest in the Nineteenth Century*. London, 1932.

Allison, Roy. "Strategic Reassertion in Russia's Central Asia Policy." *International Affairs* 80, no. 2 (2004): 277-93.

Alsulami, Mohammed. "Iranian Journals in Berlin during the Interwar Period." In *Transnational Islam in Interwar Europe: Muslim Activists and Thinkers*, edited by Götz Nordbruch and Umar Ryad, 157-80. New York: Palgrave Macmillan, 2014.

Amanat, Abbas, ed. *Cities and Trade: Consul Abbott on the Society and Economy of Iran*. Oxford Oriental Institute Monographs. London: Ithaca Press, 1983.

Amanat, Abbas. *Iran: A Modern History*. New Haven, CT: Yale University Press, 2017.

Amanat, Abbas. "Legend, Legitimacy, and Making a National Narrative in the Historiography of Qajar Iran (1785-1925)." In *Persian Historiography*, edited by Charles Melville, vol. 10 of *A History of Persian Literature*, 292-366. New York: I. B. Tauris, 2012.

Amanat, Abbas. "Nuqtavi Messianic Agnostics of Iran and the Shaping of the Doctrine of 'Universal Conciliation' (*sulh-i kull*) in Mughal India." In *Norm, Transgression and Identity in Islam: Diversity of Approaches and Interpretations / Norme, transgression et identité en Islam: Diversité d'approches et d'interprétations*, edited by Orkhan Mir-Kasimov, 367-92. Leiden: Brill, 2014.

Amanat, Abbas. "The Nuqtavi Movement of Mahmud Pasikhani and His Persian Cycle of Mystical Materialism." In *Apocalyptic Islam and Iranian Shi'ism*, 73-90. London: I. B. Tauris, 2009.

Amanat, Abbas. *Pivot of the Universe*. Los Angeles: University of California Press, 1997.

Amanat, Abbas. *Resurrection and Renewal: The Making of the Babi Movement in Iran, 1844-1850*. Ithaca, NY: Cornell University Press, 1989.

Amanat, Abbas. "'Russian Intrusion into the Guarded Domain': Reflections of a Qajar Statesman on European Expansion." *Journal of the American Oriental Society* 113, no. 1 (1993): 36-55.

Amanat, Abbas, and Assef Ashraf, eds. *The Persianate World: Rethinking a Shared Sphere*. Leiden: Brill, 2019.

Andreeva, Elena. *Russia and Iran in the Great Game: Travelogues and Orientalism*. New York: Routledge, 2007.

Andreeva, Elena. *Russian Central Asia in the Works of Nikolai Karazin (1842-1908)—Ambivalent Triumph*. Cham: Springer, 2021.

Andreyev, Alexandre. *Soviet Russia and Tibet: The Debacle of Secret Diplomacy, 1918-1930s*. Leiden: Brill, 2003.

Angiolelli, Giovanni M. degli. *A Narrative of Italian Travels in Persia in the Fifteenth and Sixteenth Centuries*. Edited by C. Grey. London, 1873.

Ansari, K. Humayun. "Maulana Barakatullah Bhopali's Transnationalism: Pan-Islamism, Colonialism, and Radical Politics." In *Transnational Islam in Interwar Europe: Muslim Activists and Thinkers*, edited by Götz Nordbruch and Umar Ryad, 181-210. New York: Palgrave Macmillan, 2014.

Ansari, K. Humayun. "Pan-Islam and the Making of the Early Indian Muslim Socialists." *Modern Asian Studies* 20, no. 3 (1986): 509-37.

Antonova, K. A., et al., eds. *Russko-indiĭskie otnosheniia v XVII v. Sbornik dokumentov*. Moscow: Izdatel'stvo Vostochnoĭ Literatury, 1958.

Arabadzhi̐an, Zaven Artëmovich. *Iran: Protivostoi̐anie imperii̐am (1918-1941)*. Moscow: IV RAN, 1996.

Aṛakʿel of Tabriz. *Book of History*. Translated by G. Bournoutian. Costa Mesa: Mazda, 2010.

Aristotle. *Meteorologica*. Text with English translation by H. D. P. Lee. Cambridge, MA: Harvard University Press, 1952.

"Arjangi Family History," accessed January 30, 2012, http://arjangi.org/rassam.

Arjomand, Saïd Amir. *The Shadow of God and the Hidden Imam: Religion, Political Order, and Societal Change*. Chicago: University of Chicago Press, 1984.

"Arrangements for Collection of Customs Duties in the Transcaspian Region." *Board of Trade Journal*, July–December 1889, 625–26.

Artizov, A. N., ed. *Iz istorii rossiĭsko-gruzinskikh otnosheniĭ k 230-letiiu zakliuncheniia Georgievskogo traktata: Sbornik dokumentov*. Moscow: Drevlekhranilishche, 2014.

Aslanian, Sebouh. *From the Indian Ocean to the Mediterranean: The Global Trade Networks of Armenian Merchants from New Julfa*. Berkeley: University of California Press, 2011.

Astarābādi, Mirzā Mahdi Khān. *Tārikh-e Jahāngoshā-ye Nāderi*. Edited by ʿAbdallah Anvār. Tehran: Chāp-e Bahman, 1341/1962–63.

Astarābādi, Mirzā Mahdi Khān. *Tārikh-e Jahāngoshā-ye Nāderi*. Edited by ʿAbdallāh Anvār. Tehran: Kiyānush, 1377/1998.

Atabaki, Touraj. *Azerbaijan: Ethnicity and Autonomy in Twentieth-Century Iran*. London: British Academic Press, 1993.

Atabaki, Touraj. *Beyond Essentialism: Who Writes Whose Past in the Middle East and Central Asia?* Amsterdam: Aksant Academic Publishers, 2012.

Atabaki, Touraj. "Disgruntled Guests: Iranian Subaltern on the Margins of the Tsarist Empire." *International Review of Social History* 48, no. 3 (2003): 401–26.

Atabaki, Touraj. "Going East: The Ottomans' Secret Service Activities in Iran." In *Iran and the First World War: Battleground of the Great Powers*, edited by Touraj Atabaki, 29–42. London: I. B. Tauris, 2006.

Atabaki, Touraj. "Incommodious Hosts, Invidious Guests: The Life and Times of Iranian Revolutionaries in the Soviet Union, 1921–1939." In *Reformers and Revolutionaries in Modern Iran: New Perspectives on the Iranian Left*, edited by Stephanie Cronin, 147–64. London: Routledge Curzon, 2004.

Atabaki, Touraj, ed. *Iran and the First World War: Battleground of the Great Powers*. London: I. B. Tauris, 2006.

Atabaki, Touraj. "Pan-Turkism and Iranian Nationalism." In *Iran and the First World War: Battleground of the Great Powers*, edited by Touraj Atabaki, 121–36. London: I. B. Tauris, 2006.

Atabaki, Touraj, and Lana Ravandi-Fadaʾi. *Zhertvy Vremeni: Zhizn' i sud'ba iranskikh politicheskikh deĭateleĭ i trudovykh migrantov v mezhvoennyĭ period*. Moscow: IV RAN, 2020.

Atabaki, Touraj, and Denis V. Volkov. "Flying away from the Bolshevik Winter: Soviet Refugees across the Southern Borders (1917–30)." *Journal of Refugee Studies* 34, no. 2 (2001): 1900–1922.

Ataev, Kh. A. *Torgovo-ėkonomicheskie sviazi Irana s Rossieĭ v XVIII–XIX vv*. Moscow: Nauka, 1991.

Atkin, Muriel. *Russia and Iran, 1780–1828*. Minneapolis: University of Minnesota Press, 1980.

Aubin, Jean. "L'avènement des Safavides reconsidéré (Études safavides III)." *Moyen Orient et Océan Indien* 5 (1988): 1–130.

Averʾianov, K. A. "Russkaia diplomatiia i kontrrazvedka v XVII veke." In *Rossiĭskaia diplomatiia: Istoriia i sovremennost'*, edited by I. S. Ivanov et al., 110–20. Moscow: Rosspen, 2001.

Avrich, P. *Russian Rebels, 1600–1800*. London: Norton, 1972.
Axworthy, Michael. "Nader Shah and Persian Naval Expansion in the Persian Gulf, 1700–1747." *Journal of the Royal Asiatic Society* 21, no. 1 (2011): 34–39.
Axworthy, Michael. *The Sword of Persia: Nader Shah, from Tribal Warrior to Conquering Tyrant*. London: I. B. Tauris, 2006.
Āẓar, ʿAbd al-Ḥosayn Nāhidi, ed. *Ruznāmeh-ye Āẓarbāijān, 1324, 1906: Nakhostin Ruznāmeh-ye Fokāhi va Tanz-e Tasviri dar Irān*. Tabriz: Nashr-e Akhtar, 2015.
Babaie, Sussan. "Nader Shah, the Delhi Loot, and the 18th-Century Exotics of Empire." In *Crisis, Collapse, Militarism & Civil War: The History and Historiography of 18th Century Iran*, edited by Michael Axworthy, 215–34. Oxford: Oxford University Press, 2018.
Babayan, Kathryn. *Mystics, Monarchs and Messiahs: Cultural Landscape of Early Modern Iran*. Cambridge, MA: Harvard University Center for Middle Eastern Studies, 2003.
Babinger, Fr., and R. M. Savory. "Ṣafī al-Din Audabīlī [sic]." *Encyclopaedia of Islam*, 2nd edition. https://referenceworks.brill.com/display/entries/EIEO/SIM-6446.xml.
Baddeley, John F. *The Russian Conquest of the Caucasus*. London: Longmans, Green, 1908.
Bāghbidi, H. Reżā'i. "Katibeha-ye Pahlavi-Kufi-ye Borj-e Lājim." *Nāmeh-ye Irān-e Bāstān* 4, no. 1 (1383/2004): 9–21.
Bahgat, Gawdat. "Europe's Energy Security: Challenges and Opportunities." *International Affairs* 82, no. 5 (2006): 961–75.
Baĭkova, N. B. *Rol' Sredneĭ Azii v russko-indiĭskikh torgovykh svi͡aziakh (pervai͡a polovina XVI–vtorai͡a polovina XVIII v.)*. Tashkent: Nauka, 1964.
Bailey, Frederick M. *Mission to Tashkent*. London: J. Cape, 1946.
Bailey, Frederick M. "A Visit to Bokhara in 1919." *Geographical Journal* 57, no. 2 (1921): 75–87.
Balaghi, Shiva. "Political Culture in the Iranian Revolution of 1906 and the Cartoons of Kashkul." In *Political Cartoons in the Middle East*, edited by Fatma Müge Göçek, 51–73. Princeton, NJ: Princeton University Press, 1998.
Balkovai͡a, V. G. "Organizatsii͡a tamozhennogo deloproizvodstva v Rossiĭskoĭ imperii v XVIII veke." *Vestnik saratovskoĭ gosudarstvennoĭ i͡uridicheskoĭ akademii*, no. 5 (2012): 11–17.
Bartol'd, Vasily. "Istorii͡a izuchenii͡a Vostoka v Evrope i Rossii." In V. V. Bartol'd, *Sochinenii͡a*, 9:374. 199–466. Moscow: Nauka, 1977.
Bashir, Shahzad. *Fazlullah Astarabadi and the Hurufis*. Makers of the Muslim World Series. London: Oneworld, 2005.
Bashir, Shahzad. "Shah Ismaʿil and the Qizilbash: Cannibalism in the Religious History of Early Safavid Iran." *History of Religion* 45 (2006): 234–56.
Bassin, Mark. "Russia between Europe and Asia: The Ideological Construction of Geographical Space." *Slavic Review* 50, no. 1 (1991): 1–17.

Bast, Oliver. *Les Allemands en Perse pendant la Première Guerre mondiale: D'après les sources diplomatiques françaises*. Paris: Peeters, 1997.

Bast, Oliver. "Cecil John Edmonds. East and West of Zagros: Travel, War and Politics in Persia and Iraq, 1913–1921." *Abstracta Iranica*, 34–35–36 (2017), https://doi.org/10.4000/abstractairanica.48458.

Bast, Oliver. "The Council for International Propaganda and the Establishment of the Iranian Communist Party." In *Iran and the First World War: Battleground of the Great Powers*, edited by Touraj Atabaki, 163–80. London: I. B. Tauris, 2006.

Bast, Oliver. "Germany ix. Germans in Persia." *Encyclopaedia Iranica*, X/6, 567–72. https://iranicaonline.org/articles/germany-ix.

Bast, Oliver. *La Perse et la Grande Guerre: Etudes réunies et présentées*. Tehran: Inst. Français de Recherche en Iran, 2002.

Bast, Oliver. "Putting the Record Straight: Vosuq al-Dowleh's Foreign Policy in 1918/19." In *Men of Order: Authoritarian Modernization under Atatürk and Reza Shah*, edited by Touraj Atabaki and Erik J. Zürcher, 260–81. London: I. B. Tauris, 2004.

Bates, Michael L. "Arab-Sasanian Coins." *Encyclopaedia Iranica*, II/3, 225–29. https://iranicaonline.org/articles/arab-sasanian-coins.

Baud, Michiel, and Willem Van Schendel. "Toward a Comparative History of Borderlands." *Journal of World History* 8, no. 2 (1997): 211–42.

Bausani, A. "Hurufiyya." *Encyclopaedia of Islam*. 2nd edition. https://referenceworks.brill.com/display/entries/EIEO/COM-0303.xml.

Bayāt, Kāveh, ed. *Irān dar Jang-e Jahāni-ye Avval: Asnād-e vezārat-e dākheleh*. Tehran: Enteshārāt-e Sāzemān-e Asnād-e Melli-ye Irān, 1381/2002.

Bayat, Mangol. *Iran's Experiment with Parliamentary Governance: The Second Majles, 1909–1911*. Syracuse: Syracuse University Press, 2020.

Bazin, Frère. "Mémoires sur les dernières années du règne de Thamas-Koulikan." In *Lettres édifiantes et curieuses, écrites des missions etrangères*, vol. 4, *Mémoires du Levant*. Toulouse: Noel-Etienne Sens, 1810.

Bazin, Marcel. "Gilan i: Geography and Ethnography." *Encyclopaedia Iranica*, X/6, 617–25. https://iranicaonline.org/articles/gilan-i-geography.

Bazin, Marcel, and C. Bromberger. "Abrīšam ii. Trade and Production of Silk and Its Use in Crafts." *Encyclopaedia Iranica*, I/3, 229–47. https://iranicaonline.org/articles/abrisam-silk-index#pt2.

Behrooz, Maziar. "From Confidence to Apprehension: Early Iranian Interaction with Russia." In *Iranian-Russian Encounters: Empires and Revolutions since 1800*, edited by Stephanie Cronin, 49–68. New York: Routledge, 2013.

Behrooz, Maziar. *Iran at War: Interaction with the Modern World and Struggle with Imperial Russia*. London: I. B. Tauris, 2023.

Behzād, Karim Ṭāherzādeh. *Qiyām-e Āzarbāijān dar Enqelāb-e Mashrutiat-e Irān*. Tehran: Eqbāl, 1334/1954.

Beiranvand, A., et al. "The Study of Causes and Factors of Illegal Logging in Caspian Forests." *Majaleh-ye Jangal-e Iran* 15, no. 2 (2023): 35–51.

Beli͡akov, A. V. *Sluzhashchie Posol'skogo prikaza 1645–1682 gg*. St. Petersburg: Nestor-Istoriia, 2017.

Bell, John, of Antermony. *Travels from St. Petersburgh in Russia to Various Parts of Asia*. Vol. 1. Edinburgh: W. Creech, 1788.
Belokurov, S. A. *O posol'skom prikaze*. Moscow, 1906.
Bennigsen, Alexandre, et al. *Le Khanat de Crimée dans les Archives de Musée du Palais de Topkapı*. Paris: Mouton, 1978.
Beradze, Grigol. "Looking Back and Ahead: An Insight into Iranian Influence in the Caucasus." Paper presented at the Conference of the G. Tsereteli Institute of Oriental Studies of the Ilia State University, Tbilisi, October 1-2, 2014.
Berberian, Houri. *Roving Revolutionaries: Armenians and the Connected Revolutions in the Russian, Iranian, and Ottoman Worlds*. Oakland: University of California Press, 2019.
Berg, Lev S. "Pervye russkie karty Kaspiĭskogo morīa (s sviazi s voprosam ob urovne ego v XVII i XVIII vekakh)." *Izvestiia Akademii Nauk SSSR, Seriia geograficheskaia i geofizicheskaia* 3 (1940): 159-78.
Berry, Lloyd E., and Robert O. Crummey, eds. *Rude and Barbarous Kingdom: Russia in the Accounts of Sixteenth-Century English Voyagers*. Madison: University of Wisconsin Press, 1968.
Bezhan, Faridullah. "Pan-Islamism in Afghanistan in the Early Twentieth Century: From Political Discourse to Government Policy, 1906-22." *Islam and Christian-Muslim Relations* 25, no. 2 (2014): 193-210.
Bezugol'nyĭ, Alekseĭ. *General Bicherakhov i ego Kavkazskaia armiia*. Moscow: Tsentrpoligraf, 2011.
Blank, Stephen. "The Future of Caspian Security." *Problems of Post-Communism* 50, no. 1 (2003): 8-21.
Blank, Stephen. "Soviet Politics and the Iranian Revolution of 1919-1921." *Cahiers du Monde russe et soviétique* 21, no. 2 (1980): 173-94.
Bobrovnikov, Vladimir, and Irina Babich, eds. *Severnyi Kavkaz v sostave Rossiiskoi imperii*. Moscow: Novoe literaturnoe obozrenie, 2007.
Bogoĭavlenskiĭ, S. K. *Moskovskiĭ prikaznyĭ apparat i deloproizvodstvo v XVI–XVII vekakh*. Moscow: Iazyki slavianskoĭ kul'tury, 2006.
Bohlen, Avis. "Changes in Russian Diplomacy under Peter the Great." *Cahiers du Monde Russe et Soviétique* 7, no. 3 (1966): 341-58.
Bohler, Alexandre. *Safarnāmeh-ye Bohler*. Edited by 'Ali Akbar Khodāparast. Tehran: Enteshārāt-e Ṭus, 1977.
Bosse, H. "Iran under the Buyids." In *The Cambridge History of Iran*, vol. 4, *The Period from the Arab Invasion to the Saljuqs*, edited by R. N. Frye, 250-304. Cambridge: Cambridge University Press, 1975.
Boterbloem, Kees. *The Fiction and Reality of Jan Struys: A Seventeenth-Century Dutch Globetrotter*. New York: Palgrave Macmillan, 2008.
Bournoutian, G. "The Armenian Church and Czarist Russia." In *Between Paris and Fresno: Armenian Studies in Honor of Dickran Kouymjian*, 431-36. Costa Mesa: Mazda, 2008.
Bournoutian, G., ed. *Armenians and Russia, 1626–1796: A Documentary Record*. Costa Mesa: Mazda, 2001.
Bournoutian, George. *From the Kur to the Aras: A Military History of Russia's Move into the South Caucasus and the First Russo-Iranian War, 1801–1813*. Leiden: Brill, 2020.

Bournoutian, George A. "The Role of the Armenians in the Russian Move into the South Caucasus." In *From the Kur to the Aras: A Military History of Russia's Move into the South Caucasus and the First Russo-Iranian War, 1801–1813*, 237–48. Leiden: Brill, 2020.

Brain, Stephen. "The Great Plan for the Transformation of Nature." *Environmental History* 15, no. 4 (2010): 670–700.

Braudel, Fernand. *The Mediterranean and the Mediterranean World in the Age of Philip II*. Vol. 1. Translated by Siân Reynolds. London: Fortuna/Collins, 1975.

Bregel, Yuri. *An Historical Atlas of Central Asia*. Leiden: Brill, 2003.

Bregel, Yuri. "Introduction." In Shīr Muḥammad Mīrāb Mūnis and Muḥammad Riżā Āgahī, *Firdaws al-iqbāl: History of Khorezm*, edited by Yuri Bregel, 1. Leiden: Brill, 1988.

Bregel, Yuri. "The Russian Conquest of Central Asia and the First Decades of Russian Rule." Section II of "Central Asia vii. In the 18th–19th Centuries." *Encyclopaedia Iranica*, V/2, 193–205. https://iranicaonline.org/articles/central-asia-vii.

Brinegar, Sara. "The Oil Deal: Nariman Narimanov and the Sovietization of Azerbaijan." *Slavic Review* 76, no. 2 (2017): 372–94.

Brinegar, Sara. *Power and the Politics of Oil in the Soviet South Caucasus: Periphery Unbound, 1920–29*. London: Bloomsbury Publishing, 2024.

Bromberger, Christian. *Un autre Iran: Un anthropologue au Gilān*. Paris: Armand Colin, 2013.

Brower, Daniel. *Turkestan and the Fate of the Russian Empire*. London: Routledge-Curzon, 2003.

Brown, Peter B. "Bureaucratic Administration in Seventeenth-Century Russia." In *Modernizing Muscovy: Reform and Social Change in Seventeenth Century Russia*, edited by Jarmo Kotilaine and Marshall Poe, 54–75. London: Routledge Curzon, 2005.

Browne, E. G. *The Press and Poetry of Modern Persia*. Cambridge: Cambridge University Press, 1914; repr. 1983.

Browne, E. G. *A Year Amongst the Persians*. London: Black, 1893.

Browne, Edward Granville. *The New History (tarikh-i-jadid) of Mirza 'Ali Mohammad the Bab*. London: Cambridge University Press, 1893.

Bruce, Peter Henry. *Memoirs*. London, 1782.

Burrell, R. M., and Robert L. Jarman, eds. *Iran Political Diaries 1881–1965*. Vol. 13, *1946–1951*. London: Archive Edition, 1997.

Burton, Audrey. *The Bukharans: A Dynastic, Diplomatic and Commercial History, 1550–1702*. New York: St. Martin's Press, 1997.

Bushev, P. P. *Istoriĩa posol'stv i diplomaticheskikh otnosheniĩ Russkogo i Iranskogo gosudarstv v 1586–1612 gg. (po russkim arkhivam)*. Moscow: Nauka, 1975.

Bushev, P. P. *Posol'stvo Artemiĩa Volynskogo v Iran v 1715–1718 gg. (po russkim arkhivam)*. Moscow: Izd. Nauka, Glavnaĩa Redaktsiĩa Vostochnoĩ Literatury, 1978.

Butkov, P. G. *Materialy dlĩa novoĩ istorii Kavkaza c–1722 po 1803 body*. Vols. 1–2. St. Petersburg, 1869.

BIBLIOGRAPHY

Carley, Michael J. *A Hidden History of Early Soviet-Western Relations.* Lanham: Rowman & Littlefield, 2014.
Carr, Edward. *The Russian Revolution: From Lenin to Stalin, 1917–1929.* New York: Free Press, 1979.
Carr, Edward. *The Twenty Years' Crisis, 1919–1939: An Introduction to the Study of International Relations.* London: Macmillan, 1946.
Carré, François. "Les Pêches en Mer Caspienne." *Annales de Géographie* 87, no. 479 (1978): 1–39.
Carter, Paul. "Dark with Excess of Bright: Mapping the Coastlines of Knowledge." In *Mappings*, edited by Denis Cosgrove, 125–47. London: Reaction Books, 1999.
Çelebi, Evliya. *Evliya Çelebi seyahatnamesi.* Vol. 7. Edited by Yücel Dağlı, Seyit Ali Kahraman, and Robert Dankof. Istanbul: Yapı Kredi Yayınları, 2003.
Chalfin, Brenda. "Global Customs Regimes and the Traffic in Sovereignty." *Current Anthropology* 47, no. 2 (2006): 243–76.
Champonnois, Sylvain. "Les projets Franco-Britanniques de bombardement aérien de l'industrie pétrolière Soviétique du Caucase (1939–1940)." *Guerres mondiales et conflits contemporains* 1, no. 269 (2018): 33–55.
Chaquèri, Cosroe. *The Russo-Caucasian Origins of the Iranian Left: Social Democracy in Modern Iran.* Richmond: Curzon, 2001.
Chaquèri, Cosroe. *The Soviet Socialist Republic of Iran, 1920–1921: Birth of the Trauma.* Pittsburgh: University of Pittsburgh Press, 1995.
Chernushevich, P. *Sluzhba v mirnoe vremya.* Saint Petersburg, 1900.
Chistiakov, O. I., and T. E. Novitzkaia. *Zakaonodatel'stvo Ekaterini II.* Vol. 2. Moscow: Izd. iuridicheskaia literatura, 2001.
Christian, David. "Silk Roads or Steppe Roads? The Silk Road in World History." *Journal of World History* 11, no. 1 (2000): 1–26.
Chulkov, Mikhaïl Dmitrievich. *Istoricheskoe opisanie rossiĭskoĭ komertsii pri vsekh portakh i granitsakh.* Vol. 2, pt. 2. Moscow: Universitetskaia tipografiia, 1785.
Chuloshnikov, A. N. "Torgovlia Moskovskogo gosudarstva s Sredneĭ Azieĭ v XVI–XVII vekakh." In *Materialy po istorii Uzbekskoĭ, Tadzhikskoĭ i Turkmenskoĭ SSR. Chast' 1: Torgovlia s Moskovskim gosudarstvom i mezhdunarodnoe polozhenie Sredneĭ Azii v XVI–XVII vv.*, edited by A. Samoĭlovich et al., 73–76. Leningrad: Izdatel'stvo AN SSSR, 1932.
Clark, James D. "Constitutionalists and Cossacks: The Constitutional Movement and Russian Intervention in Tabriz, 1907–11." *Iranian Studies* 39, no. 2 (2006): 199–225.
Coakley, Robert W. *The Persian Corridor as a Route for Aid to the USSR.* Washington, DC: Center of Military History, US Army, 1990.
Cole, Juan. "Millenarianism in Modern Iran History." In *Imagining the End: Visions of Apocalypse from the Ancient Middle East to Modern America*, edited by Abbas Amanat and Magnus Bernhardsson, 282–311. London: I. B. Tauris, 2002.

Conterio, Johanna. "'Our Black Sea Coast': The Sovietization of the Black Sea Littoral under Khrushchev and the Problem of Overdevelopment." *Kritika: Explorations in Russian and Eurasian History* 19, no. 2 (2018): 327-61.

Cordier, Bruno de. "Central Asia's Maritime Dimension? The Historical Position and Role of the Aral-Caspian Basin in the Modern Shaping of the Region." *Region: Regional Studies of Russia, Eastern Europe, and Central Asia* 8, no. 2 (2019): 149-72.

Cracraft, James. *The Revolution of Peter the Great*. Cambridge, MA: Harvard University Press, 2003.

Cronin, Stephanie. *The Army and the Creation of the Pahlavi State in Iran, 1910–1926*. London: I. B. Tauris, 1997.

Cronin, Stephanie. "Introduction." In *Iranian-Russian Encounters: Empires and Revolutions since 1800*, edited by Stephanie Cronin, 1-10. London: Routledge, 2013.

Cronin, Stephanie, ed. *Iranian-Russian Encounters: Empires and Revolutions since 1800*. London: Routledge, 2013.

Cronin, Stephanie. "Re-interpreting Modern Iran: Tribe and State in the Twentieth Century." *Iranian Studies* 42, no. 3 (2009): 357-88.

Cronin, Stephanie. *Soldiers, Shahs and Subalterns in Iran: Opposition, Protest and Revolt, 1921–1941*. New York: Palgrave Macmillan, 2014.

Csirkés, Ferenc Peter. "'Chaghatay Oration, Ottoman Eloquence, Qizilbash Rhetoric': Turkic Literature in Ṣafavid Persia." PhD thesis, University of Chicago, 2016.

Curzon, G. "The Transcaspian Railway. By the Hon. G. Curzon, M. P." *Proceedings of the Royal Geographical Society and Monthly Record of Geography*, New Monthly Series 11, no. 5 (May 1889): 273-95.

Dabiri, Moṣṭafā. *Engelestān va Rusiyeh dar 'Irān, 1919–1922: Jelve-hā-ye az solṭe-ye ānhā va talāsh barāyeh rahāyi az ān*. Tehran: Sokhan, 1386/2007.

Dailami, Pezhmann. "The Bolshevik Revolution and the Genesis of Communism in Iran, 1917-1920." *Central Asian Survey* 11, no. 3 (1992): 51-82.

Dailami, Pezhmann. "The Bolsheviks and the Jangali Revolutionary Movement, 1915-1920." *Cahiers du Monde russe et soviétique* 31, no. 1 (1990): 43-59.

Dailami, Pezhmann. "The First Congress of Peoples of the East and the Iranian Soviet Republic of Gilan, 1920-21." In *Reformers and Revolutionaries in Modern Iran: New Perspectives on the Iranian Left*, edited by Stephanie Cronin, 87-106. London: Routledge Curzon, 2004.

Dailami, Pezhmann. "Nationalism and Communism in Iran: The Case of Gilan, 1915-1921." PhD diss., University of Manchester, 1994.

Dailami, Pezhmann. "Pan-Islamism and the Role of the Central Powers." In *Iran and the First World War: Battleground of the Great Powers*, edited by Touraj Atabaki, 137-62. London: I. B. Tauris, 2006.

Daniel, Elton L. "Golestan Treaty." *Encyclopaedia Iranica*, XI/1, 86-90. https://iranicaonline.org/articles/golestan-treaty.

David-Fox, Michael. "The Implications of Transnationalism." *Kritika: Explorations in Russian and Eurasian History* 12, no. 4 (2011), 885-904.

Deepak, B. R. "The Colonial Connections: Indian and Chinese Nationalists in Japan and China." *China Report* 48, no. 147 (2012): 147-70.

Deĭaniĭa Petra Velikago, mudrago preobrazitelĭa Rossii i sobranyĭa iz dostovernykh istochnikov i raspolozhenyĭa po godam. Vol. 2. Moscow, 1788.

Dekmejian, R. Hrair, and Hovann H. Simonian. *Troubled Waters: The Geopolitics of the Caspian Region*. London: I. B. Tauris, 2001.

Demin, Aleksandr Ivanovich, and Vladimir Vladimirovich Trubetskoĭ. "Vnutrennaĭa i vneshnaĭa politika monarkhii Pekhlevi v 1925-1928 gg." In *Iran: Ocherki noveĭsheĭ istorii*, edited by Artëm Zavenovich Arabadzhĭan, 66-76. Moscow: Nauka, 1976.

Demin, Iurii A. "Sovetskaĭa diplomatiĭa i eë rol' v sozdanii i deĭatel'nosti natsional'nogo bloka v Irane (1922-1924)." *Vestnik Volgogradskogo gosudarstvennogo universiteta. Seriĭa 4, Istoriĭa. Regionovedenie. Mezhdunarodnye otnosheniĭa* 22, no. 4 (2017): 67-72, https://doi.org/10.15688/jvolsu4.2017.4.7.

Denikin, Anton. *Ocherki Russkoĭ smuty*. Paris: J. Povolozky & Co. Editeurs, 1921.

Denison, Michael John. "Why Do Sultanistic Regimes Arise and Persist? A Study of Government in the Republic of Turkmenistan, 1992-2006." PhD diss., University of Leeds, 2006.

Deutschmann, Moritz. "Cultures of Statehood, Cultures of Revolution: Caucasian Revolutionaries in the Iranian Constitutional Movement 1906-1911." *Ab Imperio*, 2013, no. 2, 165-90.

Deutschmann, Moritz. *Iran and Russian Imperialism: The Ideal Anarchists, 1800-1914*. New York: Routledge, 2016.

DeWeese, Devin. "Persian and Turkic from Kazan and Tobolsk: Literary Frontiers in Muslim Inner Asia." In *The Persianate World: The Frontiers of a Eurasian Lingua Franca*, edited by Nile Green, 131-55. Oakland: University of California Press, 2019.

Diba, Layla. "The Formation of Modern Iranian Art: From Kamal al Molk to Zenderoudi." In *Iran Modern*, edited by Fereshteh Daftari and Layla Diba, 45-65. New York: Asia Society Museum, 2013.

Diba, Layla. "The Making of a Modern Iranian Artist: Hossain Taherzadeh Behzad and the Illustrated Constitutional Press." Delivered at the International Congress of Iranian Studies, Vienna 2016, the subject of a forthcoming publication.

Diba, Layla, ed. *Royal Persian Paintings: The Qajar Epoch, 1785–1925*. New York: Brooklyn Museum of Art in association with I. B. Tauris, 1998.

Diba, Layla, with Ahmad Ashraf. "Kamal-al-Molk, Mohammad Ḡaffari." *Encyclopaedia Iranica*, XV/4, 417-33. https://iranicaonline.org/articles/kamal-al-molk-mohammad-gaffari.

Dikovitskaia, Margaret. "Central Asia in Early Photographs: Russian Colonial Attitudes and Visual Culture." In "Empire, Islam and Politics in Central Asia," edited by Uyama Tomohiko, special issue, *Slavic Eurasian Studies* 14 (2007): 104-8.

Diplomatic and Consular Reports, Annual Series. "No. 1607, Persia: Report on the Trade and Commerce of Khorasan for the Financial Year 1894-95." London: H. M. Stationery Office, 1895.

Dmitriev, G. L. *Indian Revolutionaries in Central Asia*. Delhi: Hope Greenwich Millenium Press, 2002.
Dowbakhshari, Nāṣer ʿAẓimi. *Revāyat-e now az jonbesh va enqelāb-e Jangal*. Tehran: Zharf, 1394/2015.
Dunsterville, Lionel. *The Adventures of Dunsterforce*. London: Edward Arnold, 1920.
Dunsterville, Lionel. "From Baghdad to the Caspian, 1918." *Geographical Journal* 57, no. 3 (1921): 153–64.
Dunsterville, Lionel. *More Yarns by "Stalky."* London: Stalky & Co., 1931.
Dunsterville, Lionel. *Stalky's Reminiscences*. London: Jonathan Cape, 1928.
Ebrāhim, Mirzā (last name unknown). *Safarnāmeh-ye Astarābād va Māzandarān va Gilān*. Edited by Masʿud Golzāri. Tehran: Enteshārāt-e Bonyād-e Farhang-e Irān, 1977.
Eden, Jeff. *Slavery and Empire in Central Asia*. Cambridge: Cambridge University Press, 2018.
Edgar, Adrienne. *Tribal Nation: The Making of Soviet Turkmenistan*. Princeton, NJ: Princeton University Press, 2006.
Edmonds, C. J. *East and West of Zagros: Travel, War and Politics in Persia and Iraq, 1913–1921*. Edited by Yann Richard. Leiden: Brill, 2010.
Edmonds, C. J. *Kurds, Turks and Arabs: Politics, Travel and Research in North-Eastern Iraq, 1919–1925*. London: Oxford University Press, 1957.
Efendi, Tanburi Arutin. *Tahmas Kulu Han'ın Tevarihi*. Edited by Esat Uras. Ankara: Türk Tarih Kurumu Basımevi, 1942.
Ekhtiar, Maryam. "An Encounter with the Russian Czar: The Image of Peter the Great in Early Qajar Historical Writings." *Iranian Studies* 29, no. 1–2 (1996): 57–70.
Elie, Marc, and Carole Ferret. "Verte, la steppe? Agriculture et environnement en Asie Centrale." *Études rurales*, no. 200 (2017): 64–79.
Ellis, Charles. "Russian Calendar (988–1917)." In *The Literary Encyclopedia*, vol. 2.2.1.00, *Slavic and Russian Writing and Culture: Old, Medieval and Tsarist, 700–1917*. First published September 25, 2008. https://www.litencyc.com/php/stopics.php?rec=true&UID=5547.
Elton, John, and Thomas Woodroofe. "A Plain Chart of the Caspian Sea" (1745). SOAS University of London. Accessed January 10, 2021. https://digital.soas.ac.uk/LOAC000204/00001/citation.
Emin, Joseph. *Life and Adventures of Joseph Emin, 1726–1809, Written by Himself*. Calcutta: Baptist Mission Press, 1918.
Encyclopaedia Iranica and Reza Rezazadeh Langaroudi. "Gilan vi. History in the 18th Century." *Encyclopaedia Iranica*, X/6, 642–45. https://iranicaonline.org/articles/gilan-vi.
Engerman, David C., et al., eds. *Staging Growth, Modernization, Development, and the Global Cold War*. Amherst: University of Massachusetts Press, 2003.
Entner, Marvin. *Russo-Persian Commercial Relations, 1828–1914*. Gainesville: University of Florida Press, 1965.
Ereshko, E. V. "Rossiĭskoe zakonodatel'stvo kontsa XIX–nachala XX v.v. bor'be c kontrabandoĭ." *Istoricheskaiā i sotsial'no-obrazovatel'naiā misl'*, no. 3 (2011): 111–19.

Ershādi, Minā Zahir Nejād, ed. *Gozideh-ye asnād-e daryā-ye khazar va manāṭeq-e shomāli-e Irān dar Jang-e Jahāni-e Dovvom*. Tehran: Daftar-e motāle'āt-e siyāsi va bayn-al-melali, 1375/1997.
Esayi Hasan Jalaleants', Katʻoghikos. *A Brief History of the Aghuank՝ Region (Patmut՝iwn Hamarot Aghuanitsʻ Erkri): A History of Karabagh and Ganje from 1702–1723*. Translated by George A. Bournoutian. Costa Mesa: Mazda, 2009.
Ettehadieh, Mansour. "Constitutional Revolution iv. Aftermath." *Encyclopaedia Iranica*, VI/2, 193–99. https://iranicaonline.org/articles/constitutional-revolution-iv.
Ettehadieh, Mansour. "Constitutional Revolution v. Political Parties of the Constitutional Period." *Encyclopaedia Iranica*, VI/2, 199–202. https://iranicaonline.org/articles/constitutional-revolution-v.
Ezov', G. A. *Nachalo snoshenii Echmiadzinskago patriarshago prestola s russkim pravitelstvom*. Tiflis: Martirosyants, 1901.
Ezov', G. A. *Snosheniia Petra Velikago s armianskim narodom*. St. Petersburg: Imperatorskaia Akademiia Nauk, 1898.
Fakhrā'i, Ebrāhim. *Sardār-e Jangal*. Tehran: Jāvidān Publishers, 1997.
Fatemi, Nasrollah Saifpour. *Diplomatic History of Persia, 1917–1923: Anglo-Russian Power-Politics in Iran*. New York: Moore, 1952.
Fawcett, Louise. *Iran and the Cold War: The Azerbaijan Crisis of 1946*. Cambridge: Cambridge University Press, 1992.
Fawcett, Louise. "Revisiting the Iranian Crisis of 1946: How Much More Do We Know?" *Iranian Studies* 47, no. 3 (2014): 379–99.
Fel', Sergei F. *Kartografiia Rossii XVIII veka*. Moscow: Izdatel'stvo Geodezicheskoĭ Literatury, 1960.
Ferdowsi, A. *The Shahnameh*. General ed. E. Yarshater. Vol. 2. Edited by J. Khaleqi-Motlaq. New York: Persian Heritage Foundation, 1366/1987.
Ferdowsi, A. *Shahnameh: The Persian Book of Kings*. Translated by Dick Davis. New York: Penguin Classics, 2007.
Ferguson-Cradler, Gregory. "Forecasting Fisheries: Prediction and the Planned Economy in the Interwar Soviet Union." *Cahiers du Monde russe* 58, no. 4 (2017): 615–38.
Ferrier, R. W. "The Terms and Conditions under which English Trade Was Transacted with Safavid Persia." *Bulletin of the School of Oriental and African Studies* 49, no. 1 (1986): 48–66.
Ferrier, Ronald. "Trade from the Mid-14th Century to the End of the Safavid Period." In *The Cambridge History of Iran*, vol. 6, *The Timurid and Safavid Periods*, edited by Peter Jackson and Laurence Lockhart, 412–490. Cambridge: Cambridge University Press, 1986.
Finley, Carmel. *All the Boats on the Ocean: How Government Subsidies Led to Global Overfishing*. Chicago: University of Chicago Press, 2017.
Firuz, Eskandar. *Khāṭerāt-e Eskandar Firuz*. Bethesda: Ibex Publishers, 2012.
Fitzpatrick, Sheila. *The Russian Revolution*. Oxford: Oxford University Press, 2008.
Fleury, Antoine. *La Pénétration Allemande au Moyen-Orient 1919–1939: Le cas de la Turquie, de l'Iran et de l'Afghanistan*. Geneva: Institut Universitaire des Hautes Etudes Internationales; Leiden: Sijthoff, 1977.

Floor, Willem. "Edmonds C. J., *East and West of Zagros: Travel, War and Politics in Persia and Iraq 1913-1921*, ed. with intro. by Yann Richard [review]," *Bulletin critique des Annales islamologiques* 28 (2013), https://www.ifao.egnet.net/bcai/28/58.

Floor, Willem. "The Iranian Navy in the [Persian] Gulf during the Eighteenth Century." *Iranian Studies* 20, no. 1 (1987): 31-53.

Floor, Willem. "The Persian Economy in the Eighteenth Century: A Dismal Record." In *Crisis, Collapse, Militarism & Civil War: The History and Historiography of 18th Century Iran*, edited by Michael Axworthy, 125-50. Oxford: Oxford University Press, 2018.

Floor, Willem. *The Persian Textile Industry in Historical Perspective, 1500-1925*. Paris: Societé de l'Histoire de l'Orient, L'Harmattan, 1999.

Floor, Willem, and Mansoureh Ettehadieh. "Concessions ii. In the Qajar Period." *Encyclopaedia Iranica*, VI/2, 119-22. https://iranicaonline.org/articles/concessions#pt2.

Foran, J. "The Long Fall of the Safavid Dynasty: Moving beyond the Standard Views." *International Journal of Middle East Studies* 24, no. 2 (1992): 281-304.

Forestier-Peyrat, Etienne. "Fighting Locusts Together: Pest Control and the Birth of Soviet Development Aid, 1920-1939." *Global Environment* 7, no. 2 (2014): 536-71.

Forestier-Peyrat, Etienne. "Red Passage to Iran: The Baku Trade Fair and the Unmaking of the Azerbaijani Borderland (1922-1930)." *Ab Imperio*, no. 4 (2013): 79-112.

Fowkes, Ben, and Bülent Gökay. "Unholy Alliance: Muslims and Communists—An Introduction." *Journal of Communist Studies and Transition Politics* 25, no. 1 (2009): 1-31.

Fragner, Bert. "Ardabil zwischen Sultan und Schah: Zehen urkunden Schah Tahmāsps II." *Turcica* 6 (1975): 177-225.

Fraser, James B. *Travels and Adventures in the Persian Provinces*. London: Longman, Rees, Orme, Brown, and Green, 1826.

Fraser, James B. *A Winter's Journey (Tâtar), from Constantinople to Tehran*. London: R. Bentley, 1838.

Fraser, James Baillie. *An Historical and Descriptive Account of Persia*. Edinburgh: Oliver & Boyd, Tweeddale Court; London: Simpkin & Marshall, 1834.

Fursov, V. N., and V. N. Testov. "Vozvedenie i funktsionirovanie transkaspiĭskoĭ magistrali v 80-x—nachale 90-x gg. XIX V." *Nauch'ie vedomosti BelGU ser. istoriiā, politologiiā. ėkonomika, informatika* 15, no. 27 (2013): 113-18.

[Gablits, Karl Ivanovich]. *Istoricheskiĭ zhurnal byvshikh v 1781 i 1782 godakh na Kaspiĭskom more Rossiiskoĭ ėskadry pod komandoĭu flota kapitana vtorago ranga Grafa Voĭnovicha*. Moscow: Tipografīia S. Selivanovskogo, 1809.

Gammer, Moshe, ed. *The Caspian Region*. Vol. 1, *A Re-emerging Region*. London: Routledge, 2004.

Gammer, Moshe, ed. *The Caspian Region*. Vol. 2, *The Caucasus*. London: Routledge, 2004.

Gasanly, Dzhamil'. *Sovetskaiā politika po rasshireniiu iūzhnykh granits: Stalin i Azerbaĭdzhanskaiā karta v bor'be za zeft' (1939-45)*. Moscow: ROSSPEN, 2017.

BIBLIOGRAPHY

Gasratian, Manvel. *Kurdy Turtsii v noveĭshee vremia.* Erevan: Aĭastan, 1990.
Geifman, Anna. *Thou Shalt Kill: Revolutionary Terrorism in Russia: 1894–1917.* Princeton, NJ: Princeton University Press, 1993.
Gelibolulu Mustafa Ali ve Künhü'l-ahbar'ında II. Selim, III. Murat ve III. Mehmet devirleri. Edited by Faris Çerçi. Kayseri: Erciyes Üniversitesi Yayınları, 2000.
Gelibolulu Mustafa ʿÂli. *Nusret-nâme.* Edited by Mustafa Eravcı. Ankara: Türk Tarih Kurumu, 2014.
General Map of the Russian Empire, Compiled to the Best of His Abilities by Ivan Kirilov, Ober-secretary to the Governing Senate. St. Petersburg, 1745.
Genis, Vladimir. *Krasnaia Persiia: Bol'sheviki v Giliane, 1920–1921. Dokumental'naia khronika.* Moscow: MNPI, 2000.
Genis, Vladimir. "Krasnyĭ shantazh." *Rodina*, no. 5 (2001): 107–11.
Genis, Vladimir. *Vitse—Konsul Vvedenskiĭ.* Moscow: MYSL', 2003.
Genis, Vladimir L. "Les Bolcheviks au Guilan: La chute du gouvernement de Koutchek Khan (Juin-Juillet 1920)." *Cahiers du Monde russe* 40, no. 3 (1999): 459–96.
Gestwa, Klaus. "Das Besitzergreifen von Natur in Gesellschaft im Stalinismus: Enthusiastischer Umgestaltungswille und Katastrophischer Fortschritt." *Saeculum* 56, no. 1 (2005): 105–38.
Geyer, Dietrich. *Russian Imperialism: The Interaction of Domestic and Foreign Policy, 1860–1914.* Oxford: Berg, 1987.
Girault, René. "Les relations Franco-Soviétiques après Septembre 1939." *Cahiers du Monde russe et soviétique* 17, no. 1 (1976): 27–42.
Giul', K. K. *Kaspiĭskoe More.* Baku: Azerbaĭdzhanskoe Gosudarstvennoe Izdatel'stvo Neftianoĭ i Nauchno-Technicheskoĭ Literatury, 1956.
Gledhill, Kevin. "The Caspian State: Regional Autonomy, International Trade, and the Rise of Qājār Iran, 1722–1797." PhD diss., Yale University, 2020.
Gledhill, Kevin. "The 'Persian State' and the Safavid Inheritance: Views from the Caspian, 1722–1781." In *The Idea of Iran*, vol. 11, *Transition to a New World Order*, edited by Charles Melville, 57–79. London: Bloomsbury, 2022.
Glinka, S., ed. *Sobranie aktov otnoshiashchikhsia k obozrniiu istorii armianskogo naroda.* Vol. 2. Moscow: Lazarian, 1838.
Gmelin, Samuel Gottlieb. *Travels through Northern Persia, 1770–1774.* Translated by Willem Floor. Washington: Mage, 2007.
Gobineau, Arthur comte de. *Les religions et les philosophies dans l'Asie centrale.* Paris: Didier et cie, 1866.
Gocheleishvili, Iago. "Georgian Sources on the Iranian Constitutional Revolution, 1905–1911: Sergo Gamdlishvili's Memoirs of the Gilan Resistance." In *Iranian-Russian Encounters: Empires and Revolutions since 1800*, edited by Stephanie Cronin, 207–23. New York: Routledge, 2013.
Goebel, Michael. "Geopolitics, Transnational Solidarity or Diaspora Nationalism? The Global Career of M.N. Roy, 1915–1930." *European Review of History* 21, no. 4 (2014): 485–99.
Goff, Krista. *Nested Nationalism: Making and Unmaking Nations in the Soviet Caucasus.* Ithaca, NY: Cornell University Press, 2021.
Gökbilgin, Tayyib. "L'expédition ottomane contre Astrakhan en 1569." *Cahiers du monde russe et soviétique* 11, no. 1 (1970): 118–23.

Gol'dberg, N. M. "Predislovie." In *Russko-indiĭskie otnosheniia v XVII v. Sbornik dokumentov*, edited by K. A. Antonova et al., 5–22. Moscow: Izdatel'stvo Vostochnoĭ Literatury, 1958.

Gol'denberg, Leonid A. *Kartozhanin-Sibirskiĭ gubernator: Zhiznʻ i trudy F.I. Soĭmonova*. Magadan: Magadanskoe Knizhnoe Izdatel'stvo, 1979.

Goldner, Loren. "'Socialism in One Country' before Stalin, and the Origins of Reactionary 'Anti-Imperialism': The Case of Turkey, 1917–1925." *Critique* 38, no. 4 (2010): 631–61.

Goncharov, Vladimir G. *F.I. Soĭmonov—pervyĭ russkiĭ gidrograf*. Moscow: Gosudarstvennoe Izdatel'stvo Geograficheskoĭ Literatury, 1954.

Gorokhov, I. M., et al. *Documenty vneshneĭ politiki SSSR*. Vol. 10. Moscow: Gospolitizdat, 1965.

Graham, Loren R. *Science in Russia and the Soviet Union: A Short History*. Cambridge: Cambridge University Press, 1993.

Granat, M. "Organizatsiia torgovli SSSR s Vostokom." In *Torgovlia SSSR s Vostokom (sbornik stateĭ i materialov)*, edited by V. Ksandrova et al. Moscow: AO "Promizdat," 1927.

Green, Nile. "Introduction: The Frontiers of the Persianate World (ca. 800–1900)." In *The Persianate World: The Frontiers of a Eurasian Lingua Franca*, edited by Nile Green, 1–72. Oakland: California University Press, 2019.

Green, Nile. "Introduction: Writing Travel, and the Global History in Central Asia." In *Writing Travel in Central Asian History*, edited by Nile Green, 1–40. Bloomington: Indiana University Press, 2014.

Green, Nile. *The Love of Strangers: What Six Muslim Students Learned in Jane Austen's London*. Princeton, NJ: Princeton University Press, 2015.

Greenwood, Phoebe. "Landmark Caspian Sea Deal Signed by Five Coastal Nations." *The Guardian*, August 12, 2018. https://www.theguardian.com/world/2018/aug/12/landmark-caspian-sea-deal-signed-among-five-coastal-nations.

Gupta, Sobhanlal D. *Comintern and the Destiny of Communism in India, 1919–1943: Dialectics of Real and Possible History*. Kolkata: Seribaan, 2006.

Gusarova, Elena Vasil'evna. *Astrakhanskie nakhodki: Istoriia, arckitektura, gradostroitel'stvo Astrakhani XVI–XVIII vv. Po dokumentam iz sobranii Peterburga*. St. Petersburg: Nestor-Istoriia, 2009.

Haghayeghi, Mehrdad. "The Coming of Conflict to the Caspian Sea." *Problems of Post-Communism* 50, no. 3 (2003): 32–41.

Haithcox, John P. *Communism and Nationalism in India: M. N. Roy and Comintern Policy, 1920–1939*. Princeton, NJ: Princeton University Press, 1971.

Hakimian, Hassan. "Wage Labor and Migration: Persian Workers in Southern Russia, 1880–1914." *International Journal of Middle East Studies* 17, no. 4 (1985): 443–62.

Hambly, Gavin. "Āghā Muḥammad Khān and the Establishment of the Qājār Dynasty." In *Cambridge History of Iran*, vol. 7, *From Nader Shah to the Islamic Republic*, edited by Peter Avery, Gavin Hambly, and Charles Melville, 104–43. Cambridge: Cambridge University Press, 1991.

Hamed-Troyansky, Vladimir. *Empire of Refugees: North Caucasian Muslims and the Late Ottoman State*. Stanford, CA: Stanford University Press, 2024.

Hanway, Jonas. *An Historical Account of the British Trade over the Caspian Sea*. London: Dodsley, 1753.
Hasanli, Jamil. *The Sovietization of Azerbaijan: The South Caucasus in the Triangle of Russia, Turkey, and Iran, 1920–1922*. Salt Lake City: University of Utah Press, 2019.
Hausmann, Guido. *Mütterchen Wolga: Ein Fluss als Erinnerungsort vom 16. bis ins frühe 20. Jahrhundert*. Frankfurt: Campus, 2009.
Hausmann, Guido. "Die Unterwerfung der Natur als imperiale Veranstaltung: Bau und Eröffnung des Ladoga-Kanals in Russland im frühen 18. Jahrhundert." *Frühneuzeit-Info*, no. 2 (2008): 59–72.
Hedāyat, Reżā-Qoli Khān. *Tārikh-e Rowżat al-Ṣafā-ye Nāṣeri*. Vol. 9, part 1. Edited by Jamshid Kiānfar. Tehran: Esāṭir, 1380/2002–3.
Herzfeld, F. *The Persian Empire: Studies in Geography and Ethnography of the Ancient Near East*. Wiesbaden: F. Steiner, 1968.
Herzig, Edmund. "The Armenian Merchants of New Julfa, Isfahan: A Study in Pre-modern Asian Trade." PhD diss., University of Oxford, 1991.
Herzig, Edmund. "Regionalism, Iran and Central Asia." *International Affairs* 80, no. 3 (2004): 503–17.
Həsənli, Cəmil. *İkinci Dünya Müharibəsi Illərində Azərbaycan Hərbi, Siyasi və Diplomatik Münasibətlərində (1939–1945)*. Baku: Yazıçı, 2015.
Həsənov, Müsəllim. *Azərbaycanda Gəmiçilik: Sənədli Tarix*. Baku: Azərbaycan Xəzər Dəniz Gəmiçiliyi, 2018.
Hess, M. R. "Nəsimi, İmadəddin. *Encyclopaedia of Islam*, 3rd edition. https://referenceworks.brill.com/display/entries/EI3O/COM-40738.xml.
Higgins, Patricia. "Minority-State Relations in Contemporary Iran." *Iranian Studies* 17, no. 1 (1984): 37–71.
Hinz, Walter. *Irans Aufstieg zum Nationalstaat im Fünfzehnten Jahrhundert*. Berlin: Walter de Gruyter, 1936.
Hirschfeld, Yair P. *Deutschland und Iran im Spielfeld der Mächte: Internationale Beziehungen unter Reza Schah, 1921–1941*. Dusseldorf: Droste Verlag, 1980.
Hirst, Samuel J. "Transnational Anti-Imperialism and the National Forces: Soviet Diplomacy and Turkey, 1920–23." *Comparative Studies of South Asia, Africa and the Middle East* 33, no. 2 (2013): 214–26.
Hobsbawm, E. J. *Primitive Rebels*. New York: W. W. Norton, 1959.
Hodgson, Marshall G. S. *The Venture of Islam: The Expansion of Islam in the Middle Periods*. Vol. 2. Chicago: University of Chicago Press, 1974.
Högselius, Per. *Red Gas: Russia and the Origins of European Energy Dependence*. Basingstoke: Palgrave Macmillan, 2013.
Hokanson, Katya. *Writing at Russia's Border*. Toronto: University of Toronto Press, 2008.
Holquist, Peter. *Making War, Forging Revolution: Russia's Continuum of Crisis, 1914–1921*. Cambridge, MA: Harvard University Press, 2002.
Homann, Johann Baptist. *Atlas Major*. Vol. 47, Tafel 19, *Geographica nova ex Oriente gratiosissima, duabus tabulis specialissimis contenta, quarum una mare Caspium, altera Kantzadalium seu Terram Jedso curiose exhibet*.

Hopkirk, Peter. *The Great Game: On Secret Service in High Asia.* London: Kodansha, 1994.
Hopkirk, Peter. *On Secret Service East of Constantinople: The Plot to Bring down the British Empire.* Oxford: Oxford University Press, 1994.
Hopkirk, Peter. *Setting the East Ablaze: Lenin's Dream of an Empire in Asia.* London: Kodansha International, 1984.
Horden, Peregrine, and Nicholas Purcell. *The Corrupting Sea: A Study of Mediterranean History.* Oxford: Blackwell, 2000.
Hughes, Lindsey. *Russia in the Age of Peter the Great.* New Haven, CT: Yale University Press, 1998.
Hurewitz, J. C. *Diplomacy in the Near and Middle East: A Documentary Record.* Princeton, NJ: Van Nostrand, 1956.
Husain, Iqbal. "Barakatullah—a Half-Forgotten Revolutionary." *Proceedings of the Indian History Congress* 66 (2005-2006): 1061-72.
Igolkin, A. *Sovetskaia neftianaia politika v 1940-1950 godakh.* Moscow: Institut Rossiĭskoĭ Istorii, 2009.
İnalcık, Halil. "The Origin of the Ottoman-Russian Rivalry and the Don-Volga Canal (1569)." *Annales de l'Universite d'Ankara* 1 (1947): 47-110.
İnalcık, Halil. "Ottoman Methods of Conquest." *Studia Islamica* 2 (1954): 103-29.
İnalcık, Halil. "The Question of the Closing of the Black Sea under the Ottomans." Αρχείον Πόντου 35 (1979): 74-110.
İnalcık, Halil. *Sources and Studies on the Ottoman Black Sea.* Vol. 1, *The Customs Register of Caffa, 1487-1490.* Cambridge, MA: Harvard University Press, 1996.
Irons, William. "Nomadism as a Political Adaptation: The Case of the Yomut Turkmen." In "Uses of Ethnohistory in Ethnographic Analysis," special issue, *American Ethnologist* 1, no. 4 (1974): 635-58.
Iskhanov, Anton. "A.N. Samoilovich (1880-1938) i ego polevye informanty: Konstruirovanie Turkmenskoĭ kul'turnoĭ identichnosti." PhD diss., Higher School of Economics, Moscow, 2021.
Issawi, Charles Philip. *The Economic History of Iran, 1800-1914.* Chicago: University of Chicago Press, 1971.
Iukht, A. I. "Russko-Armianskaia kompaniia 'Persidskogo torga' v seredine XVIII veka." *Patma-banasirakan handes* 2/3 (1983): 224-39.
Iukht, A. I. "Torgovlia Rossii so stranami vostoka vo vtoroĭ polovine XVIII v. i armianskoe kupechestvo." *Istoriko-filologicheskiĭ zhurnal Akademii Nauka Armianskoĭ SSR*, no. 2 (1981): 87-106.
Iukht, A. I. "Uchastie rossiĭskogo kupechestva v torgovle Rossii s Zakavkaz'em i Iranom v 1725-1750, gg." In *Torgovlia i predprinimatel'stvo v feodal'noĭ Rossii*, edited by L. A. Timoshina and I. A. Tikhoniuk, 230-51. Moscow: Arkheograficheskiĭ tsentr, 1994.
Iuzefovich, T., ed. *Dogovory Rossii s" Vostokom": Politicheskie i torgovye.* St. Petersburg: Baksta, 1869.
Ivanov, Mikhail Sergeevich. *Noveĭshaia istoriia Irana.* Moscow: Mysl', 1965.
Ivanov, Mikhail Sergeevich, and Viacheslav Zaĭtsev, eds. *Novaia istoriia Irana.* Moscow: Nauka, 1988.

Jacobson, Jon. "Essay and Reflection: On the Historiography of Soviet Foreign Relations in the 1920s." *International History Review* 18, no. 2 (1996): 336–57.

Jāhān Ārā, Nāser. *Tārikh-e ravābeṭ-e tejāri-ye Irān va Showravi az enqelab-e oktobr tā soquṭ-e Reżā shāh*. Amol: Vāreshvā, 1390/2011.

Jahānbāni, Amanollāh. *Marzhā-ye Irān va Showravi*. Tehran: Chāpkhāne-ye melli, 1336/1957.

Jaktāji, Moḥammad Puraḥmad, ed. *Gilān-nāmeh: Majmu'-eh-ye maqālāt-e Gilānshenāsi*. Vol. 3. Rasht: Enteshārāt-e tā'ati, 1369/1990.

Javādi, Roqayya. "Sāzmān-e Jahāngardi va Ta'asir-e ān bar Tosʻe-ye Gardeshgari dar dowreh-ye Pahlavi-e dovvom." *Ganjineh-ye asnād* 23, no. 1 (Spring 1392/2013): 40–61.

Josephson, Paul, et al. *An Environmental History of Russia*. Cambridge: Cambridge University Press, 2013.

Kaempfer, Engelbert. *Kritische Ausgabe in Einzelbänden*. Edited by Detlef Haberland. Vol. 2, *Briefe 1683–1715*. Munich: Iudicium, 2001.

Kaempfer, Engelbert. *Rußlandtagebuch 1683*. Edited by Michael Schippan. Munich: Iudicium Verlag, 2003.

Kalinovsky, Artemy M. *Laboratory of Socialist Development: Cold War Politics and Decolonization in Soviet Tajikistan*. Ithaca, NY: Cornell University Press, 2018.

Kandiyoti, Rafael. "What Price Access to the Open Seas? The Geopolitics of Oil and Gas Transmission from the Trans-Caspian Republics." *Central Asian Survey* 27, no. 1 (2008): 75–93.

Kappeler, Andreas. *The Russian Empire: A Multiethnic History*. Translated by Alfred Clayton. Harlow: Longman, 2001.

Kappeler, Andreas. *Russland als Vielvölkerreich: Entstehung, Geschichte, Zerfall*. Munich: Beck Verlag, 1992.

Kapur, Harish. *Soviet Russia and Asia 1917–1927: A Study of Soviet Policy towards Turkey, Iran and Afghanistan*. Geneva: Geneva Graduate Institute of International Studies, 1966.

Karazin, N. N. "Na puti v Indiĭu." *Niva* 38 (1888): 943; *Niva* 39 (1888): 967; *Niva* 40 (1888): 988.

Karazin, Nikolaĭ. *Dvunogiĭ volk*. Translated by Boris Lanin as *The Two-legged Wolf: A Romance*. University of California Libraries, 1894.

Karazin, Nikolaĭ. *Na dalekikh okrainakh*. Translated by Anthony W. Sariti as *In the Distant Confines*. Authorhouse, 2007.

Karazin, Nikolaĭ. "Samarskaīa uchënaīa ekspeditsiīa." *Vsemirnaīa illīustratsīa* 576 (1880): 75.

Kardanova, N. B. "Paleograficheskoe oformlenie tsarskikh poslaniĭ k dozham Venetsii." *Izvestiīa Volgogradskogo gosudarstvennogo pedagogicheskogo universiteta* 3 (2012): 53–54.

Karimi, Pamela. "Tourism and Urbanism in Iran: Top-Down and Ad-Hoc Developments in the Caspian Region." In *Routledge Handbook on Middle East Cities*, edited by Haim Yacobi and Mansour Nasara, 177–95. London: Routledge, 2020.

Kāshāni, Ḥāji Mirzā Jāni. *Noqṭat al-Kāf.* Leiden: Brill, 1910.
Katouzian, Homa. "The Revolt of Shaykh Muḥammad Khiyabani." *Iran* 37 (1999): 155–72.
Katouzian, Homa. *State and Society in Iran: The Eclipse of the Qajars and the Emergence of the Pahlavis.* London: I. B. Tauris, 2000.
Kāzembiki, Moḥammad ʿAli. *Daryā-ye Khazar va qodrathā-ye bozorg: Imperiyālizm-e Britāniyā (1335–1338 h.q.).* Tehran: Markaz-e asnād va tārikh-e diplomasi, 1384/2005.
Kazemzadeh, Firuz. "Iranian Relations with Russia and the Soviet Union, to 1921." in *The Cambridge History of Iran*, vol. 7, *From Nader Shah to the Islamic Republic*, edited by Peter Avery, Gavin Hambly, and Charles Melville, 314–49. Cambridge: Cambridge University Press, 1991.
Kazemzadeh, Firuz. *Russia and Britain in Persia, 1865–1914: A Study in Imperialism.* New Haven, CT: Yale University Press, 1968.
Kazemzadeh, Firuz. "Russian Penetration of the Caucasus." In *Russian Imperialism from Ivan the Great to the Revolution*, edited by T. Hunczak, 239–63. New Brunswick: Rutgers University Press, 1974.
Kazemzadeh, Firuz. *The Struggle for Transcaucasia, 1917–1921.* New York: Philosophical Library, 1951.
Keddie, Nikki N. *Roots of Revolution: An Interpretive History of Modern Iran.* New Haven, CT: Yale University Press, 2006.
Keikāvusi, Nemʾatollāh. *Promenade in the Picture Gallery: An Album of Iranian and European Paintings from the Sadābād Museum of Fine Arts, Tehrān.* Tehran: Negar Books, 1992.
Kellner-Heinkele, Barbara. "St. Petersburg and the Steppe People: Diplomatic Correspondences of the 18th Century from the Arkhiv Vneshnej Politiki Rossijskoj Imperii in Moscow." In *Proceedings of the 38th Permanent International Altaistic Conference (PIAC). Kawasaki, Japan August 7–12, 1995*, edited by Giovanni Stary, 219–36. Wiesbaden: Harrassowitz Verlag, 1995.
Kelly, Saul. "'A Man on a Watchtower': Malleson and the British Military Mission to Turkistan, 1918–20." *Middle Eastern Studies* 58, no. 3 (2022): 341–53.
Kelly, Sean. "How Far West? Lord Curzon's Transcaucasian (Mis)Adventure and the Defence of British India, 1918–23." *International History Review* 35, no. 2 (2013): 274–93.
Kemper, Michael. "Red Orientalism: Mikhail Pavlovich and Marxist Oriental Studies in Early Soviet Russia." In "A Muslim Interwar Soviet Union," special issue, *Die Welt des Islams* 50, no. 3-4 (2010): 435–76.
Khachatrīan, A [H] N., ed. *Armīanskoe voĭsko v XVIII veke.* Yerevan: Akademiīa Nauk Armīanskoĭ SSR, 1968.
Khān, Moḥammad Ḥasan. *Tārikh-e Montʿaẓam Nāṣeri.* Vol. 3. Boston: Harvard University, 1990.
Khatib-Shahidi, Rashid. *German Foreign Policy towards Iran before World War II: Political Relations, Economic Influence and the National Bank of Persia.* London: I. B. Tauris, 2013.

Khodarkovsky, Michael. *Where Two Worlds Met: The Russian State and the Kalmyk Nomads, 1600–1771.* Ithaca, NY: Cornell University Press, 1992.
Khosravi, Mohammad 'Ali Malek. *Eqlim-e Nur.* Tehran: Mo'asseseh-ye Maṭbu'āt-e 'Amri, 1958.
Khosrawshāhi, Hādi. *Nehżat-e Āzādestān va shahid Shaykh Moḥammad Khiyābāni.* Tehran: Markaz-e Asnād-e Enqelāb-e Eslāmī, 2011.
Khuzāni Esfahāni, Fażli Beg. *A Chronicle of the Reign of Shah Abbas.* Edited by K. Ghereghlou. 2 vols. Cambridge: Gibb Memorial Trust, 2015.
Kireev, Fedor. "Osetinskiĭ fenomen v istorii Terskogo kazach'ego voĭska." *Dar'ial* 5 (2003): 270–84.
Kirpichnikov, Anatoli N. *Rossiia XVII veka v risunkakh i opisaniiakh gollandskogo puteshestvennika Nikolasa Vitsena.* St. Petersburg, 1995.
Kırzıoğlu, Fahrettin. *Osmanlıların Kafkas ellerini fethi (1451–1590).* Ankara: Sevinç Matbaası, 1976.
Kivelson, Valerie. *Cartographies of Tsardom: The Land and Its Meanings in Seventeenth-Century Russia.* Ithaca, NY: Cornell University Press, 2006.
Kivelson, Valerie A., and Ronald G. Suny. *Russia's Empires.* Oxford: Oxford University Press, 2017.
Klaproth, Julius von. *Travels in the Caucasus and Georgia Performed in the Years 1807 and 1808.* London, 1814.
Kluchevsky, V. O. *A History of Russia.* Vol. 2. New York, 1912.
Kniazhetskaia, E. A. "Petr I—organizator issledovanii Kaspiĭskogo moria." In *Voprosy geografii Petrovskogo vremeni*, edited by M. I. Belova, 24–38. Leningrad, 1975.
Kniazhetskaia, E. A. *Sud'ba odnoĭ karty.* Moscow, 1964.
Kobenko, Dmitriĭ. *Nakaz TSaria Alekseia Mikhaĭlovicha Makhmetu Iusupu Kasymovu, poslannomu v 1675 godu k Velikomu Mogolu Aurenzebu.* St. Petersburg: Tipografiia V. Kirshbauma, 1884.
Kocheshkov, Alekseĭ. "Severoiranskaia neft': Iz istorii diplomaticheskikh bataliĭ." In "Russian Oil in the XXI Century," special issue, *Mezhdunarodnaia zhizn'* 14 (2010): 149–60.
Kollmann, Nancy S. "Tracking the Travels of Adam Olearius." In *Word and Image in Russian History: Essays in Honor of Gary Marker*, edited by Maria Di Salvo, Daniel H. Kaiser, and Valerie A. Kivelson, 133–46. Boston: Academic Studies Press, 2015. https://doi.org/10.2307/j.ctt1zxsht1.15.
Kollmann, Nancy Shields. *The Russian Empire 1450–1801.* Oxford: Oxford University Press, 2017.
Kołodzieczyk, Dariusz. *The Crimean Khanate and Poland-Lithuania: International Diplomacy on the European Periphery (15th–18th Century).* Leiden: Brill, 2011.
Kołodzieczyk, Dariusz. "Tibet in the Crimea? Polish Embassy to the Kalmyks of 1653 and a Project of Anti-Muslim Alliance." *Acta Poloniae Historica* 114 (2016): 231–53.
Kopelevich, Iuliia. *Iogan Anton Gil'denshtedt.* St. Petersburg, 1997.
Koriche, Sifan A., Joy S. Singarayer, and Hannah L. Cloke. "The Fate of the Caspian Sea under Projected Climate Change and Water Extraction during

the 21st Century." *Environmental Research Letters* 16 (2021): 094024. https://doi.org/10.1088/1748-9326/ac1af5.

Kotoshikhin, Grigory. *O Rossii v tsarstvovanie Aleksiia Mikhaĭlovicha*. St. Petersburg: Izdanie Arkheograficheskoĭ Komissii, 1884.

Krusinski, T. *The History of the Late Revolutions of Persia*. Vol. 1. London: J. Pemberton, 1733.

Kukanova, N. G. *Ocherki po istorii Russko-iranskikh torgovykh otnosheniĭ v XVII–pervoĭ polovine XIX veka: Po materialam russkikh arkhivov*. Saransk: Mordovskoe knizhnoe izdatel'stvo, 1977.

Kukanova, N. G. *Torgovo-ėkonomicheskie otnosheniia Rossii i Irana v period pozdnego feodalizma*. Saransk: Izdatel'stvo Mordovskogo Universiteta, 1994.

Kulagina, Liudmila. *Rossiia i Iran (XIX—nachalo XX veka)*. Moscow: Kliuch-S, 2010.

Kulakov, V. V. *Astrakhan' v persidskoĭ politike Rossii v pervoĭ polovine XVIII veka*. Astrakhan: Astrakhanskiĭ universitet, 2012.

Kulmamatov, D. S. "Offitsial'nye pis'mennye iazyki Sredneĭ Azii i dvuiazychnye bukharskie chelobitnye XVII v." *Oʻzbekistonda xorijiy tillar* 21, no. 2 (2018): 29–35.

Kurat, Akdes Nimet. "The Turkish Expedition to Astrakhan in 1569 and the Problem of the Don–Volga Canal." *Slavonic and East European Review* 40 (1961): 7–23.

Kurat, Akdes Nimet. *Türkiye ve İdil boyu*. Ankara: Türk Tarih Kurumu, 1966.

Kurochkin, A. P., and V. T. Tatarenko. *Apsheronskiĭ meridian: Dokumental'naia povest'*. Baku: Azerbaĭdzhanskoe gosudarstvennoe izdatel'stvo, 1989.

Kurukin, I. V. *Persidskiĭ pokhod Petra Velikogo: Nizavoĭ korpus na beregakh Kaspiia (1722–1735)*. Moscow: Kvadriga, 2010.

Kwon, Heonik. *The Other Cold War*. New York: Columbia University Press, 2010.

Lapradelle, Pierre. *La frontière: Etude de droit international*. Paris: Les Editions Internationales, 1928.

Lavrov, Sergei. "Politika Anglii na Kavkaze i v Sredneĭ Azii v 1917–1921 gg." *Voprosy istorii* 5 (1979): 78–92.

Lawrence, B. "'Abd-al-Qader Jilani." *Encyclopaedia Iranica*, I/2, 132–33. https://iranicaonline.org/articles/abd-al-qader-jilani.

Lawson, Todd. "Exegesis vi. In Akbari and Post-Safavid Esoteric Shi'ism." *Encyclopaedia Iranica*, IX/2, 123–25. https://iranicaonline.org/articles/exegesis-iv.

Layton, Susan. *Russian Literature and Empire: Conquest of the Caucasus from Pushkin to Tolstoy*. Cambridge: Cambridge University Press, 1994.

Lazarev, Mikhail. *Kurdistan i Kurdskiĭ vopros (1923–1945)*. Moscow: Vostochnaia literatura, 2005.

LeDonne, John P. *The Grand Strategy of the Russian Empire, 1650–1831*. New York: Oxford University Press, 2004.

Lee, Yusin. "Toward a New International Regime for the Caspian Sea." *Problems of Post-Communism* 52, no. 3 (2005): 37–48.

Lemańczyk, Szczepan. "The Transiranian Railway: History, Context, Consequences." *Middle Eastern Studies* 49, no. 2 (2013): 237–45.

Leo. *Hovsep katoghikos Arghutean*. Tiflis: Rotinants, 1902.
Létoille, René. "Les expeditions de Bekovitch-Tcherkassy (1714–1717) en Turkestan et le début de l'infiltration russe en Asie Centrale." In *Boukhara-la-Noble*, Cahiers d'Asie Centrale 5-6, 259-84. Tashkent: Cahiers d'Asie Centrale, 1998.
Levent, Sinan. "Common Asianist Intellectual History in Turkey and Japan: Turanism." *Central Asian Survey* 35, no. 1 (2016): 121-35.
Levi, Scott C. *The Bukharan Crisis: A Connected History of 18th-Century Central Asia*. Pittsburgh: University of Pittsburgh Press, 2020.
Levi, Scott C. *The Indian Diaspora in Central Asia and Its Trade, 1550–1900*. Leiden: Brill, 2002.
Levi, Scott C. *The Rise and Fall of Khoqand, 1709–1876*. Pittsburgh: University of Pittsburgh Press, 2017.
Lieven, Dominic. "The Russian Empire and the Soviet Union as Imperial Polities." *Journal of Contemporary History* 30, no. 4 (1995): 607-36.
Liseĭtsev, D. V. *Posol'skiĭ prikaz v epokhu Smuty*. Moscow: Institut Rossiĭskoĭ Istorii RAN, 2003.
Lishin, Nikolai. *Na Kaspiĭskom more: God Beloĭ bor'by*. Prague: Morskoĭ zhurnal, 1938.
Li͡ubomirov, L. *O zaselenii Astrakhanskoĭ gubernii v XVIII veke*. Astrakhan: Astrakhanskiĭ gubernskiĭ plan, 1926.
Locatelli, Catherine. "Russian and Caspian Hydrocarbons: Energy Supply Stakes for the European Union." *Europe-Asia Studies* 62, no. 6 (2010): 959-71.
Lockhart, Laurence. *The Fall of the Safavi Dynasty and the Afghan Occupation of Persia*. Cambridge: Cambridge University Press, 1958.
Lockhart, Laurence. *Nadir Shah: A Critical Study Based Mainly on Contemporary Sources*. London: Luzac, 1938.
Lockhart, Laurence. "The Navy of Nadir Shah." *Proceedings of the Iran Society* 1 (1938): 3-18.
Lodyzhenskiĭ, Konstantin Nikolaevich. *Istori͡ia Russkogo tamozhennogo tarifa*. St. Petersburg: V. C. Balasheva, 1866.
Logan, Donald Frances. *The Viking in History*. Abingdon: Routledge, 1992.
Lubimenko, Inna. "The Struggle of the Dutch with the English for the Russian Market in the Seventeenth Century." *Transactions of the Royal Historical Society*, 4th ser., 7 (1924): 27-51.
Luxemburg, Rosa. *The Mass Strike, the Political Party and the Trade Unions* (1906). Rosa Luxemburg Internet Archive, 1999. https://www.marxists.org/archive/luxemburg/1906/mass-strike/ch03.htm.
Lystsov, V. P. *Persidskiĭ pokhod Petra I, 1722–1723*. Moscow: Izd. Moskovskogo Universiteta, 1951.
MacDowell, Laurel Sefton. *An Environmental History of Canada*. Vancouver: UBC Press, 2012.
MacEion, D. M. "Bāb, 'Alī Moḥammad Šīrāzī." *Encyclopaedia Iranica*, III/3, 278-84. https://iranicaonline.org/articles/bab-ali-mohammad-sirazi.
MacKenzie, David. "The Conquest and Administration of Turkestan, 1860-85." In *Russian Colonial Expansion to 1917*, edited by Michael Rywkin, 208-34. London: Mansell Publishing, 1988.

MacLean, Fitzroy. *Eastern Approaches*. London: Four Square Books, 1967.
Mahdavi, 'Abdol-Rezā Hushang. *Siyāsat-e khāreji-ye Irān dar dowrān-e Pahlavi*. Tehran: Nashr-e Alborz, 1374/1995.
Maḥmud, Moḥammad-'Ali. *Pazhuhesh dar tārikh-e diplomāsi-ye Irān*. Tehran: Mitrā, 1361/1982.
Maitra, K. "Comintern, Roy and the Possibility of an Armed Revolution in India." *Proceedings of the Indian History Congress* 39, no. 2 (1978): 652–59.
Makhdiĭan, Mokhammad Khasan. *Istoriia mezhdunarodnykh otnoshenii Irana i Rossii (XIX–nachalo XXI veka)*. Moscow: IV RAN, 2014.
"Malek Qāsem Mirzā." *Bānk-e Eṭṭelā'āt-e Rejāl*. Last updated September 22, 2013. http://rijaldb.com/fa/12275/میرزا+قاسم+ملک.
Malov, A. V. "Trinadtsataia posol'skaia kniga v deloproizvodstve Posol'skogo prikaza: sostav, struktura, formirovanie." In *Posol'skaia kniga po sviaziam Moskovskogo gosudarstva s Krymom, 1567–1572*, edited by A. V. Vinogradov et al, 4–33. Moscow: Russkie Vitiazi, 2016
Mamedova, Aĭnura Mamed Gizi. "Torgovo-tamozhennaia politka tsarizma v severom Azerbaĭdzhane v pervoĭ polovine XIX veka." PhD diss., Baku State University, 2013.
Mandrillon, Marie-Hélène. "L'expertise d'etat, creuset de l'environnement en URSS." *Vingtième siècle: Revue d'histoire*, no. 113 (2012): 107–16.
Manshur-Gorgāni, Moḥammad-'Ali. *Siyāsat-e dowlat-e Showravi dar Irān az 1296 tā 1306*. Vol. 1. Tehran: Maẓāheri, 1326/1947.
Mar'ashi, Mirzā Moḥammad Khalil. *Mojma' al-Tavārikh, dar Tārikh-e Enqerāż-e Ṣafavieh va Vaqāie'-e Ba'ad*. Edited by 'Abbās Eqbāl. Tehran: Ketābkhāneh-e Sanā'i-e Ketābkhāneh-e Ṭahvari, 1362/1983.
Marshall, Alex. *The Russian General Staff and Asia, 1800–1917*. London: Routledge, 2014.
Martin, Terry. *The Affirmative Action Empire: Nations and Nationalisms in the Soviet Union, 1923–1939*. Ithaca, NY: Cornell University Press, 2001.
Martin, Terry. "The Origins of Soviet Ethnic Cleansing." *Journal of Modern History* 70, no. 4 (1998): 813–61.
Martin, Vanessa. "Constitutional Revolution ii. Events." *Encyclopaedia Iranica* VI/2, 176-87. https://iranicaonline.org/articles/constitutional-revolution-ii.
Matin-Asgari, Afshin. "The Impact of Imperial Russia and the Soviet Union on Qajar and Pahlavi Iran." In *Iranian-Russian Encounters: Empires and Revolutions since 1800*, edited by Stephanie Cronin, 11–46. New York: Routledge, 2013.
Matthee, Rudi. "Anti-Ottoman Politics and Transit Rights: The Seventeenth-Century Trade in Silk between Safavid Iran and Muscovy." *Cahiers du Monde Russe* 35, no. 4 (1994): 739–61.
Matthee, Rudi. "Between Aloofness and Fascination: Safavid Views of the West." In "Historiography and Representation in Safavid and Afsharid Iran," special issue, *Iranian Studies* 31, no. 2 (1998): 219–46.
Matthee, Rudi. "Facing a Rude and Barbarous Neighbor: Iranian Perceptions of Russia and Russians from the Safavids to the Qajars." In *Iran Facing Others: Identity Boundaries in a Historical Perspective*, edited by Abbas Amanat and Farzin Vejdani, 101–26. New York: Palgrave Macmillan, 2012.

Matthee, Rudi. "Firearms i. History." *Encyclopaedia Iranica*, IX/6, 619-28. https://iranicaonline.org/articles/firearms-i-history.
Matthee, Rudi. "Infidel Aggression: The Russian Assault on the Holy Shrine of Imam Reza, Mashhad, 1912." In *Russians in Iran: Diplomacy and Power in the Qajar Era and Beyond*, edited by Rudi Matthee and Elena Andreeva, 143-76. London: I. B. Tauris, 2018.
Matthee, Rudi. *Persia in Crisis: Safavid Decline and the Fall of Isfahan*. London: I. B. Tauris, 2012.
Matthee, Rudi. *The Politics of Trade in Safavid Iran: Silk for Silver, 1600-1730*. Cambridge: Cambridge University Press, 1999.
Matthee, Rudi, and Elena Andreeva, eds. *Russians in Iran: Diplomacy and Power in the Qajar Era and Beyond*. London: I. B. Tauris, 2018.
Matthews, G. V. T. *The Ramsar Convention on Wetlands: Its History and Development*. Gland: Ramsar Convention Bureau, 1993.
Māzandarāni, Asadollāh Fāżel. *Tārikh-e Ẓohur al-Ḥaqq*, vol. 2. https://www.academia.edu/42358413/Tarikh_Zuhur_Al_Haqq_Volume_2_ظهورالحق_جلد2, 59-257.
Mazzaoui, Michael. *The Origins of the Ṣafawids: Shiʿism, Ṣufism, and the Gulat*. Wiesbaden: F. Steiner, 1972.
McIlroy, John, and Alan Campbell, "Bolshevism, Stalinism and the Comintern: A Historical Controversy Revisited." *Labor History* 60, no. 3 (2019): 165-92.
McKay, John. "Baku Oil and Transcaucasian Pipelines, 1883-1891: A Study in Tsarist Economic Policy." *Slavic Review* 43, no. 4 (1984): 604-23.
Meleady, Conor. "Negotiating the Caliphate: British Responses to Pan-Islamic Appeals, 1914-1924." *Middle Eastern Studies* 52, no. 2 (2016): 182-97.
Melville, Firuza I. "Khosrow Mirza's Mission to St. Peterburg in 1829." In *Iranian-Russian Encounters: Empires and Revolutions since 1800*, edited by Stephanie Cronin, 69-94. New York: Routledge, 2013.
Minorsky, V., ed. and trans. *Hodud al-ʿĀlam*. London: Gibb Memorial, 1970.
Minovi, M. "Avallin Kāravān-e Maʾrefat." *Yaghmā*, no. 62 (1953): 181-85.
Mirfendereski, Guive. "Caspian Sea, ii. Diplomatic History in Modern Times." In *Encyclopaedia Iranica Online*, https://www.iranicaonline.org/articles/caspian-sea-ii-diplomatic-history-in-modern-times.
Mirfendereski, Guive. *A Diplomatic History of the Caspian Sea: Treaties, Diaries and Other Stories*. Basingstoke: Palgrave, 2001.
Mirnye peregovory v Brest-Litovske s 9(22) dekabria 1917 g. po 3(16) marta 1918 g. Vol. 1. Moscow, 1920.
Mirzā, Solṭān Ḥāshem. *Zabur-e Āl-e Dāvud: Sharḥ-e erṭebāt-e Marʿashi bā selāṭin-e Ṣafavieh*. Edited by ʿAbd al-Ḥossein Navāi. Tehran: Mirās-e Maktub, 1379.
Moberly, Frederick J. *Operations in Persia: 1914-1919*. Edited by the Imperial War Museum. London: HMSO, 1987.
Mochiri, Malek Iradj. *Étude de numismatique iranienne sous les Sassanides et Arabe-Sassanides*. Vol. 2. Rev. ed. Louvain: Impremerie Orientaliste, 1983.
Mohammad Ḥosayni, Noṣratollāh. *Ḥażrat-e Bāb*. Ontario: Moʾasseseh-ye Maṭbuʿāt-e Bahāʾi, 1995.

Moiseev, M. B. "Teneshevy-Baksheevy: Sem'i︠a︡ perevodchikov i tolmacheĭ vtoroĭ poloviny XVI v." In *Perevodchiki i perevody v Rossii kontsa XVI–nachala XVIII stoletii︠a︡*, edited by A. V. Beli︠a︡kov et al., 83–87. Moscow: Institut Rossiĭskoĭ Istorii RAN, 2019.

Mokri, Mohammad. *Les frontières du nord de l'Iran: Caucase, Asie Centrale.* Paris: Geuthner, 2004.

Mokri, Mohammad. *Na sharqi, na gharbi, Jomhuri-ye Eslāmi: Majmu'-e-ye sokhanrānihā va akhbār-e montasher shodeh dar jarā'id darbāreh-ye ravābeṭ-e Irān.* Tehran: Mo'asaseh-ye enteshārāt-e Amir Kabir, 1362/1983-84.

Mollā Nasreddin (1906–1931). Vol. 1, *1906–1907.* Baku: Azerbaijan Academy of Sciences, 1988.

Mollā Nasreddin (1906–1931). Vol. 2, *1908–1909.* Baku: Azerbaijan Dovlet Neshriyyat, 2002.

Mollā Nasreddin (1906–1931). Vol. 3, *1909–1910.* Baku: Çinar-Çap Neshriyyati, 2005.

Morgan, David O. "The Mongols and the Eastern Mediterranean." *Mediterranean Historical Review* 4, no. 1 (1989): 198–211.

Morgan, E. Delmar, and C. H. Coote, eds. *Early Voyages and Travels to Russia and Persia by Anthony Jenkinson and Other Englishmen.* Vol. 2. London: Hakluyt Society, 1886.

Morozov, Aleksandr. "Parusnyĭ master Ian Streĭs i ego puteshestvie." In *I︠A︡. I︠A︡. Streĭs: Tri puteshestvii︠a︡*, 31–52. Ri︠a︡zan: Aleksandrii︠a︡, 2006.

Morris, L. P. "British Secret Missions in Turkestan, 1918–19." *Journal of Contemporary History* 12, no. 2 (1977): 363–79.

Morrison, A. S. *Russian Rule in Samarkand, 1868–1910: A Comparison with British India.* Oxford: Oxford University Press, 2008.

"Moscow School of Painting, Sculpture and Architecture." Wikipedia. Last edited October 24, 2024. https://en.wikipedia.org/wiki/Moscow_School_of_Painting,_Sculpture_and_Architecture.

Moshkin, Sergeĭ Vi︠a︡cheslavovich. *Revoli︠u︡tsii︠a︡ izvne: Istoriko-politologicheskie ocherki.* Ekaterinburg: Uro RAN, 1997.

Mottahedeh, Roy P. "The Abbasid Caliphate in Iran." In *The Cambridge History of Iran*, vol. 4, *The Period from the Arab Invasion to the Saljuqs*, edited by R. N. Frye, 57–89. Cambridge: Cambridge University Press, 1975.

Mozayyan al-Dowleh, Mirzā ʿAli Akbar. *Still Life*, AH 1325 / AD 1907-8. Christie's "Art of the Islamic and Indian Worlds," sale 7843, lot 159. Closed April 13, 2010. http://www.christies.com/lotfinder/paintings/still-life-signed-mozayen-al-dowleh-qajar-5303064-details.aspx.

Multiple Authors. "Caspian Sea." *Encyclopaedia Iranica*, V/1, 48. https://www.iranicaonline.org/articles/caspian-sea-index.

Münster, Sebastian. *Die Länder Asie nah ihrer gelegenheit biß in India werden in dieser Tafel verzeichnet.* 1540.

Mustafa-Zade, Rakhman. *Dve respubliki: Azerbaĭdzhano-rossiĭskie otnoshenii︠a︡ v 1918–1922.* Moscow: MIK, 2006.

Mustafina, D. A., and V. V. Trepalov, eds. *Posol'skie knigi po svi︠a︡zi︠a︡m Rossii s Nogaĭskoĭ Ordoĭ. 1551–1561 gg.* Kazan: Tatarskoe Knizhnoe Izdatel'stvo, 2006.

"N. Karazin. Camp on the Amu Daria." Translated by Elena Andreeva and Mark Woodcock. *Metamorphosis*, Spring 2010.

Naser al-Din Shah. *Diary of H.M. the Shah of Persia during His Tour through Europe in A.D. 1873*. Translated by James Redhouse. London: J. Murray, 1874.

Naser al-Din Shah. *Ruznāmeh-e Safar-e Farangestān*. Edited by Moḥammad Ḥasan Khan E'temād al-Salṭaneh. Tehran: Dār al-Ṭeba'-e Dawlati, 1291/1874.

Naumkin, V. V. "Nekotorye aspekty diplomaticheskogo sopernichestva Sovetskogo Soīuza i Velikobritanii v Aravii v 1920-e gg." *Vostok*, no. 2 (2018): 6–19.

Nazarov, Mikhail. *Apparat i liudi: Zapiski o moem vremeni*. Baku: Apostrof, 2010.

Nejad, Kayhan. "From the Oilfield to the Battlefield: Transcaucasian Labor and Iranian Constitutionalism, 1904–11." Virtual Lecture, April 16, 2021. Iran Colloquium, Yale University.

Nejad, Kayhan A. "From the Oilfield to the Battlefield: The Internationalization of Northern Iranian Revolution." PhD diss., Yale University, 2021.

Nejad, Kayhan A. "Kuchek Khan Jangali." *Encyclopaedia Iranica Online*, forthcoming

Nejad, Kayhan A. "Provincial Revolution and Regional Anti-Colonialism: The Soviets in Iran, 1920–1921." *Slavic Review* 82, no. 2 (2023): 378–400.

Nejad, Kayhan A. "To Break the Feudal Bonds: The Soviets, Reza Khan, and the Iranian Left, 1921–25." *Middle Eastern Studies* 57, no. 5 (2021): 758–76.

Nersisīan, M. G., ed. *Armīano-russkie otnosheniīa v XVIII veke*. Vol. 4. Yerevan: Akademiīa Nauk Armīanskoĭ SSR, 1990.

Nikonov, Oleg A. *Iran vo vneshnepoliticheskoĭ strategii Rossiĭskoĭ Imperii v XVIII v.* Vladimir: Vladimir University Press, 2009.

Noack, Christian. "Coping with the Tourist: Planned and 'Wild' Mass Tourism on the Soviet Black Sea Coast." In *Turizm: The Russian and East European Tourist under Capitalism and Socialism*, edited by Anne E. Gorsuch and Diane P. Koenker, 281–304. Ithaca, NY: Cornell University Press, 2006.

Nogaevskaīa, E. V. "Nikolaĭ Nikolaevich Karazin, 1842–1908." In *Russkoe iskusstvo: Ocherki o zhizni i tvorchestve khudozhnikov. Vtoraīa polovina devīatnadtsatogo veka II*, edited by A. I. Leonov, 357–68. Moscow: Iskusstvo, 1971.

Nokandeh, Jebrael, et al. "Linear Barriers of Northern Iran: The Great Wall of Gorgan and the Wall of Tammishe." *Iran* 44 (2006): 121–73.

Noradounghian, G. *Recueil d'actes internationaux de l'Empire Ottoman*. Vol. 1. Paris, 1897.

Nova et accurata Wolgae fluminis, olim Rha dicti delineatio auctore Adamo Oleario. Amsterdam, 1666.

Nuri, Mostafā. *Ruzgār-e biqarāri-ye Māzandarān va Gorgān dar eshqāl-e Artesh-e Sorkh, 1320–1325*. Tehran: Sāzemān-e Asnād va Ketābkhāne-ye Melli-e Jomhuri-ye Eslāmi, 1394/2015.

Nuri, Mostafa. *Sardār Savādkuhi: Sargozasht-e Esmā'il Khan Amir Mo'ayyed Bāvand*. Tehran: Shirāzeh Ketab, 1397/2018–19.

O'Rourke, Shane. *The Cossacks*. Manchester: Manchester University Press, 2007.

Obertreis, Julia. "Der 'Angriff auf die Wüste' in Zentralasien: Zur Umweltgeschichte der Sowjetunion." *Osteuropa*, no. 4–5 (2008): 37–56.

Ocherk istorii Ministerstva inostrannykh del: 1802–1902. St. Petersburg: Tovarishchestvo R. Golike i A. Vil'borg, 1902.

Olearius, Adam. *Vermehrte Newe Beschreibung der Muscowitischen und Persischen Reyse*. Schleswig, 1656. Facsimile reprint, edited by Dieter Lohmeier. Tübingen: Niemeyer, 1971.

Olson, Robert. "The Turkoman Rebellion in Eastern Iran, 1924–5: Its Consequences and the Soviet Reaction." *Die Welt des Islams* 31, no. 2 (1991): 216–27.

Omrani Rekavandi, Hamid, et al. "An Imperial Frontier of the Sasanian Empire: Further Fieldwork at the Great Wall of Gorgan." *Iran* 45 (2007): 95–136.

Orishev, Aleksandr. *Iranskiĭ uzel. skhvatka razvedok, 1936–1945 gg*. Moscow: Vech, 2009.

Osborn, Patrick R. *Operation Pike: Britain versus the Soviet Union, 1939–1941*. Westport: Greenwood Press, 2000.

Ozdamirova, Ėliza Musatovna. "Vostochnoe kupechestvo v Russko-Aziatskoĭ torgovle cherez Astrakhan v pervoĭ polovine XIX veka." PhD diss., Chechen State University, 2016.

Pallas, Peter S., ed. *Reisen durch Russland und im Caucasischen Gebürge*. St. Petersburg, 1787.

Parsamian, V. A., ed. *Armiano-russkie otnosheniia v XVII veke*. Yerevan: Izd. Akademii Nauk Armiamskoĭ SSR, 1953.

Pearce, Brian. "A Falsifier of History." *Revolutionary Russia* 1, no. 1 (1988): 20–23.

Peçevi, İbrahim. *Peçevi tarihi*. Edited by Fahri Derin and Vahit Çabuk. Istanbul: Enderun, 1980.

Peri, Benedek. "Turkish Language and Literature in Medieval and Early Modern India." In *Turks in the Indian Subcontinent, Central and West Asia: The Turkish Presence in the Islamic World*, edited by Ismail K. Poonawala, 227–62. Oxford: Oxford University Press, 2017.

Perry, John R. "Ḥaydari and Ne'mati." *Encyclopaedia Iranica*, XII/2, 70–73. https://www.iranicaonline.org/articles/haydari-and-nemati.

Perry, John R. *Karim Khan Zand: A History of Iran, 1747–1779*. Chicago: University of Chicago Press, 1979.

Persits, M. A. *Persidskiĭ front mirovoĭ revoliutsii: Dokumenty o Sovetskom vtorzhenii v Gilian (1920–1921)*. Moscow: Kvadriga, 2009.

Persits, M. A. *Zastenchivaia interventsiia: O Sovetskom vtorzhenii v Iran*. Moscow: Muraveĭ-gaĭd, 1999.

Petrov, A. M. "Foreign Trade of Russia and Britain with Asia in the Seventeenth to Nineteenth Centuries." *Modern Asian Studies* 21, no. 4 (1987): 625–37.

Peyrat, Etienne. *Histoire du Caucase au XXe siècle*. Paris: Fayard, 2020.

Pickett, James. *Polymaths of Islam: Power and Networks of Knowledge in Central Asia*. Ithaca, NY: Cornell University Press, 2020.

Pierce, Richard A. *Russian Central Asia 1867–1917: A Study in Colonial Rule*. Berkeley: University of California Press, 1960.

Piliaeva, Valentina. *Istoriia tamozhennogo dela i tamozhennoĭ politiki Rossii*. Moscow: Litres, 2017.

Planhol, Xavier de. "Caspian Sea i. Geography." *Encyclopaedia Iranica*, V/1, 48-50. https://iranicaonline.org/articles/caspian-sea-i.
Poe, Marshall. "The Muscovite State and Its Personnel." In *Cambridge History of Russia*, vol. 1, *From Early Rus to 1689*, edited by Maureen Perrie, 435-63. Cambridge: Cambridge University Press, 2003.
Poghosyan, F. G. *Datastanagirk Astrakhani Hayots*. Yerevan: Akademiia Nauk Armi͡anskoĭ SSR, 1967.
Polievktov, M. A. *Ėkonomicheskoe i politicheskoe razvitie Moskovskogo gosudarstva XVII v. na Kavkaze*. Tiflis: Akademiia Nauk Gruzinskoĭ SSR, 1932.
Pollock, Sean. "Empire by Invitation? Russian Empire-Building in the Caucasus in the Reign of Catherine II." PhD diss., Harvard University, 2006.
Pollock, Sheldon. *The Language of the Gods in the World of Men: Sanskrit, Culture, and Power in Pre-modern India*. Berkeley: University of California Press, 2006.
Polnoe sobranie zakonov Rossiĭskoĭ Imperii. Series 1. St. Petersburg, 1830.
Postnikov, A. V. *Russia in Maps: A History of the Geographical Study and Cartography of the Country*. Moscow: Nash Dom, 1996.
Postnikov, Aleksey V. "The Russian Navy as Chartmaker in the Eighteenth Century." *Imago mundi* 52 (2000): 79-95.
Prishchepova, V. A. *Illi͡ustrativnye kollektsii po narodam Tsentral'noĭ Azii vtoroĭ poloviny XIX-nachala XX veka v sobranii͡akh Kunstkamery*. St. Petersburg: Nauka, 2011.
Qajar, Naser al-Din Shah. *Ruznāmeh-ye Safar-e Māzandarān*. Tehran: Enteshārāt-e Farhang-e Irān Zamin, 1977.
Qulmamatov, Doʻsmamat. "XVI-XVII asrlarda Moskva elchilik devoni sharq tarjimonlari va tilmochlari maktabining shakllanishi tarixi haqida." *Oʻzbekistonda xorijiy tillar* 13, no. 5 (2016): 120-26.
Rabino, H. L. *Mazandaran and Astarabad*. London: Luzac, 1928.
Rading. "O proisshestvii͡akh sluchivshikhsi͡a pri osnovanii Russkago selenii͡a na beregu Astrabadskago zaliva v 1781 godu." In *Zhurnal" Ministerstva Vnutrennikh Del*," edited by P. B. Butkov, 21. St. Petersburg, 1839.
Räsänen, Tuomas, and Simo Laakkonen. "Cold War and the Environment: The Role of Finland in International Environmental Politics in the Baltic Sea Region." *Ambio* 36, no. 2-3 (2007): 229-36.
Rashtiani, Goodarz. "Iranian-Russian Relations in the Eighteenth Century." In *Crisis, Collapse, Militarism & Civil War: The History and Historiography of 18th Century Iran*, edited by Michael Axworthy, 163-82. Oxford: Oxford University Press, 2018.
Rasizade, Alec. "The Mythology of Munificent Caspian Bonanza and Its Concomitant Pipeline Geopolitics." *Central Asian Survey* 21, no. 1 (2002): 37-54.
Ravāsāni, Shāpur. *Nehżat-e Jangal: Zamine-hā-ye ejtemāʻi*. Tehran: Daftar-e pazhuhesh-hā-ye farhangi, 1381/2002.
Renner, Andreas. "Peter der Grosse und Russlands Fenster nach Asien." *Historische Zeitschrift* 306, no. 1 (2018): 71-96. https://doi.org/10.1515/hzhz-2018-0003.

Reza-Jalili, Mohammad. *Diplomatie Islamique: Stratégie internationale du Khomeynisme*. Paris: Presses universitaires de France, 1989.
Richard, Yann. "Foreword." In C. J. Edmonds, *East and West of Zagros: Travel, War and Politics in Persia and Iraq, 1913–1921*, ed. by Richard, xi–xviii. Leiden: Brill, 2010.
Richard, Yann, and Willem M. Floor. *Iran: A Social and Political History since the Qajars*. Cambridge: Cambridge University Press, 2019.
Ringer, Monica. *Education, Religion, and the Discourse of Cultural Reform in Qajar Iran*. Costa Mesa: Mazda, 2001.
Rodzevich, A. I. *Ocherki postroĭki Zakaspīskoĭ voennoĭ zheleznoĭ dorogi i eīa znacheniīa dlīa russko-sredneaziatskoĭ promyshlennosti i torgovli*. St. Petersburg: Parovaīa tipografīīa Muller i Bogel'man, 1891.
Rogozhin, Ĭa. M. "Dela Posol'skie." In *"Oko vseĭ velikoĭ Rosii": Ob istorii russkoĭ diplomaticheskoĭ sluzhby XVI–XVII vekov*, edited by E. V. Chistīakova et al., 19–30. Moscow: Mezhdunarodnye otnosheniīa, 1989.
Rogozhin, N. M. *Posol'skie knigi Rossii kontsa XV–nachala XVII vv*. Moscow: Institut Rossiiskoĭ Istorii, 1994.
Rogozhin, N. M. *Posol'skiĭ prikaz-kolybel' rossiiskoĭ diplomatii*. Moscow: Mezhdunarodnye otnosheniīa, 2003.
Rogozhin, N. M. *U gosudarevykh del byt' ukazano*. Moscow: RAGS, 2002.
Romaniello, Matthew P. *Enterprising Empires: Russia and Britain in Eighteenth-Century Eurasia*. Cambridge: Cambridge University Press, 2019.
Rorlich, Azade-Ayse. "Fellow Travelers: Enver Pasha and the Bolshevik Government 1918–1920." *Asian Affairs* 13, no. 3 (1982): 288–96.
Rosenthal, Franz. *The History of al-Tabari*. Vol. 1, *General Introduction and from the Creation to the Flood*. Edited by F. Rosenthal and E. Yarshater. Albany: State University of New York Press, 1989.
Rothman, Nathalie. *Brokering Empire: Trans-Imperial Subjects between Venice and Istanbul*. Ithaca, NY: Cornell University Press, 2012.
Rothman, Nathalie. "Interpreting Dragomans: Boundaries and Crossings in the Early Modern Mediterranean." *Comparative Studies in Society and History* 51, no. 4 (2009): 771–800.
Ruban, L. S. *Kaspiĭ—more problem*. Moscow: Nauka, 2003.
Sablin, Ivan. *Governing Post-Imperial Siberia and Mongolia, 1911–1924*. London: Routledge, 2017.
Sadeghian, Saghar. "The Caspian Forests of Northern Iran during the Qajar and Pahlavi Periods: Deforestation, Regulation, and Reforestation." *Iranian Studies* 49, no. 6 (2016): 973–96.
Sadikov, P. A. "Pokhod Tatar i Turok na Astrakhan' v 1569." *Istoricheskie zapiski* 22 (1947): 153–64.
Safaralieva, D. "Iranskiĭ uchënik Akademii" [An Iranian student of the academy]. *Khudozhnik*, no. 8 (1991): 56–58.
Safiri, Floreeda. "South Persia Rifles." *Encyclopaedia Iranica Online*, https://www.iranicaonline.org/articles/south-persia-rifles-militia.
Safvet. "Hazar denizinde Osmanlı sancağı." *Tarih-i Osmani Encümeni Mecmuası* 3 (1912): 857–61.

Sahadeo, Jeff. *Russian Colonial Society in Tashkent, 1865–1923*. Bloomington: Indiana University Press, 2010.
Said, Edward. *Orientalism*. New York: Vintage Books, 1979.
Samoĭlovich, A., et al., eds. *Materialy po istorii Uzbekskoĭ, Tadzhikskoĭ i Turkmenskoĭ SSR. Chast' 1: Torgovlia s Moskovskim gosudarstvom i mezhdunarodnoe polozhenie Sredneĭ Azii v XVI–XVII vv*. Leningrad: Izdatel'stvo AN SSSR, 1932.
Sardāriniyā, Ṣamad. *Naqsh-e Markaz-e Ghaybi-e Tabriz dar enqelāb-e Mashruṭiyat-e Irān*. Tehran: Akhtar, 2015/16 [1984].
Sartor, Wolfgang. "Der armenische Rohseidenhandel im 17. und 18. Jahrhundert: Die Russland-Route." In *Armenier im östlichen Europa: Eine Anthologie*, edited by Tamara Ganjalyan, Bálint Kovács, and Stefan Troebst, 252-75. Vienna: Boehlau Verlag, 2018.
Sartori, Paolo. "From the Demotic to the Literary: The Ascendance of the Vernacular Turkic in Central Asia (Eighteenth–Nineteenth Centuries)." *Eurasian Studies* 18 (2020): 213-54.
Savich, N. G. "Iz istorii russko-nemetskikh kul'turnykh sviazeĭ v XII v. (Nemetsko-russkiĭ slovar'-razgovornik G. Nevenburga 1629 g.)." *Istoricheskie zapiski* 102 (1978): 246-86.
Savory, Roger M. "Ešīk-Āqāsī-Bāšī." *Encyclopaedia Iranica*, VIII/6, 600-601. https://iranicaonline.org/articles/esik-aqasi-basi.
Sayfutdinova, Leyla. "Mapping the Mobility of Azerbaijani Soviet Engineers." *Labor History* 59, no. 3 (2018): 316-30.
Schimmelpennick van der Oye, David. *Russian Orientalism: Asia in the Russian Mind from Peter the Great to the Emigration*. New Haven, CT: Yale University Press, 2010.
Scott, James C. *The Art of Not Being Governed*. New Haven, CT: Yale University Press, 2009.
Sevost'ianov, G. N., et al. *Rossiiu i SSHA: Ėkonomicheskie otnosheniia 1917–1933, sbornik dokumentov*. Moscow: Nauka, 1997.
Shablovskaia, Alisa. "Russian Hubris in Iran: Diplomacy, Clientelism, and Intervention (1907–1912)." *Ab Imperio*, 2019, no. 1, 79-103.
Shafei, Bijan, Sohrab Soroushiani, and Victor Daniel. *Karim Taherzadeh Behzad Architecture: Architecture of Changing Times in Iran*. Tehran: Did Publications, 2004.
Shafranovskiĭ, K. I. "Rukopisnye karty Kaspiĭskogo moria F.I. Soimonova." In *Geograficheskiĭ sbornik III: Istoriia geograficheskikh znanii i geograficheskikh otkrytii*, 100-116. Moscow: Izdatel'stvo Akademii Nauka SSSR, 1954.
Shafranovskiĭ, K. I., and E. A. Kniazhetskaia. "Karty Kaspiĭskogo i Aral'skogo more, sostavlennye v rezul'tate ėkspeditsii Aleksandra Bekovicha-Cherkasskogo 1715 g." *Izvestiia Vsesoiuznogo Geograficheskogo Obshchestva*, no. 6 (1952): 539-51.
Shanavaz, Shahbaz. "Karun River iii. The Opening of the Karun." *Encyclopaedia Iranica*, XV/6, 633-40. https://iranicaonline.org/articles/karun_3.
Shcheglova, Olimpiada P. "Lithography i. In Persia," *Encyclopaedia Iranica Online*. http://www.iranicaonline.org/articles/lithography-i-in-persia.
Shishov, Aleksandr. *Persidskiĭ front (1909–1918)*. Moscow: Izdatel'skiĭ dom Veche, 2010.

Shklovskii, Viktor. *Sentimental'noe puteshestvie*. St. Petersburg: Azbuka-klassika, 2006.
Shkuro, Andreĭ. *Zapiski belogo partizana*. Buenos Aires: Seiatel', 1961.
Shumiatskii, Boris. *Na postu sovetskoĭ diplomatii: Pervyĭ sovetskiĭ diplomat v Irane I. O. Kolomiitsev*. Moscow: IVR, 1960.
Simeon of Erevan. *Jambr*. Translated by G. Bournoutian. Costa Mesa: Mazda, 2009.
Slavs and Tatars Presents Molla Nasreddin: The Magazine that Would've Could've Should've. Zurich: JRP Ringier, 2011.
Slezkine, Yuri. "Imperialism as the Highest Stage of Socialism." *Russian Review* 59, no. 2 (2000): 227–34.
Slezkine, Yuri. "Naturalists versus Nations: Eighteenth-Century Russian Scholars Confront Ethnic Diversity." In *Russia's Orient: Imperial Borderlands and Peoples, 1700–1917*, edited by Daniel R. Brower and Edward J. Lazzerini, 27–57. Bloomington: Indiana University Press, 1997.
Smith, Jeremy. *The Bolsheviks and the National Question, 1917–23*. New York: Palgrave Macmillan, 1999.
Smith, Peter, and Moojan Momen. "Martyrs, Babi." *Encyclopaedia Iranica Online*. https://iranicaonline.org/articles/martyrs-babi-babi.
Sneddon, Christopher. *Concrete Revolution: Large Dams, Cold War Geopolitics, and the US Bureau of Reclamation*. Chicago: University of Chicago Press, 2015.
Sobotsinskiĭ, Lev. *Persiia: Statistiko-ėkonomicheskiĭ ocherk*. St. Petersburg: "Ėlektropech" Ia. Krovitskogo, 1913.
Soĭmonov, F. I. *Opisanie Kaspiĭskogo moria i chinennykh na onom rossiĭskikh zavoevanie, iako chast' istorii Gosudaria Imperatora Petra Velikago*. St. Petersburg: Imperatorskaia Akademiia Nauk, 1763.
Soĭmonov, Fëdor I. *Opisanie Kaspiĭskogo moria ot ust'ia reki Volgi, ot protoka Iarkovskago, do ust'ia reki Astrabatskoĭ, polozhenie zapadnogo i vostochnago beregov, glubiny, grunty, i vidy znatnykh gor*. O.O., 1783.
Solonchenko, E. A. "Aziatskiĭ tarif i tamozheniĭ ustav 1817g. i popitki ikh peresmotra v pervoĭ polovine XIX V." *Vestnik OGU* 16, no. 35 (2013): 570–72.
Solov'ev, Sergeĭ M. *Istoria Rossii*. Vol. 18. Moscow, 1868.
Sonyel, Salahi R. "Enver Pasha and the Basmaji Movement in Central Asia." *Middle Eastern Studies* 26, no. 1 (1990): 52–64.
Sotavov, N. A. "The Circum-Caspian Areas within the Eurasian International Relationships at the Time of Peter the Great and Nadir-Shah Afshar." *Iran & the Caucasus* 5 (2001): 93–100.
Sotudeh, Manouchehr. *Az Āstārā tā Astarābād*. 1st ed. 5 vols. Tehran, 1349/1970.
Sotudeh, Manouchehr. *Az Āstārā tā Astarābād*. 4th ed. 10 vols. Tehran, 1375–80/1996–2001.
Stadelbauer, Jörg. "Der Fremdenverkehr in Sowjet-Kaukasien: Gesamtstaatliche Bedeutung, Räumliche Strukturen und Entwicklungsprobleme." *Zeitschrift für Wirtschaftsgeographie* 30, no. 1 (1986): 1–21.
Stolte, Carolien, and Harald Fisher-Tiné. "Imagining Asia in India: Nationalism and Internationalism (ca. 1905–1940)." *Comparative Studies in Society and History* 54, no. 1 (2012): 65–92.

BIBLIOGRAPHY

Stoyanov, A. "Russia Marches South: Army Reform and Battlefield Performance in Russia's Southern Campaigns, 1695–1739." PhD diss., Leiden University, 2017.
Straußen, Johann Jansz. *Sehr schwere / widerwertige und Denckwürdige Reysen* . . . Amsterdam, 1678.
Sunderland, Willard. "Shop Signs, Monuments, Souvenirs: Views of the Empire in Everyday Life." In *Picturing Russia: Explorations in Visual Culture*, edited by Valerie A. Kivelson and Joan Neuberger, 104–8. New Haven, CT: Yale University Press, 2008.
Suny, Ronald Grigor. *The Baku Commune, 1917–1918: Class and Nationality in the Russian Revolution*. Princeton, NJ: Princeton University Press, 1972.
Swietochowski, Tadeusz. *Russian Azerbaijan, 1905–1920: The Shaping of National Identity in a Muslim Community*. London: Cambridge University Press, 2004.
Swinson, Arthur. *Beyond the Frontiers: The Biography of Colonel F.M. Bailey, Explorer and Special Agent*. London: Hutchinson of London, 1971.
Sykes, Percy, and Lionel Dunsterville. "From Baghdad to the Caspian in 1918: Discussion." *Geographical Journal* 57, no. 3 (1921): 164–66.
Sykes, Percy M., and Ella C. Sykes. *Through Deserts and Oases of Central Asia*. London: Macmillan, 1920.
Tabrizi, Mohammad Mahdi Za'im al-Dawleh. *Meftāḥ-e Bāb al-Abvāb yā Tārikh-e Bāb va Bahā'*. Translated to Persian by Hasan Farid Golpāyegāni. Isfahan: Markaz-e Taḥqiqāt-e Rāyāneh'i-ye Qā'emiyeh, n.d.
Ṭāheraḥmadi, Mahmud, ed. *Asnād-e ravābeṭ-e Irān va Showravi dar dowreh-ye Reżā Shāh (1304–1318)*. Tehran: Sāzemān-e Asnād-e Melli-ye Irān, 1374/1995.
Ṭāheraḥmadi, Maḥmud. *Ravābeṭ-e Irān va Showravi dar dowreh-ye Reżā Shāh*. Tehran: Vezārat-e Omur-e Khārejeh, Markaz-e Chāp va Enteshārāt, 1384/2005.
Ṭāheraḥmadi, Maḥmud, ed. *Tārikh-e ravābeṭ-e Irān va ettehād-e Jamāhir-e Showravi 1325–1345*. Tehran: Edāreh-ye asnād va tārikh-e diplomāsi, 1393/2014.
Taqizādeh, Ḥasan. *Zendegi-ye ṭufāni: Khāṭerāt-e Sayyed Ḥasan Taqizādeh*. Edited by Iraj Afshār. Tehran: Enteshārāt-e 'elmi, 1372/1993.
Taran, P. Y., and B. V. Zmerzly. "Establishment and Activity of Customs Offices in Siberia, Far East and Middle East from the Second Half of the XVIII Century to Beginning of the XIX Century." *Uchenie zapiski tavricheskogo natsional'nogo universiteta im. V. I. Vernadskogo, seriā iuridicheskie nauka* 26 (65), no. 2-1 (2013): 130–36.
Taskin, George A. "The Falling Level of the Caspian Sea in Relation to Soviet Economy." *Geographical Review* 44, no. 4 (1954): 508–27.
"Tbilisi State Academy of Arts." Wikipedia. Last edited July 8, 2024. https://en.wikipedia.org/wiki/Tbilisi_State_Academy_of_Arts.
Teague-Jones, Reginald. *The Spy Who Disappeared: Diary of a Secret Mission to Russian Central Asia in 1918*. London: Gollancz, 1990.
Ter Minassian, Taline. *Colporteurs du Komintern: L'Union Soviétique et les minorités au Moyen-Orient*. Paris: Presses de Sciences Po, 1997.

Ter Minassian, Taline. "Some Fresh News about the 26 Commissars: Reginald Teague-Jones and the Transcaspian Episode." *Asian Affairs* 45, no. 1 (2014): 65-78.

Ter Minassian, Taline, and Tom Rees. *Most Secret Agent of Empire: Reginald Teague-Jones, Master Spy of the Great Game*. London: Hurst, 2014.

Ter-Oganov, Nugzar. "Letters from Officer/Orientalist K.N. Smirnov from the Caucasian Front as a Source for the Study of the Military/Political Situation in Turkey and Iran in 1914-1917." *Voennyĭ sbornik* 6, no. 4 (2014): 209-35.

Ter-Oganov, Nugzar. *Persidskai͡a kazach'i͡a brigada, 1879-1921 gg*. Moscow: IV RAN, 2012.

Ter-Oganov, Nugzar. "A Russian Officer's Letters on Russian and British Activities in Iran during World War I." In *Russians in Iran: Diplomacy and Power in the Qajar Era and Beyond*, edited by Rudi Matthee and Elena Andreeva, 173-85. London: I. B. Tauris, 2018.

Ter-Oganov, Nugzar. "Two Iranian Authors, Majd Os-Saltananeh and Yahya Dowlatabadi, on Tblisi." In *Typological Researches*, vol. 4, 399-408. Tbilisi: Georgian Academy of Sciences, 2000.

Thomas, Nikolai Alun. *Nomads and Soviet Rule: Central Asia under Lenin and Stalin*. London: I. B. Tauris, 2018.

Thomas, Nikolai Alun. "Revisiting the 'Transcaspian Episode': British Intervention and Turkmen Statehood, 1918-1919." *Europe-Asia Studies* 75, no. 1 (2023): 131-53.

Tikhonov, Iu. N. *Sovetskai͡a Rossiĭ v bor'be za "Afganskiĭ Koridor" (1919-1925): Sbornik Dokumentov*. Moscow: Kvadriga, 2017.

Timofeeva, A. A. *Istorii͡a predprinimatel'stva v Rossii: uchebnoe posobie*. Moscow: Flinta, 2011.

Tolz, Vera. *Russia's Own Orient: The Politics of Identity and Oriental Studies in the Late Imperial and Early Soviet Periods*. Oxford: Oxford University Press, 2011.

Torkmān, Eskandar Beg (Monshi). *Tārikh-e ʿalam ārā-ye ʿAbbāsi*. 2 vols. Tehran: Amir Kabir, 2003.

Toutant, Marc. "De-Persifying Court Culture: The Khanate of Khiva's Translation Program." In *The Persianate World: The Frontiers of a Eurasian Lingua Franca*, edited by Nile Green, 243-58. Oakland: California University Press, 2019.

Troebst, Stefan. "Isfahan-Moskau-Amsterdam: Zur Entstehungsgeschichte des moskauischen Transitprivilegs für die Armenische Handelskompanie in Persien (1666-1676)." In *Zwischen Arktis, Adria und Armenien: Das östliche Europa und seine Ränder. Aufsätze, Essays und Vorträge 1983-2016*, 35-69. Cologne: Boehlau Verlag, 2017.

Truvorov, A. N., ed. "Nakaz Pazukhinym, poslannym v Bukharu, Balkh i I͡urgench, 1669." *Russkai͡a istoricheskai͡a biblioteka* 15 (1894): 1-91.

Tsutsiev, A. *Atlas of the Ethno-Political History of the Caucasus*. New Haven, CT: Yale University Press, 2014.

Tucker, Ernest. *Nadir Shah's Quest for Legitimacy in Post-Safavid Iran*. Gainesville: University Press of Florida, 2006.

Tucker, Ernest. "Persian Historiography in the 18th and Early 19th Century." In *Persian Historiography*, edited by Charles Melville, vol. 10 of *A History of Persian Literature*, edited by Ehsan Yarshater, 258-91. New York: I. B. Tauris, 2012.
Ulianitskiĭ, V. A. *Snosheniia Rossii s Sredneĭ Azieiu i Indeiu v XVI-XVII vv. Po dokumentam Moskovskogo Glavnogo Arkhiva Ministerstva Inostrannykh Del.* Moscow: Universitetskaia Tipografiia, 1889.
Ulozhenie o nakazaniiakh ugolovnykh i ispravitel'nykh 1885 g. St. Petersburg, 1904.
Unvala, Jamshedji M. *Coins of Tabaristan and Some Sassanian Coins from Susa.* Paris, 1938.
Ushakov, N. M., ed. *Istoriia Astrakhanskogo kraia.* Astrakhan: Izdatel'stvo Astrakhanskogo gosudarstvennogo pedagogicheskogo universiteta, 2000.
Usmanov, M. A. "O dokumentakh russko-vostochnoĭ perepiski na tiurkskikh iazykakh v XV-XVIII vv. i ikh istochnikovedcheskom znachenii." In *Vostochnoe istoricheskoe istochnikovedenie i spetsial'nye istoricheskie distsipliny*, 2:126-29. Moscow: Nauka, 1994.
Vatslik, I. Ia. *Zakaspiĭskaia zheleznaia doroga: Eia znachenie i budushchnost'.* St. Petersburg: Parovaia Skoropechatnaia Iablonskiĭ i Perrot, 1888.
Veselovsky, Nikolay. *Pamiatniki diplomaticheskikh i torgovykh snosheniĭ Moskovskoĭ Rusi s Persieĭ.* Vol. 2, *TSarstvovanie Borisa Godunova, Vasiliia Shuĭskogo i nachalo tsarstvovaniia Mikhaila Feodorovicha.* St. Petersburg: Tovarishchestvo Parovoĭ Skoropechatni Iablonskiĭ i Perott, 1890-98.
Vinogradov, A. V., et al., eds. *Posol'skaia kniga po sviaziam Moskovskogo gosudarstva s Krymom, 1567-1572.* Moscow: Russkie Vitiazi, 2016.
Vitchevskiĭ, V. *Torgovaia, tamozhennaia i promyshlennaia politika Rossii co vremen Petra Velikogo do nashikh dnei.* St. Petersburg, 1909.
Vitsen, Nicolaas. *Puteshestvie v Moskoviiu, 1664-1665: Dnevnik.* Translated by V. G. Trisman. St. Petersburg, 1996.
Vneshniaia politika Rosii (XIX-nachale XX vv.) dokumenti Rossiĭskogo MIDa. Vol. 7. Moscow, 1970.
Volkov, Denis V. *Russia's Turn to Persia: Orientalism in Diplomacy and Intelligence.* Cambridge: Cambridge University Press, 2018.
Volkov, Denis V. "Vladimir Minorsky (1877-1966) and the Iran-Iraq War (1980-8)." In *Russians in Iran: Diplomacy and Power in the Qajar Era and Beyond*, edited by Rudi Matthee and Elena Andreeva, 188-216. London: I. B. Tauris, 2018.
Volodarsky, Mikhail. *Sovety i ikh iuzhnye sosedi Iran i Afganistan (1917-33 gg.).* London: Overseas Publications Interchange, 1985.
Volodarsky, Mikhail. *The Soviet Union and Its Neighbours: Iran and Afghanistan, 1917-1933.* Portland, OR: F. Cass, 1994.
Von Baer, Karl. *Peters des Grossen Verdienste um die Erweiterung der geographischen Kenntnisse.* St. Petersburg, 1872.
Von Niedermayer, Oskar. *Unter der Glutsonne Irans: Kriegserlebnisse des deutschen Expedition nach Persien und Afganistan.* Dachau bei München: Einhorverlag, 1925.
Voskanian, V. K., ed. *Armiano-Russkie otnosheniia vo vtorom tritsatiletii XVIII veka.* Vol. 3. Yerevan: Akademiia Nauk Armianskoĭ SSR, 1978.

Voskanīan, V. K., Dzh. O. Galustīan, and V. M. Martirosīan, eds. *Armīano-russkie otnosheniīa vo vtorom tridtsatiletii XVIII veka: sbornik dokumentov*. Vol. 3. Yerevan: Izd. Akademiīa Nauk Armīanskoĭ SSR, 1978.

Vucinich, Wayne S., ed. *Russia and Asia: Essays on the Influence of Russia on the Asian Peoples*. Stanford, CA: Hoover Institution Press, 1972.

Vuurman, Corien J. M., and L. A. Fereydoun Barjesteh van Waalwijk van Doorn (Khosrovani). "Vividly Painted Watercolours: Artistic Purchases from Persian Bazaars." *Journal of the International Qajar Studies Association* 12–13 (2013): 53–141.

Wageman, P., and Inessa Kouteinikova, eds. *Russia's Unknown Orient: Orientalist Paintings 1850–1920*. Groningen: Groninger Museum, 2010.

Waltz, Kenneth. *Theory of International Politics*. Reading, MA: Addison-Wesley, 1979.

Wasti, Syed Tanvir. "The Political Aspirations of Indian Muslims and the Ottoman Nexus." *Middle Eastern Studies* 42, no. 5 (2006): 709–22.

Wilson, Arnold. *Loyalties: Mesopotamia, 1914–1917. A Personal and Historical Record*. London: Oxford University Press, 1930.

Wilson, Arnold. *Mesopotamia, 1917–1920: A Clash of Loyalties. A Personal and Historical Record*. London: Oxford University Press, 1931.

Wilson, Arnold, A. C. Wratislaw, and Percy Sykes. "The Demarcation of the Turco-Persian Boundary in 1913 1914: Discussion." *Geographical Journal* 66, no. 3 (1925): 237–42.

Winn, Antony. *Persia in the Great Game: Sir Percy Sykes, Explorer, Consul, Soldier, Spy*. London: John Murrey, 2004.

Witzenrath, Christoph. *Cossacks and the Russian Empire, 1598–1725: Manipulation, Rebellion and Expansion into Siberia*. London: Routledge, 2007.

Wladimiroff, Igor. "Andries Vitsen and Nikolaas Witsen, Tsar Peter's Dutch Connection." In *Around Peter the Great: Three Centuries of Russian-Dutch Relations*, edited by Carel Horstmeier et al., 5–23. Groningen: INOS, 1997.

Wortman, Richard S. *Scenarios of Power: Myth and Ceremony in Russian Monarchy from Peter the Great to the Abdication of Nicholas II*. Princeton, NJ: Princeton University Press, 2006.

Wright, Denis. "Ironside, William Edmund." *Encyclopaedia Iranica Online*. https://iranicaonline.org/articles/ironside-william-edmund.

Wright, Denis. *The Persians amongst the English: Episodes in Anglo-Persian History*. London: I. B. Tauris, 1985.

Wright, Denis. "Sykes, Percy Molesworth." *Encyclopaedia Iranica Online*. https://iranicaonline.org/articles/sykes-percy.

Yaşar, Murat. "North Caucasus between the Ottoman Empire and the Tsardom of Muscovy: The Beginnings, 1552–1570." *Iran & the Caucasus* 20 (2016): 105–25.

Yaşar, Murat, and Chong Jin Oh. "The Ottoman Empire and the Crimean Khanate in the North Caucasus: A Case Study of the Ottoman-Crimean Relations in the Mid-Sixteenth Century." *Turkish Historical Review* 9 (2018): 86–103.

Ye'or, B. *The Dhimmi: Jews and Christians under Islam*. Rutherford: Farleigh Dickinson University Press, 1985.

Yenen, Alp. "Internationalism, Diplomacy and the Revolutionary Origins of the Middle East's 'Northern Tier.'" *Contemporary European History* 30, no. 4 (2021): 497–512.
Yilmaz, Şuhnaz. "An Ottoman Warrior Abroad: Enver Paşa as an Expatriate," *Middle Eastern Studies* 35, no. 4 (1999): 40–69.
Zabihi-Moghaddam, Siyamak. "The Babi-State Conflict at Shaykh Tabarsi." *Iranian Studies* 35, no. 1–3 (2002): 87–112.
Zabihi-Moghaddam, Siyamak. *Vāqeʻeh-ye Qalʻeh-ye Shaykh Ṭabarsi*. Darmstadt: Mo'asseseh-ye 'Aṣr-e Jadid, 2002.
Zak`aria of Agulis. *The Journal of Zak`aria of Agulis*, Translated by G. Bournoutian. Costa Mesa: Mazda, 2003.
Zak`aria of K`anak`er. *The Chronicle of Zak`aria of K`anak`er*. Translated by George Bournoutian. Costa Mesa: Mazda, 2004.
Zanjani, Habibullah. "Gorgan i. Geography." *Encyclopaedia Iranica*, XI/2, 139–42. https://iranicaonline.org/articles/gorgan-i.
Zarandi, Nabil. *The Dawn-Breakers*. Translated by Shoghi Effendi. Wilmette, IL: U.S. Baha'i Publishing Trust, 1992.
Zargarinezhād, Gholām Reżā. *Tārikh-e Irān dar Dowreh-ye Qājārieh, ʻAṣr-e Āqā Mohammad Khān*. Tehran: Sāzmān-e Moṭālaʻeh va Tadvin-e Kotob-e ʻolum-e ensāni-e Dāneshgāhā, 1395/2017–18.
Zeyrek, Yunus, ed. *Tarih-i Osman Paşa*. Ankara: Kültür Bakanlığı Yayınları, 2001.
Zhizneopisaniia pervykh Rossiĭskikh admiralov ili opyt istorii Rossiĭskago flota. St. Petersburg, 1831.
Zimin, A. A. *Gosudarstvennyĭ arkhiv Rossii XVI stoletiia: Opyt rekonstruktsii*. Moscow: Institut Istorii AN SSSR, 1978.
Zirinsky, Michael. "Imperial Power and Dictatorship: Britain and the Rise of Reza Shah, 1921–1926." *International Journal of Middle East Studies* 24, no. 4 (1992): 647–48.
Zoghi, Iraj. *Tārikh-e Ravābeṭ-e Siyāsi-ye ʻIrān va Qodrathā-ye Bozorg, 1900–1925*. Tehran: Pazhang, 1368/1989.
Zonn, Igor, Aleksey Kosarev, Michael Glantz, and Andrey Kostianoy. *The Caspian Sea Encyclopedia*. Berlin: Springer, 2014.

Contributors

Ulfat Abdurasulov is a research fellow at the Institute of Iranian Studies at the Austrian Academy of Sciences.

Abbas Amanat is the William Graham Sumner Professor of History Emeritus and former director of the Yale Program in Iranian Studies at Yale University.

Elena Andreeva is professor of history at the Virginia Military Institute.

George Bournoutian (1943–2021) was senior professor of history at Iona College.

Iurii Demin is associate professor and leading research fellow, HSE University, Moscow; associate professor, Irkutsk State University.

Layla S. Diba is an independent scholar in New York specializing in nineteenth- and twentieth-century Iranian art.

Etienne Forestier-Peyrat is assistant professor of contemporary history and director of Sciences Po Lille.

Kevin Gledhill is an assistant teaching professor in the Department of History at Sacred Heart University.

Guido Hausmann is professor of southeast and east European history at the University of Regensburg, and head of the History Division of the Leibniz-Institute for East and Southeast European Studies, Regensburg, Germany.

Kayhan A. Nejad is the Farzaneh Family Assistant Professor of Iranian Studies at the University of Oklahoma.

Matthew P. Romaniello is professor and chair of history at Weber State University.

Saghar Sadeghian is associate professor of history at Willamette University.

Alisa Shablovskaia is a postdoctoral fellow at the Department of Culture Studies and Oriental Languages, the University of Oslo.

Ernest Tucker is professor of history at the United States Naval Academy.

Denis V. Volkov is head of the Institute for Oriental and Classical Studies, HSE University, Moscow.

Murat Yaşar is associate professor of history at the State University of New York at Oswego.

Rustin Zarkar is the field director for the Library of Congress Overseas Office in Cairo, Egypt.

Index

'Abbas I, 25, 26, 63, 93, 138, 187n23, 198
'Abbas II, 94
'Abbas III, 141
'Abbās Mirza, 172, 249, 250fig, 251, 254
'Abbas Qoli Khan Lārijāni, 192-193, 194, 196, 197
Abbasid caliphate, 20
Abdullah Khan of Bukhara, 61
Abiz, Davlat Moḥammad, 79-82
Abu al-Ghāzi Khan, 81
Abukov, Batyrbek Lokmanovich, 303
Academy of Sciences, St. Petersburg, 116, 127, 128fig, 171, 210
Achaemenids, 17
Acts of Navigation, 7, 152, 153, 155, 157, 158
Adalat, 319
Adamova, Adel, 249
Afary, Janet, 264n2, 268n45, 322n12
Afghanistan
  boundaries of, 231
  British and Russian expansion and, 232, 276
  Nader Shah and, 139, 143
  trade and, 218, 219-222
  US invasion of, 13
Afsharid rulers, 6-7
Ahl-e Ḥaqq, 23, 25, 37
Alborz Mountains, 4, 18, 19, 196
Alexander I, 105
Alexander II, 60
Alexander of Macedonia, 17
Alexandrian Barrier, 17
Alexei Mikhaïlovich, Tsar, 66, 74, 80, 94, 97
Alexidze, Marina, 251, 253
Allahverdi Afshār, 249, 250-251, 252, 263
All-Russia Constituent Assembly, 283
All-Russia Provisional Government, 290n68

Amanat, Abbas, 186n17, 195
Amanullah, Emir, 313, 314
ambassadorial logs, 83n6
Amlash, 17
Amu-Darya, 1, 4, 9, 126, 232, 240
Anglo-Persian Agreement, 299, 328
Anglo-Persian Oil Company, 332
Anglo-Russian Agreement, 34-35
Anglo-Russian Commercial Treaty of 1734, 151, 153, 159, 161
Anjoman-e Āzarbāyejān (Anjoman of Azerbaijan), 294
Anna, Empress of Russia, 102, 140, 142
Annenkov, Mikhaïl Nikolaevich, 230, 232
anti-Ententism, 295, 297, 298-299
antigovernmental movements, 338-341
anti-imperialist movements, 310
antisemitism, 195
Anzali, 4, 29, 31, 32, 100, 147, 177, 179, 278, 353
Anzali landing, 292, 302, 303, 330, 332, 342, 352
Apraksin, Fëdor, 137
Āqā Ebrāhim, 252, 253
Āqā Moḥammad Khan Qajar, 8, 30, 169-170, 171, 173, 179, 181, 183-185, 187n23
Arab Revolt, 296
Arapov, Semën, 160, 161
Argutinskiĭ, Iosif, 103, 104, 111n78
Aristotle, 17
Armenia/Armenians, 6, 35, 37, 38, 91-112, 115, 135, 138, 143, 144, 151-166, 170, 216, 243, 249
Armenian Revolutionary Party (Dashnaktsutyun), 35, 216, 282
Armeno-Russian treaty, 104
art, Karazin and, 227-246
Arzhangi, 'Abbās Rassām, 10, 248, 248fig, 252, 253-255, 254fig, 257-258, 261, 263-264

405

INDEX

Arzhangi, Mir Ḥosayn Mosavvar, 252, 253–255, 263–264
Ashgabat, 32. *See also* Ashkabad
Ashkhabad, 240, 242–243
Astarabad, 8, 19, 28, 29, 100, 138, 144, 146, 153, 170, 171, 173, 176, 181–183, 221, 315, 332
Astarābādi, Mahdi Khan, 150n35, 178, 179
Astrakhan, 4, 79–81, 92, 96, 98, 99, 104, 113–133, 136–137, 153, 154–155, 159–163, 176, 180–182, 208–214, 236, 358
Astrakhan Campaign (1569), 50–51, 52–56
Asvebekov, 'Abdurraḥim Bek (Abreimbek), 72, 73
Atabaev, K. S., 339
Atkin, Muriel, 170
Āẕarbāijān, 258
Azerbaijan, region of Iran, 39, 191, 192, 248, 249, 263, 293–296, 298, 300, 301, 302, 332, 339, 342, 353, 354
Azerbaijan, Soviet Union, 293, 300, 302, 310, 319, 328, 332, 339, 350, 355–358. *See also* Baku
Azerbaijan Democratic Republic, 300, 301, 302, 316
Azerbaijani Democratic Party (ADP), 353
Azeri revolutionaries, 317–319
'Aẓimzādeh, 'Aẓim, 258
Azizbekov Oil Institute, 355

Bābā, Mirza, 249
Bābi movement, 33–34
Bābi resistance, 8–9, 191–206
Baghavard, Battle of, 141
Baghdad Pact, 355
Bahá'u'lláh, 200–201
Bahr-i Kolzum Kapudanlığı, 60
Bailey, Frederick M., 273
Bakharden underground lake, 241
Baku
  art and, 236–237
  customs and, 207–208, 213–214, 215, 216–217
  defense of, 281–282
  Iran and, 26, 29, 34, 39, 252, 339
  naval school in, 350
  Russia and, 29, 100
  Soviet Union and, 299, 300–301
Baku Commissars, 10, 273, 288

Baku Committee of the Russian Social Democratic Labor Party (RSDRP), 294
Baku Commune, 281, 312, 317–318
Barakatullah, Mohammad Moulavi, 313–314, 315, 318
Baratov, Nikolay, 274, 275, 277, 278–279, 281
Bārforush, 32, 192–198, 201, 202
Barg, Abdul Rab, 313
Bartol'd, Vasily, 87n50
Baskakov, Nikita, 170, 173, 184
Bassin, Mark, 122
Bast, Oliver, 273–274, 311
Baud, Michiel, 225n48
Behrooz, Maziar, 172
Behzād, Ḥosayn, 255, 264
Behzād, Ḥosayn Ṭāherzādeh, 10, 255–256, 256*fig*, 258–261, 261*fig*, 262*fig*, 263, 264
Behzād, Karim, 255, 256, 258–261, 263
Bekovich-Cherkasskiĭ, Aleksandr, 123, 125–126, 176
Beliākov, Andrey, 77
Beradze, Grigol, 253
Berberian, Houri, 253
Bicherakhov, Lazar', 11, 274, 276, 277–278, 279–285
Binich, 258, 259, 261*fig*, 262*fig*
Black Death, 23
Black Sea, 51–52
Blank, Stephen, 15n15, 293, 311
Board of Trade and Plantations, 153, 158
Bohlen, Avis, 88n67
Bokhardemskoe podzemnoe ozero (Karazin), 242*fig*
"Bolshevik Ideas and the Islamic Republic" (Barakatullah), 313
Bolshevik networks, 309–325
Bolshevik Revolution, 32, 271
Bolshevism, opposition to, 10, 274, 285, 293, 302
Braudel, Fernand, 2
Bravin, Nikolai, 312
Brest-Litovsk peace agreement, 312
bridges, railroad and, 239
Brinegar, Sara, 293
British East India Company, 7, 26–27, 146, 151–158, 163, 180
Bronze Age, 17
Browne, E. G., 199–200, 256, 257, 259
Bruce, Peter Henry, 109n48

INDEX 407

Burke, Edmund, 102
Burlaki na Volge (Barge Hauleres on the Volga; Repin), 240
Burnish, Onslow, 7, 151–152, 156–158, 163
Bushev, P. P., 87n50, 187n24
Buyids, 20, 37

canal projects, 50–51, 54
Cantemir, Dmitriĭ, 99, 174
Carr, E., 327–328
cartography, 6, 8, 115, 116–130, 147, 169–190
Caspian Hyatt Hotel, 356
Caspian Sea
  description of, 1, 3
  fisheries and, 330–332, 342, 353, 355, 357–358
  surface area of, 3
  water levels in, 3, 357
Caspian State Navigation Company (Kaspar), 355
Catherine I, 101
Catherine II, 102–105, 128, 172, 182, 184, 211
Caucasian Bureau of the Russian Communist Party, 303, 328
Caucasian Caspian Alliance Government, 272, 273, 274, 275, 276, 277, 282–284, 290n68
Caucasus
  Iran and, 38–39
  Russia and, 27
  slaves from, 26
Çelebi, Evliya, 58
Central-Caspian Dictatorship, 282
Chalfin, Brenda, 209
Chaquèri, Cosroe, 306n33, 310–311
Charjew, oasis of, 243
Chekalevskiĭ, Peter, 180
Cherkasov, Fëdor Lvovich, 162
Chernushevich, P., 213
Chicherin, Georgii V., 311, 318–319, 329, 331, 335, 337
China, regional role of, 13
Chinese revolutionary movement, 312
Chinggisid Empire, 114
Choban, Shamkhāl, 55
"Chronology of the Persian Revolution" (Browne), 256
Clark, James, 257
climate, 19

climate change, 3
Cold War, 12, 39, 351, 354, 357
commenda agents, 93
Commerce College, 180, 181, 210
Commercial Code of 1653, 209
Constantinople, Treaty of, 101, 178, 179
Constitutional Revolution, 9, 34–35, 36, 45n36, 216, 257, 259, 263, 264, 271, 294–295, 304, 310, 317, 319, 328
Convention on the Legal Status of the Caspian Sea, 13
Cordier, Bruno de, 14n1
Cossacks, 28–29, 51, 92–93, 122, 276, 277, 280, 284
Council of Propaganda and Action of the Peoples of the East, 339
Cox, Percy, 273, 279–280, 284
Crimean War, 228
Criminal and Correctional Penal Code, 216
Cronin, Stephanie, 264n2, 293
Csirkés, Ferenc Peter, 87n49
Curzon, George, 230, 232, 239, 278, 279–280, 284
customs, 207–226

Dagestan, 17, 29, 49, 55–59, 62, 93, 99, 100, 173, 175, 208, 318
Dailami, Pezhmann, 293, 298, 301, 311
Danilovich, R., 208
Dār al-Fonun School of Fine Arts, 248
D'Arcy Concession, 332
Darius III, 17
Darius the Great, 17
al-Dawleh, Ḥasan Pirniyā Moshir, 300
de Gobineau, Arthur comte, 206n66
Denikin, Anton, 274, 283–284, 285, 299, 303, 350
Derbent, 17, 59–63, 97, 99, 100, 102, 114, 127, 134, 141, 147, 155, 174, 212, 236, 282
DeWeese, Devin, 85n28
Diamond Throne, 94
Diplomatic History of the Caspian Sea, A (Mirfendereski), 351–352
Dobycha s berega (Loot from the shore; Karazin), 233–234, 233*fig*
al-Dowleh, Mirza 'Ali Akbr Mozayyan, 248
dragomans, 76–82
Druze nomads, 340
Dunsterforce, 274
Dunsterville, Lionel C., 272, 274, 276, 277, 278, 280, 283–284

INDEX

Dustdār, Ehsān-Allah Khan, 281, 341
Dutch East India Company, 26–27, 146
Duval, Pierre, 119*fig*

Echmiadzin, 91, 102–103
Edirne, Treaty of, 27–28
Edmonds, Cecil J., 273
Ehsān-Allah Khan Dustdār, 36, 281
Ejtemā'iyyun-e 'Āmiyyun (Social Democrats), 294
Ekhtiar, Maryam, 172
Elizabeth (Elizaveta Petrovna), Empress of Russia, 102, 210
Elton, John, 7, 29–30, 136, 144, 145–147, 154–163
'Emād al-Din Nasimi, 23
Emin, Joseph (Hovsep), 102
Emir Mirza, Shamkhāl, 56–57
Endereī, fort of, 92
English Muscovy Company, 114, 117
Erekle II, 102, 104, 181
Ereshko, E. V., 214–215
Ermakov, Dmitriĭ, 253
Ermolov, Alekseĭ Petrovich, 249–250
Esma'il Beg, 100
Ettehād-e Eslām committee, 281
excise taxes, 222

Fabritius, Ludvig, 122
Fakhrā'i, Ebrāhim, 297
Farrokh, Mollā, 73
Fath-'Ali Khan Qajar, 138
Fath-'Ali Shah, 171, 172, 249
Fazlullah Astarābādi, 22–23
Feodor III Alekseevich, Tsar, 86n40
Ferdowsi, A., 21
Fereydun, 21–22
Ferqeh-ye Demokrāt (Democrats), 294
Firuz, Eskandar, 358
fisheries/fishing concessions, 330–332, 342, 353, 355, 357–358
Floor, Willem, 180, 185n2
forests, 196–203
Franz Ferdinand, Archduke, 272
Fraser, James B., 197, 198–199
French Communist Party, 340
frontiers, concept of, 68
funding during WWI, 279–280

Ganjeh, Treaty of, 29, 102, 138, 139, 140–143, 153, 187n23
Gates of Alexander, 17
Gelibolulu Mustafa Ali, 57, 59

Genis, Vladimir Leonidovich, 275, 310–311
geography, rise of field of, 115–116, 125
George V, King, 284
Georgia
  Iranian artists and, 247, 251–253, 255, 258, 263
  tourism and, 356
Georgian Military Road, 104
Georgievsk, Treaty of, 104, 181
Germany
  Iran and, 295–296, 351, 352
  Khiyabani and, 300
Gestwa, Klaus, 351
Ghāffari Kamāl al-Molk, Mohammad, 248
gholām army, 26
Gilan, 4, 17, 19, 20, 26, 30, 93, 97–101, 136, 139, 157, 159, 161, 172–181, 353, 356–359. *See also* Soviet Socialist Republic of Iran (SSRI)
Gilan Republic, 309, 311, 319, 330, 338, 339, 343, 353, 357
Gilāni, 'Abd al-Qāder, 22
Gilāni, Gharib Shah, 25
Gmelin, Samuel Gottlieb, 171, 180–181, 185n2
Gocheleishvili, Iago, 252
Goff, Krista, 15n14
Gök-Tepe, 241–242
Golding, Robert, 62
Golestan Treaty, 27–28
Golitsyn, Alexander, 102
Golitsyn, Sergeĭ, 141–142
Golitsyn, Vasiliĭ, 69
Gomishtappeh, Battle of, 35
Gopner, David, 314
Graeme, Mungo, 144
Great Britain
  Armenians and, 151–166
  India and, 312, 314
  Iranian artists and, 249, 251
  Iranian revolutionaries and, 293–294
  separatist movements in Iran and, 339–340
  Soviet-British accord and, 310
  trade and, 337
  Transcaspian Railroad and, 231, 232
  White Russian movement and, 293, 297
  during World War I, 271–291
Great Game, 272, 342
Great Northern War, 114, 123, 127, 175

INDEX

Great Terror, 350
Great Wall of Gorgan, 17
Green, Nile, 68, 70, 251, 265n8
Griboedov, Alexander, 251
Güldenstädt, Johann A., 128–129

Habibullah, Emir of Afghanistan, 313
Hakob of Shamakhi, 102
Hambly, Gavin, 189n60
Hamidian massacres, 216
Hanway, Jonas, 145–146, 148, 150n35, 160, 161, 162, 198
Hasan, Aga, 162
Hasanli, Jamil, 311
Hausmann, Guido, 176
Ḥāji Moḥammad Āqā 'Emrānlu, 169, 170
Ḥashārāt al-Arż, 258, 259*fig*
Ḥodud al-'Ālam, 20–21
Hirst, Samuel J., 310
Hoare, Samuel, 284
Hobsbawm, E. J., 8, 193–194, 201, 203
Hodgson, Marshall, 68
Homann, Johann Baptist, 123, 124*fig*
Horufi movement, 22–23, 25
Hümmət (Hemmat) Party, 294, 298, 317, 318
hydrography, 128
Hyrcanian Sea, 17

Ibn Sina, 20
Imperator AleksandrIII, 236, 237
imperialism, 4
İnalcık, Halil, 52
Indian Provisional Government (IPG), 312, 313
Indian revolutionaries, 312–313
interpreters, 78–79
Iomudskii, Nikolai, 316
Iran
  absence of shipbuilding tradition in, 28
  Anglo-Russian Agreement and, 34–35
  artists from, 247–268
  Caucasus and, 38–39
  firearms of, 199, 201
  regional revolutionaries in, 292–308
  revolutionary trends in, 33
  Russia and, 29–31, 38, 100, 137, 139, 140, 141–142, 169–171, 177–182
  separatist movements in, 338–341
  silk trade and, 97–99
  Soviet trade policy and, 334–337, 342–343

  Soviet Union and, 326–364
  trade and, 151–153, 157–159, 161–163, 218, 219–221
  transnationalism in, 309–325
  World War II and, 351, 352–353
Iranian Communist Party (ICP), 309, 319–320, 320–321n5, 321n12, 341
Iranian Democratic Party (IDP), 314, 319
"Iranian Operation," 350–351
Iranian Provisional Government, 314
Iranian-Azeri Socio-Democratic Party, 318
Iranian-Russian treaties, 135
Iranian-Turkmen border convention, 220
Iron Curtain, 17
Isfahan, 22, 74, 93, 97–98, 100, 115, 135, 138, 154, 156, 157, 174, 175, 178, 181, 194, 272
Islamic Revolution, 359
Islamization, 91
Isma'il I, 24–25
Istanbul, Treaty of, 63
Iūkht, A. I., 153, 179
Iurenev, K. K., 331
Ivan III, 91–92
Ivan IV, 92
Ivan V Alekseevich, Tsar, 67, 72–73

Jadid, 315
Ja'far Moḥammad, 249–251, 250*fig*, 252, 263
Jahānbāni, Amān-Allāh, 355
Jangal Movement, 11, 34, 35–36, 45n36, 196, 278, 280–281, 285, 292–308, 329
Jāvidān-nāmeh (Fazlullah Astarābādi), 23
Jenkinson, Anthony, 117, 117*fig*, 118*fig*
jihad, concept of, 315
Julfa, 93

Kaempfer, Engelbert, 121*fig*, 122
kaikchi, 240
Kalmyk, 89n75, 122
Kamāl al-Molk, 260, 264
Kapur, H., 327–328
Karakum Desert, 28, 135, 218, 232
Karazin, Nikolaï, 9, 227–246
Karim Khan Zand, 102, 104, 171, 179, 181
Karimov, Laṭif, 263
Karnal, Battle of, 143
Kasım Pasha, 54–55
Kasimov, 358

INDEX

Kasymov, Muhammad Iūsuf, 74–75
Kaufman, Konstantin Petrovich von, 229, 231, 243
Kavkaz i Merkuriĭ steamship company, 8, 215
Kayānid Dynasty, 21
Kaykavus, 21
Kazan, 78, 80, 92, 113, 147, 157
Kazım Bey, Mehmed, 315–316, 318
Kelly, Sean, 276
Kevir-Khurian Limited, 334
Khan, Yeprem, 35
Khan Devlet Girey, 54
Khatami, Mohammad, 15n18
Khazar people, 18
Khilafat movement, 313, 314
Khivan route, 84n13
Khivinets, Peter, 78–79
Khiyabani, Moḥammad, 299–302
Khodarkovsky, Michael, 89n75, 122
Khorasan, Nader Shah and, 134, 135, 138, 142, 144–145
Khoshtariya, 332–333
Khosrow II, 17
Khosrow Mirza Qajar, Prince, 251
Khrushchev, Nikita, 356
Kiā Esmā'il, tomb of, 18
Kidekov, Sutur, 80
Kirilov, Ivan, 154
Konkurenty (Rivals; Karazin), 238–239
Konstantin Kaufman, 236
Kotoshkhin, Grigory, 76
Koussis brothers, 31
Kozhin, Aleksandr, 123, 125
Kuchek Khan, Mirza, 11, 35–36, 297, 298, 299, 302, 303, 317
Küçük Kaynarca, Treaty of, 27
Kulmamatov, Dusmamat, 72
Kurdish uprisings, 340, 340t
Kuropatkin, A. N., 230
Kurukin, I.V., 175, 176
Kuznetsov, N., 350
Kyzyl-Arvat, 241
Kyzyl-Arvat (Karazin), 241fig

Lāhuti, 'Abol-Qāsem, 301
Lala Mustafa Pasha, 56–58, 60
language
  in Muscovite court documents, 66–69, 70–73
  terminology of, 71–72
Laṭif Khan, Moḥammad, 145
Latin, 74–75

Lazarev, Ivan, 103
Lazarev family, 103
LeDonne, John P., 52
Lenin, Vladimir, 312, 323n22
Levant Company, 152, 153–154, 158, 159, 163
"leveling prices," 337
Lezhava, A. M., 334
Lianozov, Martin, 331
Lianozov, S. M., 330–331
Lianozov, Stepan, 31
Lisle, Guillaume de, 123
localism, 4
Lomakin, Mikhaĭl Pavlovich, 230
Luxemburg, Rosa, 253

Maclean, Fitzroy, 351
Mahdi Khan, 150n35
Mahdi Qoli Mirza, 192–193, 197, 200
Maḥmud Pasikhāni, 24
Makhachkala (formerly Petrovsk), 9, 236, 258
malaria, 19, 29
Malen'kiĭ (Malenkov), Semën, 73–74, 75–76
Malleson, Wilfrid, 10, 282
Mamluk, 26
Mangyshlak, 84n13
Mar'ashi movement, 25
Mar'ashi revolt, 25
marine life, 16
Markaz-e Ghaybi, 294, 301
Marlik, 17
Marshall, William, 277, 278, 279, 284
Martha, 207–208
Mathee, Rudi, 171–172, 186n17
Matin-Asgari, Afshin, 263, 264n2
Matiūshkin, Mikhaĭl, 176–177
Matveev, Artamon, 69
Matveev, Maksim, 69–70
Mazandaran, 4, 17, 19, 21, 22, 29, 30, 32, 33, 100, 104, 114, 136, 139, 169–172, 181, 184, 191–202, 296, 298, 331, 353
Mediterranean and the Mediterranean World in the Age of Philip II, The (Braudel), 2
Mediterranean history, field of, 2
Mehmāndust, Battle of, 139
Mehmed Bey, 60
Mehmed Girey II, 63
Mehmed II, 51
Meier, Eremej, 123
Melikov, Devlet Abyz, 79–82
Mensheviks, 282

INDEX

Mercator, Gerardus, 120*fig*
Merk, Grigoriĭ, 180
Merv, 230–231, 239, 240, 243, 276
Meteorologica (Aristotle), 17
Mierop, Martin Kuychkan, 163
Mikhail Feodorovich, Tsar, 67
Minas, 96, 99
Minorsky, Vladimir, 273, 282–283, 284, 290n68
Mirfendereski, Guive, 13n1, 351–352
Mirza Abu al-Qāsem Farāhāni Qā'em Maqām, 186n17
Mirza Ja'far Ṭabib, 251
Mirza Moḥammad Khalil Mar'ashi, 179
mixed-capital enterprises, 335–336, 337
Moḥammad 'Ali Shah, 217, 257, 294
Moḥammad Ḥasan Khan Qajar, 29, 118n48, 138, 147–148, 179, 180–181, 183
Moḥammad Saydal Khan, 139
Moiseev, M., 76
Mokri, Mohammad, 359–360
Molla Ḥosayn Boshruyev, 191–193, 199, 200–202
Mollā Nāṣr al-Din, 257*fig*, 258
Molotov-Ribbentrop Pact, 352
Mongol Khanate, 4. *See also* Chinggisid Empire
Mongols, Russia and, 91–92
Mossadegh, 354–355
Mount Damavand, 21–22
Moẓaffar al-Din Shah, 252, 253
Mudros, Armistice of, 283
Münster, Sebastian, 126*fig*
Murad III, Sultan, 57, 62–63
Müsavat Party (Equality), 294
Muscovy
  Astrakhan Campaign and, 51, 53–54
  courts of, 66–90
  expansion and, 49
  map of, 117*fig*, 118*fig*
  trade and, 209–210
Mustafa-Zade, Rakhman, 339

"Na puti v Indiiū" (On the way to India; Karazin), 234, 235
Nader Shah, 6–7, 19, 29, 102, 103, 134–150, 152–153, 155–156, 162, 177, 179
Nafisi, Hoseyn, 353
Narimanov, Nariman, 301, 317, 318, 319
Narodnyĭ Komissariat Vnutrennikh Del (NKID, People's Commissariat of Internal Affairs), 318, 319

Naser al-Din Shah, 31, 192, 197–199, 253
National Academy (Iran), 260
National Bloc, 338
National Committee for the Defense of Iranian Independence, 300
National Museum of Georgia, 253
naval supremacy, 28, 30
naval training, 350
Naẓar 'Ali Khan, 202
Nazarov, Mikail, 356
Nazis, Iran and, 351, 352
Nefes, Khoja, 126
New Commercial code of 1667, 209
New Economic Policy, 334
New Julfa, 93, 94, 97, 115, 138, 144
Nezāmi of Ganjeh, 23
Nicholas II, Tsar, 35
Nikonov, Oleg, 186n17, 187n24
Niva, 238
nomenclature, 18
Noqtavi movement, 22, 24, 25
Norperforce, 36, 273

O'Hara, James, 160
Oil Syndicate, 336
oil/oil industry, 9, 182, 236, 237, 252, 278, 281, 293, 294, 303, 328, 332–334, 342, 355, 357
Olearius, Adam, 117–119, 118*fig*, 122
"On Measures to Prevent Pollution in the Caspian Sea," 357
Operation Barbarossa, 352
Ordin-Nashchokin, Afanasiĭ, 69
Ordzhonikidze, G. K., 329
Organization for the Protection of Environment, 359
Ori, Israyel, 6, 96
Ortelius, Abraham, 118*fig*
Ottoman Triumvirate, 315
Ottomans
  Armenians and, 216
  Iran and, 295–296
  Nader Shah and, 140, 141, 142
  occupation of Tabriz by, 298
  propaganda from, 314–315
  relationships with, 5
  Russia and, 101, 129, 137
  Safavids and, 93
  silk trade and, 96–97
  in sixteenth century, 49–65
  trade and, 153
  treaties with, 27–28
  World War I and, 281, 283

INDEX

Ottoman-Safavid War, 56, 59, 63
Ovnatanian, Akop, 253
Özdemiroğlu Osman Pasha, 50, 57–58, 59–61, 62–63

Pahlavān Qoli Bek, 66–67
Pahlavi dynasty, 19
Pahlavi style, 261, 264
Pallas, Peter Simon, 129
Pamir Treaty, 231
Pan-Islamic Committees, 296
Pasha, Enver, 315
Pasha, Nuri, 315
Peri, Benedek, 87–88n60
Persian (language), 67–69, 70–71, 72, 76–78
Persian Cossack Brigade, 316
Persian Front, 272, 274, 276
Persian-Tatar Committee, 296
Persidskiĭ front Pervoĭ mirovoĭ (The Persian Front of WWI; Baratov), 274
Persographia, 68
Pesiyan, Moḥammad Taqi Khan, 299, 302
Peter I
   Armenia and, 6
   court documents and, 67, 72–73, 74
   expansion and, 28–29, 95–100, 123, 125–127, 137, 139, 152, 172, 173–175, 179, 183, 227
   Ottomans and, 101
   trade and, 96–97, 115–116, 143, 210
Peter II, 101
Petrovsk. *See* Makhachkala (formerly Petrovsk)
Petrovsk Customs Department, 208, 217
Piātakov, G. L., 333
Planhol, Xavier de, 3
Poe, Marshall, 84n19
pollution, 357, 358
Poltava, 108n34
Popov, Ivan, 128
Posol'skiĭ Prikaz, 66–90
Potemkin, Grigoriĭ, 103–104, 182
Potemkin, Pavel, 103
Pratap, "Prince," 313
Press and Poetry of Modern Persia, The (Browne), 256
"Primitive Rebel" theory, 8, 193–194, 203
Provisional Executive Committee of the Soviet, 282

Qajars/Qajar Iran
   Bābi uprisings and, 33–34, 191–206
   cartography and, 169–190
   emergence of, 7
   Nader Shah and, 138
   nomenclature and, 19
   power of, 30–31
   Russia and, 6, 38, 169–171, 177–178, 183–184
   trade and, 173
   treaties with, 27–28
Qizilbash Turkoman Afshārs, 135
Qoddus, 191, 192, 193, 195–196, 201
Quadripartite Boundary Commission, 273

Rabino, H. L., 195
Rasht, 24, 30, 32, 35, 100, 137, 147, 151, 154, 155, 157, 159, 160, 162, 171, 177–180, 183, 295, 297, 301, 332, 356, 359
Rasht, Treaty of, 29, 102, 139, 140–143, 153, 177, 187n23
Rashtiani, Goodarz, 186n17
Rasulzadeh, Mohammad Amin, 45n36
Razin, Sten'ka, 66, 95, 107n25
Religion of Love ("Prince" Pratap), 313
Rentel, Jean-Christophe, 123
Repin, Il'iā, 240
Revolutionary Military Council, 331
Reżā Shah (Reżā Khan), 36, 260–261, 263, 299, 304, 316, 338, 341, 342, 351, 356
Reżā-Qoli Khan Hedāyat, 170
Reżā-Qoli Mirza, 144, 146
"rice riots," 353
Richard, Yann, 273
Robert Wenkhaus and Co., 336
Rodzevich, A. I., 232
Romaniello, Matthew, 180
Rostam, 21
Rothman, Nathalie, 81
Rotter, Joseph, 258
Roy, M. N., 314, 323n27
Russia
   Astrakhan and, 113–133, 136–137
   Britain and, 151
   cartographic expeditions and, 6
   cartography and, 8, 113–133, 169–190
   Caucasus and, 27
   contraband and, 9
   Cossacks and, 28–29

Elton and, 147
expansion and, 6, 8, 27–29, 32–33, 113–114, 127–128, 172–173, 174–176, 218, 227–229
interests of, 91–112
Iran and, 20, 21, 29–31, 38, 137, 139, 140, 141–142, 169–171, 177–182
Iranian artists and, 247–268
naval supremacy of, 28, 30
silk trade and, 127, 143, 175
trade and, 31–32, 38, 114–115, 136–138, 143, 152–153, 173, 184, 207–226
Volga and, 5
during World War I, 271–291
See also Soviet Union
Russia Company, 7, 29–30, 144, 145–146, 151–154, 155, 156–159, 161–162, 163, 180
Russian All-Military Union, 274
Russian Civil War, 10–11, 292, 295, 297, 299, 310
Russian Legation, 282–283
Russian nationalist realism, 254
Russian Revolution, 10, 32, 216, 276, 296–297
Russian Revolution (1905), 35, 253
Russian Social Democratic Labor Party (RSDLP), 312, 317
Russo-Georgian treaty (Treaty of Georgievsk), 103, 104, 181
Russo-Ottoman wars, 103, 104, 182
Russo-Persian Wars, 8, 30, 38, 137, 212, 251
Ruznāmeh-ye Āzarbāijān, 260*fig*

Safarilieva, D., 249
Safavids
collapse of, 137
emergence of, 4
messianic instincts and, 37
Muscovy and, 74, 78
Nader Shah and, 138–139
nomenclature and, 19
Ottomans and, 5, 49, 50, 52–53, 56–59, 61, 93
Peter I and, 143
power of, 24–25, 26
Russia and, 174, 175
Safi, Shah, 25, 93
Sakharotrest, 336
Saleh, Jahanshah, 358–359
al-Salṭaneh, Neẓām, 314

Samanid Empire, 20
Samarskai͡a uchënai͡a ėkspeditsii͡a (Samara Scholarly Expedition), 231–232
Sarafov, Moses, 103
Sarbedāari movement, 25
Sarkis, Khoja, 180
Sartori, Paolo, 85n27, 90n98
Sāru'i, Moḥammad-Taqi, 170, 179, 183
Sasanian Empire, 17
Savādkuhi, Amir Mo'ayyed, 296, 298
Sayyed 'Ali Moḥammad, 191
Schendel, Willem Van, 225n48
Schmerling, Oskar Ivanovich, 258
Scott, James, 196, 203
Second Constitutional Majles, 294, 295
Sekachev, Pavel, 211
Selim II, 50, 51
separatist movements, 338–341
Shadrin, Andreĭ, 92
Shah Aurangzeb, 74–75, 77
Shah Jahan, 74
Shah Solṭān Ḥosayn, 74, 139, 174, 175
Shahamirean family, 103
Shāhnāmeh (Ferdowsi), 21–22
Shaidā, 259, 261*fig*, 262*fig*
Shaykh Ṭabarsi, fort of, 8, 9, 34, 35, 191–206
Shaykhi movement, 33, 35, 195, 196
Shcherbatov, Prince, 160, 161
Shekāk, Semko, 299
Shi'ism, 20, 22, 25, 33–34, 37, 56, 91, 191, 195
ship building, 60, 62, 136, 147, 159–160, 161
Shir Ghāzi Khan, 176
Shirāzi, Moḥammad-Taqi Khan, 145
Shirvan, 5, 50, 56–60, 93, 98–101, 115, 152, 173, 174, 175, 212
Shirvanov, Luka, 180
Shkuro, Andrei, 274, 277
Shumiatskii, Boris, 332, 340
Shuster, Morgan, 259–260
silk/silk trade, 26–27, 93–98, 103, 114–115, 127, 143, 146, 152–158, 175, 180–181, 208, 210, 211, 216, 263
Simeon of Yerevan, 102, 103
Sinclair, H., 333
Sinclair, Ronald, 273
Sinclair company, 333
Skobelev, Mikhaĭl Dmitrievich, 230, 242
slavery, 26, 232–233

INDEX

Sluzhba v mirnoe vremiia (Service in peacetime; Chernushevich), 213
Smirnov, Konstantin, 279
smuggling, 207–209, 210, 211, 213–217, 221–222
Snesarev, Andrei, 278
Social Democrats, 35–36, 294, 298
Society of Islamic Unity, 35
Soĭmonov, Fëdor I., 123, 125, 125*fig*, 127, 129, 176
Sokullu Mehmed Pasha, 50–51, 53, 54, 55, 56, 59–61, 63
Solṭān Ḥāshem Mirza, 179
Solṭānzādeh (Mikaelian), Avetis, 319, 321n12
Sophia Alekseevna, 83n10
Sorkhāi Khan I, 141
Sotavov, N. A., 14n1
Sotudeh, Manuchehr, 200, 206n62
South Persia Rifles, 272
Soviet Socialist Republic of Iran (SSRI), 292–293, 300, 303, 309, 320, 328–330, 338, 339, 343
Soviet Union
  collapse of, 12, 13
  Iran and, 326–364
  naval training and, 350
  trade policy of, 334–337, 342–343
  See also Russia
Soviet-Iranian Treaty of 1921, 328, 329, 330, 332
St. Petersburg Academy of Fine Arts, 249
St. Petersburg, Treaty of, 100, 137, 139, 176
Stalin, Josef, 288n18, 318, 351, 353
Standard Oil, 332–333
Still Life with Melons, Peaches and a Spoon (Arzhangi), 248*fig*
Struys, Johann Janszoon, 119
sugar, trade in, 336
Süleyman I, 51–52
Sultan-Galiev, Mirsaid, 307n54, 315
Suvorov, Aleksandr, 104, 182
Sweden, Russia and, 114, 115, 123, 127, 175
Sykes, Ella Constance, 273
Sykes, Percy M., 272–273
Syroezhin, Nikita, 74

Tabarestān, 17, 20, 37
Tabari, Mohammad Jarir, 22
Tabaristan, 17, 18, 37
Tabriz
  constitutionalists in, 294, 295
  Khiyabani and, 300
  Ottoman occupation of, 298
  siege of, 256–257
Tabrizi, Mirza Ja'far, 249, 251
Tabrizi, Za'im al-Dawleh, 200, 201
Tahmasb, 26
Tahmasb II, 101, 137, 138, 139, 140, 141, 144, 174, 176, 178
Tahmasb Qoli. *See* Nader Shah
Taqizadeh, Hassan, 34, 263, 314
tariffs, 98, 139, 140, 159, 161, 207, 208, 209–213, 215–216, 220
Tārikh-e Moḥammadi (Sāru'i), 179
Tāriverdi, Ḥaydar Khan 'Amu-Oghlu, 36, 294, 319, 320–321n12, 329
Tarki, 5, 55, 92, 175
Tarumov, Zolner, 211
Tashkent
  Bolshevik headquarters in, 312, 315
  fall of to Russia, 218, 229
  Indian revolutionaries and, 312, 313, 314
  Turkkomissia and, 319
Tatar, use of term, 71
Tatishchev, Vasiliĭ Nikitich, 119
Teague-Jones, Reginald, 273
Teapot Dome Scandal, 333
Tekke, 135
terrain, 19
Teymuraz II, 102
Third Majles, 295
Thomson, Ringler, 218
Through the Deserts and Oases of Central Asia (Sykes), 273
Tiflis Academy of Art and Sculpture, 252–253
Tiflis Museum, 261
Tiflis School of Drawing and Sculpture, 258
Tiflis Secondary School of Painting and Sculpture, 252–253
Timur, 134
Timurids, 22, 23
Tonekāboni, Moḥammad Vali Khan (Sepahsālār), 294
tourism, 356
trade
  Afghanistan and, 218, 219–221
  agreements regarding, 94–98
  Anglo-Russian Commercial Treaty and, 151–152
  Astrakhan and, 114, 115

INDEX 415

Azerbaijan and, 356
balanced, 337
Bārforush and, 194
Black Sea and, 52
Britain and, 151–166
customs and, 207–226
encouragement of, 62
Great Britain and, 337
growth of, 134–135
Iran and, 97–99, 151–153, 157–159, 161–163, 218, 219–221, 334–337, 342–343
Muscovy and, 209–210
Ottomans and, 96–97, 153
Peter I and, 96–97, 115–116, 143, 210
Qajars/Qajar Iran and, 173
routes for, 92*map*
Russia and, 31–32, 38, 114–115, 127, 136–138, 143, 152–153, 173, 175, 184, 207–226
silk trade, 26–27, 93–96, 103, 114–115, 127, 143, 154–155, 175, 180–181
Soviet policy on, 334–337, 342–343
Soviet Union and, 334–337, 342–343
in sugar, 336
volume of, 179–181
World War II and, 353
Transcaspian Military Railroad, 8, 9, 215, 218, 219, 227, 231, 232–241, 243, 276
Transcaspian Provisional Government, 282
Transcaspian railway, 215, 227–246
Transcaucasian railway, 215
translators, in Muscovy, 76–82
Treaty of Warranties and Neutrality, 329
Triple Alliance, 312
Trotsky, Leon, 319, 350
TSarskiĭ tituliārnik, 74
Tuchalav Burhaneddin, 58
Tucker, Ernest, 178, 188n45
Tudeh Party, 39, 196–197, 353, 354
Turkestan, 228*map*, 229–230, 234, 273, 301–302, 312, 314, 315, 320
Turkic (language), 66–69, 71, 72, 73, 75–77, 78, 82
Turkistanov, Boris, 99
Turkkomissia, 319
Turkmen
  Bolsheviks and, 315–317
  Nader Shah and, 6, 139, 145, 147, 148, 149n5
  Qajars and, 30, 138, 181, 184

raiding and, 135, 183
revolt of, 339
Russia and, 126, 218
Turkmen *jigit*, 220–221
Turkmenchay Treaty, 27–28, 30–31, 213
Tushkanov, Vasiliĭ, 74
Twelver Shi'ism, 91

Uzun Ada (Karazin), 238*fig*

Vahidi, Iraj, 359
Vakhtang VI, King, 99, 101
van Verden, Karl, 123, 124*fig*, 125, 176
Vatslik, Ivan, 232
Vendor of Crockery (Arzhangi), 261
Vendor of Crockery (Behzād), 256*fig*, 261
Veselovsky, Nikolay, 87n50
Vidy goroda Baku (Karazin), 237*fig*
Vikings, 20
Voĭnovich, Marko, 112n81, 169–170, 171–172, 173, 177, 181, 182–184, 187n23
Volga
  cartography and, 116, 117–119
  dams on, 351, 357
  exploration of, 125
  Russian control of, 5
  silk trade, 94, 114
Volga River Delta, 3
Volkov, Denis V., 293
Volynskiĭ, Artemiĭ, 97–99, 100, 175, 176
von Hablitz, Karl, 169–170, 182, 183
Vorontsov, Mikhaĭl, 102
Voṣuq al-Dawleh, Ḥasan, 299, 303

water levels, dropping, 357
White Russian movement, 293, 297, 302–303
White Voluntary Army, 274
Wison, Arnold T., 273
Witsen, Nicolaas, 119, 120*fig*, 121*fig*, 122
Woodroofe, Thomas, 147
World War I, 271–291, 293, 295, 298
World War II, 342, 350, 352–354
Wrangel, Maria, 274
Wrangel, Pyotr, 274
Wright, Dennis, 251
Wustrow, Kurt, 300

Yokhāribāsh Qajars, 145, 148
Yomut, 135, 138, 148, 149n5, 181, 182, 221, 315
Young Turks, 35–36, 301, 339

Zakaspiĭskaia zheleznaia doroga (The Transcaspian railroad; Karazin), 234
Zapiski belogo partizana (Notes of a White Guerrilla Warrior; Shkuro), 274
Zavvāreh'i, 200
Zavvāreh'i, Sayyed Ḥosayn Mahjur, 199
Ziyarids, 20
Zohāb, Treaty of, 93
Zverev, Poluekht, 79

www.ingramcontent.com/pod-product-compliance
Lightning Source LLC
Chambersburg PA
CBHW021148230426
43667CB00006B/299